INCLUDES COMPREHENSIVE 2000 U.S. CENSUS RESULTS

21ST CENTURY
Atlas
OF THE UNITED STATES,
CANADA, AND THE WORLD

Maps created by
MapQuest.com, Inc.

MAPQUEST.COM

Gareth Stevens Publishing
A WORLD ALMANAC EDUCATION GROUP COMPANY

**World Almanac Education
Group Staff**

Editorial Director
William A. McGeveran, Jr.

Director–Purchasing and Production
Edward A. Thomas

Managing Editor
Lori Wiesenfeld

Associate Editors
Mette Bahde, David M. Faris, Kevin Seabrooke

Desktop Production Manager
Lisa Lazzara

Publisher
Ken Park

Cover Design
Eileen Svajger

**MapQuest.com/Digital Mapping
Services Staff**

Project Managers
Keith Winters, Robert Woolley

Project Coordinators
Matt DiBerardino, Andrew Green, Matt Tharp

Research & Compilation
Marley Amstutz, Laura Hartwig, Bill Truninger

Research Librarian
Craig Haggit

GIS
Dave Folk, Mark Leitzell

Cartographers
Brian Goudreau, Kendall Marten, Jeff Martz,
Hylon Plumb

Editors
Robert Harding, Dana Wolf

Production Support
Shawna Roberts

Gareth Stevens Staff

Cover Design and Photo Research
Karen Knutson, Joel Bucaro, Scott Krall,
Diane Laska-Swanke

Production
Susan Ashley

Copyright © 2001
MAPQUEST.COM

Cover: © CORBIS

Please visit our web site at:
www.garethstevens.com
For a free color catalog describing Gareth
Stevens' list of high-quality books and
multimedia programs, call 1-800-542-2595
(USA) or 1-800-461-9120 (Canada).
Gareth Stevens Publishing's Fax:
(414) 332-3567.

Library of Congress Cataloging-in-Publication Data

MapQuest.com, Inc.
        21st century atlas of the United States,
    Canada, and the world / maps created by
    MapQuest.com, Inc.
        p. cm.
        ISBN 0-8368-2919-0 (lib. bdg.)
        1. Children's atlases. 2. United States—Maps
    for children. 3. Canada—Maps for children.
    [1. Atlases.] I. Title: Twenty-first century atlas
    of the United States, Canada, and the world.
    II. Title.
    G1021.M2488 2001
    912—dc21   2001018241

This edition first published in 2001 by
Gareth Stevens Publishing
A World Almanac Education Group Company
330 West Olive Street, Suite 100
Milwaukee, WI 53212 USA

Printed in the United States of America

1 2 3 4 5 6 7 8 9 05 04 03 02 01

TABLE OF CONTENTS

PORTRAIT OF THE U.S., CENSUS 2000

THE WORLD IN THE 21ST CENTURY

4 WORLD

6 ASIA and OCEANIA

8 Japan
9 North Korea, South Korea, Taiwan
10 China
11 Vietnam, Laos, Cambodia, Mongolia
12 Thailand, Myanmar (Burma), Philippines
13 Indonesia, Brunei, Singapore, Malaysia
14 Australia
15 Papua New Guinea, New Zealand,
     Federated States of Micronesia
16 Marshall Is., Nauru, Solomon Is., Tuvalu
17 Kiribati, Fiji, Palau, Tonga
18 Vanuatu, New Caledonia &
     Dependencies, Samoa, American Samoa
19 Nepal, Maldives, Bhutan, Sri Lanka
20 India
21 Bangladesh, Pakistan
22 Afghanistan, Iran, Turkmenistan
23 Kazakhstan, Uzbekistan, Kyrgyzstan,
     Tajikistan
24 Iraq, Kuwait, Saudi Arabia
25 Bahrain, Qatar,
     United Arab Emirates, Yemen, Oman
26 Lebanon, Israel, Jordan
27 Turkey, Cyprus, Syria

28 EUROPE

30 Great Britain & Northern Ireland
31 Republic of Ireland
32 Denmark, Netherlands
33 Belgium, Liechtenstein, Luxembourg
34 France
35 Monaco, Switzerland
36 Portugal, Malta, Gibraltar, Andorra
37 Spain
38 Italy
39 Austria, Vatican City, San Marino
40 Germany
41 Poland
42 Czech Republic, Slovakia
43 Hungary, Romania
44 Russia
45 Armenia, Georgia, Azerbaijan
46 Estonia, Latvia, Lithuania
47 Belarus, Ukraine
48 Slovenia, Croatia,
     Bosnia & Herzegovina,
     F.Y.R. Macedonia
49 Albania, Yugoslavia
50 Moldova, Bulgaria
51 Greece
52 Iceland, Norway
53 Sweden, Finland

54 AFRICA

56 Egypt, Libya
57 Algeria, Tunisia, Morocco
58 Western Sahara, Cape Verde,
     Mali, Mauritania
59 Chad, Niger, Sudan
60 Eritrea, Djibouti, Ethiopia, Somalia
61 Kenya, Uganda, Rwanda, Burundi
62 Senegal, The Gambia, Guinea,
     Guinea-Bissau
63 Sierra Leone, Côte d'Ivoire,
     São Tomé & Príncipe, Liberia
64 Ghana, Burkina Faso, Benin, Togo
65 Nigeria, Cameroon
66 Equatorial Guinea, Republic of the
     Congo, Gabon, Central African Republic
67 Comoros, Democratic Republic of the
     Congo, Zambia
68 Tanzania, Malawi, Mozambique
69 Mauritius, Zimbabwe, Botswana,
     Madagascar
70 Angola, Namibia, Seychelles
71 South Africa, Swaziland, Lesotho

72 SOUTH AMERICA

74 Argentina
75 Paraguay, Uruguay
76 Chile
77 Peru, Bolivia
78 Colombia
79 Ecuador, Venezuela
80 Guyana, Suriname, French Guiana
81 Brazil

82 NORTH AMERICA

84 Mexico
85 Belize, Guatemala
86 Honduras, El Salvador, Costa Rica
87 Nicaragua, Panama
88 Cuba, Jamaica
89 Dominican Republic, Haiti, Bahamas,
     Turks & Caicos Is.
90 Puerto Rico, Antigua & Barbuda,
     St. Kitts & Nevis, Dominica
91 St. Lucia, Barbados,
     St. Vincent & the Grenadines,
     Grenada, Trinidad & Tobago
92 Canada
93 Canadian Provincial & Territorial Flags
94 Alberta
95 British Columbia
96 Manitoba
97 New Brunswick
98 Newfoundland
99 Northwest Territories, Nunavut
100 Nova Scotia, Prince Edward Island
101 Ontario, Québec
102 Southern Ontario
103 Southern Québec
104 Saskatchewan
105 Yukon Territory

POLAR REGIONS
106 Arctic Regions, Greenland
107 Antarctica

108 WORLD INDEX

UNITED STATES
126 U.S. Political
127 U.S. Physical
128 Alabama
129 Alaska
130 Arizona
131 Arkansas
132 California
133 Colorado
134 Connecticut
135 Delaware
136 Florida
137 Georgia
138 Hawaii
139 Idaho
140 Illinois
141 Indiana
142 Iowa
143 Kansas
144 Kentucky
145 Louisiana
146 Maine
147 Maryland
148 Massachusetts
149 Michigan
150 Minnesota
151 Mississippi
152 Missouri
153 Montana
154 Nebraska
155 Nevada
156 New Hampshire
157 New Jersey
158 New Mexico
159 New York
160 North Carolina
161 North Dakota
162 Ohio
163 Oklahoma
164 Oregon
165 Pennsylvania
166 Rhode Island
167 South Carolina
168 South Dakota
169 Tennessee
170 Texas
171 Utah
172 Vermont
173 Virginia
174 Washington
175 West Virginia
176 Wisconsin
177 Wyoming

178 STATE INDEXES

General

⍟ National Capital

★ Territorial Capital

• Other City

▭ International Boundary (subject area)

▭ International Boundary (non-subject)

▭ Internal Boundary (state, province, etc.)

- - - - Disputed Boundary

﹏ Perennial River

······· Intermittent River

⊥⊥⊥⊥ Canal

╱ Dam

U.S. States, Canadian Provinces & Territories
(additions and changes to general legend)

★ State Capital

• County Seat

▭ Built Up Area

▭ State Boundary

▭ County Boundary

▭ National Park

▭ Other Park, Forest, Grassland

▭ Indian, Other Reservation

▪ Point of Interest

▲ Mountain Peak

·········· Continental Divide

········ Time Zone Boundary

—— Limited Access Highway

—— Other Major Road

⑨⓪ Highway Shield

PROJECTION

The only true representation of the Earth, free of distortion, is a globe. Maps are flat, and the process by which the geographic locations (latitude and longitude) are transformed from a three-dimensional sphere to a two-dimensional flat map is called a Projection.

For a detailed explanation of Projections, see *MapScope* in Volume 2 of *Funk & Wagnalls New Encyclopedia.*

TYPES OF SCALE

VISUAL SCALE
Every map has a bar scale, or a Visual Scale, that can be used for measuring. It shows graphically the relationship between map distance and ground distance.

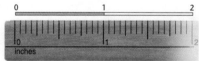

One inch represents 1 mile

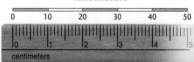

One centimeter represents 10 kilometers

REPRESENTATIVE FRACTION
The scale of a map, expressed as a numerical ratio of map distance to ground distance, is called a Representative Fraction (or RF). It is usually written as 1/50,000 or 1:50,000, meaning that one unit of measurement on the map represents 50,000 of the same units on the ground.

This example is used on pages 20, 21 for India, Bangladesh, and Pakistan.

The Globe is centered on the continent of Asia, as shown on pages 6, 7.

The subject countries are shown in a stronger red/brown color.

LOCATOR

U.S. CENSUS 2000

The following four pages look at results from Census 2000. Some highlights:
- The U.S. population increased a remarkable 13.2% over 1990.
- Most growth was in the South and West. California had the largest increase (4,111,627) and Nevada had the largest percentage increase (66.3%).
- The Hispanic population grew 57.9% since 1990, reaching 35.3 million, or 12.5% of the total population.

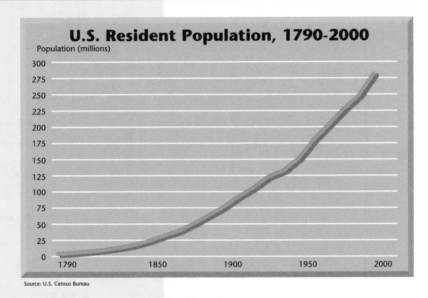

U.S. Resident Population, 1790-2000

Population (millions)

Source: U.S. Census Bureau

United States Resident Population per Census

Year	Population
2000	281,421,906
1990	248,709,873
1980	226,542,199
1970	203,302,031
1960	179,323,175
1950	151,325,798
1940	132,164,569
1930	123,202,624
1920	106,021,537
1910	92,228,496
1900	76,212,168
1890	62,979,766
1880	50,189,209
1870	38,558,371
1860	31,443,321
1850	23,191,876
1840	17,063,353
1830	12,860,702
1820	9,638,453
1810	7,239,881
1800	5,308,483
1790	3,929,214

Source: U.S. Census Bureau

Population Density, 2000
(persons per sq. mi., land area only)

© MapQuest.com, Inc.

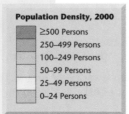

Population Density, 2000
- ≥500 Persons
- 250–499 Persons
- 100–249 Persons
- 50–99 Persons
- 25–49 Persons
- 0–24 Persons

Most People per Sq. Mi.
Washington, D.C.	9,378.0
New Jersey	1,134.5
Rhode Island	1,003.2
Massachusetts	809.8
Connecticut	702.9

Fewest People per Sq. Mi.
Alaska	1.1
Wyoming	5.1
Montana	6.2
North Dakota	9.3
South Dakota	9.9

New Apportionment in U.S. House of Representatives

© MapQuest.com, Inc.

Apportionment is the process of dividing the 435 seats in the U.S. House of Representatives among the states. The apportionment calculation is based upon the total resident population of each state as determined by the latest U.S. Census.

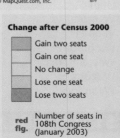

Change after Census 2000
- Gain two seats
- Gain one seat
- No change
- Lose one seat
- Lose two seats

red fig. Number of seats in 108th Congress (January 2003)

Percent Change in State Population, 1990-2000

Percent Change, 1990–2000

	≥30.0% increase
	25.0–29.9% increase
	20.0–24.9% increase
	15.0–19.9% increase
	10.0–14.9% increase
	5.0–9.9% increase
	0–4.9% increase
	decrease

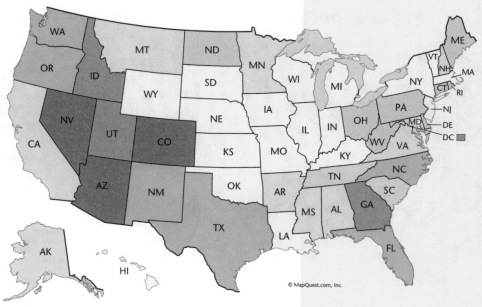

© MapQuest.com, Inc.

Population by State, 1990-2000

Source: U.S. Census Bureau

State	2000 Pop.	1990 Pop.	Percent Change
...bama	4,447,100	4,040,587	10.1
...ska	626,932	550,043	14.0
...ona	5,130,632	3,665,228	40.0
...ansas	2,673,400	2,350,725	13.7
...fornia	33,871,648	29,760,021	13.8
...rado	4,301,261	3,294,394	30.6
...nnecticut	3,405,565	3,287,116	3.6
...aware	783,600	666,168	17.6
...rict of Columbia	572,059	606,900	-5.7
...ida	15,982,378	12,937,926	23.5
...rgia	8,186,453	6,478,216	26.4
...vaii	1,211,537	1,108,229	9.3
...o	1,293,953	1,006,749	28.5
...ois	12,419,293	11,430,602	8.6
...ana	6,080,485	5,544,159	9.7
...a	2,926,324	2,776,755	5.4
...sas	2,688,418	2,477,574	8.5
...tucky	4,041,769	3,685,296	9.7
...siana	4,468,976	4,219,973	5.9
...ne	1,274,923	1,227,928	3.8
...yland	5,296,486	4,781,468	10.8
...sachusetts	6,349,097	6,016,425	5.5
...higan	9,938,444	9,295,297	6.9
...nesota	4,919,479	4,375,099	12.4
...issippi	2,844,658	2,573,216	10.5
...ouri	5,595,211	5,117,073	9.3
...ntana	902,195	799,065	12.9
...raska	1,711,263	1,578,385	8.4
...ada	1,998,257	1,201,833	66.3
...Hampshire	1,235,786	1,109,252	11.4
...Jersey	8,414,350	7,730,188	8.9
...Mexico	1,819,046	1,515,069	20.1
...York	18,976,457	17,990,455	5.5
...h Carolina	8,049,313	6,628,637	21.4
...h Dakota	642,200	638,800	0.5
...	11,353,140	10,847,115	4.7
...homa	3,450,654	3,145,585	9.7
...gon	3,421,399	2,842,321	20.4
...sylvania	12,281,054	11,881,643	3.4
...de Island	1,048,319	1,003,464	4.5
...h Carolina	4,012,012	3,486,703	15.1
...h Dakota	754,844	696,004	8.5
...essee	5,689,283	4,877,185	16.7
...	20,851,820	16,986,510	22.8
...ont	2,233,169	1,722,850	29.6
...mont	608,827	562,758	8.2
...nia	7,078,515	6,187,358	14.4
...ington	5,894,121	4,866,692	21.1
...Virginia	1,808,344	1,793,477	0.8
...onsin	5,363,675	4,891,769	9.7
...ming	493,782	453,588	8.9

Distribution of Population by Region, 1900, 1950, 2000

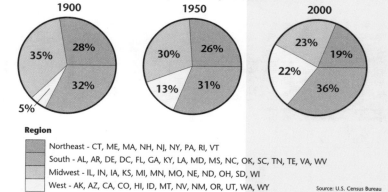

1900

35% 28% 32% 5%

1950

30% 26% 13% 31%

2000

23% 19% 22% 36%

Region

	Northeast - CT, ME, MA, NH, NJ, NY, PA, RI, VT
	South - AL, AR, DE, DC, FL, GA, KY, LA, MD, MS, NC, OK, SC, TN, TE, VA, WV
	Midwest - IL, IN, IA, KS, MI, MN, MO, NE, ND, OH, SD, WI
	West - AK, AZ, CA, CO, HI, ID, MT, NV, NM, OR, UT, WA, WY

Source: U.S. Census Bureau

U.S. Center of Population

© MapQuest.com, Inc.

Source: U.S. Census Bureau

U.S. Center of Population = center of population gravity, or the point on which the U.S. would balance if it were a rigid plane, assuming all individuals weigh the same and exert influence proportional to their distance from a central point

Population Breakdown by Race and Hispanic or Latino Origin

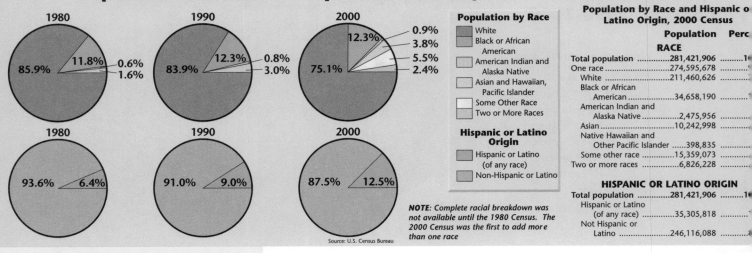

1980
85.9%
11.8%
0.6%
1.6%

1990
83.9%
12.3%
0.8%
3.0%

2000
12.3%
75.1%
0.9%
3.8%
5.5%
2.4%

1980
93.6%
6.4%

1990
91.0%
9.0%

2000
87.5%
12.5%

Population by Race
- White
- Black or African American
- American Indian and Alaska Native
- Asian and Hawaiian, Pacific Islander
- Some Other Race
- Two or More Races

Hispanic or Latino Origin
- Hispanic or Latino (of any race)
- Non-Hispanic or Latino

NOTE: *Complete racial breakdown was not available until the 1980 Census. The 2000 Census was the first to add more than one race*

Source: U.S. Census Bureau

Population by Race and Hispanic or Latino Origin, 2000 Census

	Population	Perc
RACE		
Total population	281,421,906	1
One race	274,595,678	
White	211,460,626	
Black or African American	34,658,190	1
American Indian and Alaska Native	2,475,956	
Asian	10,242,998	
Native Hawaiian and Other Pacific Islander	398,835	
Some other race	15,359,073	
Two or more races	6,826,228	
HISPANIC OR LATINO ORIGIN		
Total population	281,421,906	1
Hispanic or Latino (of any race)	35,305,818	
Not Hispanic or Latino	246,116,088	

20 Largest Metropolitan Areas, 2000 Census

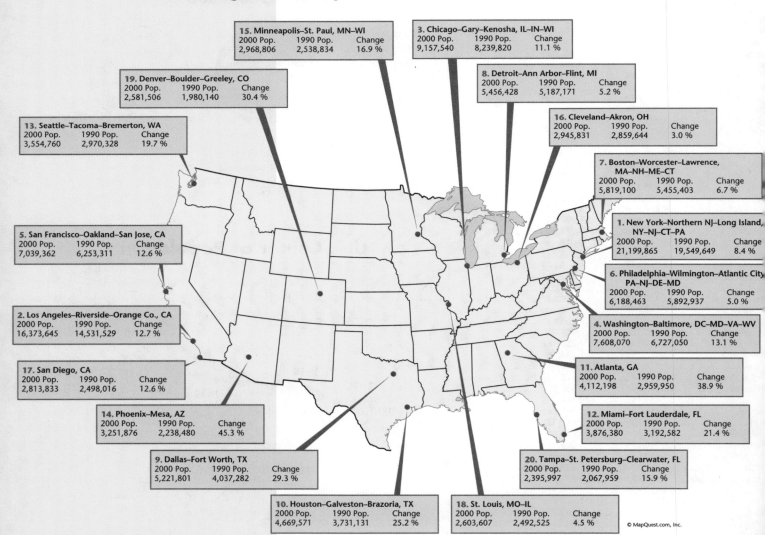

15. Minneapolis–St. Paul, MN–WI
2000 Pop.	1990 Pop.	Change
2,968,806	2,538,834	16.9 %

3. Chicago–Gary–Kenosha, IL–IN–WI
2000 Pop.	1990 Pop.	Change
9,157,540	8,239,820	11.1 %

19. Denver–Boulder–Greeley, CO
2000 Pop.	1990 Pop.	Change
2,581,506	1,980,140	30.4 %

8. Detroit–Ann Arbor–Flint, MI
2000 Pop.	1990 Pop.	Change
5,456,428	5,187,171	5.2 %

13. Seattle–Tacoma–Bremerton, WA
2000 Pop.	1990 Pop.	Change
3,554,760	2,970,328	19.7 %

16. Cleveland–Akron, OH
2000 Pop.	1990 Pop.	Change
2,945,831	2,859,644	3.0 %

7. Boston–Worcester–Lawrence, MA–NH–ME–CT
2000 Pop.	1990 Pop.	Change
5,819,100	5,455,403	6.7 %

5. San Francisco–Oakland–San Jose, CA
2000 Pop.	1990 Pop.	Change
7,039,362	6,253,311	12.6 %

1. New York–Northern NJ–Long Island, NY–NJ–CT–PA
2000 Pop.	1990 Pop.	Change
21,199,865	19,549,649	8.4 %

6. Philadelphia–Wilmington–Atlantic City, PA–NJ–DE–MD
2000 Pop.	1990 Pop.	Change
6,188,463	5,892,937	5.0 %

2. Los Angeles–Riverside–Orange Co., CA
2000 Pop.	1990 Pop.	Change
16,373,645	14,531,529	12.7 %

4. Washington–Baltimore, DC–MD–VA–WV
2000 Pop.	1990 Pop.	Change
7,608,070	6,727,050	13.1 %

17. San Diego, CA
2000 Pop.	1990 Pop.	Change
2,813,833	2,498,016	12.6 %

11. Atlanta, GA
2000 Pop.	1990 Pop.	Change
4,112,198	2,959,950	38.9 %

14. Phoenix–Mesa, AZ
2000 Pop.	1990 Pop.	Change
3,251,876	2,238,480	45.3 %

12. Miami–Fort Lauderdale, FL
2000 Pop.	1990 Pop.	Change
3,876,380	3,192,582	21.4 %

9. Dallas–Fort Worth, TX
2000 Pop.	1990 Pop.	Change
5,221,801	4,037,282	29.3 %

20. Tampa–St. Petersburg–Clearwater, FL
2000 Pop.	1990 Pop.	Change
2,395,997	2,067,959	15.9 %

10. Houston–Galveston–Brazoria, TX
2000 Pop.	1990 Pop.	Change
4,669,571	3,731,131	25.2 %

18. St. Louis, MO–IL
2000 Pop.	1990 Pop.	Change
2,603,607	2,492,525	4.5 %

© MapQuest.com, Inc.

20 Largest Cities, 2000 Census

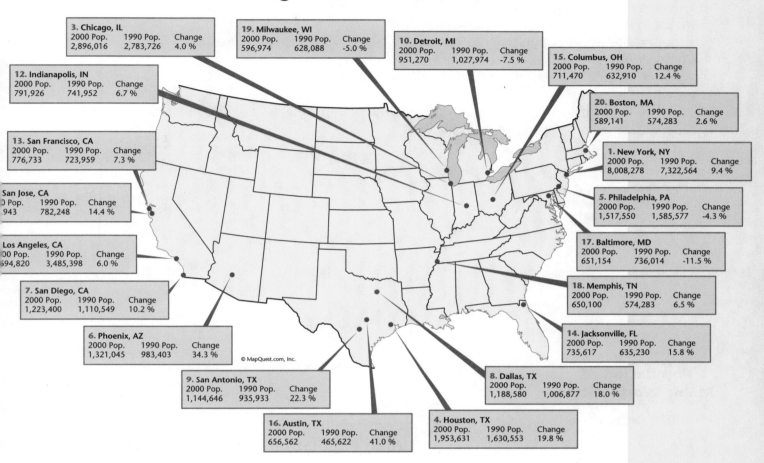

3. Chicago, IL
| 2000 Pop. | 1990 Pop. | Change |
| 2,896,016 | 2,783,726 | 4.0 % |

19. Milwaukee, WI
| 2000 Pop. | 1990 Pop. | Change |
| 596,974 | 628,088 | -5.0 % |

10. Detroit, MI
| 2000 Pop. | 1990 Pop. | Change |
| 951,270 | 1,027,974 | -7.5 % |

15. Columbus, OH
| 2000 Pop. | 1990 Pop. | Change |
| 711,470 | 632,910 | 12.4 % |

12. Indianapolis, IN
| 2000 Pop. | 1990 Pop. | Change |
| 791,926 | 741,952 | 6.7 % |

20. Boston, MA
| 2000 Pop. | 1990 Pop. | Change |
| 589,141 | 574,283 | 2.6 % |

13. San Francisco, CA
| 2000 Pop. | 1990 Pop. | Change |
| 776,733 | 723,959 | 7.3 % |

1. New York, NY
| 2000 Pop. | 1990 Pop. | Change |
| 8,008,278 | 7,322,564 | 9.4 % |

San Jose, CA
| Pop. | 1990 Pop. | Change |
| 943 | 782,248 | 14.4 % |

5. Philadelphia, PA
| 2000 Pop. | 1990 Pop. | Change |
| 1,517,550 | 1,585,577 | -4.3 % |

Los Angeles, CA
| Pop. | 1990 Pop. | Change |
| 694,820 | 3,485,398 | 6.0 % |

17. Baltimore, MD
| 2000 Pop. | 1990 Pop. | Change |
| 651,154 | 736,014 | -11.5 % |

7. San Diego, CA
| 2000 Pop. | 1990 Pop. | Change |
| 1,223,400 | 1,110,549 | 10.2 % |

18. Memphis, TN
| 2000 Pop. | 1990 Pop. | Change |
| 650,100 | 574,283 | 6.5 % |

6. Phoenix, AZ
| 2000 Pop. | 1990 Pop. | Change |
| 1,321,045 | 983,403 | 34.3 % |

© MapQuest.com, Inc.

14. Jacksonville, FL
| 2000 Pop. | 1990 Pop. | Change |
| 735,617 | 635,230 | 15.8 % |

9. San Antonio, TX
| 2000 Pop. | 1990 Pop. | Change |
| 1,144,646 | 935,933 | 22.3 % |

8. Dallas, TX
| 2000 Pop. | 1990 Pop. | Change |
| 1,188,580 | 1,006,877 | 18.0 % |

16. Austin, TX
| 2000 Pop. | 1990 Pop. | Change |
| 656,562 | 465,622 | 41.0 % |

4. Houston, TX
| 2000 Pop. | 1990 Pop. | Change |
| 1,953,631 | 1,630,553 | 19.8 % |

Percent of Population by Race and Hispanic or Latino Origin for the 20 Largest Cities

City		2000 Population	White	Black or African American	American Indian, Alaska Native	Asian	Hawaiian & Other Pacific Islander	Some Other Race	Two or More Races	Hispanic or Latino (of any race)
New York	NY	8,008,278	44.7	26.6	0.5	9.8	0.1	13.4	4.9	27.0
Los Angeles	CA	3,694,820	46.9	11.2	0.8	10.0	0.2	25.7	5.2	46.5
Chicago	IL	2,896,016	42.0	36.8	0.4	4.3	0.1	13.6	2.9	26.0
Houston	TX	1,953,631	49.3	25.3	0.4	5.3	0.1	16.5	3.1	37.4
Philadelphia	PA	1,517,550	45.0	43.2	0.3	4.5	0.0	4.8	2.2	8.5
Phoenix	AZ	1,321,045	71.1	5.1	2.0	2.0	0.1	16.4	3.3	34.1
San Diego	CA	1,223,400	60.2	7.9	0.6	13.6	0.5	12.4	4.8	25.4
Dallas	TX	1,188,580	50.8	25.9	0.5	2.7	0.0	17.2	2.7	35.6
San Antonio	TX	1,144,646	67.7	6.8	0.8	1.6	0.1	19.3	3.7	58.7
Detroit	MI	951,270	12.3	81.6	0.3	1.0	0.0	2.5	2.3	5.0
San Jose	CA	894,943	47.5	3.5	0.8	26.9	0.4	15.9	5.0	30.2
Indianapolis	IN	791,926	69.3	25.3	0.3	1.4	0.0	2.0	1.6	3.9
San Francisco	CA	776,733	49.7	7.8	0.4	30.8	0.5	6.5	4.3	14.1
Jacksonville	FL	735,617	64.5	29.0	0.3	2.8	0.1	1.3	2.0	4.2
Columbus	OH	711,470	67.9	24.5	0.3	3.4	0.1	1.2	2.6	2.5
Austin	TX	656,562	65.4	10.0	0.6	4.7	0.1	16.2	3.0	30.5
Baltimore	MD	651,154	31.6	64.3	0.3	1.5	0.0	0.7	1.5	1.7
Memphis	TN	650,100	34.4	61.4	0.2	1.5	0.0	1.5	1.0	3.0
Milwaukee	WI	596,974	50.0	37.3	0.9	2.9	0.1	6.1	2.7	12.0
Boston	MA	589,141	54.5	25.3	0.4	7.5	0.1	7.8	4.4	14.4

Source: U.S. Census Bureau

THE WORLD IN THE 21ST CENTURY

The following four pages look at the growing world population and the latest trends in health and mortality. Some highlights:

- The world population has passed 6.1 billion, with 1.3 billion people in China alone.
- By 2050 the world population may pass 11 billion, with most of the growth in urban areas and developing countries.
- The highest life expectancies and lowest infant mortality rates are in North America, Western Europe, and Australia.

Percent Increase in Urban Population, 2000–2015

- 55 and over
- 35–54
- 20–34
- 10–19
- 0–9
- No data

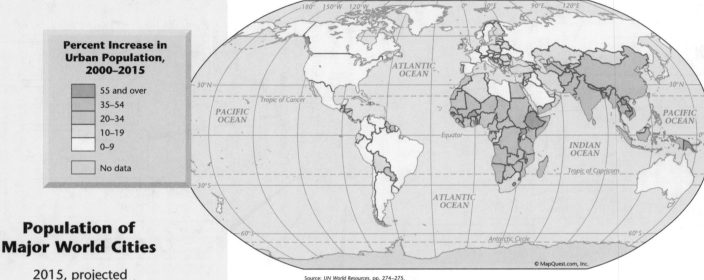

Source: *UN World Resources*, pp. 274–275.

© MapQuest.com, Inc.

Population of Major World Cities

2015, projected

1	Tokyo	28,887,000
2	Mumbai	26,218,000
3	Lagos	24,640,000
4	São Paulo	20,320,000
5	Mexico City	19,180,000
6	Shanghai	17,969,000
7	New York	17,602,000
8	Kolkata	17,305,000
9	Delhi	16,860,000
10	Beijing	15,572,000
11	Los Angeles	14,217,000
12	Buenos Aires	13,856,000
13	Seoul	12,980,000
14	Rio de Janeiro	11,860,000
15	Osaka	10,609,000

These figures are for "urban agglomerations," which are densely populated urban areas, larger than the cities by themselves.

Source: UN, Dept. for Economic and Social Information and Policy Analysis

© MapQuest.com, Inc.

Urban Population Growth, 2000–2015

The world population will become increasingly urbanized in the early 21st century. It is predicted that the largest increases in urban population will occur in Africa and southern and eastern Asia.

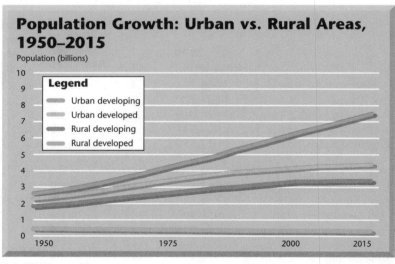

Population Growth: Urban vs. Rural Areas, 1950–2015

Population (billions)

Legend
- Urban developing
- Urban developed
- Rural developing
- Rural developed

Source: *UN World Resources*, p. 146.

Population growth in rural areas will taper off where it has not already. But urban growth will increase, especially in the developing nations.

Developed regions include United States, Canada, Japan, Europe, and Australia and New Zealand.

Developing regions include Africa, Asia (excluding Japan), South America and Central America, Mexico, and Oceania (excluding Australia and New Zealand). The European successor states of the former Soviet Union are classified as developed regions, while the Asian successor states are classified as developing regions.

Population Density, 2000

Population

Persons per sq. mi.	Persons per sq. km.
and over	200 and over
260–519	100–199
130–259	50–99
25–129	10–49
1–24	1–9
under 1	under 1

© MapQuest.com, Inc.

World population total (May 1, 2001): 6,144,488,802

Source: International Programs Center, U.S. Census Bureau

Population Density, Largest Countries

2000

People per square mile

China	330
India	800
United States	70
Indonesia	290
Brazil	50
Russia	20

2050

People per square mile

China	360
India	1,400
United States	100
Indonesia	450
Brazil	70
Russia	20

The world is becoming more crowded in the 21st century. In mid-2000, China already had the highest population in the world, with an estimated 1.3 billion inhabitants, more than one-fifth of the total population. India had passed 1 billion, while the United States had the world's third-largest population, with about 281 million, followed by Indonesia, Brazil, and Pakistan.

Source: U.S. Census Bureau

Anticipated World Population Growth

Population (billions)

Fertility rates
- High
- Medium
- Low

Developing regions

Developed regions

| 1950 | 2000 | 2050 |

Source: *UN World Resources*, p. 143.

The world population has grown from about 2 billion in 1950 to more than 6 billion today, and could almost double by 2050. Most of the growth will continue to occur in developing regions, where fertility rates (number of children born per woman of childbearing age) are relatively high.

Where the fertility rate is around 2 children per woman of childbearing age, the population will tend to stabilize. This figure indicates roughly that couples, over a lifetime, are replacing themselves without adding to the population.

Population experts at the United Nations actually give three different projections for future population growth. Under a **high** fertility-rate projection, which assumes rates would stabilize at an average of 2.6 in high-fertility regions and 2.1 in low-fertility regions, the global population would reach 11.2 billion by 2050. Under a **medium** projection, which assumes rates would ultimately stabilize at around replacement levels, the population would rise to 9.4 billion by 2050. Under a **low** fertility-rate projection, which assumes rates would eventually stabilize at lower-than-replacement levels, the world population would still reach about 7.7 billion by 2050.

Population Projections by Continent

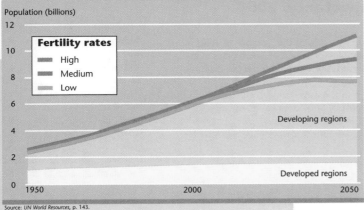

NORTH AMERICA
480,545
617,249
728,136

EUROPE*
588,240
696,838
728,982

ASIA
3,688,072
4,774,053
5,406,328

AFRICA
805,243
1,317,493
2,012,567

SOUTH AMERICA
346,504
451,641
519,878

AUSTRALIA & PACIFIC IS.
30,795
38,512
42,829

Population (in thousands)

YEAR
2000 2025 2050

Population projections based on medium fertility rate

*Including Russia

© MapQuest.com, Inc.

Source: U.S. Census Bureau, International Data Base

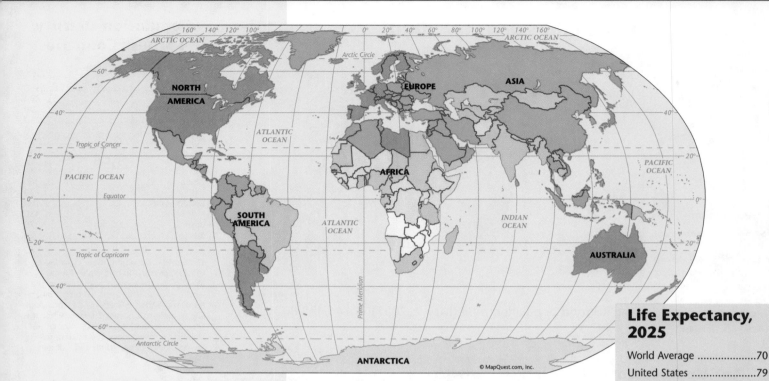

World Life Expectancy, 2000

Life Expectancy
(in years)

- 75–84
- 65–74
- 50–64
- 40–49
- Less than 40

- No data

Life expectancy at birth is a common measure of the number of years a person may expect to live. There are many factors, such as nutrition, sanitation, health and medical services, that contribute to helping people live longer.

As some of the above factors improve in the developing countries, life expectancy there should increase. But most of Sub-Saharan Africa will have less than average life expectancies.

Although it is not indicated here, females almost always have a longer life expectancy than males.

World Life Expectancy, 2025

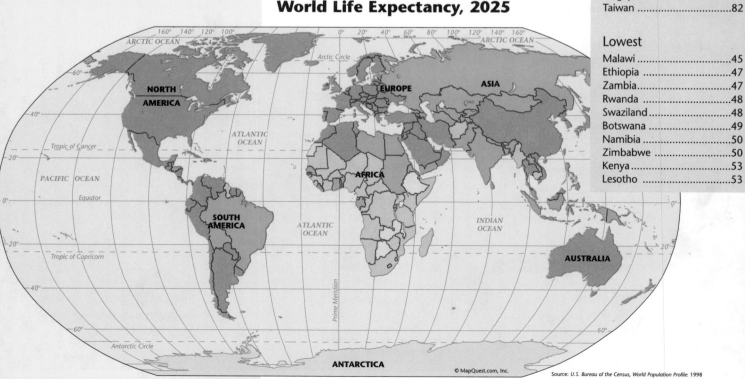

Life Expectancy, 2025

World Average	70
United States	79

Highest

Andorra	84
Austria	84
Australia	83
Canada	82
Cyprus	82
Dominica	82
Israel	82
Japan	82
Kuwait	82
Monaco	82
San Marino	82
Singapore	82
Taiwan	82

Lowest

Malawi	45
Ethiopia	47
Zambia	47
Rwanda	48
Swaziland	48
Botswana	49
Namibia	50
Zimbabwe	50
Kenya	53
Lesotho	53

Source: U.S. Bureau of the Census, World Population Profile: 1998

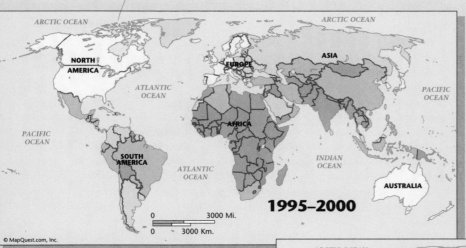

1995–2000

© MapQuest.com, Inc.

Infant Mortality Averages, 2015–2020
by continent with highest and lowest country

World Average 35

Africa 55		Europe 8	
Sierra Leone 114		Albania 20	
Mauritius 8		Austria	
		& 14 others 5	
Asia 32			
Afghanistan 118		North America 22	
Japan 4		Haiti 82	
		Canada 5	
Australia & Oceania .. 15		U.S. 5	
Papua			
New Guinea 37		South America 23	
Australia 5		Guyana 37	
		Chile 9	

Infant Mortality

Infant mortality means the number of deaths before the age of one per 1,000 live births. It is a fairly common way of judging how healthy a country is. Presently there are about 14 countries with infant mortality rates lower than that of the United States.

With improvements in sanitation and health care, it is expected that infant mortality will decline substantially in the 21st century. However, it will continue to be a serious problem especially in Sub-Saharan Africa and other developing regions

Infant Mortality Rate
(per 1,000 live births)

	85–169
	50–85
	25–49
	10–24
	Less than 10
	No data

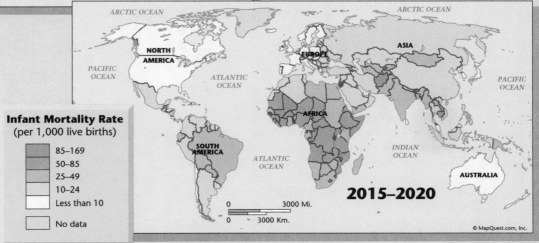

2015–2020

© MapQuest.com, Inc.

Source: UN Population Division and UN Children's Fund

Food & Nutrition

There has been a general trend towards better nutrition, but Sub-Saharan Africa remains a problem area: increasing numbers of people will be suffering from undernutrition.

On a worldwide basis, the food supply seems adequate. Unfortunately the availability of food and the distribution of people don't always match up.

Undernutrition in Developing Countries, 1969-2010

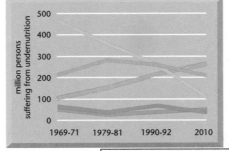

Legend
- Latin America and the Caribbean
- Near East and North Africa
- Sub-Saharan Africa
- East and Southeast Asia
- South Asia

Fertility

This rate is the number of births related to the number of women of childbearing age. Currently the rate for developed nations is about 1.6, but it is about 2.9 in developing nations.

Africa shows the slowest reduction in the fertility rate. With improvements in infant mortality and the implementation of family planning programs, the rate should stabilize.

Average Daily per Capita Calorie Supply, 1999
by continent
with highest and lowest country

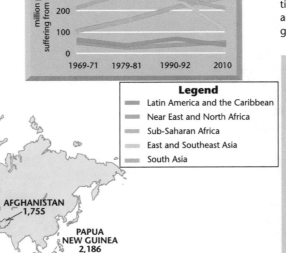

PORTUGAL 3,768
CROATIA 2,617
ISRAEL 3,542
AFGHANISTAN 1,755
UNITED STATES 3,754
HAITI 1,977
VENEZUELA 2,229
TUNISIA 3,388
SOMALIA 1,555
PAPUA NEW GUINEA 2,186
ARGENTINA 3,176
NEW ZEALAND 3,152

Source: UN Food and Agriculture Organization, UN Population Division, U.S. Department of Agriculture

© MapQuest.com, Inc.

Trends in Fertility Rates

Legend
- Africa
- Asia
- South and Central America
- Developed
- Developing

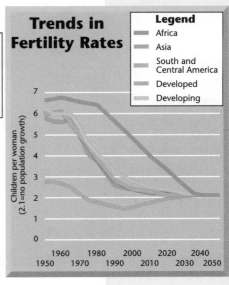

Source: UN Population Division

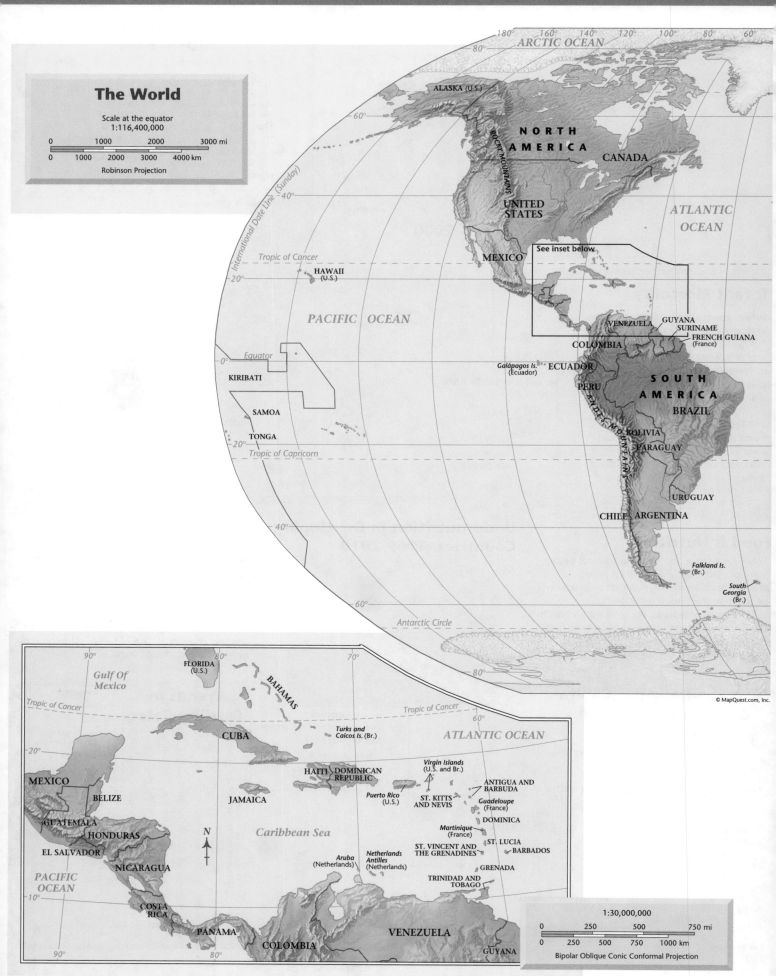

The World

Scale at the equator
1:116,400,000

0   1000   2000   3000 mi
0   1000   2000   3000   4000 km

Robinson Projection

ARCTIC OCEAN

ALASKA (U.S.)

NORTH AMERICA

CANADA

ROCKY MOUNTAINS

UNITED STATES

ATLANTIC OCEAN

MEXICO

See inset below

International Date Line (Sunday)

Tropic of Cancer

HAWAII (U.S.)

PACIFIC OCEAN

VENEZUELA   GUYANA
                SURINAME
                FRENCH GUIANA
                (France)

COLOMBIA

Equator

Galápagos Is.
(Ecuador)   ECUADOR

KIRIBATI

PERU   SOUTH AMERICA
                BRAZIL

ANDES MOUNTAINS   BOLIVIA

SAMOA

PARAGUAY

TONGA

Tropic of Capricorn

URUGUAY

CHILE   ARGENTINA

Falkland Is.
(Br.)

South
Georgia
(Br.)

Antarctic Circle

© MapQuest.com, Inc.

Inset

Gulf Of Mexico

FLORIDA (U.S.)

BAHAMAS

Tropic of Cancer

Tropic of Cancer

ATLANTIC OCEAN

Turks and
Caicos Is. (Br.)

CUBA

Virgin Islands
(U.S. and Br.)

HAITI   DOMINICAN
            REPUBLIC

ANTIGUA AND
BARBUDA

MEXICO

BELIZE

JAMAICA

Puerto Rico
(U.S.)

ST. KITTS
AND NEVIS

Guadeloupe
(France)

GUATEMALA

DOMINICA

HONDURAS

Caribbean Sea

Martinique
(France)

ST. LUCIA

EL SALVADOR

ST. VINCENT AND
THE GRENADINES

BARBADOS

NICARAGUA

PACIFIC OCEAN

Aruba
(Netherlands)

Netherlands
Antilles
(Netherlands)

GRENADA

N

TRINIDAD AND
TOBAGO

COSTA RICA

PANAMA

VENEZUELA

COLOMBIA

GUYANA

1:30,000,000

0   250   500   750 mi
0   250   500   750   1000 km

Bipolar Oblique Conic Conformal Projection

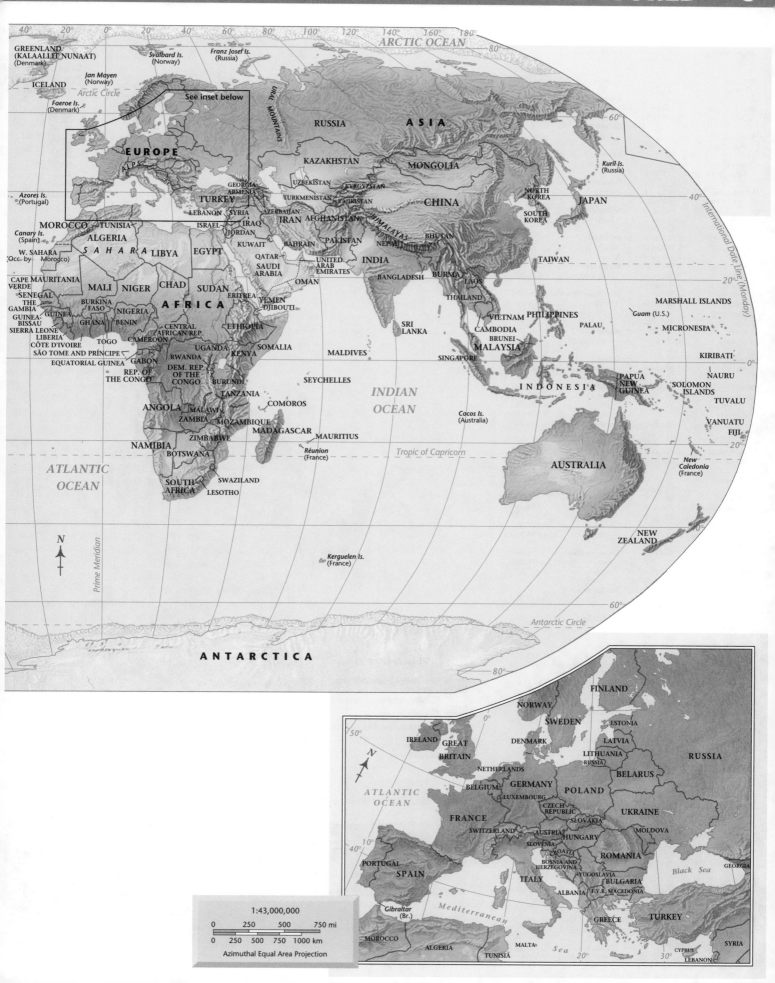

40° 20° 0° 20° 40° 60° 80° 100° 120° 140° 160° 180°

ARCTIC OCEAN

GREENLAND
(KALAALLIT NUNAAT)
(Denmark)

Svalbard Is.
(Norway)

Franz Josef Is.
(Russia)

Jan Mayen
(Norway)

80°

ICELAND

Arctic Circle

Faeroe Is.
(Denmark)

See inset below

60°

URAL MOUNTAINS

RUSSIA

ASIA

EUROPE

ALPS

Kuril Is.
(Russia)

Azores Is.
(Portugal)

GEORGIA
ARMENIA

TURKEY

40°

UZBEKISTAN KYRGYZSTAN

MONGOLIA

NORTH KOREA

JAPAN

International Date Line (Monday)

TURKMENISTAN TAJIKISTAN

LEBANON SYRIA

CHINA

SOUTH KOREA

Canary Is.
(Spain)

MOROCCO TUNISIA

ISRAEL

JORDAN

IRAQ

AZERBAIJAN

IRAN AFGHANISTAN

HIMALAYAS

TAIWAN

ALGERIA

SAHARA

LIBYA

EGYPT

KUWAIT

BAHRAIN

QATAR

PAKISTAN

NEPAL

BHUTAN

20°

W. SAHARA
(Occ. by Morocco)

UNITED ARAB EMIRATES

INDIA

BANGLADESH

BURMA

LAOS

MARSHALL ISLANDS

CAPE VERDE

MAURITANIA

MALI NIGER CHAD

SUDAN

SAUDI ARABIA

OMAN

AFRICA

ERITREA

YEMEN

THAILAND

Guam (U.S.)

MICRONESIA

SENEGAL
THE GAMBIA
GUINEA-BISSAU
SIERRA LEONE
LIBERIA
CÔTE D'IVOIRE

BURKINA FASO

NIGERIA

DJIBOUTI

VIETNAM

PHILIPPINES

PALAU

KIRIBATI

GUINEA

BENIN

CENTRAL AFRICAN REP.

ETHIOPIA

SRI LANKA

CAMBODIA

GHANA

UGANDA

SOMALIA

BRUNEI

NAURU

TOGO

CAMEROON

KENYA

MALDIVES

MALAYSIA

SÃO TOME AND PRÍNCIPE

RWANDA

SINGAPORE

0°

EQUATORIAL GUINEA

GABON

REP. OF THE CONGO

DEM. REP. OF THE CONGO

BURUNDI

SEYCHELLES

INDONESIA

PAPUA NEW GUINEA

SOLOMON ISLANDS

TANZANIA

TUVALU

ANGOLA

MALAWI

COMOROS

INDIAN OCEAN

VANUATU

ZAMBIA

MOZAMBIQUE

MADAGASCAR

MAURITIUS

FIJI

20°

ZIMBABWE

NAMIBIA

BOTSWANA

Réunion
(France)

Cacos Is.
(Australia)

Tropic of Capricorn

AUSTRALIA

New Caledonia
(France)

ATLANTIC OCEAN

SOUTH AFRICA

SWAZILAND

LESOTHO

NEW ZEALAND

0°

N

Prime Meridian

Kerguelen Is.
(France)

60°

ANTARCTICA

Antarctic Circle

80°

1:43,000,000

0 250 500 750 mi

0 250 500 750 1000 km

Azimuthal Equal Area Projection

FINLAND

NORWAY

SWEDEN

50°

ESTONIA

IRELAND

GREAT BRITAIN

DENMARK

LATVIA

LITHUANIA

RUSSIA

RUSSIA

N

NETHERLANDS

BELARUS

ATLANTIC OCEAN

BELGIUM

GERMANY

POLAND

LUXEMBOURG

FRANCE

CZECH REPUBLIC

UKRAINE

SWITZERLAND

SLOVAKIA

40°

AUSTRIA

HUNGARY

MOLDOVA

SLOVENIA

CROATIA

ROMANIA

PORTUGAL

SPAIN

ITALY

BOSNIA AND HERZEGOVINA

YUGOSLAVIA

BULGARIA

Black Sea

GEORGIA

ALBANIA

F.Y.R. MACEDONIA

Gibraltar
(Br.)

GREECE

TURKEY

Mediterranean

Sea

20°

30°

MOROCCO

ALGERIA

TUNISIA

MALTA

CYPRUS

SYRIA

LEBANON

MAJOR CITIES

Afghanistan	(metro)
Kabul	2,029,000
Bahrain	
Manama	151,000
Bangladesh	(metro)
Dhaka	8,545,000
Bhutan	
Thimphu	8,900
Brunei	
Band. Seri Begawan	51,000
Cambodia	
Phnom Penh	800,000
China	
Shanghai	7,500,000
Hong Kong	6,502,000
Beijing	5,700,000
Tianjin	4,500,000
Shenyang	3,600,000
Wuhan	3,200,000
Guangzhou	2,900,000
Chongqing	2,700,000
Harbin	2,500,000
Chengdu	2,500,000
Zibo	2,200,000
Xi'an	2,200,000
Nanjing	2,091,000
Cyprus	
Nicosia	193,000
India	(metro)
Mumbai	
(Bombay)	12,572,000
Kolkata	
(Calcutta)	10,916,000
Delhi	8,375,000
Madras	5,361,000
Hyderabad	4,280,000
Bangalore	4,087,000
Indonesia	
Jakarta	9,113,000
Surabaya	2,664,000
Bandung	2,356,000
Medan	1,844,000
Iran	
Tehran	6,750,000
Mashhad	1,964,000
Iraq	(metro)
Baghdad	4,336,000
Israel	
Jerusalem	585,000
Japan	
Tokyo	7,968,000
Yokohama	3,320,000
Osaka	2,600,000
Nagoya	2,151,000
Sapporo	1,774,000
Kyoto	1,464,000
Kobe	1,420,000
Fukuoka	1,296,000
Kawasaki	1,209,000
Hiroshima	1,115,000
Jordan	(metro)
Amman	1,183,000
Kazakhstan	
Almaty	
(Alma-Ata)	1,064,000
North Korea	
P'yŏngyang	2,741,000

South Korea	
Seoul	10,231,000
Pusan	3,814,000
Taegu	2,449,000
Kuwait	
Kuwait	29,000
Kyrgyzstan	
Bishkek	589,000
Laos	
Vientiane	377,000
Lebanon	(metro)
Beirut	1,826,000
Malaysia	(metro)
Kuala Lumpur	1,236,000
Maldives	
Male	55,000
Mongolia	
Ulaanbaatar	536,000
Myanmar (Burma)	(metro)
Yangon	
(Rangoon)	3,873,000
Nepal	
Kathmandu	419,000
Oman	
Muscat	85,000
Pakistan	(metro)
Karachi	5,181,000
Lahore	2,953,000
Faisalabad	1,104,000
Islamabad	204,000
Philippines	
Manila	1,655,000
Qatar	
Doha	236,000
Russia (Asian)	
Novosibirsk	1,368,000
Yekaterinburg	1,277,000
Omsk	1,161,000
Chelyabinsk	1,084,000
Saudi Arabia	(metro)
Riyadh	2,619,000
Jeddah	1,492,000
Singapore	
Singapore	3,737,000
Sri Lanka	
Colombo	615,000
Syria	
Damascus	1,549,000
Halab (Aleppo)	1,542,000
Taiwan	
Taipei	1,770,000
Tajikistan	
Dushanbe	529,000
Thailand	(metro)
Bangkok	6,547,000
Turkey (Asian)	
Ankara	2,938,000
İzmir	2,130,000
Turkmenistan	
Ashgabat	407,000
United Arab Emirates	
Abu Dhabi (metro)	799,000
Uzbekistan	(metro)
Tashkent	2,282,000
Vietnam	(metro)
Ho Chi Minh City	3,521,000
Hanoi	1,236,000
Yemen	(metro)
Sanaa	927,000

International comparability of city population data is limited by various data inconsistencies.

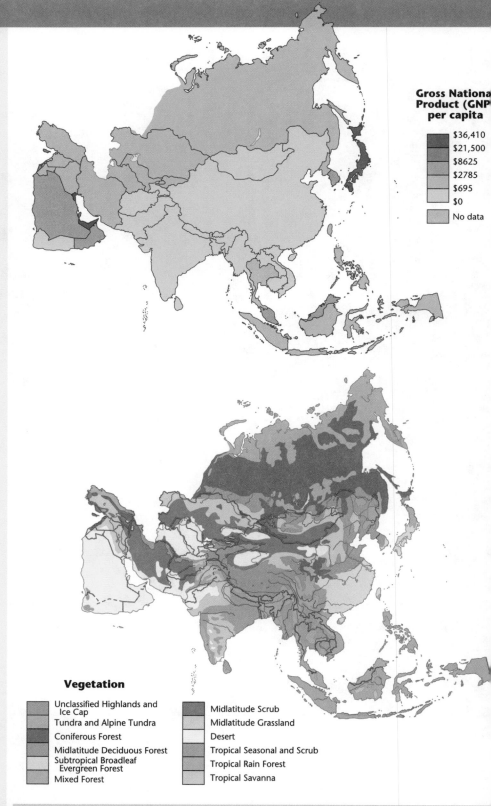

Gross National Product (GNP) per capita

- $36,410
- $21,500
- $8625
- $2785
- $695
- $0
- No data

Vegetation

- Unclassified Highlands and Ice Cap
- Tundra and Alpine Tundra
- Coniferous Forest
- Midlatitude Deciduous Forest
- Subtropical Broadleaf Evergreen Forest
- Mixed Forest
- Midlatitude Scrub
- Midlatitude Grassland
- Desert
- Tropical Seasonal and Scrub
- Tropical Rain Forest
- Tropical Savanna

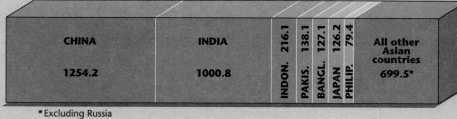

Asia: Population, by nation (in millions)*

CHINA	INDIA	INDON.	PAKIS.	BANGL.	JAPAN	PHILIP.	All other Asian countries
1254.2	1000.8	216.1	138.1	127.1	126.2	79.4	699.5*

*Excluding Russia

© MapQuest.com, Inc.

CLIMATE

Average daily temperature °F range — High / Low
Average monthly precipitation Inches

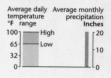

ALMATY, Kazakhstan

BEIRUT, Lebanon

COLOMBO, Sri Lanka
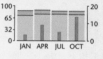

DHAKA, Bangladesh
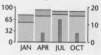

HONG KONG, China
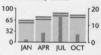

JAKARTA, Indonesia
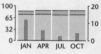

NEW DELHI, India
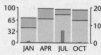

RIYADH, Saudi Arabia
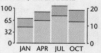

TEHRAN, Iran

TIANJIN, China
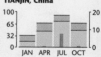

TOKYO, Japan
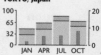

YAKUTSK, Russia
Temp. Range -53 to -45
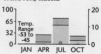

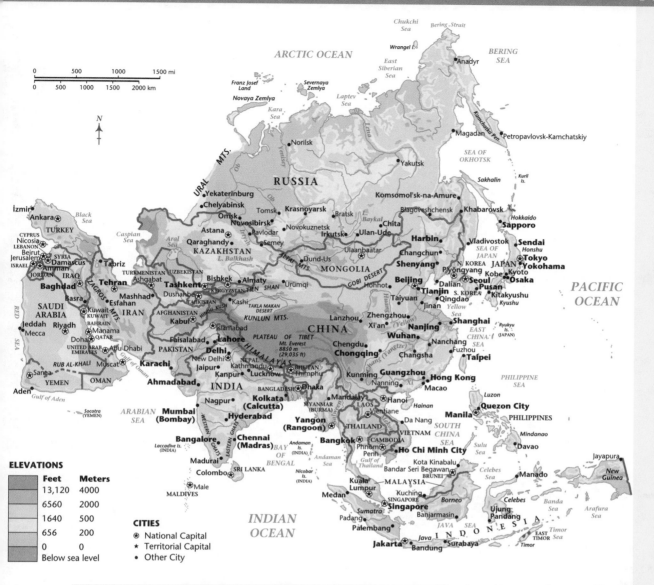

ELEVATIONS

Feet	Meters
13,120	4000
6560	2000
1640	500
656	200
0	0
Below sea level	

CITIES
⊛ National Capital
★ Territorial Capital
• Other City

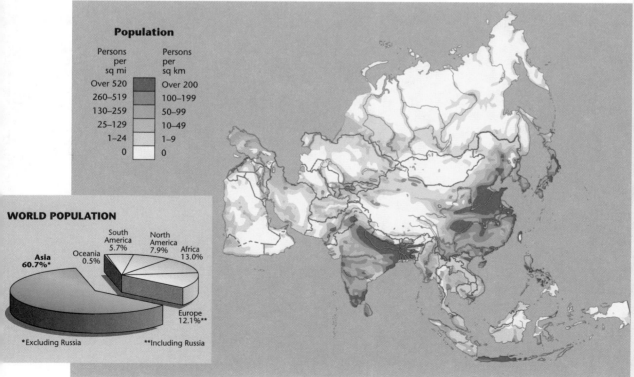

Population

Persons per sq mi	Persons per sq km
Over 520	Over 200
260–519	100–199
130–259	50–99
25–129	10–49
1–24	1–9
0	0

WORLD POPULATION

Asia 60.7%*
Oceania 0.5%
South America 5.7%
North America 7.9%
Africa 13.0%
Europe 12.1%**

*Excluding Russia
**Including Russia

Japan

- ⊛ National Capital
- • Other City

1:7,500,000

| 0 | 50 | 100 | 150 mi |
| 0 | 50 | 100 | 150 km |

Lambert Conformal Conic Projection

same scale as main map

Sea of Okhotsk

HOKKAIDO

Asahi Dake 2290 m (7513 ft)

HIDAKA MTS.

Sea of Japan

SOUTH KOREA

HONSHU

Zao 1841 m (6040 ft)

Asama 2542 m (8340 ft)

Yariga 3180 m (10,433 ft)

Shirane 3192 m (10,472 ft)

Fuji 3776 m (12,388 ft)

PACIFIC OCEAN

KYUSHU

Aso 1592 m (5223 ft)

SHIKOKU

Ishizuchi 1981 m (6499 ft)

East China Sea

RYUKYU ISLANDS (see inset)

Bonin Is. (see inset)

RYUKYU ISLANDS

Japan
Capital: Tokyo
Area: 145,850 sq. mi.
377,850 sq. km.
Population: 126,182,000
Largest City: Tokyo
Language: Japanese
Monetary Unit: Yen

© MapQuest.com, Inc.

Japan:
Map Index

Prefectures
Aichi C3
Akita D2
Aomori D1
Chiba D3
Ehime B3
Fukui C2
Fukuoka A3
Fukushima C2
Gifu C3

Gumma C2
Hiroshima B3
Hokkaido ....D1, Inset I
Hyogo B3
Ibaraki D2
Ishikawa C2
Iwate D2
Kagawa B3
Kagoshima A4
Kanagawa C3
Kochi B3
Kumamoto A3
Kyoto C3

Mie C3
Miyagi D2
Miyazaki A3
Nagano C2
Nagasaki A3
Nara B3
Niigata C2
Oita A3
Okayama B3
Okinawa ......Inset II
Osaka B3
Saga A3
Saitama C2

Shiga C3
Shimane B3
Shizuoka C3
Tochigi C2
Tokushima B3
Tokyo C3
Tottori B3
Toyama C2
Wakayama B3
Yamagata D2
Yamaguchi A3
Yamanashi C3

Cities and Towns
Aizuwakamatsu C2
Akashi B3
Akita D1
Amagasaki B3
Aomori D1
Asahikawa ......Inset I
Ashikaga C2
Awaji B3
Chiba D3
Chitose ....Inset I
Fujisawa C3
Fukue A3
Fukui C2
Fukuoka A3
Fukushima D2
Fukuyama B3
Funabashi C3
Gifu C3
Gotsu B3
Gushikawa ......Inset II
Haboro ....Inset I
Hachinohe D1
Hachioji C3
Hakodate ......D1, Inset I
Hamamatsu C3
Higashiosaka B3
Himeji B3
Hirakata B3
Hirara ....Inset II
Hirosake D1
Hiroshima B3
Hitachi D2
Ibaraki B3
Ichihara D3
Ichikawa C3
Ichinomiya C3
Ise C3
Ishinomaki D2
Iwaki D2
Iwakuni B3
Izuhara A3
Joetsu C2
Kagoshima A4
Kanazawa C2
Kashiwa D3
Kasugai C3
Kawagoe C3
Kawaguchi C3
Kawasaki C3
Kitakyushu A3
Kitami ....Inset I
Kobe B3
Kochi B3
Kofu C3
Komatsu C2
Koriyama D2
Koshigaya C3
Kumamoto A3
Kurashiki B3
Kure B3
Kurume A3
Kushiro ....Inset I
Kyoto B3
Machida C3
Maebashi C2
Maizuru B3
Masuda A3
Matsudo C3
Matsue B3
Matsumae ......D1, Inset I
Matsumoto C2
Matsuyama B3
Mito D2
Miyako D2
Miyakonojo A4
Miyazaki A4
Mombetsu ......Inset I
Morioka D2
Muroran ......D1, Inset I
Mutsu D1
Nagano C2
Nagaoka C2
Nagasaki A3
Nagoya C3
Naha ....Inset II
Nara B3
Naze ....Inset II
Nemuro ....Inset I
Neyagawa B3
Niigata C2
Niihama B3
Nikko C2
Nishinomiya B3
Nobeoka A3
Numazu C3
Obihiro ....Inset I
Oita A3
Okayama B3
Okazaki C3
Omiya C3
Omuta A3
Osaka B3
Otaru ....Inset I
Otsu B3
Ryotsu C2
Saga A3
Sagamihara B3
Sakai B3
Sapporo ....Inset I
Sasebo A3
Sendai D2
Shimizu C3
Shimonoseki A3
Shizuoka C3
Suita B3
Takamatsu B3
Takatsuki B3
Tanabe B3
Tokorozawa C3
Tokushima B3
Tokuyama A3
Tokyo, capital C3
Tomakomai ......Inset I
Tottori B3
Toyama C2
Toyohashi C3
Toyonaka B3
Toyota C3
Tsuruga C2
Tsuruoka C2
Ube A3
Urawa C3
Utsunomiya C3
Uwajima A3
Wakayama B3
Wakkanai ....Inset I
Yamagata D2
Yamaguchi A3
Yao B3
Yatsushiro A3

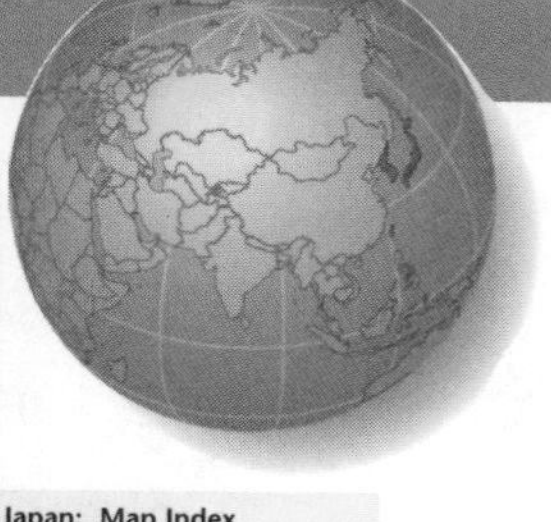

Japan: Map Index
Yokkaichi C3
Yokohama......................C3
Yokosuka C3
Yonago B3
Yubari ....Inset I

Other Features
Akuseki, *island*...................A4
Amakusa, *islands*................A3
Amami, *island*..............Inset II
Amami, *islands* ....Inset II
Asahi Dake, *mt.* ....Inset I
Asama, *mt.* C2
Ashizuri, *cape* B3
Aso, *mt.* A3
Awaji, *island* B3
Biwa, *lake* B3
Bonin, *islands*............Inset III
Boso, *peninsula*..................D3
Bungo, *channel*...................B3
Chichi, *island* ....Inset III
Chugoku, *mts.* B3
Dogo, *island* B2
Dozen, *island* B2
East China, *sea* A4
Erimo, *cape* ....Inset I
Fuji, *mt.* C3
Fukue, *island*........................A3
Hachijo, *island* C3
Haha, *island*.................Inset III
Henashi, *cape* C1
Hidaka, *mts.*.................Inset I
Hino, *cape*............................B3
Hokkaido, *island* ....D1, Inset I
Honshu, *island* C2
Iki, *island*..............................A3
Inland, *sea* B3
Iriomote, *island*...........Inset II
Ise, *bay*.................................C3
Ishigaki, *island*.............Inset II
Ishikari, *river*.................Inset I
Ishinomaki, *bay* D2
Ishizuchi, *mt.*........................B3
Iwo Jima, *island* ....Inset III
Izu, *islands* C3
Izu, *peninsula* C3
Japan, *sea* B2
Japanese Alps, *mts.* C3
Kakeroma, *island*..........Inset II
Kamui, *cape*...................Inset I
Kii, *channel* B3
Kii, *peninsula* B3
Kita, *island* ....Inset III
Kitakami, *river*......................D2
Kitami, *mts.* ....Inset I
Korea, *strait* A3
Koshiki, *islands* A4
Kozu, *island* C3
Kuchino, *island* A4
Kume, *island* ....Inset II
Kyushu, *island*......................A3
La Pérouse, *strait* ....Inset I
Mikura, *island* C3
Minami, *island* ....Inset III
Miyake, *island*.......................C3
Miyako, *island*.............Inset II
Mogami, *river*.......................D2
Muko, *island* ....Inset III
Muroto, *cape* B3
Nakadori, *island* A3
Nakano, *island* A4
Nemuro, *strait* ....Inset I
Nii, *island* C3
Nishino, *island* ....Inset III
Nojima, *cape* D3
Noto, *peninsula* C2
Okhotsk, *sea* ....Inset I
Oki, *islands* B2
Okinawa, *island* ....Inset II
Okinawa, *islands* ....Inset II
Okino Erabu, *island*......Inset II
Okushiri, *island* ......C1, Inset I
Oshima, *peninsula*..D1, Inset I
Osumi, *islands*......................A4
Osumi, *peninsula*..................A4
Osumi, *strait*.........................A4
Ou, *mts.*...............................D2
Rebun, *island*................Inset I
Rishiri, *island* ....Inset I
Ryukyu, *islands* ......A4, Inset II
Sado, *island* C2
Sagami, *bay* C3
Sakishima, *islands* ....Inset II
Sata, *cape* A4
Satsuma, *peninsula* A4
Senkaku, *islands* ....Inset II
Shikoku, *island* B3
Shimonoseki, *strait* A3
Shinano, *river* C2
Shiono, *cape* B3
Shirane, *mt.* C3
Shiretoko, *cape* ....Inset I
Soya, *point*....................Inset I
Suwanose, *island*..................A4
Takara, *island* A4
Tanega, *island*.......................A4
Tenryu, *river* C3
Teshio, *river* ....Inset I
Tokachi, *river* ....Inset I
Tokara, *islands*.....................A4
Tokuno, *island*.............Inset II
Tone, *river*............................C2
Tosa, *bay*..............................B3
Towada, *lake* D1
Toyama, *bay* C2
Tsu, *island* A3
Tsugaru, *strait* ....D1, Inset I
Uchiura, *bay* ....Inset I
Volcano, *islands* ....Inset III
Wakasa, *bay* B3
Yaku, *island*..........................A4
Yariga, *mt.* C2
Yonaguni, *island* ....Inset II
Yoron, *island* ....Inset II
Yoshino, *river*.......................B3
Zao, *mt.*................................D2

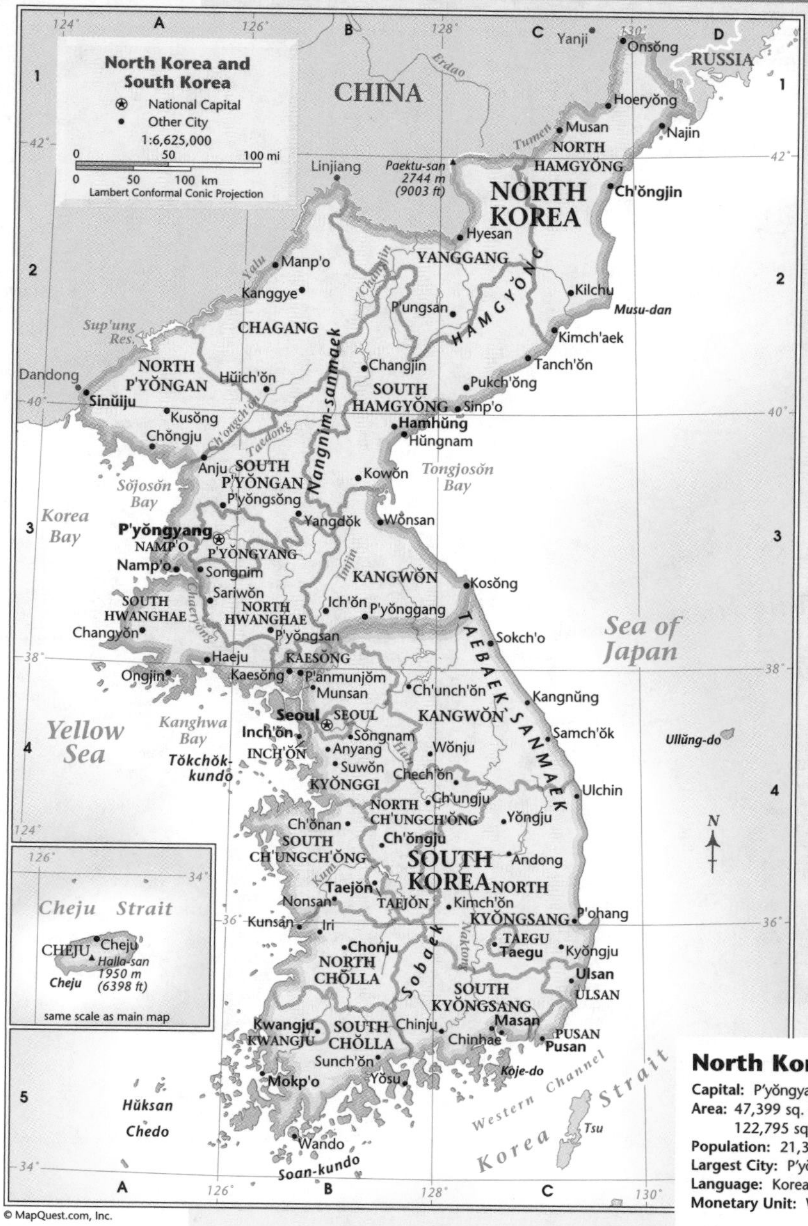

North Korea and South Korea
National Capital
Other City
1:6,625,000
0 50 100 mi
0 50 100 km
Lambert Conformal Conic Projection
CHINA
RUSSIA
NORTH KOREA
SOUTH KOREA
Korea Bay
Yellow Sea
Sea of Japan
Korea Strait
Western Channel
Cheju Strait
same scale as main map

© MapQuest.com, Inc.

North Korea: Map Index

Provinces
Chagang B2
Kaesŏng B3
Kangwŏn..............................B3
Namp'o.................................A3
North Hamgyŏng C1
North Hwanghae...................B3
North P'yŏngan A2
P'yŏngyang..........................A3
South Hamgyŏng..................B2
South Hwanghae...................A3
South P'yŏngan....................B3
Yanggang B2

Cities and Towns
Anju A3
Changjin B2
Changyŏn A3
Ch'ŏngjin C2
Chŏngju A3
Haeju A3
Hamhŭng B3
Hoeryŏng C1
Hŭich'ŏn B2
Hŭngnam B3
Hyesan C2
Ich'ŏn B3
Kaesŏng B4
Kanggye B2
Kilchu C2
Kimch'aek C2
Kosŏng C3
Kowŏn B3
Kusŏng A3
Manp'o B2
Musan C1
Najin D1
Namp'o A3
Ongjin A4
Onsŏng C1
P'anmunjŏm B4
Pukch'ŏng C2
P'ungsan C2
P'yŏnggang B3
P'yŏngsan B3
P'yŏngsŏng A3
P'yŏngyang, *capital*..............A3
Sariwŏn A3
Sinp'o C2
Sinŭiju A2
Songnim A3
Tanch'ŏn C2
Wŏnsan B3
Yangdŏk B3

Other Features
Chaeryŏng, *river* A3
Changjin, *river* B2
Ch'ongch'ŏn, *river*................A3
Hamgyŏng, *mts.* C2
Imjin, *river* B3
Kanghwa, *bay* A4
Korea, *bay*............................A3
Musu-dan, *point* C2
Nangnim-sanmaek, *mts.*.......B3
Paektu-san, *mt.* C2
Sŏjosŏn, *bay* A3
Sup'ung, *reservoir* A2
Taedong, *river* B3
Tongjosŏn, *bay* B3
Tumen, *river* C1
Yalu, *river*............................B2

South Korea: Map Index

Provinces
Cheju ....Inset
Inch'ŏn B4
Kangwŏn...............................B4
Kwangju B5
Kyŏnggi B4
North Chŏlla B5
North Ch'ungch'ŏng B4
North Kyŏngsang C4
Pusan C5
Seoul B4
South Chŏlla B5
South Ch'ungch'ŏng B4
South Kyŏngsang C5
Taegu C5
Taejŏn B4
Ulsan C5

Cities and Towns
Andong..................................C4
Anyang B4
Chech'ŏn C4
Cheju ....Inset
Chinhae.................................C5
Chinju C5
Chonju B5
Ch'ŏnan B4
Ch'ŏngju B4
Ch'unch'ŏn B4
Ch'ungju B4
Inch'ŏn B4
Iri B5
Kangnŭng C4
Kimch'ŏn C4
Kunsan B5
Kwangju B5
Kyŏngju C5
Masan C5
Mokp'o B5
Munsan B4
Nonsan B4
P'ohang C4
Pusan C5
Samch'ŏk C4
Seoul, *capital*.......................B4
Sokch'o C3
Sŏngnam B4
Sunch'ŏn B5
Suwŏn B4
Taegu C5
Taejŏn B4
Ulchin C4
Ulsan C5
Wŏnju B4
Wando B5
Yŏngju C4
Yŏsu B5

Other Features
Cheju, *island*....................Inset
Cheju, *strait* ....Inset
Halla-san, *mt.* ....Inset
Han, *river* B4
Hŭksan Chedo, *islands*.........A5
Kanghwa, *bay*......................A4
Koje-do, *island* C5
Korea, *strait*.........................C5
Kum, *river* B4
Naktong, *river*......................C5
Soan-kundo, *islands* B5
Sobaek, *mts.* B5
Taebaek-Sanmaek, *mts.* C3
Tŏkchŏk-kundo, *islands* A4
Ullŭng-do, *island*..................D4
Western, *channel* C5

North Korea

Capital: P'yŏngyang
Area: 47,399 sq. mi.
122,795 sq. km.
Population: 21,386,000
Largest City: P'yŏngyang
Language: Korean
Monetary Unit: Won

South Korea

Capital: Seoul
Area: 38,330 sq. mi.
99,301 sq. km.
Population: 46,885,000
Largest City: Seoul
Language: Korean
Monetary Unit: Won

Taiwan
National Capital
Other City
1:10,292,000
0 30 60 mi
0 30 60 km
Lambert Conformal Conic Projection
CHINA
East China Sea
Taiwan Strait
South China Sea
Philippine Sea
Luzon Strait

© MapQuest.com, Inc.

Taiwan

Capital: Taipei
Area: 13,969 sq. mi.
36,189 sq. km.
Population: 22,113,000
Largest City: Taipei
Language: Mandarin Chinese
Monetary Unit: New Taiwan dollar

Taiwan: Map Index

Cities and Towns
Changhua..............................B1
Chiai B2
Chilung B1
Chunan B1
Chungho B1
Chungli B1
Fangliao B2
Fengshan B2
Fengyüan..............................B1
Hengch'un.............................B2
Hsinchu B1
Hsinchuang B1
Hsintien B1
Hsinying B2
Hualien B2
Ilan B1
Kangshan..............................B2
Kaohsiung.............................B2
Makung A2
Miaoli B1
Nant'ou B2
Panch'iao B1
P'ingtung...............................B2
Shanchung B1
T'aichung B1
T'ainan B2
Taipei, *capital*.......................B1
T'aitung B2
Tanshui B1
T'aoyüan................................B1
Touliu B2
Yungho B1

Other Features
Choshui, *river*........................B2
Chungyang, *range*..................B2
East China, *sea*......................B1
Kaop'ing, *river* B2
Lan, *island* B2
Lü, *island* B2
Luzon, *strait* B3
P'enghu (Pescadores), *islands*...............................A2
Pescadores, *channel*...............A2
Philippine, *sea*........................B2
South China, *sea* A2
Taiwan, *strait* A1
Tanshui, *river*...........................B1
Tsengwen, *river*........................B2
Yü Shan, *mt.* B2

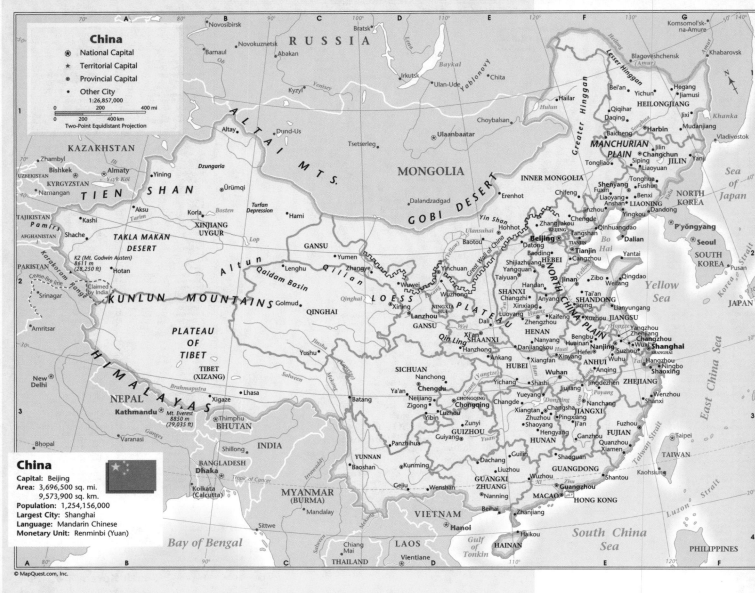

China

- ⊕ National Capital
- ★ Territorial Capital
- ⊛ Provincial Capital
- • Other City

1:26,857,000

0   200   400 mi

0 200 400 km

Two-Point Equidistant Projection

China

Capital: Beijing
Area: 3,696,500 sq. mi.
9,573,900 sq. km.
Population: 1,254,156,000
Largest City: Shanghai
Language: Mandarin Chinese
Monetary Unit: Renminbi (Yuan)

© MapQuest.com, Inc.

Hong Kong S.A.R.

- • City

1:1,800,000

0   10   20 mi

0 10 20 km

Transverse Mercator Projection

© MapQuest.com, Inc.

China:
Map Index

Internal Divisions
Provinces
Anhui E2
Fujian E3
Gansu C1, D2
Guangdong E3
Guizhou D3
Hainan D4
Hebei E2
Heilongjiang F1
Henan E2
Hubei E3
Hunan E3
Jiangsu E2
Jiangxi E3
Jilin F1
Liaoning F1
Qinghai C2
Shaanxi D2
Shandong E2
Shanxi D2
Sichuan D2
Yunnan C3
Zhejiang E3

Autonomous Regions
Guangxi Zhuang D3
Inner Mongolia E1
Ningxia Hui D2
Tibet (Xizang) B2
Xinjiang Uygur B1

Independent Municipalities
Beijing E1
Chongqing D3
Shanghai F2
Tianjin E2

**Special Administrative
Regions (S.A.R.)**
Hong Kong ....E3, Inset
Macao E3

Cities and Towns
Aberdeen ....Inset
Aksu B1
Altay B1
Ankang D2
Anqing E2
Anshan F1

Anyang E2
Baicheng F1
Baoding E2
Baoshan C3
Baotou E1
Batang C3
Bei'an F1
Beihai D3
Beijing, capital E2
Bengbu E2
Benxi F1
Cangzhou E2
Changchun F1
Changde E3
Changsha E3
Changzhi E2
Changzhou F2
Chek Keng ....Inset
Chengde E1
Chengdu D2
Chifeng E1
Chongqing D3
Chung Hau ....Inset
Dachang D3
Dali D3
Dalian F2
Dandong F1
Danjiangkou E2
Daqing F1
Datong E1
Erenhot E1
Fushun F1
Fuxin F1
Fuzhou E3
Ganzhou E3
Gejiu D3
Golmud C2
Guangzhou E3
Guilin D3
Guiyang D3
Haikou E4
Hailar E1
Hami C1
Handan E2
Hangzhou F2
Hanzhong D2
Harbin F1
Hefei E2
Hegang G1
Hengyang E3
Hohhot E1
Hotan A2

Huainan E2
Jiamusi G1
Ji'an E3
Jilin F1
Jinan E2
Jingdezhen E3
Jinzhou F1
Jiujiang E3
Jixi G1
Kaifeng E2
Kashi A2
Korla B1
Kowloon ....Inset
Kunming D3
Lanzhou D2
Lenghu C2
Lhasa C3
Lianyungang E2
Liaoyang F1
Liaoyuan F1
Liuzhou D3
Lo Wu ....Inset
Luoyang E2
Luzhou D3
Mudanjiang G1
Nanchang E3
Nanchong D2
Nanjing E2
Nanning D3
Nanyang E2
Neijiang D2
New Kowloon ....Inset
Ningbo F3
Panzhihua D3
Pingxiang E3
Qingdao F2
Qinhuangdao F2
Qiqihar F1
Quanzhou E3
Sai Kung ....Inset
Shache A2
Shanghai F2
Shantou E3
Shanxi E3
Shaoguan E3
Shaoxing E3
Shaoyang E3
Sha Tin ....Inset
Shek Pik ....Inset
Shenyang F1

Shijiazhuang E2
Siping F1
Suzhou F2
Tai'an E2
Taiyuan E2
Tangshan E2
Tianjin E2
Tonghua F1
Tongliao E2
Tsuen Wan ....Inset
Tuen Mun ....Inset
Ürümqi B1
Weifang E2
Wenshan D3
Wenzhou F3
Wuhan E2
Wuhu E2
Wuwei D2
Wuxi F2
Wuzhong D2
Xiamen E3
Xi'an D2
Xiangfan E2
Xiangtan E3
Xigaze B3
Xining D2
Xinxiang E2
Xinyang E2
Xuzhou E2
Ya'an D2
Yangquan E2
Yangzhou E2
Yanji F1
Yantai F2
Yibin D3
Yichang E2
Yichun F1
Yinchuan D2
Yingkou F1
Yining B1
Yuen Long ....Inset
Yueyang E3
Yumen C2
Yushu C2
Zhangjiakou E2
Zhangye D2
Zhanjiang D3
Zhengzhou E2
Zhenjiang E2
Zhuzhou E3
Zibo E2

Zigong D3
Zunyi D3

Other Features
Altai, mts. B1
Altun, range B2
Bayan Har, range C2
Bo Hai, gulf E2
Bosten, lake B1
Brahmaputra, river B3
Chang (Yangtze), river .D2, E2
Deep, bay ....Inset
Dongting, lake E3
Dzungaria, desert basin B1
East China, sea F3
Fen, river E2
Gan, river E3
Gobi, desert D1
Greater Hinggan, range F1
Great Wall of China D2
Han, river E2
Heilong (Amur), river F1
Himalayas, mts. B3
Hong Kong, island ......Inset
Hongze, lake E2
Huai, river E2
Huang (Yellow), river ..D2, E2
Hulun, lake E1
Indus, river A2
Jinsha (Yangtze), river C2
Khanka, lake G1
Kunlun, mts. B2
K2 (Godwin Austen), mt. ..A2
Lantau, island ....Inset
Lesser Hinggan, range F1
Liao, river F1
Loess, plateau D2
Lop, lake C1
Manchurian, plain F1
Mekong, river C3
Nan Ling, mts. E3
New Territories, island ..Inset
North China, plain E2
Pamirs, region A2
Poyang, lake E3
Qaidam, basin C2
Qilian, range C2
Qinghai, lake C2
Qin Ling, mts. D2
Salween, river C3
Songhua, river F1
South China, sea ......E4, Inset

Stonecutters (S.I.), island ..Inset
Tai, lake F2
Taiwan, strait E3
Takla Makan, desert B2
Tanggula, range C2
Tarim, river B1
Tibet, plateau B2
Tien Shan, range A1
Tonkin, gulf D4
Turfan, depression C1
Ulansuhai, lake D1
Wei, river E3
Xi, river E3
Yalu, river F1
Yangtze, river C2, D2
Yellow, sea F2
Yin Shan, mts. E1
Yuan, river D3
Zhu, river E3

Vietnam:
Map Index

Cities and Towns
Bac Lieu A5
Bien Hoa B4
Buon Me Thuot B4
Ca Mau A5
Cam Ranh B4
Can Tho A4
Cao Bang B1
Chau Doc A4
Da Lat B4
Da Nang B3
Dien Bien Phu A2
Dong Hoi B3
Ha Giang A1
Haiphong B2
Hanoi, capital A2
Hoa Binh A2
Ho Chi Minh City B4
Hon Gai B2
Hue B3
Khe Sanh B3
Kontum B3
Lang Son B2
Lao Cai A1
Long Xuyen A4
My Tho B4
Nam Dinh B2
Nha Trang B4
Phan Rang B4
Phan Thiet B4
Pleiku B4
Quang Ngai B3
Quang Tri B3
Qui Nhon B4
Rach Gia A4
Soc Trang A5
Son La A2
Tay Ninh B4
Thai Nguyen A2

Thanh Hoa A2
Tuy Hoa B4
Viet Tri A2
Vinh A2
Vung Tau-Con Dao B4
Yen Bai A2

Other Features
Annam, mts. A2
Ba, river B3
Black (Da), river A2
Ca, river A2
Central, highlands B4
Con Son, islands B5
Cu Lao Thu, island B4
Dao Phu Quoc, island A4
Dong Nai, river B4
Fan Si Pan, mt. A1
Gam, river A1
Lo, river A1
Ma, river A2
Mekong, delta B5
Mekong, river A4
Mui Bai Bung, point A5
Ngoc Linh, mt. B3
Red (Hong), river A2
Tonkin, gulf B2

Vietnam

Capital: Hanoi
Area: 127,246 sq. mi.
    329,653 sq. km.
Population: 77,311,000
Largest City: Ho Chi Minh City
Language: Vietnamese
Monetary Unit: Dong

Vietnam
- ⊛ National Capital
- • Other City

1:14,333,000

0 50 100 150 200 mi
0 50 100 150 200 km

Lambert Conformal Conic Projection

Laos:
Map Index

Cities and Towns
Attapu D4
Ban Houayxay A1
Champasak C4
Louang Namtha A1
Luang Prabang B2
Muang Khammouan C3
Muang Khong C4
Muang Khôngxédôn C4
Muang Paklay A2
Muang Pakxan B2
Muang Vangviang B2
Muang Xaignabouri A2
Muang Xay A1
Muang Xépôn D3
Muang Xon B1
Pakse C4
Phôngsali B1
Saravan D4
Savannakhet C3
Vientiane, capital B2
Xam Nua B1
Xiangkhoang B2

Other Features
Annam, range C3
Banghiang, river C3
Bolovens, plateau D4
Kong, river D4
Luang Prabang, range A3
Mekong, river A1, C3
Nam Ngum, reservoir B2
Ou, river B1
Phou Bia, mt. B2
Xiangkhoang, plateau B2

Laos

Capital: Vientiane
Area: 91,429 sq. mi.
    236,085 sq. km.
Population: 5,407,000
Largest City: Vientiane
Language: Lao
Monetary Unit: New kip

Laos
- ⊛ National Capital
- • Other City

1:14,533,000

0 50 100 mi
0 50 100 km

Lambert Conformal Conic Projection

© MapQuest.com, Inc.

Mongolia

Capital: Ulaanbaatar
Area: 604,800 sq. mi.
    1,566,839 sq. km.
Population: 2,617,000
Largest City: Ulaanbaatar
Language: Mongolian
Monetary Unit: Tughrik

Mongolia:
Map Index

Cities and Towns
Altay B2
Arvayheer C2
Baruun-Urt D2
Bayanhongor C2
Bulgan C2
Buyant-Uhaa D3
Choybalsan D2
Dalandzadgad C3
Darhan C2
Dund-Us B2

Erdenet C2
Mandalgovĭ C2
Mörön C2
Ölgiy A2
Öndörhaan D2
Sühbaatar C2
Tamsagbulag D2
Tsetserleg C2
Ulaangom B2
Ulaan-Uul C2
Ulaanbaatar, capital C2
Uliastay B2

Other Features
Altai, mts. B2
Bööntsagaan, lake B2
Dörgön, lake B2
Dzavhan, river B2
Gobi, desert C3
Hangayn, mts. B2
Har Us, lake B2
Hovd, river B2
Hövsgöl, lake C1
Hyargas, lake B2
Ih Bogd Uul, mt. C3
Kerulen, river D2
Mongolian, plateau C2
Onon, river D2
Orhon, river C2
Selenge Mörön, river C2
Tavan Bogd Uul, mt. A2
Tesiyn, river B2
Tuul, river C2
Uvs, lake B1

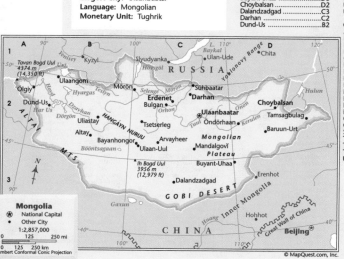

Mongolia
- ⊛ National Capital
- • Other City

1:2,857,000

0 125 250 mi
0 125 250 km

Lambert Conformal Conic Projection

© MapQuest.com, Inc.

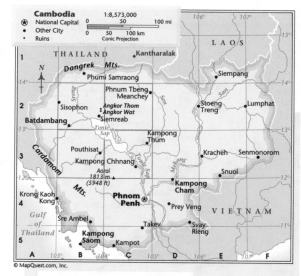

Cambodia
- ⊛ National Capital
- • Other City
- • Ruins

1:8,573,000

0 50 100 mi
0 50 100 km

Conic Projection

© MapQuest.com, Inc.

Cambodia

Capital: Phnom Penh
Area: 70,238 sq. mi.
    181,964 sq. km.
Population: 11,627,000
Largest City: Phnom Penh
Language: Khmer
Monetary Unit: New riel

Cambodia:
Map Index

Cities and Towns
Batdambang B2
Kampong Cham D4
Kampong Chhnang C3
Kampong Saom B5
Kampong Thum C3
Kampot C5
Kracheh E3
Krong Kaoh Kong B4
Lumphat F2
Phnom Penh, capital C4
Phnum Tbeng Meanchey C2
Phumi Samraong B1
Pouthisat B3

Prey Veng D4
Senmonorom F3
Siempang E1
Siemreab B2
Sisophon B2
Snuol E3
Sre Ambel B2
Stoeng Treng D2
Svay Rieng D4
Takev C5

Other Features
Angkor Thom, ruins B2
Angkor Wat, ruins B2
Aoral, mt. C3
Cardamom, mts. A3
Dangrek, mts. B1
Mekong, river D3
San, river E2
Sen, river D2
Sreng, river B2
Thailand, gulf A4
Tonle Sap, lake B2, C3
Tonle Sap, river B3

Thailand

Capital: Bangkok
Area: 198,115 sq. mi.
513,251 sq. km.
Population: 60,609,000
Largest City: Bangkok
Language: Thai
Monetary Unit: Baht

Thailand: Map Index

Cities and Towns

Aranyaprathet	C3
Bangkok, *capital*	B3
Ban Phai	C2
Buriram	C3
Chaiyaphum	C3
Chiang Mai	B2
Chiang Rai	B2
Chon Buri	B3
Chumphon	B4
Hat Yai	B5
Hua Hin	B3
Khon Kaen	C2
Lampang	B2
Lamphun	B2
Loei	B2
Lop Buri	B3
Nakhon Phanom	C2
Nakhon Ratchasima	C3
Nakhon Sawan	B3
Nakhon Si Thammarat	B4
Nam Tok	B3
Nan	B2
Narathiwat	B5
Nong Khai	C2
Nonthaburi	B3
Pattani	B5
Phatthalung	B4
Phayao	B2
Phetchabun	B2
Phetchaburi	B3
Phichit	B2
Phitsanulok	B2
Phrae	B2
Phra Nakhon Si Ayutthaya	B3
Phuket	B5
Prachuap Khiri Khan	B4
Ranong	B4
Ratchaburi	B3
Rayong	B3
Roi Et	C2
Sakon Nakhon	C2
Sara Buri	B3
Sattahip	B3
Sisaket	C3
Songkhla	B5
Sukhothai	B2
Surat Thani	B4
Surin	C3
Tak	B2
Takua Pa	B4
Trang	B5
Trat	C3
Ubon Ratchathani	C3
Udon Thani	C2
Uttaradit	B2
Yala	B5

Other Features

Bilauktaung, *range*	B3
Chao Phraya, *river*	B3
Chi, *river*	C2
Dangrek, *mts.*	C3
Dawna, *range*	B2
Inthanon, *mt.*	B2
Khorat, *plateau*	C3
Ko Chang, *island*	C3
Ko Kut, *island*	C4
Ko Phangan, *island*	B4
Ko Samui, *island*	B4
Ko Tarutao, *island*	B5
Kra, *isthmus*	B4
Laem, *mt.*	B3
Lam Pao, *reservoir*	C2
Luang, *mt.*	B4
Mae Klong, *river*	B3
Malacca, *strait*	B5
Malay, *peninsula*	B4
Mekong, *river*	C2
Mun, *river*	C3
Nan, *river*	B2
Pa Sak, *river*	B3
Phetchabun, *range*	B3
Ping, *river*	B3
Salween, *river*	A2
Sirinthorn, *reservoir*	C3
Srinagarind, *reservoir*	B3
Tanen, *range*	B2
Thailand, *gulf*	B4
Thale Luang, *lagoon*	B5
Yom, *river*	B2

Thailand

⊛ National Capital
• Other City

1:14,667,000

0   100   200 km
0   100   200 mi

Lambert Conformal Conic Projection

© MapQuest.com, Inc.

Myanmar (Burma): Map Index

States and Divisions

Chin, *state*	B2
Irrawaddy, *division*	B3
Kachin, *state*	C1
Karen, *state*	C3
Kayah, *state*	C2
Magwe, *division*	B2
Mandalay, *division*	B2
Mon, *state*	C3
Pegu, *division*	B3
Rakhine, *state*	B2
Sagaing, *division*	B2
Shan, *state*	C2
Tenasserim, *division*	C3
Yangon (Rangoon), *division*	C3

Cities and Towns

Bassein	B3
Bhamo	C1
Haka	B2
Henzada	B3
Kawthaung	C4
Keng Tung	C2
Kyaukpyu	B2
Lashio	C2
Loi-kaw	C2
Mandalay	C2
Maymyo	C2
Meiktila	C2
Mergui	C3
Monywa	B2
Moulmein	C3
Myingyan	B2
Myitkyina	C1
Pa-an	C3
Pegu	C3
Prome	B2
Putao	C1
Sagaing	B2
Shwebo	B2
Sittwe	B2
Tamu	B1
Taunggyi	C2
Tavoy	C3
Toungoo	C2
Yangon (Rangoon), *capital*	C3
Ye	C3

Other Features

Andaman, *sea*	B3
Arakan Yoma, *mts.*	B2
Bengal, *bay*	B3
Bilauktaung, *range*	C3
Cheduba, *island*	B2
Chin, *hills*	B2
Chindwin, *river*	B1
Coco, *islands*	B3
Hkakabo Razi, *mt.*	C1
Irrawaddy, *river*	B2
Martaban, *gulf*	C3
Mekong, *river*	C2
Mergui, *archipelago*	C4
Mouths of the Irrawaddy, *delta*	B3
Preparis, *island*	B3
Ramree, *island*	B2
Salween, *river*	C2
Shan, *plateau*	C2
Sittang, *river*	C2
Tavoy, *point*	C3
Thailand, *gulf*	C4

Myanmar (Burma)

Capital: Yangon (Rangoon)
Area: 261,228 sq. mi.
676,756 sq. km.
Population: 48,081,000
Largest City: Yangon (Rangoon)
Language: Burmese
Monetary Unit: Kyat

Myanmar (Burma)

⊛ National Capital
• Other City

1:24,054,000

0   100   200 km
0   100   200 mi

Lambert Conformal Conic Projection

© MapQuest.com, Inc.

Philippines

⊛ National Capital
• Other City

1:16,000,000

0   100   200 km
0   100   200 mi

Lambert Conformal Conic Projection

Philippines

Capital: Manila
Area: 115,860 sq. mi.
300,155 sq. km.
Population: 79,346,000
Largest City: Manila
Languages: Pilipino, English
Monetary Unit: Philippine peso

Philippines: Map Index

Regions

Bicol	B3
Cagayan Valley	B2
Central Luzon	A3
Central Mindanao	C5
Central Visayas	B4
*Cordillera Autonomous Region	B2
Eastern Visayas	C4
Ilocos	C3
*Moslem Mindanao Autonomous Region	B5
National Capital Region	B3
Northern Mindanao	C4
Southern Mindanao	C5
Southern Tagalog	B3
Western Mindanao	B5
Western Visayas	B3

Cities and Towns

Angeles	B3
Bacolod	B4
Baguio	B3
Basilan	B5
Batangas	B3
Bislig	C4
Butuan	C4
Cabanatuan	B3
Cadiz	B4
Cagayan de Oro	C4
Calapan	B3
Calbayog	C3
Cebu	B4
Cotabato	C5
Dagupan	B2
Davao	C5
Dipolog	B4
Dumaguete	B4
General Santos	C5
Iligan	C4
Iloilo	B4
Jolo	B5
Laoag	B2
Laoang	C3
Legazpi	B3
Lipa	B3
Lucena	B3
Mamburao	B3
Mandaue	B4
Manila, *capital*	B3
Masbate	B3
Naga	B3
Olongapo	B3
Ormoc	C4
Pagadian	B5
Puerto Princesa	A4
Quezon City	B3
Roxas	B4
San Carlos	B4
San Fernando	B2
San Pablo	B3
Silay	B4
Surigao	C4
Tacloban	C4
Tuguegarao	B2
Vigan	B2
Zamboanga	B5

Other Features

Agusan, *river*	C4
Apo, *volcano*	C5
Babuyan, *channel*	B2
Babuyan, *islands*	B2
Balabac, *island*	A5
Balabac, *strait*	A5
Bashi, *channel*	B1
Basilan, *island*	B5
Bataan, *peninsula*	B3
Batan, *islands*	B1
Bohol, *island*	B4
Bohol, *sea*	C4
Cagayan, *islands*	B4
Cagayan, *river*	B2
Cagayan Sulu, *island*	A5
Calamian, *islands*	A3
Caramoan, *peninsula*	B3
Catanduanes, *island*	C3
Cebu, *island*	B4
Celebes, *sea*	B5
Cordillera Central, *mts.*	B2
Corregidor, *island*	B3
Cuyo, *islands*	B4
Davao, *gulf*	C5
Dinagat, *island*	C4
Diuata, *mts.*	C4
Jolo, *island*	B5
Laguna de Bay, *lake*	B3
Lamon, *bay*	B3
Leyte, *island*	C4
Lingayen, *gulf*	B2
Luzon, *island*	B3
Luzon, *strait*	B2
Manila, *bay*	B3
Marinduque, *island*	B3
Masbate, *island*	B3
Mayon, *volcano*	B3
Mindanao, *island*	C5
Mindoro, *island*	B3
Mindoro, *strait*	B3
Moro, *gulf*	B5
Negros, *island*	B4
Palawan, *island*	A4
Panay, *gulf*	B4
Panay, *island*	B4
Philippine, *sea*	C3
Pulangi, *river*	C5
Samar, *island*	C4
Samar, *sea*	C4
Siargao, *island*	C4
Sibuyan, *island*	B3
Sibuyan, *sea*	B3
Sierra Madre, *mts.*	B2
South China, *sea*	A3
Sulu, *archipelago*	B5
Sulu, *sea*	A4
Tablas, *island*	B3
Tawi Tawi, *island*	A5
Visayan, *islands*	B4
Visayan, *sea*	B4
Zambales, *mts.*	B2
Zamboanga, *peninsula*	B5

*Not on map

© MapQuest.com, Inc.

Indonesia: Map Index

Cities and Towns
Amahai	D2
Ambon	D2
Balikpapan	C2
Banda Aceh	A1
Bandar Lampung	B2
Bandung	B2
Banjarmasin	C2
Baubau	D2
Bengkulu	B2
Bogor	B2
Cilacap	B2
Cirebon	B2
Denpasar	C2
Ende	D2
Fakfak	E2
Gorontalo	D1
Jakarta, capital	B2
Jambi	B2
Jayapura	F2
Kediri	C2
Kendari	D2
Kupang	D3
Madiun	C2
Magelang	C2
Malang	C2
Manado	D1
Manokwari	E2
Mataram	C2
Medan	A1
Merauke	F2
Padang	B2
Palangkaraya	C2
Palembang	B2
Palu	C2
Pangkalpinang	B2
Parepare	C2
Pekalongan	B2
Pekanbaru	B1
Pematangsiantar	A1
Pontianak	B2
Raba	C2
Samarinda	C2
Semarang	C2
Sorong	E2
Sukabumi	B2
Surabaya	C2
Surakarta	C2
Tanjungpinang	B1
Tarakan	C1
Tasikmalaya	B2
Tegal	B2
Ternate	D1
Ujung Pandang	C2
Waingapu	D2
Yogyakarta	C2

Other Features
Agung, mt.	C2
Alor, island	D2
Arafura, sea	E2
Aru, islands	E2
Babar, island	D2
Bali, island	C2
Banda, sea	D2
Bangka, island	B2
Belitung, island	B2
Biak, island	E2
Borneo, island	C1
Buru, island	D2
Celebes (Sulawesi), island	D2
Celebes, sea	D1
Ceram, island	D2
Ceram, sea	D2
Digul, river	E2
Enggano, island	B2
Flores, island	C2
Flores, sea	C2
Greater Sunda, islands	B2
Halmahera, island	D1
Irian Jaya, region	E2
Java, island	C2
Java, sea	C2
Jaya, mt.	E2
Kahayan, river	C2
Kai, islands	E2
Kalimantan, region	C2
Kerinci, mt.	B2
Krakatau, island	B2
Lesser Sunda, islands	C2
Lingga, island	B2
Lombok, island	C2
Madura, island	C2
Makassar, strait	C2
Malacca, strait	A1
Mentawai, islands	A2
Misool, island	E2
Moa, island	D2
Molucca, sea	D2
Moluccas, islands	D2
Morotai, island	D1
Muna, island	D2
Natuna Besar, island	B1
New Guinea, island	E2
Nias, island	A1
Obi, island	D2
Peleng, island	D2
Savu, sea	C2
Semeru, mt.	C2
Siberut, island	A2
Simeulue, island	A1
South China, sea	C1
Sudirman, range	E2
Sula, islands	D2
Sulu, sea	D1
Sumatra, island	B2
Sumba, island	C2
Sumbawa, island	C2
Talaud, islands	D1
Tanimbar, islands	E2
Timor, island	D3
Timor, sea	D3
Waigeo, island	E2
Wetar, island	D2
Yapen, island	E2

Indonesia
Capital: Jakarta
Area: 741,052 sq. mi.
1,919,824 sq. km.
Population: 216,108,000
Largest City: Jakarta
Language: Bahasa Indonesian
Monetary Unit: New rupiah

©MapQuest.com, Inc.

Brunei
Capital: Bandar Seri Begawan
Area: 2,226 sq. mi.
5,767 sq. km.
Population: 323,000
Largest City: Bandar Seri Begawan
Language: Malay
Monetary Unit: Brunei dollar

Brunei: Map Index

Cities and Towns
Badas	A2
Bandar Seri Begawan, capital	B2
Bangar	C2
Batang Duri	C2
Jerudong	B2
Kerangan Nyatan	B3
Kuala Abang	B2
Kuala Belait	A2
Labi	A3
Labu	C2
Lumut	B2
Medit	B2
Muara	C1
Seria	A2
Sukang	B3
Tutong	B2

Other Features
Belait, river	B3
Brunei, bay	C1
Brunei, river	B2
Bukit Pagon, mt.	C3
Pandaruan, river	C2
South China, sea	A2
Temburong, river	C2
Tutong, river	B2

Singapore: Map Index

Cities and Towns
Bedok	B1
Bukit Panjang	B1
Bukit Timah	B1
Changi	B1
Choa Chu Kang	A1
Jurong	A1
Kranji	A1
Nee Soon	B1
Punggol	B1
Queenstown	B1
Sembawang	B1
Serangoon	B1
Singapore, capital	B1
Tampines	B1
Thong Hoe	A1
Toa Payoh	B1
Tuas	A1
Woodlands	B1

Other Features
Ayer Chawan, island	A1
Bukum, island	B2
Johor, strait	B1
Keppel, harbor	B2
Pandan, strait	A2
Semakau, island	B2
Senang, island	A2
Sentosa, island	B2
Singapore, island	B1
Singapore, strait	B2
Tekong, island	C1
Timah, hill	B1
Ubin, island	B1

Singapore
Capital: Singapore
Area: 247 sq. mi.
640 sq. km.
Population: 3,532,000
Largest City: Singapore
Languages: Mandarin Chinese, English, Malay, Tamil
Monetary Unit: Singapore dollar

© MapQuest.com, Inc.

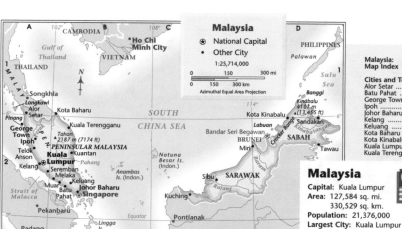
© MapQuest.com, Inc.

Malaysia
Capital: Kuala Lumpur
Area: 127,584 sq. mi.
330,529 sq. km.
Population: 21,376,000
Largest City: Kuala Lumpur
Language: Malay
Monetary Unit: Ringgit

Malaysia: Map Index

Cities and Towns
Alor Setar	A1
Batu Pahat	A2
George Town	A2
Ipoh	B2
Johor Baharu	B2
Kelang	B2
Keluang	B2
Kota Baharu	B1
Kota Kinabalu	D2
Kuala Lumpur, capital	B2
Kuala Terengganu	B2
Kuantan	B2
Kuching	C2
Melaka	B2
Miri	D2
Muar	A2
Sandakan	D2
Seremban	A2
Sibu	C2
Tawau	D2
Telok Anson	A2

Other Features
Banggi, island	D1
Baram, river	D2
Crocker, range	D1
Kinabalu, mt.	D1
Kinabatangan, river	D2
Labuan, island	D2
Langkawi, island	A1
Malacca, strait	A2
Malay, peninsula	A1
Pahang, river	B2
Peninsular Malaysia, region	B2
Perak, river	A2
Pinang, island	A2
Rajang, river	C2
Sabah, state	D2
Sarawak, state	C2
Tahan, mt.	B2

AUSTRALIA

Australia: Map Index

States and Territories
Australian Capital Territory ... D3
New South Wales ... D3
Northern Territory ... C2
Queensland ... D2
South Australia ... C2
Tasmania ... D4
Victoria ... D3
Western Australia ... B2

Aboriginal Lands
Alawa-Ngandji ... C1
Balwina ... B2
Central Australia ... B2
Central Desert ... C2
Daly River ... B1
Haasts Bluff ... C2
Lake Mackay ... B2
Nganyatjara ... B2
Petermann ... B2
Pitjantjatjara ... C2
Waani/Garawa ... C1
Yandeyarra ... A2
Unnamed ... B2
Unnamed ... C1
Unnamed ... D1

Cities and Towns
Adelaide, S.A., *capital* ... C3, Inset II
Albany, W.A. ... A3
Albury, N.S.W. ... D3
Alice Springs, N.T. ... C2
Altona, Vic. ... Inset V
Armadale, W.A. ... Inset I
Armidale, N.S.W. ... E3
Asquith, N.S.W. ... Inset IV
Auburn, N.S.W. ... Inset IV
Balcatta, W.A. ... Inset I
Bald Hills, Qld. ... Inset III
Ballarat, Vic. ... D3
Bankstown, N.S.W. ... Inset IV
Bayswater, W.A. ... Inset I
Beenleigh, Qld. ... Inset III
Belmont, W.A. ... Inset I
Bendigo, Vic. ... D3
Berwick, Vic. ... Inset V
Blacktown, N.S.W. ... Inset IV
Botany, N.S.W. ... Inset IV
Bourke, N.S.W. ... D3
Bowen, Qld. ... D2
Box Hill, Vic. ... Inset V
Brighton, S.A. ... Inset II
Brighton, Qld. ... Inset III
Brighton, Vic. ... Inset V
Brisbane, Qld., *capital* ... E2, Inset III
Broadmeadows, Vic. ... Inset V
Broken Hill, N.S.W. ... D3
Broome, W.A. ... B1
Brown Plains, Qld. ... Inset III
Bunbury, W.A. ... A3
Bundaberg, Qld. ... E2
Burnside, S.A. ... Inset II
Byford, W.A. ... Inset I
Cairns, Qld. ... D1
Campbelltown, S.A. ... Inset II
Campbelltown, N.S.W. ... Inset IV
Canberra, A.C.T., *national capital* ... D3
Cannington, W.A. ... Inset I
Canterbury, N.S.W. ... Inset IV
Carnarvon, W.A. ... A2
Castle Hill, N.S.W. ... Inset IV
Caulfield, Vic. ... Inset V
Ceduna, S.A. ... C3
Charleville, Qld. ... D2
Charters Towers, Qld. ... D2
Chelsea, Vic. ... Inset V
Chermside, Qld. ... Inset III
City Beach, W.A. ... Inset I
Cleveland, Qld. ... Inset III
Cloncurry, Qld. ... D2
Coburg, Vic. ... Inset V
Coober Pedy, S.A. ... C2
Coopers Plains, Qld. ... Inset III
Cranbourne, Vic. ... Inset V
Cronulla, N.S.W. ... Inset IV
Dampier, W.A. ... A2
Dandenong, Vic. ... Inset V
Darwin, N.T., *capital* ... C1
Dee Why, N.S.W. ... Inset IV
Devonport, Tas. ... D4
Doncaster, Vic. ... Inset V
Dubbo, N.S.W. ... D3
Elizabeth, S.A. ... Inset II
Eltham, Vic. ... Inset V
Emerald, Qld. ... D2
Enfield, S.A. ... Inset II
Epping, N.S.W. ... Inset IV
Esperance, W.A. ... B3
Essendon, Vic. ... Inset V
Fairfield, N.S.W. ... Inset IV
Ferntree Gully, Vic. ... Inset V
Ferny Grove, Qld. ... Inset III
Frankston, Vic. ... Inset V
Fremantle, W.A. ... A3, Inset I
Geelong, Vic. ... D3
Geraldton, W.A. ... A2
Gladstone, Qld. ... E2
Glenelg, S.A. ... Inset II
Glen Forrest, W.A. ... Inset I
Gold Coast, Qld. ... E2
Goodna, Qld. ... Inset III
Gosford, N.S.W. ... E3
Gosnells, W.A. ... Inset I
Grafton, N.S.W. ... E2
Grange, S.A. ... Inset II
Greenslopes, Qld. ... Inset III
Griffith, N.S.W. ... D3
Gympie, Qld. ... E2
Heidelberg, Vic. ... Inset V
Hobart, Tas., *capital* ... D4
Holland Park, Qld. ... Inset III
Holroyd, N.S.W. ... Inset IV
Hornsby, N.S.W. ... Inset IV
Hurstville, N.S.W. ... Inset IV
Inala, Qld. ... Inset III
Ipswich, Qld. ... Inset III
Kalamunda, W.A. ... Inset I
Kalgoorlie-Boulder, W.A. ... B3
Katherine, N.T. ... C1
Keilor, Vic. ... Inset V
Kelmscott, W.A. ... Inset I
Kersbrook, S.A. ... Inset II
Kwinana, W.A. ... Inset I
Kwinana Beach, W.A. ... Inset I
La Perouse, N.S.W. ... Inset IV
Launceston, Tas. ... D4
Leichhardt, N.S.W. ... Inset IV
Lilydale, Vic. ... Inset V
Lismore, N.S.W. ... E2
Liverpool, N.S.W. ... Inset IV
Lobethal, S.A. ... Inset II
Logan, Qld. ... Inset III
Longreach, Qld. ... D2
Mackay, Qld. ... D2
Mandurah, W.A. ... A3
Manly, Qld. ... Inset III
Manly, N.S.W. ... Inset IV
Marion, S.A. ... Inset II
Maryborough, Qld. ... E2
Melbourne, Vic., *capital* ... D3, Inset V
Melville, W.A. ... Inset I
Merredin, W.A. ... A3
Midland, W.A. ... Inset I
Mildura, Vic. ... D3
Mitcham, S.A. ... Inset II
Mona Vale, N.S.W. ... Inset IV
Moorabbin, Vic. ... Inset V
Mordialloc, Vic. ... Inset V
Moree, N.S.W. ... D2
Morningside, Qld. ... Inset III
Mosman Park, W.A. ... Inset I
Mount Barker, S.A. ... Inset II
Mount Gambier, S.A. ... D3
Mount Gravatt, Qld. ... Inset III
Mount Isa, Qld. ... C2
Mount Nebo, Qld. ... Inset III
Mullaloo, W.A. ... Inset I
Narrogin, W.A. ... A3
Nedlands, W.A. ... Inset I
Newcastle, N.S.W. ... E3
Newman, W.A. ... A2
Newmarket, Qld. ... Inset III
Noarlunga, S.A. ... Inset II
North Adelaide, S.A. ... Inset II
Northcote, Vic. ... Inset V
North Sydney, N.S.W. ... Inset IV
Nunawading, Vic. ... Inset V
Oakleigh, Vic. ... Inset V
Orange, N.S.W. ... D3
Parramatta, N.S.W. ... Inset IV
Perth, W.A., *capital* ... A3, Inset I
Petrie, Qld. ... Inset III
Pickering Brook, W.A. ... Inset I
Port Adelaide, S.A. ... Inset II
Port Augusta, S.A. ... C3
Port Hedland, W.A. ... A2
Port Lincoln, S.A. ... C3
Port Macquarie, N.S.W. ... E3
Port Pirie, S.A. ... C3
Prahran, Vic. ... Inset V
Preston, Vic. ... Inset V
Queenstown, Tas. ... D4
Randwick, N.S.W. ... Inset IV
Redcliffe, Qld. ... Inset III
Redland Bay, Qld. ... Inset III
Reynella, S.A. ... Inset II
Ringwood, Vic. ... Inset V
Rockdale, N.S.W. ... Inset IV
Rockhampton, Qld. ... E2
Roma, Qld. ... D2
Ryde, N.S.W. ... Inset IV
St. Ives, N.S.W. ... Inset IV
St. Kilda, S.A. ... Inset II
St. Kilda, Vic. ... Inset V
Salisbury, S.A. ... Inset II
Samford, Qld. ... Inset III
Sandgate, Qld. ... Inset III
Scarborough, W.A. ... Inset I
Spearwood, W.A. ... Inset I
Springvale, Vic. ... Inset V
Stirling, W.A. ... Inset I
Stirling, S.A. ... Inset II
Sunshine, Vic. ... Inset V
Sutherland, N.S.W. ... Inset IV
Sydney, N.S.W., *capital,* ... E3, Inset IV
Tamworth, N.S.W. ... E3
Taree, N.S.W. ... E3
Tea Tree Gully, S.A. ... Inset II
Tennant Creek, N.T. ... C1
Tom Price, W.A. ... A2
Toowoomba, Qld. ... E2
Townsville, Qld. ... D1
Unley, S.A. ... Inset II
Victoria Park, W.A. ... Inset I
Victoria Point, Qld. ... Inset III
Wagga Wagga, N.S.W. ... D3
Wanneroo, W.A. ... Inset I
Warrnambool, Vic. ... D3
Waverley, Vic. ... Inset V
Weipa, Qld. ... D1
Whyalla, S.A. ... C3
Willoughby, N.S.W. ... Inset IV
Wollongong, N.S.W. ... E3
Woodside, S.A. ... Inset II
Woodville, S.A. ... Inset II
Woomera, S.A. ... C3
Wyndham, W.A. ... B1
Wynnum, Qld. ... Inset III

Other Features
Arafura, *sea* ... C1
Arnhem, *cape* ... C1
Arnhem Land, *region* ... C1
Ashburton, *river* ... A2
Ashmore and Cartier, *islands* ... B1
Australian Alps, *mts.* ... D3
Barkly, *tableland* ... C1
Bass, *strait* ... D3
Bate, *bay* ... Inset IV
Blue, *mts.* ... E3
Botany, *bay* ... Inset IV
Brisbane, *river* ... Inset III
Burdekin, *river* ... D1
Canning, *river* ... Inset I
Cape York, *peninsula* ... D1
Carpentaria, *gulf* ... C1
Coral, *sea* ... E1
Daly, *river* ... C1
Darling, *range* ... A3
Darling, *river* ... D3
Drysdale River Natl. Park ... B1
Eyre, *lake* ... C2
Eyre, *peninsula* ... C3
Fitzroy, *river* ... B1
Flinders, *range* ... C3
Flinders, *river* ... D1
Frome, *lake* ... D2
Gairdner, *lake* ... C3
Garden, *island* ... Inset I
Gascoyne *river* ... A2
Gibson, *desert* ... B2
Gilbert, *river* ... D1
Great Artesian, *basin* ... D2
Great Australian, *bight* ... B3
Great Barrier, *reef* ... D1
Great Dividing, *range* ... D1, D3
Great Sandy, *desert* ... B2
Great Victoria, *desert* ... B2
Gregory Natl. Park ... C1
Grey, *range* ... D2
Groote Eylandt, *island* ... C1
Hamersley, *range* ... A2
Hobsons, *bay* ... Inset V
Jackson, *port* ... Inset IV
Kakadu Natl. Park ... C1
Kangaroo, *island* ... C3
Kimberley, *plateau* ... B1
King Leopold, *range* ... B1
Kosciusko, *mt.* ... D3
Lakefield Natl. Park ... D1
Leeuwin, *cape* ... A3
Leichhardt, *river* ... D1
Leveque, *cape* ... B1
Logan, *river* ... Inset III
Macdonnell, *ranges* ... C2
Melville, *island* ... C1
Mitchell, *river* ... D1
Moreton, *bay* ... Inset III
Murchison, *river* ... A2
Murray, *river* ... D3
Murrumbidgee, *river* ... D3
Musgrave, *ranges* ... C2
New England, *range* ... E3
North West, *cape* ... A2
Nullarbor, *plain* ... B3
Port Phillip, *bay* ... Inset V
Roper, *river* ... C1
Rudall River Natl. Park ... B2
St. Vincent, *gulf* ... Inset II
Samsonvale, *lake* ... Inset III
Simpson, *desert* ... C2
Simpson Desert Natl. Park ... C2
Spencer, *gulf* ... C3
Swan, *river* ... Inset I
Tasman, *sea* ... E3
Timor, *sea* ... B1
Torrens, *lake* ... C2
Torrens, *river* ... Inset II
Torres, *strait* ... D1
Uluru (Ayers Rock) ... C2
Victoria, *river* ... C1
Witjira Natl. Park ... C2
Yampi, *sound* ... B1
York, *cape* ... D1

Australia

Capital: Canberra
Area: 2,966,200 sq. mi.
7,684,456 sq. km.
Population: 18,784,000
Largest City: Sydney
Language: English
Monetary Unit: Australian dollar

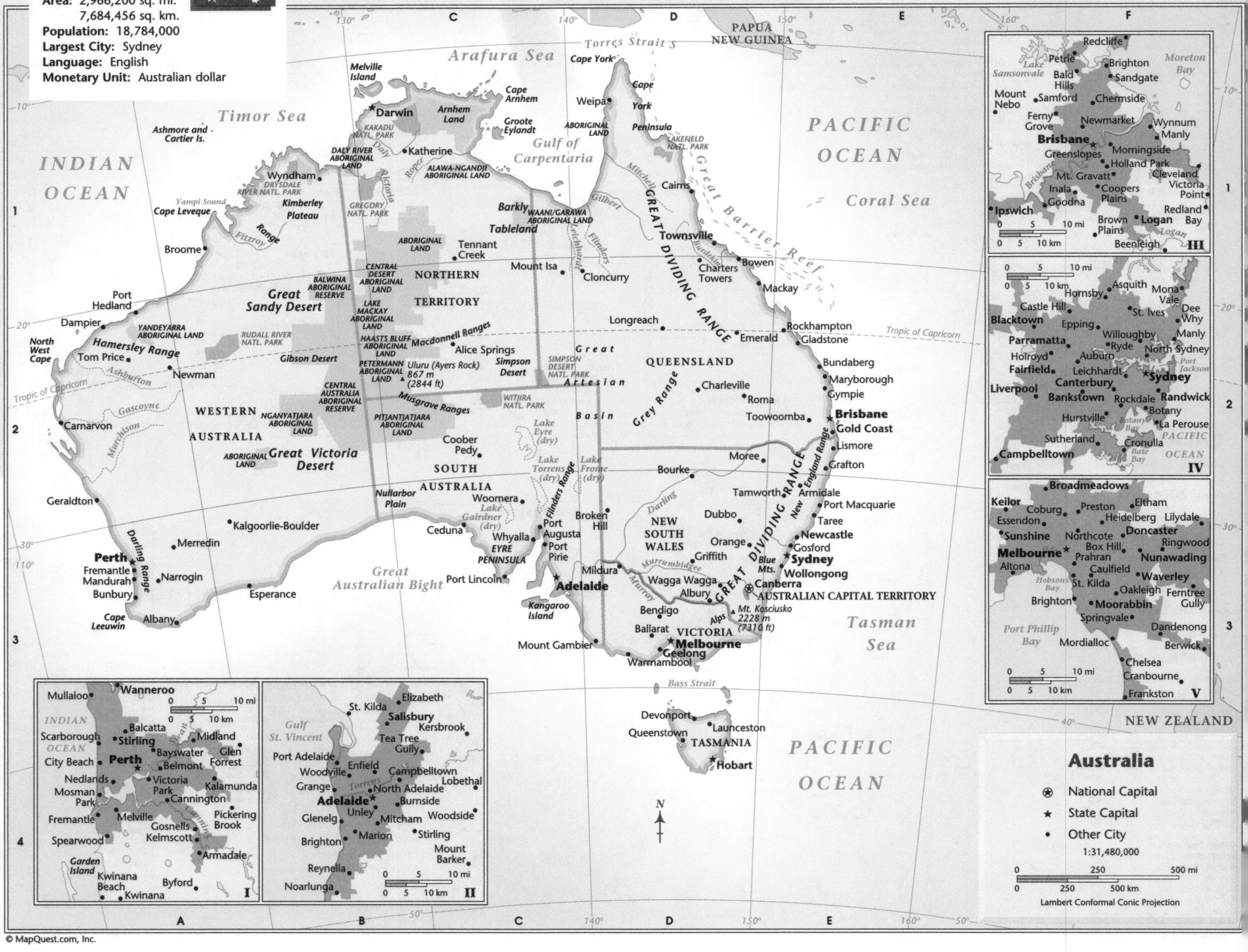
Arafura Sea
Timor Sea
INDIAN OCEAN
PACIFIC OCEAN
Coral Sea
Tasman Sea
Torres Strait
PAPUA NEW GUINEA
NEW ZEALAND
Gulf of Carpentaria
Great Australian Bight
Bass Strait
NORTHERN TERRITORY
QUEENSLAND
WESTERN AUSTRALIA
SOUTH AUSTRALIA
NEW SOUTH WALES
VICTORIA
TASMANIA
AUSTRALIAN CAPITAL TERRITORY
GREAT DIVIDING RANGE
Great Barrier Reef
Great Sandy Desert
Gibson Desert
Great Victoria Desert
Simpson Desert
Nullarbor Plain
Great Artesian Basin
Macdonnell Ranges
Musgrave Ranges
Hamersley Range
Kimberley Plateau
Barkly Tableland
Arnhem Land
Cape York Peninsula
Uluru (Ayers Rock) 867 m (2844 ft)
Mt. Kosciusko 2228 m (7310 ft)
Darwin
Perth
Adelaide
Melbourne
Sydney
Brisbane
Canberra
Hobart
Tropic of Capricorn
Australia
National Capital
State Capital
Other City
1:31,480,000
Lambert Conformal Conic Projection

Papua New Guinea: Map Index

Cities and Towns
Alotau.................................B3
Arawa.................................B2
Daru..................................A2
Goroka................................A2
Kavieng...............................B2
Kerema................................A2
Kimbe.................................B2
Lae...................................A2
Lorengau..............................A2
Madang................................A2
Morehead..............................A2
Mount Hagen...........................A2
Popondetta............................A2
Port Moresby, *capital*...............A2
Rabaul................................B2
Vanimo................................A2
Wabag.................................A2
Wau...................................A2
Wewak.................................A1

Other Features
Admiralty, *islands*..................A2
Bismarck, *archipelago*...............A2
Bismarck, *range*.....................A2
Bismarck, *sea*.......................A2
Bougainville, *island*................B2
Buka, *island*........................B2
Central, *range*......................A2
Coral, *sea*..........................A3
D'Entrecasteaux, *islands*............B2
Feni, *islands*.......................B2
Fly, *river*..........................A2
Gazelle, *peninsula*..................B2
Green, *islands*......................B2
Huon, *peninsula*.....................A2
Karkar, *island*......................A2
Lihir, *group*........................B2
Louisiade, *archipelago*..............B3
Manus, *island*.......................A2
Markham, *river*......................A2

Milne, *bay*..........................B3
Murray, *lake*........................A2
Mussau, *island*......................A2
New Britain, *island*.................B2
New Guinea, *island*..................A2
New Hanover, *island*.................B2
New Ireland, *island*.................B2
Ninigo, *group*.......................A2
Nuguria, *islands*....................A2
Owen Stanley, *range*.................A2
Papua, *gulf*.........................A2
Purari, *river*.......................A2
Ramu, *river*.........................A2
Rossel, *island*......................B3
St. George's, *channel*...............A2
Sepik, *river*........................A2
Solomon, *sea*........................B2
Tabar, *islands*......................B2
Tagula, *island*......................B3
Tanga, *islands*......................B2
Tauu, *islands*.......................B2
Torres, *strait*......................A2
Trobriand, *islands*..................B2
Umboi, *island*.......................A2
Whiteman, *range*.....................A2
Wilhelm, *mt.*........................A2
Witu, *island*........................A2
Woodlark (Muyua), *island*............B2

Papua New Guinea

Capital: Port Moresby
Area: 178,704 sq. mi.
  462,964 sq. km.
Population: 4,705,000
Largest City: Port Moresby
Language: English
Monetary Unit: Kina

New Zealand

Capital: Wellington
Area: 104,454 sq. mi.
  270,606 sq. km.
Population: 3,662,000
Largest City: Auckland
Language: English
Monetary Unit: New Zealand dollar

New Zealand: Map Index

Cities and Towns
Alexandra.............................A4
Ashburton.............................B3
Auckland..............................B2
Blenheim..............................B3
Christchurch..........................B3
Collingwood...........................B3
Dunedin...............................B4
East Coast Bays.......................B2
Gisborne..............................C2
Greymouth.............................B3
Hamilton..............................C2
Hastings..............................C2
Hicks Bay.............................C2
Invercargill..........................A4
Kaeo..................................B2
Kaikoura..............................B3
Kaitaia...............................B2
Kawhia................................B2
Lower Hutt............................B3
Manukau...............................B2
Milford Sound.........................A3
Napier................................C2
Nelson................................B3
New Plymouth..........................B2
Oamaru................................B4
Palmerston North......................C3
Queenstown............................A3
Rotorua...............................C2
Taumaruni.............................C2
Taupo.................................C2
Tauranga..............................C2
Timaru................................B3
Waimamaku.............................B2
Wanganui..............................C2
Wellington, *capital*.................B3
Westport..............................B3
Whakatane.............................C2
Whangarei.............................B2

Other Features
Aspiring, *mt.*.......................A3
Banks, *peninsula*....................B3
Canterbury, *bight*...................B3
Canterbury, *plains*..................B3
Clutha, *river*.......................A4
Cook, *mt.*...........................B3
Cook, *strait*........................B3
Coromandel, *peninsula*...............C2
East, *cape*..........................C2
Egmont, *cape*........................B2
Egmont, *mt.*.........................B2
Farewell, *cape*......................B3
Foveaux, *strait*.....................A4
Great Barrier, *island*...............C2
Hawea, *lake*.........................A3
Hawke, *bay*..........................C2
Ngauruhoe, *mt.*......................C2
North, *cape*.........................B1
North, *island*.......................B2
North Taranaki, *bight*...............C2
Palliser, *cape*......................C3
Pegasus, *bay*........................B3
Plenty, *bay*.........................C2
Puysegur, *point*.....................A4
Rangitikei, *river*...................C2
Raukumara, *range*....................C2
Ruahine, *range*......................C2
Ruapehu, *mt.*........................C2
South, *island*.......................A3
Southern Alps, *mts.*.................A3
Southland, *plains*...................A4
South Taranaki, *bight*...............B2
South West, *cape*....................A4
Stewart, *island*.....................A4
Tararua, *range*......................C3
Tasman, *bay*.........................B3
Tasman, *sea*.........................A2
Taupo, *lake*.........................C2
Te Anau, *lake*.......................A4
Tekapo, *lake*........................B3
Three Kings, *islands*................B1
Tongariro, *mt.*......................C2
Waikato, *river*......................C2
Wairau, *river*.......................B3
Waitaki, *river*......................B3
Wanaka, *lake*........................A3

MAJOR CITIES

Australia	
Sydney	3,935,000
Melbourne	3,322,000
Brisbane	1,548,000
Perth	1,319,000
Adelaide	1,083,000

New Zealand	
Auckland	998,000
Wellington	335,000
Christchurch	331,000
Hamilton	159,000
Dunedin	112,000

Papua New Guinea	(metro)
Morobe	439,725
Western Highlands	398,376
Southern Highlands	390,240
Eastern Highlands	316,802
Madang	288,317
Port Moresby	271,813

Micronesia: Map Index

Cities and Towns
Colonia...............................A2
Kosrae................................D2
Palikir, *capital*....................C2
Weno..................................C2

Other Features
Caroline, *islands*...................B2
Chuuk, *islands*......................C2
Eauripik, *atoll*.....................B2
Faraulep, *atoll*.....................B2

Kapingamarangi, *atoll*...............C2
Kosrae, *island*......................D2
Mortlock, *islands*...................C2
Murilo, *atoll*.......................C2
Namoluk, *atoll*......................C2
Namonuito, *atoll*....................C2
Ngulu, *atoll*........................A2
Nukuoro, *atoll*......................C2
Oroluk, *atoll*.......................C2
Pohnpei, *island*.....................D2
Pulusuk, *island*.....................B2
Ulithi, *atoll*.......................B2
Weno, *island*........................C2
Yap, *islands*........................A2

Micronesia

Capital: Palikir
Area: 271 sq. mi.
  702 sq. km.
Population: 132,000
Largest City: Palikir
Language: English
Monetary Unit: U.S. dollar

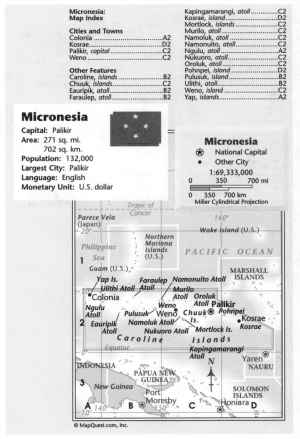

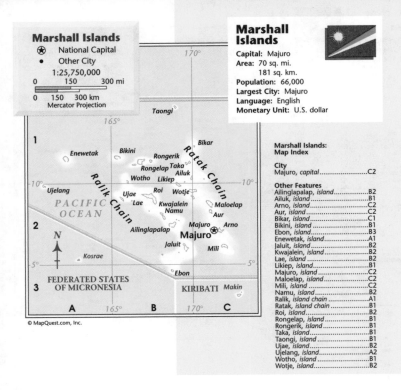

Marshall Islands
* ⊛ National Capital
* • Other City

1:25,750,000

0   150   300 mi

0   150   300 km
Mercator Projection

© MapQuest.com, Inc.

Marshall Islands
Capital: Majuro
Area: 70 sq. mi.
181 sq. km.
Population: 66,000
Largest City: Majuro
Language: English
Monetary Unit: U.S. dollar

Marshall Islands:
Map Index

City
Majuro, capital C2

Other Features
Ailinglapalap, island B2
Ailuk, island B1
Arno, island C2
Aur, island C2
Bikar, island C1
Bikini, island B1
Ebon, island B3
Enewetak, island A1
Jaluit, island B2
Kwajalein, island B2
Lae, island B2
Likiep, island B1
Majuro, island C2
Maloelap, island C2
Mili, island C2
Namu, island B2
Ralik, island chain A1
Ratak, island chain B1
Roi, island B2
Rongelap, island B1
Rongerik, island B1
Taka, island B1
Taongi, island B1
Ujae, island B2
Ujelang, island A2
Wotho, island B1
Wotje, island B2

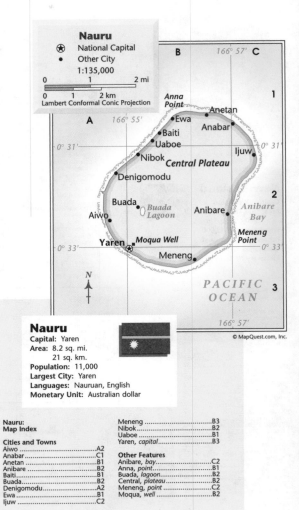

Nauru
* ⊛ National Capital
* • Other City

1:135,000

0   1   2 mi

0   1   2 km
Lambert Conformal Conic Projection

© MapQuest.com, Inc.

Nauru
Capital: Yaren
Area: 8.2 sq. mi.
21 sq. km.
Population: 11,000
Largest City: Yaren
Languages: Nauruan, English
Monetary Unit: Australian dollar

Nauru:
Map Index

Cities and Towns
Aiwo A2
Anabar C1
Anetan B1
Anibare B2
Baiti B1
Buada B2
Denigomodu A2
Ewa B1
Ijuw C2

Meneng B3
Nibok B2
Uaboe B1
Yaren, capital B3

Other Features
Anibare, bay C2
Anna, point B1
Buada, lagoon B2
Central, plateau B2
Meneng, point C2
Moqua, well B2

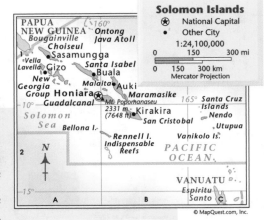

Solomon Islands
* ⊛ National Capital
* • Other City

1:24,100,000

0   150   300 mi

0   150   300 km
Mercator Projection

© MapQuest.com, Inc.

Solomon Islands:
Map Index

Cities and Towns
Auki B1
Buala A1
Gizo A1
Honiara, capital A1
Kirakira B2
Sasamungga A1

Other Features
Bellona, island A2
Choiseul, island A1
Guadalcanal, island A1
Indispensable, reefs B2
Malaita, island B1
Maramasike, island B1
Nendo, island C2
New Georgia Group,
islands A1
Ontong Java, island A1
Popomanaseu, mt. B1
Rennell, island B2
San Cristobal, island B2
Santa Cruz, islands C2
Santa Isabel, island A1
Solomon, sea A2
Utupua, island C2
Vanikolo, islands C2
Vella Lavella, island A1

Solomon Islands
Capital: Honiara
Area: 10,954 sq. mi.
28,378 sq. km.
Population: 455,000
Largest City: Honiara
Language: English
Monetary Unit: Dollar

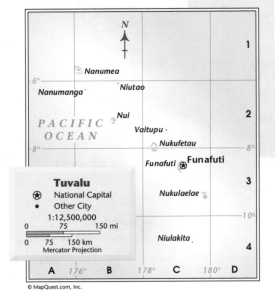

© MapQuest.com, Inc.

Tuvalu
* ⊛ National Capital
* • Other City

1:12,500,000

0   75   150 mi

0   75   150 km
Mercator Projection

Tuvalu
Capital: Funafuti
Area: 9.4 sq. mi.
24.4 sq. km.
Population: 11,000
Largest City: Funafuti
Languages: Tuvaluan, English
Monetary Unit: Tuvalu dollar,
Australian dollar

Tuvalu:
Map Index

City
Funafuti, capital C3

Other Features
Funafuti, island C3
Nanumanga, island B2
Nanumea, island B1
Niulakita, island C4
Niutao, island B2
Nui, island B2
Nukufetau, island C2
Nukulaelae, island C3
Vaitupu, island C2

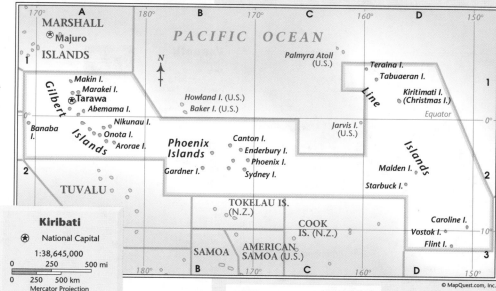

MARSHALL ISLANDS · Majuro

PACIFIC OCEAN

N

Gilbert Islands
Makin I.
Marakei I.
⊛ Tarawa
Abemama I.
Nikunau I.
Banaba I.
Onota I.
Arorae I.

Palmyra Atoll (U.S.)

Teraina I.
Tabuaeran I.
Kiritimati I. (Christmas I.)

Howland I. (U.S.)
Baker I. (U.S.)

Line Islands

Equator

Phoenix Islands
Canton I.
Enderbury I.
Phoenix I.
Gardner I.
Sydney I.

Jarvis I. (U.S.)

Malden I.
Starbuck I.

TUVALU

Caroline I.
Vostok I.
Flint I.

TOKELAU IS. (N.Z.)
COOK IS. (N.Z.)
SAMOA
AMERICAN SAMOA (U.S.)

© MapQuest.com, Inc.

Fiji: Map Index

Cities and Towns
Galoa B3
Labasa B2
Lami B3
Lautoka A2
Lomawai A3
Nabouwalu A3
Nadi A2
Naduri B2
Nakodu B2
Navua B3
Suva, *capital* B3
Vunisea B3

Other Features
Beqa, *island* B3
Bligh Water, *sound* B2
Cicia, *island* C2
Cikobia, *island* C1
Gau, *island* B3
Great Sea, *reef* B2
Kadavu, *island* B3
Kadavu, *passage* A3
Kioa, *island* C2

Koro, *island* B2
Koro, *sea* B2
Lakeba, *island* C3
Lakeba, *passage* C3
Lau, *island group* C2
Laucala, *island* C2
Moala, *island group* B3
Nadi, *bay* A3
Navua, *river* A3
Ono, *island* B3
Ovalau, *island* B2
Qamea, *island* C2
Qelelevu, *island* C2
Rabi, *island* C2
Soso, *bay* B3
Taveuni, *island* C2
Tomanivi, *mt.* B2
Udu, *point* C2
Vanua Balavu, *island* C2
Vanua Levu, *island* B2
Vatu Lele, *island* A3
Vetauua, *island* C1
Viti Levu, *island* A2
Vunaniu, *bay* A3
Washington, *cape* A3
Yasawa, *island group* A2

Kiribati

⊛ National Capital

1:38,645,000

0   250   500 mi

0   250   500 km

Mercator Projection

Fiji 🇫🇯

Capital: Suva
Area: 7,056 sq. mi.
18,280 sq. km.
Population: 813,000
Largest City: Suva
Languages: Fijian, Hindi, English
Monetary Unit: Fiji dollar

Kiribati

Capital: Tarawa
Area: 313 sq. mi.
811 sq. km.
Population: 86,000
Largest City: Tarawa
Languages: I-Kiribati (Gilbertese), English
Monetary Unit: Australian dollar

Kiribati: Map Index

City
Tarawa, *capital* A1

Other Features
Abemama, *island* A1
Arorae, *island* A2

Banaba, *island* A2
Canton, *island* B2
Caroline, *island* D2
Enderbury, *island* B2
Flint, *island* D3
Gardner, *island* B2
Gilbert, *islands* A1
Kiritimati (Christmas), *island* D1
Line, *islands* D1
Makin, *island* A1
Malden, *island* D2
Marakei, *island* A1
Nikunau, *island* A2
Onota, *island* A2
Phoenix, *island* B2
Phoenix, *islands* B2
Starbuck, *island* D2
Sydney, *island* B2
Tabuaeran, *island* D1
Teraina, *island* D1
Vostok, *island* D3

Fiji

⊛ National Capital
• Other City

1:8,900,000

0   50   100 mi

0   50   100 km

Azimuthal Equal Area Projection

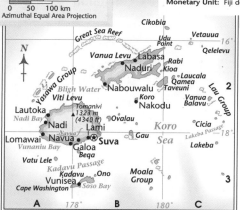

N

Cikobia
Great Sea Reef
Udu Point
Vetauua
Qelelevu
Vanua Levu · Labasa
Naduri
Rabi
Kioa
Laucala
Qamea
Taveuni
Nabouwalu
Yasawa Group
Bligh Water
Viti Levu
Koro
Nakodu
Vanua Balavu
Lau Group
Lautoka
Nadi Bay
Tomanivi 1323 m (4340 ft)
Ovalau
Nadi
Lami
Navua
Koro Sea
Gau
Cicia
Lomawai
Navua
⊛ Suva
Galoa
Beqa
Lakeba Passage
Lakeba
Vunaniu Bay
Vatu Lele
Kadavu Passage
Kadavu
Ono
Moala Group
Vunisea
Soso Bay
Cape Washington

© MapQuest.com, Inc.

Tonga

⊛ National Capital
• Other City

1:11,000,000

0   75   150 mi

0   75   150 km

Mercator Projection

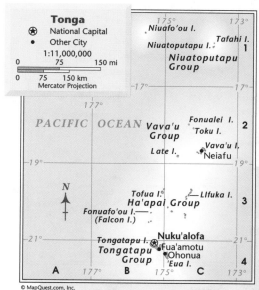

Niuafo'ou I.
Niuatoputapu I.
Tafahi I.
Niuatoputapu Group

PACIFIC OCEAN

Vava'u Group
Fonualei I.
Toku I.
Late I.
Vava'u I.
Neiafu

N

Tofua I.
Lifuka I.
Ha'apai Group
Fonuafo'ou I. (Falcon I.)

Tongatapu I.
Tongatapu Group
Nuku'alofa
Fua'amotu
Ohonua
'Eua I.

© MapQuest.com, Inc.

Tonga

Capital: Nuku'alofa
Area: 301 sq. mi.
780 sq. km.
Population: 109,000
Largest City: Nuku'alofa
Languages: Tongan, English
Monetary Unit: Pa'anga

Palau: Map Index

Cities and Towns
Kloulklubed B3
Koror, *capital* B3
Melekeok C3
Meyungs B3
Ngaramasch B4
Ngerkeel B3
Ngermechau C2
Ngetbong C2
Ollei C2

Other Features
Angaur, *island* B4
Arakabesan, *island* B3
Arekalong, *peninsula* C2

Babelthuap, *island* C3
Cormoran, *reef* B2
Eli Malk, *island* B3
Helen, *reef* .... Inset
Kayangel, *islands* C1
Kossol, *passage* C2
Kossol, *reef* C2
Merir, *island* .... Inset
Ngemelis, *islands* B3
Peleliu, *island* B4
Philippine, *sea* B2
Pulo Anna, *island* .... Inset
Sar, *passage* B3
Sonsoral, *island* .... Inset
Tobi, *island* .... Inset
Urukthapel, *island* B3

Palau

⊛ National Capital
• Other City

1:1,900,000

0   5   10 mi

0   5   10 km

Lambert Conformal Conic Projection

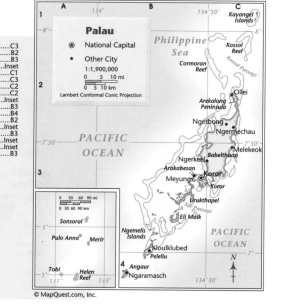

Kayangel Islands
Philippine Sea
Kossol Reef
Kossol Passage
Cormoran Reef
Arekalong Peninsula
Ollei
Ngetbong
Ngermechau
Melekeok
Ngerkeel
Babelthuap
Arakabesan
Koror
Meyungs
Koror
Urukthapel
Eli Malk
Ngemelis Islands
Kloulklubed
Peleliu
PACIFIC OCEAN

N

Sonsoral
Pulo Anna
Merir
Tobi
Helen Reef
Angaur
Ngaramasch

© MapQuest.com, Inc.

Palau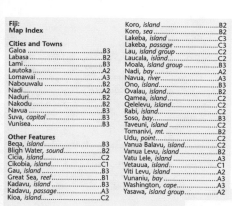

Capital: Koror
Area: 177 sq. mi.
458 sq. km.
Population: 18,000
Largest City: Koror
Languages: English, Sonsorolese, Angaur, Japanese, Tobi, Palauan
Monetary Unit: U.S. dollar

Tonga: Map Index

Cities and Towns
Fua'amotu B4
Neiafu C2
Nuku'alofa, *capital* B4
Ohonua C4

Other Features
'Eua, *island* C4
Fonuafo'ou (Falcon), *island* B3
Fonualei, *island* C2

Ha'apai, *island group* B3
Late, *island* C2
Lifuka, *island* C3
Niuafo'ou, *island* B1
Niuatoputapu, *island* C1
Niuatoputapu, *island group* C1
Tafahi, *island* C1
Tofua, *island* B3
Toku, *island* C2
Tongatapu, *island* B4
Tongatapu, *island group* B4
Vava'u, *island* C2
Vava'u, *island group* C2

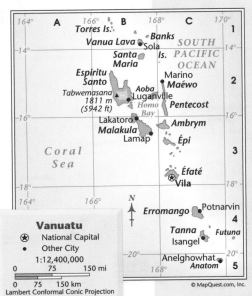

Torres Is.
Banks
Vanua Lava · Sola
SOUTH
Santa Maria
PACIFIC
OCEAN
Espiritu Santo
Marino
Tabwemasana 1811 m (5942 ft)
Aoba Maéwo
Luganville
Homo Bay
Pentecost
Lakatoro
Ambrym
Malakula
Lamap
Épi
Coral Sea
Éfaté
Vila
Erromango
Potnarvin
Tanna
Isangel
Futuna
Anelghowhat
Anatom

Vanuatu

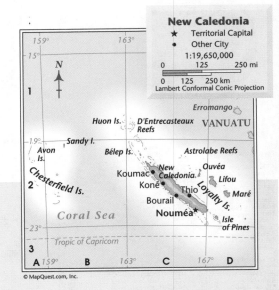

Capital: Vila
Area: 4,707 sq. mi.
12,194 sq. km.
Population: 189,000
Largest City: Vila
Languages: French, English, Bislama
Monetary Unit: Vatu

Vanuatu: Map Index

Cities and Towns
Anelghowhat C5
Isangel C4
Lakatoro B3
Lamap B3
Luganville B2
Marino C2
Potnarvin C4
Sola B1
Vila, capital C3

Other Features
Ambrym, island C3
Anatom, island C5
Aoba, island B2
Banks, islands B1
Coral, sea C3
Éfaté, island C3
Épi, island C3
Erromango, island C4
Espiritu Santo, island. B2
Futuna, island C4
Homo, bay. B2
Maéwo, island C2
Malakula, island B3
Pentecost, island C3
Santa Maria, island B2
Tabwemasana, mt. B2
Tanna, island C4
Torres, islands B1
Vanua Lava, island B1

Vanuatu

⊛ National Capital
● Other City
1:12,400,000

0 · 75 · 150 mi
0 · 75 · 150 km
Lambert Conformal Conic Projection

New Caledonia

★ Territorial Capital
● Other City
1:19,650,000

0 · 125 · 250 mi
0 · 125 · 250 km
Lambert Conformal Conic Projection

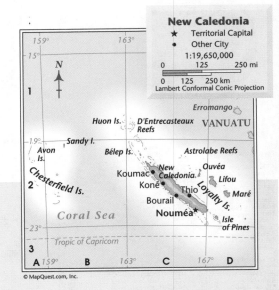

Erromango
Huon Is.
D'Entrecasteaux Reefs
VANUATU
Sandy I.
Avon Is.
Bélep Is.
Astrolabe Reefs
Chesterfield Is.
Koumac
New Caledonia
Ouvéa
Lifou
Koné
Thio
Loyalty Is.
Maré
Bourail
Nouméa
Isle of Pines
Coral Sea
Tropic of Capricorn

New Caledonia: Map Index

Cities and Towns
Bourail C2
Koné C2
Koumac C2
Nouméa, capital. C2
Thio C2

Other Features
Astrolabe, reefs C2

Avon, islands A2
Bélep, islands C2
Chesterfield, islands A2
Coral, sea B2
D'Entrecasteaux, reefs C1
Huon, islands B1
Lifou, island D2
Loyalty, islands C2
Maré, island D2
New Caledonia, island C2
Ouvéa, island C2
Pines, island D2
Sandy, island B2

New Caledonia

Capital: Nouméa
Area: 8,548 sq. mi.
21,912 sq. km.
Population: 197,000
Largest City: Nouméa
Language: French
Monetary Unit: CFA Franc

Samoa

⊛ National Capital
● Other City
1:3,000,000

0 · 20 · 40 mi
0 · 20 · 40 km
Mercator Projection

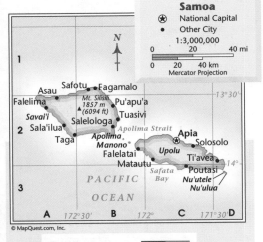

Asau
Safotu
Fagamalo
Falelima
Mt. Silisili 1857 m (6094 ft)
Pu'apu'a
Tuasivi
Savai'i
Saleloga
Sala'ilua
Apolima Strait
Apia
Taga
Apolima
Manono
Upolu
Solosolo
Falelatai
Ti'avea
Matautu
Poutasi
Safata Bay
Nu'utele
Nu'ulua
PACIFIC OCEAN

Samoa

Capital: Apia
Area: 1,093 sq. mi.
2,832 sq. km.
Population: 230,000
Largest City: Apia
Languages: Samoan, English
Monetary Unit: Tala

Samoa: Map Index

Cities and Towns
Apia, capital C2
Asau A2
Fagamalo B1
Falelatai B2
Falelima A2
Matautu B2
Poutasi C3
Pu'apu'a B2
Safotu B1
Sala'ilua A2
Saleloga B2
Solosolo C2
Taga A2
Ti'avea D2
Tuasivi B2

Other Features
Apolima, island B2
Apolima, strait. B2
Manono, island B2
Nu'ulua, island D3
Nu'utele, island D3
Safata, bay C3
Savai'i, island A2
Silisili, mt. B2
Upolu, island C2

American Samoa

★ Territorial Capital
● Other City
1:1,429,000

0 · 10 · 20 mi
0 · 10 · 20 km
Conformal Conic Projection

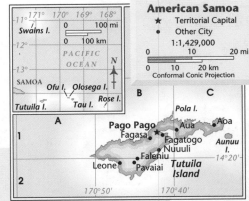

Swains I.
PACIFIC OCEAN
SAMOA
Ofu I.
Olosega I.
Tutuila I.
Tau I.
Rose I.
Pola I.
Pago Pago
Aua
Aoa
Fagasa
Fagatogo
Aunuu I.
Nuuuli
Leone
Faleniu
Pavaiai
Tutuila Island

American Samoa: Map Index

Cities and Towns
Aoa C1
Aua C1
Fagasa B1
Fagatogo B1
Faleniu B1
Leone B2
Nuuuli B1
Pago Pago, capital B1
Pavaiai B2

Other Features
Aunuu, island C1
Ofu, island A1
Olosega, island A1
Pola, island C1
Rose, island B1
Swains, island A1
Tau, island A1
Tutuila, island A1, C2

American Samoa

Capital: Pago Pago
Area: 77 sq. mi.
199 sq. km.
Population: 64,000
Largest City: Pago Pago
Language: Samoan, English
Monetary Unit: U.S. dollar

© MapQuest.com, Inc.

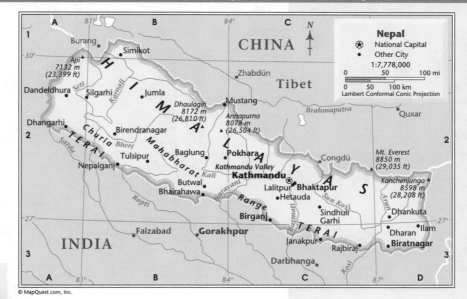

© MapQuest.com, Inc.

Nepal:
Map Index

Cities and Towns
Baglung B2
Bhairahawa B2
Bhaktapur C2
Biratnagar D3
Birendranagar B2
Birganj C2
Butwal B2
Dandeldhura A2
Dhangarhi A2
Dhankuta D2
Dharan D3
Hetauda C2
Ilam D3
Janakpur C3
Jumla B2
Kathmandu, *capital* C2
Lalitpur C2
Mustang B2
Nepalganj B2
Pokhara B2
Rajbiraj C3
Silgarhi B2
Simikot B1
Sindhuli Garhi C2
Tulsipur B2

Other Features
Annapurna, *mt.* B2
Api, *mt.* A2
Arun, *river* D2
Bagmati, *river* C2
Bheri, *river* B2
Churia, *mts.* B2
Dhaulagiri, *mt.* B2
Everest, *mt.* C2
Himalayas, *mts.* B2
Kali, *river* B2
Kanchenjunga, *mt.* D2
Karnali, *river* B2
Kathmandu, *valley* C2
Mahabharat, *range* B2
Narayani, *river* B2
Rapti, *river* B2
Sarda, *river* A2
Seti, *river* A2
Sun Kosi, *river* C2
Terai, *region* A2, C3

Maldives

Capital: Male
Area: 115 sq. mi.
298 sq. km.
Population: 300,000
Largest City: Male
Language: Divehi
Monetary Unit: Rufiyaa

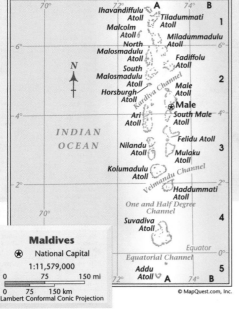

© MapQuest.com, Inc.

Maldives:
Map Index

City
Male, *capital* A2

Other Features
Addu, *atoll* A5
Ari, *atoll* A3
Equatorial, *channel* A5
Fadiffolu, *atoll* A2
Felidu, *atoll* A3
Haddummati, *atoll* A4
Horsburgh, *atoll* A2
Ihavandiffulu, *atoll* A1
Kardiva, *channel* A2
Kolumadulu, *atoll* A3
Malcolm, *atoll* A1
Male, *atoll* A2
Miladummadulu, *atoll* A1
Mulaku, *atoll* A3
Nilandu, *atoll* A3
North Malosmadulu, *atoll* ..A2
One and Half Degree, *channel* ..A4
South Male, *atoll* A2
South Malosmadulu, *atoll* ..A2
Suvadiva, *atoll* A4
Tiladummati, *atoll* A1
Veimandu, *channel* A3

Nepal

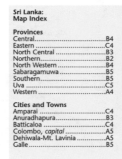

Capital: Kathmandu
Area: 56,827 sq. mi.
147,220 sq. km.
Population: 24,303,000
Largest City: Kathmandu
Language: Nepali
Monetary Unit: Rupee

Sri Lanka:
Map Index

Provinces
Central B4
Eastern C4
North Central B3
Northern B2
North Western B4
Sabaragamuwa B5
Southern B5
Uva C5
Western A4

Cities and Towns
Amparai C4
Anuradhapura B3
Batticaloa C4
Colombo, *capital* A5
Dehiwala-Mt. Lavinia A5
Galle B5
Hambantota C5
Jaffna B2
Kalutara A5
Kandy B4
Kilinochchi B2
Kurunegala B4
Mankulam B2
Mannar A3
Matale B4
Matara B6
Moratuwa A5
Mullaittivu B2
Negombo A4
Nuwara Eliya B5
Point Pedro B2
Polonnaruwa C4
Pottuvil C5
Puttalam A3
Ratnapura B5
Sri Jayawardenepura, *capital* A5
Trincomalee C3
Vavuniya B3

Other Features
Adam's, *peak* B4
Adam's Bridge, *shoal* A3
Aruvi, *river* B3
Bengal, *bay* C3
Delft, *island* A2
Dondra Head, *cape* B6
Jaffna, *lagoon* B2
Kala, *river* B5
Kelani, *river* B4
Mahaweli Ganga, *river* C4
Mannar, *gulf* A3
Mannar, *island* A2
Palk, *strait* A2
Pidurutalagala, *mt.* B4
Trincomalee, *harbor* C3
Yan, *river* B3

Sri Lanka

Capital: Colombo,
Sri Jayawardenepura
Area: 25,332 sq. mi.
65,627 sq. km.
Population: 19,145,000
Largest City: Colombo
Language: Sinhalese
Monetary Unit: Rupee

© MapQuest.com, Inc.

© MapQuest.com, Inc.

Bhutan

Capital: Thimphu
Area: 18,147 sq. mi.
47,013 sq. km.
Population: 1,952,000
Largest City: Thimphu
Language: Dzongkha
Monetary Unit: Ngultrum

Bhutan:
Map Index

Cities and Towns
Chhukha A2
Geylegphug B3
Lhuntshi C2
Lingshi B2
Louri C2
Paro A2
Phuntsholing A3
Punakha A2
Sarbhang B3
Shamgong B2
Tashigang C2

Thimphu, *capital* A2
Tongsa B2

Other Features
Chomo Lhari, *mt.* A1
Dangme, *river* C2
Duars, *plain* A3
Himalayas, *mts.* B1
Kula Kangri, *mt.* B1
Kuru, *river* C2
Lhobrak, *river* B2
Sankosh, *river* B2
Tongsa, *river* B2
Wong, *river* A2

India:
Map Index

Internal Divisions

Andaman and Nicobar
 Islands (territory) F6
Andhra Pradesh (state)........C5
Arunachal Pradesh (state)....F3
Assam (state)......................F3
Bihar (state).......................E3
Chandigarh (territory).........C2
Chhattisgarh (state).............D4
Dadra and Nagar
 Haveli (territory)...............B4
Daman and Diu (territory)....B4
Delhi (territory)..................C3
Goa (state).........................B5
Gujarat (state)....................B4
Haryana (state)...................C3
Himachal Pradesh (state)......C2
Jammu and Kashmir (state)....C2

Jharkhand (state) E4
Karnataka (state) C6
Kerala (state) C6
Lakshadweep (territory) B6
Madhya Pradesh (state) C4
Maharashtra (state) B5
Manipur (state) F4
Meghalaya (state) F3
Mizoram (state) F4
Orissa (state) D4
Pondicherry (territory) C6
Punjab (state) C2
Rajasthan (state) B3
Sikkim (state) E3
Tamil Nadu (state) C6
Tripura (state) F4
Uttar Pradesh (state) C3
Uttaranchal (state) C3
West Bengal (state) E4

Cities and Towns

Agartala F4
Agra C3
Ahmadabad B4
Aizawl F4
Ajmer B3
Akola C4
Alampur ....Inset II
Aligarh C3
Allahabad D3
Alleppey (Alappuzha) C7
Amdanga ....Inset II
Amravati C4
Amritsar B2
Andheri ....Inset I
Ara D3
Asansol E4
Aurangabad C5
Babu Bheri ....Inset II
Baidyabati ....Inset II
Bally ....Inset II

Bamangachi ....Inset II
Bananga F7
Bandra ....Inset I
Bangalore C6
Bansaria ....Inset II
Barakpur ....Inset II
Baranagar ....Inset II
Barasat ....Inset II
Bareilly C3
Bargachia ....Inset II
Bauria ....Inset II
Behala ....Inset II
Belapurpada ....Inset I
Belgaum B5
Bellary C5
Bhadrakh E4
Bhadreswar ....Inset II
Bhagalpur E3
Bhamapur D5
Bhandup ....Inset I
Bharatpur C3

Bhatpara D4
Bhatpara ....Inset II
Bhavnagar B4
Bhayandar ....Inset I
Bhimpur ....Inset I
Bhiwandi ....Inset I
Bhopal C4
Bhubaneswar E4
Bhuj A4
Bihar E3
Bijapur C5
Bikaner B3
Bilaspur D4
Bishnupur ....Inset II
Borivli ....Inset I
Buj-Buj ....Inset II
Burdwan E4
Burhanpur C4
Chandannagar ....Inset II
Chandigarh C2
Chandrapur C5

Chembur ....Inset I
Chene ....Inset I
Chennai (Madras) D6
Cherrapunji F3
Chirner ....Inset I
Cochin (Kochi) C7
Coimbatore C6
Cuddalore C6
Cuttack E4
Daman B4
Darbhanga E3
Darjiling E3
Dehra Dun C2
Delhi C3
Dhulagarh ....Inset II
Dibrugarh F3
Dispur F3
Diu B4
Dum-Dum ....Inset II
Dumjor ....Inset II
Faizabad D3
Gandhinagar B4
Gangaganar B3
Gangtok E3
Garden Reach ....Inset II
Garulia ....Inset II
Gauhati F3
Gaya E4
Ghatkopar ....Inset I
Gorakhpur D3
Gulbarga C5
Guntur D5
Gwalior C3
Halisahar ....Inset II
Haora ....E4, Inset II
Hisapur ....Inset II
Hubli-Dharwar C5
Hugli-Chunchura ....Inset II
Hyderabad C5
Imphal F4
Indore C4
Itanagar F3
Jabalpur C4
Jadabpur ....Inset II
Jagdalpur D5
Jaipur C3
Jammu B2
Jamnagar B4
Jampur ....Inset II
Jamshedpur E4
Janai ....Inset II
Jejur ....Inset II
Jhansi C3
Jodhpur B3
Joka ....Inset II
Jullundur C2
Junagadh B4
Kakinada D5
Kalwa ....Inset I
Kaman ....Inset I
Kamarhati ....Inset II
Kanchipuram C6
Kanchrapara ....Inset II
Kanpur D3
Kansaripara ....Inset II
Kasinathpur ....Inset II
Kathgodam C3
Kharagpur E4
Kohima F3
Kolhapur B5
Kolkata (Calcutta)......E4, Inset II
Kolshet ....Inset I
Konnagar ....Inset II
Kota C3
Kozhikode C6
Kurla ....Inset I
Kurnool C5
Lakhpat A4
Lucknow D3
Ludhiana C2
Madurai C7
Malad ....Inset I
Malegaon B4
Mangalore B6
Mathura C3
Meerut C3
Moradabad C3
Mulund ....Inset I
Mumbai (Bombay) ......B5, Inset I
Mumbra ....Inset I
Mysore C6
Nagpur C4
Naihati ....Inset II
Nalikul ....Inset II
Nanded C5
Nangi ....Inset II
Nanole ....Inset II
Nasik B4
Nellore C6
New Delhi, capital C3
Nizamabad C5
Ongole C5
Panaji B5
Panihati ....Inset II
Patiala C2
Patna E3
Paye ....Inset I
Polba ....Inset II
Pondicherry C6
Port Blair F6
Pune B5
Raipur D4
Rajkot B4
Ramanbati ....Inset II
Ranchi E4
Raurkela D4
Rishra ....Inset II
Saharanpur Panipat C3
Salem C6
Sambalpur D4
Sankrail ....Inset II
Sasaram D4
Sheva ....Inset I
Shillong F3
Sholapur C5
Shrirampur ....Inset II
Silvassi B4
Simla C2
Singur ....Inset II
Sonarpur ....Inset II
South Dum-Dum ....Inset II
Srinagar B2
Sugandha ....Inset II
Surat B4
Thane ....Inset I
Thanjavur C6
Tiruchchirappalli C6
Titagarh ....Inset II
Trivandrum
 (Thiruvananthapuram) C7

India

⊛ National Capital

● Other City

1:20,000,000

0   100   200   300   400 mi
0   100 200 300 400 km
Lambert Conformal Conic Projection

India

Capital: New Delhi
Area: 1,222,559 sq. mi.
 3,167,251 sq. km.
Population: 1,000,849,000
Largest City: Mumbai (Bombay)
Languages: Hindi, English
Monetary Unit: Rupee

© MapQuest.com, Inc.

Bangladesh

* National Capital
* Other City

1:7,491,000

0   50   100 mi
0 50 100 km
Azimuthal Equal Area Projection

Bangladesh
Capital: Dhaka
Area: 57,295 sq. mi.
148,433 sq. km.
Population: 127,118,000
Largest City: Dhaka
Language: Bengali
Monetary Unit: Taka

Bangladesh: Map Index

Cities and Towns
Barisal D6
Bogra C4
Brahmanbaria E5
Chalna C6
Chandpur D5
Chittagong E6
Comilla E5
Cox's Bazar E7
Dhaka, capital D5
Dinajpur B3
Faridpur C5
Jaipurhat B3
Jamalpur C4
Jessore C5
Khulna C6
Kushtia C5
Mymensingh D4
Narayanganj D5
Noakhali E6
Pabna C4
Patuakhali D6
Rajshahi B4
Rangamati F6
Rangpur C3
Saidpur B3
Sirajganj C4
Sylhet E4
Tangail C4

Other Features
Atrai, river B4
Barind, region B4
Bengal, bay D7
Brahmaputra, river D3
Chittagong Hills, region F5
Ganges, river B4
Jamuna, river C4
Karnaphuli, reservoir F6
Karnaphuli, river E6
Keokradong, mt. F7
Madhumati, river C5
Madhupur Tract, region D4
Meghna, river D5
Mouths of the Ganges,
delta C7
Old Brahmaputra, river C4
Padma, river D5
Sundarbans, region C7
Surma, river E3
Tista, river C2

India: Map Index
Trombay .... Inset I
Tuticorin C7
Udaipur B4
Ujjain C4
Ulubaria .... Inset II
Uran .... Inset I
Utan .... Inset I
Vadodara B4
Varanasi D3
Vasai .... Inset I
Vellore C6
Vijayawada D5
Visakhapatnam D5
Warangal C5

Other Features
Amindivi, islands B6
Andaman, islands F6
Androth, island B6
Arabian, sea .... A5, Inset I
Aravalli, range B3
Bengal, bay E5
Bhima, river C5
Brahmaputra, river F3
Car Nicobar, island F7
Cauvery, river C6
Chambal, river C3
Chata Nagpur, plateau D4
Comorin, cape C7
Coromandel, coast D6
Deccan, plateau C5
Eastern Ghats, mts. C6
Elephanta, island .... Inset I
False Divi, point D5
Ganges, river E3
Ghaghara, river D3
Godavari, river C5
Great Indian, desert B3
Great Nicobar, island F7
Himalayas, mts. C2, E3
Hirakud, reservoir D4
Hugli, river .... Inset II
Indus, river C2
Kalpeni, island B7
Kamet, mt. C2
Kanchenjunga, mt. E3
Karakoram, range C1
Kathiawar, peninsula B4
Kavaratti, island B6
Khambhat, gulf B4
Khasi, hills F3
Kolar, gold fields C6
Krishna, river C5
Kutch, gulf A4
Laccadive, islands B6
Little Andaman, island F6
Mahanadi, river D4
Mahim, bay .... Inset I
Malabar, coast B6
Malabar, point .... Inset I
Mannar, gulf C7
Manori, point .... Inset I
Middle Andaman, island F6
Minicoy, island B7
Mizo, hills F4
Mouths of the Ganges, delta .. F4
Mumbai, harbor .... Inset I
Naga, hills F3
Nanda Devi, mt. C2
Narmada, river C4
Nicobar, islands F7
Nilgiri, hills C6
North Andaman, island F6
Palk, strait C7
Rann of Kutch, mud flat B4
Ritchies, archipelago F6
Salsette, island .... Inset I
Salt Water, lake .... Inset II
Satpura, range C4
Son, river D4
South Andaman, island F6
Sutlej, river C2
Ten Degree, channel F7
Ulhas, river .... Inset I
Vasai, creek .... Inset I
Vindhya, range C4
Western Ghats, mts. B5
Yamuna, river C3

Pakistan
Capital: Islamabad
Area: 339,697 sq. mi.
880,044 sq. km.
Population: 138,123,000
Largest City: Karachi
Languages: Urdu, English
Monetary Unit: Pakistani rupee

Pakistan: Map Index

Internal Divisions
Azad Kashmir Province D2
Baluchistan Province B4
Federally Administrated
Tribal Areas C3
Islamabad Capital Territory .. D3
Northern Areas D2
North-West Frontier Province .. D2
Punjab Province D3
Sind Province C5

Cities and Towns
Bahawalpur D4
Bela C4
Chiniot D3
Chitral D2
Dadu C4
Dera Ghazi Khan D3
Dera Ismail Khan D3
Faisalabad D3
Gilgit E2
Gujranwala E3
Gujrat E3
Gwadar B5
Hyderabad C5
Islamabad, capital D3
Jhang Sadar D3
Jhelum D3
Karachi C5
Kasur E3
Khuzdar C4
Lahore E3
Larkana C4
Mardan D2
Mianwali D3
Mirpur Khas C5
Multan D3
Muzaffarabad D2
Nawabshah C4
Nok Kundi B4

Okara D3
Panjgur B4
Peshawar D2
Quetta C3
Rahimyar Khan D4
Rawalpindi D3
Sahiwal D3
Sargodha D3
Shikarpur C4
Sialkot E3
Sukkur C4
Surab C4

Other Features
Arabian, sea B6
Central Makran, range B4
Chagai, hills B4
Chenab, river D3
Hindu Kush, mts. D2
Indus, river C4, D3
Jhelum, river D3
Karakoram, range E2
Khojak, pass C3
Khyber, pass D2
Kirthar, range C4
Konar, river D2
K2 (Godwin Austen), mt. E2
Makran Coast, range B5
Mouths of the Indus, delta ... C5
Nal, river B4
Nanga Parbat, mt. E2
Nara, canal C4
Nowshak, mt. D2
Rakaposhi, mt. E2
Ravi, river D3
Safed Koh, range D3
Siahan, range B4
Sulaiman, range D4
Sutlej, river D4
Thar, desert D4
Tirich Mir, mt. D2
Toba Kakar, range C3
Zhob, river C3

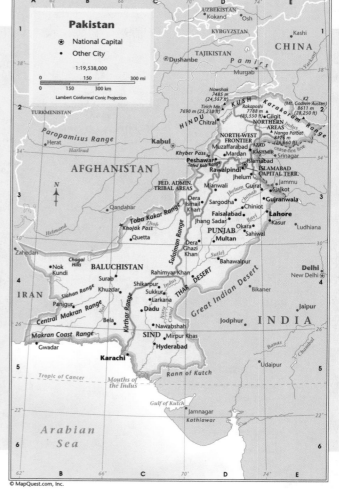

Pakistan
* National Capital
* Other City

1:19,538,000

0   150   300 mi
0 150 300 km
Lambert Conformal Conic Projection

© MapQuest.com, Inc.

Afghanistan: Map Index

Cities and Towns

Asadabad	C2
Baghlan	B1
Balkh	B1
Bamian	B2
Baraki Barak	B2
Chaghcharan	B2
Charikar	B2
Farah	A2
Feyzabad	C1
Gardez	B2
Ghazni	B2
Herat	A2
Jalalabad	C2
Kabul, *capital*	B2
Khowst	B2
Konduz	B1
Kowt-e Ashrow	B2
Lashkar Gah	A2
Mazar-e Sharif	B1
Meymaneh	A1
Qalat	B2
Qaleh-ye Now	A2
Qaleh-ye Panjeh	C1
Qandahar	B2
Samangan	B1
Sar-e Pol	B1
Sheberghan	B1
Shindand	A2
Taloqan	B1
Tarin Kowt	B2
Zaranj	A2
Zareh Sharan	B2

Other Features

Amu Darya, *river*	B1
Arghandab, *river*	B2
Farah, *river*	A2
Fuladi, *mt.*	B2
Gowd-e Zereh, *lake*	A3
Hamun-e Saberi, *lake*	A2
Harirud, *river*	A2
Helmand, *river*	A2
Hindu Kush, *range*	B1
Kabul, *river*	B2
Khojak, *pass*	B2
Khyber, *pass*	C2
Konar, *river*	C1
Konduz, *river*	B1
Morghab, *river*	A1
Nowshak, *mt.*	C1
Panj, *river*	C1
Paropamisus, *range*	A2
Registan, *region*	A2
Shibar, *pass*	B2
Vakhan, *region*	C1

Afghanistan

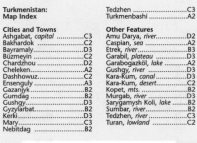

Capital: Kabul
Area: 251,825 sq. mi.
652,396 sq. km.
Population: 25,825,000
Largest City: Kabul
Languages: Pashto, Dari Persian
Monetary Unit: Afghani

Iran

Capital: Tehran
Area: 632,457 sq. mi.
1,638,490 sq. km.
Population: 65,180,000
Largest City: Tehran
Languages: Persian, Turkic, Luri, Kurdish
Monetary Unit: Rial

Iran: Map Index

Cities and Towns

Abadan	B3
Ahvaz	B3
Arak	B3
Ardabil	B2
Bakhtaran	B3
Bam	D4
Bandar Beheshti	E4
Bandar-e Abbas	D4
Bandar-e Anzali	B2
Bandar-e Bushehr	C4
Bandar-e Khomeyni	B3
Bandar-e Torkeman	C2
Birjand	D3
Dezful	B3
Esfahan	C3
Hamadan	B3
Ilam	B3
Iranshahr	E4
Jask	D4
Karaj	C2
Kashan	C3
Kerman	D3
Khorramabad	B3
Khorramshahr	B3
Khvoy	A2
Mashhad	D2
Neyshabur	D2
Orumiyeh (Urmia)	A2
Qazvin	B2
Qom	C3
Rasht	B2
Sabzevar	D2
Sanandaj	B2
Sari	C2
Shahr-e Kord	C3
Shiraz	C4
Sirjan	D4
Tabriz	B2
Tehran, *capital*	C2
Yasuj	C3
Yazd	C3
Zabol	E3
Zahedan	E4
Zanjan	B2

Other Features

Aras, *river*	B2
Atrak, *river*	D2
Azerbaijan, *region*	B2
Bakhtiari, *region*	B3
Baluchistan, *region*	E4
Caspian, *sea*	C1
Damavand, *mt.*	C2
Dasht-e Kavir, *desert*	D3
Dasht-e Lut, *desert*	D3
Elburz, *mts.*	C2
Halil, *river*	D4
Hamun-e Jaz Murian, *lake*	D4
Hashtadan, *region*	E3
Hormuz, *strait*	D4
Karun, *river*	B3
Kavir-e Namak, *desert*	D3
Kerman, *region*	D4
Kharg, *island*	C4
Khorasan, *region*	D2
Khuzestan, *region*	B3
Kopet, *mts.*	D2
Kul, *river*	C4
Larestan, *region*	C4
Mand, *river*	C4
Mazandaran, *region*	C2
Oman, *gulf*	D5
Persian, *gulf*	C4
Qareh, *river*	C4
Qeshm, *island*	D4
Shatt al-Arab, *river*	B3
Urmia, *lake*	B2
Yazd, *region*	C3
Zagros, *mts.*	B3

Afghanistan

⊛ National Capital
• Other City

1:10,870,000

0 50 100 150 mi

0 50 100 150 km

Lambert Conformal Conic Projection

© MapQuest.com, Inc.

Turkmenistan: Map Index

Cities and Towns

Ashgabat, *capital*	C3
Bakhardok	C2
Bayramaly	D3
Büzmeyin	C2
Chardzhou	D2
Cheleken	A2
Dashhowuz	C2
Ensenguly	A3
Gazanjyk	B2
Gumdag	B2
Gushgy	D3
Gyzylarbat	C2
Kerki	D3
Mary	C3
Nebitdag	B2

Tedzhen	C3
Turkmenbashi	A2

Other Features

Amu Darya, *river*	D2
Caspian, *sea*	A2
Etrek, *river*	B3
Garabil, *plateau*	D3
Garabogazköl, *lake*	A2
Gushgy, *river*	D3
Kara-Kum, *canal*	D3
Kara-Kum, *desert*	C2
Kopet, *mts.*	B2
Murgab, *river*	D3
Sarygamysh Koli, *lake*	B2
Sumbar, *river*	B2
Tedzhen, *river*	C3
Turan, *lowland*	C2

Turkmenistan

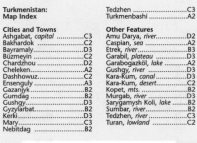

Capital: Ashgabat
Area: 188,417 sq. mi.
488,127 sq. km.
Population: 4,366,000
Largest City: Ashgabat
Languages: Turkmen, Russian, Uzbek
Monetary Unit: Manat

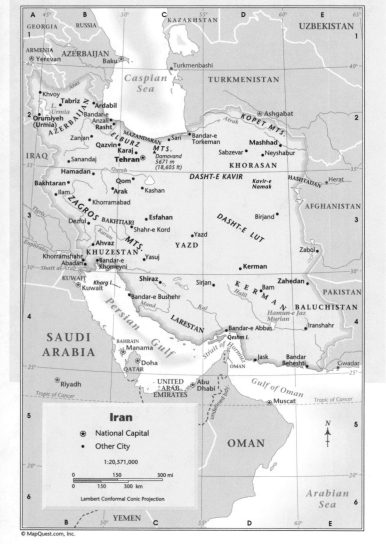

Iran

⊛ National Capital
• Other City

1:20,571,000

0 150 300 mi

0 150 300 km

Lambert Conformal Conic Projection

© MapQuest.com, Inc.

Turkmenistan

⊛ National Capital
• Other City

1:16,929,000

0 100 200 mi

0 100 200 km

Lambert Conformal Conic Projection

© MapQuest.com, Inc.

Kazakhstan

Capital: Astana (Aqmola)
Area: 1,049,200 sq. mi.
 2,718,135 sq. km.
Population: 16,825,000
Largest City: Almaty (Alma-Ata)
Language: Kazakh
Monetary Unit: Tenge

Kazakhstan: Map Index

Cities and Towns

Astana (Aqmola), *capital*	D1
Almaty (Alma-Ata)	D2
Aqtau	B2
Aqtobe	B1
Aral	C2
Arqalyq	C1
Atbasar	C1
Atyrau	B2
Ayagöz	E2
Balkhash	D2
Beyneu	B2
Ekibastuz	D1
Embi	B2
Esil	C1
Kokshetau	C1
Leninsk	C2
Lepsi	D2
Oral	B1
Öskemen (Ust-Kamenogorsk)	E1
Pavlodar	D1
Petropavl	C1
Qaraghandy (Karaganda)	D2
Qostanay	C1
Qyzylorda	C2
Rudnyy	C1
Saryshaghan	D2
Semey (Semipalatinsk)	E1
Shalqar	B2
Shymkent (Chimkent)	C2
Taldyqorghan	D2
Temirtau	D1
Zaysan	E2
Zhambyl (Dzhambul)	D2
Zhezqazgham	C2

Other Features

Alakol, *lake*	E2
Aral, *sea*	B2
Balkhash, *lake*	D2
Betpak Dala, *plain*	C2
Caspian, *depression*	B2
Caspian, *sea*	A2
Ili, *river*	D2
Irtysh, *river*	D1
Ishim, *river*	C1
Kazakh Upland *region*	C2
Khan-Tengri, *mt.*	E2
Muyun Kum, *desert*	D2
Syrdarya, *river*	C2
Tengiz, *lake*	C1
Tobol, *river*	C1
Torghay, *plateau*	C1
Ural, *river*	B2
Ustyurt, *plateau*	A2
Zaysan, *lake*	E2

Kazakhstan

⊛ National Capital
• Other City

1:26,667,000

0 — 125 — 250 mi
0 — 125 — 250 km
Lambert Conformal Conic Projection

© MapQuest.com, Inc.

Uzbekistan

Capital: Tashkent
Area: 172,700 sq. mi.
 447,409 sq. km.
Population: 24,102,000
Largest City: Tashkent
Languages: Uzbek, Russian
Monetary Unit: Ruble

Uzbekistan: Map Index

Cities and Towns

Andizhan	D2
Bukhara	B3
Farghona	D2
Gulistan	C2
Jizzakh	C2
Khujayli	A2
Muynoq	A2
Namangan	D2
Nawoiy	B2
Nukus	A2
Olmaliq	C2
Qarshi	C3
Qunghirot	A2
Quqon	D2
Samarqand	C3
Tashkent, *capital*	C2
Termiz	C3
Uchquduq	B2
Urganch	B2
Zarafshon	B2

Other Features

Amu Darya, *river*	B2
Aral, *sea*	A2
Chirchiq, *river*	C2
Fergana, *valley*	D2
Kyzylkum, *desert*	B2
Syrdarya, *river*	D2
Turan, *lowland*	A2
Ustyurt, *plateau*	A2
Zeravshan, *river*	B2

Uzbekistan

⊛ National Capital
• Other City

1:14,725,000

0 — 40 — 80 mi
0 — 40 — 80 km
Lambert Conformal Conic Projection

Kyrgyzstan: Map Index

Cities and Towns

At-Bashy	D2
Balykchy	E1
Bishkek, *capital*	D1
Cholpon-Ata	E1
Jalal-Abad	C2
Jangy-Bazar	B2
Karakol	F1
Kara-Say	F2
Kyzyl-Kyya	C2
Naryn	E2
Osh	C2
Özgön	C2
Sary Tash	C3
Songköl	D2
Sülüktü	A3
Talas	C1
Tash Kömür	C2
Tokmok	D1
Toktogul	C2

Other Features

Alay, *mts.*	C3
Chatkal, *river*	B2
Chu, *river*	D1
Jengish Chokusu, *mt.*	G1
Kyzyl-Suu, *river*	C3
Naryn, *river*	E2
Tien Shan, *mts.*	E2
Toxkan, *river*	E2
Ysyk-Köl, *lake*	E1

Kyrgyzstan

Capital: Bishkek
Area: 76,642 sq. mi.
 198,554 sq. km.
Population: 4,546,000
Largest City: Bishkek
Language: Kirghiz
Monetary Unit: Som

Kyrgyzstan

⊛ National Capital
• Other City

1:14,286,000

0 — 75 — 150 mi
0 — 75 — 150 km
Lambert Conformal Conic Projection

© MapQuest.com, Inc.

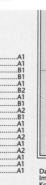

Tajikistan

Capital: Dushanbe
Area: 55,300 sq. mi.
 143,264 sq. km.
Population: 6,103,000
Largest City: Dushanbe
Language: Tajik
Monetary Unit: Ruble

Tajikistan: Map Index

Cities and Towns

Dangara	A1
Dushanbe, *capital*	A1
Jirgatol	B1
Kalai Khum	B1
Kansay	A1
Khorugh	B2
Khudzhand	A1
Konibodom	B1
Kulob	A2
Morghob	B1
Navabad	A1
Norak	A1
Panj	A2
Panjakent	A1
Qurghonteppa	A1
Tursunzoda	A1
Uroteppa	A1
Zarafobod	A1

Other Features

Alay, *mts.*	B1
Bartang, *river*	B1
Darya, *river*	A2
Imeni Ismail Samani, *mt.*	B1
Kofarnihon, *river*	A2
Morghob, *river*	B1
Oqsu, *river*	C2
Pamirs, *mts.*	B2
Panj, *river*	B2
Pyandzh, *river*	B1
Qarokul, *lake*	B1
Surkhob, *river*	B1
Syrdarya, *river*	A1, B1
Turkeston, *mts.*	A1
Vahsh, *river*	A1
Zeravshan, *mts.*	A1
Zeravshan, *river*	A1

Tajikistan

⊛ National Capital
• Other City

1:7,622,000

0 — 40 — 80 mi
0 — 40 — 80 km
Lambert Conformal Conic Projection

© MapQuest.com, Inc.

Iraq: Map Index

Cities and Towns

Amarah, al-..............C2
Baghdad, *capital*........B2
Baqubah...............B2
Basra.................C2
Dahuk.................B1
Diwaniyah, ad-.........C2
Fallujah, al-...........B2
Hadithah, al-..........B2
Hillah, al-............B2
Irbil..................B1
Karbala...............B2
Khanaqin.............C2
Kirkuk................B1
Kut, al-...............C2
Mosul.................B1
Najaf, an-............B2
Nasiriyah, an-.........C2
Qayyarah, al-.........B1
Ramadi, ar-...........B2
Rutbah, ar-...........B2

Samarra...............B2
Samawah, as-..........C2
Sulaymaniyah, as-......C1
Tall Afar..............B1
Tikrit.................B2
Umm Qasr.............C2

Other Features

Babylon, *ruins*.........B2
Diyala, *river*..........C2

Euphrates, *river*........C2
Great Zab, *river*.......B1
Haji Ibrahim, *mt.*.......B1
Little Zab, *river*.......B1
Mesopotamia, *region*....B2
Milh, *lake*............B2
Persian, *gulf*.........C3
Shatt al-Arab, *river*....C2
Syrian, *desert*........B2
Tigris, *river*..........B1

Iraq

Capital: Baghdad
Area: 167,975 sq. mi.
435,169 sq. km.
Population: 22,427,000
Largest City: Baghdad
Language: Arabic
Monetary Unit: Dinar

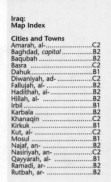

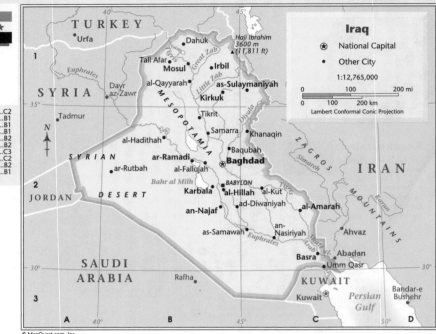

Iraq

⊛ National Capital
• Other City

1:12,765,000

0   100   200 mi
0   100   200 km

Lambert Conformal Conic Projection

© MapQuest.com, Inc.

Kuwait

⊛ National Capital
• Other City

1:4,667,000

0   25   50 mi
0   25   50 km

Lambert Conformal Conic Projection

© MapQuest.com, Inc.

Kuwait

Capital: Kuwait
Area: 6,880 sq. mi.
17,924 sq. km.
Population: 1,991,000
Largest City: Kuwait
Language: Arabic
Monetary Unit: Dinar

Kuwait: Map Index

Cities and Towns

Abdali................B1
Ahmadi, al-...........C2
Fuhayhil, al-..........C2
Hawalli...............C2
Jahrah, al-............B2
Khiran, al-............C3
Kuwait, *capital*......B2
Qasr as-Sabiyah........C2
Rawdatayn, ar-.........B2
Sulaybikhat, as-.......B2
Wafrah, al-............B3

Other Features

Bubiyan, *island*......C2
Faylakah, *island*.....C2
Kuwait, *bay*.........B2
Persian, *gulf*........C2
Wadi al-Batin, *river*..A2
Warbah, *island*......C1

Saudi Arabia

Capital: Riyadh
Area: 865,000 sq. mi.
2,240,933 sq. km.
Population: 21,505,000
Largest City: Riyadh
Language: Arabic
Monetary Unit: Riyal

Saudi Arabia: Map Index

Cities and Towns

Abha..................B2
Badanah...............B1
Buqayq................B1
Buraydah..............B1
Dammam, ad-..........C1
Dhahran...............C1
Hail...................B1
Harad.................C1
Hillah, al-.............B1
Hufuf, al-.............C1
Jawf, al-..............A1
Jeddah.................A2
Jizan.................B2
Jubayl, al-............C1

Khamis Mushayt.......B2
Kharj, al-.............B1
Mecca.................A2
Medina................A1
Najran................B2
Qalat Bishah...........B1
Qunfudhah, al-........B2
Rafha.................B1
Ras al-Khafji..........C1
Ras Tanura............C1
Riyadh, *capital*......B1
Sulayyil, as-..........B2
Tabuk.................A1
Taif, at-..............B2
Turayf................A1
Unayzah...............B1
Wajh, al-.............A1
Yanbu al-Bahr.........A1

Other Features

Asir, *region*..........B2
Dahna, ad-, *desert*....B1
Farasan, *islands*......B2
Hasa, al-, *region*......C1
Hijaz, al-, *region*......A1
Jabal Tuwayq, *mts.*....B2
Nafud, an-, *desert*.....B1
Najd, *region*.........B1
Persian, *gulf*.........C1
Red, *sea*............A1
Rub al-Khali
(Empty Quarter), *desert*..C2
Sabkhat Matti, *salt flat*...C2
Sawda, *mt.*..........B2
Syrian, *desert*........A1
Umm as-Samim, *salt flat*...C2
Wadi al-Hamd, *river*....A1

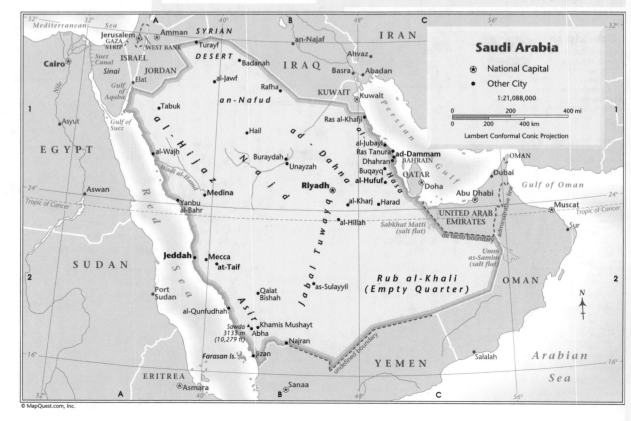

Saudi Arabia

⊛ National Capital
• Other City

1:21,088,000

0   200   400 mi
0   200   400 km

Lambert Conformal Conic Projection

© MapQuest.com, Inc.

Bahrain and Qatar: Map Index

Bahrain
Cities and Towns
Askar B1
Mamtalah, al- B2
Manama, *capital* B1
Mina Salman B1

Other Features
Bahrain, *gulf* A2
Hawar, *islands* B2
Jiddah, *island* A1
Muharraq, al-, *island* ...B1
Ras al-Barr, *cape* B2
Sitrah, *island* B1
Umm an-Nasan, *island* ...A1

Qatar
Cities and Towns
Doha, *capital* D3
Dukhan B3
Jumayliyah, al- C2
Khawr, al- D2
Ruways, ar- C1
Umm Bab B3
Umm Said (Musayid) D4
Wakrah, al- D3

Other Features
Dawhat as-Salwa, *bay* ...B3
Ras Laffan, *cape* D2
Ras Rakan, *cape* C1
Tuwayyir al-Hamir, *hill* ...C4

Bahrain and Qatar
⊛ National Capital
• Other City
1:2,842,000
0   10   20 mi
0   10 20 km
Transverse Mercator Projection

Bahrain
Capital: Manama
Area: 268 sq. mi.
    694 sq. km.
Population: 629,000
Largest City: Manama
Language: Arabic
Monetary Unit: Dinar

Qatar
Capital: Doha
Area: 4,412 sq. mi.
    11,430 sq. km.
Population: 724,000
Largest City: Doha
Language: Arabic
Monetary Unit: Riyal

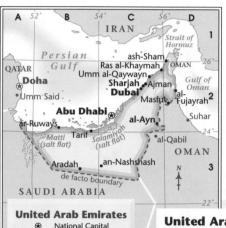

United Arab Emirates
⊛ National Capital
• Other City
1:11,579,000
0   50   100 150 mi
0   50 100 150 km
Lambert Conformal Conic Projection
© MapQuest.com, Inc.

United Arab Emirates (U.A.E.)
Capital: Abu Dhabi
Area: 30,000 sq. mi.
    77,720 sq. km.
Population: 2,344,000
Largest City: Abu Dhabi
Language: Arabic
Monetary Unit: Dirham

United Arab Emirates: Map Index

Cities and Towns
Abu Dhabi, *capital* C2
Ajman C2
Aradah B3
Ayn, al- C2
Dubai C2
Fujayrah, al- D2
Masfut D2
Nashshash, an- C3
Ras al-Khaymah C2

Ruways, ar- B2
Sham, ash- D1
Sharjah C2
Tarif B2
Umm al-Qaywayn C2

Other Features
Hormuz, *strait* D1
Matti, *salt flat* B3
Oman, *gulf* D2
Persian, *gulf* B1
Salamiyah, *salt flat* C3

Yemen: Map Index

Cities and Towns
Aden B2
Ahwar B2
Amran A1
Ataq B2
Balhaf B2
Bayda, al- B2
Dhamar A2
Ghaydah, al- C1
Habarut C1
Hadiboh C2
Hajjah A1
Hawf C1
Hazm, al- A1
Hudaydah, al- A2
Ibb A2
Lahij A2
Madinat ash-Shab A2
Marib B1
Maydi A1

Mocha (Mukha, al-) A2
Mukalla, al- B2
Qalansiyah C2
Qishn C1
Rida A2
Sadah A1
Sanaa, *capital* A1
Sanaw C1
Sayhut C1
Saywun B1
Shabwah B1
Taizz A2
Zabid A2

Other Features
Abd al-Kuri, *island* C2
Aden, *gulf* B2
Arabian, *sea* C2
Bab al-Mandab, *strait* ...A2
Hadhramaut, *district* B1
Jabal an-Nabi Shuayb, *mt.* ...A1
Jabal Zuqar, *island* A2
Kamaran, *island* A1

Perim, *island* A2
Ras al-Kalb, *cape* B2
Ras Fartak, *cape* C1
Red, *sea* A2
Socotra, *island* C2
The Brothers, *islands* C2
Wadi al-Masilah, *river* ...B1

Yemen
Capital: Sanaa
Area: 205,356 sq. mi.
    532,010 sq. km.
Population: 16,942,000
Largest City: Sanaa
Language: Arabic
Monetary Unit: Riyal

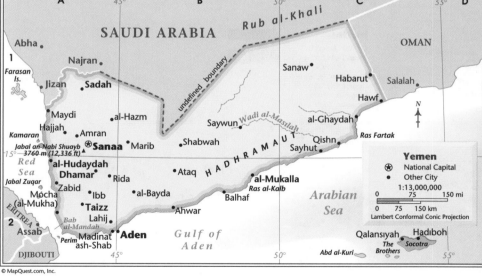

Yemen
⊛ National Capital
• Other City
1:13,000,000
0   75   150 mi
0   75 150 km
Lambert Conformal Conic Projection
© MapQuest.com, Inc.

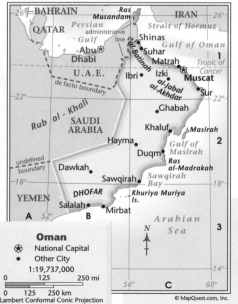

Oman
⊛ National Capital
• Other City
1:19,737,000
0   125   250 mi
0   125 250 km
Lambert Conformal Conic Projection
© MapQuest.com, Inc.

Oman: Map Index

Cities and Towns
Dawkah B2
Duqm C2
Ghabah C2
Hayma C2
Ibri C1
Izki C1
Khaluf C2
Matrah C1

Mirbat B3
Muscat, *capital* C1
Salalah B3
Sawqirah C2
Shinas C1
Suhar C1
Sur C1

Other Features
Arabian, *sea* C3
Batinah, al-, *region* C1
Dhofar, *region* B3

Hormuz, *strait* C1
Jabal al-Akhdar, al-, *mts.* ...C1
Khuriya Muriya, *islands* ...C3
Masirah, *gulf* C2
Masirah, *island* C2
Oman, *gulf* C1
Persian, *gulf* C1
Ras al-Madrakah, *cape* ...C2
Ras Musandam, *cape* C1
Sawqirah, *bay* C2

Oman
Capital: Muscat
Area: 118,150 sq. mi.
    305,829 sq. km.
Population: 2,447,000
Largest City: Muscat
Language: Arabic
Monetary Unit: Rial Omani

Lebanon

Capital: Beirut
Area: 3,950 sq. mi.
10,233 sq. km.
Population: 3,563,000
Largest City: Beirut
Languages: Arabic, French
Monetary Unit: Pound

Lebanon: Map Index

Cities and Towns

Amyun	A1
Baalbek	B1
Babda	A2
Batrun, al-	A1
Beirut, *capital*	A2
Bint Jubayl	A2
Bsharri	B1
Damur, ad-	A2
Duma	A1
Halba	B1
Hirmil, al-	B1
Jazzin	A2
Jubayl	A1
Juniyah	A2
Marj Uyun	A2
Nabatiyah at-Tahta, an-	A2
Qubayyat, al-	B1
Rashayya	A2
Riyaq	B2
Sidon (Sayda)	A2
Sur (Tyre)	A2
Tripoli (Tarabulus)	A1
Zahlah	A2

Other Features

Anti-Lebanon, *mts.*	B1
Awwali, *river*	A2
Bekaa, *valley*	A2
Byblos, *ruins*	A1
Hermon, *mt.*	A2
Ibrahim, *river*	A1
Kebir, *river*	B1
Lebanon, *mts.*	B1
Litani, *river*	A2
Orontes, *river*	B1
Qurnat as-Sawda, *mt.*	B1

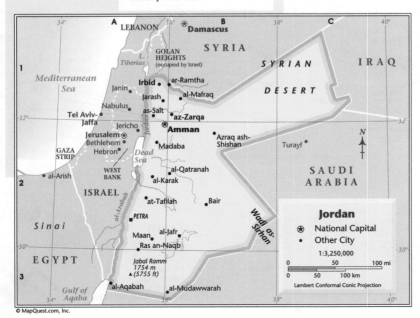

Jordan: Map Index

Cities and Towns

Amman, *capital*	A2
Aqabah, al-	A3
Azraq ash-Shishan	B2
Bair	B2
Irbid	A1
Jafr, al-	B2
Jarash	A1
Karak, al-	A2
Maan	A2
Madaba	A2
Mafraq, al-	B1
Mudawwarah, al-	B3
Qatranah, al-	B2
Ramtha, ar-	B1
Ras an-Naqb	A2
Salt, as-	A1
Tafilah, al-	A2
Zarqa, az-	B1

Other Features

Aqaba, *gulf*	A3
Arabah, al-, *river*	A2
Dead Sea, *lake*	A2
Jabal Ramm, *mt.*	A3
Jordan, *river*	A2
Petra, *ruins*	A2
Syrian, *desert*	B1
Tiberias, *lake*	A1
Wadi as-Sirhan, *depression*	B2

Jordan

Capital: Amman
Area: 34,342 sq. mi.
88,969 sq. km.
Population: 4,561,000
Largest City: Amman
Language: Arabic
Monetary Unit: Dinar

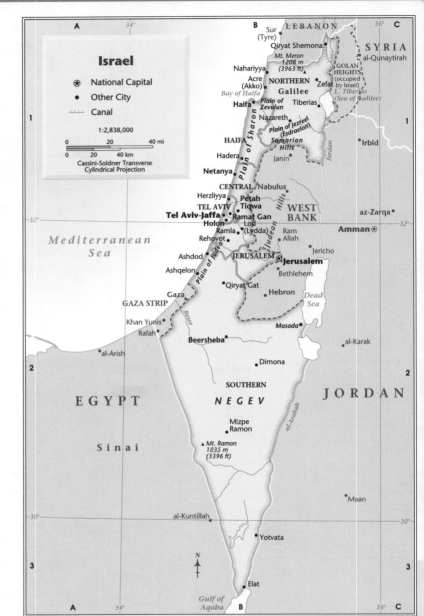

Israel

Capital: Jerusalem
Area: 7,992 sq. mi.
20,705 sq. km.
Population: 5,750,000
Largest City: Jerusalem
Languages: Hebrew, Arabic
Monetary Unit: New Shekel

Israel: Map Index

Districts

Central	B1
Haifa	B1
Jerusalem	B2
Northern	B1
Southern	B2
Tel Aviv	B1

Cities and Towns

Acre (Akko)	B1
Ashdod	B2
Ashqelon	B2
Beersheba	B2
Dimona	B2
Elat	B3
Hadera	B1
Haifa	B1
Herzliyya	B1
Holon	B1
Jerusalem, *capital*	B2
Lod (Lydda)	B2
Mizpe Ramon	B2
Nahariyya	B1
Nazareth	B1
Netanya	B1
Petah Tiqwa	B1
Qiryat Gat	B2
Qiryat Shemona	B1
Ramat Gan	B1
Ramla	B2
Rehovot	B2
Tel Aviv-Jaffa	B1
Tiberias	B1
Yotvata	B3
Zefat	B1

Other Features

Aqaba, *gulf*	B3
Arabah, al-, *river*	B2
Besor, *river*	B2
Dead, *sea*	B2
Galilee, *region*	B1
Haifa, *bay*	B1
Jezreel (Esdraelon), *plain*	B1
Jordan, *river*	B1
Judea, *plain*	B2
Masada, *ruins*	B2
Meron, *mt.*	B1
Negev, *region*	B2
Ramon, *mt.*	B2
Samarian, *hills*	B1
Sharon, *plain*	B1
Tiberias (Galilee), *lake*	B1
Zevulun, *plain*	B1

© MapQuest.com, Inc.

BULGARIA
Black Sea
GEORGIA
Tbilisi
AZERBAIJAN
ARMENIA
Burgas
Edirne
Thrace
Sinope
Batumi
Kura
Tekirdağ
Eyüp
Bosporus
Zonguldak
Samsun
Ordu
Giresun
Trabzon
Artvin
Kars
İstanbul
Üsküdar
Bolu
Pontic
Mountains
L. Sevan
Kadıköy
(Gallipoli)
İzmit
Adapazarı
Çankırı
Amasya
Çorum
Yeşilırmak
Erzincan
Erzurum
Ağrı
Yerevan
Gelibolu
Çanakkale
Bursa
Sakarya
Ankara
Tokat
Sivas
Mt. Ararat (Ağrı Dağı) 5165 m (16,946 ft)
Balıkesir
Ulu Dağ (Mt. Olympus) 2543 m (8343 ft)
Eskişehir
Kırıkkale
Divriği
Keban Res.
Muş
Van
Khvoy
Kütahya
Kırşehir
Kızıl Irmak
Kayseri
Elâzığ
Murat
AZERBAIJAN
Manisa
Uşak
Afyon
ANATOLIA
Malatya
Diyarbakır
Van L.
IRAN
İzmir
Tuz L.
Erciyas Dağı 3916 m (12,848 ft)
Atatürk Res.
Batman
Orumiyeh (Urmia)
Aydın
Büyük Menderes
Denizli
Isparta
Aksaray
Niğde
Maraş
Urfa
Mardin
Siirt
Tigris
L. Urmia
Aegean Sea
Burdur L.
Beyşehir L.
Konya
Karaman
Cilician Gates
Tarsus
Adana
Gaziantep
Great Zab
IRAQ
Muğla
Antalya
Taurus Mts.
Mersin
Çukurova
İskenderun
Halab (Aleppo)
Assad Res.
Fethiye
Alanya
Silifke
Gulf of İskenderum
al-Ladhiqiyah (Latakia)
Rhodes
Gulf of Antalya
Antioch (Antakya)
Crete
CYPRUS
Nicosia
Homs
SYRIA
Mediterranean Sea
LEBANON
Beirut
Damascus
ISRAEL
JORDAN

Turkey

Capital: Ankara
Area: 300,948 sq. mi.
779,658 sq. km.
Population: 65,599,000
Largest City: İstanbul
Language: Turkish
Monetary Unit: Lira

Turkey

⊛ National Capital
• Other City

1:11,125,000

0   75   150 mi
0   75   150 km

Lambert Conformal Conic Projection

© MapQuest.com, Inc.

Turkey: Map Index

Cities and Towns
Adana C3
Adapazarı B2
Afyon B2
Ağrı E2
Aksaray C2
Alanya C3
Amasya C2
Ankara, capital C2
Antalya B3
Antioch (Antakya) ...D3
Artvin E2
Aydın A3
Balıkesir A2
Batman E3
Bolu B2
Bursa B2
Çanakkale A2
Çankırı C2
Çorum C2
Denizli B3
Divriği D2
Diyarbakır E3
Edirne A2
Elâzığ D2
Erzincan D2
Erzurum E2
Eskişehir B2
Eyüp B2
Fethiye B3
Gaziantep D3
Gelibolu (Gallipoli) ..A2
Giresun D2
İskenderun B3
Isparta B3
İstanbul B2
İzmir B2
İzmit B2
Kadıköy B2
Karaman C3
Kars E2
Kastamonu C2
Kayseri C2
Kırıkkale C2
Kırşehir C2
Konya C3
Kütahya B2
Malatya D2

Manisa A2
Maraş D3
Mardin E3
Mersin C3
Muğla B3
Muş E2
Niğde C3
Ordu D2
Samsun D2
Siirt E3

Silifke C3
Sinope C2
Sivas D2
Tarsus C3
Tekirdağ A2
Thrace A2
Tokat D2
Trabzon D2
Urfa D3
Uşak B2
Üsküdar B2
Van E2
Zonguldak C2

Other Features
Aegean, sea A3
Anatolia, region A3
Antalya, gulf B3
Ararat (Ağrı Dağı), mt. ..E2
Aras, river E2

Atatürk, reservoir D3
Beyşehir, lake B3
Black, sea C1
Bosporus, strait B2
Burdur, lake B3
Büyük Menderes, rivers ..A3
Ceyhan, river D3
Cilician Gates, pass ...C3
Çoruh, river E2
Çukurova, region C3

Eğridir, lake B2
Erciyas Dağı, mt. C2
Euphrates, river D2
Great Zab, river E3
İskenderum, gulf B3
Keban, reservoir D2
Kızıl Irmak, river C2
Kura, river E2
Marmara, sea B2
Mediterranean, sea ...B4

Murat, river E2
Pontic, mts. C2
Sakarya, river B2
Seyhan, river C3
Taurus, mts. B3
Tigris, river E2
Tuz, lake C2
Ulu Dağ (Mt. Olympus), mt. ..B2
Van, lake E2
Yesilırmak, river D2

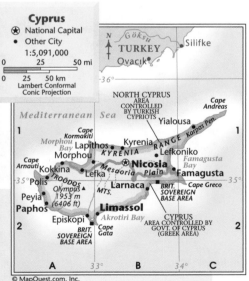

Cyprus

⊛ National Capital
• Other City

1:5,091,000

0   25   50 mi
0   25   50 km

Lambert Conformal Conic Projection

TURKEY
Göksu
Silifke
Ovacık
Mediterranean Sea
Cape Kormakiti
Morphou Bay
Lapithos
Cape Andreas
Karpas Pen.
Yialousa
KYRENIA RANGE
Kyrenia
Lefkoniko
Cape Arnauti
Morphou
Nicosia
Mesaoria Plain
Famagusta Bay
Kokkina
Lefka
Famagusta
Polis
TROODOS MTS.
Olympus 1953 m (6406 ft)
Larnaca
Cape Greco
Peyia
BRIT. SOVEREIGN BASE AREA
Paphos
Limassol
Episkopi
Akrotiri Bay
CYPRUS AREA CONTROLLED BY GOVT. OF CYPRUS (GREEK AREA)
Cape Gata
BRIT. SOVEREIGN BASE AREA

NORTH CYPRUS AREA CONTROLLED BY TURKISH CYPRIOTS

© MapQuest.com, Inc.

Cyprus:
Map Index

Cities and Towns
Episkopi A2
Famagusta B1
Kokkina A1
Kyrenia B1
Lapithos B1
Larnaca B2
Lefka A1
Lefkoniko B1
Limassol B2
Morphou A1
Nicosia, capital A2
Paphos A2
Peyia A1
Polis A1

Yialousa C1

Other Features
Akrotiri, bay B2
Andreas, cape C1
Arnauti, cape A1
British Sovereign Base Area ..A2, B2
Famagusta, bay C1
Gata, cape B2
Greco, cape C1
Karpas, peninsula C1
Kormakiti, cape A1
Kyrenia, range B1
Mesaoria, plain B1
Morphou, bay A1
Olympus, mt. A2
Troödos, mts. A2

Cyprus

Capital: Nicosia
Area: 3,572 sq. mi.
9,254 sq. km.
Population: 754,000
Largest City: Nicosia
Languages: Greek, Turkish
Monetary Unit: Pound

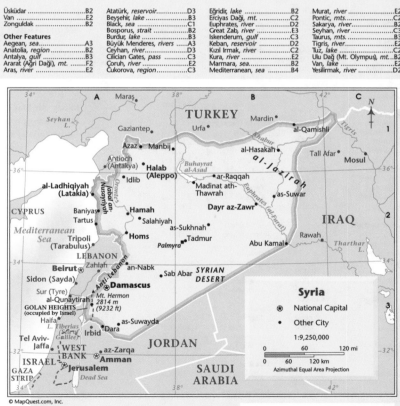

TURKEY
Maraş
Seyhan L.
Gaziantep
Urfa
Mardin
al-Qamishli
Tigris
Azaz
Manbij
al-Hasakah
Tall Afar
Mosul
Antioch (Antakya)
Halab (Aleppo)
Buhayrat al-Asad
ar-Raqqah
al-Jazirah
Idlib
Madinat ath-Thawrah
as-Suwar
al-Ladhiqiyah (Latakia)
Jabal an-Nusayriyah
Euphrates (al-Furat)
Dayr az-Zawr
IRAQ
Baniyas
Hamah
Salahiyah
as-Sukhnah
Tartus
CYPRUS
Mediterranean Sea
Homs
as-Sukhnah
Rawah
Tharthar L.
Tripoli (Tarabulus)
Palmyra
Tadmur
Abu Kamal
LEBANON
Beirut
Zahlah
an-Nabk
Sab Abar
SYRIAN DESERT
Sidon (Sayda)
Anti-Lebanon
Damascus
Sur (Tyre)
al-Qunaytirah
Mt. Hermon 2814 m (9232 ft)
Haifa
GOLAN HEIGHTS (occupied by Israel)
as-Suwayda
L. Tiberias (Galilee)
Dara
Tel Aviv-Jaffa
Irbid
JORDAN
WEST BANK
az-Zarqa
Jerusalem
Amman
ISRAEL
GAZA STRIP
Dead Sea
SAUDI ARABIA

Syria

⊛ National Capital
• Other City

1:9,250,000

0   60   120 mi
0   60   120 km

Azimuthal Equal Area Projection

© MapQuest.com, Inc.

Syria:
Map Index

Cities and Towns
Abu Kamal B2
Azaz A1
Baniyas A2
Damascus, capital A3
Dara A3
Dayr az-Zawr B2
Halab (Aleppo) A1
Hamah A2
Hasakah, al- B1
Homs A2
Idlib A2
Ladhiqiyah, al- (Latakia) ..A2
Madinat ath-Thawrah ..B2
Manbij A1
Nabk, an- A2
Qamishli, al- B1

Qunaytirah, al- A3
Raqqah, ar- B2
Sab Abar A3
Salahiyah A2
Sukhnah, as- B2
Suwar, as- B2
Suwayda, as- A3
Tadmur A2
Tartus A2

Other Features
Anti-Lebanon, mts. ...A3
Buhayrat al-Asad, lake ..B2
Euphrates (al-Furat), river ..B2
Golan Heights, occupied territory ..A3
Hermon, mt. A3
Jabal an-Nusayriyah, mts. ..A2
Jazirah, al-, region B1
Khabur, river B1

Mediterranean, sea ...A2
Orontes, river A2
Palmyra, ruins B2
Syrian, desert B3
Tigris, river C1

Syria

Capital: Damascus
Area: 71,498 sq. mi.
185,228 sq. km.
Population: 17,214,000
Largest City: Damascus
Language: Arabic
Monetary Unit: Pound

MAJOR CITIES

Albania		**Italy**	
Tirana	244,000	Rome	2,645,000
		Milan	1,304,000
Andorra		Naples	1,046,000
Andorra la Vella	16,000	Turin	920,000
		Palermo	688,000
Armenia	(metro)	Genoa	654,000
Yerevan	1,278,000		
		Latvia	
Austria		Riga	821,000
Vienna	1,540,000		
		Liechtenstein	
Azerbaijan	(metro)	Vaduz	5,000
Baku	1,848,000		
		Lithuania	
Belarus	(metro)	Vilnius	580,000
Minsk	1,708,000		
		Luxembourg	
Belgium	(metro)	Luxembourg	77,000
Brussels	948,000		
Antwerp	456,000	**F.Y.R. Macedonia**	
		Skopje	430,000
Bosnia and Hercegovina			
Sarajevo	416,000	**Malta**	
		Valletta	7,000
Bulgaria			
Sofia	1,117,000	**Moldova**	
		Chişinău	656,000
Croatia	(metro)		
Zagreb	981,000	**Monaco**	
		Monaco	27,000
Czech Republic			
Prague	1,200,000	**Netherlands**	
		Amsterdam	717,000
Denmark		Rotterdam	591,000
Copenhagen	632,000		
		Norway	
Estonia		Oslo	492,000
Tallinn	424,000		
		Poland	
Finland		Warsaw	1,633,000
Helsinki	532,000	Łódź	820,000
		Kraków	745,000
France		Wrocław	642,000
Paris	2,152,000		
Lyon	1,260,000	**Portugal**	
Marseille	1,200,000	Lisbon	582,000
Georgia	(metro)	**Romania**	
Tbilisi	1,342,000	Bucharest	2,037,000
Germany		**Russia (European)**	
Berlin	3,458,000	Moscow	8,368,000
Hamburg	1,708,000	St. Petersburg	4,232,000
Munich	1,226,000	Nizh. Novgorod	1,376,000
Cologne	964,000	Samara	1,184,000
Frankfurt	647,000	Ufa	1,093,000
Essen	612,000	Kazan	1,076,000
Dortmund	597,000	Perm	1,031,000
Stuttgart	586,000	Rostov-na-Donu	1,014,000
Düsseldorf	571,000	Volgograd	999,000
Leipzig	549,000		
		San Marino	
Great Britain		San Marino	3,000
London	7,074,000		
Birmingham	1,021,000	**Slovakia**	
Leeds	727,000	Bratislava	452,000
Glasgow	616,000		
Sheffield	530,000	**Slovenia**	
Bradford	483,000	Ljubljana	273,000
Liverpool	468,000		
Edinburgh	449,000	**Spain**	
		Madrid	2,867,000
Greece	(metro)	Barcelona	1,509,000
Athens	3,073,000	Valencia	747,000
		Seville	697,000
Hungary			
Budapest	1,897,000	**Sweden**	
		Stockholm	718,000
Iceland			
Reykjavík	105,000	**Switzerland**	
		Zürich	342,000
Ireland		Bern	129,000
Dublin	482,000		
		Turkey (European)	
		İstanbul	6,620,000
		Ukraine	
		Kiev	2,630,000
		Kharkiv	1,555,000
		Dnipropetrovsk	1,147,000
		Donetsk	1,088,000
		Odesa	1,046,000
		Yugoslavia	(metro)
		Belgrade	1,204,000

International comparability of city population data is limited by various data inconsistencies.

Gross National Product (GNP) per capita

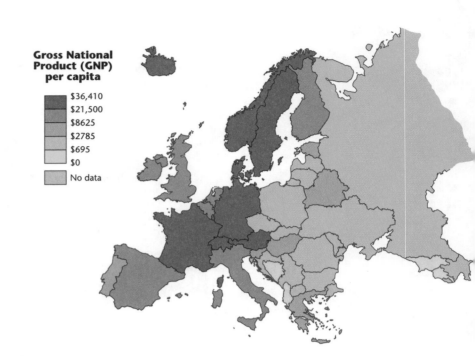

- $36,410
- $21,500
- $8625
- $2785
- $695
- $0
- No data

Vegetation

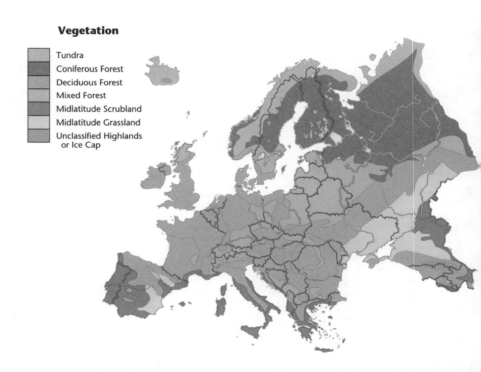

- Tundra
- Coniferous Forest
- Deciduous Forest
- Mixed Forest
- Midlatitude Scrubland
- Midlatitude Grassland
- Unclassified Highlands or Ice Cap

Europe: Population, by nation (in millions)*

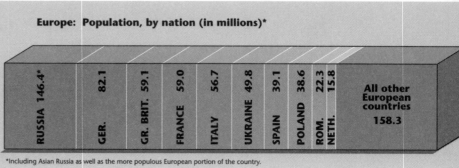

| RUSSIA 146.4* | GER. 82.1 | GR. BRIT. 59.1 | FRANCE 59.0 | ITALY 56.7 | UKRAINE 49.8 | SPAIN 39.1 | POLAND 38.6 | ROM. 22.3 | NETH. 15.8 | All other European countries 158.3 |

*Including Asian Russia as well as the more populous European portion of the country.

© MapQuest.com, Inc.

CITIES

⊗ National Capital
★ Territorial Capital
• Other City

ELEVATIONS

Feet	Meters
13,120	4000
6560	2000
1640	500
656	200
0	0
Below sea level	

CLIMATE

Average daily temperature °F range
Average monthly precipitation Inches

High
Low

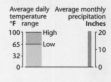

ARKHANGELSK, Russia

ATHENS, Greece

COPENHAGEN, Denmark
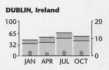

DUBLIN, Ireland

LISBON, Portugal

MOSCOW, Russia
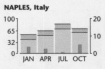

NAPLES, Italy

ODESA, Ukraine
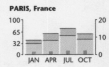

PARIS, France

REYKJAVÍK, Iceland
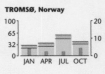

TROMSØ, Norway
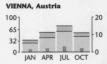

VIENNA, Austria

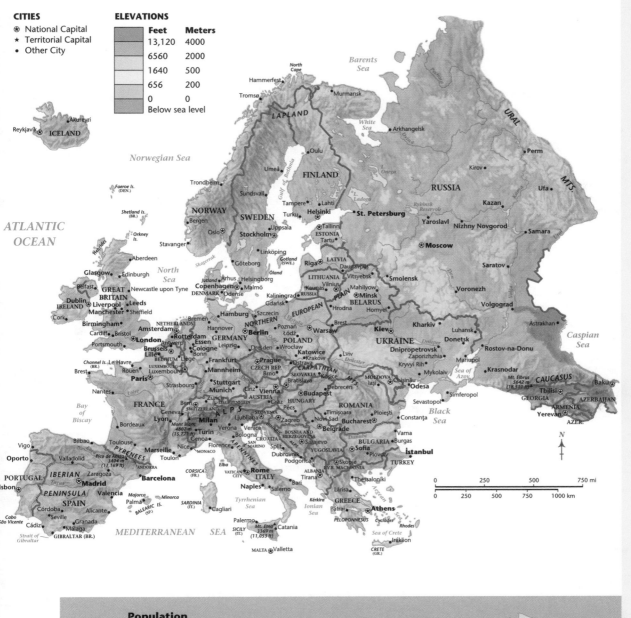

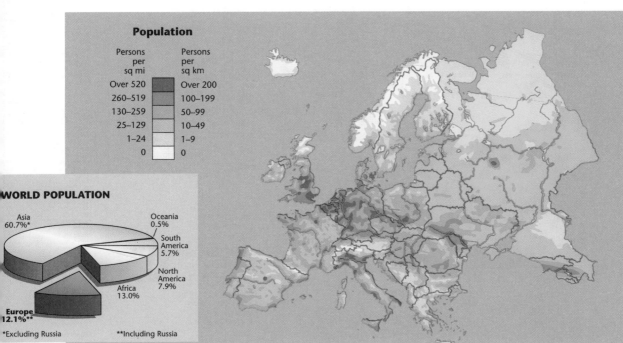

Population

Persons per sq mi	Persons per sq km
Over 520	Over 200
260–519	100–199
130–259	50–99
25–129	10–49
1–24	1–9
0	0

WORLD POPULATION

Asia 60.7%*
Oceania 0.5%
South America 5.7%
North America 7.9%
Africa 13.0%
Europe 12.1%**

*Excluding Russia   **Including Russia

Great Britain:
Map Index

CHANNEL ISLANDS
Features
Alderney, island ....Inset II
Guernsey, island ....Inset II
Jersey, island ....Inset II
St. Malo, gulf ....Inset II
Sark, island ....Inset II

ENGLAND
Cities and Towns
Aylesbury ....Inset III
Banbury C3
Barnsley C3
Barnstaple B3
Barrow-in-Furness B2
Bath C3
Bedford C3
Berwick-upon-Tweed C2
Birkenhead B3
Birmingham C3
Blackburn C3
Blackpool C3
Bolton C3
Boston C3
Bournemouth C4
Bradford C3
Braintree ....Inset III
Brentwood ....Inset III
Brighton C4
Bristol C3
Burnley C3
Bury C3
Bury St. Edmunds D3
Buxton C3
Camberley ....Inset III
Cambridge D3
Canterbury D3
Carlisle C2
Chatham ....Inset III
Chelmsford ....D3, Inset III
Cheltenham C3
Chester C3
Chesterfield C3
Chichester C4
Colchester D3
Coventry C3
Cowes C4
Crawley ....Inset III
Crewe C3
Darlington C2
Derby C3
Doncaster C3
Dorchester C4
Dorking ....Inset III
Dover D3
Dudley C3
Dunstable ....Inset III
Durham C2
Eastbourne D4
Ely D3
Epsom ....Inset III
Ewell ....Inset III
Exeter B4
Farnham ....Inset III
Felixstowe D3
Fleetwood C3
Folkestone D3
Gateshead C2
Gillingham D3
Glastonbury C3
Gloucester C3
Gosport C4
Grantham C3
Gravesend ....Inset III
Great Yarmouth D3
Grimsby C3
Guildford C3
Halifax C3
Harlow ....Inset III
Harrogate C2
Haslemere ....Inset III
Hastings D4
Hereford C3
Hertford ....Inset III
High Wycombe ....Inset III
Hove C4
Huddersfield C3
Ipswich D3
Kendal C2
Kenilworth C3
Kidderminster C3
King's Lynn D3
Kingston upon Hull C3
Kingston upon Thames .....Inset III
Lancaster C2
Launceston B4
Leeds C3
Leicester C3
Lewes D4
Lichfield C3
Lincoln C3
Liverpool C3
London, capital ....C3, Inset III
Lowestoft D3
Luton C3
Maidstone D3
Manchester C3
Margate D3
Matlock C3
Middlesbrough C2
Newcastle-under-Lyme C3
Newcastle upon Tyne C2
Newmarket D3
Newquay B4
Northallerton C2
Northampton C3
North Shields C2
Norwich D3
Nottingham C3
Oldham C3
Oxford C3
Penrith C2
Penzance B4
Peterborough C3
Plymouth B4
Poole C4
Portsmouth C4
Preston C3
Reading C3
Reigate ....Inset III
Rochdale C3
Rotherham C3
St. Albans ....C3, Inset III

Great Britain

⊛ National Capital

• Other City

1:4,375,000

0 25 50 75 100 mi

0 25 50 75 100 125 150 km

Lambert Conformal Conic Projection

Great Britain
Capital: London
Area: 94,251 sq. mi.
 244,174 sq. km.
Population: 59,133,000
Largest City: London
Language: English
Monetary Unit: Pound

Republic of Ireland
Capital: Dublin
Area: 27,137 sq. mi.
70,303 sq. km.
Population: 3,632,000
Largest City: Dublin
Languages: English, Irish
Monetary Unit: Punt, Euro

Republic of Ireland:
Map Index

Counties
Carlow C2
Cavan C2
Clare B2
Cork B3
Donegal B1
Dún Laoghaire-Rathdown ...C2
Fingal C2
Galway B2
Kerry B2
Kildare C2
Kilkenny C2
Laois C2
Leitrim B1
Limerick B2
Longford C2
Louth C2
Mayo B2
Meath C2
Monaghan C1
Offaly C2
Roscommon B2
Sligo B1
South Dublin C2
Tipperary North Riding B2
Tipperary South Riding B2
Waterford C2
Westmeath C2
Wexford C2
Wicklow C2

County Boroughs
Cork B3
Dublin D2
Galway B2
Limerick B2
Waterford C2

Cities and Towns
Ardara B1
Arklow C2
Athlone C2
Ballina B1
Bantry B3
Blarney B3
Carlingford C1
Carlow C2
Carrick-on-Shannon B2
Cashel C2
Castlebar B2
Cavan C2
Clara C2
Clifden A2
Clonmel C2
Cóbh B3
Cork B3
Dingle A2
Donegal B1
Drogheda C2
Dublin, capital C2
Dundalk C2
Dungarvan C2
Dún Laoghaire C2
Ennis B2
Ennistymon B2
Galway B2
Kildare C2
Kilkee B2
Kilkenny C2
Killarney B2
Letterkenny C1
Lifford C1
Limerick B2
Longford C2
Mallow B2
Maynooth C2

Monaghan C1
Mullingar C2
Naas C2
Nenagh B2
Port Laoise C2
Roscommon B2
Roscrea C2
Rosslare C2
Shannon B2
Sligo B1
Swords C2
Tipperary B2
Tralee B2
Trim C2
Tuam B2
Tullamore C2
Waterford C2
Westport B2
Wexford C2
Wicklow C2
Youghal C3

Other Features
Achill, island A2
Allen, lake B1
Aran, islands B2
Bantry, bay B3
Barrow, river C2
Benwee Head, cape B1
Blackwater, river B2
Blackwater, river C1
Boggeragh, mts. B2
Boyne, river C2
Caha, mts. B3
Carlingford, lake C1
Carnsore, point C2
Carrantuohill, mt. B3
Celtic, sea B3
Clear, cape B3
Conn, lake B1
Connaught, province B2
Connemara, region B2
Corrib, lake B2
Derg, lake B2
Dingle, bay A2
Donegal, bay B1
Erne, river B1
Errigal, mt. C1
Finn, river C1
Foyle, inlet C1
Galway, bay B2
Grand, canal C2
Irish, sea D2
Killala, bay B1
Knockboy, mt. B3
Lee, river B3
Leinster, province C2
Loop Head, cape B2
Malin Head, cape C1
Mask, lake B2
Maumturk, mts. B2
Mizen Head, cape B3
Moher, cliffs B2
Munster, province B2
Ree, lake C2
Royal, canal C2
Saint George's, channel C3
Shannon, river C2
Suir, river C2
Twelve Pins, mt. B2
Ulster, province C1
Wicklow, mts. C2
Wicklow Head, cape D2

Great Britain: Map Index
St. Austell B4
St. Helens C3
Salford C3
Salisbury C3
Scarborough C2
Scunthorpe C3
Sheffield C3
Shrewsbury C3
Slough ....Inset III
Solihull C3
Southampton C4
Southend-on-Sea D3
Southport C3
South Shields C3
Stafford C3
Stevenage ....Inset III
Stoke-on-Trent C3
Stratford-upon-Avon C3
Sunderland C2
Swindon C3
Taunton C3
Telford C3
Tewkesbury C3
Thetford D3
Tiverton B4
Tonbridge ....Inset III
Torbay B4
Trowbridge C3
Truro A4
Tunbridge Wells D3
Wakefield C3
Walsall C3
Warrington C3
Warwick C3
Watford ....Inset III
Westminster ....Inset III
Whitehaven B2
Wigan C3
Winchester C3
Windsor ....Inset III
Wolverhampton C3
Worcester C3
Yeovil C4
York C3

Other Features
Avon, river C3
Black Country, region C3
Bristol, channel B3
Cheviot, hills C2
Cotswold, hills C3
Cumbrian, mts. C2
Dartmoor, plateau B4
Dee, river B3
Dover, strait D4
English, channel C4
Exmoor, plateau B4
Fens, region D3
Flodden Field, plain C2
Humber, river D3
Irish, sea B2
Lake, district B2
Land's End, promontory B4
Liverpool, bay B3
Lyme, bay C3
Mersey, river C3
Midlands, region C3
North, sea D2
North Downs, hills C3
North Foreland,
  promontory D3
Ouse, river C2, D3
Pennines, mts. C2
Scafell Pike, mt. B2
Scilly, islands A4
Severn, river C3
South Downs, hills C3
Spithead, channel C4
Start, point B4
Tees, river C2
Thames, river ....C3, Inset III
Trent, river C3
Tweed, river C2
Tyne, river C2
Wash, bay D3
Wight, island C4
Wye, river C3
Yare, river D3

ISLE OF MAN
City
Douglas B2

NORTHERN IRELAND
Cities and Towns
Armagh A2
Ballymena A2
Bangor B2
Belfast B2
Coleraine A2
Holywood B2
Larne B2
Londonderry A2
Newry A2
Omagh A2
Portadown A2
Strangford B2

Other Features
Antrim, mts. A2

Bann, river A2
Erne, river A2
Foyle, lake A2
Foyle, river A2
Giant's Causeway,
  headland A2
Irish, sea B3
Lough Erne, lake A2
Mourne, mts. A2
Neagh, lake A2
North, channel A2
Rathlin, island A2
Slieve Donard, mt. B2
Sperrin, mts. A2
Upper Lough Erne, lake A2

SCOTLAND
Cities and Towns
Aberdeen C1
Aviemore B1
Ayr B2
Campbeltown B2
Clydebank B2
Cupar B1
Dornoch B1
Dumfries C2
Dundee B2
Dunfermline B2
Elgin B1
Fort William B1
Fraserburgh C1
Glasgow B2
Greenock B2
Hamilton B2
Hawick C2
Inverness B1
Kilmarnock B2
Kirkcaldy B2
Kirkwall ....Inset I
Kyle of Lochalsh B1
Lairg B1

Lerwick ....Inset I
Mallaig B1
Montrose C2
Motherwell B2
Newtown St. Boswells C2
Oban B2
Paisley B2
Perth B2
Peterhead C1
Pitlochry B2
Portree A1
St. Andrews C2
Scone B2
Sconser A1
Stirling B2
Stornoway A1
Stranraer B2
Thurso B1
Ullapool B1
Wick B1

Other Features
Arran, island B2
Barra, island A2
Bass Rock, islet C2
Bell Rock (Inchcape),
  reef C2
Ben Nevis, mt. B2
Bute, island B2
Cheviot, hills C2
Clyde, estuary B2
Clyde, river B2
Coll, island A2
Colonsay, island A2
Dee, river C1
Dornoch, estuary B1
Duncansby, cape B1
Dunsinane, mt. B2
Eigg, island A2
Fair, island ....Inset I
Forth, estuary B2
Forth, river B2

Grampian, mts. B2
Hebrides, sea A1
Hoy, island ....Inset I
Inner Hebrides, islands A2
Islay, island A2
Jura, island B2
Katrine, lake B2
Kinnairds, cape C1
Lammermuir, hills C2
Lewis, island A1
Linnhe, lake A2
Lomond, lake B2
Lorne, estuary A2
Mainland, island ....Inset I
Merrick, mt. B2
Minch, strait A1
Moray, estuary B1
Mull, island A2
Ness, lake B1
North Uist, island A1
Ochil, hills B2
Orkney, islands ....Inset I
Outer Hebrides, islands A1
Rhum, island A2
Sanday, island ....Inset I
Shetland, islands ....Inset I
Sidlaw, hills B2
Skye, island A1
Solway, estuary B2
Southern Uplands, mts. B2
South Ronaldsay,
  island ....Inset I
South Uist, island A1
Spey, river B1
Stronsay, island ....Inset I
Tay, estuary C2
Tay, lake B2
Tay, river B2
Tiree, island A2
Tweed, river C2
Unst, island ....Inset I
Westray, island ....Inset I

Wrath, cape B1
Yell, island ....Inset I

WALES
Cities and Towns
Aberystwyth B3
Bangor B3
Caerleon C3
Caernarfon B3
Cardiff B3
Carmarthen B3
Conwy B3
Fishguard B3
Holyhead B3
Lampeter B3
Llandrindod Wells B3
Merthyr Tydfil B3
Milford Haven B3
Mold B3
Newport C3
Pembroke B3
Port Talbot B3
Rhondda B3
St. David's B3
Swansea B3
Welshpool B3

Other Features
Anglesey, island B3
Bala, lake B3
Brecon Beacons, mts. B3
Bristol, channel B3
Cambrian, mts. B3
Cardigan, bay B3
Dee, river B3
Lleyn, peninsula B3
Menai, strait B3
Snowdon, mt. B3
Teifi, river B3
Tywi, river B3
Usk, river C3
Wye, river C3

Ireland

⊛ National Capital

• Other City

1:3,960,000

0   30   60 mi
0 30 60 km
Lambert Conformal Conic Projection

© MapQuest.com, Inc.

ATLANTIC OCEAN

GREAT BRITAIN

Irish Sea

Celtic Sea

Saint George's Channel

DONEGAL
ULSTER
CONNAUGHT
LEINSTER
MUNSTER
Dublin

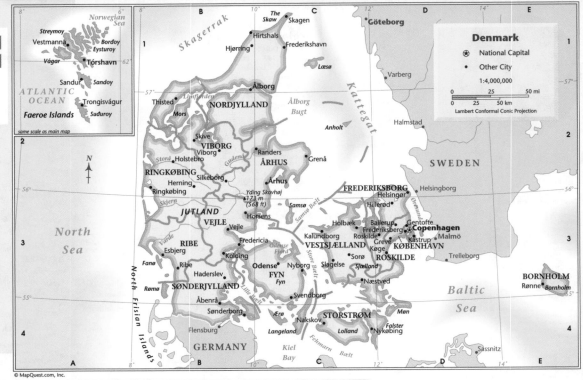

Denmark

Capital: Copenhagen
Area: 16,639 sq. mi.
43,080 sq. km.
Population: 5,357,000
Largest City: Copenhagen
Language: Danish
Monetary Unit: Krone

Denmark: Map Index

Counties
Århus C2
Bornholm E3
Frederiksborg D2
Fyn C3
København D3
Nordjylland B2
Ribe B3
Ringkøbing B2
Roskilde D3
Sønderjylland B3
Storstrøm C4
Vejle C3
Vestsjælland C3
Viborg B2

Cities and Towns
Åbenrå B3
Ålborg B1
Århus C2
Ballerup D3
Copenhagen, *capital* .. D3
Esbjerg B3
Fredericia B3
Frederiksberg D3
Frederikshavn C1
Gentofte D3
Grenå C2
Greve D3
Haderslev B3
Helsingør D2
Herning B3
Hillerød D3
Hirtshals B1
Hjørring B1
Holbæk C3
Holstebro B2
Horsens B3
Kalundborg C3
Kastrup D3
Køge D3
Kolding B3
Næstved C3
Nakskov C4
Nyborg C3
Nykøbing C4
Odense C3
Randers C2
Ribe B3
Ringkøbing B2
Rønne E3
Roskilde D3
Sandur .... Inset
Silkeborg B2
Skagen C1
Skive B2
Slagelse C3
Sønderborg B4
Sorø C3
Svendborg C3
Thisted B2
Tórshavn .... Inset
Trongisvágur .... Inset
Vejle B3
Vestmanna .... Inset
Viborg B2

Other Features
Ærø, *island* C4
Ålborg, *bay* C2
Anholt, *island* C2
Baltic, *sea* D3
Bordoy, *island* ...... Inset
Bornholm, *island* E3
Eysturoy, *island* .... Inset
Faeroe, *islands* ..... Inset
Falster, *island* D4
Fanø, *island* B3
Fehmarn, *strait* C4
Fyn, *island* C3
Gudenå, *river* B2
Jutland, *peninsula* .. B3
Kattegat, *strait* C2
Læsø, *island* C1
Langeland, *island* ... C4
Lille, *strait* B3
Limfjorden, *channel* . B2
Lolland, *island* C4
Møn, *island* D4
Mors, *island* B2
North, *sea* A3
North Frisian, *islands* B4
Norwegian, *sea* ...... Inset
Odense, *fjord* C3
Øresund, *sound* D3
Rømø, *island* B3
Samsø, *island* C3
Samsø, *island* C3
Sandoy, *island* ...... Inset
Sjælland, *island* C3
Skagerrak, *strait* B1
Skaw, *cape* C1
Skjern, *river* B3
Storå, *river* B2
Store, *strait* C3
Streymoy, *island* .... Inset
Suduroy, *island* ..... Inset
Vágar, *island* .... Inset
Varde, *river* B3
Yding Skovhøj, *hill* .. B2

Netherlands

Capital: Amsterdam
Area: 16,033 sq. mi.
41,536 sq. km.
Population: 15,808,000
Largest City: Amsterdam
Language: Dutch
Monetary Unit: Guilder, Euro

Netherlands: Map Index

Provinces
Drenthe D2
Flevoland C2
Friesland C1
Gelderland D2
Groningen D1
Limburg C3
North Brabant C3
North Holland B2
Overijssel D2
South Holland B2
Utrecht C2
Zeeland A3

Cities and Towns
Alkmaar B2
Almelo D2
Amersfoort C2
Amsterdam, *capital* .. B2
Apeldoorn C2
Arnhem C3
Assen D2
Bergen op Zoom B3
Breda B3
Delft B2
Delfzijl D1
Den Helder B2
Deventer C2
Doetinchem D3
Dordrecht B3
Edam C2
Ede C2
Eindhoven C3
Emmeloord C2
Emmen D2
Enschede D2
Gouda B2
Groningen D1
Haarlem B2
Heerenveen C2
Heerlen C4
Hengelo D2
Hilversum C2
Hoogeveen D2
Hoorn C2
Leeuwarden C1
Leiden B2
Lelystad C2
Maastricht C4
Meppel D2
Middelburg A3
Nijmegen C3
Oss C3
Otterlo C2
Roermond D3
Rotterdam B3
Scheveningen B2
Schiedam B3
's Hertogenbosch C3
Sittard C4
Sneek C1
The Hague B2
Tilburg C3
Utrecht C2
Venlo D3
Vlaardingen B3
Vlissingen A3
Weert C3
Zaandam B2
Zwolle D2

Other Features
Ameland, *island* C1
Eems, *river* D1
Flevoland, *polder* D2
Ijssel, *river* D2
Ijsselmeer, *sea* C2
Maas, *river* C3, D3
Neder Rijn, *river* C3
New Waterway, *channel* B3
Northeast, *polder* ... C2
North Holland, *canal* . B2
North Sea, *canal* B2
Oosterschelde, *channel* A3
Overflakkee, *island* .. B3
Princess Margriet, *canal* C1
Schiermonnikoog, *island* D1
Schouwen, *island* A3
Terschelling, *island* .. C1
Texel, *island* B1
Tholen, *island* B3
Vaalserberg, *mt.* D4
Vlieland, *island* B1
Waal, *river* C3
Waddenzee, *sound* ... C1
Walcheren, *island* ... A3
Westerschelde, *channel* A3
West Frisian, *islands* . C1
Wilhelmina, *canal* B3
Zuid-Willemsvaart, *canal* C3

Map (Belgium)

North Sea

Middleburg • NETHERLANDS
Eindhoven •
Breda •
Venlo •

GERMANY

Knokke
Zeebrugge
Oostende
Dunkirk

Turnhout •
Antwerp
ANTWERP
KEMPENLAND
LIMBURG
Genk •

FLANDERS
Sint-Niklaas
Brugge
WEST FLANDERS
Ghent
Mechelen •

Albert Canal
Maas
Cologne
Bonn

Roeselare •
EAST FLANDERS
Aalst •
BRUSSELS CAPITAL REGION
Schaerbeek
Leuven
FLEMISH BRABANT
Hasselt •
Maastricht •

Ypres
Kortrijk
Poperinge •
Anderlecht
Brussels
Ixelles Uccle
Halle
Wavre •
Sint-Truiden •
Aachen •

Mouscron
Lille •
Tournai •
Ath •
WALLOON BRABANT
Senne
Gembloux •
Namur
Liège
Verviers •
Limbourg •

FRANCE
Valenciennes •
HAINAUT
Mons •
Binche •
La Louvière •
Charleroi
NAMUR
WALLONIA
LIÈGE
Spa •
Botrange 694 m (2277 ft)
Malmédy •

Sambre
Dinant •
ARDENNES
Bastogne •

Chimay •
LUXEMBOURG
Neufchâteau •
LUXEMBOURG

Oise
Fumay •
Meuse
Semois
Moset

Charleville Mézières •
Arlon •
Luxembourg

Belgium Legend

⊛ National Capital
• Other City
⊥⊥⊥ Canal

1:2,381,000

0   20   40 mi
0   20   40 km
Lambert Conformal Conic Projection

© MapQuest.com, Inc.

Belgium: Map Index

Internal Divisions
Antwerp (province)..........C1
Brussels Cap. Region......C2
East Flanders (province)...B2
Flanders (region)............C1
Flemish Brabant (province) C2
Hainaut (province).........B2
Liège (province)..............D2
Limburg (province).........D1
Luxembourg (province)....D3
Namur (province)...........C2
Walloon Brabant (province)...........C2
Wallonia (region)...........C2
West Flanders (province)...B1

Cities and Towns
Aalst C2
Anderlecht C1
Antwerp C1
Arlon D3
Ath B2
Bastogne D2
Binche C2
Brugge B1

Brussels, *capital*............C2
Charleroi....................C2
Chimay.......................C2
Dinant.......................C2
Gembloux.....................C2
Genk.........................D2
Ghent........................B1
Halle........................C2
Hasselt......................D2
Ixelles......................C2
Knokke.......................B1
Kortrijk.....................B2
La Louvière..................C2
Leuven.......................C2
Liège........................D2
Limbourg.....................D2
Malmédy......................E2
Mechelen.....................C1
Mons.........................B2
Mouscron.....................B2
Namur........................C2
Neufchâteau..................D3
Oostende.....................A1
Poperinge....................A2
Roeselare....................B2
Schaerbeek...................C2
Sint-Niklaas.................C1
Sint-Truiden.................D2

Spa..........................D2
Tournai......................B2
Turnhout.....................C1
Uccle........................C2
Verviers.....................D2
Wavre........................C2
Ypres........................A2
Zeebrugge....................B1

Other Features
Albert, *canal*...............C1
Ardennes, *plateau*..........D2
Botrange, *mt.*..............E2
Brugge-Ghent, *canal*.......B1
Dender, *river*..............B2
Kempenland, *region*........D1
Leie, *river*................B2
Maas, *river*................D2
Meuse, *river*...............D2
Oostende-Brugge, *canal*.....B1
Ourthe, *river*..............D2
Rupel, *river*...............C1
Sambre, *river*..............C2
Schelde, *river*.............B2
Semois, *river*..............D3
Senne, *river*...............C2

Belgium

Capital: Brussels
Area: 11,787 sq. mi.
　　　30,536 sq. km.
Population: 10,182,000
Largest City: Brussels
Languages: Flemish, French, German
Monetary Unit: Belgian franc, Euro

Map (Luxembourg)

BELGIUM
Ardennes
Buurgplaatz 559 m (1835 ft)
Troisvierges
Clervaux
Wiltz
Vianden
Sûre
Diekirch
Ettelbruck
Sûre
Echternach
Mersch
Larochette
Redange
Bon Pays
Luxembourg
Grevenmacher
GERMANY
Differdange
Remich
Esch-sur-Alzette
Dudelange
FRANCE
Moset
Our
Clerve
Alzette

Luxembourg Legend

⊛ National Capital
• Other City

1:1,700,000

0   10   20 mi
0   10   20 km
Azimuthal Equal Area Projection

© MapQuest.com, Inc.

Liechtenstein

Capital: Vaduz
Area: 62 sq. mi.
　　　161 sq. km.
Population: 32,000
Largest City: Vaduz
Language: German
Monetary Unit: Swiss franc

Map (Liechtenstein)

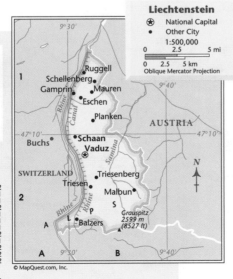

Liechtenstein Legend

⊛ National Capital
• Other City

1:500,000

0   2.5   5 mi
0   2.5   5 km
Oblique Mercator Projection

Ruggell
Schellenberg
Gamprin
Mauren
Eschen
Planken
Buchs
Schaan
Vaduz
AUSTRIA
SWITZERLAND
Triesenberg
Triesen
Malbun
Rhine Canal
Rhine
Samina
Grauspitz 2599 m (8527 ft)
ALPS
Balzers

© MapQuest.com, Inc.

Liechtenstein: Map Index

Cities and Towns
Balzers......................B2
Eschen.......................B1
Gamprin......................B1
Malbun.......................B2
Mauren.......................B1
Planken......................B1
Ruggell......................B1
Schaan.......................B2
Schellenberg.................B1
Triesen......................B2
Triesenberg..................B2
Vaduz, *capital*.............B2

Other Features
Alps, *range*................A2
Grauspitz, *mt.*.............A2
Rhine, *canal*...............B1, B2
Rhine, *river*...............A1, A2
Samina, *river*..............B2

Luxembourg

Capital: Luxembourg
Area: 999 sq. mi.
　　　2,588 sq. km.
Population: 429,000
Largest City: Luxembourg
Languages: French, German
Monetary Unit: Luxembourg franc, Euro

Luxembourg: Map Index

Cities and Towns
Clervaux.....................B1
Diekirch.....................B2
Differdange..................A2
Dudelange....................B2
Echternach...................B2
Esch-sur-Alzette.............A2
Ettelbruck...................B2
Grevenmacher.................B2
Larochette...................B2
Luxembourg, *capital*........B2
Mersch.......................B2
Redange......................A2
Remich.......................B2
Troisvierges.................B1
Vianden......................B2
Wiltz........................A2

Other Features
Alzette, *river*.............B2
Ardennes, *plateau*..........A1
Bon Pays, *region*...........B2
Buurgplaatz, *mt.*...........B1
Clerve, *river*..............B1
Mosel, *river*...............B2
Our, *river*.................B2
Sûre, *river*................A2, B2

France

⊛ National Capital

• Other City

1:5,625,000

0   50   100 mi

0   50   100 km

Lambert Conformal Conic Projection

Same scale as main map

CORSICA
CORSE

N

© MapQuest.com, Inc.

Switzerland

Capital: Bern
Area: 15,943 sq. mi.
41,303 sq. km.
Population: 7,275,000
Largest City: Zürich
Languages: German, French, Italian
Monetary Unit: Swiss franc

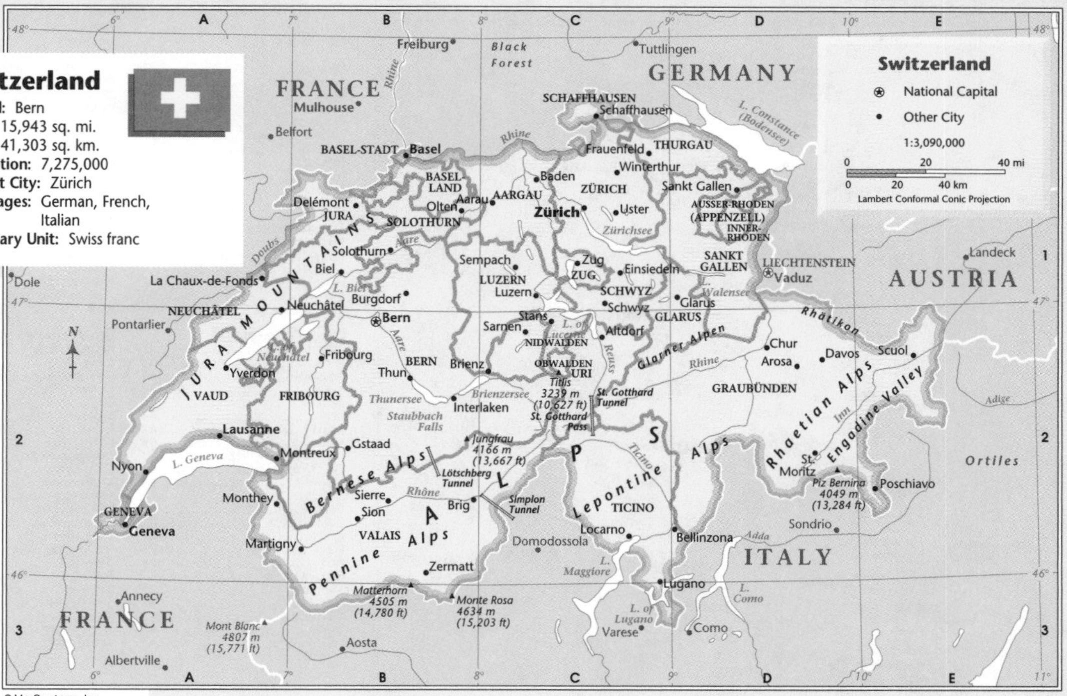

Switzerland
National Capital
Other City
1:3,090,000
0 20 40 mi
0 20 40 km
Lambert Conformal Conic Projection
FRANCE
GERMANY
AUSTRIA
ITALY
LIECHTENSTEIN
Freiburg
Black Forest
Tuttlingen
Mulhouse
Belfort
SCHAFFHAUSEN
Schaffhausen
L. Constance (Bodensee)
BASEL-STADT
Basel
Rhine
Frauenfeld
THURGAU
Winterthur
BASEL-LAND
Baden
ZÜRICH
Sankt Gallen
Delémont
JURA
Olten
Aarau
AARGAU
Zürich
Uster
AUSSER-RHODEN (APPENZELL)
INNER-RHODEN
SOLOTHURN
Zürichsee
Solothurn
Sempach
Zug
Einsiedeln
SANKT GALLEN
Vaduz
Landeck
Dole
La Chaux-de-Fonds
Biel
L. Biel
LUZERN
ZUG
SCHWYZ
L. Walensee
Luzern
Schwyz
Glarus
NEUCHÂTEL
Neuchâtel
Burgdorf
Bern
GLARUS
Rhätikon
Pontarlier
Stans
Sarnen
NIDWALDEN
L. of Lucerne
Altdorf
Chur
Davos
Scuol
JURA MOUNTAINS
L. Neuchâtel
Fribourg
BERN
Brienz
OBWALDEN
URI
Glarner Alpen
Arosa
Yverdon
Thun
Reuss
Titlis 3239 m (10,627 ft)
Rhine
GRAUBÜNDEN
VAUD
FRIBOURG
Thunersee
Brienzersee
Interlaken
St. Gotthard Tunnel
St. Gotthard Pass
Staubbach Falls
Rhaetian Alps
Engadine Valley
Inn
Adige
Lausanne
Gstaad
Jungfrau 4166 m (13,667 ft)
A L P S
Ticino
Ortiles
Nyon
L. Geneva
Montreux
Bernese Alps
Lötschberg Tunnel
Lepontine
St. Moritz
Piz Bernina 4049 m (13,284 ft)
Poschiavo
Monthey
Sierre
Rhône
Simplon Tunnel
TICINO
GENEVA
Sion
Brig
Sondrio
Geneva
VALAIS
Alps
Locarno
Bellinzona
Adda
Martigny
Domodossola
Pennine
Zermatt
L. Maggiore
Lugano
L. Como
Annecy
Matterhorn 4505 m (14,780 ft)
Monte Rosa 4634 m (15,203 ft)
L. of Lugano
FRANCE
Mont Blanc 4807 m (15,771 ft)
Varese
Como
Aosta
Albertville

© MapQuest.com, Inc.

Monaco
National Capital
1:74,470
0 0.5 1 mi
0 0.5 1 km
Lambert Conformal Conic Projection
FRANCE
Sporting Club
Monte Carlo
Casino
La Condamine
Port of Monaco
Monaco
Palace
Mediterranean Sea
Fontvieille
Port of Fontvieille

© MapQuest.com, Inc.

Monaco: Map Index

Districts
Fontvieille A2
La Condamine....B1
Monaco, *capital* B1
Monte Carlo B1

Other Features
Casino....B1
Fontvieille, *port* B2
Monaco, *port* B1
Palace B2
Sporting Club C1

Monaco

Capital: Monaco
Area: 0.75 sq. mi.
1.94 sq. km.
Population: 32,000
Language: French
Monetary Unit: French franc or Monégasque franc

Switzerland: Map Index

Cantons
Aargau C1
Appenzell Ausser-Rhoden D1
Appenzell Inner-Rhoden D1
Basel-Land B1
Basel-Stadt B1
Bern B2
Fribourg B2
Geneva A2
Glarus....D2
Graubünden....D2
Jura....B1
Lucerne C1
Neuchâtel A2
Nidwalden C2
Obwalden C2
Sankt Gallen....D1
Schaffhausen C1
Schwyz....C1
Solothurn B1
Thurgau C1
Ticino C2
Uri C2
Valais B2
Vaud....A2
Zug C1
Zürich....C1

Cities and Towns
Aarau C1
Altdorf C2
Baden....C1
Basel B1
Bellinzona....D2
Bern, *capital* B2
Biel B1
Bolligen B2
Bulle B2
Chur....D2
Davos....D2
Einsiedeln C1
Fribourg B2
Frutigen B2
Geneva A2
Horgèn....C1
Interlaken B2
La Chaux-de-Fonds....A1
Lausanne A2
Locarno C2
Lucerne C1
Lugano....C3
Montreux A2
Morges....A2
Neuchâtel....A2
St. Moritz....D2
Sankt Gallen....D1
Schaffhausen C1
Schwyz....C1
Sempach C1
Sion B2
Thun....B2
Uster C1
Winterthur C1
Yverdon A2
Zermatt B2
Zug C1
Zürich....C1

Other Features
Aare, *river* B1, B2
Alps, *mts.* B2
Bernese Alps, *mts.*....B2
Biel, *lake* B1
Brienzersee, *lake* B2
Constance (Bodensee), *lake* D1
Doubs, *river* A1
Dufourspitze, *mt.* B3
Engadine, *valley* D2
Geneva, *lake* A2
Inn, *river*....D2
Jungfrau, *mt.*....B2
Jura, *mts.* A2
Lepontine Alps, *mts.* C2
Lucerne, *lake* C2
Lugano, *lake* C3
Maggiore, *lake* C2
Matterhorn, *mt.* B3
Neuchâtel, *lake*....A2
Pennine Alps, *mts.* B2
Reuss, *river* C2
Rhaetian Alps, *mts.*....D2
Rhine, *river*....C1, D2
Rhône, *river*....B2
St. Gotthard, *pass*....C2
St. Gotthard, *tunnel* C2
Splügen, *pass*....D2
Staubbach, *falls*....B2
Thunersee, *lake*....B2
Ticino, *river*....C2
Walensee, *lake* D1
Zürichsee, *lake* C1

France

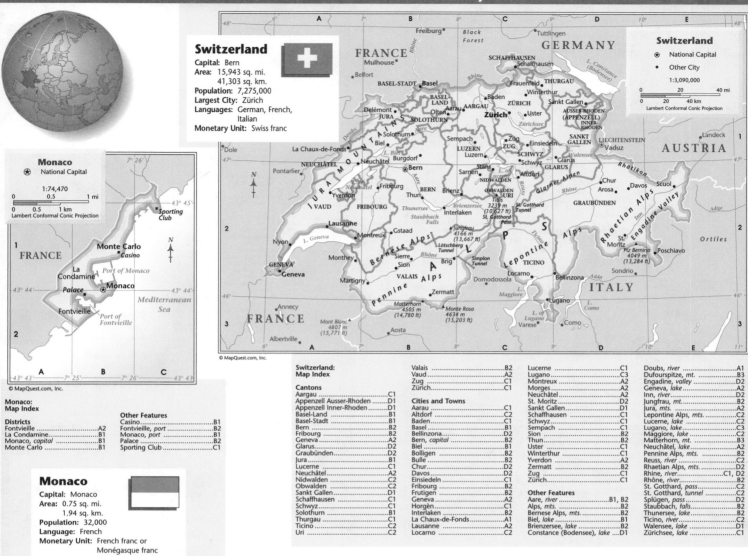

Capital: Paris
Area: 210,026 sq. mi.
544,109 sq. km.
Population: 58,978,000
Largest City: Paris
Language: French
Monetary Unit: Franc, Euro

France: Map Index

Regions
Alsace D2
Aquitaine....B4
Auvergne C4
Basse-Normandie B2
Bourgogne....C3
Bretagne B2
Centre....C3
Champagne-Ardenne....D2
Corse ....Inset I
Franche-Comté....D3
Haute-Normandie C2
Île-de-France C2
Languedoc-Roussillon....C5
Limousin C4
Lorraine D2
Midi-Pyrénées C5
Nord-Pas-de-Calais....C1
Pays De La Loire B3
Picardie....C2
Poitou-Charentes C3
Provence-Alpes-Côte-d'Azur....D4
Rhône-Alpes....D4

Cities and Towns
Abbeville....C1
Agen....C4
Aix-en-Provence....D5
Aix-les-Bains....D4
Ajaccio ....Inset I
Albi C5
Alençon C2
Alès....D4
Amiens....C2
Angers....B3
Angoulême C4
Annecy D4
Arachon B4
Argenteuil ....Inset II
Arles D5
Arpajon ....Inset II
Arras C1
Auch C5
Aurillac....C4
Auxerre C3
Avignon D5
Ballancourt-sur-Essonne....Inset II
Bar-le-Duc....D2
Bastia ....Inset I
Bayeux B2
Bayonne B5
Beauvais....C2
Belfort....D3
Bergerac C4
Besançon D3
Béziers C5
Biarritz....B5
Blois....C3
Bondy ....Inset II
Bordeaux....B4
Boulogne-Billancourt....Inset II
Boulogne-sur-Mer C1
Bourg-en-Bresse....D3
Bourges C3
Brest....A2
Briançon D4
Brive-la-Gallarde....C4
Caen B2
Cahors C4
Calais C1
Calvi ....Inset I
Cambrai....C1
Cannes D5
Carcassonne....C5
Carnac B3
Châlons-sur-Marne D2
Chambéry....D4
Chamonix-Mont-Blanc....D4
Chantilly C2
Charleville Mézières D2
Chartres....C2
Châteauroux C3
Châtellerault C3
Chaumont D2
Chelles....Inset II
Cherbourg....B2
Chevreuse ....Inset II
Choisy-le Roi ....Inset II
Cholet....B3
Clermont-Ferrand C4
Clichy....Inset II
Cluny....D3
Cognac B4
Colmar D2
Compiègne....C2
Conflans-Sainte-Honorine....Inset II
Corbeil-Essonnes ....Inset II
Coubert ....Inset II
Créteil ....Inset II
Dammartin-en-Goële ....Inset II
Deauville....C2
Dieppe....C2
Digne D4
Dijon D3
Dôle....D3
Domont ....Inset II
Douai....C1
Draguignan D5
Dreux....C2
Dunkirk (Dunkerque) C1
Épinal D2
Étrechy....Inset II
Évreux....C2
Évry....Inset II
Foix....C5
Fontainebleau C2
Fréjus....D5
Gap D4
Gentilly ....Inset II
Grenoble D4
Guéret C3
Laon C2
La Rochelle....B3
La-Roche-sur-Yon....B3
Laval....B2
Le Creusot D3
Le Havre C2
Le Mans C2
Lens....C1
Le Puy....C4
Les Ulis....Inset II
Levallois-Perret ....Inset II
Lille....C1
Limoges....C4
Limours....Inset II
L'Isle-Adam ....Inset II
Lorient....B3
Lourdes B5
Louvres ....Inset II
Luzarches ....Inset II
Lyon D4
Mâcon....D3
Maisons-Laffitte....Inset II
Marseille....D5
Massy....Inset II
Maurepas....Inset II
Melun ....Inset II
Mende....C4
Mennecy....Inset II
Metz....D2
Meulan ....Inset II
Montargis C2
Montauban....C4
Montélimar....D4
Montluçon....C3
Montpellier C5
Montreuil ....Inset II
Mont-Saint-Michel B2
Morlaix....B2
Mulhouse D3
Nancy....D2
Nanterre ....Inset II
Nantes B3
Narbonne C5
Nevers C3
Nice....D5
Nîmes....D5
Niort B3
Orléans C3
Ozoir-la-Ferrière ....Inset II
Palaiseau ....Inset II
Paris, *capital*....C2, Inset II
Pau....B5
Périgueux....C4
Perpignan C5
Poissy ....Inset II
Poitiers....C3
Pontchartrain ....Inset II
Pontoise ....Inset II
Porto-Vecchio....Inset I
Privas D4
Quimper A2
Reims....D2
Rennes B2
Roanne D3
Rochefort B4
Rodez....C4
Roubaix C1
Rouen C2
Saint-Brieuc B2
Saint-Cloud ....Inset II
Saint-Denis....Inset II
Saint-Dizier D2
Saintes....B4
Saint-Étienne....D4
Saint-Germain-en-Laye....Inset II
Saint-Lô....B2
Saint-Malo....B2
Saint-Nazaire....B3
Saint-Tropez....D5
Sarcelles ....Inset II
Saumur B3
Savigny-sur-Orge ....Inset II
Sedan D2
Sevran....Inset II
Sèvres ....Inset II
Soissons C2
Strasbourg D2
Tarbes C5
Taverny ....Inset II
Toulon D5
Toulouse C5
Tourcoing C1
Tours....C3
Trouville C2
Troyes D2
Valence....D4
Valenciennes C1
Vannes B3
Verdun....D2
Versailles....C2, Inset II
Vesoul D3
Vichy....C3
Vierzon C3
Villeneuve-Saint-Georges....Inset II
Vincennes....Inset II

Other Features
Adour, *river*....B5
Aisne, *river* D2
Allier, *river* C3
Alps, *range*....D4
Ardennes, *region* D1
Argonne, *forest* D2
Aube, *river* D3
Belfort, *gap* D3
Belle, *island* B3
Biscay, *bay*....B4
Blanc, *mt.* D4
Cévennes, *mts.*....C4
Charente, *river*....B4
Corsica, *island* ....Inset I
Cotentin, *peninsula*....B2
Dordogne, *river*....C4
Dover, *strait* C1
Durance, *river* D5
English, *channel*....B2
Garonne, *river* C4
Geneva, *lake* D3
Gironde, *river* B4
Hague, *cape* B2
Isère, *river* D4
Jura, *mts.* D3
Landes, *region* B5
Lion, *gulf*....D5
Little St. Bernard, *pass* D4
Loire, *river*....C3
Lot, *river*....C4
Maritime Alps, *range*....D4
Marne, *river* ....C2, Inset II
Massif Central, *plateau* C4
Meuse, *river*....D2
Moselle, *river* D2
Oise, *river* ....C2, Inset II
Oléron, *island*....B4
Omaha, *beach*....B2
Orne, *river*....B2
Pyrenees, *range*....C5
Rance, *river*....B2
Raz, *point* A3
Ré, *island*....B3
Rhine, *river*....D2
Rhône, *river* D4
Saint-Malo, *gulf*....B2
Sambre, *river*....C1
Saône, *river*....D3
Seine, *river*....C2, Inset II
Somme, *river*....C2
Utah, *beach*....B2
Vienne, *river* C3
Vignemale, *mt.* B5
Vilaine, *river*....B3
Vosges, *mts.*....D2
Yeu, *island*....B3
Yonne, *river*....C2

© MapQuest.com, Inc.

**Portugal:
Map Index**

Districts
Aveiro A2
Beja A4
Braga A2
Bragança B2
Castelo Branco B3
Coimbra A2
Évora B3
Faro A4
Guarda B2
Leiria A3
Lisbon A3
Oporto (Porto) A2
Portalegre B3
Santarém A3
Setúbal A3
Viana do Castelo A2
Vila Real B2
Viseu B2

Cities and Towns
Abrantes A3
Almada A3
Amadora A3
Aveiro A2
Barreiro A3
Beja B3
Braga A2
Bragança B2
Caidasm da Rainha A3
Castelo Branco B3
Chaves B2
Coimbra A2
Covilhã B2
Elvas B3
Estoril A3
Évora B3
Faro B4
Figueira da Foz A2
Grândola A3
Guarda B2
Guimarães A2
Lagos A4
Leiria A3

Leixões A2
Lisbon, *capital* A3
Mafra A3
Moura B3
Odemira A4
Oeiras A3
Oporto (Porto) A2
Peniche A3
Portalegre B3
Portimão A4
Queluz A3
Santarém A3
Setúbal A3
Sines A4
Valença A1
Viana do Castelo A2
Vila do Conde A2
Vila Nova de Gaia A2
Vila Real B2
Vila Real
  de Santo Antonio..................B4
Viseu B2

Other Features
Algarve, *region* A4
Cádiz, *gulf* B4
Carvoeiro, *cape* A3
Chança, *river* B4
Douro, *river* B2
Espichel, *cape* A3
Estrela, *mt.* B2
Estrela, *mts.* B2
Guadiana, *river* B3
Lima, *river* A2
Minho, *river* A1
Mondego, *cape* A2
Mondego, *river* B2
Roca, *cape* A3
Sado, *river* A3
São Vicente, *cape* A4
Seda, *river* B3
Setúbal, *bay* A3
Sor, *river* B3
Sorraia, *river* A3
Tagus, *river* A3
Tâmega, *river* B2
Zêzere, *river* A3

**Malta:
Map Index**

Cities and Towns
Birkirkara B2
Birzebbuga C3
Dingli B2
Mellieha B2
Nadur B1
Qormi B2
Rabat B2
San Pawl il-Bahar B2
Siggiewi B2
Sliema B2
Valletta, *capital* C2
Victoria A1
Zabbar C2
Zebbug A1
Zurrieq B2

Other Features
Comino, *island* B1
Cominotto, *island* B1
Filfla, *island* B3
Gozo, *island* A1
Grand, *harbor* C2
Malta, *island* B2
Marsaxlokk, *bay* C3
Mellieha, *bay* B2
North Comino, *channel* B1
Saint Paul's, *bay* B2
South Comino, *channel* B2

© MapQuest.com, Inc.

**Gibraltar:
Map Index**

Features
Catalan, *bay* A2
Detached, *mole* A2
Eastern, *beach* A2
Fortress Headquarters A3
Gibraltar, *bay* A2
Gibraltar, *harbor* A2
Gibraltar, *strait* A4
Governor's Residence A2
Great Europa, *point* A4
Highest point A3
Little, *bay* A4
Mediterranean, *sea* A2
North, *mole* A2
North Front, *airfield* A1
Rosia, *bay* A3
Saint Michael's, *cave* A3
Sandy, *bay* A2
Signal, *hill* A2
South, *mole* A3
The Rock, *prom.* A2

**Andorra:
Map Index**

Cities and Towns
Andorra la Vella, *capital* B2
Anyos B2
Arinsal A2
El Serrat B1
Les Escaldes B2
Llorts B1
Ordino B2
Pas de la Casa C2
Sant Julià de Lòria A3
Soldeu B2

Other Features
Coma Pedrosa, *mt.* A1
Estany d'Engolasters, *lake* B2
Inclés, *river* C1
La Coma, *river* B1
Madriu, *river* B3
Os, *river* A3
Pyrenees, *range* A1
Valira, *river* B2
Valira d'Orient, *river* B2

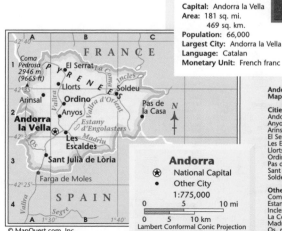

© MapQuest.com, Inc.

Spain:
Map Index

Regions

Andalusia	D4
Aragón	F2
Asturias	C1
Balearic Islands	G3
Basque Country	E1
Canary Islands	Inset I
Cantabria	D1
Castile-La Mancha	E3
Castile-León	D1, E1
Catalonia	G2
Estremadura	C3
Galicia	C1
La Rioja	E1
Madrid	E2
Murcia	F4
Navarra	F1
Valencia	F2, F3

Cities and Towns

Águilas	F4
Albacete	F3
Alcalá de Henares	Inset II
Alcañiz	F2
Alcázar de San Juan	E3
Alcira	F3
Alcobendas	Inset II
Alcorcón	E2, Inset II
Alcoy	F3
Algeciras	D4
Alicante	F3
Almadén	D3
Almansa	F3
Almendralejo	C3
Almería	E4
Antequera	D4
Aranda de Duero	E2
Aranjuez	E2
Astorga	C1
Ávila	D2
Avilés	D1
Badajoz	C3
Badalona	H2
Baracaldo	E1
Barcelona	H2
Baza	E4
Béjar	D2
Benavente	D1
Benidorm	F3
Bilbao	E1
Burgos	E1
Cáceres	C3
Cádiz	C4
Calatayud	F2
Cartagena	F4
Castellón de la Plana	F3
Ceuta	D5
Cieza	F3
Ciudad Real	D3
Ciudad Rodrigo	C2
Córdoba	D4
Cornellá de Llobregat	G2
Coslada	Inset II
Cuenca	E2
Don Benito	D3
Dos Hermanas	D4
Écija	D4
Elche	F3
El Ferrol	B1
Figueras	H1
Fuenlabrada	Inset II
Gerona	H2
Getafe	E2, Inset II
Gijón	D1
Granada	E4
Guadalajara	E2
Guecho	E1
Guernica y Luno	E1
Hellín	F3
Hospitalet	H2
Huelva	C4
Huesca	F1
Ibiza	G3
Jaén	E4
Jerez de la Frontera	C4
La Coruña	B1
La Laguna	Inset I
Las Palmas	Inset I
Leganés	Inset II
León	D1
Lérida	G2
Linares	E3
Logroño	E1
Loja	D4
Lorca	F4
Lucena	D4
Lugo	C1
Madrid, capital	E2, Inset II
Mahón	J3
Málaga	D4
Marbella	D4
Mataró	H2
Medina del Campo	D2
Mérida	C3
Mieres	D1
Miranda de Ebro	E1
Monforte	C1
Morón de la Frontera	D4
Móstoles	Inset II
Murcia	F4
Orense	C1
Oviedo	D1
Palencia	D1
Palma	H3
Pamplona	F1
Plasencia	C2
Ponferrada	C1
Pontevedra	B1
Puertollano	D3
Reinosa	D1
Reus	G2
Sabadell	H2
Sagunto	F3
Salamanca	D2
San Baudilio de Llobregat	G2
San Fernando	C4
San Sebastián	F1
Santa Coloma de Gramanet	H2
Santa Cruz de Tenerife	Inset I
Santander	E1
Santiago de Compostela	B1
Segovia	D2
Seville	D4
Soria	E2
Talavera de la Reina	D3
Tarragona	G2
Tarrasa	H2
Telde	Inset I
Teruel	F2
Toledo	D3
Tomelloso	E3
Torrejón de Ardoz	Inset II
Torrelavega	D1
Torrente	G1
Tortosa	G2
Úbeda	E3
Valdepeñas	E3
Valencia	F3
Valladolid	D2
Vich	H2
Vigo	B1
Villarreal de los Infantes	F3
Vitoria	E1
Yecla	F3
Zafra	C3
Zamora	D2
Zaragoza	F2

Other Features

Alarcón, reservoir	E3
Alborán, sea	E4
Alcántara, reservoir	C2
Almendra, reservoir	C2
Aneto, mt.	G1
Balearic, islands	G3
Balearic, sea	G2
Béticos, mts.	D4
Biscay, bay	D1
Brava, coast	H2
Buendía, reservoir	E2
Cabrera, island	H3
Cádiz, gulf	C4
Canary, islands	Inset I
Cantábrica, mts.	C1
Cijara, reservoir	D3
Duero, river	D2
Ebro, river	F1
Esla, river	D2
Finisterre, cape	B1
Formentera, island	G3
Fuerteventura, island	Inset I
Gata, cape	E4
Gibraltar, strait	D5
Gomera, island	Inset I
Gran Canaria, island	Inset I
Gredos, mts.	D2
Guadalquivir, river	D4
Guadarrama, mts.	D2
Guadiana, river	C3
Hierro, island	Inset I
Ibérico, mts.	E2
Ibiza, island	G3
Jarama, river	Inset II
Júcar, river	F3
Lanzarote, island	Inset I
La Palma, island	Inset I
Majorca, island	H3
Mediterranean, sea	E4
Mequinenza, reservoir	F2
Meseta, plateau	D3
Miño, river	B1
Minorca, island	H2
Morena, mts.	D3
Mulhacén, mt.	E4
Nao, cape	G3
Nevada, mts.	E4
Orellana, reservoir	D3
Ortegal, cape	C1
Palos, cape	F4
Pyrenees, mts.	F1
Ricobayo, reservoir	D2
Segura, river	E3
Sol, coast	D4
Tagus, river	D3
Tenerife, island	Inset I
Toledo, mts.	D3
Tormes, river	D2
Tortosa, cape	G2
Valdecañas, reservoir	D3
Valencia, gulf	G3
Zújar, reservoir	D3

Spain

Capital: Madrid
Area: 194,898 sq. mi.
504,917 sq. km.
Population: 39,168,000
Largest City: Madrid
Language: Spanish
Monetary Unit: Peseta, Euro

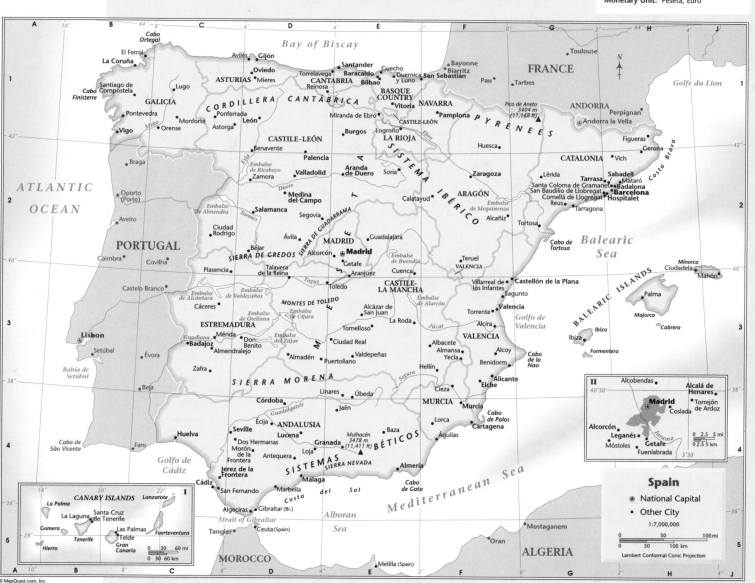

Italy

⊛ National Capital

• Other City

1:5,614,000

| 0   50   100   150 mi |
| 0   50   100   150 km |

Lambert Conformal Conic Projection

Italy
Capital: Rome
Area: 116,333 sq. mi.
            301,381 sq. km.
Population: 56,735,000
Largest City: Rome
Language: Italian
Monetary Unit: Lira, Euro

© MapQuest.com, Inc.

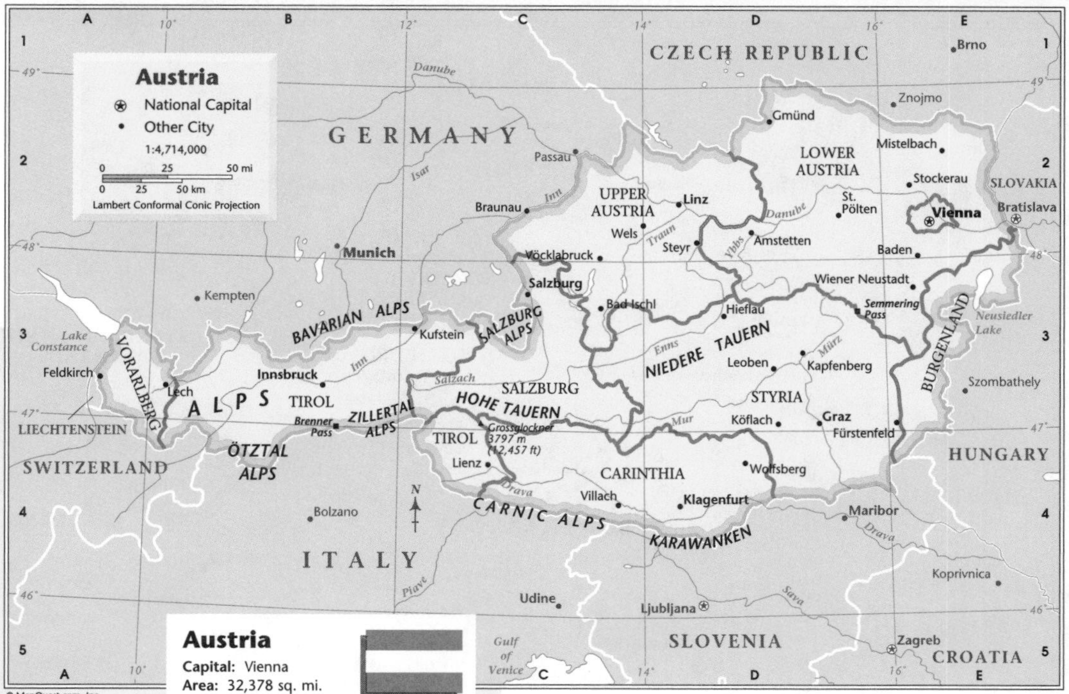
Austria
National Capital
Other City
1:4,714,000
0 25 50 mi
0 25 50 km
Lambert Conformal Conic Projection
CZECH REPUBLIC
GERMANY
SLOVAKIA
HUNGARY
SWITZERLAND
LIECHTENSTEIN
ITALY
SLOVENIA
CROATIA
LOWER AUSTRIA
UPPER AUSTRIA
SALZBURG
TIROL
STYRIA
CARINTHIA
VORARLBERG
BURGENLAND
ALPS
BAVARIAN ALPS
SALZBURG ALPS
NIEDERE TAUERN
HOHE TAUERN
ZILLERTAL ALPS
ÖTZTAL ALPS
CARNIC ALPS
KARAWANKEN
Grossglockner 3797 m (12,457 ft)
Vienna
Linz
Salzburg
Innsbruck
Graz
Klagenfurt
Munich
Bratislava
Ljubljana
Zagreb
© MapQuest.com, Inc.

Austria

Capital: Vienna
Area: 32,378 sq. mi.
83,881 sq. km.
Population: 8,139,000
Largest City: Vienna
Language: German
Monetary Unit: Schilling, Euro

Austria: Map Index

Provinces
Burgenland E3
Carinthia C4
Lower Austria D2
Salzburg C3
Styria D3
Tirol B3, C4
Upper Austria C2
Vienna E2
Vorarlberg A3

Cities and Towns
Amstetten D2
Baden E2
Bad Ischl C3
Braunau C2
Feldkirch A3
Fürstenfeld E3
Gmünd D2
Graz D3
Hieflau D3
Innsbruck B3
Kapfenberg D3
Klagenfurt D4
Köflach D3
Kufstein C3
Lech B3
Leoben D3
Lienz C4
Linz D2
Mistelbach E2
Salzburg C3
Sankt Pölten D2
Steyr D2
Stockerau E2
Vienna, *capital* E2
Villach C4
Vöcklabruck C2
Wels C2
Wiener Neustadt E3
Wolfsberg D4

Other Features
Alps, *range* B3
Bavarian Alps, *range* B3
Brenner, *pass* B3
Carnic Alps, *range* C4
Constance, *lake* A3
Danube, *river* D2
Drava, *river* C4
Enns, *river* D3
Grossglockner, *mt.* C3
Hohe Tauern, *mts.* C3
Inn, *river* B3, C2
Karawanken, *range* D4
Mur, *river* D3
Mürz, *river* D3
Neusiedler, *lake* E3
Niedere Tauern, *range* D3
Ötztal Alps, *range* B4
Salzach, *river* C3
Salzburg Alps, *range* C3
Semmering, *pass* D3
Traun, *river* D2
Ybbs, *river* D2
Zillertal Alps, *range* B3

Italy: Map Index

Regions
Abruzzi C2
Apulia C2
Basilicata C2
Calabria D3
Campania C2
Emilia-Romagna B1
Friuli-Venezia Giulia C1
Latium C2
Liguria B1
Lombardy B1
Marche C2
Molise C2
Piedmont A1
Puglia C2
Sardinia B3
Sicily C3
Trentino-Alto Adige B1
Tuscany B2
Umbria C2
Valle d'Aosta A1
Veneto B1

Cities and Towns
Agrigento C3
Alessandria B1
Alghero B2
Ancona C2
Aosta A1
Aquileia C1
Arezzo B2
Ascoli Piceno C2
Asti B1
Avellino C2
Bari D2
Barletta D2
Belluno C1
Benevento C2
Bergamo B1
Bologna B1
Bolzano B1
Brescia B1
Brindisi D2
Cagliari B3
Caltanissetta C3
Campobasso C2
Canossa B1
Capua C2
Carbonia B3
Caserta C2
Castel Gandolfo C2
Catania C3
Catanzaro D3
Cefalù C3
Chieti C2
Chioggia C1
Civitavecchia B2
Como B1
Cortina d'Ampezzo C1
Cortona B2
Cosenza D3
Cremona B1
Crotone D3
Cuneo A1
Enna C3
Faenza B1
Ferrara B1
Florence B2
Foggia C2
Forlì C1
Frosinone C2
Gaeta C2
Gela C3
Genoa B1
Gorizia C1
Grosseto B2
Isernia C2
L'Aquila C2
La Spezia B1
Latina C2
Lecce D2
Livorno B2
Lucca B2
Macerata C2
Manfredonia C2
Mantova B1
Mantua (Mantova) B1
Marsala C3
Matera D2
Merano B1
Messina C3
Milan B1
Modena B1
Monopoli D2
Montepulciano B2
Monza B1
Naples C2
Novara B1
Nuoro B2
Olbia B2
Oristano B3
Otranto D2
Padova B1
Padua (Padova) B1
Palermo C3
Parma B1
Pavia B1
Perugia C2
Pesaro C2
Pescara C2
Pisa B2
Pistoia B2
Placenza B1
Potenza C2
Prato B2
Ragusa C3
Ravenna C1
Reggio di Calabria C3
Reggio nell'Emilia B1
Rieti C2
Rimini C1
Rome, *capital* C2
Rovigo B1
Salerno C2
San Gimignano B2
San Remo A2
San Severo C2
Sassari B2
Savona B1
Siena B2
Siracusa C3
Sondrio B1
Sorrento C2
Spoleto C2
Syracuse (Siracusa) C3
Taranto D2
Teramo C2
Termoli C2
Terni C2
Torre del Greco C2
Trapani C3
Trento B1
Treviso C1
Trieste C1
Turin A1
Udine C1
Venice C1
Ventimiglia A2
Vercelli B1
Verona B1
Vicenza B1
Viterbo C2

Other Features
Adige, *river* B1
Adriatic, *sea* C2
Alps, *mts.* A1, B1
Apennines, *range* B1
Arno, *river* B2
Asinara, *island* B2
Blanc, *mt.* A1
Bolsena, *lake* B2
Botte Donato, *mt.* D3
Bracciano, *lake* C2
Brenner, *pass* B1
Cagliari, *gulf* B3
Campagna di Roma, *region* C2
Caprara, *point* B2
Capri, *island* C2
Carbonara, *cape* B3
Cervati, *mt.* C2
Cimone, *mt.* B1
Como, *lake* B1
Corno, *mt.* C2
Dolomites, *range* B1
Egadi, *islands* C3
Elba, *island* B2
Etna, *mt.* C3
Garda, *lake* B1
Gennargentu, *mts.* B2
Genoa, *gulf* B1
Giglio, *island* B2
Ionian, *sea* D3
Ischia, *island* C2
Ligurian, *sea* B2
Lipari, *islands* C3
Lombardy, *plain* B1
Lugano, *lake* B1
Maggiore, *lake* B1
Maremma, *region* B2
Mediterranean, *sea* C3
Messina, *strait* C3
Montalto, *mt.* C3
Montecristo, *island* B2
Naples, *bay* C2
Oglio, *river* B1
Pantelleria, *island* C3
Passero, *cape* C3
Pianosa, *island* B2
Piave, *river* C1
Po, *river* A1, B1
Pontine, *islands* C2
Pontine, *marshes* C2
Rosa, *mt.* A1
Salerno, *gulf* C2
Sangro, *river* C2
San Pietro, *island* B3
Santa Maria di Leuca, *cape* D3
Sant'Antioco, *island* B3
San Vito, *cape* C3
Sardinia, *island* B2
Sicily, *island* C3
Sicily, *strait* B3
Spartivento, *cape* D3
Stromboli, *island* C3
Taranto, *gulf* D2
Testa del Gargano, *point* D2
Teulada, *cape* B3
Tiber, *river* C2
Tirso, *river* B2
Trasimeno, *lake* C2
Tyrrhenian, *sea* B2
Ustica, *island* C3
Venice, *gulf* C1
Vesuvius, *volcano* C2

Vatican City

Area: 108.7 acres
Population: 811
Languages: Italian, Latin
Monetary Unit: Lira

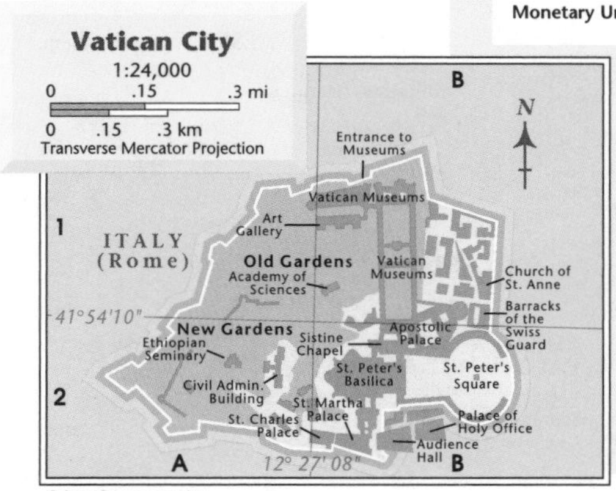
Vatican City
1:24,000
0 .15 .3 mi
0 .15 .3 km
Transverse Mercator Projection
ITALY (Rome)
Entrance to Museums
Vatican Museums
Art Gallery
Old Gardens
Academy of Sciences
Church of St. Anne
Barracks of the Swiss Guard
New Gardens
Ethiopian Seminary
Sistine Chapel
Apostolic Palace
St. Peter's Basilica
St. Peter's Square
Civil Admin. Building
St. Martha Palace
St. Charles Palace
Palace of Holy Office
Audience Hall
41°54'10"
12° 27' 08"

© MapQuest.com, Inc.

Vatican City: Map Index

Features
Academy of Sciences B1
Apostolic Palace B2
Art Gallery B1
Audience Hall B2
Barracks of the Swiss Guard B1
Church of St. Anne B1
Civil Administration Building A2
Entrance to Museums B1
Ethiopian Seminary A2
New Gardens A2
Old Gardens A1
Palace of Holy Office B2
St. Charles Palace B2
St. Martha Palace B2
St. Peter's Basilica B2
St. Peter's Square B2
Sistine Chapel B2
Vatican Museums B1

San Marino

Capital: San Marino
Area: 24 sq. mi.
62 sq. km.
Population: 25,000
Largest City: San Marino
Language: Italian
Monetary Unit: Italian lira

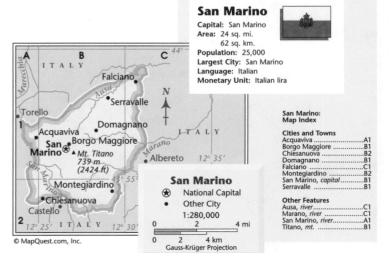

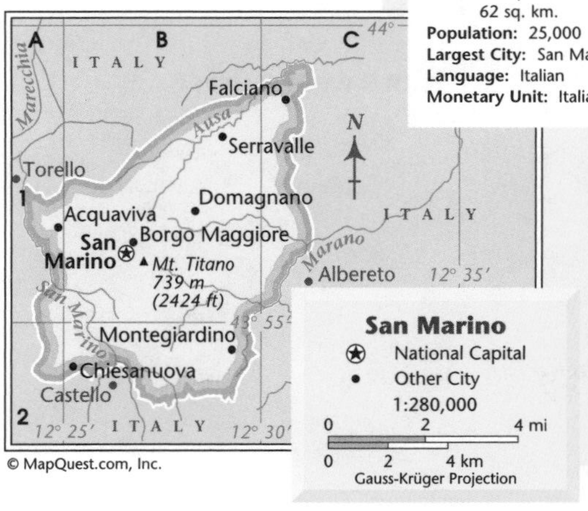
ITALY
Falciano
Serravalle
Torello
Domagnano
Acquaviva
Borgo Maggiore
San Marino
Mt. Titano 739 m (2424 ft)
Albereto
Montegiardino
Chiesanuova
Castello
Ausa
Marano
Marecchia
San Marino
44°
43° 55'
12° 25'
12° 30'
12° 35'
San Marino
National Capital
Other City
1:280,000
0 2 4 mi
0 2 4 km
Gauss-Krüger Projection

© MapQuest.com, Inc.

San Marino: Map Index

Cities and Towns
Acquaviva A1
Borgo Maggiore B1
Chiesanuova B2
Domagnano B1
Falciano C1
Montegiardino B2
San Marino, *capital* B1
Serravalle B1

Other Features
Ausa, *river* C1
Marano, *river* C1
San Marino, *river* A1
Titano, *mt.* B1

Germany

Capital: Berlin
Area: 137,735 sq. mi.
356,826 sq. km.
Population: 82,087,000
Largest City: Berlin
Language: German
Monetary Unit: Mark, Euro

Germany

⊛ National Capital
● Other City

1:4,066,000

| 0 | 25 | 50 | 75 mi |

| 0 | 25 | 50 | 75 km |

Lambert Conformal Conic Projection

© MapQuest.com, Inc.

Poland

Capital: Warsaw
Area: 120,727 sq. mi.
312,764 sq. km.
Population: 38,609,000
Largest City: Warsaw
Language: Polish
Monetary Unit: Zloty

Poland: Map Index

Cities and Towns

Biała Podlaska	F2
Białystok	F2
Bielsko-Biała	D4
Bydgoszcz	C2
Bytom	D3
Chełm	F3
Chojnice	C2
Chorzów	D3
Ciechanów	E2
Częstochowa	D3
Darłowo	C1
Elbląg	D1
Ełk	F2
Gdańsk	D1
Gdynia	D1
Gliwice	D3
Głogów	C3
Gorzów Wielkopolski	B2
Grudziądz	D2
Hel	D1
Jelenia Góra	B3
Katowice	D3
Kielce	E3
Kołobrzeg	B1
Konin	D2
Koszalin	C1
Kraków	D3
Krosnow	E4
Kutno	D2
Legnica	C3
Leszno	C3
Łódź	D3
Łomża	F2
Lublin	F3
Nowy Sącz	E4
Nysa	C3
Olsztyn	E2
Opole	C3
Ostrołęka	E2
Piła	C2
Piotrków Trybunalski	D3
Płock	D2
Poznań	C2
Przemyśl	F4
Puck	D1
Puławy	E3
Radom	E3
Ruda Śląska	D3
Rybnik	D3
Rzeszów	F3
Sczecinek	C2
Siedlce	F2
Sieradz	D3
Skierniewice	E3
Słupsk	C1
Sosnowiec	D3
Suwałki	F1
Świnoujście	B2
Szczecin	B2
Tarnobrzeg	E3
Tarnów	E3
Toruń	D2
Tychy	D3
Ustka	C1
Wałbrzych	C3
Warsaw, capital	E2
Władysławowo	D1
Włocławek	D2
Wodzisław Śląski	D3
Wrocław	C3
Zabrze	D3
Zakopane	D4
Zamość	F3
Zielona Góra	B3

Other Features

Baltic, sea	B1
Beskid, mts.	D4
Bug, river	E2, F3
Carpathian, mts.	E4
Frisches Haff, bay	D1
Gdańsk, gulf	D1
High Tatra, mts.	D4
Mamry, lake	E1
Narew, river	E2
Neisse, river	B3
Noteć, river	C2, D2
Oder, river	B2, C3
Pilica, river	E3
Pomeranian, bay	B1
Rysy, mt.	E4
San, river	F3
Silesia, region	C3
Śniardwy, lake	E2
Sudeten, mts.	B3
Vistula, river	D2, E3
Warta, river	B2, C2
Wieprz, river	F3

Map legend:

Poland

- ⊛ National Capital
- • Other City
- ⊥⊥⊥ Canal

1:6,687,500

0 50 100 mi
0 50 100 km

Lambert Conformal Conic Projection

© MapQuest.com, Inc.

Germany: Map Index

States

Baden-Württemberg	B4
Bavaria	B4
Berlin	C2
Brandenburg	C2
Bremen	B2
Hamburg	B2
Hesse	B3
Lower Saxony	B2
Mecklenburg-Western Pomerania	C2
North Rhine-Westphalia	A3
Rhineland-Palatinate	A4
Saarland	A4
Saxony	C3
Saxony-Anhalt	B3
Schleswig-Holstein	B2
Thuringia	B3

Cities and Towns

Aachen	A3
Amberg	B4
Ansbach	B4
Arnsberg	B3
Augsburg	B4
Bad Ems	A3
Baden-Baden	A4
Bad Kreuznach	A4
Bad Reichenhall	C5
Bamberg	B4
Bautzen	C3
Bayreuth	B4
Bergisch Gladbach	A3
Berlin, capital	C2
Bernburg	B3
Bielefeld	B2
Bingen	A4
Bocholt	A3
Bochum	A3
Bonn	A3
Bottrop	A3
Brandenburg	C2
Bremen	B2
Bremerhaven	B2
Brunswick	B2
Büren	B3
Chemnitz	C3
Coburg	B3
Cologne	A3
Constance	B5
Cottbus	C3
Cuxhaven	B2
Dachau	B4
Darmstadt	B4
Dessau	C3
Detmold	B3
Dortmund	A3
Dresden	C3
Duisburg	A3
Düsseldorf	A3
Eberswalde	C2
Eisenach	B3
Eisenhüttenstadt	C2
Eisleben	B3
Emden	A2
Erfurt	B3
Erlangen	B4
Essen	A3
Esslingen	B4
Flensburg	B1
Frankfurt am Main	B3
Frankfurt an der Oder	C2
Freiberg	C3
Freiburg	A5
Friedrichshafen	B5
Fulda	B3
Fürth	B4
Garmisch-Partenkirchen	B5
Gelsenkirchen	A3
Gera	B3
Giessen	B3
Göppingen	B4
Görlitz	C3
Goslar	B3
Gotha	B3
Göttingen	B3
Greifswald	C1
Guben	C3
Güstrow	C2
Hagen	A3
Halberstadt	B3
Halle	B3
Hamburg	B2
Hameln	B2
Hamm	A3
Hanau	B3
Hannover	B2
Heidelberg	B4
Heidenheim	B4
Heilbronn	B4
Herne	A3
Hildesheim	B2
Hindelang	B5
Hof	B3
Ingolstadt	B4
Jena	B3
Kaiserslautern	A4
Karlsruhe	A4
Kassel	B3
Kaufbeuren	B5
Kempten	B5
Kiel	B1
Kleve	A3
Koblenz	A3
Krefeld	A3
Kulmbach	B3
Landshut	C4
Leipzig	B3
Leverkusen	A3
Lindau	B5
Lippstadt	B3
Lübeck	B2
Luckenwalde	C2
Ludwigsburg	B4
Ludwigshafen am Rhein	B4
Lüneburg	B2
Lünen	A3
Magdeburg	B2
Mainz	B4
Mannheim	B4
Marburg	B3
Marl	A3
Meissen	C3
Memmingen	B5
Moers	A3
Mönchengladbach	A3
Mühlhausen	B3
Mülheim an der Ruhr	A3
Munich	B4
Münster	A3
Naumburg	B3
Neubrandenburg	C2
Neumünster	B1
Neunkirchen	A4
Neuss	A3
Neustrelitz	C2
Nienburg	B2
Nordenham	B2
Nordhausen	B3
Nordhorn	A2
Northeim	B3
Nuremberg	B4
Oberammergau	B5
Oberhausen	A3
Offenbach	B3
Oldenburg	B2
Osnabrück	B2
Paderborn	B3
Passau	C4
Pforzheim	B4
Pirmasens	A4
Plauen	B3
Potsdam	C2
Puttgarden	B1
Ratingen	A3
Ravensburg	B5
Recklinghausen	A3
Regensburg	C4
Remagen	A3
Remscheid	A3
Reutlingen	B4
Riesa	C3
Rosenheim	C5
Rostock	C1
Saarbrücken	A4
Salzgitter	B2
Sassnitz	C1
Schleswig	B1
Schwäbisch Gmünd	B4
Schwedt	C2
Schweinfurt	B3
Schwerin	B2
Siegen	B3
Singen	B5
Solingen	A3
Spandau	C2
Speyer	B4
Stendal	B2
Stralsund	C1
Straubing	C4
Stuttgart	B4
Suhl	B3
Trier	A4
Tübingen	B4
Uelzen	B2
Ulm	B4
Weiden	C4
Weimar	B3
Wetzlar	B3
Wiesbaden	B3
Wilhelmshaven	B2
Wismar	B2
Witten	A3
Wittenberg	C3
Wittenberge	B2
Wolfsburg	B2
Worms	B4
Wuppertal	A3
Würzburg	B4
Zittau	C3
Zwickau	C3

Other Features

Ammersee, lake	B4
Baltic, sea	C1
Bavarian Alps, mts.	B5
Bayerischer Wald, mts.	C4
Black, forest	A4
Bohemian, forest	C4
Chiem, lake	C5
Constance, lake	B5
Danube, river	B4
East Frisian, islands	A2
Eifel, plateau	A3
Elbe, river	B2, C3
Ems, river	A2
Erzgebirge, mts.	C3
Fehmarn, island	B1
Fichtelberg, mts.	C3
Fichtelgebirge, mts.	B4
Franconian Jura, mts	B4
Frankenwald, mts.	B3
Fulda, river	B3
Harz, mts.	B3
Havel, river	C2
Helgoland, island	A1
Hünsruck, mts.	A4
Inn, river	C4
Isar, river	C4
Kiel, bay	B1
Lahn, river	B3
Lech, river	B4
Lüneburger Heide, region	B2
Main, river	B4
Main-Danube, canal	B4
Mecklenburg, bay	B1
Mittelland, canal	B2
Mosel, river	A4
Mulde, river	C3
Müritz, lake	C2
Neckar, river	B4
Neisse, river	C3
Nord-Ostsee, canal	B1
North, sea	A1
Northern European, plain	B2
North Frisian, islands	B1
Oberpfälzer Wald, mts.	C4
Odenwald, forest	B4
Oder, river	C2
Oderhaff, lake	C2
Pomeranian, bay	C1
Rhine, river	A3, A4
Rügen, island	C1
Ruhr, river	B3
Saale, river	B3
Saar, river	A4
Salzach, river	C4
Schweriner, lake	B2
Spessart, mts.	B4
Spree, river	C3
Starnberg, lake	B5
Swabian Jura, mts.	B4
Taunus, mts.	B3
Thuringian, forest	B3
Werra, river	B3
Weser, river	B2
Zugspitze, mt.	B5

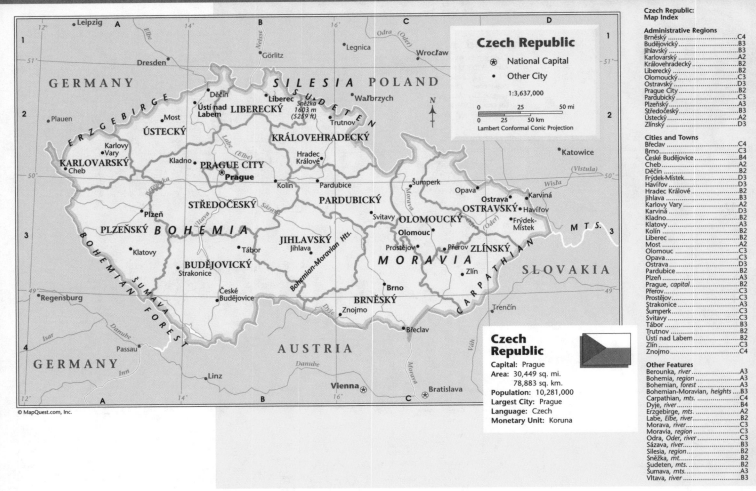

Czech Republic

National Capital
Other City

1:3,637,000

0   25   50 mi
0   25   50 km
Lambert Conformal Conic Projection

Czech Republic

Capital: Prague
Area: 30,449 sq. mi.
78,883 sq. km.
Population: 10,281,000
Largest City: Prague
Language: Czech
Monetary Unit: Koruna

© MapQuest.com, Inc.

Czech Republic:
Map Index

Administrative Regions
Brněský C4
Budějovický B3
Jihlavský B3
Karlovarský A2
Královehradecký B2
Liberecký B2
Olomoucký C3
Ostravský D3
Prague City B2
Pardubický C3
Plzeňský A3
Středočeský B3
Ústecký A2
Zlínský D3

Cities and Towns
Břeclav C4
Brno C3
České Budějovice B4
Cheb A2
Děčín B2
Frýdek-Místek D3
Havířov D3
Hradec Králové B2
Jihlava B3
Karlovy Vary A2
Karviná D3
Kladno B2
Klatovy A3
Kolín B2
Liberec B2
Most A2
Olomouc C3
Opava C3
Ostrava D3
Pardubice B2
Plzeň A3
Prague, *capital* B2
Přerov C3
Prostějov C3
Strakonice A3
Šumperk C3
Svitavy C3
Tábor B3
Trutnov B2
Ústí nad Labem A2
Zlín C3
Znojmo C4

Other Features
Berounka, *river* A3
Bohemia, *region* A3
Bohemian, *forest* A3
Bohemian-Moravian, *heights* .. B3
Carpathian, *mts.* C4
Dyje, *river* B4
Erzgebirge, *mts.* A2
Labe, *Elbe, river* B2
Morava, *river* C3
Moravia, *region* C3
Odra, *Oder, river* C3
Sázava, *river* B3
Silesia, *region* B2
Sněžka, *mt.* B2
Šudeten, *mts.* B2
Šumava, *mts.* A3
Vltava, *river* B3

Slovakia

Capital: Bratislava
Area: 18,933 sq. mi.
49,049 sq. km.
Population: 5,396,000
Largest City: Bratislava
Language: Slovak
Monetary Unit: New Koruna

Slovakia:
Map Index

Regions
Banskobystrický C2
Bratislavský A2
Košický C2
Nitriansky B2
Prešovský C2
Trenčiansky A2
Trnavský A2
Žilinský B2

Cities and Towns
Banská Bystrica B2
Bardejov C2
Bratislava, *capital* A2
Humenné C2
Komárno B3
Košice C2
Levice B2
Liptovský Mikuláš B2
Lučenec B2
Martin B2
Michalovce C2
Nitra B2
Nové Zámky B3
Piešťany A2
Poprad C2
Považská Bystrica B2
Prešov C2
Prievidza B2
Ružomberok B2
Spišská Nová Ves C2
Trenčín B2
Trnava A2
Žilina B2
Zvolen B2

Other Features
Biele Karpaty, *mts.* A2
Carpathian, *mts.* C2
Danube, *river* A3
Gerlachovka, *mt.* C2
Hornád, *river* B2
Hron, *river* B2
Ipeľ, *river* B2
Laborec, *river* C2
Male Karpaty, *mts.* A2
Morava, *river* A2
Ondava, *river* C2
Slaná, *river* C2
Slovenskérudohorie, *mts.* B2
Tatra, *range* B2
Váh, *river* A2

Slovakia

National Capital
Other City

1:4,353,000

0   25   50   75 mi
0   25   50   75 km
Lambert Conformal Conic Projection

© MapQuest.com, Inc.

Romania:
Map Index

Cities and Towns
Alba Iulia B2
Alexandria C4
Arad A2
Bacău D2
Baia Mare B2
Bîrlad D2
Bistriţa C2
Botoşani D2
Brăila D3
Braşov C3
Bucharest, *capital* D3
Buzău D3
Călăraşi D3
Cernavodă E3
Cluj-Napoca C2
Constanţa E3
Craiova B3
Dej C2
Deva B3
Dorohoi D2
Drobeta-Turnu Severin B3
Făgăras C3
Feteşti D3
Focşani D3
Galaţi E3
Giurgiu C4
Hunedoara B3
Iaşi D2
Lugoj A3
Lupeni B3
Medgidia E3
Mediaş C2
Miercurea Ciuc C2
Oltenita D3
Oneşti D2
Oradea A2
Petrila B3
Petroşani B3
Piatra Neamţ D2
Piteşti C3
Ploieşti D3
Rădăuţi C2
Reghin C2
Reşiţa A3
Rîmnicu Vîlcea C3
Roman D2
Salonta A2
Satu Mare B2
Sfîntu Gheorghe C3
Sibiu C3
Sighetul Marmaţiei B2

Hungary
Capital: Budapest
Area: 35,919 sq. mi.
93,054 sq. km.
Population: 10,186,000
Largest City: Budapest
Language: Hungarian
Monetary Unit: Forint

Hungary
⊛ National Capital
• Other City
1:4,187,000
0   40   80 mi
0   40   80   120 km
Lambert Conformal Conic Projection

Hungary:
Map Index

Counties

Bács-Kiskun	B2
Baranya	B3
Békés	C2
Békéscsaba	C2
Borsod-Abaúj-Zemplén	C1
Budapest (city)	B2
Csongrád	C2
Debrecen	C2
Dunaújváros	B2
Eger	C1
Fejér	B2
Győr	A2
Győr-Moson-Sopron	A2
Hajdú-Bihar	C2
Heves	C2
Hódmezővásárhely	C2
Jász-Nagykun-Szolnok	C2
Kaposvár	A2
Kecskemét	B2
Komárom-Esztergom	B2
Miskolc	C1
Nagykanizsa	A2
Nógrád	B2
Nyíregyháza	C2
Pécs	B2
Pest	B2
Somogy	A2
Sopron	A2
Szabolcs- Szatmár-Bereg	C1
Szeged	C2
Székesfehérvár	B2
Szolnok	C2
Szombathely	A2
Tatabánya	B2
Tolna	B2
Vas	A2
Veszprém	A2
Zala	A
Zalaegerszeg	A2

Cities and Towns

Ajka	A2
Baja	B2
Békéscsaba	C2
Budapest, capital	B2
Cegléd	B2
Debrecen	C2
Dunaújváros	B2
Eger	C2
Érd	B2
Esztergom	B2
Gyöngyös	B2
Győr	A2
Hajdúböszörmény	C2
Hódmezővásárhely	C2
Jászberény	B2
Kaposvár	A2
Karcag	C2
Kazincbarcika	C1
Kecskemét	B2
Keszthely	A2
Kiskunhalas	B2
Komárom	B2
Miskolc	C1
Mohács	B2
Nagykanizsa	A2
Nyíregyháza	C2
Oroszháza	C2
Ózd	C1
Paks	B2
Pápa	A2
Pécs	B2
Salgótarján	B1
Siófok	B2
Sopron	A2
Szeged	C2
Székesfehérvár	B2
Szekszárd	B2
Szentes	C2
Szolnok	C2
Szombathely	A2
Tatabánya	B2
Tokaj	C1
Vác	B2
Veszprém	A2
Zalaegerszeg	A2

Other Features

Bakony, mts.	A2
Balaton, lake	A2
Bükk, mts.	C1
Danube, river	A2, B2
Drava, river	A2
Great Alföld, plain	B2
Hernád, river	C1
Ipoly, river	B1
Kékes, mt.	C2
Kiskörei-víztároló, lake	C2
Körös, river	C2
Little Alföld, plain	A2
Maros, river	C2
Mátra, mts.	B2
Mecsek, mts.	B2
Neusiedler (Fertő), lake	A2
Rába, river	A2
Sió, river	B2
Tisza, river	C2
Zala, river	A2

Romania
Capital: Bucharest
Area: 91,699 sq. mi.
267,174 sq. km.
Population: 22,334,000
Largest City: Bucharest
Language: Romanian
Monetary Unit: Leu

Sighişoara	C2
Siret	D2
Slatina	C3
Slobozia	D3
Suceava	D2
Tecuci	D3
Timişoara	A3
Tîrgovişte	C3
Tîrgu Jiu	B3
Tîrgu-Mureş	C2
Tîrgu Neamţ	D2
Tîrgu Ocna	D2
Tulcea	E3
Turda	B2
Turnu Măgurele	C4
Vaslui	D2
Zalău	B2

Other Features

Apuseni, mts.	B2
Argeş, river	C3
Banat, region	A3
Bicaz, reservoir	D2
Bihor, mts.	B2
Bistriţa, river	C2
Carpathian, mts.	B1
Danube, river	B3, D3, E3
Dobruja, region	E4
Ialomiţa, river	D3
Iron Gate, reservoir	B3
Jiu, river	B3
Moldavia, region	D2
Moldoveanu, mt.	C3
Mouths of the Danube, delta	E3
Mureş, river	C2
Olt, river	C3
Prut, river	E2
Razelm, lake	E3
Siret, river	D2
Someş, river	B2
Transylvanian Alps, mts.	B3
Walachia, region	B3

Romania
⊛ National Capital
• Other City
1:5,750,000
0   40   80 mi
0   40   80 km
Lambert Conformal Conic Projection

© MapQuest.com, Inc.

Armenia

Capital: Yerevan
Area: 11,500 sq. mi.
29,793 sq. km.
Population: 3,409,000
Largest City: Yerevan
Language: Armenian
Monetary Unit: Dram

Armenia: Map Index

Cities and Towns

Alaverdi	B1
Ararat	B3
Artashat	B3
Artik	A2
Artsvashen	C2
Dilijan	B2
Ejmiatsin	B2
Gavarr	C2
Goris	D3
Gyumri	A2
Hoktemberyan	B2
Hrazdan	B2
Ijevan	C2
Kafan	D3
Kirovakan	B2
Martuni	C2
Meghri	D4
Sisian	D3
Sotk	C2
Stepanavan	B2
Tashir	B1
Vardenis	C2
Vayk	C3
Yerevan, *capital*	B2

Other Features

Akhuryan, *river*	A2
Aragats, *mt.*	B2
Aras, *river*	B2
Arpa, *river*	C3
Debed, *river*	B2
Hrazdan, *river*	B2
Lesser Caucasus, *mts.*	B1
Sevan, *lake*	C2
Vorotan, *river*	C3

Georgia: Map Index

Cities and Towns

Akhalkalaki	B4
Akhaltsikhe	B4
Akhmeta	C3
Batumi	A4
Bolnisi	C4
Borjomi	B4
Chiatura	B3
Gagra	A2
Gori	C4
Gudauta	A2
Jvari	B3
Khashuri	C4
Kobuleti	A4
Kutaisi	B3
Lagodekhi	D4
Marneuli	C4
Mtskheta	C4
Ochamchire	A3
Ozurgeti	A4
Poti	A3
Rustavi	C4
Samtredia	B3
Senaki	B3
Sukhumi	A3
Tbilisi, *capital*	C4
Telavi	C4
Tqvarcheli	A3
Tsiteli-Tsqaro	D4
Tskhinvali	B3
Tsnori	C4
Zestaponi	B3
Zugdidi	A3

Other Features

Abkhazia, *autonomous republic*	A3
Ajaria, *autonomous republic*	A4
Alazani, *river*	C4
Caucasus, *mts.*	A2
Enguri, *river*	A3
Iori, *river*	C4
Lesser Caucasus, *mts.*	B4
Mqinvartsveri, *mt.*	C3
Mtkvari, *river*	C4
Rioni, *river*	B3
Shkhara, *mt.*	B3
South Ossetia, *region*	B3

Georgia

Capital: Tbilisi
Area: 26,900 sq. mi.
69,689 sq. km.
Population: 5,067,000
Largest City: Tbilisi
Language: Georgian
Monetary Unit: Lari

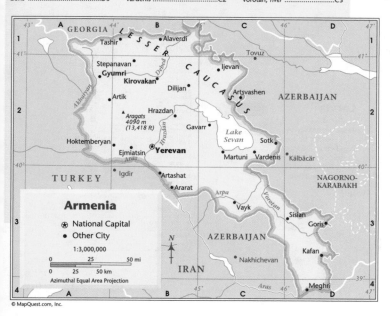

Azerbaijan

Capital: Baku
Area: 33,400 sq. mi.
86,528 sq. km.
Population: 7,908,000
Largest City: Baku
Language: Azerbaijani
Monetary Unit: Manat

Azerbaijan: Map Index

Cities and Towns

Ağcabädi	B2
Ağdam	B3
Ağstafa	A2
Älät	C3
Äli Bayramli	C3
Astara	C3
Baku, *capital*	C2
Balakän	B2
Bärdä	B2
Biläsuvar	C3
Gäncä	B2
Göyçay	B2
Kälbäcär	B2
Länkäran	C3
Mingäçevir	B2
Nakhichevan	A3
Quba	C2
Şahbuz	A3
Şaki	B2
Salyan	C3
Sumqayit	C2
Tovuz	A2
Xaçmaz	C2
Xankändi	B3
Yevlax	B2
Zaqatala	B2

Other Features

Abşeron, *peninsula*	C2
Aras, *river*	B3
Bazardüzü Daği, *mt.*	B1
Caucasus, *range*	A1
Karabakh, *canal*	A2, C2
Kür, *river*	A2, C2
Kür-Aras, *lowland*	A2
Lesser Caucasus, *range*	A2
Mingäçevir, *reservoir*	B2
Nagorno-Karabakh, *autonomous region*	B2
Samur, *river*	B2
Talish, *mts.*	C3

**Estonia:
Map Index**

Cities and Towns
Haapsalu B2
Kärdla B1
Keila C1
Kohtla-Järve D1
Kunda D1
Kuressaare B2
Mustvee D2
Narva E1
Paldiski C1
Pärnu C2
Rapla C1
Tallinn, *capital* C1
Tapa C1
Tartu D2
Törva C2
Türi C2

Valga D3
Viljandi C2
Virtsu B2
Võru D3

Other Features
Baltic, *sea* A1
Finland, *gulf* C1
Hiiumaa, *island* B2
Irbe, *strait* A3
Munamägi, *mt.* D3
Narva, *river* D1
Pärnu, *river* C2
Pedja, *river* D2
Peipus, *lake* D2
Pskov, *lake* D3
Riga, *gulf* B3
Saaremaa, *island* B2
Võrts Järv, *lake* D2

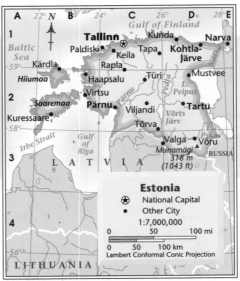

Estonia
National Capital ✪
Other City ●
1:7,000,000
0   50   100 mi
0   50   100 km
Lambert Conformal Conic Projection

© MapQuest.com, Inc.

Estonia
Capital: Tallinn
Area: 17,413 sq. mi.
45,111 sq. km.
Population: 1,409,000
Largest City: Tallinn
Language: Estonian
Monetary Unit: Kroon

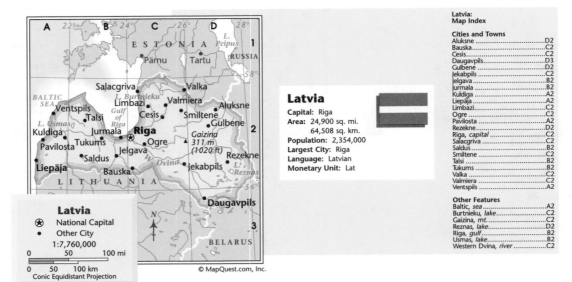

Latvia
National Capital ✪
Other City ●
1:7,760,000
0   50   100 mi
0   50   100 km
Conic Equidistant Projection

© MapQuest.com, Inc.

Latvia
Capital: Riga
Area: 24,900 sq. mi.
64,508 sq. km.
Population: 2,354,000
Largest City: Riga
Language: Latvian
Monetary Unit: Lat

**Latvia:
Map Index**

Cities and Towns
Aluksne D2
Bauska C2
Cesis C2
Daugavpils D3
Gulbene D2
Jekabpils C2
Jelgava B2
Jurmala B2
Kuldiga A2
Liepãja A2
Limbazi C2
Ogre C2
Pavilosta A2
Rezekne D2
Riga, *capital* C2
Salacgriva C2
Saldus B2
Smiltene C2
Talsi B2
Tukums B2
Valka C2
Valmiera C2
Ventspils A2

Other Features
Baltic, *sea* A2
Burtnieku, *lake* C2
Gaizina, *mt.* C2
Reznas, *lake* D2
Riga, *gulf* B2
Usmas, *lake* B2
Western Dvina, *river* ...C2

Lithuania
Capital: Vilnius
Area: 25,213 sq. mi.
65,319 sq. km.
Population: 3,585,000
Largest City: Vilnius
Language: Lithuanian
Monetary Unit: Litas

Lithuania
National Capital ✪
Other City ●
1:4,600,000
0   30   60 mi
0   30   60 km
Conic Equidistant Projection

© MapQuest.com, Inc.

**Lithuania:
Map Index**

Cities and Towns
Alytus C2
Biržai C1
Druskininkai B2
Jonava C2
Jurbarkas B2
Kaunas B2
Kedainiai B2
Klaipeda A2
Kretinga A2
Kuršenai B1
Marijampole B2
Mažeikiai B1
Naujoji Akmene B1
Palanga A2
Panevežys C2
Radviliškis B2
Šiauliai B2
Šilalė B2

Šilutė A2
Tauragė B2
Telšiai B2
Ukmergė C2
Utena C2
Vilkaviškis B2
Vilnius, *capital* C2

Other Features
Baltic, *sea* A2
Courland, *lagoon* A2
Dubysa, *river* B2
Juozapines, *mt.* C2
Jura, *river* A2
Merkys, *river* C2
Minija, *river* A2
Mūša, *river* B1
Nemunas, *river* A2, C2
Neris, *river* C2
Nevėžis, *river* B2
Šventoji, *river* C2
Venta, *river* B1

© MapQuest.com, Inc.

Belarus

Capital: Minsk
Area: 80,134 sq. mi.
207,601 sq. km.
Population: 10,402,000
Largest City: Minsk
Languages: Belarussian, Russian
Monetary Unit: Belarus ruble

Belarus:
Map Index

Cities and Towns

Asipovichy	D3
Babruysk	D3
Baranavichy	C3
Brest	A3
Homyel	E3
Hrodna	A3
Krychaw	E3
Lida	B3
Mahilyow	E3
Maladzyechna	C2
Mazyr	D3
Minsk, capital	C3
Orsha	E2
Pastavy	C2
Pinsk	C3
Polotsk	D2
Rechytsa	E3
Salihorsk	C3
Smilovichi	D3
Smolevichi	D2
Vawkavysk	B3
Vitsyebsk	E2
Zhlobin	D3

Other Features

Bug, river	A3
Byarezina, river	D3
Byelaruskaya Hrada, range	C3
Dnepr, river	E3
Dnepr-Bug, canal	B3
Dzyarzhynskaya Hara, mt.	C3
Nyoman, river	B3
Pripyats, marshes	C4
Pripyats, river	C3
Ptsich, river	D3
Sozh, river	E3
Western Dvina, river	D2

Ukraine:
Map Index

Cities and Towns

Balaklava	C4
Belaya Tserkov	C2
Berdyansk	D3
Cherkassy	C2
Chernigov	C1
Chernivtsi	B2
Chornobyl'	C1
Dneprodzerzhinsk	C2
Dnipropetrovsk	D2
Donetsk	D2
Feodosiya	D3
Gorlovka	D2
Ivano-Frankovsk	A2
Izmail	B3
Kachovka	C3
Kerch	D3
Kharkiv	D1
Kherson	C3
Khmelnytskyy	B2
Khust	A2
Kiev, capital	C1
Kirovograd	C2
Konotop	C1
Korosten	B1
Kotovsk	B2
Kovel	A1
Kramatorsk	D2
Kremenchug	C2
Kryvyi Rih	C2
Lisichansk	D2
Luhansk	D2
Lutsk	B1
Lviv	A2
Makeyevka	D2
Mariupol	D3
Melitopol	D3
Mogilev Podolskiy	B2
Mykolaiv	C3
Nikopol	C2
Odesa	C3
Pervomaysk	C2
Poltava	C2
Priluki	C1
Rovno	B1
Sevastopol	C4
Shostka	C1
Simferopol	C3
Sumy	C1
Ternopol	B2
Uman	C2
Uzhgorod	A2
Vinnitsa	B2
Yalta	C4
Yevpatoriya	C3
Zaporizhzhia	D2
Zhitomir	B1

Other Features

Azov, sea	D3
Black, sea	C3
Bug, river	A1
Carpathian, mts.	A2
Crimean, mts.	C4
Crimean, peninsula	C3
Desna, river	C1
Dneprodzerzhinsk, reservoir	C2
Dnieper, river	C1,C3
Dniester, river	B2
Donets, basin	D2
Donets, river	D2
Hoverla, mt.	A2
Kakhovka, reservoir	C3
Karkinit, bay	C3
Kerch, strait	D3
Kiev, reservoir	C1
Kremenchug, reservoir	C2
Pripyat, river	A1
Prut, river	B2
Psel, river	C1
Sluch, river	B1
Southern Bug, river	B2
Taganrog, gulf	D3
Tisza, river	A2
Volyno-Podol'skaya Vozvyshennost, uplands	B2
Vorskla, river	C1

© MapQuest.com, Inc.

Ukraine

Capital: Kiev
Area: 233,100 sq. mi.
603,886 sq. km.
Population: 49,811,000
Largest City: Kiev
Languages: Ukrainian, Russian
Monetary Unit: Hryvnya

Slovenia

Capital: Ljubljana
Area: 7,821 sq. mi.
20,262 sq. km.
Population: 1,971,000
Largest City: Ljubljana
Languages: Slovenian, Serbo-Croatian
Monetary Unit: Tolar

Slovenia:
Map Index

Cities and Towns
Celje C2
Idrija B2
Jesenice B2
Kočevje B3
Koper A3
Kranj B2
Krško C3
Ljubljana, *capital* B2
Maribor C2
Murska Sobota D2
Nova Gorica A3
Novo Mesto C3
Postojna B3
Ptuj C2

Other Features
Adriatic, *sea* A3
Drava, *river* C2
Julian Alps, *mts.* A2
Krka, *river* B3
Kupa, *river* B3
Mura, *river* B2
Sava, *river* B2
Savinja, *river* B2
Trieste, *gulf* A3
Triglav, *mt.* A2

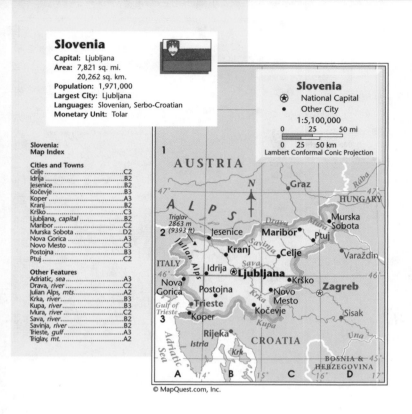

Slovenia
⊛ National Capital
● Other City
1:5,100,000
0   25   50 mi
0   25   50 km
Lambert Conformal Conic Projection

© MapQuest.com, Inc.

Croatia

⊛ National Capital
● Other City
1:9,700,000
0   50   100 mi
0   50   100 km
Lambert Conformal Conic Projection

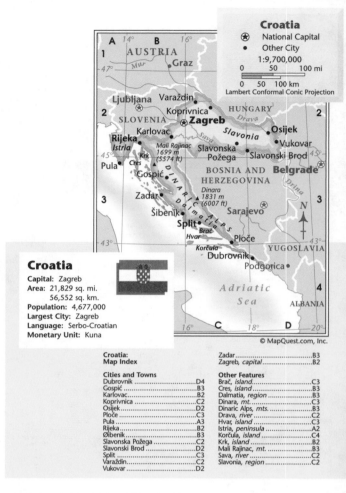

© MapQuest.com, Inc.

Croatia

Capital: Zagreb
Area: 21,829 sq. mi.
56,552 sq. km.
Population: 4,677,000
Largest City: Zagreb
Language: Serbo-Croatian
Monetary Unit: Kuna

Croatia:
Map Index

Cities and Towns
Dubrovnik D4
Gospić B3
Karlovac B2
Koprivnica C2
Osijek D2
Ploče C3
Pula A3
Rijeka B2
Øibenik B3
Slavonska Požega C2
Slavonski Brod D2
Split C3
Varaždin C2
Vukovar D2

Zadar B3
Zagreb, *capital* B2

Other Features
Brač, *island* C3
Cres, *island* B3
Dalmatia, *region* B3
Dinara, *mt.* C3
Dinaric Alps, *mts.* B3
Drava, *river* C2
Hvar, *island* C3
Istria, *peninsula* A2
Korčula, *island* C4
Krk, *island* B2
Mali Rajinac, *mt.* B3
Sava, *river* C2
Slavonia, *region* C2

Bosnia and Hercegovina:
Map Index

Cities and Towns
Banja Luka B1
Bihać A1
Bijeljina C1
Bosanska Gradiška B1
Bosanska Krupa A1
Brčko B1
Bugojno B1
Derventa B1
Doboj B1
Foča B2
Gacko B2
Goražde B2
Gračanica B1
Jajce B1
Livno B2
Mostar B2
Pale B2
Prijedor A1
Sanski Most A1
Sarajevo, *capital* B2
Srebrenica C1
Teslić B1
Trebinje B2
Tuzla B1
Zavidovići B1
Zenica B1
Zvornik C1

Other Features
Bosna, *river* B1
Dinara, *mt.* A2
Dinaric Alps, *mts.* A1
Drina, *river* C1
Neretva, *river* B2
Sava, *river* B1
Una, *river* A1
Vrbas, *river* B1

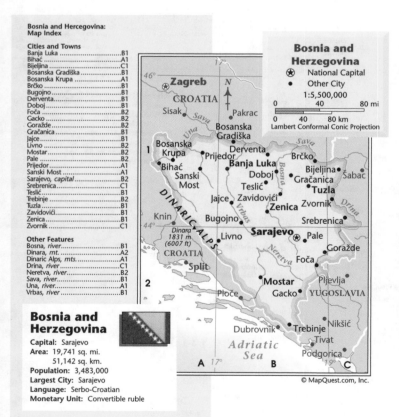

Bosnia and Herzegovina
⊛ National Capital
● Other City
1:5,500,000
0   40   80 mi
0   40   80 km
Lambert Conformal Conic Projection

© MapQuest.com, Inc.

Bosnia and Herzegovina

Capital: Sarajevo
Area: 19,741 sq. mi.
51,142 sq. km.
Population: 3,483,000
Largest City: Sarajevo
Language: Serbo-Croatian
Monetary Unit: Convertible ruble

F.Y.R. Macedonia

Capital: Skopje
Area: 9,928 sq. mi.
25,720 sq. km.
Population: 2,023,000
Largest City: Skopje
Languages: Macedonian, Albanian, Serbo-
Croatian, Turkish
Monetary Unit: Denar

F.Y.R. Macedonia:
Map Index

Cities and Towns
Bitola B2
Blatec C2
Debar A2
Gevgelija C2
Kavadarci C2
Kičevo A2
Kočani C2
Kruševo B2
Kumanovo B1
Ohrid A2
Prilep B2
Skopje, *capital* B2
Štip C2
Struga A2
Strumica C2
Tetovo A1
Titov Veles B2

Other Features
Belasica, *mts.* C2
Bregalnica, *river* C2
Crna, *river* B2
Crna Gora, *mts.* B1
Doiran, *lake* C2
Jakupica, *mts.* B2
Korab, *mt.* A2
Kožuf, *mts.* B2
Nidže, *mts.* B3
Ogražden, *mts.* C2
Ohrid, *lake* A3
Prespa, *lake* B3
Treska, *river* B2
Vardar, *river* C2

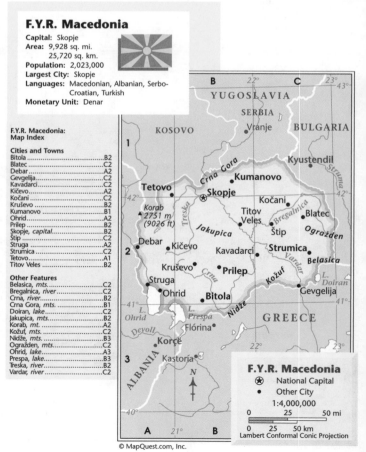

F.Y.R. Macedonia
⊛ National Capital
● Other City
1:4,000,000
0   25   50 mi
0   25   50 km
Lambert Conformal Conic Projection

© MapQuest.com, Inc.

Albania

★ National Capital
● Other City

1:3,750,000

0   15   30 mi
0   15   30 km

Lambert Conformal
Conic Projection

© MapQuest.com, Inc.

Federal Republic of Yugoslavia

★ National Capital
● Other City

1:3,682,000

0   30   60 mi
0   30   60 km

Lambert Conformal Conic Projection

© MapQuest.com, Inc.

Albania:
Map Index

Cities and Towns
Berat	A3
Durrës	A2
Elbasan	B2
Ersekë	B3
Fier	A3
Gjirokastër	B3
Kavajë	A2
Korçë	B3
Krujë	A2
Kukës	B1
Laç	A2
Lushnjë	A3
Peshkopi	B2
Pogradec	B3
Pukë	A1
Sarandë	A4
Shëngjin	A2
Shkodër	A1
Tirana, *capital*	A2
Vlorë	A3

Other Features
Adriatic, *sea*	A2
Buene, *river*	A2
Devoll, *river*	B3
Drin, *river*	A1
Erzen, *river*	A2
Ionian, *sea*	A4
Korab, *mt.*	B2
Mat, *river*	A2
North Albanian Alps, *range*	A1
Ohrid, *lake*	B2
Osum, *river*	B3
Otranto, *strait*	A3
Prespa, *lake*	C3
Scutari, *lake*	A1
Seman, *river*	A3
Shkumbin, *river*	A2
Vijosë, *river*	A3

Albania

Capital: Tirana
Area: 11,100 sq. mi.
28,756 sq. km.
Population: 3,365,000
Largest City: Tirana
Languages: Albanian, Greek
Monetary Unit: Lek

Yugoslavia:
Map Index

Internal Divisions
Kosovo (province)	B3
Montenegro (republic)	A3
Serbia (republic)	B2
Vojvodina (province)	A2

Cities and Towns
Bačka Palanka	A2
Bar	A3
Bečej	B2
Belgrade, *capital*	B2
Bor	C2
Čačak	B3
Cetinje	A3
Đakovica	B3
Kikinda	B2
Kosovska Mitrovica	B3
Kragujevac	B2
Kraljevo	B3
Kruševac	B3
Leskovac	B3
Nikšić	A3
Niš	B3
Novi Pazar	B3
Novi Sad	B2
Pančevo	B2
Peć	B3
Pirot	C3
Pljevlja	A3
Podgorica	A3
Požarevac	B2
Priboj	A3
Priština	B3
Prizren	B3
Prokuplje	B3
Šabac	A2
Senta	B2
Smederevo	B2
Sombor	A2
Sremska Mitrovica	A2
Subotica	A1
Svetozarevo	B3
Uroševac	B3
Užice	A3
Valjevo	A2
Vranje	B3
Vrbas	B2
Vršac	B2
Zaječar	C3
Zrenjanin	B2

Other Features
Adriatic, *sea*	A4
Balkan, *mts.*	C3
Beli Drim, *river*	B3
Crna Gora, *mts.*	A3
Danube, *river*	A2, B2
Đaravica, *mt.*	B3
Dinaric Alps, *mts.*	A3
Drina, *river*	A2
Durmitor, *mts.*	A3
Fruška Gora, *mts.*	A2
Ibar, *river*	B3

Jastrebac, *mts.*	B3
Južna, *river*	B3
Kopaonik, *mts.*	B3
Kotor, *gulf*	A3
Morava, *river*	B3
Nišava, *river*	C3
North Albanian Alps, *mts.*	B3
Šar Planina, *mts.*	B3
Sava, *river*	A2
Scutari, *lake*	A3
Tara, *river*	A3
Tisa, *river*	B2
Velika Morava, *river*	B2
Veliki, *canal*	A2
Zapandna Morava, *river*	B3
Zeta, *river*	A3
Zlatibor, *mts.*	A3

Yugoslavia

Capital: Belgrade
Area: 39,449 sq. mi.
102,199 sq. km.
Population: 11,207,000
Largest City: Belgrade
Language: Serbo-Croatian
Monetary Unit: New Yugoslav dinar

Moldova

★ National Capital
• Other City

1:4,800,000

0   35   70 mi
0   35   70 km

Lambert Conformal Conic Projection

© MapQuest.com, Inc.

Moldova

Capital: Chişinău
Area: 13,012 sq. mi.
     33,710 sq. km.
Population: 4,461,000
Largest City: Chişinău
Languages: Moldovan, Russian
Monetary Unit: Moldovan leu

Moldova:
Map Index

Cities and Towns

Bălţi	A2
Basarabeasca	B2
Bender (Tighina)	B2
Briceni	A1
Cahul	B3
Căuşeni	B2
Chişinău, *capital*	B2
Comrat	B2
Dubăsari	B2
Făleşti	A2
Floreşti	B2
Leova	B2
Orhei	B2
Rîbniţa	B2
Rîşcani	A2
Soroca	B1
Tiraspol	B2
Ungheni	A2

Other Features

Botna, *river*	B2
Bugeac, *region*	B3
Codri, *region*	A3
Cogalnic, *river*	B2
Dnestr, *river*	B2
Ialpug, *river*	B2
Prut, *river*	A1, B3
Raut, *river*	B2

Bulgaria:
Map Index

Administrative Regions

Blagoevgrad	B4
Burgas	F3
Dobrich	F2
Gabrovo	D3
Haskovo	D4
Jambol	E3
Kardzhali	D4
Kjustendil	A3
Lovech	C3
Montana	B2
Pazardzhik	C3
Pernik	A3
Pleven	C2
Plovdiv	C3
Razgrad	E2
Ruse	D2
Shumen	F2
Silistra	F2
Sliven	E3
Smoljan	C4
Sofia	B3
Sofia City	B3
Stara Zagora	D3
Targovishte	E2
Varna	F2
Veliko Tarnovo	D2
Vidin	A2
Vraca	B2

Cities and Towns

Asenovgrad	C3
Aytos	F3
Blagoevgrad	B4
Burgas	F3
Dimitrovgrad	D3
Dobrich	F2
Elkhovo	E3
Gabrovo	D3
Haskovo	D4
Jambol	E3
Kardzhali	D4
Kazanlŭk	D3
Kjustendil	A3
Kozloduy	B2
Lom	B2
Lovech	C2
Madan	C4
Montana	B2
Oryakhovo	B2
Panagyurishte	C3
Pazardzhik	C3
Pernik	B3
Petrich	B4
Pleven	C2
Plovdiv	C3
Primorsko	F3
Razgrad	E2
Ruse	D2
Samokov	B3
Shumen	E2
Silistra	F1
Sliven	E3
Smoljan	C4
Sofia, *capital*	B3
Stara Zagora	D3
Svilengrad	E4
Svishtov	D2
Targovishte	E2
Varna	F2
Veliko Tarnovo	D2
Vidin	A2
Vratsa	B2

Other Features

Arda, *river*	C4
Balkan, *mts.*	B2
Danube, *river*	B2
Golyama Kamchiya, *river*	E2
Iskŭr, *river*	C2
Kamchiya, *river*	F2
Luda Kamchiya, *river*	E3
Ludogorie, *region*	E2
Maritsa, *river*	D3
Mesta, *river*	B4
Musala, *mt.*	B3
Ogosta, *river*	B2
Osŭm, *river*	C3
Rhodope, *mts.*	C4
Rila, *mts.*	B3
Sredna Gora, *mts.*	C3
Struma, *river*	A3
Stryama, *river*	C3
Thrace, *region*	D4
Thracian, *plain*	C3
Tundzha, *river*	D3
Yantra, *river*	D2

Bulgaria

Capital: Sofia
Area: 42,855 sq. mi.
     111,023 sq. km.
Population: 8,195,000
Largest City: Sofia
Language: Bulgarian
Monetary Unit: Lev

Bulgaria

★ National Capital
• Other City

1:3,210,000

0   25   50   75 mi
0   25   50   75 km

Lambert Conformal Conic Projection

Greece

⊛ National Capital

● Other City

1:6,500,000

| 0 | 75 | 150 mi |
| 0 | 75 | 150 km |

Lambert Conformal Conic Projection

© MapQuest.com, Inc.

Greece:
Map Index

Regions
Attica B2
Central Greece B2
Central Macedonia B1
Crete..........................C4
Eastern Macedonia and
  Thrace C1
Epirus B2
Ionian Islands B2
Northern Aegean C2
Peloponnesus B3
Southern Aegean C3
Thessaly.....................B2
Western Greece B3
Western Macedonia.......B1

Cities and Towns
Agrínion B2
Akharnaí......................Inset
Alexandroúpolis C1
Árgos B3
Asprópirgos..................Inset
Athens, capital.....B3, Inset
Áyios Dhimítrios...........Inset
Corinth B3
Dháfni ....Inset
Elevsís........................Inset
Ellinikón ....Inset
Glifádha ....Inset
Ioánnina B2
Iráklion C4
Kalámai B3

Kalamáki ....Inset
Kallithéa ....Inset
Kastoría B1
Kateríni B1
Kavála C1
Keratsínion ....Inset
Kérkira........................A2
Khalándrion ....Inset
Khalkís B2
Khaniá........................B4
Kifisiá ....Inset
Komotiní C1
Kozáni B1
Lamía B2
Lárisa B2
Mándra ....Inset
Mesolóngion B2
Mitilíni C2
Néa Liósia ....Inset
Neápolis B3
Níkaia ....Inset
Paianía ....Inset
Pátrai B2
Peristéri ....Inset
Pílos B3
Piraiévs...............B3, Inset
Préveza B2
Rhodes D3
Selínia ....Inset
Sérrai B1
Sparta B3
Thásos C1
Thessaloníki B1
Tríkala B2
Véroia B1

Vólos B2
Xánthi C1

Other Features
Aegean, sea C2
Aigáleo, mts. ....Inset
Aíyina, island B3
Akhelóös, river B2
Alifiós, river B3
Aliákmon, river B1
Ándros, island C3
Astipálaia, island C3
Áthos, mt. C1
Corinth, gulf B2
Corinth, isthmus B3
Crete, island C4
Crete, sea C4
Cyclades, islands C3
Delos, island C3
Dodecanese, islands C3
Elevsís, bay ....Inset
Euboea, island B2
Idhra, island B3
Ikaría, island C3
Ionian, islands B2
Ionian, sea...................A2
Itháki, island B2
Kárpathos, island...........C4
Kefallinía, island B2
Kérkira, island A2
Khalkidhikí, peninsula......B1
Khíos, island C2
Kifissós, river B2
Kíthira, island B3
Kos, island...................C3

Lésvos, island C2
Límnos, island C2
Míkonos, island C3
Mílos, island C3
Náxos, island................C3
Northern Sporades, islands B2
Olympus, mt..................B1
Páros, island C3
Pindus, mts..................B2
Piniós, river B2
Prespa, lake B1
Rhodes, island D3
Salamís, island ....Inset
Sámos, island C3
Samothráki, island..........C1
Saronic, gulf.................Inset
Skíros, island C2
Struma, river B1
Thásos, island C1
Thíra, island C3
Zákinthos, island B3

Greece

Capital: Athens
Area: 50,949 sq. mi.
  131,992 sq. km.
Population: 10,707,000
Largest City: Athens
Language: Greek
Monetary Unit: Drachma

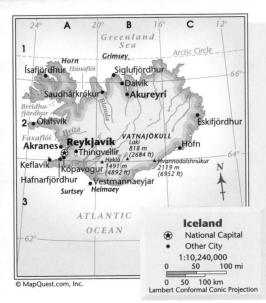

Iceland

Capital: Reykjavík
Area: 36,699 sq. mi.
95,075 sq. km.
Population: 273,000
Largest City: Reykjavík
Language: Icelandic
Monetary Unit: New Icelandic króna

Iceland
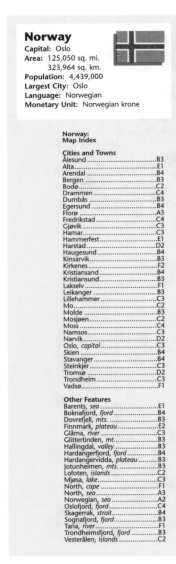

(★) National Capital

• Other City

1:10,240,000

0   50   100 mi

0 50 100 km
Lambert Conformal Conic Projection

© MapQuest.com, Inc.

Iceland:
Map Index

Cities and Towns

Akranes	A2
Akureyri	B2
Dalvík	B2
Eskifjördhur	C2
Hafnarfjördhur	A3
Höfn	C2
Ísafjördhur	A1
Keflavík	A3
Kópavogur	A2
Ólafsvík	A2
Reykjavík, capital	A2
Saudhárkrókur	B2
Siglufjördhur	B1
Thingvellir	A2
Vestmannaeyjar	A3

Other Features

Blanda, river	B2
Breidhafjördhur, fjord	A2
Faxaflói, bay	A2
Greenland, sea	B1
Grímsey, island	B1
Heimaey, island	A3
Hekla, volcano	B3
Horn, cape	A1
Húnaflói, bay	A2
Hvannadalshnúkur, mt.	B3
Hvítá, river	A2
Laki, volcano	B2
Surtsey, island	A3
Vatnajökull, ice cap	B2

Norway

Capital: Oslo
Area: 125,050 sq. mi.
323,964 sq. km.
Population: 4,439,000
Largest City: Oslo
Language: Norwegian
Monetary Unit: Norwegian krone

Norway:
Map Index

Cities and Towns

Ålesund	B3
Alta	E1
Arendal	B4
Bergen	B3
Bodø	C2
Drammen	C4
Dumbås	B3
Egersund	B4
Florø	A3
Fredrikstad	C4
Gjøvik	C3
Hamar	C3
Hammerfest	E1
Harstad	D2
Haugesund	B4
Kinsarvik	B3
Kirkenes	F2
Kristiansand	B4
Kristiansund	B3
Lakselv	F1
Leikanger	B3
Lillehammer	C3
Mo	C2
Molde	B3
Mosjøen	C2
Moss	C4
Namsos	C3
Narvik	D2
Oslo, capital	C3
Skien	B4
Stavanger	B4
Steinkjer	C3
Tromsø	D2
Trondheim	C3
Vadsø	F1

Other Features

Barents, sea	E1
Boknafjord, fjord	B4
Dovrefjell, mts.	B3
Finnmark, plateau	E2
Glåma, river	C3
Glittertinden, mt.	B3
Hallingdal, valley	B3
Hardangerfjord, fjord	B4
Hardangervidda, plateau	B3
Jotunheimen, mts.	B3
Lofoten, islands	C2
Mjøsa, lake	C3
North, cape	F1
North, sea	A3
Norwegian, sea	A2
Oslofjord, fjord	C4
Skagerrak, strait	B4
Sognafjord, fjord	B3
Tana, river	F1
Trondheimsfjord, fjord	B3
Vesterålen, islands	C2

Norway

(★) National Capital

• Other City

1:12,075,000

0   50   100   150   200 mi

0   100   200   300 km
Lambert Conformal Conic Projection

© MapQuest.com, Inc.

Finland: Map Index

Internal Divisions

Eastern Finland (province)........C2
Lapland (province)....................C1
Oulu (province).........................C1
Southern Finland (province)......B2
Western Finland (province)........B2
Central Finland (region)............C2
Central Ostrobothnia (region)...B2
Etelä-Savo (region)..................C2
Häme (region)...........................B2
Itä-Uusimaa (region)................C2
Kainuu (region).........................C2
Kymenlaakso (region)...............C2
North Karelia (region)..............C2
Northern Ostrobothnia
  (region)..................................B2
Ostrobothnia (region)..............B2
Päijät Häme (region)................C2
Pirkanmaa (region)..................B2
Satakunta (region)...................B2
Savo (region)............................C2
South Karelia (region)..............C2
South Ostrobothnia (region).....B2
South-West Finland (region).....B2
Uusimaa (region)......................B2

Cities and Towns

Espoo..B2

Hämeenlinna..............................B2
Hangö...B3
Helsinki, capital.........................B2
Hyvinkää.....................................B2
Iisalmi...C2
Imatra...C2
Ivalo..C1
Jakobstad...................................B2
Jämsä..C2
Joensuu.......................................C2
Jyväskylä....................................C2
Kajaani..C2
Kemi...B1
Kemijärvi....................................C1
Kokkola.......................................B2
Kolari...C1
Kotka...C2
Kouvola.......................................C2
Kuopio...C2
Lahti..C2
Lappeenranta.............................C2
Lieksa..D2
Mariehamn (Maarianhamina).....A2
Mikkeli...C2
Muonio..B1
Oulu...C1
Pori..B2
Raahe..B2
Rauma..B2
Rovaniemi....................................C1
Salo..C2
Savonlinna...................................C2

Seinäjoki......................................B2
Tampere......................................B2
Tornio..B1
Turku..B2
Vaasa...B2
Vantaa...B2
Varkaus.......................................C2
Ylivieska......................................B2

Other Features

Åland, islands............................A2
Baltic, sea...................................B3
Bothnia, gulf...............................B2
Finland, gulf................................C3
Haltiatunturi, mt.........................B1
Iijoki, river.................................C1
Inari, lake....................................C1
Kemijoki, river............................C1
Kivi, lake.....................................C2
Lapland, region..........................B1
Lokka, reservoir.........................C1
Muoniojoki, river........................B1
Näsi, lake....................................B2
Oulu, lake....................................C2
Oulujoki, river............................C2
Ounasjoki, river..........................B1
Päijänne, lake.............................C2
Pielinen, lake..............................C2
Saimaa, lake...............................C2
Temojoki, river...........................C1
Torniojoki, river..........................B1
Ylikitka, lake...............................C1

Finland

- ⊛ National Capital
- ● Other City

1:10,000,000

0 50 100 150 mi
0 50 100 150 200 km

Lambert Conformal Conic Projection

Finland

Capital: Helsinki
Area: 130,559 sq. mi.
 338,236 sq. km.
Population: 5,158,000
Largest City: Helsinki
Languages: Finnish, Swedish
Monetary Unit: Markka, Euro

Sweden

- ⊛ National Capital
- ● Other City

1:11,333,000

0 50 100 150 mi
0 50 100 150 km

Lambert Conformal Conic Projection

Sweden

Capital: Stockholm
Area: 173,732 sq. mi.
 450,083 sq. km.
Population: 8,911,000
Largest City: Stockholm
Language: Swedish
Monetary Unit: Krona

Sweden: Map Index

Counties

Blekinge.......................................C3
Dalarna.......................................B2
Gävleborg...................................C2
Gotland..C3
Halland...B3
Jämtland.......................................B2
Jönköping....................................B3
Kalmar...B3
Kronoberg....................................B3
Malmöhus....................................B3
Norrbotten...................................C1
Örebro...B3
Östergötland...............................C3
Skåne...B3
Södermanland.............................C3
Stockholm....................................C3
Uppsala..C2
Värmland.....................................B2
Västerbotten...............................C2
Västernorrland............................C2

Västmanland...............................C3
Västra Götaland..........................B3

Cities and Towns

Borås...B3
Eskilstuna....................................C3
Falun..C2
Gällivare......................................D1
Gävle..C2
Göteborg.....................................B3
Halmstad......................................B3
Haparanda...................................D1
Härnösand...................................C2
Helsingborg.................................B3
Hudiksvall...................................C2
Jönköping....................................B3
Kalmar...C3
Karlskrona...................................C3
Karlstad.......................................B3
Kiruna..D1
Kristianstad.................................B3
Kristinehamn...............................B3
Linköping.....................................C3
Luleå..D1
Lund...B3
Malmberget.................................D1
Malmö..B3
Norrköping..................................C3
Örebro...C3
Örnsköldsvik...............................C2
Orrefors......................................C3
Östersund....................................B2
Sarjektjakko................................C1
Skellefteå....................................D2
Söderhamn..................................C2
Stockholm, capital.....................C3
Sundsvall.....................................C2
Trollhättan...................................B3
Uddevalla.....................................B3
Umeå..D2
Uppsala..C3

Västerås......................................C3
Växjö..B3
Visby..C3

Other Features

Ångermanälven, river.................C2
Baltic, sea...................................C3
Bothnia, gulf...............................D2
Dalälven, river............................C2
Faxälven, river............................C2
Göta, canal.................................B3
Gotland, island...........................C3
Hornavan, lake...........................C1
Indalsälven, river........................C2
Kalixälven, river..........................D1
Kattegat, strait...........................B3
Kebnekaise, mt...........................C1
Kjölen, mts..................................C1
Klarälven, river...........................B2
Ljusnanälven, river.....................B2
Luleälven, river...........................D1
Mälaren, lake..............................C3
Muonioälven, river......................D1
Norra Storfjället, mt....................C1
Öland, island..............................C3
Öresund, sound..........................B3
Österdalälven, river....................B2
Skagerrak, strait.........................A3
Skellefteälven, river....................C1
Småland, region.........................B3
Storavan, lake.............................C1
Storsjön, lake..............................B2
Torneälven, river.........................D1
Uddjaur, lake...............................C1
Umeälven, river..........................C2
Vänern, lake................................B3
Vättern, lake...............................B3
Vindelälven, river........................C2

MAJOR CITIES

Algeria
Algiers 1,483,000
Oran 590,000
Constantine 483,000

Angola (metro)
Luanda 2,081,000

Benin
Cotonou 402,000
Porto-Novo 144,000

Botswana
Gaborone 183,000

Burkina Faso
Ouagadougou 824,000

Burundi
Bujumbura 235,440

Cameroon (metro)
Douala 1,320,000
Yaoundé 1,119,000

Cape Verde
Praia 61,000

Central African Republic
Bangui 474,000

Chad (metro)
N'Djamena 826,000

Comoros (metro)
Moroni 30,000

Congo, Democratic Republic of the
Kinshasa 3,800,000
Lubumbashi 739,000

Congo, Republic of the
Brazzaville (metro) 1,004,000

Côte d'Ivoire
Abidjan 2,793,000
Yamoussoukro 107,000

Djibouti (metro)
Djibouti 450,000

Egypt
Cairo 6,789,000
Alexandria 3,328,000
Port Said 470,000
Suez 418,000

Equatorial Guinea
Malabo 38,000

Eritrea
Asmara 358,000

Ethiopia
Addis Ababa 2,085,000

Gabon
Libreville 275,000

The Gambia
Banjul 40,000

Ghana (metro)
Accra 1,673,000

Guinea (metro)
Conakry 1,558,000

Guinea-Bissau
Bissau 138,000

Kenya
Nairobi 959,000
Mombasa 401,000

Lesotho
Maseru 109,000

Liberia (metro)
Monrovia 962,000

Libya (metro)
Tripoli 1,682,000

Madagascar (metro)
Antananarivo 876,000

Malawi
Blantyre 332,000
Lilongwe 234,000

Mali
Bamako 810,000

Mauritania
Nouakchott 550,000

Mauritius
Port Louis 146,000

Morocco
Casablanca 2,943,000
Fez 564,000
Rabat 1,220,000

Mozambique (metro)
Maputo 2,212,000

Namibia
Windhoek 114,000

Niger
Niamey 392,000

Nigeria
Lagos 1,300,000
Ibadan 1,300,000
Abuja 250,000

Rwanda
Kigali 237,000

São Tomé & Príncipe
São Tomé 43,000

Senegal
Dakar 1,641,000

Seychelles (metro)
Victoria 24,000

Sierra Leone
Freetown 470,000

Somalia
Mogadishu 997,000

South Africa
Cape Town 2,350,000
Johannesburg 1,916,000
Durban 1,137,000
Pretoria 1,080,000
Port Elizabeth 853,000
Bloemfontein 300,000

Sudan
Omdurman 1,271,000
Khartoum 947,000

Swaziland
Mbabane 38,000

Tanzania (metro)
Dar es-Salaam 1,747,000

Togo
Lomé 600,000

Tunisia
Tunis 674,000

Uganda (metro)
Kampala 954,000

Western Sahara
el-Aaiún 90,000

Zambia (metro)
Lusaka 1,317,000

Zimbabwe (metro)
Harare 1,410,000

International comparability of city population data is limited by various data inconsistencies.

© MapQuest.com, Inc.

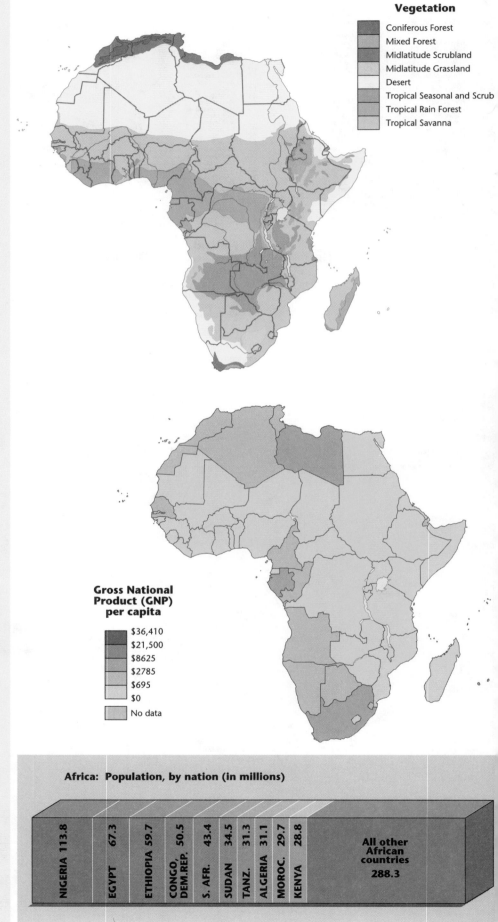

Vegetation

- Coniferous Forest
- Mixed Forest
- Midlatitude Scrubland
- Midlatitude Grassland
- Desert
- Tropical Seasonal and Scrub
- Tropical Rain Forest
- Tropical Savanna

Gross National Product (GNP) per capita

- $36,410
- $21,500
- $8625
- $2785
- $695
- $0
- No data

Africa: Population, by nation (in millions)

| NIGERIA 113.8 | EGYPT 67.3 | ETHIOPIA 59.7 | CONGO, DEM.REP. 50.5 | S. AFR. 43.4 | SUDAN 34.5 | TANZ. 31.3 | ALGERIA 31.1 | MOROC. 29.7 | KENYA 28.8 | All other African countries 288.3 |

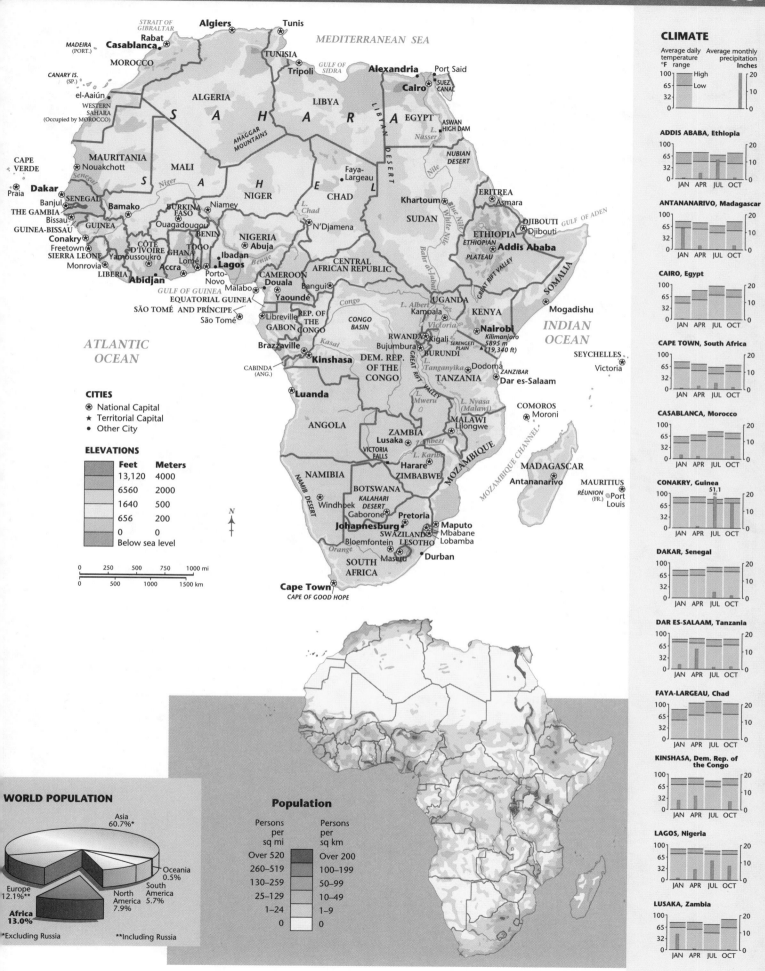

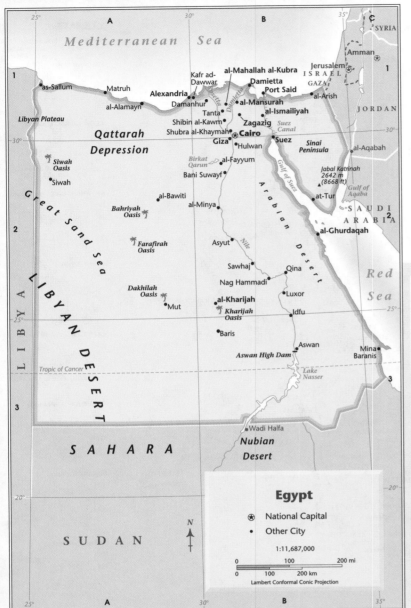

Mediterranean Sea

as-Sallum • Matruh • Kafr ad-Dawwar • al-Mahallah al-Kubra • Damietta • Port Said • al-Arish • SYRIA • Amman

ISRAEL • GAZA • Jerusalem

Alexandria • Damanhur • Tanta • al-Mansurah • al-Ismailiyah • JORDAN

Libyan Plateau • al-Alamayn • Shibin al-Kawm • Zagazig • Suez Canal

Qattarah • Shubra al-Khaymah • Cairo • Suez

Depression • Giza • Hulwan • Sinai • al-Aqabah

Siwah Oasis • al-Fayyum • Birkat Qarun • Peninsula

Siwah • Bani Suwayf • Jabal Katrinah 2642 m (8668 ft) • Gulf of Aqaba

Great Sand Sea • al-Bawiti • al-Minya • SAUDI ARABIA

Bahriyah Oasis • Asyut • al-Ghurdaqah

LIBYA • Farafirah Oasis • Nile • Arabian Desert • Red Sea

Dakhilah Oasis • Sawhaj • Qina

Mut • Nag Hammadi • Luxor

LIBYAN DESERT • al-Kharijah • Idfu

Kharijah Oasis • Baris

Tropic of Cancer • Aswan • Mina Baranis

Aswan High Dam • Lake Nasser

Wadi Halfa

SAHARA • Nubian Desert

SUDAN

Egypt

⊛ National Capital
• Other City

1:11,687,000

| 0 | 100 | 200 mi |
| 0 | 100 | 200 km |

Lambert Conformal Conic Projection

© MapQuest.com, Inc.

Egypt

Capital: Cairo
Area: 385,229 sq. mi.
998,003 sq. km.
Population: 67,273,906
Largest City: Cairo
Language: Arabic
Monetary Unit: Pound

Egypt:
Map Index

Cities and Towns
Alamayn, al- A1
Alexandria A1
Arish, al- B1
Aswan B3
Asyut B2
Bani Suwayf B2
Baris B3
Bawiti, al- A2
Cairo, capital B1
Damanhur B1
Damietta B1
Fayyum, al- B2
Ghurdaqah, al- B2
Giza B2
Hulwan B2
Idfu B3
Ismailiyah, al- B1
Kafr ad-Dawwar B1
Kharijah, al- B2
Luxor B2
Mahallah al-Kubra, al- ..B1
Mansurah, al- B1
Matruh A1
Mina Baranis C3
Minya, al- B2
Mut A2
Nag Hammadi B2
Port Said B1
Qina B2
Sallum, as- A1

Sawhaj B2
Shibin al-Kawm B1
Shubra al-Khaymah B1
Siwah A2
Suez B2
Tanta B1
Tur, at- B2
Zagazig B1

Other Features
Aqaba, gulf B2
Arabian, desert B2
Aswan High, dam B3
Bahriyah, oasis B2
Birkat Qarun, lake B2
Dakhilah, oasis A2
Damietta, river B1
Farafirah, oasis A2
Great Sand Sea, desert ..A2
Jabal Katrinah, mt. B2
Kharijah, oasis B2
Libyan, desert A2
Libyan, plateau A1
Nasser, lake B3
Nile, river B2
Qattarah, depression ...A2
Red, sea C2
Rosetta, river B1
Sahara, desert A3
Sinai, peninsula B2
Siwah, oasis A2
Suez, canal B1
Suez, gulf B2

Libya

Capital: Tripoli
Area: 679,359 sq. mi.
1,759,997 sq. km.
Population: 4,992,838
Largest City: Tripoli
Language: Arabic
Monetary Unit: Dinar

Libya:
Map Index

Cities and Towns
Ajdabiya D1
Awbari B2
Bani Walid B1
Bayda, al- D1
Benghazi D1
Birak B2
Darnah D1
Ghadamis A1
Gharyan B1
Ghat B3
Jaghbub, al- D2
Jalu D2
Jawf, al- D3
Khums, al- B1
Marj, al- D1
Marsa al-Burayqah C1
Misurata C1
Murzuq B2
Qaryah ash-Sharqiyah, al- ..B1

Qatrun, al- B3
Sabha B2
Surt C1
Tobruk D1
Tripoli, capital B1
Uwaynat, al- B2
Waddan C2
Yafran B1
Zillah C2
Zuwarah B1

Other Features
Bette, mt. C3
Cyrenaica, region D2
Fezzan, region B2
Hamra, al-, plateau B1
Haruj al-Aswad, al-, hills ..C2
Jabal Akakus, mts. B2
Jabal al-Uwaynat, mt. ...D3
Libyan, desert D2
Sahara, desert C2
Sidra, gulf C1
Tripolitania, region B1

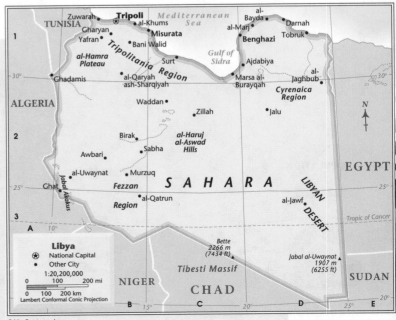

Mediterranean Sea

Zuwarah • Tripoli • al-Khums • al-Bayda • Darnah

TUNISIA • Gharyan • Misurata • al-Marj • Benghazi • Tobruk

Yafran • Bani Walid • Tripolitania Region • Gulf of Sidra • Ajdabiya

al-Hamra Plateau • Surt • Marsa al-Burayqah • al-Jaghbub

Ghadamis • al-Qaryah ash-Sharqlyah • Cyrenaica Region

ALGERIA • Waddan • Zillah • Jalu

Birak • al-Haruj al-Aswad Hills • EGYPT

Awbari • Sabha

al-Uwaynat • Murzuq • SAHARA • al-Jawf

Ghat • Fezzan • al-Qatrun • LIBYAN DESERT

Jabal Akakus • Region • Tropic of Cancer

Libya

⊛ National Capital
• Other City

1:20,200,000

| 0 | 100 | 200 mi |
| 0 | 100 | 200 km |

Lambert Conformal Conic Projection

Bette 2266 m (7434 ft)

Jabal al-Uwaynat 1907 m (6255 ft)

Tibesti Massif

NIGER • CHAD • SUDAN

© MapQuest.com, Inc.

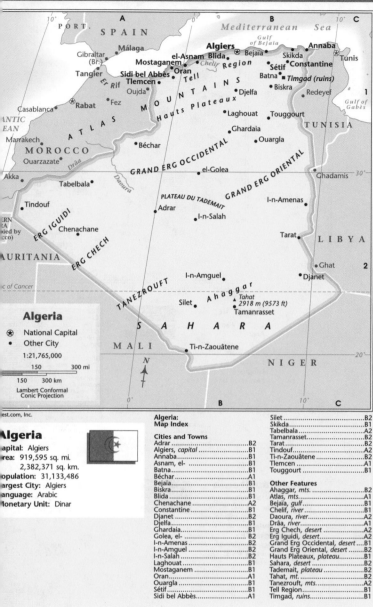

Algeria Map
PORT. SPAIN
Mediterranean Sea
Gulf of Bejaia
Gibraltar (Br.)
Málaga
Algiers
Bejaia
Annaba
Mostaganem
el-Asnam
Blida
Skikda
Tunis
Tangier
Oran
Tlemcen
Sidi bel Abbès
Oujda
Sétif
Constantine
Batna
Timgad (ruins)
Casablanca
Rabat
Fez
Biskra
Redeyef
Marrakech
Djelfa
Laghouat
Touggourt
Ouarzazate
Akka
Ghardaia
Ouargla
Tabelbala
Béchar
Ghadamis
Tindouf
el-Golea
Chenachane
Adrar
I-n-Salah
I-n-Amenas
Tarat
Ghat
I-n-Amguel
Djanet
Silet
Tahat 2918 m (9573 ft)
Tamanrasset
Ti-n-Zaouâtene
MALI
NIGER
LIBYA
TUNISIA
SAHARA
MOROCCO
MAURITANIA
ATLAS MOUNTAINS
Hauts Plateaux
Tell Region
GRAND ERG OCCIDENTAL
GRAND ERG ORIENTAL
PLATEAU DU TADEMAIT
ERG IGUIDI
ERG CHECH
TANEZROUFT
Ahaggar
Chelif
Daoura
Drâa

Algeria
⊛ National Capital
● Other City
1:21,765,000
0   150   300 mi
0   150   300 km
Lambert Conformal Conic Projection

MapQuest.com, Inc.

Algeria
Capital: Algiers
Area: 919,595 sq. mi.
      2,382,371 sq. km.
Population: 31,133,486
Largest City: Algiers
Language: Arabic
Monetary Unit: Dinar

Algeria:
Map Index

Cities and Towns
Adrar	B2
Algiers, capital	B1
Annaba	B1
Asnam, el-	B1
Batna	B1
Béchar	A1
Bejaïa	B1
Biskra	B1
Blida	B1
Chenachane	A2
Constantine	B1
Djanet	B2
Djelfa	B1
Ghardaia	B1
Golea, el-	B2
I-n-Amenas	B2
I-n-Amguel	B2
I-n-Salah	B2
Laghouat	B1
Mostaganem	B1
Oran	A1
Ouargla	B1
Sétif	B1
Sidi bel Abbès	A1

Silet	B2
Skikda	B1
Tabelbala	A2
Tamanrasset	B2
Tarat	B2
Tindouf	A2
Ti-n-Zaouâtene	A1
Tlemcen	A1
Touggourt	B1

Other Features
Ahaggar, mts.	B2
Atlas, mts.	A1
Bejaïa, gulf	B1
Chelif, river	B1
Daoura, river	A2
Drâa, river	A1
Erg Chech, desert	A2
Erg Iguidi, desert	A2
Grand Erg Occidental, desert	B1
Grand Erg Oriental, desert	B2
Hauts Plateaux, plateau	B1
Sahara, desert	B2
Tademait, plateau	B2
Tahat, mt.	B2
Tanezrouft, mts.	A2
Tell Region	B1
Timgad, ruins	B1

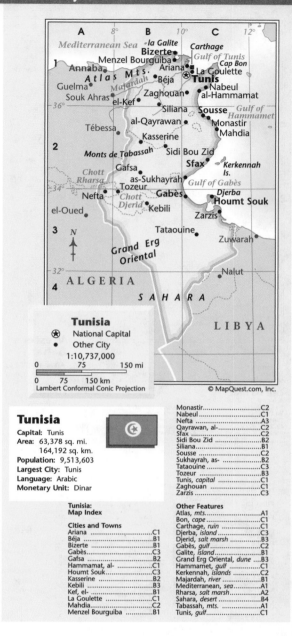

Tunisia Map
Mediterranean Sea
la Galite
Bizerte
Carthage
Menzel Bourguiba
Cap Bon
Annaba
Ariana
La Goulette
Guelma
Atlas Mts.
Béja
Tunis
Souk Ahras
el-Kef
Zaghouan
Nabeul
al-Hammamat
Siliana
Sousse
Gulf of Hammamet
Tébessa
al-Qayrawan
Monastir
Mahdia
Kasserine
Monts de Tabassah
Sidi Bou Zid
Sfax
Kerkennah Is.
Gafsa
as-Sukhayrah
Chott Rharsa
Tozeur
Gabès
Djerba
Nefta
Houmt Souk
el-Oued
Kebili
Chott Djerid
Zarzis
Tataouine
Zuwarah
Grand Erg Oriental
Nalut
ALGERIA
SAHARA
LIBYA
Majardah
Gulf of Tunis
Gulf of Gabès

Tunisia
⊛ National Capital
● Other City
1:10,737,000
0   75   150 mi
0   75   150 km
Lambert Conformal Conic Projection

© MapQuest.com, Inc.

Tunisia
Capital: Tunis
Area: 63,378 sq. mi.
      164,192 sq. km.
Population: 9,513,603
Largest City: Tunis
Language: Arabic
Monetary Unit: Dinar

Tunisia:
Map Index

Cities and Towns
Ariana	C1
Béja	B1
Bizerte	B1
Gabès	C3
Gafsa	B2
Hammamat, al-	C1
Houmt Souk	C3
Kasserine	B2
Kebili	B3
Kef, el-	B1
La Goulette	C1
Mahdia	C2
Menzel Bourguiba	B1

Monastir	C2
Nabeul	C1
Nefta	A3
Qayrawan, al-	C2
Sfax	C2
Sidi Bou Zid	B2
Siliana	B1
Sousse	C2
Sukhayrah, as-	B2
Tataouine	C3
Tozeur	B3
Tunis, capital	C1
Zaghouan	C1
Zarzis	C3

Other Features
Atlas, mts.	A1
Bon, cape	C1
Carthage, ruin	C1
Djerba, island	C3
Djerid, salt marsh	B3
Gabès, gulf	C2
Galite, island	B1
Grand Erg Oriental, dune	B3
Hammamet, gulf	C1
Kerkennah, islands	C2
Majardah, river	B1
Mediterranean, sea	A1
Rharsa, salt marsh	A2
Sahara, desert	B4
Tabassah, mts.	A1
Tunis, gulf	C1

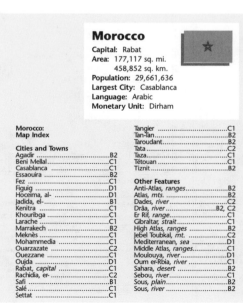

Morocco
Capital: Rabat
Area: 177,117 sq. mi.
      458,852 sq. km.
Population: 29,661,636
Largest City: Casablanca
Language: Arabic
Monetary Unit: Dirham

Morocco:
Map Index

Cities and Towns
Agadir	B2
Beni Mellal	C1
Casablanca	C1
Essaouira	B2
Fez	C1
Figuig	D1
Hoceima, al-	D1
Jadida, el-	B1
Kenitra	C1
Khouribga	C1
Larache	C1
Marrakech	B2
Meknès	C1
Mohammedia	C1
Ouarzazate	C2
Ouezzane	C1
Oujda	D1
Rabat, capital	C1
Rachidia, er-	D1
Safi	B1
Salé	C1
Settat	C1

Tangier	C1
Tan-Tan	B2
Taroudant	B2
Tata	C2
Taza	C1
Tétouan	C1
Tiznit	B2

Other Features
Anti-Atlas, ranges	B2
Atlas, mts.	C1
Dades, river	C2
Drâa, river	B2, C2
Er Rif, range	C1
Gibraltar, strait	C1
High Atlas, ranges	C1
Jebel Toubkal, mt.	C1
Mediterranean, sea	D1
Middle Atlas, ranges	C1
Moulouya, river	D1
Oum er-Rbia, river	C1
Sahara, desert	B2
Sebou, river	C1
Sous, plain	B2
Sous, river	B2

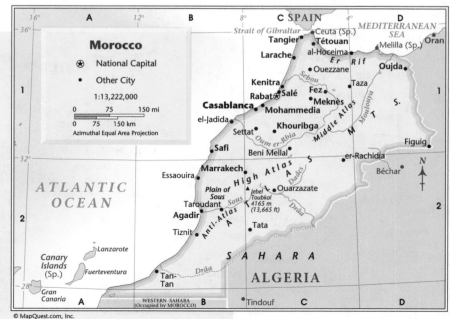

Morocco Map
SPAIN
MEDITERRANEAN SEA
Strait of Gibraltar
Ceuta (Sp.)
Tangier
Tétouan
Melilla (Sp.)
al-Hoceima
Oran
Larache
Er Rif
Oujda
Ouezzane
Taza
Kenitra
Rabat
Salé
Fez
Meknès
Casablanca
Mohammedia
el-Jadida
Khouribga
Settat
Figuig
Safi
Beni Mellal
Middle Atlas
er-Rachidia
Béchar
Essaouira
Marrakech
Plain of Sous
Jebel Toubkal 4165 m (13,665 ft)
Ouarzazate
Taroudant
Agadir
Tata
Tiznit
ATLAS
High Atlas
Anti-Atlas
ATLANTIC OCEAN
Canary Islands (Sp.)
Lanzarote
Fuerteventura
Gran Canaria
Tan-Tan
SAHARA
ALGERIA
WESTERN SAHARA (Occupied by MOROCCO)
Tindouf
Sebou
Oum er-Rbia
Moulouya
Dades
Sous
Drâa

Morocco
⊛ National Capital
● Other City
1:13,222,000
0   75   150 mi
0   75   150 km
Azimuthal Equal Area Projection

© MapQuest.com, Inc.

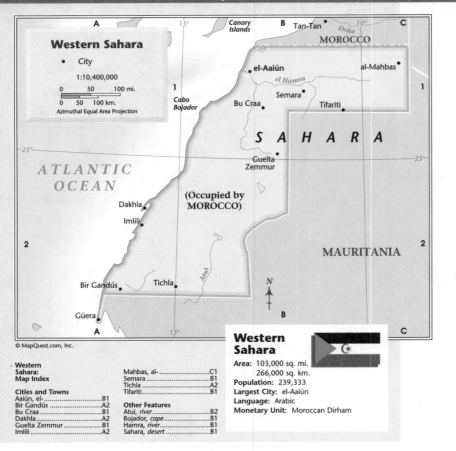

Western Sahara

- • City
- 1:10,400,000
- 0   50   100 mi.
- 0   50   100 km.
- Azimuthal Equal Area Projection

MOROCCO
Canary Islands
Tan-Tan
Drâa
el-Aaiún
al-Mahbas
Cabo Bojador
Semara
Tifariti
el Hamra
Bu Craa
S A H A R A
ATLANTIC OCEAN
Guelta Zemmur
Dakhla
(Occupied by MOROCCO)
Imlili
MAURITANIA
Atui
Bir Gandús
Tichla
Güera
N

© MapQuest.com, Inc.

Western Sahara:
Map Index

Cities and Towns
Aaiún, el- B1
Bir Gandús A2
Bu Craa B1
Dakhla A2
Guelta Zemmur B1
Imlili A2

Mahbas, al- C1
Semara B1
Tichla A2
Tifariti B1

Other Features
Atui, river B2
Bojador, cape B1
Hamra, river B1
Sahara, desert B1

Western Sahara

Area: 103,000 sq. mi.
266,000 sq. km.
Population: 239,333
Largest City: el-Aaiún
Language: Arabic
Monetary Unit: Moroccan Dirham

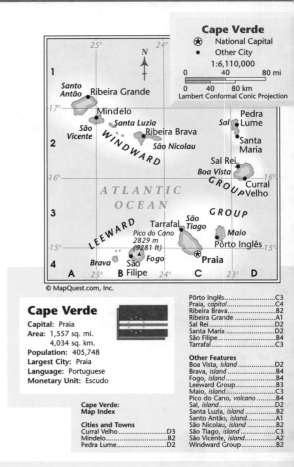

Cape Verde

- ⊛ National Capital
- • Other City
- 1:6,110,000
- 0   40   80 mi
- 0   40   80 km
- Lambert Conformal Conic Projection

N
Santo Antão
Ribeira Grande
São Vicente
Mindelo
Santa Luzia
Pedra Lume
Sal
Ribeira Brava
São Nicolau
Santa Maria
WINDWARD GROUP
Sal Rei
Boa Vista
ATLANTIC OCEAN
Curral Velho
LEEWARD GROUP
Tarrafal
São Tiago
Maio
Pico do Cano 2829 m (9281 ft)
Pôrto Inglês
Brava
São Filipe
Fogo
Praia

© MapQuest.com, Inc.

Cape Verde

Capital: Praia
Area: 1,557 sq. mi.
4,034 sq. km.
Population: 405,748
Largest City: Praia
Language: Portuguese
Monetary Unit: Escudo

Cape Verde:
Map Index

Cities and Towns
Curral Velho D3
Mindelo B2
Pedra Lume D2

Pôrto Inglês C3
Praia, capital C4
Ribeira Brava B2
Ribeira Grande A1
Sal Rei D2
Santa Maria D2
São Filipe B4
Tarrafal C3

Other Features
Boa Vista, island D2
Brava, island B4
Fogo, island B4
Leeward Group B3
Maio, island C3
Pico do Cano, volcano .B4
Sal, island D2
Santa Luzia, island B2
Santo Antão, island ...A1
São Nicolau, island B2
São Tiago, island C3
São Vicente, island A2
Windward Group B2

Mali:
Map Index

Cities and Towns
Ansongo D2
Bafoulabé A3
Bamako, capital B3
Bougouni B3
Bourem C2
Djenné C3
Gao D2
Goundam C2
Kayes A3
Kidal D2
Kita B3
Koulikoro B3
Koutiala B3
Ménaka D2
Mopti C3
Niono B3
Nioro du Sahel B2

San C3
Ségou B3
Sikasso B3
Taoudenni C1
Tessalit D1
Timbuktu C2

Other Features
Adrar des Iforas, massif ...D2
Azaouâd, region C2
Bani, river B3
Baoulé, river B3
Djouf, el-, desert B1
Erg Chech, desert C1
Hombori, mts. C1
Hombori Tondo, mt. ...C2
Niger, river B3
Sahara, desert C1
Sahel, region C2
Senegal, river A3

Mali

Capital: Bamako
Area: 482,077 sq. mi.
1,248,904 sq. km.
Population: 10,429,124
Largest City: Bamako
Language: French
Monetary Unit: Franc

Mauritania

Capital: Nouakchott
Area: 398,000 sq. mi.
1,031,088 sq. km.
Population: 2,581,738
Largest City: Nouakchott
Languages: Arabic, Wolof
Monetary Unit: Ouguiya

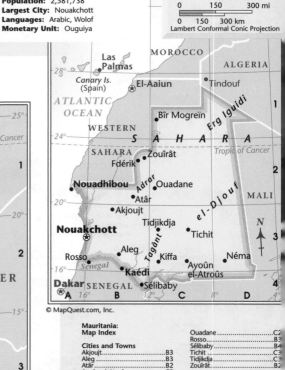

Mauritania

- ⊛ National Capital
- • Other City
- 1:2,350,000
- 0   150   300 mi
- 0   150   300 km
- Lambert Conformal Conic Projection

MOROCCO
Las Palmas
Canary Is. (Spain)
El-Aaiun
ALGERIA
Tindouf
ATLANTIC OCEAN
WESTERN SAHARA
Bîr Mogreïn
Erg Iguidi
Tropic of Cancer
SAHARA
Fdérik
Zouîrât
Nouadhibou
Adrar
Ouadane
Atâr
MALI
el-Djouf
Akjoujt
Tidjikdja
Nouakchott
Tichit
Tagânt
Rosso
Aleg
Kiffa
Ayoûn el-Atroûs
Néma
Senegal
Kaédi
Dakar
SENEGAL
Sélibaby

© MapQuest.com, Inc.

Mauritania:
Map Index

Cities and Towns
Akjoujt B3
Aleg B3
Atâr B2
Ayoûn el-Atroûs C3
Bîr Mogreïn C1
Fdérik B2
Kaédi B3
Kiffa C3
Néma D3
Nouadhibou A2
Nouakchott, capital ...A3

Ouadane C2
Rosso B3
Sélibaby C3
Tichit C3
Tidjikdja C2
Zouîrât B2

Other Features
Adrar, region B2
Djouf, el-, desert C1
Erg Iguidi, desert D1
Sahara, desert C1
Senegal, river B3
Tagânt, region C3

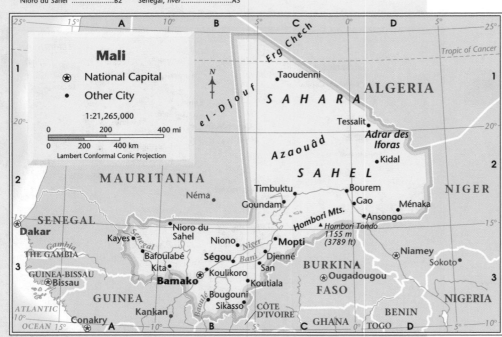
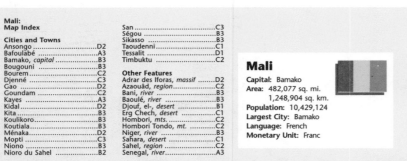

Mali

- ⊛ National Capital
- • Other City
- 1:21,265,000
- 0   200   400 mi
- 0   200   400 km
- Lambert Conformal Conic Projection

N
Erg Chech
el-Djouf
Taoudenni
SAHARA
ALGERIA
Tropic of Cancer
Tessalit
Adrar des Iforas
Azaouâd
Kidal
SAHEL
MAURITANIA
Néma
Timbuktu
Bourem
Gao
Ménaka
Goundam
NIGER
Hombori Mts.
Hombori Tondo 1155 m (3789 ft)
SENEGAL
Dakar
Nioro du Sahel
Niono
Niger
Mopti
Djenné
Niamey
THE GAMBIA
Kayes
Bani
Ségou
San
Sokoto
GUINEA-BISSAU
Bafoulabé
Kita
Koulikoro
BURKINA FASO
Bissau
Bamako
Koutiala
Ougadougou
NIGERIA
Baoulé
Bougouni
Sikasso
GUINEA
Kankan
CÔTE D'IVOIRE
BENIN
ATLANTIC OCEAN
Conakry
GHANA
TOGO

© MapQuest.com, Inc.

Niger:
Map Index

Cities and Towns
Agadès B2
Arlit B2
Bilma C2
Birni Nkonni B3
Diffa C3
Djado C1
Dogondoutchi A3
Dosso A3
Gaya A3
Gouré C3
Maradi B3
Nguigmi C3
Niamey, *capital* A3
Tahoua B3
Téra A3
Tessaoua B3
Tillabéry A3
Zinder B3

Other Features
Air, *mts.* B2
Bagzane, *mt.* B2
Chad, *lake* C3
Dallol Bosso, *river* A3
Dillia, *river* C2
Djado, *plateau* C1
Erg du Ténéré, *desert* B2
Grand Erg de Bilma,
  desert C2
Gréboun, *mt.* B1
Komadugu Yobe, *river* ...C3
Manga, *region* C3
Niger, *river* A3
Sahara, *desert* A1
Sahel, *region* A3
Talak, *region* B2
Ténéré, *desert* C1

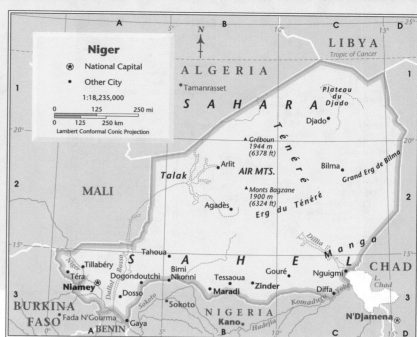

Niger

⊛ National Capital
● Other City

1:18,235,000

0 — 125 — 250 mi
0 — 125 — 250 km
Lambert Conformal Conic Projection

© MapQuest.com, Inc.

Niger

Capital: Niamey
Area: 497,000 sq. mi.
  1,287,565 sq. km.
Population: 9,962,242
Largest City: Niamey
Language: French
Monetary Unit: CFA franc

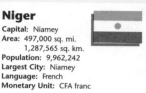

Chad

⊛ National Capital
● Other City

1:23,122,000

0 — 150 — 300 mi
0 — 150 — 300 km
Lambert Conformal Conic Projection

© MapQuest.com, Inc.

Chad:
Map Index

Cities and Towns
Abéché C4
Abou Deïa B5
Am Timan C5
Aozou B2
Ati B4
Bardaï B2
Berdoba C4
Biltine C4
Bol A4
Bongor A5
Bousso B5
Doba B5
Fada C3
Faya-Largeau B3
Koro Toro B4
Laï B5
Mao A4
Massenya B5
Melfi B5
Mongo B4
Moundou B5
N'Djamena, *capital* A4
Pala B5
Sarh B5
Zouar B2

Other Features
Bahr Salamat, *river* B5
Batha, *river* C4
Bodélé, *depression* B3
Chad, *lake* A4
Chari, *river* A5
Emi Koussi, *mt.* B3
Ennedi, *plateau* C3
Enneri Ke, *river* B3
Ghazal, *river* B4
Grand Erg de Bilma,
  desert A3
Logone, *river* A5
Ouadi Maba, *river* C4
Sahara, *desert* A2
Tibesti, *massif* B2

Chad

Capital: N'Djamena
Area: 495,755 sq. mi.
  1,248,339 sq. km.
Population: 7,557,436
Largest City: N'Djamena
Languages: French, Arabic
Monetary Unit: CFA franc

Sudan:
Map Index

Cities and Towns
Atbarah C2
Babanusah B3
Damazin, ad- C1
Dunqulah C1
Fashir, al- B2
Halaib D1
Juba C4
Junaynah, al- A2
Kaduqli B3
Kassala D2
Khartoum, *capital* C2
Khartoum North C2
Khashm al-Qirbah C2
Kuraymah C1
Kusti C2
Malakal C3
Nuhud, an- B2
Nyala B2
Omdurman C2
Pibor Post C3
Port Sudan D1
Qadarif, al- C2
Rumbek B3
Sannar C2
Ubayyid, al- C2
Wadi Halfa C1
Wad Madani C2
Waw B3
Yambio B4

Other Features
Akobo, *river* C3
Atbarah, *river* C2
Bahr al-Arab, *river* B3
Bahr al-Ghazal, *river* C3
Bahr al-Jabal, *river* C3
Blue Nile, *river* C2
Kangen, *river* C3
Kinyeti, *mt.* C4
Libyan, *desert* B1
Lol, *river* B3
Nasser, *lake* C1
Nile, *river* C1, C2
Nuba, *mts.* C3
Nubian, *desert* C1
Red, *sea* D1
Red Sea, *hills* D1
Sobat, *river* C3
Sudd, *region* B3
Sue, *river* B3
Wadi al-Malik, *river* B2
Wadi Howar, *river* B2
White Nile, *river* C3

Sudan

Capital: Khartoum
Area: 966,757 sq. mi.
  2,530,459 sq. km.
Population: 34,475,690
Largest City: Khartoum
Language: Arabic
Monetary Unit: Pound

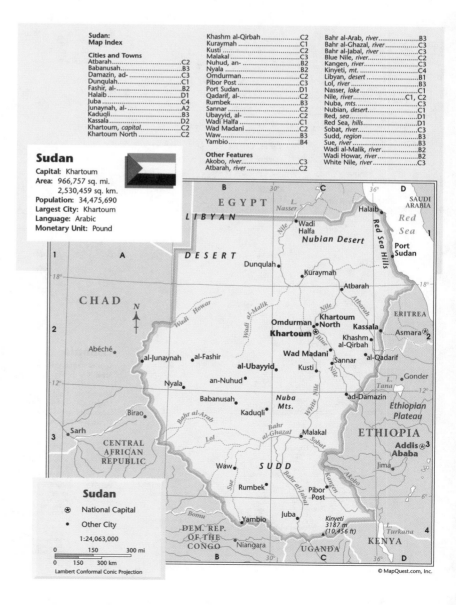

Sudan

⊛ National Capital
● Other City

1:24,063,000

0 — 150 — 300 mi
0 — 150 — 300 km
Lambert Conformal Conic Projection

© MapQuest.com, Inc.

Eritrea

Capital: Asmara
Area: 45,300 sq. mi.
117,358 sq. km.
Population: 3,984,723
Largest City: Asmara
Language: Tigrinya
Monetary Unit: Ethiopian birr

Eritrea

⊛ National Capital
• Other City
1:13,000,000
0   90   180 mi
0   90   180 km
Mercator Projection

Eritrea:
Map Index

Cities and Towns
Adi Keyih B2
Adi Ugri B2
Akordat A2
Asmara, capital B2
Assab D3
Ed C3
Keren B2
Massawa B2
Nakfa B1
Teseney A2
Tio C2

Other Features
Bab al-Mandab, strait D3
Dahlak, archipelago C2
Danakil, desert C2
Gash, river B2
Red, sea C1

Djibouti

⊛ National Capital
• Other City
1:5,500,000
0   25   50 mi
0   25   50 km
Transverse Mercator Proj.

Djibouti:
Map Index

Cities and Towns
Alayli Dadda ....B
Ali Adde ....B
Ali-Sabieh ....B
Arta ....B
As Ela ....B
Balho ....B
Dikhil ....B
Djibouti, capital C
Dorra ....B
Holhol C
Khor Angar C
Loyada C
Obock ....B
Randa ....B
Tadjoura ....B
Yoboki ....B

Other Features
Abhé, lake ....A
Aden, gulf ....B
Assal, lake ....B
Bab al-Mandab, strait C
Gaggade, plain ....B
Mabla, mts. ....B
Moussa Ali, mt. ....B
Red, sea C
Tadjoura, gulf ....B

Djibouti

Capital: Djibouti
Area: 8,950 sq. mi.
23,187 sq. km.
Population: 447,439
Largest City: Djibouti
Languages: Cushitic languages
Monetary Unit: Franc

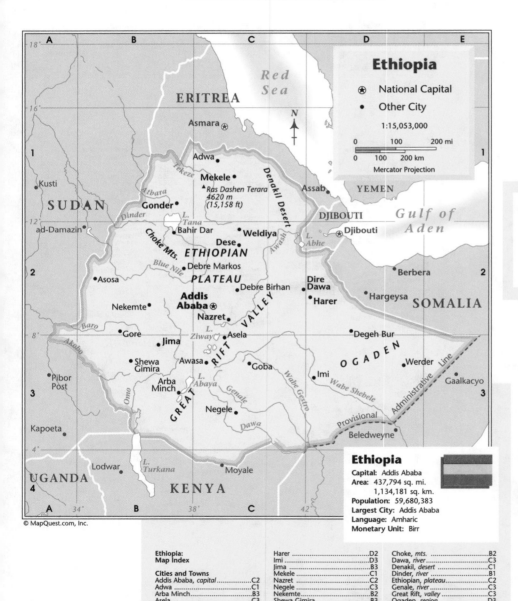

Ethiopia

⊛ National Capital
• Other City
1:15,053,000
0   100   200 mi
0   100   200 km
Mercator Projection

Ethiopia

Capital: Addis Ababa
Area: 437,794 sq. mi.
1,134,181 sq. km.
Population: 59,680,383
Largest City: Addis Ababa
Language: Amharic
Monetary Unit: Birr

Somalia:
Map Index

Cities and Towns
Baraawe A3
Baydhabo A3
Beledweyne B3
Benderbeyla C2
Berbera B1
Boosaaso B1
Burco B2
Ceerigaabo B1
Dhuusamareeb B2
Eyl B2
Gaalkacyo B2
Garoowe B2
Hargeysa A2
Hobyo B2
Jamaame A3
Jawhar A3
Jilib A3
Kismayu A4
Luuq A3
Marka A3
Mogadishu, capital B3
Qardho B2
Xuddur A3

Other Features
Aden, gulf B1
Gees Gwardafuy, cape C1
Juba, river A3
Nugaal, valley B2
Raas Xaafun, cape C1
Surud Ad, mt. B1
Webi Shabeelle, river B3

Somalia

Capital: Mogadishu
Area: 246,300 sq. mi.
638,083 sq. km.
Population: 7,140,643
Largest City: Mogadishu
Language: Somali, Arabic
Monetary Unit: Shilling

Somalia

⊛ National Capital
• Other City
1:22,100,000
0   150   300 mi
0   150   300 km
Miller Cylindrical Projection

Ethiopia:
Map Index

Cities and Towns
Addis Ababa, capital C2
Adwa C1
Arba Minch B3
Asela C2
Asosa B2
Awasa C3
Bahir Dar B2
Debre Birhan C2
Debre Markos C2
Degeh Bur D2
Dese C2
Dire Dawa D2
Goba C3
Gonder B1
Gore B2
Harer D2
Imi D3
Jima B3
Mekele C1
Nazret C2
Negele C3
Nekemte B2
Shewa Gimira B3
Weldiya C2
Werder D3

Other Features
Abaya, lake B3
Abhe, lake C2
Akobo, river A3
Atbara, river B1
Awash, river C2
Baro, river B2
Blue Nile, river B2
Choke, mts. B2
Dawa, river C3
Denakil, desert C1
Dinder, river B1
Ethiopian, plateau C2
Genale, river C3
Great Rift, valley C3
Ogaden, region D3
Omo, river B3
Provisional
Administrative Line D3
Ras Dashen, mt. C1
Tana, lake B1
Tekeze, river B1
Turkana, lake B3
Wabe Gestro, river C3
Wabe Shebele, river D3
Ziway, lake C3

© MapQuest.com, Inc.

Kenya

Capital: Nairobi
Area: 224,961 sq. mi.
          582,801 sq. km.
Population: 28,808,658
Largest City: Nairobi
Language: Swahili, English
Monetary Unit: Shilling

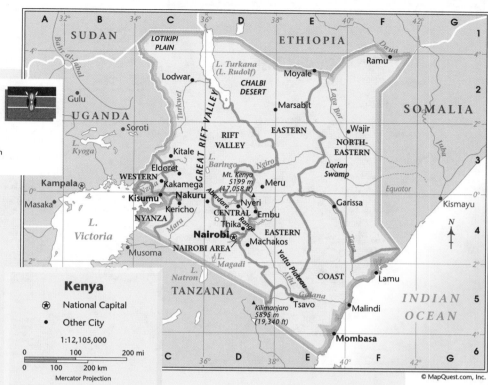

**Kenya:
Map Index**

Provinces
Central D4
Coast E5
Eastern E3
Nairobi Area D4
North-Eastern F3
Nyanza C4
Rift Valley D3
Western C3

Cities and Towns
Eldoret C3
Embu D4
Garissa E4
Kakamega C4
Kericho C4
Kisumu C4
Kitale C3
Lamu F5
Lodwar C2
Machakos D4
Malindi F5
Marsabit E2
Meru D3
Mombasa E5
Moyale E2

Nairobi, capital D4
Nakuru D4
Nyeri D4
Ramu F2
Thika D4
Tsavo E5
Wajir F3

Other Features
Aberdare, range D4
Athi, river E5
Baringo, lake D3
Chalbi, desert D2
Daua, river F1
Galana, river E5
Great Rift, valley C3
Kenya, mt. D4
Laga Bor, river E2
Lorian, swamp E3
Lotikipi, plain C1
Magadi, lake D4
Mara, river C4
Ngiro, river D3
Nzoia, river C3
Tana, river F4
Turkana (Rudolf), lake ..D2
Turkwel, river D2
Victoria, lake B4
Yatta, plateau E5

Kenya

⊛ National Capital
• Other City

1:12,105,000

0   100   200 mi
0   100   200 km
Mercator Projection

© MapQuest.com, Inc.

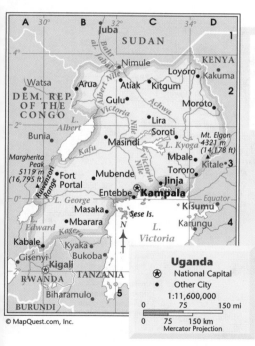

Uganda

Capital: Kampala
Area: 93,070 sq. mi.
          241,114 sq. km.
Population: 22,804,973
Largest City: Kampala
Language: English
Monetary Unit: Shilling

**Uganda:
Map Index**

Cities and Towns
Arua B2
Atiak C2
Entebbe C3
Fort Portal B3
Gulu C2
Jinja C3
Kabale A4
Kampala, capital C3
Kitgum C2
Lira C2
Loyoro D2
Masaka B4
Masindi B3
Mbale D3
Mbarara B4
Moroto D2

Mubende B3
Soroti C3
Tororo D3

Other Features
Achwa, river C2
Albert, lake B3
Albert Nile, river B2
Bahr al-Jabal, river B2
Edward, lake A4
Elgon, mt. D3
George, lake B4
Kafu, river B3
Kagera, river B4
Kyoga, lake C3
Margherita, peak A3
Ruwenzori, range B3
Sese, islands C4
Victoria, lake C4
Victoria Nile, river B2,C3

Uganda

⊛ National Capital
• Other City

1:11,600,000

0   75   150 mi
0   75   150 km
Mercator Projection

© MapQuest.com, Inc.

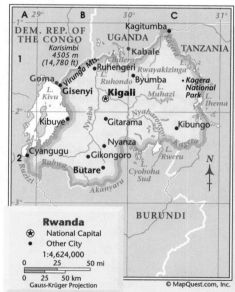

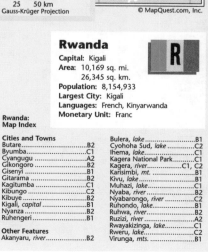

Rwanda

Capital: Kigali
Area: 10,169 sq. mi.
          26,345 sq. km.
Population: 8,154,933
Largest City: Kigali
Languages: French, Kinyarwanda
Monetary Unit: Franc

Rwanda

⊛ National Capital
• Other City

1:4,624,000

0   25   50 mi
0   25   50 km
Gauss-Krüger Projection

© MapQuest.com, Inc.

**Rwanda:
Map Index**

Cities and Towns
Butare B2
Byumba C1
Cyangugu A2
Gikongoro B2
Gisenyi B1
Gitarama B2
Kagitumba C1
Kibungo C2
Kibuye B2
Kigali, capital B2
Nyanza B2
Ruhengeri B1

Bulera, lake B1
Cyohoha Sud, lake C2
Ihema, lake C1
Kagera National Park ..C1
Kagera, river C1, C2
Karisimbi, mt. B1
Kivu, lake A2
Muhazi, lake C1
Nyaba, lake B2
Nyabarongo, river C2
Ruhondo, lake B1
Ruhwa, river B2
Ruzizi, river A2
Rwayakizinga, lake C1
Rweru, lake C2
Virunga, mts. B1

Burundi

Capital: Bujumbura
Area: 10,740 sq. mi.
          27,824 sq. km.
Population: 5,735,937
Largest City: Bujumbura
Languages: French, Kirundi
Monetary Unit: Franc

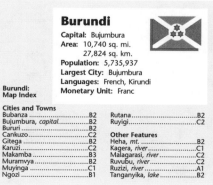

**Burundi:
Map Index**

Cities and Towns
Bubanza B2
Bujumbura, capital B2
Bururi B2
Cankuzo C2
Gitega B2
Karuzi B2
Makamba B3
Muramvya B2
Muyinga C1
Ngozi B1

Rutana B2
Ruyigi C2

Other Features
Heha, mt. B2
Kagera, river C1
Malagarasi, river C2
Ruvubu, river C2
Ruzizi, river A1
Tanganyika, lake B2

Burundi

⊛ National Capital
• Other City

1:6,548,000

0   50   100 mi
0   50   100 km
Conic Equidistant Projection

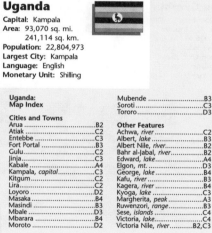

© MapQuest.com, Inc.

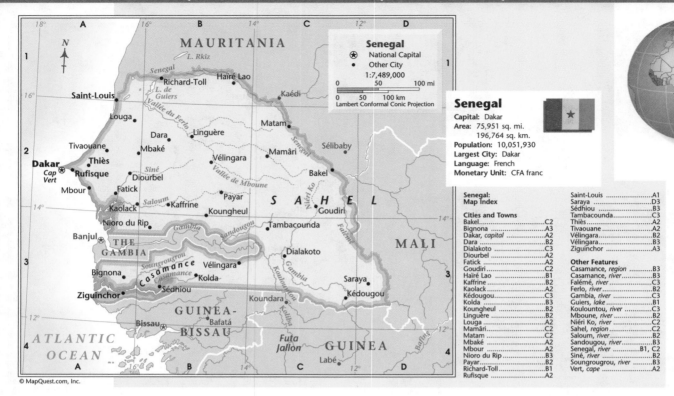

Senegal
- ⊛ National Capital
- • Other City

1:7,489,000

0 50 100 mi
0 50 100 km
Lambert Conformal Conic Projection

Senegal
Capital: Dakar
Area: 75,951 sq. mi.
196,764 sq. km.
Population: 10,051,930
Largest City: Dakar
Language: French
Monetary Unit: CFA franc

Senegal: Map Index

Cities and Towns
Bakel C2
Bignona A3
Dakar, *capital* A2
Dara B2
Dialakoto C3
Diourbel A2
Fatick A2
Goudiri C2
Haïré Lao B1
Kaffrine B2
Kaolack A2
Kédougou C3
Kolda B3
Koungheul B2
Linguère B2
Louga A2
Mamâri C2
Matam C2
Mbaké A2
Mbour A2
Nioro du Rip B3
Payar B2
Richard-Toll B1
Rufisque A2

Saint-Louis A1
Saraya D3
Sédhiou B3
Tambacounda C3
Thiès A2
Tivaouane A2
Vélingara B2
Vélingara B3
Ziguinchor A3

Other Features
Casamance, *region* .. B3
Casamance, *river* B3
Falémé, *river* C3
Ferlo, *river* B2
Gambia, *river* C3
Guiers, *lake* B1
Koulountou, *river* ... C3
Mboune, *river* C2
Niéri Ko, *river* C2
Sahel, *region* C2
Saloum, *river* B2
Sandougou, *river* B3
Senegal, *river* B1, C2
Siné, *river* A2
Soungrougrou, *river* . B3
Vert, *cape* A2

© MapQuest.com, Inc.

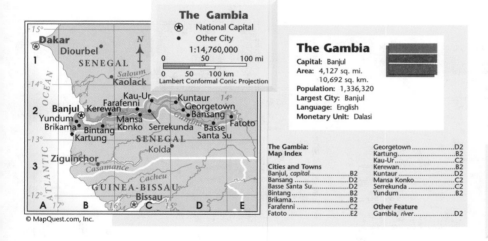

The Gambia
- ⊛ National Capital
- • Other City

1:14,760,000

0 50 100 mi
0 50 100 km
Lambert Conformal Conic Projection

The Gambia
Capital: Banjul
Area: 4,127 sq. mi.
10,692 sq. km.
Population: 1,336,320
Largest City: Banjul
Language: English
Monetary Unit: Dalasi

The Gambia: Map Index

Cities and Towns
Banjul, *capital* B2
Bansang D2
Basse Santa Su D2
Bintang B2
Brikama B2
Farafenni C2
Fatoto E2

Georgetown D2
Kartung B2
Kau-Ur C2
Kerewan B2
Kuntaur C2
Mansa Konko C2
Serrekunda B2
Yundum B2

Other Feature
Gambia, *river* D2

© MapQuest.com, Inc.

Guinea-Bissau
- ⊛ National Capital
- • Other City

1:7,100,000

0 40 80 mi
0 40 80 km
Lambert Conformal Conic Projection

© MapQuest.com, Inc.

Guinea-Bissau

Capital: Bissau
Area: 13,948 sq. mi.
36,135 sq. km.
Population: 1,234,555
Largest City: Bissau
Language: Portuguese
Monetary Unit: CFA franc

Guinea-Bissau: Map Index

Cities and Towns
Bafatá C1
Bambadinca C1
Barro B1
Bissau, *capital* B2
Bissorã B1
Bolama B2
Buba C2
Bubaque B2
Bula B1
Cacheu A1
Cacine B2
Canchungo A1
Catió B2
Farim B1
Fulacunda B2
Gabú C1
Ondame C2
Pirada C1
Quebo C2
Quinhámel B2
São Domingos A1

Other Features
Bijagós, *islands* A2
Cacheu, *river* B1
Corubal, *river* D1
Gêba, *river* C1

Guinea: Map Index

Cities and Towns
Beyla D3
Conakry, *capital* B3
Coyah B3
Dabola C2
Fria B2
Guéckédou C3
Kailahun C3
Kali C1
Kamsar A2
Kankan D2
Kérouané D3
Kindia B2
Kissidougou C3
Kouroussa D2
Labé B2
Lélouma B2
Macenta D3
Mamou B2
Niagassola D1
Nzérékoré D4
Siguiri D2
Tougué C2
Yomou D4

Other Features
Bafing, *river* C2
Futa Jallon, *plateau* . B1
Gambia, *river* B2
Los, *islands* A3
Milo, *river* D3
Niger, *river* C2
Nimba, *mts.* D4
Tinkissa, *river* C2

Guinea
Capital: Conakry
Area: 94,926 sq. mi.
245,922 sq. km.
Population: 7,538,953
Largest City: Conakry
Language: French
Monetary Unit: Guinea franc

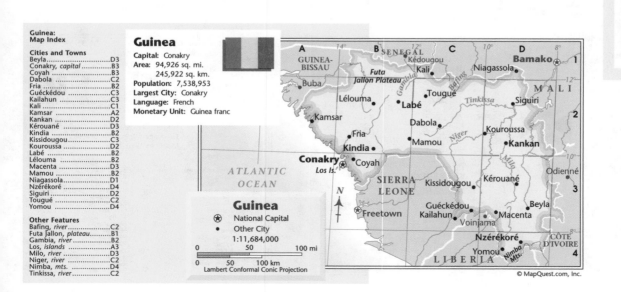

Guinea
- ⊛ National Capital
- • Other City

1:11,684,000

0 50 100 mi
0 50 100 km
Lambert Conformal Conic Projection

© MapQuest.com, Inc.

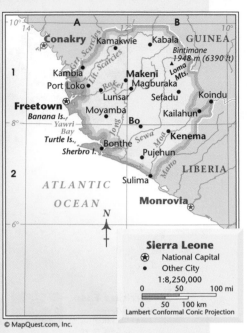

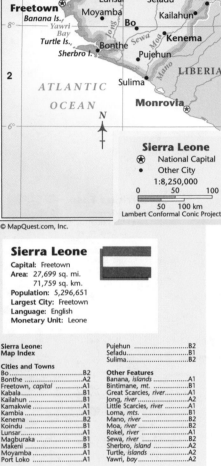

Côte d'Ivoire (Ivory Coast)

- ⊛ National Capital
- • Other City

1:9,789,000

0   75   150 mi
0   75   150 km

Lambert Conformal Conic Projection

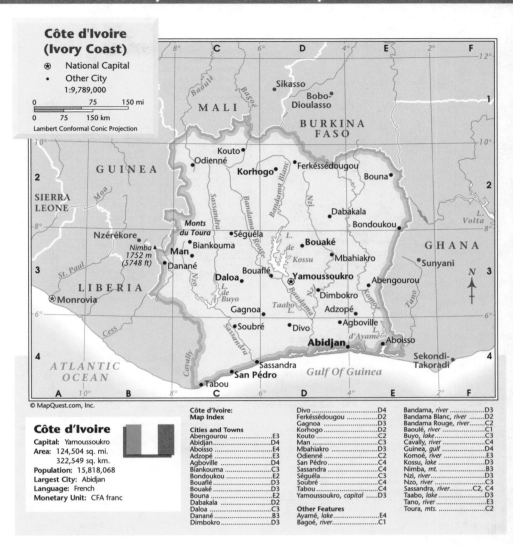

© MapQuest.com, Inc.

Sierra Leone

- ⊛ National Capital
- • Other City

1:8,250,000

0   50   100 mi
0   50   100 km

Lambert Conformal Conic Projection

© MapQuest.com, Inc.

Sierra Leone

Capital: Freetown
Area: 27,699 sq. mi.
  71,759 sq. km.
Population: 5,296,651
Largest City: Freetown
Language: English
Monetary Unit: Leone

Sierra Leone: Map Index

Cities and Towns

Bo	B2
Bonthe	A2
Freetown, *capital*	A1
Kabala	B1
Kailahun	B1
Kamakwie	B1
Kambia	A1
Kenema	B2
Koindu	B1
Lunsar	B1
Magburaka	B1
Makeni	B1
Moyamba	A1
Port Loko	A1

Pujehun	B2
Sefadu	B1
Sulima	B2

Other Features

Banana, *islands*	A1
Bintimane, *mt.*	B1
Great Scarcies, *river*	A1
Jong, *river*	A1
Little Scarcies, *river*	A1
Loma, *mts.*	B1
Mano, *river*	B2
Moa, *river*	B2
Rokel, *river*	A1
Sewa, *river*	B2
Sherbro, *island*	A2
Turtle, *islands*	A2
Yawri, *bay*	A2

Côte d'Ivoire

Capital: Yamoussoukro
Area: 124,504 sq. mi.
  322,549 sq. km.
Population: 15,818,068
Largest City: Abidjan
Language: French
Monetary Unit: CFA franc

© MapQuest.com, Inc.

Côte d'Ivoire: Map Index

Cities and Towns

Abengourou	E3
Abidjan	D4
Aboisso	E4
Adzopé	E3
Agboville	D4
Biankouma	C3
Bondoukou	E2
Bouaflé	D3
Bouaké	D3
Bouna	E2
Dabakala	D2
Daloa	C3
Danané	C3
Dimbokro	D3

Divo	D4
Ferkéssédougou	D2
Gagnoa	D3
Korhogo	D2
Kouto	C2
Man	C3
Mbahiakro	D3
Odienné	C2
San Pédro	C4
Sassandra	C4
Séguéla	C3
Soubré	C3
Tabou	C4
Yamoussoukro, *capital*	D3

Other Features

Ayamé, *lake*	E4
Bagoé, *river*	C1

Bandama, *river*	D3
Bandama Blanc, *river*	D2
Bandama Rouge, *river*	C2
Baoulé, *river*	C1
Buyo, *lake*	C3
Cavally, *river*	C4
Guinea, *gulf*	D4
Komoé, *river*	E3
Kossu, *lake*	D3
Nimba, *mt.*	B3
Nzi, *river*	D3
Nzo, *river*	C3
Sassandra, *river*	C2, C4
Taabo, *lake*	D3
Tano, *river*	E3
Toura, *mts.*	C2

Liberia

Capital: Monrovia
Area: 38,250 sq. mi.
  99,093 sq. km.
Population: 2,923,725
Largest City: Monrovia
Language: English
Monetary Unit: Dollar

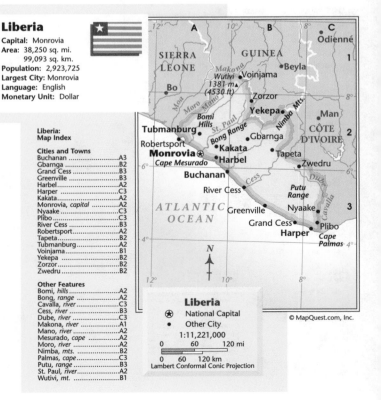

© MapQuest.com, Inc.

Liberia: Map Index

Cities and Towns

Buchanan	A3
Gbarnga	B2
Grand Cess	B3
Greenville	B3
Harbel	A2
Harper	C3
Kakata	A2
Monrovia, *capital*	A2
Nyaake	C3
Plibo	C3
River Cess	B3
Robertsport	A2
Tapeta	B2
Tubmanburg	A2
Voinjama	B1
Yekepa	B2
Zorzor	B2
Zwedru	B2

Other Features

Bomi, *hills*	A2
Bong, *range*	A2
Cavalla, *river*	C3
Cess, *river*	B3
Dube, *river*	C3
Makona, *river*	A1
Mano, *river*	A2
Mesurado, *cape*	A2
Moro, *river*	A2
Nimba, *mts.*	B2
Palmas, *cape*	C3
Putu, *range*	B3
St. Paul, *river*	A2
Wutivi, *mt.*	B1

Liberia

- ⊛ National Capital
- • Other City

1:11,221,000

0   60   120 mi
0   60   120 km

Lambert Conformal Conic Projection

São Tomé & Príncipe

Capital: São Tomé
Area: 386 sq. mi.
  1,000 sq. km.
Population: 154,878
Largest City: São Tomé
Language: Portuguese
Monetary Unit: Dobra

São Tomé & Príncipe: Map Index

Cities and Towns

Jou	B4
Neves	B4
Porto Alegre	B4
São Tomé, *capital*	B4
Sundi	C1
Terreiro Velho	C1

Other Features

Príncipe, *island*	C1
São Tomé, *island*	B4
São Tomé, *mt.*	B4

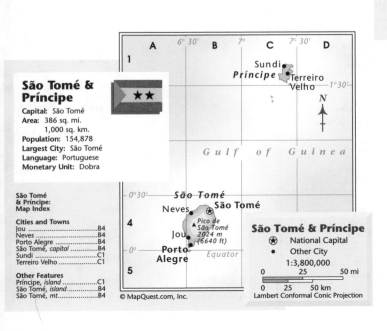

São Tomé & Príncipe

- ⊛ National Capital
- • Other City

1:3,800,000

0   25   50 mi
0   25   50 km

Lambert Conformal Conic Projection

© MapQuest.com, Inc.

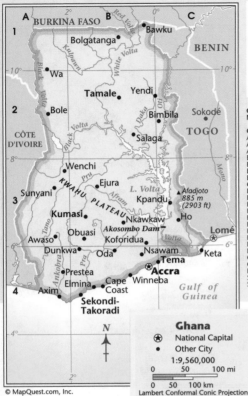

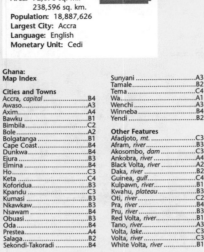

Ghana

Capital: Accra
Area: 92,098 sq. mi.
238,596 sq. km.
Population: 18,887,626
Largest City: Accra
Language: English
Monetary Unit: Cedi

Ghana: Map Index

Cities and Towns

Accra, *capital*	B4
Awaso	A3
Axim	A4
Bawku	B1
Bimbila	C2
Bole	A2
Bolgatanga	B1
Cape Coast	B4
Dunkwa	B4
Ejura	B3
Elmina	B4
Keta	C4
Koforidua	B3
Kpandu	C3
Kumasi	B3
Nkawkaw	B3
Nsawam	B4
Obuasi	B3
Oda	B4
Prestea	A4
Salaga	B2
Sekondi-Takoradi	B4

Sunyani	A3
Tamale	B2
Tema	C4
Wa	A1
Wenchi	A3
Winneba	B4
Yendi	B2

Other Features

Afadjoto, *mt.*	C3
Afram, *river*	B3
Akosombo, *dam*	C3
Ankobra, *river*	A4
Black Volta, *river*	A2
Daka, *river*	B2
Guinea, *gulf*	C4
Kulpawn, *river*	B1
Kwahu, *plateau*	B3
Oti, *river*	C2
Pra, *river*	B4
Pru, *river*	B3
Red Volta, *river*	B1
Tano, *river*	A3
Volta, *lake*	C3
Volta, *river*	C3
White Volta, *river*	B1

Ghana

⊛ National Capital
• Other City
1:9,560,000
0 50 100 mi
0 50 100 km
Lambert Conformal Conic Projection

© MapQuest.com, Inc.

Burkina Faso

Capital: Ouagadougou
Area: 105,946 sq. mi.
274,472 sq. km.
Population: 11,575,898
Largest City: Ouagadougou
Language: French
Monetary Unit: CFA franc

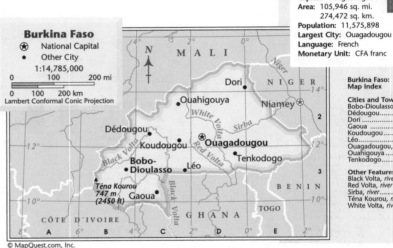

Burkina Faso

⊛ National Capital
• Other City
1:14,785,000
0 100 200 mi
0 100 200 km
Lambert Conformal Conic Projection

Burkina Faso: Map Index

Cities and Towns

Bobo-Dioulasso	B3
Dédougou	C2
Dori	D1
Gaoua	C3
Koudougou	C2
Léo	C3
Ouagadougou, *capital*	D2
Ouahigouya	C2
Tenkodogo	D3

Other Features

Black Volta, *river*	B3
Red Volta, *river*	D3
Sirba, *river*	D2
Téna Kourou, *mt.*	B3
White Volta, *river*	D2

© MapQuest.com, Inc.

Benin

⊛ National Capital
• Other City
1:14,800,000
0 100 200 mi
0 100 200 km
Lambert Conformal Conic Projection

© MapQuest.com, Inc.

Benin

Capital: Porto-Novo
Area: 43,500 sq. mi.
112,694 sq. km.
Population: 6,305,567
Largest City: Cotonou
Language: French
Monetary Unit: CFA franc

Benin: Map Index

Cities and Towns

Abomey	A4
Bassila	A3
Cotonou	B4
Djougou	A3
Kandi	B2
Lokossa	A4
Malanville	B2
Natitingou	A2
Nikki	B3
Ouidah	B4
Parakou	B3
Pobé	B4

Porto-Novo, *capital*	B4
Savalou	A3
Savé	B3
Segbana	B2
Tchaourou	B3

Other Features

Alibori, *river*	B2
Chaîne de l'Atacora, *mts.*	A2
Couffo, *river*	B4
Guinea, *gulf*	A4
Mékrou, *river*	A2
Mono, *river*	A4
Niger, *river*	B1
Ouémé, *river*	B3
Sota, *river*	B2

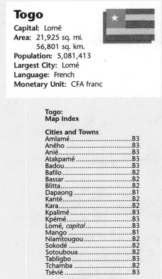

Togo

Capital: Lomé
Area: 21,925 sq. mi.
56,801 sq. km.
Population: 5,081,413
Largest City: Lomé
Language: French
Monetary Unit: CFA franc

Togo: Map Index

Cities and Towns

Amlamé	B3
Aného	B3
Anié	B3
Atakpamé	B3
Badou	B3
Bafilo	B2
Bassar	B2
Blitta	B2
Dapaong	B1
Kanté	B2
Kara	B2
Kpalimé	B3
Kpémé	B3
Lomé, *capital*	B3
Mango	B1
Niamtougou	B2
Sokodé	B2
Sotouboua	B2
Tabligbo	B3
Tchamba	B2
Tsévié	B3

Other Features

Agou, *mt.*	B3
Benin, *bight*	B4
Mono, *river*	B3
Oti, *river*	B1

Togo

⊛ National Capital
• Other City
1:8,600,000
0 50 100 mi
0 50 100 km
Lambert Conformal Conic Projection

© MapQuest.com, Inc.

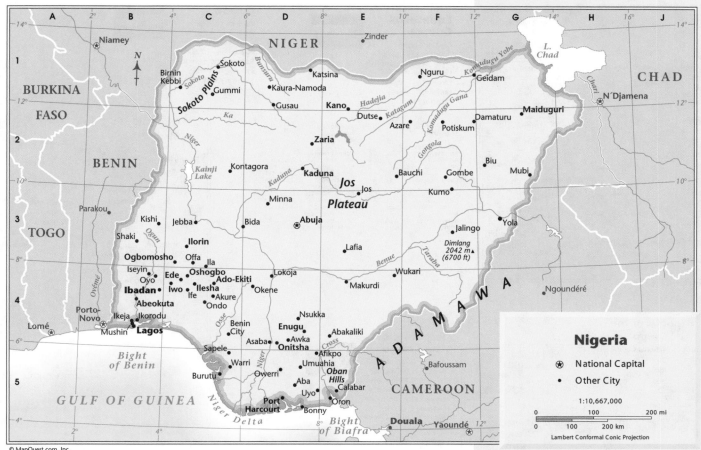

© MapQuest.com, Inc.

Nigeria

* National Capital
* Other City

1:10,667,000

| 0 | 100 | 200 mi |
| 0 | 100 | 200 km |

Lambert Conformal Conic Projection

Nigeria

Capital: Abuja
Area: 356,669 sq. mi.
924,013 sq. km.
Population: 113,828,587
Largest City: Lagos
Language: English
Monetary Unit: Naira

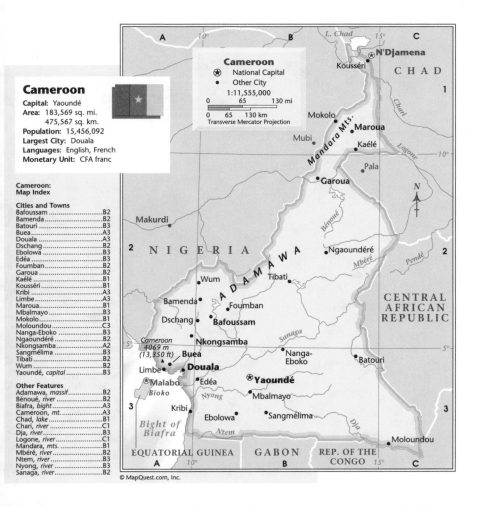

© MapQuest.com, Inc.

Cameroon

* National Capital
* Other City

1:11,555,000

| 0 | 65 | 130 mi |
| 0 | 65 | 130 km |

Transverse Mercator Projection

Cameroon

Capital: Yaoundé
Area: 183,569 sq. mi.
475,567 sq. km.
Population: 15,456,092
Largest City: Douala
Languages: English, French
Monetary Unit: CFA franc

Cameroon:
Map Index

Cities and Towns
Bafoussam B2
Bamenda B2
Batouri B3
Buea A3
Douala A3
Dschang B2
Ebolowa B3
Edéa B3
Foumban B2
Garoua B2
Kaélé B1
Kousséri B1
Kribi A3
Limbe A3
Maroua B1
Mbalmayo B3
Mokolo B1
Moloundou C3
Nanga-Eboko B3
Ngaoundéré B2
Nkongsamba A2
Sangmélima B3
Tibati B2
Wum B2
Yaoundé, *capital* B3

Other Features
Adamawa, *massif* B2
Bénoué, *river* B2
Biafra, *bight* A3
Cameroon, *mt.* A3
Chad, *lake* B1
Chari, *river* C1
Dja, *river* B3
Logone, *river* C1
Mandara, *mts.* B1
Mbéré, *river* B3
Ntem, *river* B3
Nyong, *river* B3
Sanaga, *river* B2

Nigeria:
Map Index

Cities and Towns
Aba D5
Abakaliki E4
Abeokuta B4
Abuja, *capital* D3
Ado-Ekiti C4
Afikpo D5
Akure C4
Asaba D4
Awka D4
Azare F2
Bauchi E2
Benin City C4
Bida D3
Birnin Kebbi C1
Biu G2
Bonny D5
Burutu C5
Calabar E5
Damaturu F2
Dutse E2
Ede C4
Enugu D4
Geidam F1
Gombe F2
Gummi C1
Gusau D1
Ibadan B4
Ife C4
Ikeja B4
Ikorodu B4
Ila C3
Ilesha C4
Ilorin C3
Iseyin B4
Iwo C4
Jalingo F3
Jebba C3
Jos E3
Kaduna D2
Kano E1
Katsina D1
Kaura-Namoda D1
Kishi B3
Kontagora C2
Kumo F2
Lafia E3
Lagos B4
Lokoja D4
Maiduguri G2

Makurdi E4
Minna D3
Mubi G2
Mushin B4
Nguru F1
Nsukka D4
Offa C3
Ogbomosho C3
Okene D4
Ondo C4
Onitsha D4
Oron E5
Oshogbo C4
Owerri D5
Oyo B4
Port Harcourt D5
Potiskum F2
Sapele C5
Shaki B3
Sokoto C1
Umuahia D5
Uyo D5
Warri C5
Wukari E4
Yola G3
Zaria D2

Other Features
Adamawa, *massif* E5
Benin, *bight* B5
Benue, *river* E3
Bunsuru, *river* D1
Chad, *lake* G1
Cross, *river* E4
Dimlang, *mt.* F3
Gongola, *river* F2
Guinea, *gulf* B5
Hadejia, *river* E1
Jos, *plateau* E2
Ka, *river* C2
Kaduna, *river* D2
Kainji, *lake* C2
Katagum, *river* F2
Komadugu Gana, *river* ..F2
Komadugu Yobe, *river* ..F1
Niger, *delta* C5
Niger, *river* C2, D5
Oban, *hills* E5
Ogun, *river* B5
Osse, *river* C4
Sokoto, *plains* C1
Sokoto, *river* C1
Taraba, *river* F3

Equatorial Guinea

⊛ National Capital
• Other City

1:6,250,000

0   40   80 mi
0   40   80 km

Transverse Mercator Projection

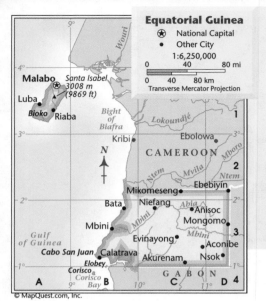

© MapQuest.com, Inc.

Equatorial Guinea

Capital: Malabo
Area: 10,831 sq. mi.
28,060 sq. km.
Population: 465,746
Largest City: Malabo
Language: Spanish
Monetary Unit: CFA franc

Equatorial Guinea:
Map Index

Cities and Towns
Aconibe C3
Akurenam C3
Añisoc C3
Bata B3
Calatrava C3
Ebebiyín D2
Evinayong C3
Luba A1
Malabo, *capital* A1
Mbini B3
Mikomeseng C2
Mongomo D3

Niefang C3
Nsok D3
Riaba A1

Other Features
Abia, *river* C3
Biafra, *bight* B1
Bioko, *island* A1
Corisco, *bay* B4
Corisco, *island* B4
Elobey, *islands* B3
Guinea, *gulf* A3
Mbini, *river* C3
Mboro, *river* D4
San Juan, *cape* B3
Santa Isabel, *peak* ...A1

Gabon

Capital: Libreville
Area: 103,347 sq. mi.
267,738 sq. km.
Population: 1,225,853
Largest City: Libreville
Language: French
Monetary Unit: CFA franc

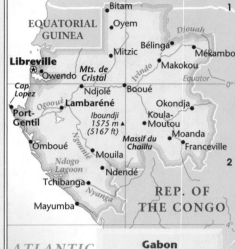

© MapQuest.com, Inc.

Gabon

⊛ National Capital
• Other City

1:11,850,000

0   75   150 mi
0   75   150 km

Azimuthal Equal Area Projection

Gabon:
Map Index

Cities and Towns
Bélinga B1
Bitam A1
Booué B2
Franceville B2
Koula-Moutou B2
Lambaréné A2
Libreville, *capital* ...A1
Makokou B1
Mayumba A2
Mékambo B1
Mitzic A1
Moanda B2
Mouila A2
Ndendé A2
Ndjolé A2

Okondja B2
Omboué A2
Owendo A1
Oyem A1
Port-Gentil A2
Tchibanga A2

Other Features
Chaillu, *mts.* B2
Cristal, *mts.* A1
Djouah, *river* B1
Iboundji, *mt.* B2
Ivindo, *river* B1
Lopez, *cape* A2
Ndogo, *lagoon* A2
Ngounié, *river* A2
Nyanga, *river* A2
Ogooué, *river* A2

Republic of the Congo

⊛ National Capital
• Other City

1:18,000,000

0   100   200 mi
0   100   200 km

Azimuthal Equal Area Projection

© MapQuest.com, Inc.

Republic of the Congo

Capital: Brazzaville
Area: 132,047 sq. mi.
342,091 sq. km.
Population: 2,716,814
Largest City: Brazzaville
Language: French
Monetary Unit: CFA franc

Republic of the Congo:
Map Index

Cities and Towns
Bétou E2
Brazzaville, *capital* ...C6
Djambala C5
Ewo C4
Impfondo D3
Kinkala C6
Loubomo B6
Makoua C4
Mossendjo B5
Ouesso D3
Owando C4
Pointe-Noire A6

Sembé C3
Sibiti B5

Other Features
Alima, *river* D4
Batéké, *plateau* C5
Congo, *basin* D3
Congo, *river* D4
Ivindo, *river* B3
Lékéti, *mts.* C5
Lengoué, *river* C3
Mayombé, *massif* ...B5
Niari, *river* B5
Nyanga, *river* A5
Sangha, *river* D2
Ubangi, *river* E2

Central African Republic (C.A.R.)

Capital: Bangui
Area: 240,324 sq. mi.
622,601 sq. km.
Population: 3,444,951
Largest City: Bangui
Language: French
Monetary Unit: CFA franc

Central African Republic:
Map Index

Cities and Towns
Bambari B2
Bangassou B3
Bangui, *capital* A3
Batangafo A2
Berbérati A3
Birao B1
Bossangoa A2
Bouar A2
Bria B2
Kaga Bandoro B2
Mobaye B3
Ndélé B2
Nola A3
Obo C2
Yalinga B2

Other Features
Chari, *river* A2
Chinko, *river* B2
Gribingui, *river* A2
Kadei, *river* A3
Kotto, *river* B2
Lobaye, *river* A2
Mambéré, *river* A2
Massif des Bongos, *range* ...B2
Mpoko, *river* A2
Ouaka, *river* B2
Ouarra, *river* C2
Ouham, *river* A2
Pendé, *river* A2
Toussoro, *mt.* B2
Ubangi, *river* A3

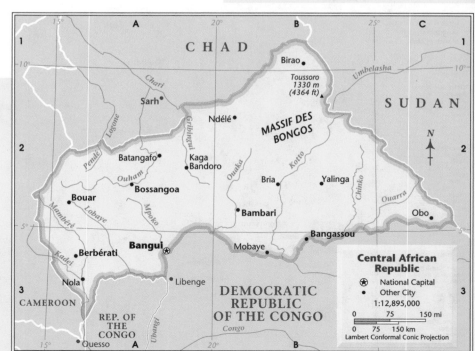

Central African Republic

⊛ National Capital
• Other City

1:12,895,000

0   75   150 mi
0   75   150 km

Lambert Conformal Conic Projection

© MapQuest.com, Inc.

Democratic Republic of the Congo

Capital: Kinshasa
Area: 905,446 sq. mi.
2,345,715 sq. km.
Population: 50,481,305
Largest City: Kinshasa
Language: French
Monetary Unit: Congolese franc

Democratic Republic of the Congo: Map Index

Regions
Bandundu B2
Bas-Congo A2
Équateur B1
Kasai-Occidental B2
Kasai-Oriental B2
Katanga C3
Kinshasa B2
Maniema C2
Nord-Kivu C2
Orientale C1
Sud-Kivu C2

Cities and Towns
Banana A2
Bandundu B2
Boende B2
Bolobo B2
Boma A2
Bondo B1
Bukavu C2
Bumba B1
Bunia C1
Buta C1
Dilolo B3
Gemena B1
Goma C2
Ikela B2
Ilebo B2
Inga A2
Isiro C1
Kabalo C2
Kahemba B2
Kalemie C2
Kamina C3
Kananga B2
Kikwit B2
Kindu C2
Kinshasa, capital A2
Kisangani C1
Kolwezi C3

Likasi C3
Lisala B1
Lodja B2
Lubumbashi C3
Lusambo B2
Manono C2
Matadi A2
Mbandaka B2
Mbanza-Ngungu A2
Mbuji-Mayi B2
Moba C2
Mwene-Ditu B2
Tshikapa B2
Uvira C2
Watsa C1
Yangambi C1

Other Features
Albert, lake C1
Aruwimi, river C1
Bomu, river C1
Congo, river B1
Congo Basin, region B1
Edward, lake C2
Kasai, river B2
Katanga, plateau B3
Kivu, lake C2
Kwa, river C2
Kwango, river B2
Lomami, river C2
Lualaba, river C2
Luapula, river C3
Lukuga, river C2
Luvua, river C2
Mai-Ndombe, lake B2
Margherita, peak C1
Mitumba, mts. C2
Mweru, lake C3
Sankuru, river B2
Tanganyika, lake C2
Tshuapa, river B2
Tumba, lake B2
Ubangi, river B1
Uele, river C1
Upemba, lake C3

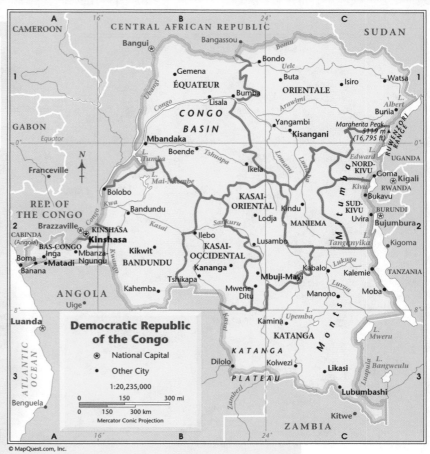

Democratic Republic of the Congo

⊛ National Capital
• Other City

1:20,235,000

0   150   300 mi
0   150   300 km
Mercator Conic Projection

© MapQuest.com, Inc.

Zambia

⊛ National Capital
• Other City

1:14,541,000

0   100   200 mi
0   100   200 km
Lambert Conformal Conic Projection

© MapQuest.com, Inc.

Zambia

Capital: Lusaka
Area: 290,586 sq. mi.
752,813 sq. km.
Population: 9,663,535
Largest City: Lusaka
Language: English
Monetary Unit: Kwacha

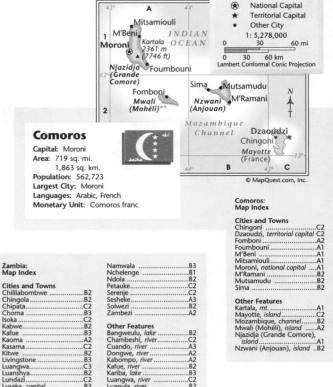

Comoros

⊛ National Capital
★ Territorial Capital
• Other City

1: 5,278,000

0   30   60 mi
0   30   60 km
Lambert Conformal Conic Projection

© MapQuest.com, Inc.

Comoros

Capital: Moroni
Area: 719 sq. mi.
1,863 sq. km.
Population: 562,723
Largest City: Moroni
Languages: Arabic, French
Monetary Unit: Comoros franc

Comoros: Map Index

Cities and Towns
Chingoni C2
Dzaoudzi, territorial capital C2
Fomboni A2
Foumbouni A1
M'Beni A1
Mitsamiouli A1
Moroni, national capital ...A1
M'Ramani B2
Mutsamudu B2
Sima B2

Other Features
Kartala, mt. A1
Mayotte, island C2
Mozambique, channel B2
Mwali (Mohéli), island ...A2
Njazidja (Grande Comore), island .A1
Nzwani (Anjouan), island ..B2

Zambia: Map Index

Cities and Towns
Chililabombwe B2
Chingola B2
Chipata C2
Choma B3
Isoka C2
Kabwe B2
Kafue B3
Kaoma A2
Kasama C2
Kitwe B2
Livingstone B3
Luanshya B2
Lundazi C2
Lusaka, capital B2
Mansa B2
Mazabuka B3
Mbala C1
Mongu A3
Mpika C2
Mporokoso C1
Mufulira B2
Mumbwa B3
Mwinilunga A2

Namwala B3
Nchelenge B1
Ndola B2
Petauke C2
Serenje C2
Sesheke A3
Solwezi B2
Zambezi A2

Other Features
Bangweulu, lake B2
Chambeshi, river C2
Cuando, river A3
Dongwe, river A2
Kabompo, river A2
Kafue, river B2
Kariba, lake B3
Luangwa, river B2
Luapula, river B2
Lunga, river B2
Lungwebungu, river A2
Luvua, river B1
Muchinga, mts. B2
Mweru, lake B1
Tanganyika, lake C1
Victoria, falls B3
Zambezi, river A3, B3

© MapQuest.com, Inc.

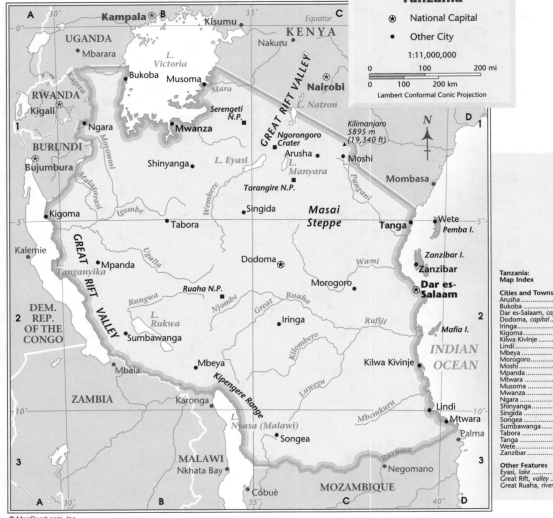

Tanzania

⊛ National Capital

• Other City

1:11,000,000

| 0 | 100 | 200 mi |
| 0 | 100 | 200 km |

Lambert Conformal Conic Projection

Tanzania

Capital: Dar es-Salaam, Dodoma
Area: 364,017 sq. mi.
943,049 sq. km.
Population: 31,270,820
Largest City: Dar es-Salaam
Languages: Swahili, English
Monetary Unit: Shilling

Tanzania:
Map Index

Cities and Towns
Arusha	C1
Bukoba	B1
Dar es-Salaam, capital	C2
Dodoma, capital	C2
Iringa	C2
Kigoma	A1
Kilwa Kivinje	C2
Lindi	C2
Mbeya	B2
Morogoro	C2
Moshi	C1
Mpanda	B2
Mtwara	D3
Musoma	B1
Mwanza	B1
Ngara	B1
Shinyanga	B1
Singida	B1
Songea	C3
Sumbawanga	B2
Tabora	B2
Tanga	C2
Wete	C1
Zanzibar	C2

Other Features
Eyasi, lake	B1
Great Rift, valley	B2, C1
Great Ruaha, river	C2

Igombe, river	B1
Kagera, river	B1
Kilimanjaro, mt.	C1
Kilombero, river	C2
Kipengere, range	B2
Luwegu, river	C2
Mafia, island	C2
Malagarasi, river	B1
Manyara, lake	C1
Mara, river	B1
Masai, steppe	C1
Mbemkuru, river	C3
Moyowosi, river	B1
Natron, lake	C1
Ngorongoro, crater	C1
Njombe, river	B2
Nyasa (Malawi), lake	B3
Pangani, river	C1
Pemba, island	C2
Ruaha Natl. Park	B2
Rufiji, river	C2
Rukwa, lake	B2
Rungwa, river	B2
Ruvuma, river	C3
Serengeti Natl. Park	B1
Tanganyika, lake	A2
Tarangire Natl. Park	C1
Ugalla, river	B2
Victoria, lake	B1
Wami, river	C2
Wembere, river	B1
Zanzibar, island	C2

© MapQuest.com, Inc.

Malawi

Capital: Lilongwe
Area: 45,747 sq. mi.
118,516 sq. km.
Population: 10,000,416
Largest City: Blantyre
Languages: English, Chichewa
Monetary Unit: Kwacha

Malawi:
Map Index

Cities and Towns
Blantyre	B3
Chitipa	B1
Dedza	B2
Karonga	B1
Kasungu	B2
Lilongwe, capital	B2
Mchinji	A2
Monkey Bay	B2
Mzimba	B2
Mzuzu	B2
Nkhata Bay	B2
Nkhotakota	B2
Nsanje	C3
Salima	B2
Zomba	C3

Other Features
Bua, river	B2
Chilwa, lake	C3
Great Rift, valley	B1
Malawi (Nyasa), lake	B2
Malombe, lake	B2
Nyika, plateau	B2
Sapitwa, mt.	B3
Shire, river	B3
Songwe, river	B1

Malawi

⊛ National Capital

• Other City

1:10,756,000

| 0 | 70 | 140 mi |
| 0 | 70 | 140 km |

Lambert Conformal Conic Projection

© MapQuest.com, Inc.

Mozambique

Capital: Maputo
Area: 313,661 sq. mi.
812,593 sq. km.
Population: 19,124,335
Largest City: Maputo
Language: Portuguese
Monetary Unit: Metical

Mozambique

⊛ National Capital

• Other City

1:25,181,000

| 0 | 150 | 300 mi |
| 0 | 150 | 300 km |

Modified Lambert Conformal Conic Projection

Mozambique:
Map Index

Cities and Towns
Angoche	C3
Beira	B3
Chimoio	B3
Chinde	C3
Cuamba	C2
Inhambane	B5
Lichinga	B2
Maputo, capital	B5
Moçambique	D2
Mocímboa da Praia	D1
Nacala	D2
Nampula	C2
Pebane	C3
Pemba	D2
Quelimane	C3
Tete	B3
Vilanculos	B4
Xai-Xai	B5

Other Features
Binga, mt.	B3
Búzi, river	B4
Cabora Bassa, dam	B3
Cabora Bassa, lake	A2
Changane, river	B4
Chilwa, lake	C3
Chire, river	C3
Lebombo, mts.	A4
Limpopo, river	B4
Lugenda, river	C2
Lúrio, river	C2
Mozambique, channel	C3
Namuli, highlands	C2
Nyasa (Malawi), lake	B2
Rovuma, river	C1
Save, river	B4
Zambezi, river	B3

© MapQuest.com, Inc.

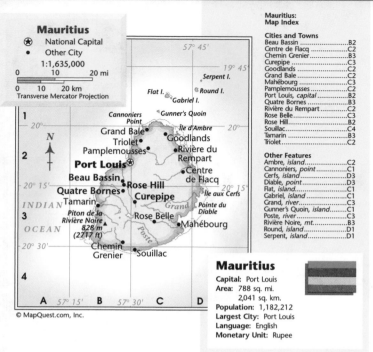

Mauritius

⭐ National Capital
● Other City

1:1,635,000

0   10   20 mi
0   10   20 km
Transverse Mercator Projection

© MapQuest.com, Inc.

Mauritius: Map Index

Cities and Towns

Beau Bassin	B2
Centre de Flacq	C2
Chemin Grenier	B3
Curepipe	C3
Goodlands	C2
Grand Baie	C2
Mahébourg	C3
Pamplemousses	B2
Port Louis, *capital*	B2
Quatre Bornes	B3
Rivière du Rempart	C2
Rose Belle	C3
Rose Hill	B2
Souillac	C4
Tamarin	B3
Triolet	C2

Other Features

Ambre, *island*	C1
Cannoniers, *point*	C1
Cerfs, *island*	D3
Diable, *point*	D3
Flat, *island*	C1
Gabriel, *island*	C1
Grand, *river*	C3
Gunner's Quoin, *island*	C1
Poste, *river*	C3
Rivière Noire, *mt.*	B3
Round, *island*	D1
Serpent, *island*	D1

Mauritius

Capital: Port Louis
Area: 788 sq. mi.
2,041 sq. km.
Population: 1,182,212
Largest City: Port Louis
Language: English
Monetary Unit: Rupee

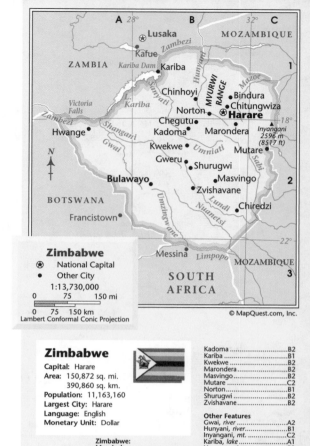

© MapQuest.com, Inc.

Zimbabwe

⭐ National Capital
● Other City

1:13,730,000

0   75   150 mi
0   75   150 km
Lambert Conformal Conic Projection

Zimbabwe

Capital: Harare
Area: 150,872 sq. mi.
390,860 sq. km.
Population: 11,163,160
Largest City: Harare
Language: English
Monetary Unit: Dollar

Kadoma	B2
Kariba	B1
Kwekwe	B2
Marondera	B2
Masvingo	B2
Mutare	C2
Norton	B1
Shurugwi	B2
Zvishavane	B2

Other Features

Gwai, *river*	A2
Hunyani, *river*	B1
Inyangani, *mt.*	C2
Kariba, *lake*	A1
Limpopo, *river*	B3
Lundi, *river*	B2
Mazoe, *river*	B1
Mvurwi, *range*	B1
Nuanetsi, *river*	B2
Sabi, *river*	C2
Sanyati, *river*	B1
Shangani, *river*	A2
Umniati, *river*	B2
Umzingwani, *river*	B2
Victoria, *falls*	A1
Zambezi, *river*	A1, B1

Zimbabwe: Map Index

Cities and Towns

Bindura	B1
Bulawayo	B2
Chegutu	B2
Chinhoyi	B1
Chiredzi	B2
Chitungwiza	B1
Gweru	B2
Harare, *capital*	B1
Hwange	A2

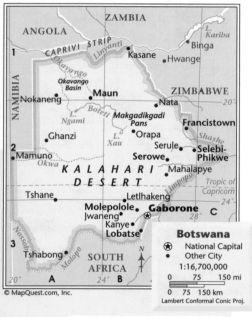

© MapQuest.com, Inc.

Botswana

⭐ National Capital
● Other City

1:16,700,000

0   75   150 mi
0   75   150 km
Lambert Conformal Conic Proj.

Botswana

Capital: Gaborone
Area: 224,607 sq. mi.
581,883 sq. km.
Population: 1,464,167
Largest City: Gaborone
Language: English
Monetary Unit: Pula

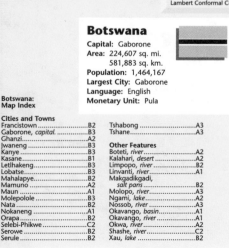

Botswana: Map Index

Cities and Towns

Francistown	B2
Gaborone, *capital*	B3
Ghanzi	A2
Jwaneng	B3
Kanye	B3
Kasane	B1
Letlhakeng	B3
Lobatse	B3
Mahalapye	B2
Mamuno	A2
Maun	A1
Molepolole	B3
Nata	B2
Nokaneng	A1
Orapa	B2
Selebi-Phikwe	C2
Serowe	B2
Serule	B2
Tshabong	A3
Tshane	A3

Other Features

Boteti, *river*	A2
Kalahari, *desert*	A2
Limpopo, *river*	B2
Linvanti, *river*	A1
Makgadikgadi, salt pans	B2
Molopo, *river*	A3
Ngami, *lake*	A2
Nossob, *river*	A3
Okavango, *basin*	A1
Okavango, *river*	A1
Okwa, *river*	A2
Shashe, *river*	C2
Xau, *lake*	B2

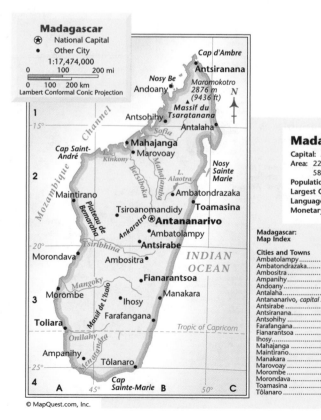

Madagascar

⭐ National Capital
● Other City

1:17,474,000

0   100   200 mi
0   100   200 km
Lambert Conformal Conic Projection

© MapQuest.com, Inc.

Madagascar

Capital: Antananarivo
Area: 226,658 sq. mi.
587,197 sq. km.
Population: 14,873,387
Largest City: Antananarivo
Languages: Malagasy, French
Monetary Unit: Malagasy franc

Madagascar: Map Index

Cities and Towns

Ambatolampy	B2
Ambatondrazaka	B2
Ambositra	B3
Ampanihy	A3
Andoany	B1
Antalaha	C1
Antananarivo, *capital*	B2
Antsirabe	B2
Antsiranana	B1
Antsohihy	B1
Farafangana	B3
Fianarantsoa	B3
Ihosy	B3
Mahajanga	B2
Maintirano	A2
Manakara	B3
Morombe	A3
Morondava	A3
Toamasina	B2
Tôlanaro	B3

Toliara	A3
Tsiroanomandidy	B2

Other Features

Alaotra, *lake*	B2
Ambre, *cape*	B1
Ankaratra, *mts.*	B2
Bemaraha, *plateau*	A2
Betsiboka, *river*	B2
Kinkony, *lake*	A2
L'Isalo, *mts.*	B3
Mahajamba, *river*	B2
Mangoky, *river*	A3
Maromokotro, *mt.*	B1
Menarandra, *river*	A3
Mozambique, *channel*	A2
Nosy Be, *island*	B1
Nosy Sainte Marie, *island*	C2
Onilahy, *river*	A3
Saint-André, *cape*	A2
Sainte-Marie, *cape*	B4
Sofia, *river*	B1
Tsaratanana, *mts.*	B1
Tsiribihina, *river*	B2

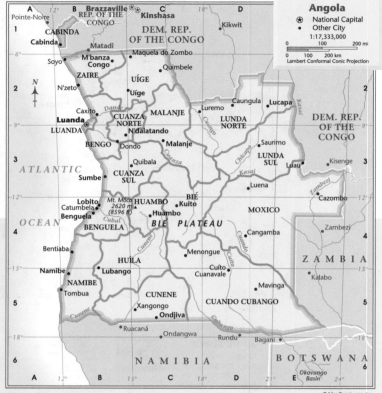

Angola
★ National Capital
• Other City
1:17,333,000
0   100   200 mi
0   100   200 km
Lambert Conformal Conic Projection

© MapQuest.com, Inc.

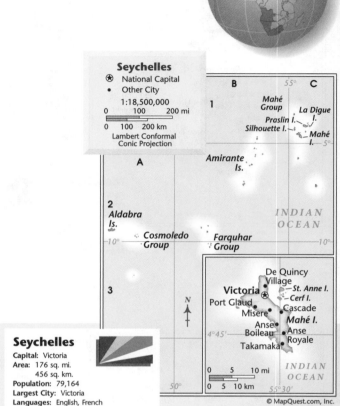

Seychelles
★ National Capital
• Other City
1:18,500,000
0   100   200 mi
0   100   200 km
Lambert Conformal Conic Projection

0   5   10 mi
0   5   10 km

© MapQuest.com, Inc.

Angola
Capital: Luanda
Area: 481,354 sq. mi.
1,247,031 sq. km.
Population: 11,177,537
Largest City: Luanda
Language: Portuguese
Monetary Unit: Kwanza

Seychelles
Capital: Victoria
Area: 176 sq. mi.
456 sq. km.
Population: 79,164
Largest City: Victoria
Languages: English, French
Monetary Unit: Rupee

Angola:
Map Index

Provinces
Bengo B3
Benguela B4
Bié C4
Cabinda B1
Cuando Cubango D5
Cuanza Norte B2
Cuanza Sul B3
Cunene C5
Huambo C4
Huíla B4
Luanda B3
Lunda Norte D2
Lunda Sul D3
Malanje C2
Moxico D4
Namibe B5
Uíge C2
Zaire B2

Cities and Towns
Benguela B4
Bentiaba B4
Cabinda B1
Cangamba D4
Catumbela B4
Caungula D2

Caxito B2
Cazombo E3
Cuíto Cuanavale D5
Dondo B3
Huambo C4
Kuíto C4
Lobito B4
Luanda, capital B2
Luau E3
Lubango B5
Lucapa D2
Luena D3
Luremo C2
Malanje C3
Maquela do Zombo B2
Mavinga D5
M'banza Congo B2
Menongue C4
Namibe B5
N'dalatando B2
N'zeto B2
Ondjiva C5
Quibala C3
Quimbele C2
Saurimo D3
Soyo B2
Sumbe B3
Tombua B5
Uíge C2
Xangongo C5

Other Features
Bié, plateau C4
Chicapa, river D3
Cuando, river D4
Cuango, river D2
Cuanza, river C3
Cubal, river B4
Cubango, river D5
Cuíto, river D4
Cunene, river B5, C4
Dande, river B2
Kasai, river D3
Môco, mt. C4
Zambezi, river E3

Seychelles:
Map Index

Cities and Towns
Anse Boileau ....Inset
Anse Royale ....Inset
Cascade ....Inset
De Quincy Village ....Inset
Misere ....Inset

Port Glaud ....Inset
Takamaka ....Inset
Victoria, capital ....Inset

Other Features
Aldabra, islands A2
Amirante, islands B2
Cerf, island ....Inset
Cosmoledo, island group ..A2

Farquhar, island group ...B2
La Digue, island C1
Mahé, island ....C1, Inset
Mahé, island group B1
Praslin, island C1
St. Anne, island ....Inset
Silhouette, island C1

Namibia
Capital: Windhoek
Area: 318,146 sq. mi.
824,212 sq. km.
Population: 1,648,270
Largest City: Windhoek
Language: English, Afrikaans
Monetary Unit: Rand

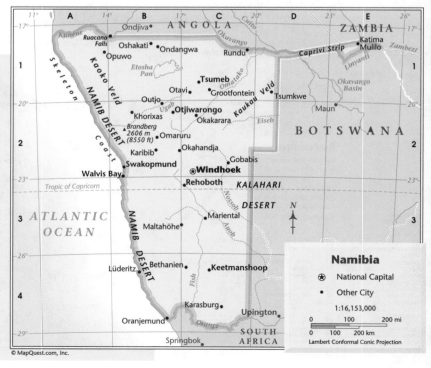

Namibia
★ National Capital
• Other City
1:16,153,000
0   100   200 mi
0   100   200 km
Lambert Conformal Conic Projection

© MapQuest.com, Inc.

Namibia:
Map Index

Cities and Towns
Bethanien C4
Gobabis C2
Grootfontein C1
Karasburg C4
Karibib B2
Katima Mulilo E1
Keetmanshoop C4
Khorixas B2
Lüderitz B4
Maltahöhe B3
Mariental C3
Okahandja B2
Okakarara C2
Omaruru B2
Ondangwa B1
Opuwo A1
Oranjemund B4
Oshakati B1
Otavi C1
Otjiwarongo B2
Outjo B2
Rehoboth B3
Rundu C1

Swakopmund B2
Tsumeb C1
Tsumkwe D1
Walvis Bay B2
Windhoek, capital C2

Other Features
Auob, river C3
Brandberg, mt. B2
Caprivi, strip D1
Eiseb, river D2
Etosha, pan B1
Fish, river C4
Kalahari, desert C3
Kaoko Veld, mts. A1
Kaukau Veld, region C2
Kunene, river A1
Linyanti, river E1
Namib, desert A1, B3
Nossob, river C3
Okavango, river C1
Omatako, river C2
Orange, river C4
Ruacana, falls B1
Skeleton, coast A1
Ugab, river B2
Zambezi, river E1

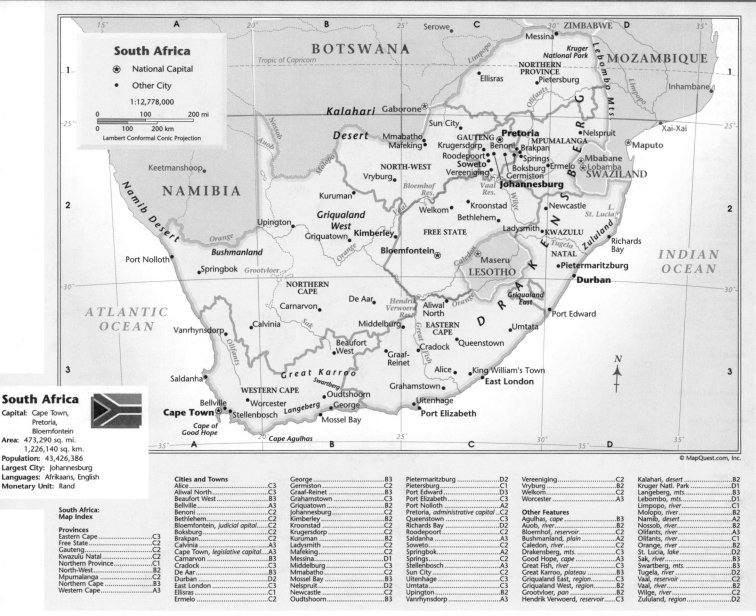

South Africa

⊛ National Capital
● Other City

1:12,778,000

0   100   200 mi
0 100 200 km

Lambert Conformal Conic Projection

South Africa

Capital: Cape Town, Pretoria, Bloemfontein
Area: 473,290 sq. mi. 1,226,140 sq. km.
Population: 43,426,386
Largest City: Johannesburg
Languages: Afrikaans, English
Monetary Unit: Rand

South Africa: Map Index

Provinces
Eastern Cape	C3
Free State	C2
Gauteng	C2
Kwazulu Natal	C2
Northern Province	C1
North-West	B2
Mpumalanga	C2
Northern Cape	B3
Western Cape	A3

Cities and Towns
Alice	C3
Aliwal North	C3
Beaufort West	B3
Bellville	A3
Benoni	C2
Bethlehem	C2
Bloemfontein, judicial apital	C2
Boksburg	C2
Brakpan	C2
Calvinia	A3
Cape Town, legislative capital	A3
Carnarvon	B3
Cradock	B3
De Aar	B3
Durban	D2
East London	C3
Ellisras	C1
Ermelo	C2
George	B3
Germiston	C2
Graaf-Reinet	B3
Grahamstown	C3
Griquatown	B2
Johannesburg	C2
Kimberley	B2
Kroonstad	C2
Krugersdorp	C2
Kuruman	B2
Ladysmith	C2
Mafeking	C2
Messina	D1
Middelburg	C3
Mmabatho	C2
Mossel Bay	B3
Nelspruit	D2
Newcastle	C2
Oudtshoorn	B3
Pietermaritzburg	D2
Pietersburg	C1
Port Edward	D3
Port Elizabeth	C3
Port Nolloth	A2
Pretoria, administrative capital	C2
Queenstown	C3
Richards Bay	D2
Roodepoort	C2
Saldanha	A3
Soweto	C2
Springbok	A2
Springs	C2
Stellenbosch	A3
Sun City	C2
Uitenhage	C3
Umtata	C3
Upington	B2
Vanrhynsdorp	A3
Vereeniging	C2
Vryburg	B2
Welkom	C2
Worcester	A3

Other Features
Agulhas, cape	B3
Auob, river	B2
Bloemhof, reservoir	B2
Bushmanland, plain	A2
Caledon, river	C2
Drakensberg, mts.	C3
Good Hope, cape	A3
Great Fish, river	C3
Great Karroo, plateau	B3
Griqualand East, region	C3
Griqualand West, region	B2
Grootvloer, pan	B2
Hendrik Verwoerd, reservoir	C3
Kalahari, desert	B2
Kruger Natl. Park	D1
Langeberg, mts.	B3
Lebombo, mts.	D1
Limpopo, river	C1
Molopo, river	B2
Namib, desert	A2
Nossob, river	B2
Olifants, river	C1
Olifants, river	A3
Orange, river	B2
St. Lucia, lake	D2
Sak, river	B3
Swartberg, mts.	B3
Tugela, river	D2
Vaal, reservoir	C2
Vaal, river	B2
Wilge, river	C2
Zululand, region	D2

© MapQuest.com, Inc.

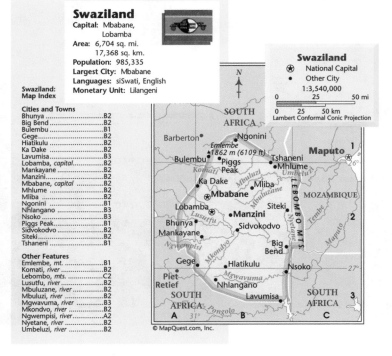

Swaziland

Capital: Mbabane, Lobamba
Area: 6,704 sq. mi. 17,368 sq. km.
Population: 985,335
Largest City: Mbabane
Languages: siSwati, English
Monetary Unit: Lilangeni

Swaziland: Map Index

Cities and Towns
Bhunya	B2
Big Bend	B2
Bulembu	B1
Gege	B2
Hlatikulu	B2
Ka Dake	B3
Lavumisa	B3
Lobamba, capital	B2
Mankayane	B2
Manzini	B2
Mbabane, capital	B2
Mhlume	B2
Mliba	B2
Ngonini	B1
Nhlangano	B3
Nsoko	B3
Piggs Peak	B1
Sidvokodvo	B2
Siteki	B2
Tshaneni	B1

Other Features
Emlembe, mt.	B1
Komati, river	B1
Lebombo, mts.	C2
Lusutfu, river	B2
Mbuluzane, river	B2
Mbuluzi, river	B2
Mgwavuma, river	B3
Mkondvo, river	B2
Ngwempisi, river	A2
Nyetane, river	B2
Umbeluzi, river	B2

Swaziland

⊛ National Capital
● Other City

1:3,540,000

0   25   50 mi
0 25 50 km

Lambert Conformal Conic Projection

© MapQuest.com, Inc.

Lesotho

Capital: Maseru
Area: 11,716 sq. mi. 30,352 sq. km.
Population: 2,128,950
Largest City: Maseru
Language: English
Monetary Unit: Loti

Lesotho: Map Index

Cities and Towns
Butha-Buthe	B1
Leribe	B1
Libono	B1
Mafeteng	A2
Maseru, capital	A2
Mohales Hoek	A3
Mokhotlong	C2
Morija	A2
Pitseng	B1
Qachas Nek	B3
Quthing	A3
Roma	A2
Sekake	A2
Teyateyaneng	A2
Thaba-Tseka	B2

Other Features
Caledon, river	A1
Central, range	B2
Drakensberg, mts.	B3
Makhaleng, river	A2
Maloti, mts.	B2
Matsoku, river	B2
Orange, river	A3, B2
Sources, mt.	B1
Thabana Ntlenyana, mt.	B3
Tsedike, river	B3

Lesotho

⊛ National Capital
● Other City

1:5,811,000

0   30   60 mi
0 30 60 km

Lambert Conformal Conic Projection

© MapQuest.com, Inc.

MAJOR CITIES

Argentina
Buenos Aires	2,961,000
Córdoba	1,148,000
Rosario	895,000

Bolivia
La Paz	739,000
Santa Cruz	833,000
El Alto	527,000

Brazil
São Paulo	10,018,000
Rio de Janeiro	5,606,000
Salvador	2,263,000
Belo Horizonte	2,097,000
Fortaleza	1,917,000
Brasília	1,738,000
Curitiba	1,409,000
Recife	1,330,000
Pôrto Alegre	1,296,000
Belém	1,168,000
Manaus	1,138,000

Chile
| Santiago | 4,641,000 |
| Puente Alto | 363,000 |

Colombia
Bogotá	4,945,000
Cali	1,666,000
Medellín	1,630,000
Barranquilla	994,000

Ecuador
| Guayaquil | 1,974,000 |
| Quito | 1,444,000 |

Falkland Islands
| Stanley | 1,200 |

French Guiana
| Cayenne | 41,000 |

Guyana
| Georgetown | 195,000 |

Paraguay
| Asunción | 547,000 |

Peru
Lima	5,682,000
Arequipa	619,000
Trujillo	509,000

Suriname
| Paramaribo | 216,000 |

Uruguay
| Montevideo | 1,303,000 |

Venezuela
Caracas	3,673,000
Maracaibo	1,221,000
Barquisimeto	954,000
Valencia	911,000

International comparability of city population data is limited by various data inconsistencies.

CITIES
⊗ National Capital
★ Territorial Capital
• Other City

ELEVATIONS
	Feet	Meters
	13,120	4000
	6560	2000
	1640	500
	656	200
	0	0
	Below sea level	

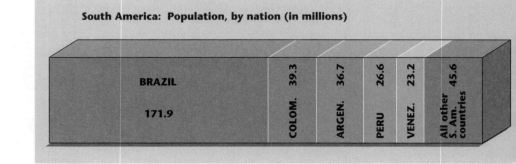

South America: Population, by nation (in millions)

| BRAZIL 171.9 | COLOM. 39.3 | ARGEN. 36.7 | PERU 26.6 | VENEZ. 23.2 | All other S. Am. countries 45.6 |

© MapQuest.com, Inc.

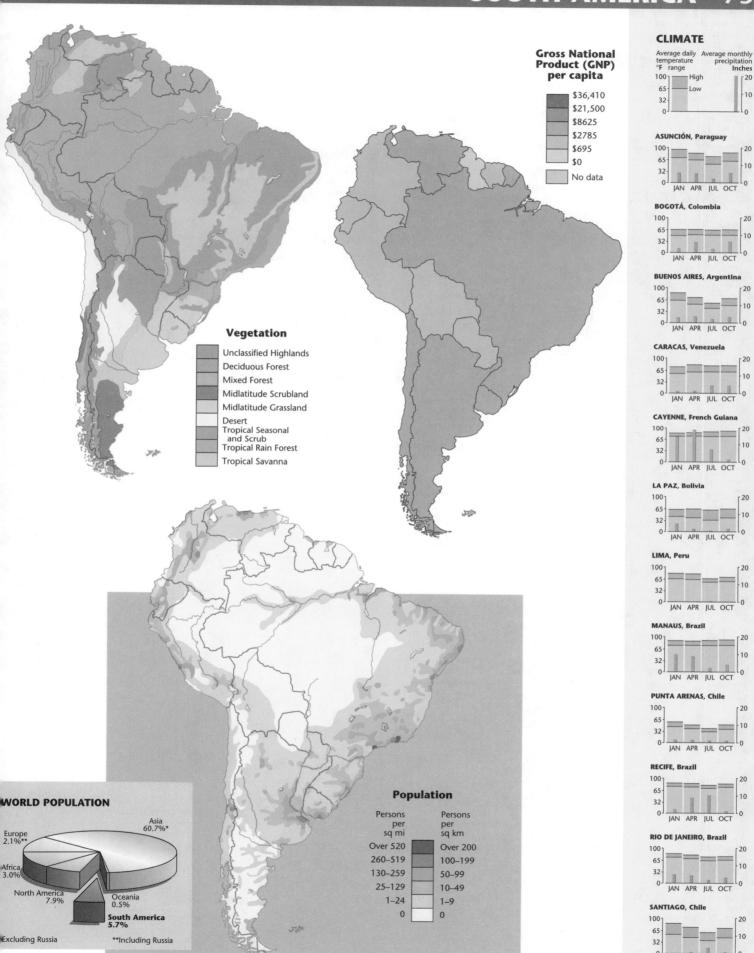

Gross National Product (GNP) per capita

- $36,410
- $21,500
- $8625
- $2785
- $695
- $0
- No data

Vegetation

- Unclassified Highlands
- Deciduous Forest
- Mixed Forest
- Midlatitude Scrubland
- Midlatitude Grassland
- Desert
- Tropical Seasonal and Scrub
- Tropical Rain Forest
- Tropical Savanna

CLIMATE

Average daily temperature °F range

Average monthly precipitation Inches

High
Low

ASUNCIÓN, Paraguay

BOGOTÁ, Colombia

BUENOS AIRES, Argentina

CARACAS, Venezuela

CAYENNE, French Guiana

LA PAZ, Bolivia

LIMA, Peru

MANAUS, Brazil

PUNTA ARENAS, Chile

RECIFE, Brazil

RIO DE JANEIRO, Brazil

SANTIAGO, Chile

Population

Persons per sq mi	Persons per sq km
Over 520	Over 200
260–519	100–199
130–259	50–99
25–129	10–49
1–24	1–9
0	0

WORLD POPULATION

- Asia 60.7%*
- Europe 2.1%**
- Africa 3.0%*
- North America 7.9%
- Oceania 0.5%
- South America 5.7%

*Excluding Russia   **Including Russia

Argentina

Capital: Buenos Aires
Area: 1,073,518 sq. mi.
2,781,134 sq. km.
Population: 36,737,664
Largest City: Buenos Aires
Language: Spanish
Monetary Unit: Peso

Argentina: Map Index

Provinces

Buenos Aires	C4
Catamarca	B2
Chaco	C2
Chubut	B5
Córdoba	C3
Corrientes	D2
Distrito Federal	D3
Entre Ríos	D3
Formosa	D1
Jujuy	B1
La Pampa	B4
La Rioja	B2
Mendoza	B3
Misiones	E2
Neuquén	B4
Río Negro	B5
Salta	B2
San Juan	B3
San Luis	B3
Santa Cruz	A6
Santa Fe	C2
Santiago del Estero	C2
Tierra del Fuego	B7
Tucumán	B2

Cities and Towns

Avellaneda	D3
Bahía Blanca	C4
Buenos Aires, *capital*	C4
Calafate	A7
Catamarca	B2
Comodoro Rivadavia	B6
Concordia	D3
Córdoba	C3
Corrientes	D2
Curuzú Cuatiá	D2
Embarcación	C1
Esquel	A5
Formosa	D2
Godoy Cruz	B3
Lanús	D3

La Plata	D4
La Rioja	B2
Lomas de Zamora	D4
Mar del Plata	D4
Mendoza	B3
Necochea	D4
Neuquén	B4
Olavarría	C4
Paraná	C3
Posadas	D2
Presidencia Roque	
Sáenz Peña	C2
Puerto Deseado	B6
Puerto Santa Cruz	B7
Rawson	B5
Reconquista	D2
Resistencia	D2
Río Cuarto	C3
Río Gallegos	B7
Rosario	C3
Salta	B1
San Antonio Oeste	B5
San Carlos de Bariloche	A5
San Francisco	C3
San Juan	B3
San Luis	B3
San Miguel de Tucumán	B2
San Nicolás	C3
San Rafael	B3
San Salvador de Jujuy	B1
Santa Fe	C3
Santa Rosa	C4
Santiago del Estero	C2
Tandil	D4
Ushuaia	B7
Viedma	C5
Villa María	C3

Other Features

Aconcagua, *mt.*	A3
Andes, *mts.*	A6–B1
Argentino, *lake*	A7
Atuel, *river*	B4
Beagle, *channel*	B7
Bermejo, *river*	C2

Blanca, *bay*	C4
Buenos Aires, *lake*	A6
Cardiel, *lake*	A6
Champaquí, *mt.*	C3
Chico, *river*	B6
Chubut, *river*	A5
Colorado, *river*	B4
Córdoba, *range*	B3
Desaguadero, *river*	B2
Deseado, *river*	B6
Domuyo, *volcano*	A4
Dungeness, *point*	B7
Estados, *island*	C7
Fitzroy, *mt.*	A6
Gallegos, *river*	A7
Gran Chaco, *region*	C1
Grande, *bay*	B7
Iguaçu, *falls*	E2
Iguaçu, *river*	E2
Lanín, *volcano*	A4
Llullaillaco, *volcano*	B1
Magellan, *strait*	B7
Mar Chiquita, *lake*	C3
Mercedario, *mt.*	A3
Negro, *river*	B4
Ojos del Salado, *mt.*	B2
Pampas, *plain*	C4
Paraguay, *river*	D2
Paraná, *river*	D2
Patagonia, *region*	A6
Pilcomayo, *river*	C1
Plata, Río de la, *estuary*	D3
Rasa, *point*	B5
Salado, *river*	B3
Salado, *river*	C2
San Antonio, *cape*	D4
San Jorge, *gulf*	B6
San Martín, *lake*	A6
San Matías, *gulf*	C5
Santa Cruz, *river*	A7
Tres Puntas, *cape*	B6
Tupungato, *mt.*	B3
Uruguay, *river*	D3
Valdés, *peninsula*	C5
Viedma, *lake*	A6

Paraguay

Capital: Asunción
Area: 157,048 sq. mi.
406,752 sq. km.
Population: 5,434,095
Largest City: Asunción
Language: Spanish
Monetary Unit: Guarani

Paraguay: Map Index

Departments

Alto Paraguay	C2
Alto Paraná	E4
Amambay	E3
Asunción	D4
Boquerón	B3
Caaguazú	D4
Caazapá	D5
Canendiyú	E4
Central	D4
Concepción	D3
Cordillera	D4
Guairá	D4
Itapúa	E5
Misiones	D5
Ñeembucú	C5
Paraguarí	D5
Presidente Hayes	C4
San Pedro	D4

Cities and Towns

Abaí	E4
Asunción, *capital*	D4
Caacupé	D4
Caaguazú	E4
Caazapá	D5
Capitán Pablo Lagerenza	B1
Ciudad del Este	E4
Concepción	D3
Coronel Oviedo	D4
Doctor Pedro P. Peña	A3
Encarnación	E5

Filadelfia	B3
Fuerte Olimpo	D2
General	
Eugenio A. Garay	A2
Mariscal Estigarribia	B3
Paraguarí	D4
Pedro Juan Caballero	E3
Pilar	C5
Pozo Colorado	C3
Puerto Bahía	C2
Puerto Pinasco	D3
Salto del Guairá	E4
San Juan Bautista	D5
San Lorenzo	D4
San Pedro	D4
Villa Hayes	D4
Villarrica	D4

Other Features

Acaray, *river*	E4
Amambay, *mts.*	E3
Apa, *river*	D3
Chaco Boreal, *region*	B2
Gran Chaco, *region*	B3
Iguazú, *falls*	E4
Itaipú, *reservoir*	E4
Jejuí-Guazú, *river*	D4
Montelindo, *river*	C3
Paraguay, *river*	C2, C5
Paraná, *river*	C5, E5
Pilcomayo, *river*	B3, C4
Tebicuary, *river*	D5
Verde, *river*	C3
Ypané, *river*	D3
Ypoá, *lake*	D4

Uruguay

Capital: Montevideo
Area: 68,037 sq. mi.
176,215 sq. km.
Population: 3,308,523
Largest City: Montevideo
Language: Spanish
Monetary Unit: New peso

Uruguay: Map Index

Cities and Towns

Artigas	B1
Bella Unión	B1
Canelones	B3
Carmelo	A2
Colonia	B3
Durazno	B2
Florida	B3
Fray Bentos	A2
Las Piedras	B3
Melo	C2
Mercedes	A2
Minas	C3
Montevideo, *capital*	B3
Nueva Palmira	A2
Pando	C3
Paso de los Toros	B2
Paysandú	A2
Piedra Sola	B2
Punta del Este	C3
Rivera	C1
Rocha	C3
Salto	B1
San Carlos	C3
San José	B3
Tacuarembó	C1
Treinta y Tres	C2
Trinidad	B2

Other Features

Arapey Grande, *river*	B1
Baygorria, *lake*	B2
Cebollatí, *river*	C2
Cuareim, *river*	B1
Daymán, *river*	B1
Grande, *range*	C2
Haedo, *range*	B2
Merín, *lagoon*	D2
Mirador Nacional, *mt.*	C3
Negra, *lagoon*	D2
Negro, *river*	C2
Paso de Palmar, *lake*	B2
Plata, *river*	B3
Queguay Grande, *river*	B2
Rincón del Bonete, *lake*	B2
Salto Grande, *reservoir*	B1
San José, *river*	A2
San Salvador, *river*	A2
Santa Ana, *range*	C1
Santa Lucía, *river*	B3
Tacuarembó, *river*	C1
Tacuarí, *river*	D2
Uruguay, *river*	A1
Yaguarí, *river*	C1
Yaguarón, *river*	D2
Yi, *river*	C2

Chile

Capital: Santiago
Area: 292,135 sq. mi.
        756,826 sq. km.
Population: 14,973,843
Largest City: Santiago
Language: Spanish
Monetary Unit: Peso

Chile:
Map Index

Regions
Aisén del General Carlos
  Ibáñez del Campo B8
Antofagasta C2
Atacama B3
Bío-Bío B6
Coquimbo B4
El Libertador General
  Bernardo O'Higgins B4
La Araucanía B6
Los Lagos B7
Magallanes y Antártica
  Chilena B9
Maule B5, B6
Región Metropolitana B4,
  Inset
Tarapacá C1
Valparaíso ....B4, Inset

Cities and Towns
Aguada de Cachinal C2
Aguas Blancas C2
Algarrobo ....Inset
Altamira C3
Ancud B7
Angol B6
Antofagasta B2
Arica B1
Balmaceda B8
Calama C2
Casablanca ....Inset
Castro B7
Cerro Castillo B9
Chaitén B7
Chañaral B3
Chiapa C1
Chile Chico B8
Chillán B6
Chuquicamata C2
Cochrane B8
Coihaique B8
Colina ....Inset
Collaguasi C2
Concepción B6
Conchalí ....Inset
Constitución B5
Copiapó B3
Coquimbo B3
Curicó B4
El Tabo ....Inset
El Trebolar ....Inset
Freirina B3
Gatico B2
Illapel B4
Iquique B1
Lampa ....Inset
La Serena B3
La Unión B7
Lebu B6
Linares B5
Los Andes B4
Los Ángeles B6
Maipú ....Inset
Mamiña C2
Melipilla ....Inset
Nuñoa ....Inset
Osorno B7
Ovalle B4
Parral B6
Pisagua B1
Porvenir B9
Potrerillos C3
Puente Alto ....Inset
Puerto Aisén B8
Puerto Cisnes B8
Puerto Montt B7
Puerto Natales B9
Puerto Varas B7
Puerto Williams C9
Punta Arenas B9
Punta Delgada B9
Putre C1
Quellón B7
Quillota B4
Quilpué ....Inset
Rancagua B4
Rungue ....Inset
San Antonio ....B4, Inset
San Bernardo ....Inset
San Félix B3
San Fernando B4
San Pedro de Atacama C2
Santa Inés ....Inset
Santiago, capital ......B4, Inset
Socompa C2
Talagante ....Inset
Talca B5
Talcahuano B6
Taltal B3
Temuco B6
Tilomonte C2
Tocopilla B2
Tomé B6
Unión C2
Valdivia B6
Vallenar B3
Valparaíso ....B4, Inset
Victoria B6
Viña del Mar ....Inset

Other Features
Aconcagua, river B4
Ancud, gulf B7
Andes, mts. B8, C4
Atacama, desert C2
Bascuñán, cape B3
Bío-Bío, river B6
Brunswick, peninsula B9
Campana, island A8
Chiloé, island B7
Chonos, archipelago B7
Cochrane, lake B8
Concepción, bay B6
Copiapó, river B3
Corcovado, gulf B7
Desolación, island B9
Domeyko, mts. C3
Dungeness, point C9
Duque de York, island A9
Elqui, river B3
Fitzroy, mt. B8
Galera, point B6
Horn, cape C9
Hoste, island C9
Imperial, river B6
Lanín, volcano B6
Lengua de Vaca, point B4
Llanquihue, lake B7
Llullaillaco, volcano C2
Loa, river B2
Madre de Dios, island A9
Magdalena, island B7
Magellan, strait B9
Maipo, river ....B4, Inset
Maule, river B5
Navarino, island C9
Occidental, mts. C1
Ojos del Salado, mt. C2
Ollagüe, volcano C2
Peñas, gulf B8
Rapel, river B4
Reina Adelaida, archipelago .B9
San Martín, lake B8
San Valentín, mt. B8
Santa Inés, island B9
Taitao, peninsula A8
Tierra del Fuego, island C9
Toltén, river B6
Wellington, island A8

Peru

Capital: Lima
Area: 496,225 sq. mi.
1,285,216 sq. km.
Population: 26,624,582
Largest City: Lima
Languages: Spanish, Quechua
Monetary Unit: Nuevo Sol

Peru Map

© MapQuest.com, Inc.

Peru:
Map Index

Cities and Towns
Abancay	C3
Arequipa	C4
Ayacucho	C3
Cajamarca	B2
Callao	B3
Cerro de Pasco	B3
Chachapoyas	B2
Chiclayo	B2
Chimbote	B2
Chincha Alta	B3
Cuzco	C3
Huacho	B3
Huancavelica	B3
Huancayo	B3
Huánuco	B2
Huaraz	B2
Ica	B3
Ilo	C4
Iquitos	C1
Juliaca	C4
La Oroya	B3
Lima, capital	B3
Mollendo	C4
Moquegua	C4

Moyobamba	B2
Nazca	C3
Pacasmayo	B2
Paita	A2
Patavilca	B3
Pisco	B3
Piura	A2
Pucallpa	C2
Puerto Maldonado	D3
Puno	C4
Salaverry	B2
San Juan	B4
Sicuani	C3
Sullana	A1
Tacna	C4
Talara	A1
Tarapoto	B2
Tingo María	B2
Trujillo	B2
Tumbes	A1
Yurimaguas	B2

Other Features
Amazon, river	C1
Andes, mts.	B1, C3
Apurímac, river	C3
Central, mts.	B2
Colca, river	C4

Coropuna, mt.	C4
Guayaquil, gulf	A1
Huallaga, river	B2
Huascarán, mt.	B2
La Montaña, region	C2
Machupicchu, ruins	C3
Madre de Dios, river	C3
Mantaro, river	B3
Marañón, river	B1, B2
Napo, river	C1
Negra, point	A2
Occidental, mts.	B2, C4
Oriental, mts.	B2, C3
Pastaza, river	B1
Purús, river	C3
Putumayo, river	C1
Santiago, river	B1
Sechura, desert	A2
Tambo, river	C3
Tambo, river	C4
Tigre, river	B1
Titicaca, lake	D4
Ucayali, river	C2
Urubamba, river	C3
Vilcabamba, mts.	C3
Yavarí, river	C1

Peru (map legend)

Peru
⊛ National Capital
• Other City
1:15,900,000
0   100   200 mi
0   100   200 km
Transverse Mercator Projection

Bolivia

Bolivia:
Map Index

Departments
Beni	A2
Chuquisaca	B4
Cochabamba	A3
La Paz	A3
Oruro	A3
Pando	A2
Potosí	A4
Santa Cruz	B3
Tarija	B4

Cities and Towns
Aiquile	A3
Camiri	B4
Cobija	A2
Cochabamba	A3
Fortín Ravelo	B3
Guaqui	A3
La Paz, capital	A3
Llallagua	A3
Magdalena	B2
Mojos	A3
Montero	B3
Oruro	A3
Potosí	A3
Puerto Suárez	C3
Riberalta	A2
Roboré	C3
San Borja	A2

San Cristóbal	B2
San Ignacio	B3
San José de Chiquitos	B3
San Matías	C3
Santa Ana	A2
Santa Cruz	B3
Santa Rosa del Palmar	B3
Sucre, capital	A3
Tarija	B4
Tarvo	B2
Trinidad	B2
Tupiza	A4
Uyuni	A4
Villazón	A4
Yacuiba	B4

Other Features
Abuná, river	A2
Altiplano, plateau	A3
Beni, river	A2
Chaparé, river	A3
Cordillera Central, mts.	A3
Cordillera Occidental, mts.	A3
Cordillera Oriental, mts.	A3
Cordillera Real, mts.	A3
Desaguadero, river	A3
Gran Chaco, region	B4
Grande, river	A3
Guaporé, river	B2
Ichilo, river	B3
Illampu, mt.	A3
Illimani, mt.	A3

Iténez, river	B2
Madre de Dios, river	A2
Mamoré, river	A2
Ollagüe, volcano	A4
Paraguá, river	B2
Paraguay, river	C4
Pilaya, river	B4
Pilcomayo, river	B3
Poopó, lake	A3
Sajama, mt.	A3
Salar de Uyuni, salt flat	A4
San Luis, lake	B2
San Pablo, river	B3
Titicaca, lake	A3
Yata, river	A2
Yungas, region	A3

Bolivia

Capital: La Paz, Sucre
Area: 424,164 sq. mi.
1,098,871 sq. km.
Population: 7,982,850
Largest City: La Paz
Languages: Spanish, Quechua, Aymara
Monetary Unit: Boliviano

Bolivia Map

Bolivia
⊛ National Capital
• Other City
1:15,400,000
0   100   200 mi
0   100   200 km
Transverse Mercator Projection

© MapQuest.com, Inc.

Inset map (upper left):

Banco Serranilla
82° 80°
Cayo de Roncador
Isla de Providencia
SAN ANDRÉS Y PROVIDENCIA
Isla de San Andrés
Cayos de Albuquerque
0 25 50 mi
0 25 50 km
A

Map grid labels: A B C D — 1 2 3 4 5 6

Caribbean Sea
PANAMA
Panamá
Gulf of Panama
PACIFIC OCEAN
VENEZUELA
BRAZIL
PERU
ECUADOR
Quito
Equator 0°
Iquitos
Amazon
Leticia

Places/features on map:
Punta Gallinas, Peninsula de la Guajira, Ríohacha, Golfo de Venezuela, Coro, Santa Marta, Pico Cristóbal Colón 5775 m (18,947 ft), LA GUAJIRA, Maracaibo, Barranquilla, ATLÁNTICO, Sierra Nevada de Santa Marta, Cartagena, CÉSAR, Valledupar, L. de Maracaibo, Barquisimeto, MAGDALENA, Mérida, Sincelejo, SUCRE, Montería, CÓRDOBA, BOLÍVAR, NORTE DE SANTANDER, Cúcuta, San Cristóbal, Apure, San Fernando de Apure, Turbo, ANTIOQUIA, Bucaramanga, Arauca, Barrancabermeja, ARAUCA, Cravo Norte, Medellín, SANTANDER, Puerto Carreño, Quibdó, CHOCÓ, RISARALDA, Manizales, BOYACÁ, Tunja, CASANARE, LLANOS, Orinoco, Yopal, CALDAS, CUNDINAMARCA, Tolima 5215 m (17,110 ft), VICHADA, Pereira, QUINDÍO, Armenia, Ibagué, Bogotá, Villavicencio, Meta, Vichada, Buenaventura, TOLIMA, Palmira, VALLE DEL CAUCA, Huila 5750 m (18,865 ft), CAPITAL DISTRICT, META, Puerto Inírida, Cali, CAUCA, Neiva, Vista Hermosa, GUAINÍA, Patía, HUILA, San José del Guaviare, Guaviare, San Felipe, Popayán, Tumaco, NARIÑO, Mocoa, Florencia, GUAVIARE, Pasto, PUTUMAYO, Miraflores, Mitú, VAUPÉS, Apaporis, Puerto Leguízamo, CAQUETÁ, Caquetá, São Gabriel de Cachoeria, AMAZONAS, El Encanto, Putumayo, Napo, Japurá, Içá, Yavarí

Legend (Colombia):
Colombia
⊛ National Capital
• Other City
1:13,825,000
0 100 200 mi
0 100 200 km
Transverse Mercator Projection

© MapQuest.com, Inc.

Colombia
Capital: Bogotá
Area: 440,831 sq. mi.
1,142,049 sq. km.
Population: 39,309,422
Largest City: Bogotá
Language: Spanish
Monetary Unit: Peso

Colombia:
Map Index

Internal Divisions
Amazonas (commissary) B5
Antioquia (dept.) B3
Arauca (intendency) C3
Atlántico (dept.) B2
Bolívar (dept.) B2
Boyacá (dept.) B3
Caldas (dept.) B3
Capital District B4
Caquetá (dept.) B4
Casanare (intendency) C3
Cauca (dept.) A4
César (dept.) B2
Chocó (dept.) A3
Córdoba (dept.) B2
Cundinamarca (dept.) B3
Guainía (commissary) C4
Guaviare (commissary) B4
Huila (dept.) A4
La Guajira (dept.) B2
Magdalena (dept.) B2
Meta (dept.) B4
Nariño (dept.) A4
Norte de Santander (dept.) B2
Putumayo (intendency) A4
Quindío (dept.) B3
Risaralda (dept.) B3
San Andrés y Providencia (intendency) ...... Inset
Santander (dept.) B2
Sucre (dept.) B2
Tolima (dept.) B4
Valle del Cauca (dept.) A4
Vaupés (commissary) C4
Vichada (commissary) C3

Cities and Towns
Arauca C3
Armenia B3
Barrancabermeja B3
Barranquilla B2
Bogotá, capital B3
Bucaramanga B3
Buenaventura A4
Cali A4
Cartagena B2
Cravo Norte C3
Cúcuta B2
El Encanto B5
Florencia B4
Ibagué B3
Leticia C6
Manizales B3
Medellín B3
Miraflores B4
Mitú C4
Mocoa A4
Montería B2
Neiva B4
Orocué C3
Palmira A4
Pasto A4
Pereira B3
Popayán A4
Puerto Carreño D3
Puerto Inírida D4
Puerto Leguízamo B5
Quibdó A3
Ríohacha B2
San Felipe D4
San José del Guaviare B4
Santa Marta B2
Sincelejo B2
Tumaco A4
Tunja B3
Turbo A2
Valledupar B2
Villavicencio B3
Vista Hermosa B4
Yopal B3

Other Features
Albuquerque, cays ...... Inset
Amazon, river C5
Andes, range A4
Apaporis, river C4
Atrato, river A3
Caquetá, river B5
Cauca, river B3
Cordillera Central, range A4
Cordillera Occidental, range A4
Cordillera Oriental, range B4
Cristóbal Colón, peak B2
Gallinas, point C1
Guainía, river C4
Guajira, peninsula C1
Guaviare, river C4
Huila, mt. A4
Llanos, prairie C3
Magdalena, river B3
Meta, river C3
Orinoco, river D3
Patía, river A4
Providencia, island ...... Inset
Putumayo, river B5
Roncador, cay ...... Inset
San Andrés, island ...... Inset
San Juan, river A3
Serranilla, bank ...... Inset
Sierra Nevada de Santa Marta, mts. B2
Tolima, mt. B3
Vaupés, river B4
Vichada, river C3

Venezuela:
Map Index

Internal Divisions
Amazonas (territory) C3
Anzoátegui (state) D2
Apure (state) C2
Aragua (state) C2
Barinas (state) C2
Bolívar (state) D2
Carabobo (state) C2
Cojedes (state) C2
Delta Amacuro (territory) D2
Dependencias Federales C1
Distrito Federal C1
Falcón (state) B1
Guárico (state) C2
Lara (state) B1
Mérida (state) B2
Miranda (state) C1
Monagas (state) D2
Nueva Esparta (state) D1
Portuguesa (state) C2
Sucre (state) D1
Táchira (state) B2
Trujillo (state) B2
Yaracuy (state) C1
Zulia (state) B2

Cities and Towns
Acarigua C2
Anaco D2
Barcelona D1
Barinas B2
Barquisimeto C1
Baruta C1
Cabimas B1
Calabozo C2
Canaima D2
Caracas, capital C1
Carora C1
Carúpano D1
Ciudad Bolívar D2
Ciudad Guayana D2
Coro C1
Cumaná D1
El Tigre D2
Guanare C2
Güiria D1
La Asunción D1
La Guaira Maiquetía C1
Los Teques C1
Maiquetía C1
Maracaibo B1
Maracay C1
Maturín D2
Mérida B2
Petare C1
Puerto Ayacucho C2
Puerto Cabello C1
Puerto La Cruz D1
Punto Fijo B1
San Cristóbal B2
San Felipe C1
San Fernando de Apure C2
San Juan de Los Morros C2
Santa Elena de Uairén D3
Trujillo B2
Tucupita D2
Valencia C1
Valera B2

Other Features
Angel, falls D2
Apure, river C2
Arauca, river C2
Bolívar, mt. B2
Caroní, river D2
Casiquiare, river C3
Caura, river D2
Cojedes, river C2
Guri, reservoir D2
Guiana, highlands D2
La Tortuga, island C1
Llanos, plain B2
Maracaibo, lake B2
Margarita, island D1
Mérida, mts. B2
Meta, river C2
Neblina, mt. C3
Negro, river B3
Orinoco, river C3, D2
Pacaraima, mts. D3
Paria, gulf D1
Parima, mts. D3
Roraima, mt. D2
Venezuela, gulf B1

Venezuela
Capital: Caracas
Area: 352,144 sq. mi.
912,050 sq. km.
Population: 23,203,466
Largest City: Caracas
Language: Spanish
Monetary Unit: Bolívar

Ecuador

Capital: Quito
Area: 105,037 sq. mi.
272,117 sq. km.
Population: 12,562,496
Largest City: Guayaquil
Language: Spanish
Monetary Unit: Sucre

Ecuador:
Map Index

Provinces
Azuay	B4
Bolívar	B3
Cañar	B4
Carchi	C2
Chimborazo	B3
Cotopaxi	B3
El Oro	B4
Esmeraldas	B2
Galápagos	Inset
Guayas	A4
Imbabura	B2
Loja	B5
Los Ríos	B3
Manabí	A3
Morona-Santiago	C4
Napo	C3
Pastaza	C3
Pichincha	B2
Sucumbíos	C3
Tungurahua	B3
Zamora-Chinchipe	B5

Cities and Towns
Ambato	B3
Azogues	B4
Babahoyo	B3
Baquerizo Moreno	Inset
Chone	A3
Cuenca	B4

Esmeraldas	B2
Guaranda	B3
Guayaquil	B4
Ibarra	B2
Jipijapa	A3
La Libertad	A4
Latacunga	B3
Loja	B4
Macas	B4
Machala	B4
Manta	A3
Milagro	B4
Nueva Loja	C2
Nuevo Rocafuerte	D3
Otavalo	B2
Portoviejo	A3
Puerto Bolívar	B4
Quevedo	B3
Quito, *capital*	B3
Riobamba	B3
San Lorenzo	B2
Santa Rosa	B4
Santo Domingo de los Colorados	B3
Tena	C3
Tulcán	C2
Zamora	B5

Other Features
Aguarico, *river*	C3
Andes, *mts.*	B4
Cayambe, *mt.*	C3

Chimborazo, *mt.*	B3
Chira, *river*	A5
Cordillera Occidental, *mts.*	B4
Cordillera Oriental, *mts.*	C4
Cotopaxi, *mt.*	B3
Curaray, *river*	C3
Daule, *river*	B3
Española, *island*	Inset
Fernandina, *island*	Inset
Galera, *point*	A2
Guaillabamba, *river*	B2
Guayaquil, *gulf*	A4
Guayas, *river*	B4
Isabela, *island*	Inset
Manta, *bay*	A3
Marchena, *island*	Inset
Napo, *river*	C3
Pastaza, *river*	C3
Pinta, *island*	Inset
Plata, *island*	A4
Puná, *island*	A4
Putumayo, *river*	D2
San Cristóbal, *island*	Inset
San Lorenzo, *cape*	A3
San Salvador, *island*	Inset
Santa Cruz, *island*	Inset
Santa Elena, *point*	A4
Santa María, *island*	Inset
Santiago, *river*	B4
Tigre, *river*	C3
Vinces, *river*	B3
Wolf, *mt.*	Inset
Zamora, *river*	B4

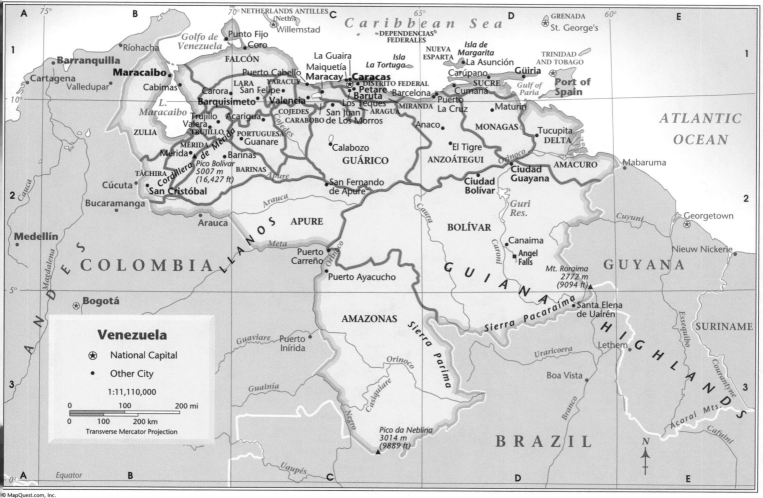

Guyana

⊛ National Capital
● Other City

1:10,660,000

0 ——— 75 ——— 150 mi
0 ——— 75 ——— 150 km
Transverse Mercator Projection

Guyana

Capital: Georgetown
Area: 83,000 sq. mi.
   214,969 sq. km.
Population: 705,156
Largest City: Georgetown
Language: English
Monetary Unit: Guyana dollar

Guyana:
Map Index

Cities and Towns

Anna Regina	B2
Apoteri	B4
Bartica	B2
Biloku	B5
Charity	B2
Georgetown, *capital*	B2
Isherton	B4
Lethem	B4
Linden	B3
Mabaruma	B1
Mahdia	B3
Matthews Ridge	A2
New Amsterdam	C2
Suddie	B2

Other Features

Acarai, *mts.*	B5
Barama, *river*	B2
Berbice, *river*	B3
Courantyne, *river*	B3
Cuyuni, *river*	A2
Demerara, *river*	B3
Essequibo, *river*	B3, B5
Kaieteur, *falls*	B3
Kanuku, *mts.*	B4
Mazaruni, *river*	A2
Merume, *mts.*	A2
New, *river*	C4
Pakaraima, *mts.*	A3
Potaro, *river*	B3
Rawa, *river*	B4
Roraima, *mt.*	A3
Takutu, *river*	B4

Suriname

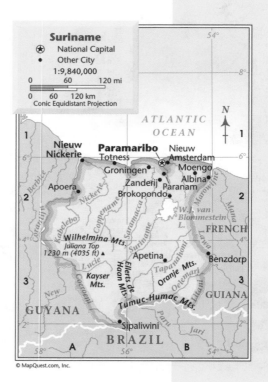

⊛ National Capital
● Other City

1:9,840,000

0 ——— 60 ——— 120 mi
0 ——— 60 ——— 120 km
Conic Equidistant Projection

Suriname

Capital: Paramaribo
Area: 63,037 sq. mi.
   163,265 sq. km.
Population: 431,156
Largest City: Paramaribo
Language: Dutch
Monetary Unit: Suriname guilder

Suriname:
Map Index

Cities and Towns

Albina	B2
Apetina	B3
Apoera	A2
Benzdorp	B3
Brokopondo	B2
Groningen	B2
Moengo	B2
Nieuw Amsterdam	B2
Nieuw Nickerie	A2
Paramaribo, *capital*	B2
Paranam	B2
Sipaliwini	A3
Totness	A2
Zanderij	B2

Other Features

Coeroeni, *river*	A3
Coppename, *river*	A2
Corantijn, *river*	A2
Ellerts de Haan, *mts.*	A3
Juliana Top, *mt.*	A3
Kabelebo, *river*	A2
Kayser, *mts.*	A3
Lawa, *river*	B2
Litani, *river*	B3
Lucie, *river*	A3
Marowijne, *river*	B2
Nickerie, *river*	A2
Oelemari, *river*	B3
Oranje, *mts.*	B3
Saramacca, *river*	B2
Suriname, *river*	B3
Tapanahoni, *river*	B3
Tumuc-Humac, *mts.*	B3
Wilhelmina, *mts.*	A2
W.J. van Blommestein, *lake*	B2

French Guiana:
Map Index

Cities and Towns

Apatou	A1
Cacao	B1
Camopi	B2
Cayenne, *capital*	B1
Grand Santi	A1
Iracoubo	B1
Kaw	B1
Kourou	B1
Mana	B1
Maripasoula	A2
Ouanary	C1
Régina	B1
Rémire	B1
Saint-Élie	B1
Saint-Georges	C2
Saint-Laurent du Maroni	A1
Saül	B2

Other Features

Camopi, *river*	B2
Devil's, *island*	B1
Lawa, *river*	A2
Litani, *river*	A2
Mana, *river*	B1
Maroni, *river*	A2
Oyapock, *river*	B2
Salut, *islands*	B1
Tampok, *river*	B2
Tumuc-Humac, *mts.*	A2

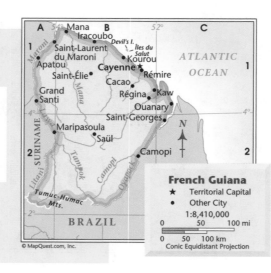

French Guiana

★ Territorial Capital
● Other City

1:8,410,000

0 ——— 50 ——— 100 mi
0 ——— 50 ——— 100 km
Conic Equidistant Projection

French Guiana

Capital: Cayenne
Area: 35,135 sq. mi.
   91,000 sq. km.
Population: 167,982
Largest City: Cayenne
Language: French
Monetary Unit: French franc

© MapQuest.com, Inc.

Brazil:
Map Index

States and Federal District

Acre A2
Alagoas E2
Amapá C1
Amazonas B2
Bahia D3
Ceará E2
Espírito Santo D3
Federal District D3
Goiás D3
Maranhão D2
Mato Grosso C3
Mato Grosso do Sul C4
Minas Gerais D3
Pará C2
Paraíba E2
Paraná C4
Pernambuco E2
Piauí D2
Rio de Janeiro ....D4, Inset I
Rio Grande do Norte E2
Rio Grande do Sul C4
Rondônia B3
Roraima B1
Santa Catarina C4
São Paulo ....C4, Inset II
Sergipe E3
Tocantins D3

Cities and Towns

Alagoinhas E3
Altamira C2
Anápolis D3
Aracaju E3
Bacabal D2
Bauru D4
Belém D2
Belford Roxo ....Inset I
Belo Horizonte D3
Boa Vista B1
Bom Jesus da Lapa D3
Brasília, capital D3

Cáceres C3
Cachimbo C2
Campina Grande E2
Campinas D4
Campo Grande C4
Campos D4
Campos Elísios ....Inset I
Carapicuíba ....Inset II
Corumbá C3
Cotia ....Inset II
Cruzeiro do Sul A2
Cubatão ....Inset II
Cuiabá C3
Curitiba D4
Diadema ....Inset II
Dourados C4
Duque de Caxias ....Inset I
Feira de Santana E3
Floriano D2
Florianópolis D4
Fortaleza E2
Foz do Iguaçu C4
Goiânia D3
Governador Valadares D3
Guajará Mirim B3
Guarujá ....Inset II
Guarulhos ....Inset II
Ilhéus E3
Imbariê ....Inset I
Imperatriz D2
Inhomirim ....Inset I
Ipiíba ....Inset I
Itabira D3
Itabuna E3
Itaipu ....Inset I
Itajaí D4
Itapecerica da Serra ....Inset II
Itapeva ....Inset II
Itaquaquecetuba ....Inset II
Jaboatão E2
Jacare-Acanga C2
Japeri ....Inset I
Jir Paraná B3
João Pessoa E2
Joinville D4

Juàzeiro D2
Juàzeiro do Norte E2
Juiz de Fora D4
Jundiaí D4
Lajes C4
Londrina C4
Macapá C1
Maceió E2
Majé ....Inset I
Manaus C2
Maraba D2
Mariana D3
Mauá ....Inset II
Mogi das Cruzes ....Inset II
Monjolo ....Inset I
Montes Claros D3
Mozzoro E2
Natal E2
Neves ....Inset I
Nilópolis ....Inset I
Niterói ....D4, Inset I
Nova Iguaçu ....Inset I
Olinda E2
Osasco ....Inset II
Palmas D3
Paranaguá D4
Parnaíba D2
Passo Fundo C4
Paulo Afonso E2
Pelotas C5
Petrólina D2
Petrópolis ....D4, Inset I
Piracicaba D4
Poá ....Inset II
Pôrto Alegre C5
Pôrto Velho B2
Queimados ....Inset I
Randonopolis C3
Recife E2
Ribeirão Pires ....Inset II
Ribeirão Prêto D4
Rio Branco B2
Rio de Janeiro ....D4, Inset I
Rio Grande C5
Rio Verde C3

Salvador E3
Santa Maria C4
Santana do Livramento C5
Santarém C2
Santo André ....Inset II
Santos ....D4, Inset II
São Bernardo do Campo ....Inset II
São Caetano do Sul ....Inset II
São Gonçalo ....Inset I
São João de Meriti ....Inset I
São José do Rio Prêto D4
São Luís D2
São Paulo ....D4, Inset II
São Vicente ....Inset II
Sobral D2
Sorocaba D4
Suzano ....Inset II
Taboão da Serra ....Inset II
Tefé B2
Teresina D2
Tubarão D4
Uberaba D3
Uberlândia D3
Vincente de Carvalho ....Inset II
Vitória D4
Vitória da Conquista D3
Volta Redonda D4

Other Features

Acaraí, range C1
Açúcar, mt. ....Inset I
Amazon, basin B2
Amazon, river B2
Araguaia, river C3
Aripuanã, river C2
Baleia, point E3
Bandeira, mt. D3
Billings, reservoir ....Inset II
Branco, river B1
Brazilian, highlands D3
Caviana, island D1
Chapada dos Parecis, range C3
Corcovado, mt. ....Inset I
Corumbau, point E3
Furnas, reservoir D4

Geral, range C4
Grande, river D3
Guandu, river ....Inset I
Guaporé, river B3
Guiana, highlands B1
Içá, river B2
Iguaçu, falls C4
Itaipu, reservoir C4
Japurá, river B2
Jari, river C1
Javari, river A2
Juruá, river B2
Juruena, river C3
Madeira, river B2
Mantiqueira, range D4
Mar, range D4
Marajó, island D2
Mato Grosso, plateau C3
Mexiana, island D1
Neblina, mt. B1
Negro, river B2
Orgãos, range ....Inset I
Pantanal, lowland C4
Pará, river C2
Paraguai, river C3
Paraná, river C4
Parima, range B1
Parnaíba, river D2
Patos, lagoon C5
Paulo Afonso, falls E2
Pedra Açu, mt. ....Inset I
Purus, river B2
Roncador, range C3
São Francisco, river D3
Selvas, region B2
Sobradinho, reservoir D3
Tapajós, river C2
Taquari, river C3
Teles Pires, river C2
Tietê, river ....Inset II
Tocantins, river D2
Tucuruí, reservoir D2
Tumucumaque, range C1
Uruguai, river C4
Xingu, river C3

Brazil

Capital: Brasília
Area: 3,286,470 sq. mi.
8,514,171 sq. km.
Population: 171,853,126
Largest City: São Paulo
Language: Portuguese
Monetary Unit: Real

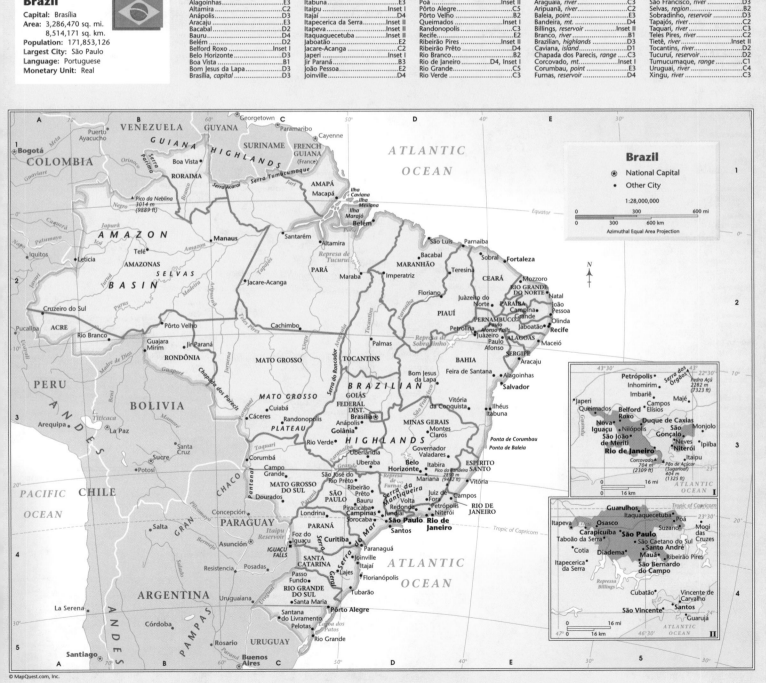

MAJOR CITIES

Antigua & Barbuda
St. Johns 27,000

Bahamas
Nassau 172,000

Barbados
Bridgetown 6,000

Belize
Belize City 45,000
Belmopan 4,000

Canada (metro)
Toronto 4,264,000
Montréal 3,327,000
Vancouver 1,832,000
Ottawa 1,010,000

Costa Rica
San José 324,000

Cuba
Havana 2,185,000

Dominica
Roseau 16,000

Dominican Republic
Santo Domingo 2,135,000

El Salvador (metro)
San Salvador 1,214,000

Grenada
St. George's 30,000

Guatemala (metro)
Guatemala 2,205,000

Haiti
Port-au-Prince 884,000

Honduras (metro)
Tegucigalpa 995,000

Jamaica (metro)
Kingston 587,000

Mexico
Mexico City 8,489,000
Guadalajara 1,633,000
Puebla 1,223,000

Nicaragua (metro)
Managua 1,124,000

Panama
Panamá 465,000

Puerto Rico
San Juan 428,000

St. Kitts & Nevis
Basseterre 15,000

St. Lucia
Castries 45,000

St. Vincent & Grenadines
Kingstown 15,000

Trinidad & Tobago
Port of Spain 43,000

United States (Census 2000)
New York 8,008,000
Los Angeles 3,695,000
Chicago 2,896,000
Houston 1,954,000
Philadelphia 1,518,000
Phoenix 1,321,000
San Diego 1,223,000
Washington, D.C. 572,000

International comparability of city population data is limited by various data inconsistencies.

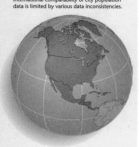

North America: Population, by nation (in millions)

UNITED STATES	MEXICO	CANADA	GUATEM.	CUBA	All other N. Am. countries
272.6	100.3	31.0	12.3	11.1	48.5

© MapQuest.com, Inc.

Gross National Product (GNP) per capita

- $36,410
- $21,500
- $8625
- $2785
- $695
- $0
- No data

Vegetation

- Ice Cap
- Tundra
- Coniferous Forest
- Deciduous Forest
- Broadleaf Evergreen Forest
- Mixed Forest
- Midlatitude Scrubland
- Midlatitude Grassland
- Desert
- Tropical Seasonal and Scrub
- Tropical Rain Forest

Population

Persons per sq mi	Persons per sq km
Over 520	Over 200
260–519	100–199
130–259	50–99
25–129	10–49
1–24	1–9
0	0

WORLD POPULATION

- Asia 60.7%*
- Europe 12.1%**
- Africa 13.0%
- South America 5.7%
- Oceania 0.5%
- North America 7.9%

*Excluding Russia   **Including Russia

CLIMATE

Average daily temperature °F range — High, Low
Average monthly precipitation Inches

ATLANTA, USA

FAIRBANKS, USA — Temp. Range -21 to -1

MEXICO CITY, Mexico

MINNEAPOLIS, USA

NUUK, Greenland

NEW YORK, USA

PHOENIX, USA

ST. JOHN'S, Canada

SAN FRANCISCO, USA

SAN JOSÉ, Costa Rica

SAN JUAN, Puerto Rico

VANCOUVER, Canada

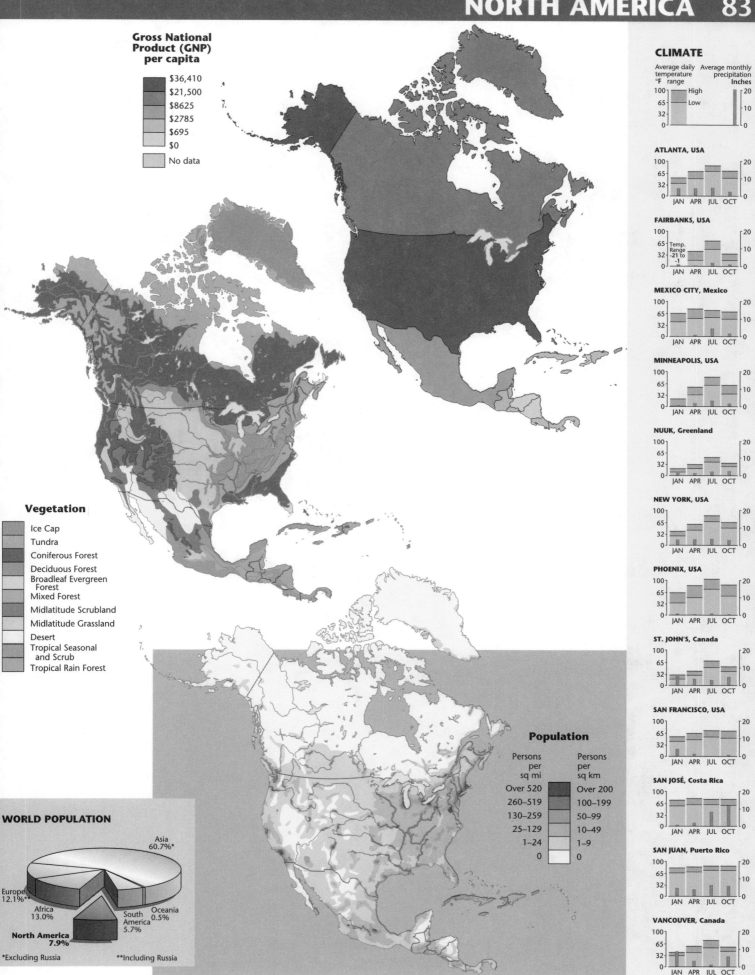

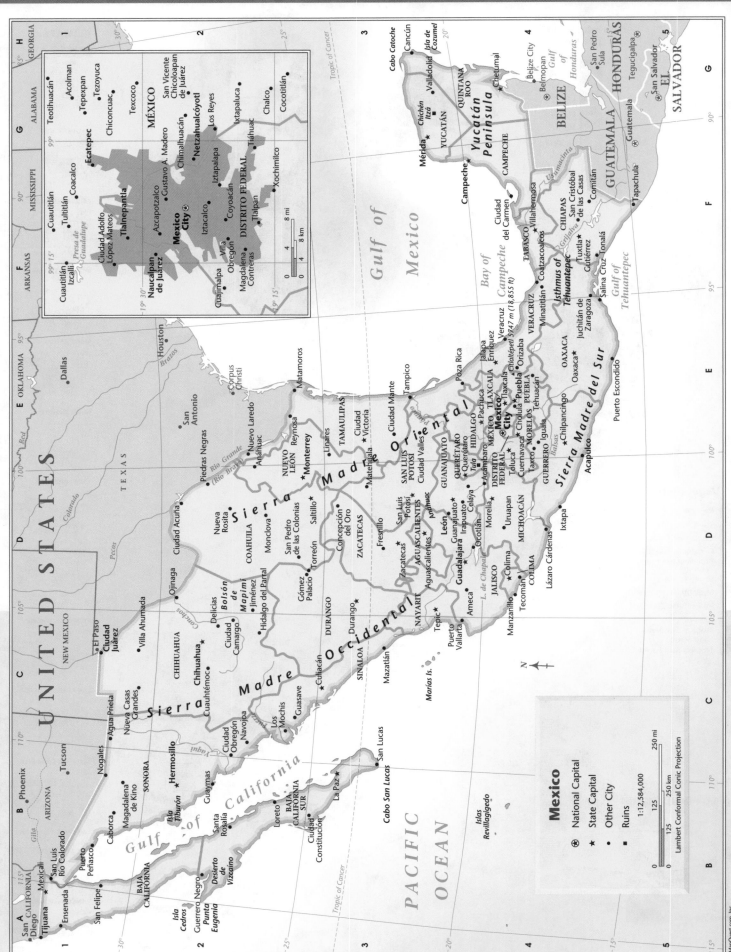

Mexico

⊛ National Capital
★ State Capital
• Other City
■ Ruins

1:12,584,000

0   125   250 mi
0   125   250 km

Lambert Conformal Conic Projection

© MapQuest.com, Inc.

Belize Map

Caribbean Sea

Corozal
Progresso
Orange Walk
Maskall   Ambergris Cay
Belize City
Hill Bank
Belmopan
Neustadt
San Ignacio
Dangriga
Turneffe Islands
Glover Reef
Placentia
▲ Victoria 1122 m (3681 ft)
Punta Gorda
San Antonio

MEXICO

Hondo R.
New R.
Belize R.
Sarstoon R.

Maya Mts.

GUATEMALA

Belize
* National Capital
* Other City

1:5,590,000
0   25   50 mi
0   25   50 km
Lambert Conformal Conic Projection

© MapQuest.com, Inc.

Belize

Capital: Belmopan
Area: 8,867 sq. mi.
22,972 sq. km.
Population: 235,789
Language: English
Monetary Unit: Belize dollar

Belize:
Map Index

Cities and Towns
Belize City	B2
Belmopan, *capital*	B2
Corozal	B1
Dangriga	B2
Hill Bank	B2
Maskall	B2
Neustadt	A2
Orange Walk	B1
Placentia	B3
Progresso	B1
Punta Gorda	B3
San Antonio	A3
San Ignacio	A2

Other Features
Ambergris Cay, *island*	C2
Belize, *river*	B2
Glover, *reef*	C3
Hondo, *river*	B1
Maya, *mts.*	A3
New, *river*	B1
Sarstoon, *river*	C2
Turneffe, *islands*	B3

Guatemala Map

MEXICO

BELIZE

Belize City
Belmopan

Gulf of Honduras

Paxbán
L. Tikal
Petén Itzá
Tikal
Flores
La Libertad
San Luis
Chinajá
Santo Tomás de Castilla
Cobán
Puerto Barrios
San Pedro Sula
L. de Izabal
Zacapa
Santa Rosa de Copán
HONDURAS
Huehuetenango
Quetzaltenango
Salamá
Santa Ana
San Salvador
Guatemala City
Antigua
Jutiapa
EL SALVADOR
Tajumulco
Mazatenango
Champerico
Escuintla
Comitán

Tacaná 4093 m (13,428 ft)
4220 m (13,845 ft)

Sierra Madre
L. de Atitlán
Sierra de los Cuchumatanes

San José

PACIFIC OCEAN

San Pedro R.
Usumacinta R.
Chixoy R.
Pasión R.
Sarstún R.
Motagua R.

Guatemala
* National Capital
* Other City

1:8,150,000
0   50   100 mi
0   50   100 km
Lambert Conformal Conic Projection

© MapQuest.com, Inc.

Guatemala

Capital: Guatemala City
Area: 42,042 sq. mi.
108,917 sq. km.
Population: 12,335,580
Largest City: Guatemala City
Language: Spanish
Monetary Unit: Quetzal

Guatemala:
Map Index

Cities and Towns
Antigua	B5
Champerico	B5
Chinajá	C4
Cobán	C4
Escuintla	B5
Flores	D3
Guatemala City, *capital*	B4
Huehuetenango	B5
Jutiapa	C5
La Libertad	D5
Mazatenango	B5
Paxbán	C3
Puerto Barrios	C4
Quetzaltenango	B5
Salamá	C4
San José	C6
San Luis	D3
Santo Tomás de Castilla	C4
Tikal	D2
Zacapa	C5

Other Features
Atitlán, *lake*	B5
Chixoy, *river*	C4
Honduras, *gulf*	E3
Izabal, *lake*	C4
Motagua, *river*	D4
Pasión, *river*	C3
Paz, *river*	C6
Petén-Itzá, *lake*	D3
San Pedro, *river*	C2
Sarstún, *river*	D4
Sierra Madre, *mts.*	A5
Suchiate, *river*	A4
Tacaná, *volcano*	B4
Tajumulco, *volcano*	B4
Usumacinta, *river*	C3

Mexico

Mexico

Capital: Mexico City
Area: 756,066 sq. mi.
1,958,720 sq. km.
Population: 100,294,036
Largest City: Mexico City
Language: Spanish
Monetary Unit: New peso

Mexico:
Map Index

States
Aguascalientes	D3
Baja California	A1
Baja California Sur	B2
Campeche	F4
Chiapas	F4
Chihuahua	C2
Coahuila	D2
Colima	D4
Distrito Federal	E4, Inset
Durango	D3
Guanajuato	D3
Guerrero	D4
Hidalgo	E3
Jalisco	D3
México	E4, Inset
Michoacán	D4
Morelos	Inset
Nayarit	C3
Nuevo León	D2
Oaxaca	E4
Puebla	E4
Querétaro	D3
Quintana Roo	G4
San Luis Potosí	D3
Sinaloa	C3
Sonora	B1
Tabasco	F4
Tamaulipas	E3
Tlaxcala	E4
Veracruz	E4
Yucatán	G3
Zacatecas	D3

Cities and Towns
Acámbaro	D4
Acapulco	E4
Acolman	Inset
Agua Prieta	C1
Aguascalientes, *state capital*	D3
Ameca	D3
Anáhuac	D2
Atzcapotzalco	Inset
Caborca	B1
Campeche, *state capital*	F4
Cancún	G3
Celaya	D3
Chalco	Inset
Chetumal, *state capital*	G4
Chiconcuac	Inset
Chihuahua, *state capital*	C2
Chilpancingo, *state capital*	E4
Chimalhuacán	Inset
Cholula	E4
Ciudad Acuña	D2
Ciudad Adolfo López Mateos	Inset
Ciudad Camargo	C2
Ciudad Constitución	B3
Ciudad del Carmen	F4
Ciudad Juárez	C1
Ciudad Mante	E3
Ciudad Obregón	C2
Ciudad Valles	E3
Ciudad Victoria, *state capital*	E3
Coacalco	Inset
Coatzacoalcos	F4
Cocotitlán	Inset
Colima, *state capital*	D4
Comitán	F4
Concepción del Oro	D3
Coyoacán	Inset
Cuajimalpa	Inset
Cuauhtémoc	C2
Cuautitlán	Inset
Cuautitlán Izcalli	Inset
Cuernavaca, *state capital*	E4
Culiacán, *state capital*	C3
Delicias	C2
Durango, *state capital*	D3
Ecatepec	Inset
Ensenada	A1
Fresnillo	D3
Gómez Palacio	D2
Guadalajara, *state capital*	D3
Guanajuato, *state capital*	D3
Guasave	C3
Guerrero Negro	B2
Gustavo A. Madero	Inset
Guaymas	B2
Hermosillo, *state capital*	B2
Hidalgo del Parral	C2
Iguala	D4
Irapuato	D3
Ixtapaluca	Inset
Ixtapalapa	Inset
Ixtapaluca	Inset
Jalapa Enríquez, *state capital*	E4
Jiménez	D2
Juchitán de Zaragoza	F4
La Paz, *state capital*	B3
Lázaro Cárdenas	D4
León	D3
Linares	E3
Loreto	B2
Los Mochis	C2
Los Reyes	Inset
Magdalena de Kino	B1
Magdalena Contreras	Inset
Manzanillo	D4
Matamoros	E2
Matehuala	D3
Mazatlán	C3
Mérida, *state capital*	G3
Mexicali, *state capital*	A1
Mexico City, *national capital*	E4, Inset
Minatitlán	F4
Monclova	D2
Monterrey, *state capital*	D2
Morelia, *state capital*	D4
Naucalpan de Juárez	Inset
Navojoa	C2
Netzahualcóyotl	Inset
Nogales	B1
Nueva Casas Grandes	C1
Nueva Rosita	D2
Nuevo Laredo	E2
Oaxaca, *state capital*	E4
Ocotlán	D3
Ojinaga	D2
Orizaba	E4
Pachuca, *state capital*	E3
Piedras Negras	D2
Puebla, *state capital*	E4
Puerto Escondido	E4
Puerto Peñasco	B1
Puerto Vallarta	C3
Querétaro, *state capital*	D3
Reynosa	E2
Salina Cruz	E4
Saltillo, *state capital*	D3
San Cristóbal de las Casas	F4
San Felipe	B1
San Lucas	C3
San Luis Potosí, *state capital*	D3
San Luis Río Colorado	B1
San Pedro de las Colonias	D2
Santa Rosalía	B2
San Vicente Chicoloapan	Inset
Tampico	E3
Tapachula	F5
Taxco	E4
Tecomán	D4
Tehuacán	E4
Teotihuacán	Inset
Tepexpan	Inset
Tepic, *state capital*	D3
Texcoco	Inset
Tijuana	A1
Tlalpan	Inset
Tlalnepantla	Inset
Tlaxcala, *state capital*	E4
Toluca, *state capital*	E4
Tonalá	F4
Torreón	D2
Tultitlán	Inset
Tuxtla Gutiérrez, *state capital*	F4
Uruapan	D4
Valladolid	G3
Veracruz	E4
Villa Ahumada	C1
Villahermosa, *state capital*	F4
Villa Obregón	Inset
Xochimilco	Inset
Zacatecas, *state capital*	D3

Other Features
Anáhuac, *depression*	D3
Balsas, *river*	E4
Bolsón de Mapimí, *depression*	D2
California, *gulf*	B1
Campeche, *bay*	F4
Catoche, *cape*	G3
Cedros, *island*	A2
Chapala, *lake*	D3
Chichén Itzá, *ruins*	G3
Citlaltépetl, *mt.*	E4
Conchos, *river*	C2
Cozumel, *island*	G3
Eugenia, *point*	A2
Fuerte, *river*	C2
Grijalva, *river*	F4
Guadalupe, *reservoir*	Inset
Marías, *islands*	C3
Pánuco, *river*	E3
Revillagigedo, *islands*	B4
Río Grande (Río Bravo), *river*	D2
San Lucas, *cape*	B3
Sierra Madre del Sur, *mts.*	D4
Sierra Madre Occidental, *mts.*	C2
Sierra Madre Oriental, *mts.*	D3
Tehuantepec, *gulf*	E4
Tehuantepec, *isthmus*	F4
Tiburón, *island*	B2
Tula, *ruins*	D3
Usumacinta, *river*	F4
Vizcaíno, *desert*	B2
Yaqui, *river*	C2
Yucatán, *peninsula*	G4

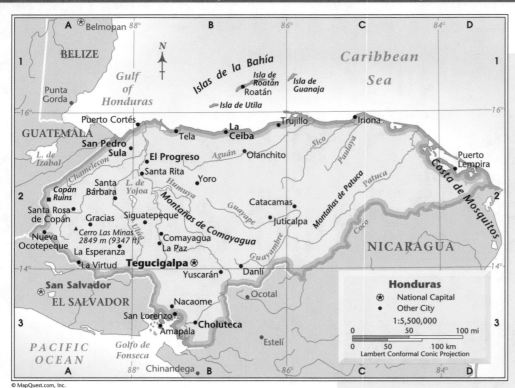

BELIZE
Belmopan
Punta Gorda
Gulf of Honduras
GUATEMALA
L. de Izabal

Islas de la Bahía
Isla de Roatán
Roatán
Isla de Guanaja
Isla de Utila
Caribbean Sea

Puerto Cortés
Tela
La Ceiba
Trujillo
Iriona
San Pedro Sula
El Progreso
Olanchito
Santa Rita
Yoro
Santa Bárbara
L. de Yojoa
Catacamas
Puerto Lempira
Copán Ruins
Gracias
Siguatepeque
Juticalpa
Montañas de Patuca
Santa Rosa de Copán
Cerro Las Minas 2849 m (9347 ft)
Comayagua
La Paz
Nueva Ocotepeque
La Esperanza
Costa de Mosquitos
La Virtud
Tegucigalpa
Yuscarán
Danlí
NICARAGUA
San Salvador
Nacaome
Ocotal
EL SALVADOR
San Lorenzo
Choluteca
Amapala
Estelí
PACIFIC OCEAN
Golfo de Fonseca
Chinandega

Aguán
Sico
Paulaya
Patuca
Humuya
Guayape
Guayambe
Coco
Chamelecon
Ulúa
Montañas de Comayagua

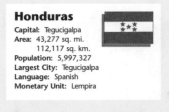

Honduras
Capital: Tegucigalpa
Area: 43,277 sq. mi.
    112,117 sq. km.
Population: 5,997,327
Largest City: Tegucigalpa
Language: Spanish
Monetary Unit: Lempira

Honduras
National Capital
Other City
1:5,500,000

0   50   100 mi
0   50   100 km
Lambert Conformal Conic Projection

Honduras: Map Index

Cities and Towns
Amapala B3
Catacamas C2
Choluteca B3
Comayagua B2
Danlí B2
El Progreso B2
Gracias A2
Iriona C2
Juticalpa B2
La Ceiba B2
La Esperanza A2
La Paz B2
La Virtud A2
Nacaome B3
Nueva Ocotepeque A2
Olanchito B2
Puerto Cortés B2
Puerto Lempira D2
Roatán B1
San Lorenzo B3
San Pedro Sula A2
Santa Bárbara A2
Santa Rita B2
Santa Rosa de Copán A2
Siguatepeque B2
Tegucigalpa, capital B2

Tela B2
Trujillo B2
Yoro B2
Yuscarán B3

Other Features
Aguán, river B2
Bahía, islands B1
Caribbean, sea C1
Chamelecon, river A2
Coco, river C2
Comayagua, mts. B2
Copán, ruins A2
Fonseca, gulf B3
Guanaja, island C1
Guayambre, river B2
Guayape, river B2
Honduras, gulf A1
Humuya, river B2
Las Minas, mt. A2
Mosquitos, coast D2
Patuca, mts. C2
Patuca, river C2
Paulaya, river C2
Roatán, island B1
Sico, river C2
Ulúa, river B2
Utila, island B1
Yojoa, lake B2

© MapQuest.com, Inc.

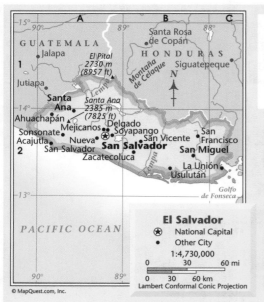

GUATEMALA
Jalapa
Santa Rosa de Copán
HONDURAS
El Pital 2730 m (8957 ft)
Montaña de Celaque
Siguatepeque
Jutiapa
Santa Ana 2385 m (7825 ft)
Santa Ana
Ahuachapán
Sonsonate
Mejicanos
Delgado
Soyapango
San Vicente
San Francisco
Acajutla
Nueva
San Salvador
San Miguel
Zacatecoluca
La Unión
Usulután
Golfo de Fonseca
Lempa
PACIFIC OCEAN

El Salvador
Capital: San Salvador
Area: 8,124 sq. mi.
    21,047 sq. km.
Population: 5,839,079
Largest City: San Salvador
Language: Spanish
Monetary Unit: Colón

El Salvador: Map Index

Cities and Towns
Acajutla A2
Ahuachapán A2
Delgado A2
La Unión C2
Mejicanos A2
Nueva San Salvador A2
San Francisco B2
San Miguel B2
San Salvador, capital A2
Santa Ana A2
San Vicente B2
Sonsonate A2
Soyapango A2
Usulután B2
Zacatecoluca B2

Other Features
El Pital, mt. A1
Fonseca, gulf B2
Lempa, river A1, B2
Santa Ana, volcano A2

El Salvador
National Capital
Other City
1:4,730,000

0   30   60 mi
0   30   60 km
Lambert Conformal Conic Projection

© MapQuest.com, Inc.

Costa Rica: Map Index

Cities and Towns
Alajuela B2
Cartago C3
Colorado C2
Golfito C4
Heredia B2
La Cruz A1
Liberia A2
Limón C3
Los Chiles B1
Puerto Jiménez C4
Puerto Quepos B3
Puntarenas B3
San José, capital B3
Santa Cruz A2

Other Features
Arenal, lake B2
Central, range B2
Chirripó, mt. C3
Chirripó, river C2
Coronado, bay B3
Dulce, gulf C4
Frío, river B2
General, river C3

Grande, river B3
Guanacaste, range A2
Irazú, volcano C3
Nicoya, gulf B3
Papagayo, gulf A2
Pirris, river B3
Reventazón, river C3
San Carlos, river B2
San Juan, river B2
Sarapiquí, river B2
Sixaola, river C3
Talamanca, range C3
Tempisque, river A2

Costa Rica
Capital: San José
Area: 19,730 sq. mi.
    51,114 sq. km.
Population: 3,674,490
Largest City: San José
Language: Spanish
Monetary Unit: Colón

L. de Nicaragua
NICARAGUA
La Cruz
Los Chiles
San Juan
Cordillera de Guanacaste
Colorado
Frío
San Carlos
Sarapiquí
Caribbean Sea
Golfo de Papagayo
Liberia
L. de Arenal
Chirripó
Santa Cruz
Tempisque
Cordillera Central
Irazú 3432 m (11,260 ft)
Limón
Puntarenas
Alajuela
Heredia
San José
Cartago
Reventazón
Sixaola
Grande
Pirris
Golfo de Nicoya
Puerto Quepos
Chirripó 3819 m (12,530 ft)
Cordillera de Talamanca
General
Bahía de Coronado
PANAMA
Golfito
Puerto Jiménez
PACIFIC OCEAN
Golfo Dulce

Costa Rica
National Capital
Other City
1:4,400,000

0   30   60 mi
0   30   60 km
Lambert Conformal Conic Projection

© MapQuest.com, Inc.

Nicaragua

Capital: Managua
Area: 50,880 sq. mi.
133,813 sq. km.
Population: 4,717,132
Largest City: Managua
Language: Spanish
Monetary Unit: Córdoba

Nicaragua: Map Index

Cities and Towns

Bluefields	C3
Boaco	B2
Bocay	B1
Chinandega	A2
Colonia Nueva Guinea	B3
Corinto	A2
Diriamba	A3
Estelí	A2
Granada	B3
Jinotega	B2
Jinotepe	A3
Juigalpa	B2
La Rosita	B2
León	A2
Managua, *capital*	A2
Masaya	A3
Matagalpa	B2
Nagarote	A2
Ocotal	A2
Prinzapolka	C2
Puerto Cabezas	C1
Puerto Sandino	A2
Rama	B2
Río Blanco	B2
Río Grande	A2
Rivas	B3
San Carlos	B3
San Juan del Norte	C3
San Juan del Sur	B2
Siuna	B2
Somoto	A2
Waspam	C1
Wiwili	B2

Other Features

Bambana, *river*	B2
Bismuna, *lagoon*	C1
Bluefields, *bay*	C3
Bocay, *river*	B2
Chontaleña, *mts.*	B2
Coco, *river*	A2, C1
Cosigüina, *mt.*	A2
Cosigüina, *point*	A2
Dariense, *mts.*	B2
Escondido, *river*	B2
Fonseca, *gulf*	A2
Gracias a Dios, *cape*	C1
Grande de Matagalpa, *river*	B2
Huapí, *mts.*	B2
Isabelia, *mts.*	B2
Kurinwás, *river*	B2
Maíz, *islands*	C2
Managua, *lake*	A2
Mico, *river*	B2
Miskitos, *cays*	C1
Mogotón, *mt.*	A2
Mosquitos, *coast*	C3
Nicaragua, *lake*	B3
Ometepe, *island*	B3
Perlas, *lagoon*	C2
Perlas, *point*	C2
Prinzapolka, *river*	B2
San Juan, *river*	B3
San Juan del Norte, *bay*	C3
Siquia, *river*	B2
Solentiname, *island*	B3
Tipitapa, *river*	A2
Tuma, *river*	B2
Wawa, *river*	B1
Zapatera, *island*	B3

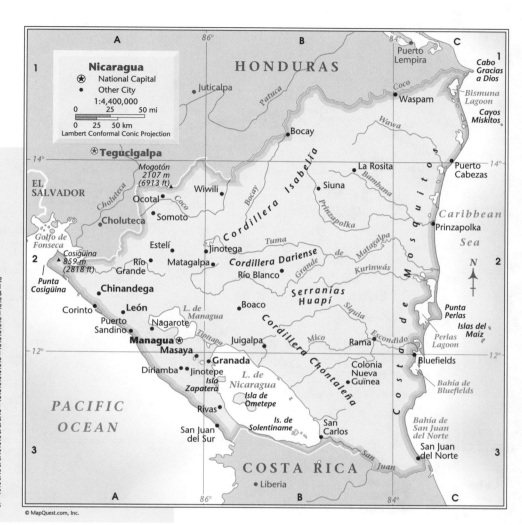

© MapQuest.com, Inc.

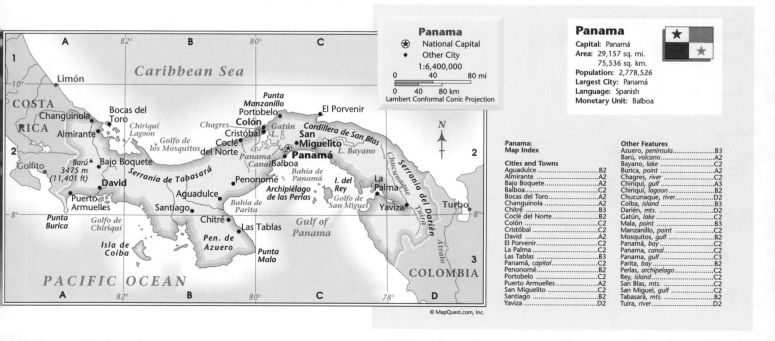

Panama

Capital: Panamá
Area: 29,157 sq. mi.
75,536 sq. km.
Population: 2,778,526
Largest City: Panamá
Language: Spanish
Monetary Unit: Balboa

Panama: Map Index

Cities and Towns

Aguadulce	B2
Almirante	A2
Bajo Boquete	A2
Balboa	C2
Bocas del Toro	A2
Changuinola	A2
Chitré	B3
Coclé del Norte	B2
Colón	C2
Cristóbal	C2
David	A2
El Porvenir	C2
La Palma	C2
Las Tablas	B3
Panamá, *capital*	C2
Penonomé	B2
Portobelo	C2
Puerto Armuelles	A2
San Miguelito	C2
Santiago	B2
Yaviza	D2

Other Features

Azuero, *peninsula*	B3
Barú, *volcano*	A2
Bayano, *lake*	C2
Burica, *point*	A2
Chagres, *river*	C2
Chiriquí, *gulf*	A3
Chiriquí, *lagoon*	B2
Chucunaque, *river*	D2
Coiba, *island*	B3
Darién, *mts.*	D2
Gatún, *lake*	C2
Mala, *point*	B3
Manzanillo, *point*	C2
Mosquitos, *gulf*	B2
Panamá, *bay*	C2
Panama, *canal*	C2
Panama, *gulf*	C3
Parita, *bay*	B2
Perlas, *archipelago*	C2
Rey, *island*	C2
San Blas, *mts.*	C2
San Miguel, *gulf*	C2
Tabasará, *mts.*	B2
Tuira, *river*	D2

© MapQuest.com, Inc.

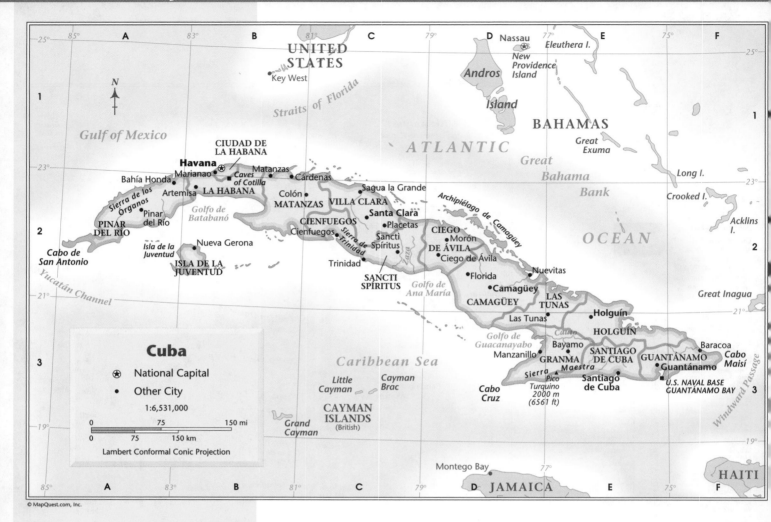

Cuba

⊛ National Capital

• Other City

1:6,531,000

| 0 | 75 | 150 mi |
| 0 | 75 | 150 km |

Lambert Conformal Conic Projection

© MapQuest.com, Inc.

Cuba

Capital: Havana
Area: 42,804 sq. mi.
110,890 sq. km.
Population: 11,096,395
Largest City: Havana
Language: Spanish
Monetary Unit: Peso

Cuba:
Map Index

Provinces

Camagüey	D2
Ciego de Ávila	D2
Cienfuegos	C2
Ciudad de La Habana	B1
Granma	E3
Guantánamo	E3
Holguín	E3
Isla de la Juventud	
(special municipality)	B2
La Habana	B2
Las Tunas	E2
Matanzas	B2
Pinar del Río	A2
Sancti Spíritus	C2
Santiago de Cuba	E3
Villa Clara	C2

Cities and Towns

Artemisa	B2
Bahía Honda	A2
Baracoa	F3
Bayamo	E3
Camagüey	D2
Cárdenas	B1
Ciego de Ávila	D2
Cienfuegos	C2
Colón	C2
Florida	D2
Guantánamo	E3
Havana, capital	B1
Holguín	E3
Las Tunas	E3

Manzanillo	D3
Marianao	B1
Matanzas	B1
Morón	D2
Nueva Gerona	B2
Nuevitas	D2
Pinar del Río	A2
Placetas	C2
Sagua la Grande	C2
Sancti Spíritus	C2
Santa Clara	C2
Santiago de Cuba	E3
Trinidad	C2

Other Features

Ana María, gulf	D2
Batabanó, gulf	B2
Camagüey, archipelago	D2
Cauto, river	E3
Cotilla, caves	B2
Cruz, cape	D3
Florida, straits	B1
Guacanayabo, gulf	D3
Juventud, island	B2
Maestra, mts.	D3
Maisí, cape	F3
Mexico, gulf	A1
Organos, mts.	A2
San Antonio, cape	A2
Trinidad, mts.	C2
Turquino, mt.	E3
U.S. Naval Base	
Guantánamo Bay	E3
Windward, passage	F3
Yucatán, channel	A2
Zaza, river	C2

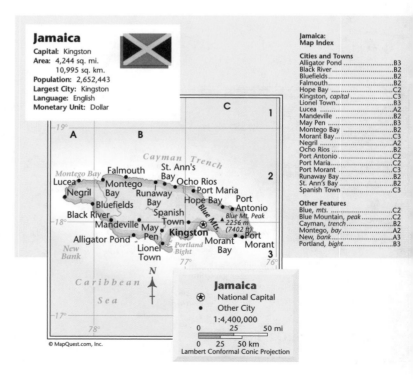

Jamaica

Capital: Kingston
Area: 4,244 sq. mi.
10,995 sq. km.
Population: 2,652,443
Largest City: Kingston
Language: English
Monetary Unit: Dollar

Jamaica
⊛ National Capital

• Other City

1:4,400,000

| 0 | 25 | 50 mi |
| 0 | 25 | 50 km |

Lambert Conformal Conic Projection

© MapQuest.com, Inc.

Jamaica:
Map Index

Cities and Towns

Alligator Pond	B3
Black River	B3
Bluefields	B2
Falmouth	B2
Hope Bay	C2
Kingston, capital	C3
Lionel Town	B3
Lucea	A2
Mandeville	B2
May Pen	B3
Montego Bay	B2
Morant Bay	C3
Negril	A2
Ocho Rios	B2
Port Antonio	C2
Port Maria	C2
Port Morant	C3
Runaway Bay	B2
St. Ann's Bay	B2
Spanish Town	C3

Other Features

Blue, mts.	C2
Blue Mountain, peak	C2
Cayman, trench	A2
Montego, bay	A2
New, bank	A3
Portland, bight	B3

Bonao	B2
Cabrera	C1
Comendador	A2
Cotuí	B1
Dajabón	A1
El Macao	D2
El Seibo	C2
Hato Mayor	C2
Higüey	D2
Jimaní	A2
La Romana	D2
La Vega	B1
Luperón	B1
Mao	A1
Miches	C2
Moca	B1
Monte Cristi	A1
Monte Plata	C2
Nagua	C1
Neiba	A2
Oviedo	A3
Pedernales	A2
Pedro Santana	A2
Puerto Plata	B1
Sabana de la Mar	C1
Sabaneta	A1
Salcedo	B1
Samaná	C1
San Cristóbal	B2
San Francisco de Macorís	B1
San José de las Matas	A1
San Juan	A2
San Pedro de Macorís	C2
Santiago	B1
Santo Domingo, capital	C2
Sousúa	B1

Other Features

Bahoruco, mts.	A2
Beata, cape	A3
Beata, island	A3
Calderas, bay	B2
Camú, river	B1
Central, range	B2
Cibao, valley	A1
Duarte, mt.	B1
Engaño, cape	D2
Enriquillo, lake	A2
Mona, passage	D2
Neiba, mts.	A2
Ocoa, bay	B2
Oriental, range	C2
Ozama, river	B2
Samaná, bay	C1
Samaná, cape	C1
Saona, island	D2
Septentrional, range	A1
Soco, river	C2
Yaque del Norte, river	A1
Yaque del Sur, river	A2
Yuna, river	B2

Dominican Republic: Map Index

Provinces

Azua	B2
Bahoruco	A2
Barahona	A2
Dajabón	A1
Distrito Nacional	B2
Duarte	C1
El Seibo	C2
Espaillat	B1
Hato Mayor	C2
Independencia	A2
La Altagracia	D2
La Estrelleta	A1
La Romana	D2
La Vega	B2
María Trinidad Sánchez	B1
Monseñor Nouel	B2
Monte Cristi	A1
Monte Plata	C2
Pedernales	A3
Peravia	B2
Puerto Plata	B1
Salcedo	B1
Samaná	C1
Sánchez Ramírez	B1
San Cristóbal	B2
San Juan	A2
San Pedro de Macorís	C2
Santiago	B1
Santiago Rodríguez	A1
Valverde	B1

Cities and Towns

Azua	B2
Baní	B2
Barahona	A2

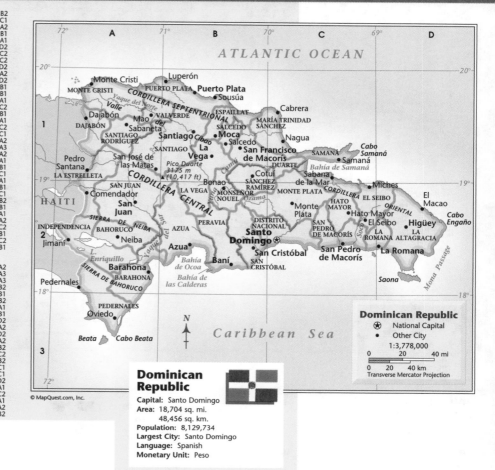

Dominican Republic
Capital: Santo Domingo
Area: 18,704 sq. mi.
48,456 sq. km.
Population: 8,129,734
Largest City: Santo Domingo
Language: Spanish
Monetary Unit: Peso

Dominican Republic
⊛ National Capital
● Other City
1:3,778,000
0   20   40 mi
0   20   40 km
Transverse Mercator Projection

Haiti
⊛ National Capital
● Other City
1:5,593,000
0   30   60 mi
0   30   60 km
Lambert Conformal Conic Projection

© MapQuest.com, Inc.

Haiti: Map Index

Departments

Artibonite	C1
Centre	D1
Grand Ande	B2
Nord	C1
Nord-Est	D1
Nord-Ouest	B1
Ouest	B2
Sud	B2
Sud-Est	C2

Cities and Towns

Anse-à-Galets	C2
Belle-Anse	C2
Cap-Haïtien	C1
Dame-Marie	A2
Ennery	C1
Gonaïves	C1
Hinche	C1
Jacmel	C2
Jérémie	A2
Léogâne	C2
Les Cayes	B2
Miragoâne	B2
Mirebalais	C1
Port-au-Prince, capital	C1
Port-de-Paix	B1
Port-Salut	B2
Saint-Marc	C1

Other Features

Artibonite, river	C1
Gonâve, gulf	B1
Gonâve, island	B2
Gravois, point	B3
Pic de la Selle, mt.	D2
Port-au-Prince, bay	C2
Tortuga, island	C1
Vache, island	B2
Windward, passage	B1

Haiti
Capital: Port-au-Prince
Area: 10,695 sq. mi.
27,614 sq. km.
Population: 6,884,264
Largest City: Port-au-Prince
Languages: French, Creole
Monetary Unit: Gourde

The Bahamas
Capital: Nassau
Area: 5,382 sq. mi.
13,943 sq. km.
Population: 283,705
Largest City: Nassau
Languages: English, Creole
Monetary Unit: Dollar

Turks and Caicos Is.
Capital: Grand Turk
Area: 193 sq. mi.
500 sq. km.
Population: 16,863
Largest City: Grand Turk
Language: English
Monetary Unit: U.S. Dollar

Bahamas and Turks & Caicos Islands: Map Index

Bahamas

Cities and Towns

Alice Town	B2
Arthur's Town	B3
Freeport	A2
Kemps Bay	B3
Marsh Harbour	B2
Matthew Town	C4
Nassau, capital	B2
Nicholls' Town	A2
Sandy Point	B2

Other Features

Acklins, island	C4
Andros, island	A3
Cat, island	B3
Crooked, island	C4
Crooked Island, passage	C4
Eleuthera, island	B2
Exuma, sound	B3
Grand Bahama, island	A2
Great Abaco, island	B2
Great Bahama, bank	A3
Great Exuma, island	B3
Great Inagua, island	C4
Harbour, island	B2
Little Inagua, island	C4
Long, island	C3
Mayaguana, island	C4
Mayaguana, passage	C4
New Providence, island	B3
Northeast Providence, channel	B2
Rum, cay	C3
Samana, cay	C3
San Salvador, island	C3
Water, cays	A3

Turks and Caicos Islands

Cities and Towns

Cockburn Harbour	D4
Grand Turk, capital	D4

Other Features

Ambergris, cay	D4
Caicos, islands	D4
Grand Turk, island	D4
Providenciales, island	C4
Salt, cay	D4
Turks, islands	D4

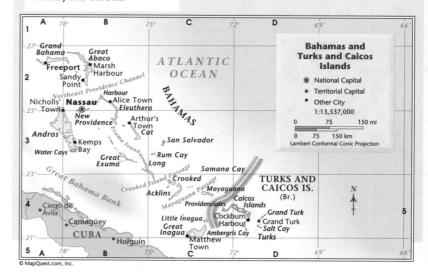

Bahamas and Turks and Caicos Islands
⊛ National Capital
★ Territorial Capital
● Other City
1:13,537,000
0   75   150 mi
0   75   150 km
Lambert Conformal Conic Projection

© MapQuest.com, Inc.

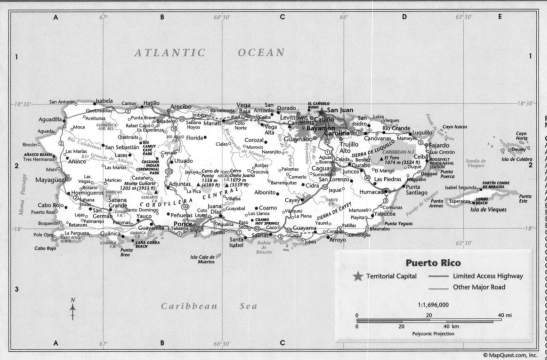

Puerto Rico

Capital: San Juan
Area: 3,492 sq. mi.
9,047 sq. km.
Population: 3,887,652
Largest City: San Juan
Languages: Spanish, English
Monetary Unit: U.S. dollar

Puerto Rico

Territorial Capital · — Limited Access Highway
· — Other Major Road

1:1,696,000

0   20   40 mi
0   20   40 km
Polyconic Projection

© MapQuest.com, Inc.

Puerto Rico: Map Index

Cities and Towns

Adjuntas	B2
Aguada	A2
Aguadilla	A2
Aguas Buenas	B2
Aguilita	B2
Aibonito	B2
Añasco	A2
Arecibo	B2
Arroyo	C3
Bajadero	B2
Barceloneta	B2
Barranquitas	C2
Bayamón	B2
Cabo Rojo	A2
Caguas	C2
Camuy	B2
Candelaria	C2
Canóvanas	D2
Carolina	C2
Cataño	C2
Cayey	C2
Ceiba	C2
Ceiba	D2
Celada	D2
Ciales	C2
Cidra	C2
Coamo	C2
Coco	C2
Comerío	C2
Coquí	C3
Corazón	C2
Corozal	C2
Coto Laurel	B2
Dorado	C2
Fajardo	D2
Florida	B2
Guánica	B3
Guayama	C2
Guayanilla	B2
Guaynabo	C2
Gurabo	D2
Hatillo	B2
Hormigueros	A2
Humacao	D2
Imbéry	B2
Isabela	A1
Jayuya	B2
Jobos	C3
Juana Díaz	C2
Juncos	D2
Lajas	A2
Lares	B2
Las Piedras	D2
Levittown	C2
Loíza	D2
Luquillo	D2
Manatí	B2
Martorell	D2
Maunabo	D2
Mayagüez	A2
Moca	A2
Naguabo	D2
Pastillo	C2
Patillas	C2
Peñuelas	B2
Ponce	B2
Puerto Real	A2
Punta Santiago	D2

Quebradillas	B2
Río Grande	D2
Sabana Grande	B2
Salinas	C3
San Antonio	A2
San Germán	A2
San Isidro	D2
San Juan, capital	C2
San Lorenzo	D2
San Sebastián	B2
Santa Isabel	C3
Santo Domingo	B2
Trujillo Alto	C2
Utuado	B2
Vega Alta	C2
Vega Baja	C2
Vieques	D2
Villalba	C2
Yabucoa	D2
Yauco	B2

Other Features

Añasco, beach	A2
Arenas, point	D2
Bayamón, river	C2
Brea, point	B3
Cabo Rojo Natl. Wildlife Refuge	A3
Caguana Indian Ceremonial Park	B2
Caja de Muertos, island	B3
Caña Gorda, beach	B3
Caribbean, sea	B3
Caribbean Natl. Forest	D2
Carite Forest Reserve	C2
Coamo Hot Springs	C2
Cordillera Central, mts.	C2
Culebra, island	E2
Culebrinas, river	A2
Doña Juana, mt.	C2
El Cañuelo, ruins	C2
El Toro, mt.	D2
Este, point	E2
Fortín Conde de Mirasol, fort	E2
Grande de Añasco, river	A2
Grande de Manatí, river	C2
Guajataca Forest Reserve	B2
Guánica Forest Reserve	B3
Guilarte, mt.	B2
Guilarte Forest Reserve	B2
Icacos, key	D2
La Plata, river	C2
Maricao Forest Reserve	B2
Mona, passage	A2
Norte, key	E2
Puerca, point	D2
Punta, mt.	C2
Rincón, bay	C3
Río Abajo Forest Reserve	B2
Río Camuy Cave Park	B2
Rojo, cape	A3
Roosevelt Roads Naval Station	D2
San Juan, passage	D2
Sierra de Cayey, mts.	C2
Sierra de Luquillo, mts.	D2
Sombe, beach	E2
Susúa Forest Reserve	B2
Toro Negro Forest Reserve	C2
Vieques, island	D2
Vieques, passage	D2
Vieques, sound	D2
Yeguas, point	D2

Antigua & Barbuda

National Capital
Other City

1:1,480,000

0   10   20 mi
0   10   20 km
Transverse Mercator Projection

© MapQuest.com, Inc.

Antigua and Barbuda

Capital: St. John's
Area: 171 sq. mi.
443 sq. km.
Population: 64,246
Largest City: St. John's
Language: English
Monetary Unit: East Caribbean dollar

Antigua and Barbuda: Map Index

Cities and Towns

Bolands	D5
Cedar Grove	E5
Codrington	E2
Falmouth	E5
Freetown	E5
Old Road	D5
St. John's, capital	D5

Other Features

Antigua, island	D4
Barbuda, island	E3
Boggy, peak	D5
Cobb, cove	E1
Codrington, lagoon	D1
Goat, point	D1
Gravenor, bay	E2
Palmetto, point	D2
Redonda, island	A6
Shirley, cape	E6
Spanish, point	E2
Willoughby, bay	E5

Dominica: Map Index

Cities and Towns

Berekua	B4
Castle Bruce	B2
Colihaut	A2
Glanvillia	A2
La Plaine	B3
Laudat	B3
Marigot	B2
Massacre	B3
Pointe Michel	B3
Pont Cassé	B3
Portsmouth	A2
Rosalie	B3
Roseau, capital	B3
Saint Joseph	A3
Salibia	A2
Salisbury	A2
Soufrière	B4
Vieille Case	B1
Wesley	B2

Other Features

Boiling, lake	B3
Dominica, passage	A1
Grand, bay	B4
Layou, river	B3
Morne Diablotin, mt.	B2
Roseau, river	B3
Toulaman, river	B2

Dominica

Capital: Roseau
Area: 290 sq. mi.
751 sq. km.
Population: 64,881
Largest City: Roseau
Language: English
Monetary Unit: East Caribbean dollar

Dominica

National Capital
Other City

1:1,076,000

0   6   12 mi
0   6   12 km
Lambert Conformal Conic Projection

© MapQuest.com, Inc.

St. Kitts & Nevis: Map Index

Cities and Towns

Basseterre, capital	B2
Bath	C3
Cayon	B1
Charlestown	C3
Cotton Ground	C2
Dieppe Bay Town	B1
Fig Tree	C3
Newcastle	C2
Old Road Town	B2
St. Paul's	A1
Sandy Point Town	A1
Zion	C3

Other Features

Great Salt, pond	C2
Nag's Head, cape	C2
Narrows, strait	C2
Nevis, island	C3
St. Kitts (St. Christopher), island	B2

St. Kitts & Nevis

National Capital
Other City

1:670,000

0   4   8 mi
0   4   8 km
Transverse Mercator Projection

St. Kitts & Nevis

Capital: Basseterre
Area: 104 sq. mi.
269 sq. km.
Population: 42,838
Largest City: Basseterre
Language: English
Monetary Unit: East Caribbean dollar

© MapQuest.com, Inc.

St. Lucia

Capital: Castries
Area: 238 sq. mi.
617 sq. km.
Population: 154,020
Largest City: Castries
Language: English
Monetary Unit: East Caribbean dollar

St. Lucia: Map Index

Cities and Towns
Canaries.............................A2
Castries, capital.................B1
Choiseul.............................A3
Dauphin..............................B1
Dennery..............................B2
Desruisseau.......................B3
Grand Anse........................B1
Gros Islet...........................B1
Laborie...............................B3
La Croix Maingot...............A2
Micoud...............................B3
Mon Repos........................B2

Other Features
Praslin................................B2
Soufrière............................A2
Vieux Fort..........................B3
Canelles, river...................B3
Cul de Sac, river................B2
Fond d'Or, river.................B2
Gimie, mt...........................A2
Maria, islands....................B3
Moule à Chique, cape.......B3
Point, cape.........................B1
Saint Lucia, channel..........B1
Saint Vincent, passage......B4
Soufrière, volcano.............A2

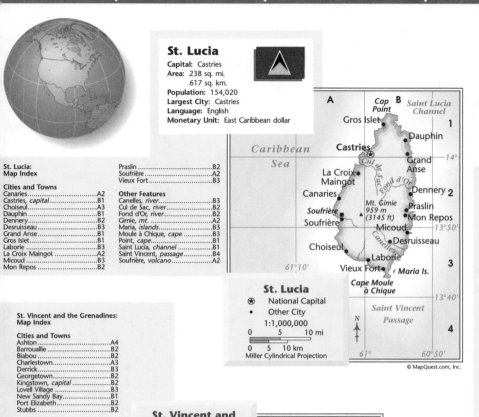

St. Lucia
⊛ National Capital
● Other City
1:1,000,000
0   5   10 mi
0   5   10 km
Miller Cylindrical Projection

© MapQuest.com, Inc.

St. Vincent and the Grenadines: Map Index

Cities and Towns
Ashton................................A4
Barrouallie.........................B2
Biabou................................B2
Charlestown.......................A3
Derrick................................B3
Georgetown.......................B2
Kingstown, capital............B2
Lovell Village.....................B3
New Sandy Bay..................B1
Port Elizabeth....................B2
Stubbs................................B2

Other Features
Baleine, bay.......................B1
Baliceaux, island...............B3
Bequia, island....................B2
Canouan, island................B3
Grenadines, islands...........A3
Mayreau, island.................A4
Mt. Wynn, bay...................B2
Mustique, island................B3
North Mayreau, channel....A3
Palm, island.......................A4
Petit Canouan, island........B3
Petit Mustique, island.......B3
Petit St. Vincent, island.....A4
St. Vincent, island.............B2
Savan, island.....................B3
Soufrière, mt......................B1
Tobago, cays......................A4
Union, island......................A4
Windward, islands.............B4

St. Vincent and The Grenadines

Capital: Kingstown
Area: 150 sq. mi.
389 sq. km.
Population: 120,519
Largest City: Kingstown
Languages: English, French patois
Monetary Unit: East Caribbean dollar

St. Vincent and the Grenadines
⊛ National Capital
● Other City
1:1,900,000
0   10   20 mi
0   10   20 km
Miller Cylindrical Projection

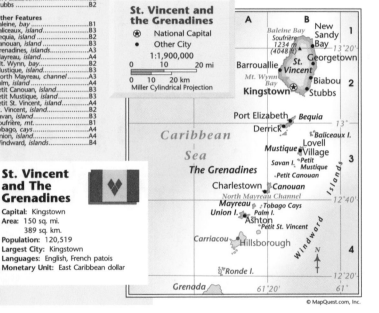

© MapQuest.com, Inc.

Barbados

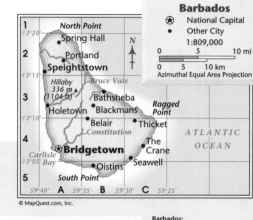

Barbados
⊛ National Capital
● Other City
1:809,000
0   5   10 mi
0   5   10 km
Azimuthal Equal Area Projection

Barbados

Capital: Bridgetown
Area: 166 sq. mi.
430 sq. km.
Population: 259,191
Largest City: Bridgetown
Language: English
Monetary Unit: Dollar

Barbados: Map Index

Cities and Towns
Bathsheba...........................B3
Belair..................................B4
Blackmans..........................B3
Bridgetown, capital...........A4
Holetown............................A3
Oistins................................B5
Portland..............................A2
Seawell...............................C4
Speightstown......................A2
Spring Hall..........................A2
The Crane...........................C4
Thicket................................C4

Other Features
Bruce Vale, river...............B3
Carlisle, bay.......................A4
Constitution, river.............B4
Hillaby, mt..........................A3
North, point........................A1
Ragged, point.....................C3
South, point........................B5

Trinidad & Tobago

Capital: Port of Spain
Area: 1,980 sq. mi.
5,130 sq. km.
Population: 1,102,096
Largest City: Port of Spain
Language: English
Monetary Unit: Dollar

Trinidad & Tobago: Map Index

Cities and Towns
Arima..................................A2
Canaan...............................B1
Chaguanas..........................A2
Charlotteville......................B1
Couva..................................A2
Fullarton.............................A2
Guayaguayare.....................A2
Matelot...............................A2
Moruga...............................A2
Pierreville...........................A2
Plymouth.............................B1
Point Fortin.........................A2
Port of Spain, capital........A2
Princes Town......................A2
Rio Claro............................A2
St. Augustine......................A2
San Fernando.....................A2
San Francique.....................A2
Sangre Grande...................A2
Scarborough.......................B1
Siparia................................A2
Toco....................................B2

Other Features
El Cerro del Aripo, mt........A2
Paria, gulf..........................A2
Pitch, lake...........................A2
Tobago, island....................B1
Trinidad, island..................A2

Trinidad & Tobago
⊛ National Capital
● Other City
1:2,700,000
0   15   30 mi
0   15   30 km
Azimuthal Equal Area Projection

© MapQuest.com, Inc.

Grenada: Map Index

Cities and Towns
Grand Bay...........................C1
Grand Roy...........................B2
Hillsborough.......................C1
Marquis...............................B2
St. David's...........................B2
St. George's, capital..........A2
Sauteurs.............................B2
Tivoli...................................B2

Other Features
Bird, island.........................B2
Caille, island......................B1
Carriacou, island...............C1
Diamond, island.................C1
Frigate, island....................C1
Grenada, island..................B2
Grenadines, island group...B1, C1
Large, island.......................C1
Les Tantes, island..............C1
Petit Martinique, island.....C1
Ronde, island.....................B1
St. Catherine, mt................B2
Salines, point......................A2
Sandy, island......................B2

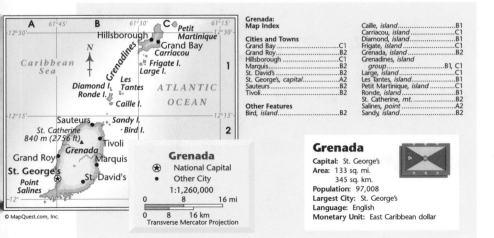

Grenada
⊛ National Capital
● Other City
1:1,260,000
0   8   16 mi
0   8   16 km
Transverse Mercator Projection

© MapQuest.com, Inc.

Grenada

Capital: St. George's
Area: 133 sq. mi.
345 sq. km.
Population: 97,008
Largest City: St. George's
Language: English
Monetary Unit: East Caribbean dollar

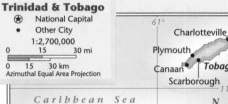

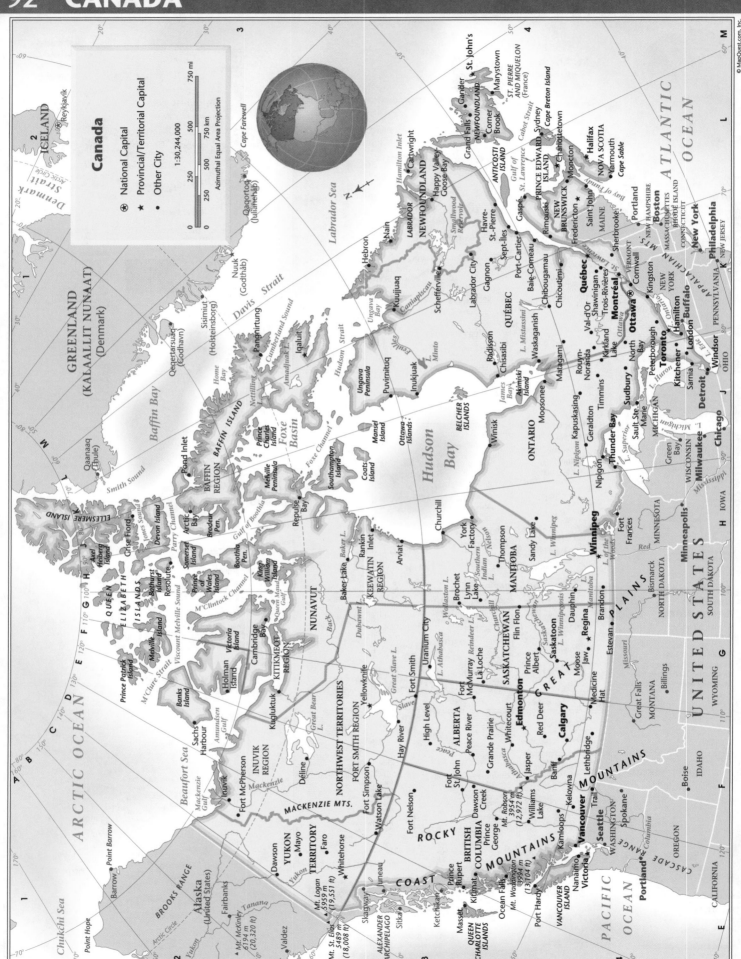

Canada: Map Index

ALBERTA
Cities and Towns
- Banff — F3
- Calgary — F3
- Edmonton, *capital* — F3
- Fort McMurray — F3
- Grande Prairie — F3
- High Level — F3
- Jasper — E3
- Lethbridge — F4
- Medicine Hat — F4
- Peace River — E3
- Red Deer — F3
- Whitecourt — F3

Other Features
- Athabasca, *river* — F3
- Peace, *river* — F3

BRITISH COLUMBIA
Cities and Towns
- Dawson Creek — E3
- Fort Nelson — E3
- Fort St. John — E3
- Kamloops — E4
- Kelowna — E4
- Kitimat — D3
- Masset — D3
- Nanaimo — E4
- Ocean Falls — E3
- Port Hardy — D3
- Prince George — E3
- Prince Rupert — D3
- Trail — E4
- Vancouver — E4
- Victoria, *capital* — E4
- Williams Lake — E4

Other Features
- Coast, *mts.* — D3
- Fraser, *river* — E3
- Queen Charlotte, *islands* — D3
- Robson, *mt.* — E3
- Rocky, *mts.* — C2
- Vancouver, *island* — E4
- Waddington, *mt.* — E3

MANITOBA
Cities and Towns
- Brandon — H4
- Brochet — G3
- Churchill — H3
- Dauphin — G3
- Flin Flon — G3
- Lynn Lake — G3
- Thompson — H3
- Winnipeg, *capital* — H4
- York Factory — H3

Other Features
- Churchill, *river* — G3
- Hudson, *bay* — H3
- Manitoba, *lake* — G3
- Nelson, *river* — H3
- Saskatchewan, *river* — G3
- Southern Indian, *lake* — G3
- Winnipeg, *lake* — H3
- Winnipegosis, *lake* — G3

NEW BRUNSWICK
Cities and Towns
- Fredericton, *capital* — L4
- Moncton — L4
- Saint John — L4

Other Feature
- Fundy, *bay* — L4

NEWFOUNDLAND
Cities and Towns
- Cartwright — M3
- Corner Brook — M4
- Gander — M4
- Grand Falls — M4
- Happy Valley-Goose Bay — M3
- Hebron — L3
- Labrador City — L3
- Marystown — M4
- Nain — L3
- St. John's, *capital* — M4

Other Features
- Hamilton, *inlet* — M4
- Labrador, *sea* — M3
- St. Lawrence, *gulf* — M3
- Smallwood, *reservoir* — L3

NORTHWEST TERRITORIES
Cities and Towns
- Arviat — H2
- Déline — E2
- Fort McPherson — D2
- Fort Simpson — F2
- Fort Smith — F2
- Hay River — F2
- Holman Island — E1
- Inuvik — D2
- Sachs Harbour — E1
- Yellowknife, *capital* — F2

Other Features
- Amundsen, *gulf* — E1
- Banks, *island* — D1
- Beaufort, *sea* — D1
- Great Bear, *lake* — E2
- Great Slave, *lake* — F2
- Inuvik, *region* — D2
- Mackenzie, *gulf* — D2
- Mackenzie, *mts.* — D2
- Mackenzie, *river* — E2
- M'Clure, *strait* — E1
- Melville, *island* — F1
- Prince Patrick, *island* — E1
- Victoria, *island* — F1
- Viscount Melville, *sound* — F1

NUNAVUT
Cities and Towns
- Arctic Bay — J1
- Baker Lake — H2
- Cambridge Bay — G2
- Grise Fiord — J1
- Iqaluit, *capital* — L2
- Keewatin — J2
- Pangnirtung — L2
- Pond Inlet — K1
- Rankin Inlet — H2
- Repulse Bay — J2
- Resolute — J1

Other Features
- Amadjuak, *lake* — K2
- Axel Heiberg, *island* — H1
- Back, *river* — G2
- Baffin, *bay* — L1
- Baffin, *island* — K1
- Baffin, *region* — K2
- Bathurst, *island* — H1
- Belcher, *islands* — J3
- Boothia, *gulf* — J2
- Boothia, *peninsula* — J1
- Brodeur, *peninsula* — J1
- Coats, *island* — J2
- Cumberland, *sound* — L2
- Davis, *strait* — M2
- Devon, *island* — J1
- Dubawnt, *lake* — G2
- Ellesmere, *island* — K1
- Foxe, *basin* — K2
- Foxe, *channel* — J2
- Home, *bay* — L2
- Hudson, *bay* — J3
- Hudson, *strait* — K2
- James, *bay* — J3
- Jones, *sound* — J1
- Keewatin, *region* — H2
- King William, *island* — H2
- Kitikmeot, *region* — F2
- Mansel, *island* — J2
- M'Clintock, *channel* — G1
- Melville, *peninsula* — J2
- Nettilling, *lake* — K2
- Ottawa, *islands* — J3
- Parry, *channel* — J1
- Prince Charles, *island* — K2
- Prince of Wales, *island* — H1
- Queen Elizabeth, *islands* — G1
- Smith, *sound* — K1
- Somerset, *island* — J1
- Southampton, *island* — J2
- Victoria, *island* — G1

NOVA SCOTIA
Cities and Towns
- Halifax, *capital* — L4
- Sydney — M4
- Yarmouth — L4

Other Features
- Cabot, *strait* — M4
- Cape Breton, *island* — M4
- Fundy, *bay* — L4
- Sable, *cape* — L4

ONTARIO
Cities and Towns
- Cornwall — K4
- Fort Frances — H4
- Geraldton — J3
- Hamilton — J4
- Kapuskasing — J3
- Kingston — K4
- Kirkland Lake — J3
- Kitchener — J4
- London — J4
- Moosonee — J3
- Nipigon — J3
- North Bay — K4
- Ottawa, *national capital* — K4
- Peterborough — K4
- Sandy Lake — H3
- Sarnia — J4
- Sault Ste. Marie — J4
- Sudbury — J4
- Thunder Bay — J3
- Timmins — J3
- Toronto, *capital* — K4
- Windsor — J4

Other Features
- Akimiski, *island* — J3
- Albany, *river* — J3
- Erie, *lake* — J4
- Huron, *lake* — J4
- James, *bay* — J3
- Nipigon, *lake* — J3
- Ontario, *lake* — K4
- Ottawa, *river* — K4
- Superior, *lake* — J3
- Woods, *lake* — H3

PRINCE EDWARD ISLAND
Cities and Towns
- Charlottetown, *capital* — L4

QUÉBEC
Cities and Towns
- Baie-Comeau — L3
- Chibougamau — K3
- Chicoutimi — K3
- Chisasibi — K3
- Gagnon — L3
- Gaspé — L3
- Havre-St-Pierre — L3
- Inukjuak — K3
- Kuujjuaq — L3
- Matagami — K3
- Montréal — K4
- Port-Cartier — L3
- Puvirnituq — K2
- Québec, *capital* — K4
- Radisson — K3
- Rimouski — L4
- Rouyn-Noranda — K4
- Schefferville — L3
- Sept-Îles — L3
- Shawinigan — K4
- Sherbrooke — K4
- Trois-Rivières — K4
- Val-d'Or — K4
- Waskaganish — J3

Other Features
- Anticosti, *island* — L4
- Caniapiscau, *river* — L3
- Feuilles, *river* — K3
- Hudson, *bay* — J3
- Hudson, *strait* — K2
- James, *bay* — J3
- Minto, *lake* — K3
- Mistassini, *lake* — K3
- Ottawa, *river* — K4
- St. Lawrence, *gulf* — L3
- St. Lawrence, *river* — K4
- Ungava, *bay* — L2
- Ungava, *peninsula* — K2

SASKATCHEWAN
Cities and Towns
- Estevan — G4
- La Loche — G3
- Moose Jaw — G4
- Prince Albert — G3
- Regina, *capital* — G4
- Saskatoon — G3
- Uranium City — G3

Other Features
- Athabasca, *lake* — G3
- Churchill, *river* — G3
- Great Plains, *plain* — G3
- Reindeer, *lake* — G3
- Saskatchewan, *river* — G3
- Wollaston, *lake* — G3

YUKON TERRITORY
Cities and Towns
- Dawson — D2
- Faro — D2
- Mayo — E2
- Watson Lake — D2
- Whitehorse, *capital* — D2

Other Features
- Beaufort, *sea* — D1
- Logan, *mt.* — C2
- St. Elias, *mt.* — C2
- Yukon, *river* — D2

Canada
Capital: Ottawa
Area: 3,849,674 sq. mi.
9,973,249 sq. km.
Population: 31,006,347
Languages: English, French
Monetary Unit: Canadian dollar

New Brunswick
Capital: Fredericton
Area: 28,355 sq. mi.
73,459 sq. km.
Population: 738,133
Largest City: Saint John

Newfoundland
Capital: St. John's
Area: 156,949 sq. mi.
406,604 sq. km.
Population: 551,792
Largest City: St. John's

Prince Edward Island
Capital: Charlottetown
Area: 2,185 sq. mi.
5,661 sq. km.
Population: 134,557
Largest City: Charlottetown

Ontario
Capital: Toronto
Area: 412,581 sq. mi.
1,068,863 sq. km.
Population: 10,753,573
Largest City: Toronto

Alberta
Capital: Edmonton
Area: 255,287 sq. mi.
661,265 sq. km.
Population: 2,696,826
Largest City: Edmonton

British Columbia
Capital: Victoria
Area: 365,947 sq. mi.
948,049 sq. km.
Population: 3,724,500
Largest City: Vancouver

Northwest Territories
Capital: Yellowknife
Area: 520,850 sq. mi.
1,349,000 sq. km.
Population: 39,672
Largest City: Yellowknife

Nova Scotia
Capital: Halifax
Area: 21,425 sq. mi.
55,505 sq. km.
Population: 909,282
Largest City: Halifax

Québec
Capital: Québec
Area: 594,860 sq. mi.
1,541,088 sq. km.
Population: 7,138,795
Largest City: Montréal

Saskatchewan
Capital: Regina
Area: 251,866 sq. mi.
652,503 sq. km.
Population: 990,237
Largest City: Saskatoon

Manitoba
Capital: Winnipeg
Area: 250,947 sq. mi.
650,122 sq. km.
Population: 1,113,898
Largest City: Winnipeg

Nunavut
Capital: Iqaluit
Area: 800,775 sq. mi.
2,074,000 sq. km.
Population: 24,730
Largest City: Iqaluit

Yukon Territory
Capital: Whitehorse
Area: 186,661 sq. mi.
483,578 sq. km.
Population: 30,766
Largest City: Whitehorse

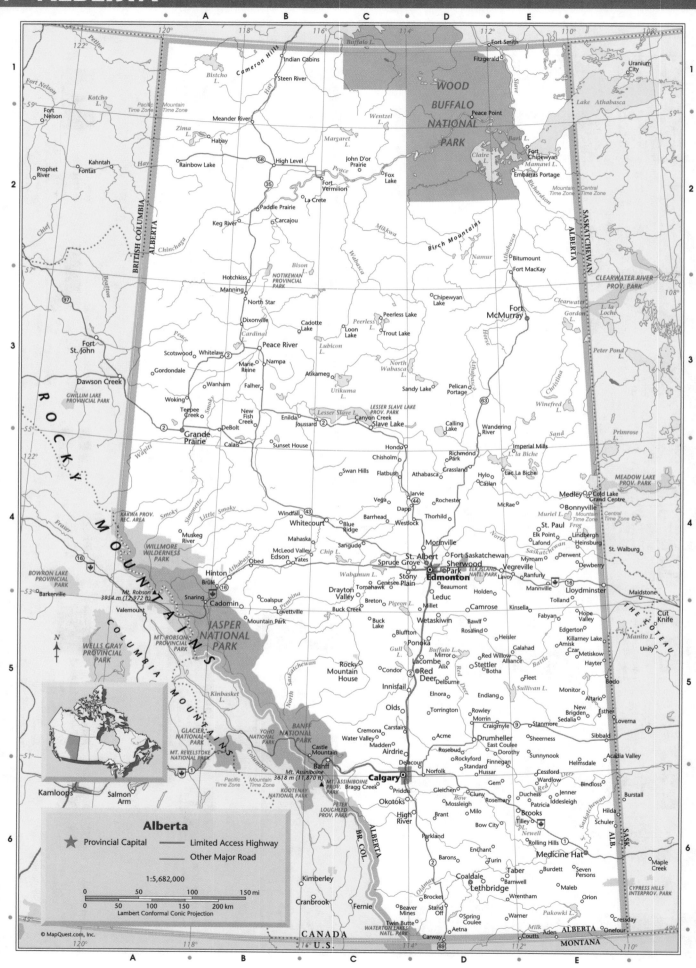

Alberta

★ Provincial Capital — Limited Access Highway
— Other Major Road

1:5,682,000

0   50   100   150 mi
0   50   100   150   200 km

Lambert Conformal Conic Projection

© MapQuest.com, Inc.

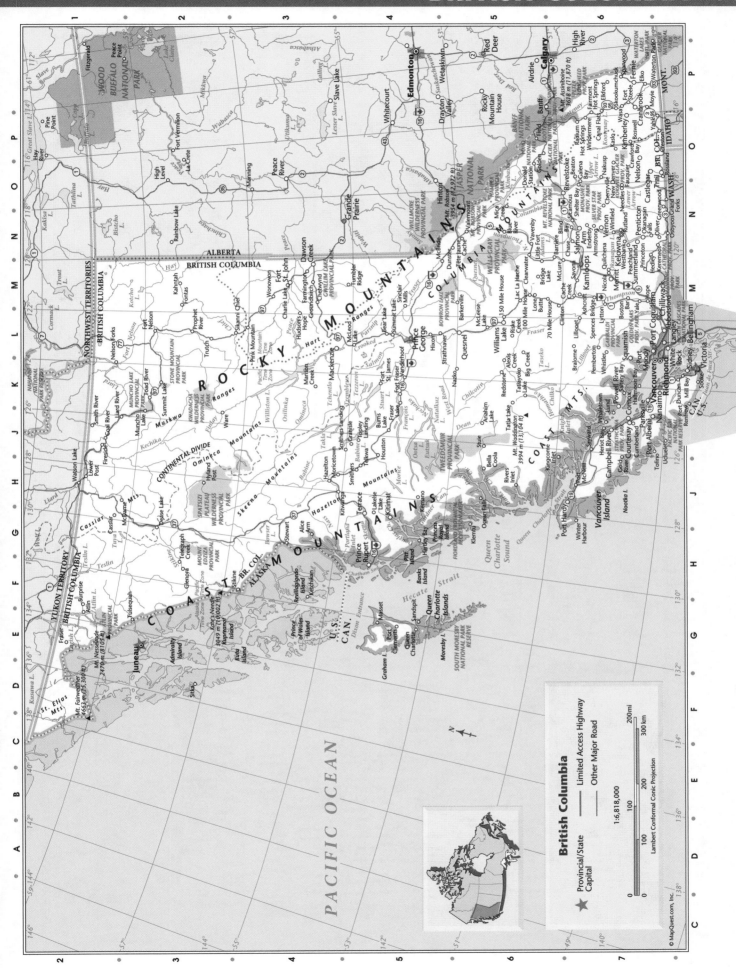

British Columbia

★ Provincial/State Capital

—— Limited Access Highway

—— Other Major Road

1:6,818,000

0   100   200mi
0   100   200   300km

Lambert Conformal Conic Projection

© MapQuest.com, Inc.

PACIFIC OCEAN

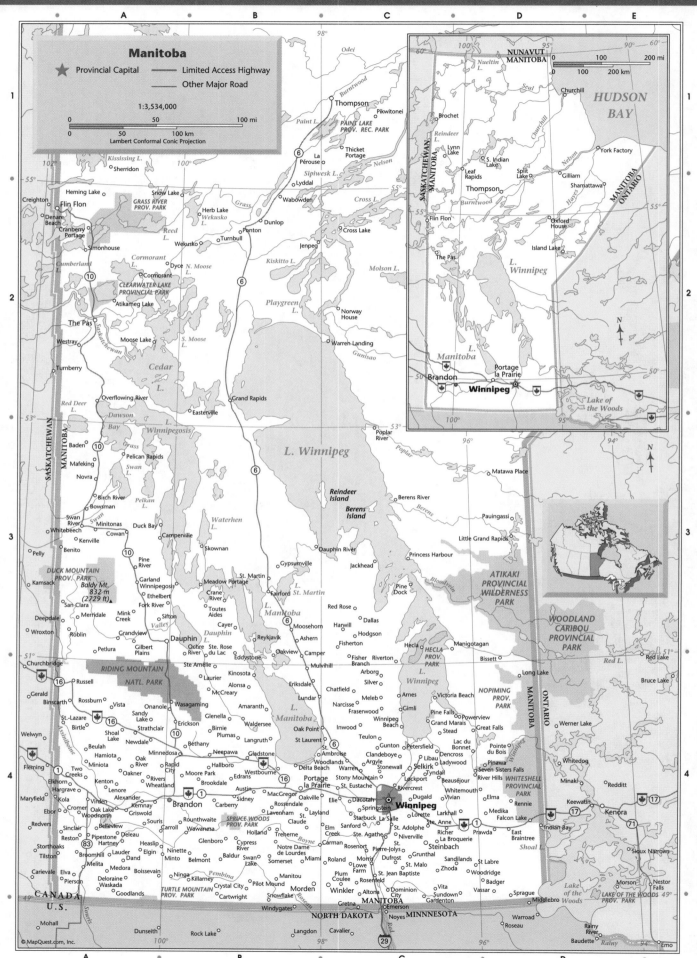

Manitoba

★ Provincial Capital ▬▬ Limited Access Highway

▬▬ Other Major Road

1:3,534,000

0   50   100 mi

0   50   100 km

Lambert Conformal Conic Projection

Odei

Thompson

Pikwitonei

PAINT LAKE PROV. REC. PARK

La Pérouse

Thicket Portage

Burntwood

Paint L.

NUNAVUT
MANITOBA

Nueltin L.

Brochet

Churchill

HUDSON BAY

Reindeer L.

Lynn Lake

S. Indian Lake

Seal

Churchill

York Factory

Sherridon

Kississing L.

Lyddal

Wabowden

Grass

Sipiwesk L.

Cross L.

Leaf Rapids

Split Lake

Gilliam

Shamattawa

Heming Lake

Snow Lake

GRASS RIVER PROV. PARK

Herb Lake

Wekusko L.

Dunlop

Burntwood

Flin Flon

Oxford House

MANITOBA ONTARIO

Creighton

Flin Flon

Denare Beach

Cranberry Portage

Herb Lake

Ponton

Jenpeg

Cross Lake

The Pas

Island Lake

Simonhouse

Reed L.

Wekusko

Turnbull

Molson L.

L. Winnipeg

Cumberland L.

Cormorant L.

Dyce

Cormorant

N. Moose L.

Playgreen L.

Kiskitto L.

CLEARWATER LAKE PROVINCIAL PARK

Atikameg Lake

S. Moose L.

Norway House

The Pas

Moose Lake

Warren Landing

Westray

Saskatchewan

Cedar L.

Gunisao

Turnberry

Red Deer L.

Dawson Bay

Overflowing River

Easterville

Grand Rapids

Poplar River

N

SASKATCHEWAN MANITOBA

Baden

Winnipegosis

Grass

Poplar

L. Winnipeg

Brandon

Portage la Prairie

Winnipeg

Lake of the Woods

Mafeking

Pelican Rapids

Swan L.

Novra

Matawa Place

Birch River

Pelkan L.

Bowsman

Reindeer Island

Berens River

Berens

Swan River

Minitonas

Duck Bay

Camperville

Berens Island

Pauingassi

Whitebeech

Cowan

Skownan

Princess Harbour

Little Grand Rapids

Kenville

Pine River

Waterhen L.

Dauphin River

Jackhead

ATIKAKI PROVINCIAL WILDERNESS PARK

Benito

Pelly

Kamsack

DUCK MOUNTAIN PROV. PARK

Baldy Mt. 832 m (2729 ft)▲

Garland

Winnipegosis

Meadow Portage

Gypsumville

St. Martin

St. Martin L.

Red Rose

Pine Dock

Bloodvein

WOODLAND CARIBOU PROVINCIAL PARK

San Clara

Ethelbert

Crane River

Fairford

Deepdale

Merridale

Mink Creek

Fork River

Toutes Aides

L. Manitoba

Wroxton

Roblin

Grandview

Sifton

Cayer

Moosehorn

Harwill

Dallas

Red L.

Hodgson

Manigotagan

Red Lake

Petlura

Gilbert Plains

Dauphin L.

Reykjavik

Ashern

Fisherton

Hecla

HECLA PROV. PARK

Bissett

Bruce Lake

Churchbridge

Dauphin

Ochre River

Ste. Rose du Lac

Eddystone

Oakview

Camper

Fisher Branch

Riverton

L. Winnipeg

Long Lake

RIDING MOUNTAIN NATL. PARK

Ste Amelie

Laurier

Alonsa

Mulvihill

Arborg

Silver

Victoria Beach

NOPIMING PROV. PARK

Werner Lake

Russell

Gerald

Vista

McCreary

Chatfield

Meleb

Arnes

Gimli

Pine Falls

MANITOBA ONTARIO

Binscarth

Rossburn

Onanole

Wasagaming

Amaranth

Lundar

Narcisse

Fraserwood

Grand Marais

Powerview

Great Falls

St-Lazare

Sandy Lake

Erickson

Glenella

L. Manitoba

Oak Point

Inwood

Winnipeg Beach

Lac du Bonnet

Birtle

Strathclair

Birnie

Plumas

Langruth

St Laurent

Teulon

Gunton

Petersfield

Stead

Pointe du Bois

Whitedog

Welwyn

Shoal Lake

Newdale

Bethany

Neepawa

St. Ambroise

Woodlands

Clandeboye

Libau

Dencross

Pinawa

Beulah

Hamiota

Oak River

Rapid City

Hallboro

Edrans

Westbourne

Delta Beach

Warren

Argyle

Stonewall

Ladywood

Tyndall

Seven Sisters Falls

River Hills

WHITESHELL PROVINCIAL PARK

Minaki

Fleming

Two Creeks

Miniota

Oakner

Rivers

Wheatland

Moore Park

Brookdale

Austin

Portage la Prairie

Stony Mountain

St. Eustache

Lockport

Selkirk

Beauséjour

Whitemouth

Rennie

Redditt

Elkhorn

Kenton

Lenore

Sidney

MacGregor

Oakville

Elie

Dacotah

Rivercrest

Vivian

Elma

Keewatin

Hargrave

Kola

Virden

Alexander

Kemnay

Griswold

Carberry

Rossendale

Lavenham

St. Claude

Layland

Starbuck

La Salle

Winnipeg

Lorette

Larkhall

Medika

Falcon Lake

Kenora

Maryfield

Ebor

Cromer

Oak Lake

Woodnorth

Souris

Carroll

Wawanesa

Holland

Treherne

Elm Creek

Sanford

St. Agathe

St. Adolphe

Richer

Ste. Anne

Prawda

East Braintree

Indian Bay

Redvers

Sinclair

Pipestone

Deleau

Glenboro

Cypress River

Notre Dame de Lourdes

Carman

Rosenort

Niverville

La Broquerie

Sandilands

Reston

Bellview

Hartney

Heaslip

Minto

Baldur

Swan Lake

Somerset

Miami

Roland

Morris

Dufrost

Grunthal

Steinbach

St Labre

Storthoaks

Tilston

Broomhill

Dand

Lauder

Elgin

Belmont

Ninette

Ninga

Pilot Mound

Manitou

Lowe Farm

St. Malo

Zhoda

Woodridge

Carievale

Elva

Melita

Medora

Boissevain

TURTLE MOUNTAIN PROV. PARK

Crystal City

Snowflake

Plum Coulee

Rosenfeld

St. Jean Baptiste

Dominion City

Vita

Badger

Sprague

Morson

Nestor Falls

Pierson

Deloraine

Waskada

Goodlands

Cartwright

Pembina

Winkler

Morden

Gretna

MANITOBA

Sundown

Gardenton

Vassar

Middlebro

LAKE OF THE WOODS PROV. PARK

CANADA U.S.

Windygates

Emerson

NORTH DAKOTA

Noyes

MINNNESOTA

Warroad

Roseau

Rainy River

Lake of the Woods

Mohall

Dunseith

Rock Lake

Langdon

Cavalier

Souris

Baudette

Rainy

Emo

©MapQuest.com, Inc.

N

CANADA

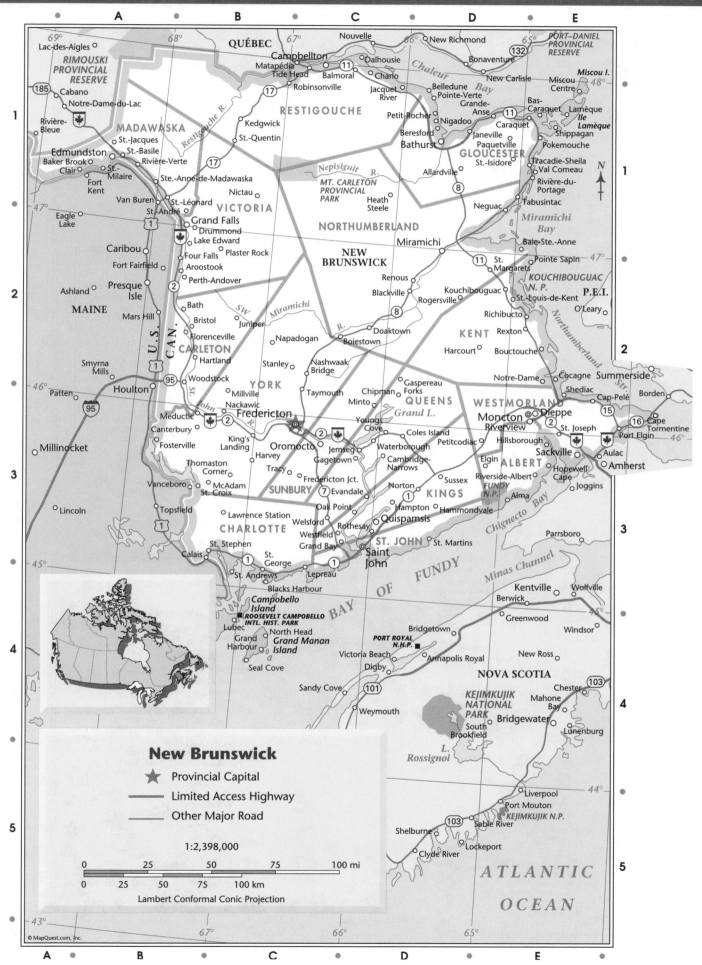

QUÉBEC

RIMOUSKI PROVINCIAL RESERVE
Lac-des-Aigles
69°
68°
67°
66°
65°

Nouvelle
Campbellton
New Richmond
Matapédia
Dalhousie
Bonaventure
Tide Head
Charlo
New Carlisle
(185)
Cabano
Balmoral
Robinsonville
Jacquet River
Miscou I.
Notre-Dame-du-Lac
Belledune
Miscou Centre
Pointe-Verte
Rivière-Bleue
Kedgwick
Petit-Rocher
Grande-Anse
Bas-Caraquet
Île Lamèque
48°
MADAWASKA
St.-Quentin
Nigadoo
Caraquet
Lamèque
Edmundston
St.-Jacques
Beresford
Janeville
Shippagan
St.-Basile
Bathurst
Paquetville
Pokemouche
Baker Brook
Rivière-Verte
GLOUCESTER
St.-Isidore
Clair
St.-Milaire
Tracadie-Sheila
Fort Kent
Ste.-Anne-de-Madawaska
Val Comeau
Van Buren
St.-Léonard
Nictau
Allardville
Rivière-du-Portage
St.-André
VICTORIA
MT. CARLETON PROVINCIAL PARK
Neguac
Tabusintac
Eagle Lake
Grand Falls
Heath Steele
47°
Drummond
Miramichi Bay
Caribou
Lake Edward
NORTHUMBERLAND
Baie-Ste.-Anne
Four Falls
Plaster Rock
KOUCHIBOUGUAC W.P.
Fort Fairfield
Aroostook
NEW BRUNSWICK
Miramichi
St. Margarets
Pointe Sapin
47°
Presque Isle
Perth-Andover
Renous
Ashland
MAINE
Bath
Blackville
Kouchibouguac
St-Louis-de-Kent
P.E.I.
Mars Hill
Bristol
Juniper
Rogersville
O'Leary
Napadogan
Doaktown
Richibucto
Smyrna Mills
Florenceville
Boiestown
KENT
Rexton
Patten
CARLETON
Hartland
Stanley
Nashwaak Bridge
Harcourt
Bouctouche
46°
Houlton
YORK
Taymouth
Gaspereau Forks
Notre-Dame
Cocagne
Summerside
(95)
Woodstock
Millville
Chipman
QUEENS
Shediac
Borden
Meductic
Nackawic
Minto
Grand L.
WESTMORLAND
Cap-Pelé
Millinocket
Canterbury
Fredericton
Youngs Cove
Moncton
Dieppe
(15)
Cape Tormentine
Fosterville
King's Landing
Oromocto
Coles Island
Riverview
St. Joseph
Port Elgin
46°
Thomaston Corner
Harvey
Jemseg
Waterborough
Petitcodiac
Hillsborough
Sackville
Vanceboro
Tracy
Gagetown
Cambridge-Narrows
Elgin
Aulac
Amherst
Lincoln
McAdam
SUNBURY
Fredericton Jct.
Sussex
Riverside-Albert
ALBERT
Hopewell Cape
Joggins
St. Croix
Evandale
Norton
KINGS
FUNDY N.P.
Topsfield
(7)
Oak Point
Hampton
Hammondvale
Alma
Parrsboro
Lawrence Station
Welsford
Quispamsis
CHARLOTTE
Westfield
Rothesay
Chignecto Bay
St. Stephen
Grand Bay
ST. JOHN
St. Martins
Calais
St. George
Saint John
Kentville
Wolfville
St. Andrews
Lepreau
Berwick
Blacks Harbour
BAY OF FUNDY
Minas Channel
Greenwood
Windsor
45°
Campobello Island
Bridgetown
ROOSEVELT CAMPOBELLO INTL. HIST. PARK
PORT ROYAL N.H.P.
New Ross
Lubec
North Head
Victoria Beach
Annapolis Royal
Grand Harbour
Grand Manan Island
Digby
NOVA SCOTIA
Chester
Seal Cove
Sandy Cove
(101)
KEJIMKUJIK NATIONAL PARK
Mahone Bay
(103)
Weymouth
South Brookfield
Bridgewater
Lunenburg
L. Rossignol
KEJIMKUJIK N.P.
44°
Liverpool
Port Mouton
(103)
Shelburne
Sable River
Lockeport
Clyde River
ATLANTIC OCEAN
43°
© MapQuest.com, Inc.

New Brunswick

★ Provincial Capital

— Limited Access Highway

— Other Major Road

1:2,398,000

0   25   50   75   100 mi

0   25   50   75   100 km

Lambert Conformal Conic Projection

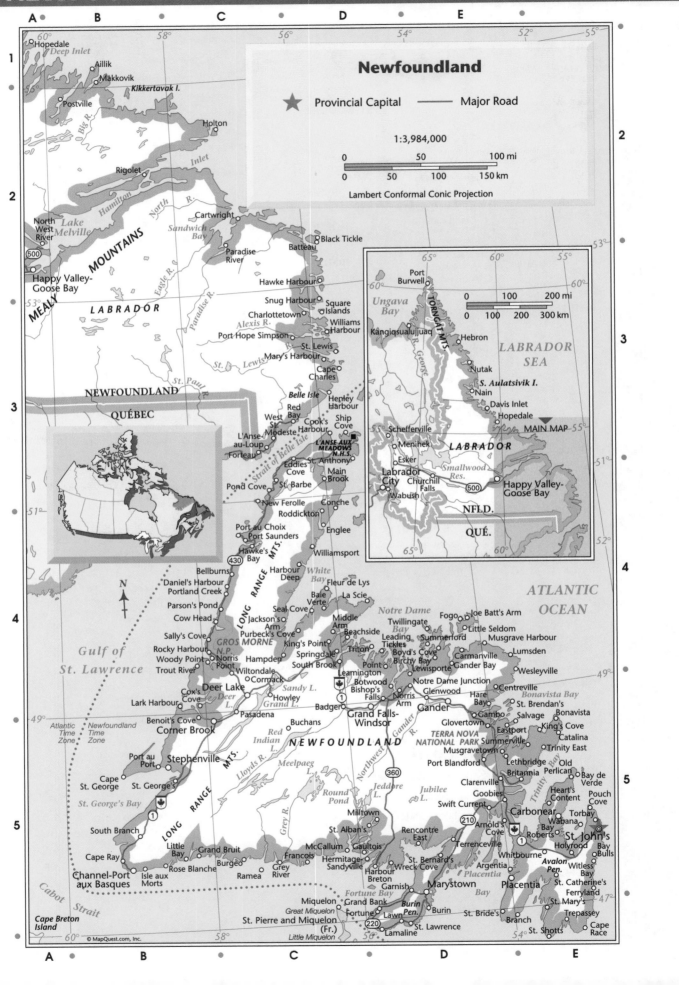

Newfoundland

★ Provincial Capital ——— Major Road

1:3,984,000

0   50   100 mi
0   50   100   150 km

Lambert Conformal Conic Projection

Hopedale
Deep Inlet
Aillik
Makkovik
Kikkertavak I.
Postville
Holton
Rigolet
Hamilton Inlet
North West River
Lake Melville
MEALY MOUNTAINS
Cartwright
Sandwich Bay
Paradise River
Batteau
Black Tickle
Happy Valley-Goose Bay
Hawke Harbour
LABRADOR
Snug Harbour
Square Islands
Williams Harbour
Charlottetown
Alexis R.
Port Hope Simpson
St. Lewis
Mary's Harbour
Cape Charles
Belle Isle
Henley Harbour
NEWFOUNDLAND
QUÉBEC
Red Bay
Cook's Harbour
Ship Cove
West St. Modeste
L'Anse-au-Loup
L'ANSE AUX MEADOWS N.H.S.
St. Anthony
Forteau
Eddies Cove
Main Brook
Pond Cove
St. Barbe
Conche
New Ferolle
Roddickton
Englee
Port au Choix
Port Saunders
Williamsport
Hawke's Bay
White Bay
Bellburns
Harbour Deep
Fleur de Lys
Daniel's Harbour
Portland Creek
Baie Verte
La Scie
Parson's Pond
Seal Cove
Cow Head
Jackson's Arm
Middle Arm
Beachside
Notre Dame Bay
Fogo
Joe Batt's Arm
Sally's Cove
Purbeck's Cove
King's Point
Twillingate
Little Seldom
Rocky Harbour
GROS MORNE N.P.
Triton
Leading Tickles
Summerford
Musgrave Harbour
Woody Point
Norris Point
Hampden
Springdale
Birchy Bay
Boyd's Cove
Carmanville
Lumsden
Trout River
Wiltondale
South Brook
Leamington
Lewisporte
Gander Bay
Wesleyville
Cormack
Botwood
Notre Dame Junction
Centreville
Deer Lake
Howley
Bishop's Falls
Glenwood
Bonavista Bay
Lark Harbour
Cox's Cove
Pasadena
Norris Arm
Gander
Hare Bay
St. Brendan's
Benoit's Cove
Badger
Grand Falls-Windsor
Gambo
Salvage
Bonavista
Corner Brook
Buchans
Glovertown
Eastport
King's Cove
NEWFOUNDLAND
TERRA NOVA NATIONAL PARK
Summerville
Catalina
Port au Port
Stephenville
Port Blandford
Musgravetown
Trinity East
Cape St. George
St. George's
Clarenville
Lethbridge
Old Perlican
St. George's Bay
Goobies
Britannia
Bay de Verde
South Branch
Swift Current
Heart's Content
Pouch Cove
Milltown
Rencontre East
Arnold's Cove
Roberts
Torbay
Little Bay
Grand Bruit
Cape Ray
St. Alban's
Carbonear
Wabana
Isle aux Morts
Rose Blanche
Burgeo
Grey River
McCallum
Gaultois
Hermitage
Sandyville
Harbour Breton
Wreck Cove
St. Bernard's
Terrenceville
Whitbourne
Holyrood
St. John's
Bay Bulls
Channel-Port aux Basques
Ramea
Francois
Garnish
Marystown
Argentia
Avalon Pen.
Witless Bay
Cabot Strait
Cape Breton Island
Miquelon
Great Miquelon
Grand Bank
Fortune
St. Pierre and Miquelon (Fr.)
Little Miquelon
Lawn
Lamaline
Burin Pen.
Burin
St. Lawrence
Placentia Bay
Placentia
Marystown
St. Bride's
Branch
St. Catherine's
Ferryland
St. Mary's
Trepassey
Cape Race
Cape St. Shotts

Gulf of St. Lawrence
LONG RANGE MTS.
Deer L.
Grand L.
Sandy L.
Red Indian L.
Lloyds R.
Meelpaeg L.
Grey R.
Round Pond
Jubilee L.
Jeddore L.
Trinity Bay
Conception Bay
Fortune Bay
ATLANTIC OCEAN

Atlantic Time Zone
Newfoundland Time Zone

Port Burwell
Ungava Bay
George R.
TORNGAT MTS.
Hebron
LABRADOR SEA
Kangiqsualujjuaq
Nutak
S. Aulatsivik I.
Nain
Davis Inlet
Hopedale
MAIN MAP
Schefferville
LABRADOR
Menihek
Esker
Smallwood Res.
Labrador City
Churchill Falls
Wabush
Happy Valley-Goose Bay
NFLD.
QUÉ.

0   100   200 mi
0   100   200   300 km

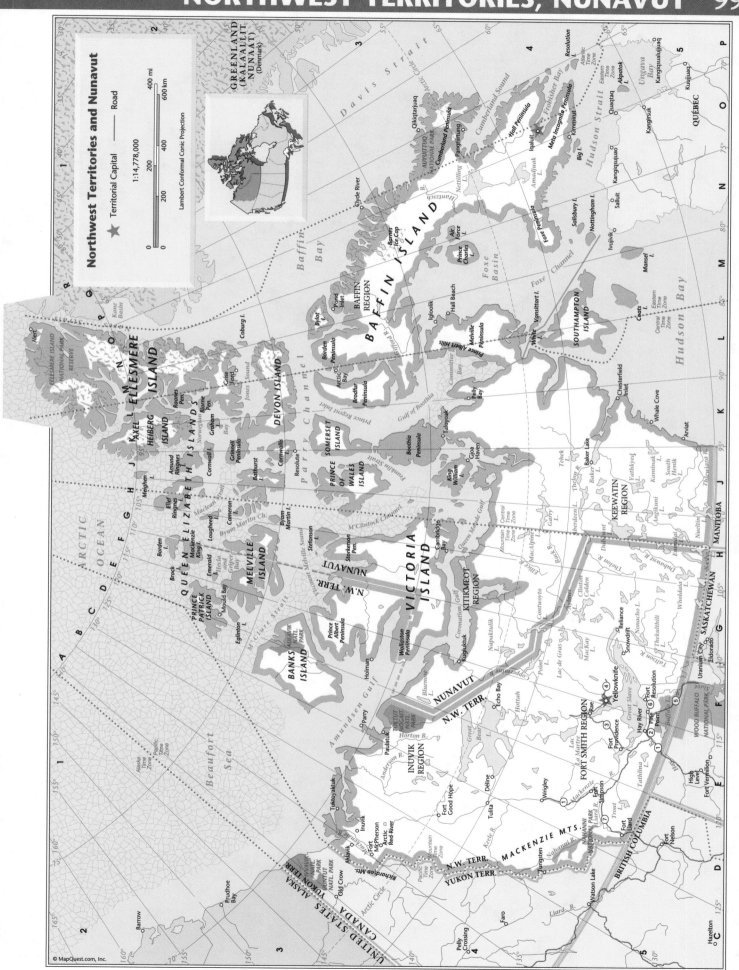

Northwest Territories and Nunavut

★ Territorial Capital ——— Road

1:14,778,000

Lambert Conformal Conic Projection

© MapQuest.com, Inc.

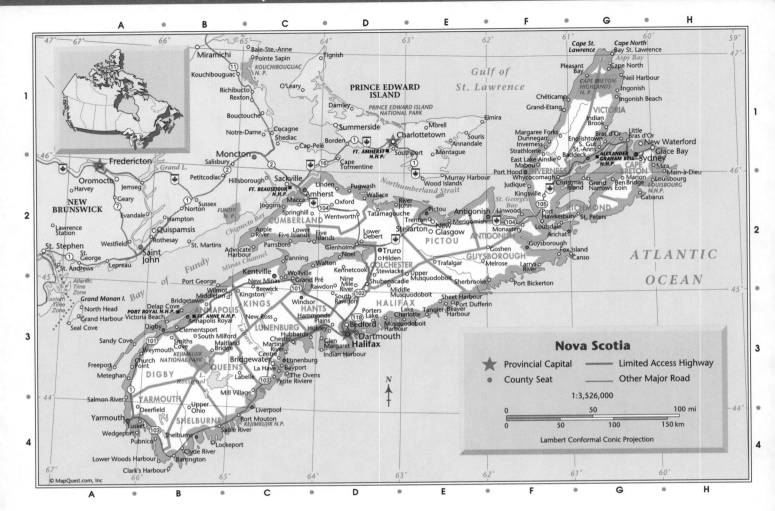

Nova Scotia

⭐ Provincial Capital   ── Limited Access Highway
● County Seat   ── Other Major Road

1:3,526,000

0   50   100 mi
0   50   100   150 km

Lambert Conformal Conic Projection

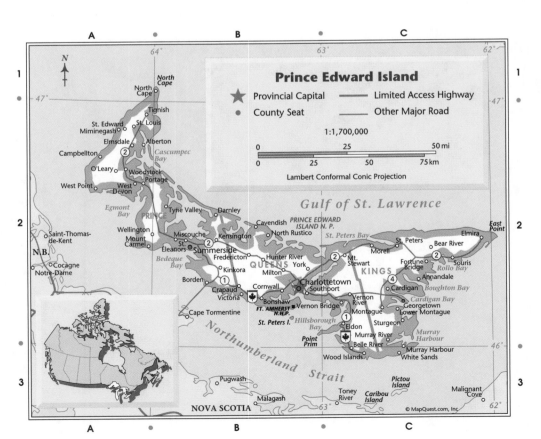

Prince Edward Island

⭐ Provincial Capital   ── Limited Access Highway
● County Seat   ── Other Major Road

1:1,700,000

0   25   50 mi
0   25   50   75 km

Lambert Conformal Conic Projection

© MapQuest.com, Inc

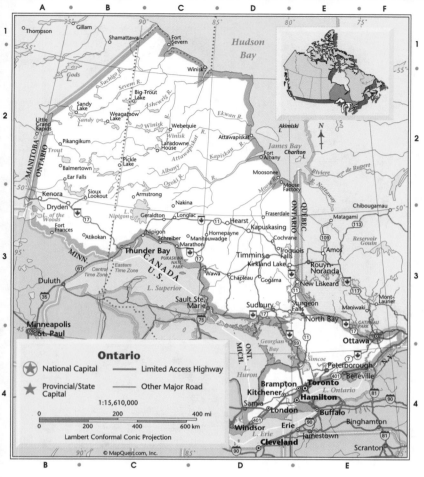

Ontario

- ⭐ National Capital
- ★ Provincial/State Capital
- ─── Limited Access Highway
- ─── Other Major Road

1:15,610,000

| 0 | 200 | 400 mi |
| 0 | 200 | 400 | 600 km |

Lambert Conformal Conic Projection

© MapQuest.com, Inc.

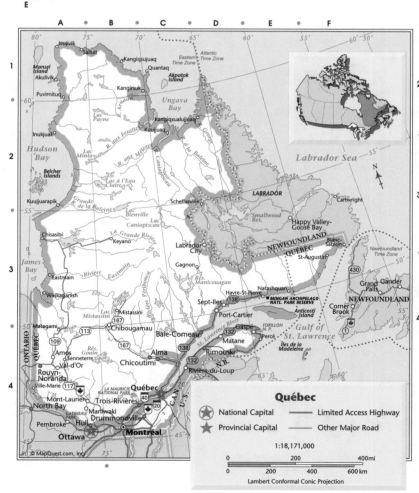

Québec

- ⭐ National Capital
- ★ Provincial Capital
- ─── Limited Access Highway
- ─── Other Major Road

1:18,171,000

| 0 | 200 | 400mi |
| 0 | 200 | 400 | 600 km |

Lambert Conformal Conic Projection

© MapQuest.com, Inc.

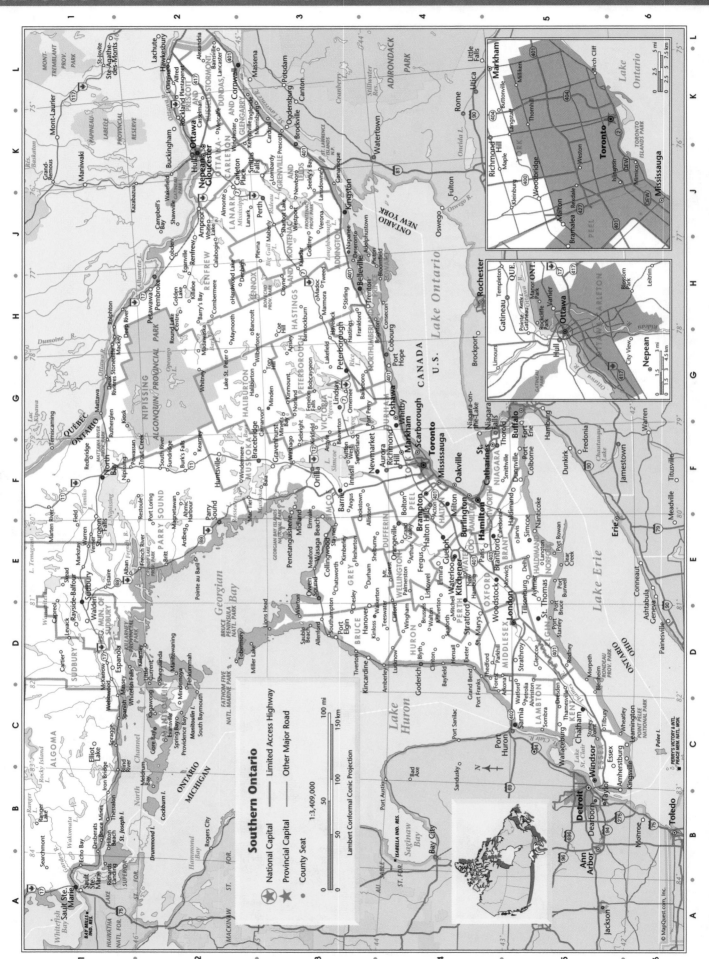

Southern Ontario

National Capital ★
Provincial Capital ★
County Seat •

—— Limited Access Highway
—— Other Major Road

1:3,409,000

Lambert Conformal Conic Projection

0   50   100 mi
0   50   100   150 km

© MapQuest.com, Inc.

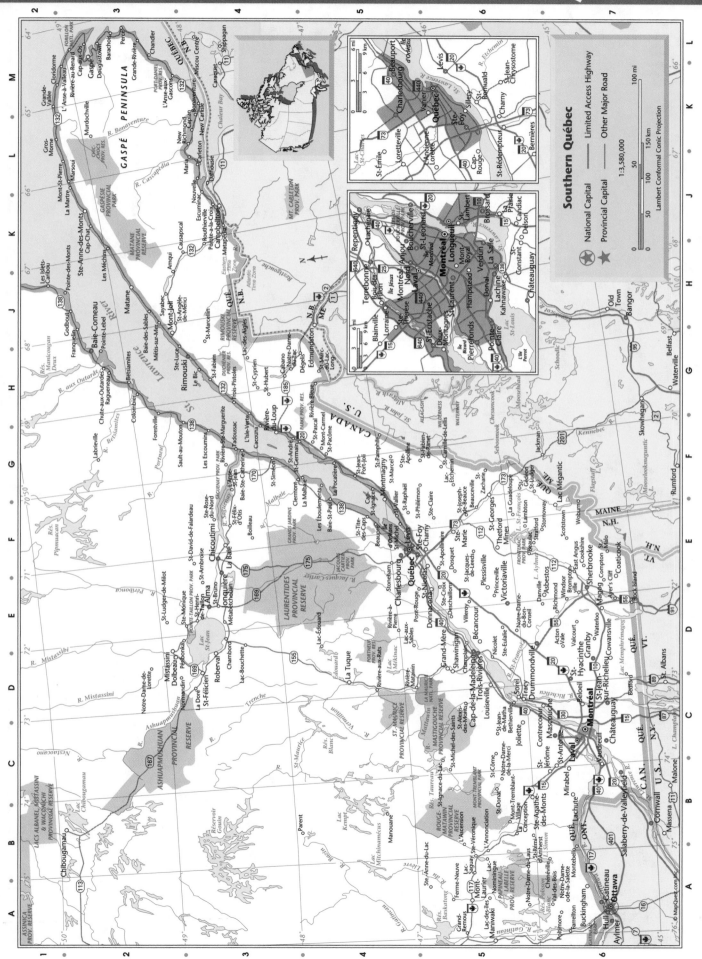

Saskatchewan
★ Provincial Capital
— Major Road
-- Unpaved Road
1:5,114,000

Lambert Conformal Conic Projection

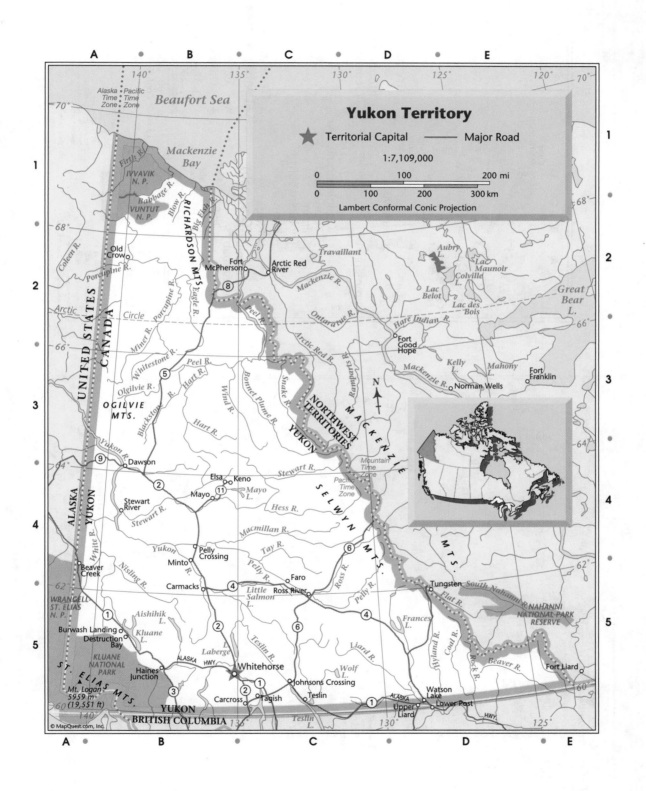

Beaufort Sea

Yukon Territory

★ Territorial Capital ——— Major Road

1:7,109,000

| 0 | 100 | 200 mi |
| 0 | 100 | 200 | 300 km |

Lambert Conformal Conic Projection

Alaska Time Zone • Pacific Time Zone

Mackenzie Bay

IVVAVIK N. P.

Babbage R.
VUNTUT N. P.
Blow R.
Big Fish R.
Firth R.

RICHARDSON MTS
Eagle R.

Coleen R.
Old Crow
Porcupine R.
Miner R.
Porcupine R.

UNITED STATES
CANADA

Arctic
Circle

Fort McPherson
8

Peel R.

Arctic Red River

Travaillant

Aubry L.
Lac Maunoir
Colville L.

Lac Belot
Lac des Bois

Great Bear L.

Mackenzie R.

Ontaratue R.

Arctic Red R.

Hare Indian R.

Fort Good Hope

Whitestone R.
Peel R.
5
Ogilvie R.
Hart R.

OGILVIE MTS.

Wind R.

Bonnet Plume R.

Snake R.

Blackstone R.

Hart R.

NORTHWEST TERRITORIES

YUKON

Kelly L.
Mahony L.
Fort Franklin

Mackenzie R.
Norman Wells

Yukon R.
9
Dawson

Stewart R.

Mountain Time Zone
Pacific Time Zone

SELWYN

MACKENZIE

Elsa • Keno
2
Mayo
11
Mayo L.

Hess R.

Stewart River
Stewart R.

White R.
YUKON
ALASKA

Beaver Creek

Nisling R.

Macmillan R.

Tay R.

Yukon R.
Pelly Crossing
Minto
R.

6

MTS.

WRANGELL ST. ELIAS N. P.

Carmacks
4

Little Salmon L.

Ross River

Pelly R.

Ross R.

Faro

Pelly R.
4

Tungsten
South Nahanni R.
Flat R.

MTS.

NAHANNI NATIONAL PARK RESERVE

Aishihik L.

2

6

Frances L.

Hyland R.
Coal R.
Rock R.
Beaver R.

Fort Liard

Burwash Landing
Destruction Bay

Kluane L.

Teslin R.

Wolf L.

Liard R.

KLUANE NATIONAL PARK

L. Laberge

ALASKA HWY.

ST. ELIAS MTS.

Haines Junction
3

Mt. Logan 5959 m (19,551 ft)

Carcross
2

Whitehorse
1

Tagish

Johnsons Crossing

Teslin

1

ALASKA HWY.
Upper Liard

Watson Lake
Lower Post

HWY.

YUKON
BRITISH COLUMBIA

Teslin L.

© MapQuest.com, Inc.

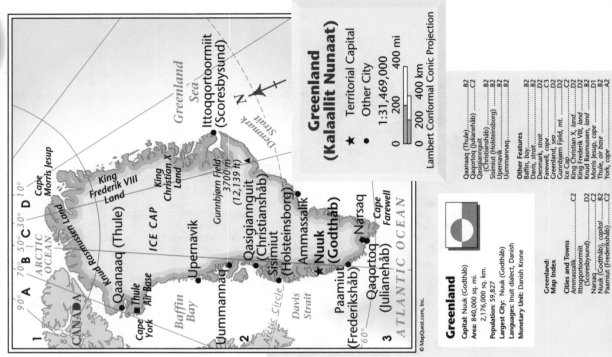

Greenland (Kalaallit Nunaat)

★ Territorial Capital
● Other City

1:31,469,000

0 200 400 km
0 200 400 mi

Lambert Conformal Conic Projection

Greenland

Capital: Nuuk (Godthåb)
Area: 840,000 sq. mi.
2,176,000 sq. km.
Population: 59,827
Largest City: Nuuk (Godthåb)
Languages: Inuit dialect, Danish
Monetary Unit: Danish Krone

Qaanaaq (Thule)........................B2
Qaqortoq (Julianehåb)............C2
Qasigiannguit
(Christianshåb)......................B2
Sisimiut (Holsteinsborg)..........B2
Upernavik..................................B2
Uummannaq..............................B2

Other Features
Baffin, bay..............................B2
Davis, strait............................B2
Denmark, strait........................C3
Farewell, cape..........................D2
Greenland, sea, mt....................D2
Gunnbjørn Fjeld, mt.................D2
Ice Cap....................................C2
King Christian X, land..............D2
King Frederik VIII, land.............B2
Knud Rasmussen, land.............B1
Morris Jesup, cape....................B2
Thule, air base..........................A2
York, cape...............................A2

Greenland:
Map Index

Cities and Towns
Ammassalik............................C2
Ittoqqortoormiit
(Scoresbysund)....................D2
Nuuk (Godthåb), capital..........B2
Paamiut (Frederikshåb)...........C2

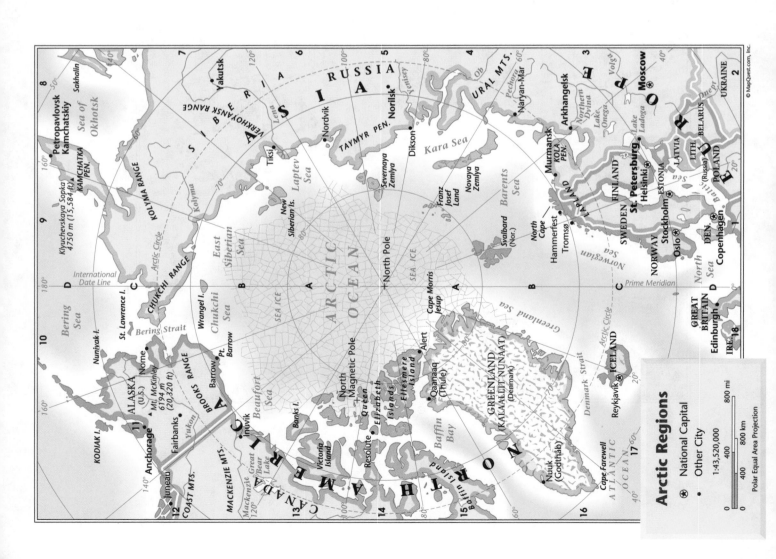

Arctic Regions

⊛ National Capital
● Other City

1:43,520,000

0 400 800 km
0 400 800 mi

Polar Equal Area Projection

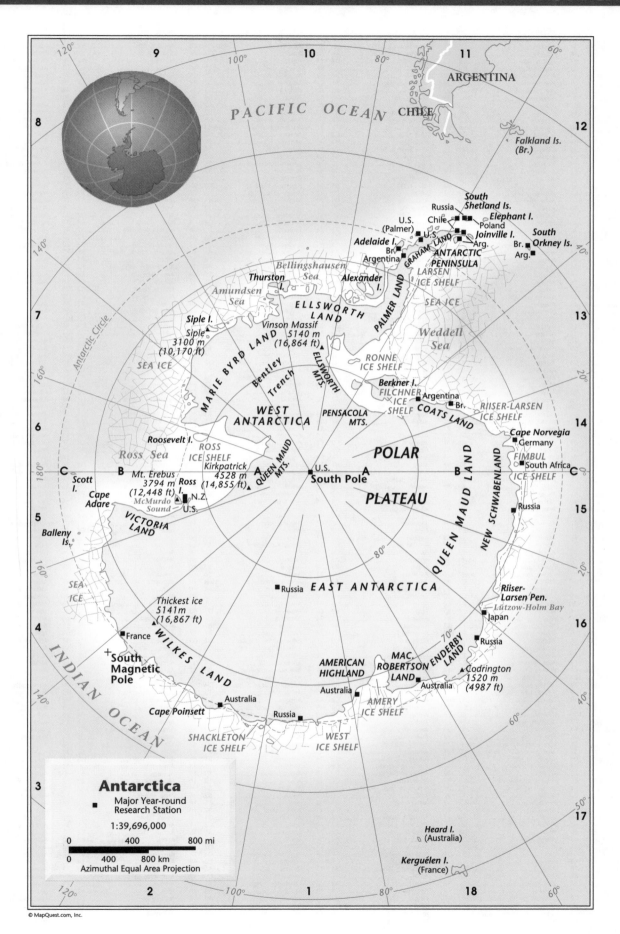

PACIFIC OCEAN

ARGENTINA

CHILE

Falkland Is. (Br.)

South Shetland Is.
Russia
Chile
U.S. (Palmer)
U.S.
Adelaide I.
Br.
Argentina
Elephant I.
Poland
Joinville I.
Arg.
South Orkney Is.
Br.
Arg.

GRAHAM LAND
ANTARCTIC PENINSULA

Bellingshausen Sea

Thurston I.

Alexander I.

LARSEN ICE SHELF

SEA ICE

Amundsen Sea

ELLSWORTH LAND

PALMER LAND

Weddell Sea

Siple I.

Siple 3100 m (10,170 ft)

Vinson Massif 5140 m (16,864 ft)

RONNE ICE SHELF

SEA ICE

MARIE BYRD LAND

Bentley

Trench

ELLSWORTH MTS.

Berkner I.

FILCHNER ICE SHELF

Argentina
Br.

RIISER-LARSEN ICE SHELF

Antarctic Circle

WEST ANTARCTICA

PENSACOLA MTS.

COATS LAND

Cape Norvegia
Germany

Roosevelt I.

ROSS ICE SHELF

Kirkpatrick 4528 m (14,855 ft)

QUEEN MAUD MTS.

POLAR

U.S. South Pole
A

FIMBUL ICE SHELF
South Africa

Ross Sea

Scott I.

Mt. Erebus 3794 m (12,448 ft)

Ross I.

N.Z.
U.S.
McMurdo Sound

C   B

QUEEN MAUD LAND

NEW SCHWABENLAND

Russia

Cape Adare

VICTORIA LAND

PLATEAU

Balleny Is.

SEA ICE

EAST ANTARCTICA

Russia

Riiser-Larsen Pen.

Lützow-Holm Bay

Japan

Thickest ice 5141m (16,867 ft)

France

WILKES LAND

Russia

South Magnetic Pole

AMERICAN HIGHLAND

MAC. ROBERTSON LAND

ENDERBY LAND

Australia

Codrington 1520 m (4987 ft)

INDIAN OCEAN

Cape Poinsett

Australia

Russia

Australia

AMERY ICE SHELF

SHACKLETON ICE SHELF

WEST ICE SHELF

Antarctica

■ Major Year-round Research Station

1:39,696,000

0   400   800 mi

0   400   800 km

Azimuthal Equal Area Projection

Heard I. (Australia)

Kerguélen I. (France)

A

	Key	Page
Aachen	A3	40
Aaiún, el-	B1	58
Aalst	C2	33
Aarau	C1	35
Aare, river	B1, B2	35
Aba	D5	65
Abadan	B3	22
Abaí	E4	75
Abakaliki	E4	65
Abakan	D6	44
Abancay	C3	77
Abaya, lake	B3	60
Abbeville	C1	34
Abbey	B10	104
Abbotsford	L6	95
Abdali	B1	24
Abéché	C4	59
Abemama, island	A1	17
Abengourou	E3	63
Abenrå	B3	32
Abeokuta	B4	65
Aberdeen	Inset	30
Aberdeen	C1	30
Aberdeen, lake	H4	99
Aberdeen, S. Dak.	D1	126
Aberystwyth	B3	30
Abha	B2	24
Abhe, lake	C2	60
Abia, river	C3	66
Abidjan	D4	63
Abilene, Tex.	D2	126
Abkhazia, autonomous republic	A3	45
Aboisso	E4	63
Abomey	A4	64
Abou Deïa	B5	59
Abrantes	A3	36
Abruzzi, peninsula	C2	38
Abşeron, peninsula	C2	45
Abu Dhabi, capital	C2	25
Abu Kamal	B2	27
Abuja, capital	D3	65
Abunã, river	A2	77
Acadia Valley	E5	94
Acajutla	A2	86
Acámbaro	D4	84
Acapulco	E4	84
Acarai, mts.	B5	80
Acaray, river	E4	75
Acarigua	C2	79
Accra, capital	B4	64
Achill, island	A2	31
Achinsk	D6	44
Achwa, river	C2	61
Acklins, island	C4	89
Acme	D5	94
Acolman	Inset	84
Aconcagua, mt.	A3	74
Aconcagua, river	B4	76
Aconibe	C3	66
Acquaviva	A1	39
Acre	A2	81
Acre (Akko)	B1	26
Acton	E4	102
Acton Vale	D6	103
Açúcar, mt.	Inset I	81
Adamawa, massif	B2, E5	65
Adams, lake	N5	95
Adana	C3	27
Adapazari	B2	27
Adare, cape	B5	107
Addis Ababa, capital	C2	60
Addu, atoll	A5	19
Adelaide, island	C11	107
Adelaide, S.A., capital	C3, Inset II	14
Aden	B2	25
Aden	E6	94
Aden, gulf	B1, C2	60
Adi Keyih	B2	60
Adi Ugri	B2	60
Adige, river	B1	38
Adirondack, mts., N.Y.	F1	126
Adjuntas	B2	90
Admiralty, islands	A2	15
Ado-Ekiti	C4	65
Adolphustown	H3	102
Adour, river	B5	34
Adrar	B2	57
Adrar des Iforas, massif	D2	58
Adriatic, sea	C2	38
Advocate Harbour	C2	100
Adwa	C1	60
Adygeya, republic	E4	44
Adzopé	E3	63
Aegean, sea	C2	51
Ærø, island	C4	32
Aetna	D6	94
Afadjoto, mt.	C3	64
Afghanistan		**22**
Afikpo	D5	65
Afram, river	B3	64
Afyon	B2	27
Agadès	B2	59
Agadir	B2	57
Agartala	F4	20
Agboville	D4	63
Ağcabädi	B2	45
Ağdam	B3	45
Agen	C4	34
Aginskiy Buryat, autonomous okrug	D7	44
Aginskoye	D7	44
Agou, mt.	B3	64
Agra	C3	20
Ağri	E2	27
Agrigento	C3	38
Agrínion	B2	51
Ağstafa	A2	45
Agua Prieta	C1	84
Aguada	A2	90
Aguadilla	A2	90
Aguadulce	B2	87
Aguán, river	B2	86
Aguarico, river	C3	79
Aguas Blancas	C2	76
Aguas Buenas	C2	90
Aguascalientes, state capital	D3	84
Águilas	F4	37
Aguilita	B2	90
Agung, mt.	C2	13
Agusan, river	C4	12
Ahmadabad	B4	20
Ahmadi, al-	C2	24
Ahmic Harbour	F2	102
Ahuachapán	A2	86
Ahvaz	B3	22
Ahwar	B2	25
Aibonito	C2	90
Aigáleo, mts.	Inset	51
Ailinglapalap, island	B2	16
Ailuk, island	B1	16
Aillik	B1	98
Aiquile	A3	77
Air Force, island	O3	99
Air Ronge	E5	104
Air, mts.	B2	59
Airdrie	C5	94
Aishihik, lake	B5	105
Aisne, river	D2	34
Aiwo	A2	16
Aix-en-Provence	D5	34
Aix-les-Bains	D4	34
Aíyina, island	B3	51
Aizawl	F4	20
Aizuwakamatsu	C2	8
Ajaccio	Inset I	34
Ajaria, autonomous republic	A4	45
Ajdabiya	D1	56
Ajka	A2	43
Ajman	C2	25
Ajmer	B3	20
Akanyaru, river	B2	61
Akashi	B3	8
Akhalkalaki	B4	45
Akhaltsikhe	B4	45
Akharnaí	Inset	51
Akhelóös, river	B2	51
Akhmeta	C3	45
Akhuryan, river	A2	45
Akita	D2	8
Akjoujt	B3	58
Aklavik	A3	99
Akobo, river	A3	60
Akola	C4	20
Akordat	A2	60
Akosombo, dam	C3	64
Akpatok, island	P4	99
Akranes	A2	52
Akron, Ohio	E1	126
Aksaray	C2	27
Aksu	B1	10
Akulivik	A1	101
Akure	C4	65
Akurenam	C3	66
Akureyri	B2	52
Akuseki, island	A4	8
Alabama	E2	126
Alagoas	E2	81
Alagoinhas	E3	81
Alajuela	B2	86
Alakol, lake	E2	23
Alamayn, al-	A1	56
Alameda	H11	104
Alampur	Inset II	20
Åland, islands	B2	53
Alanya	C3	27
Alarcón, reservoir	E3	37
Alaska	Inset I	126
Alaska, gulf, Alaska	Inset I	126
Alaska, range, Alaska	Inset I	126
Alät	C3	45
Alaverdi	B1	45
Alay, mts.	B1, C3	23
Alayli Dadda	B1	60
Alazani, river	C4	45
Alba Iulia	B2	43
Albacete	F3	37
Alban	E1	102
Albania		**49**
Albany, capital, N.Y.	F1	126
Albany, Ga.	E2	126
Albany, river	C2	101
Albany, W.A.	A3	14
Albert Nile, river	B2	61
Albert, canal	C1	33
Albert, lake	B3	61
Alberton	A2	100
Albi	C5	34
Albina	B2	80
Alboran, sea	E4	37
Ålborg	B1	32
Ålborg, bay	C2	32
Albuquerque, cays	Inset	78
Albuquerque, N. Mex.	C2	126
Albury, N.S.W.	D3	14
Alcalá de Henares	Inset II	37
Alcañiz	F2	37
Alcántara, reservoir	C3	37
Alcázar de San Juan	E3	37
Alcira	F3	37
Alcobendas	Inset II	37
Alcorcón	E2, Inset II	37
Alcoy	F3	37
Aldabra, islands	A2	70
Aldan	D8	44
Aldan, river	D8	44
Alderney, island	Inset II	30
Aleg	B3	58
Alençon	C2	34
Alert	Q1	99
Alès	D4	34
Alessandria	B1	38
Ålesund	A2	52
Aleutian islands, Alaska	Inset I	126
Alexander	A4	94
Alexander, island	B11	107
Alexandra	A4	15
Alexandria	C4	43
Alexandria	A1	56
Alexandria	L2	102
Alexandria, La.	D2	126
Alexandroúpolis	C1	51
Alexis Creek	L5	95
Alexis, river	C3	98
Alfios, river	B3	51
Alfred	L2	102
Algarrobo	Inset	76
Algarve, region	A4	36
Algeciras	D4	37
Algeria		**57**
Alghero	B2	38
Algiers, capital	B1	57
Ali Adde	C2	60
Ali Bayrami	C3	45
Ali-Sabieh	C2	60
Aliákmon, river	B1	51
Alibori, river	B2	64
Alicante	F3	37
Alice	C3	71
Alice Arm	H3	95
Alice Springs, N.T.	C2	14
Alice Town	B2	89
Aligarh	C3	20
Alima, river	D4	66
Aliwal North	C3	71
Alix	D5	94
Alkmaar	B2	32
Allahabad	D3	20
Allardville	D1	97
Allen, lake	B1	31
Allenford	D3	102
Allentown, Pa.	F1	126
Alleppey (Alappuzha)	C7	20
Alliance	E5	94
Allier, river	C3	34
Alligator Pond	B3	88
Allumette, lake	H2	102
Alma	E3	97
Alma	E3	103
Almada	A3	36
Almadén	D3	37
Almansa	F3	37
Almaty (Alma-Ata)	D2	23
Almehdralejo	C3	37
Almelo	D2	32
Almendra, reservoir	C2	53
Almería	E4	37
Almirante	A2	87
Almonte	B4	96
Almonte	J2	102
Alonsa	B4	96
Alor Setar	A1	13
Alor, island	C2	13
Alotau	B3	15
Alpena, Mich.	E1	126
Alps, mts.		29
Alsace	D2	34
Alsask	A9	104
Alta	B1	52
Altai, mts.	B1	10
Altai, republic	F4	44
Altamira	C2	81
Altamira	C3	76
Altario	E5	94
Altay	B1	10
Altay	B2	11
Altay	F4	44
Altdorf	C2	35
Altiplano, plateau	A3	77
Altona	C4	96
Altun, range	A3	10
Aluksne	D2	46
Alvinston	D5	102
Alytus	C2	46
Alzette, river	B2	33
Am Timan	C5	59
Amadjuak, lake	O4	99
Amadora	A3	36
Amagasaki	B3	8
Amahai	D2	13
Amakusa, islands	A3	8
Amambay, mts.	E3	75
Amami, island	Inset II	8
Amapá	C1	81
Amapala	A2	86
Amarah, al-	C2	24
Amaranth	B4	96
Amarillo, Tex.	C2	126
Amasya	C2	27
Amazon, basin	B2	81
Amazon, river	B2	81
Amazonas	B2	81
Ambato	B3	79
Ambatolampy	B2	69
Ambatondrazaka	B2	69
Amberg	B4	40
Ambergris Cay, island	C2	85
Ambergris, cay	C2	85
Amberley	D3	102
Ambon	D2	13
Ambositra	B3	69
Ambre, cape	A2	30
Ambrym, island	C3	18
Amdanga	Inset II	20
Ameca	D3	84
Ameland, island	C1	32
American Samoa		**18**
Amersfoort	C2	32
Amherst	C2	100
Amherstburg	B5	102
Amiens	C2	34
Amindivi, islands	B6	20
Amirante, islands	B2	70
Amisk	E5	94
Amisk, lake	H6	104
Amlamé	A4	64
Amman, capital	A2	26
Ammassalik	C2	106
Ammersee, lake	B4	40
Amos	A4	101
Ampanihy	A3	69
Amparai	C4	19
Amqui	J3	103
Amran	A1	25
Amravati	C4	20
Amritsar	B2	20
Amsterdam, capital	B2	32
Amstetten	D2	39
Amu Darya, river	B1, D2	23
Amund Ringnes, island	J1	99
Amundsen, gulf	C2	99
Amundsen, sea	B9	107
Amur, river	D8	44
Amyun	A1	26
Ana María, gulf	D2	88
Anabar	C1	16
Anaco	D2	79
Anadyr	C10	44
Anadyr, gulf	C11	44
Anahim Lake	K5	95
Anáhuac	D2	84
Anápolis	D3	81
Añasco	A2	90
Añasco, beach	A2	90
Anatolia, region	B2	27
Anatom, island	C4	18
Anchorage, Alaska	Inset I	126
Ancona	C2	38
Ancud	B7	76
Ancud, gulf	B7	76
Andalusia	D4	37
Andaman, islands	F6	20
Andaman, sea	B3	12
Anderlecht	C2	33
Anderson, river	C3	99
Andes, mts.		73
Andheri	Inset I	20
Andizhan	D2	23
Andoany	B1	69
Andong	C4	9
Andorra		**36**
Andorra la Vella, capital	B2	36
Andreas, cape	C1	27
Andros, island	A3	89
Androth, island	B6	20
Aného	B3	64
Anelghowhat	C5	18
Anetan	B1	16
Aneto, mt.	G1	37
Angara, river	D6	44
Angarsk	D7	44
Angaur	B4	17
Angel, falls	D2	79
Angeles	B3	12
Ångermanälven, river	C2	53
Angers	B3	34
Angikuni, lake	H4	99
Angkor Thom, ruins	B2	11
Angkor Wat, ruins	B2	11
Anglesey, island	B3	30
Angoche	C2	68
Angol	B6	76
Angola		**70**
Angoulême	C4	34
Angra	F3	102
Anguilla	C2	17
Anhui	E2	10
Anholt, island	C2	32
Anibare	B2	16
Anié	B3	64
Añisoc	C3	66
Anju	A3	9
Ankang	D2	10
Ankara, capital	C2	27
Ankaratra, mts.	B2	69
Ankobra, river	A4	64
Ann Arbor, Mich.	E1	126
Ann Regina	B2	80
Annaba	B1	57
Annai	A2	11
Annandale	C2	100
Annapolis Royal	B3	100
Annapolis, capital, Md.	F2	126
Annapurna, mt.	B2	19
Annecy	D4	34
Anging	E2	10
Ansbach	B4	40
Anse Boileau	Inset	70
Anse Royale	Inset	70
Anse-à-Galets	C2	89
Anshan	F1	10
Ansongo	D2	58
Antalaha	C1	69
Antalya	B3	27
Antalya, gulf	B3	27
Antananarivo, capital	B2	69
Antarctica		**107**
Antequera	D4	37
Anti-Atlas, ranges	B2	57
Anti-Lebanon, mts.	B1	26
Anticosti, island	D4	101
Antigonish	F2	100
Antigua	C5	85
Antigua	D4	90
Antigua and Barbuda		**90**
Antioch (Antakya)	D3	27
Antofagasta	B2	76
Antrim, mts.	A2	30
Antsirabe	B2	69
Antsiranana	B1	69
Antsohihy	B1	69
Antwerp	C1	33
Anuradhapura	B3	19
Anyang	E2	10
Anyos	B2	36
Aoa	C1	18
Aoba, island	B2	18
Aomori	D1	8
Aoral, mt.	C3	11
Aosta	A1	38
Aozou	B2	59
Apatou	A1	80
Apeldoorn	C2	32
Apennines, range	B1	38
Apetina	B3	80
Api, mt.	A2	19
Apia, capital	C2	18
Apo, volcano	C5	12
Apoera	A2	80
Apolima, strait	B2	18
Appalachian, mts.	E2	126
Apple River	C2	100
Apsley	G3	102
Apulia	C2	38
Apure, river	C2	79
Apurímac, river	C3	77
Aqaba, gulf	A3, B3	26
Aqaba, al-	A3	26
Aqtau	B2	23
Aqtobe	B1	23
Ara	D3	20
Arabah, al-, river	A2, B2	26
Arabian, desert	B2	56
Arabian, sea	A5, Inset I	20
Aracaju	E3	81
Arachon	A4	34
Arad	A2	43
Aradah	B3	25
Arafura, sea	E2	13
Aragats, mt.	B2	45
Aragón	F2	37
Araguaia, river	C3	81
Arak	B3	22
Arakabesan, island	B3	17
Arakan Yoma, mts.	A2	12
Aral	C2	23
Aral, sea	A2, B2	23
Aran, islands	B2	31
Aranda de Duero	E2	37
Aranjuez	E2	37
Aranyaprathet	C3	11
Arapey Grande, river	B1	75
Ararat	B3	45
Ararat (Ağri Daği), mt.	F2	27
Aras, river	E2	27
Arauca	C2	78
Arauca, river	C2	79
Aravalli, range	B3	20
Arawa	B3	15
Arba Minch	B3	60
Arborfield	G7	104
Arborg	C4	96
Archerwill	G8	104
Arctic Bay	L2	99
Arctic Red River	B3	99
Arcola	H11	104
Arda, river	C4	50
Ardabil	B2	22
Ardara	B1	31
Ardbeg	E2	102
Ardennes, plateau	D2	33
Ardennes, region	D1	34
Arecibo	B2	90
Arekalong, peninsula	C2	17
Arenal, lake	B2	86
Arenas, point	D2	90
Arendal	A4	52
Arequipa	C4	77
Arezzo	C2	38
Argenteuil	Inset II	34
Argentina		**74**
Argentino, lake	A7	74
Argeş, river	C3	43
Arghandab, river	B2	22
Argonne, forest	D2	34
Árgos	B3	51
Argyle	C4	96
Argyle	F3	102
Århus	C2	32
Ari, atoll	A3	19
Ariana	C1	57
Arica	B1	76
Arichat	F2	100
Arima	A2	91
Arinsal	A2	36
Aripuanã, river	C2	81
Arish, al-	B1	56
Arizona	B2	126
Arkansas	D2	126
Arkansas, river	D2	126
Arkhangelsk	C4	44
Arklow	C2	31
Arkona	B4	102
Arles	D5	34
Arlington	B2	59
Arlit	D3	33
Armagh	A2	30
Armenia		**45**
Armenia	B3	78
Armidale, N.S.W.	E3	14
Armstrong	N6	95
Armstrong	C2	101
Arnaud, river	B2	101
Arnes	C4	96
Arnhem	C2	32
Arnhem Land, region	C1	14
Arnhem, cape	C1	14
Arno, island	C2	16
Arno, river	B2	38
Arnold's Cove	D5	98
Arnprior	J2	102
Arorae, island	A2	17
Arorae, island	A2	17
Arpa, river	C3	45
Arpajon	Inset II	34
Arqalyq	C1	23
Arran, island	B2	30
Arras	C1	34
Arroyo	C3	90
Arta	B2	60
Artashat	B3	45
Artemisa	B2	88
Artibonite, river	B2	89
Artigas	B1	75
Artik	A2	45
Artsvashen	C2	45
Artvin	E2	27
Aru, islands	E2	13
Arua	B2	61
Aruba, island		82
Arun, river	D2	19
Arusha	C1	68
Aruvi, river	B3	19
Aruwimi, river	C1	67
Arvayheer	C2	11
As Ela	B2	60
Asaba	D4	65
Asadabad	C2	22
Asahi Dake, mt.	Inset I	8
Asahikawa	Inset I	8
Asama, mt.	C2	8
Asansol	E4	20
Asau	B1	18
Asbestos	E6	103
Ascoli Piceno	C2	38
Asela	C3	60
Asenovgrad	C3	50
Ashburton	B3	15
Ashburton, river	A2	14
Ashcroft	M6	95
Ashdod	B2	26
Ashern	B3	96
Asheville, N.C.	E2	126
Asheweig, river	C2	101
Ashgabat, capital	C3	22
Ashikaga	C2	8
Ashizuri, cape	B3	8
Ashmore and Cartier, islands	B1	14
Ashqelon	A4	91
Ashton	C2	91
Ashuapmushuan, river	C2	103
Asinara, island	D3	38
Asipovichy	D3	47
Asir, region	B2	24
Askar	B1	25
Asmara, capital	B2	60
Asnam, el-	B1	57
Aso, mt.	A3	8
Asosa	A3	15
Aspiring, mt.	A3	15
Asprópirgos	Inset	51
Asquith	C8	104
Assab	D3	60
Assal, lake	B2	60
Assam	B2	60
Assiniboia	D11	104
Assiniboine, mts.	P6	95
Assiniboine, river	A4	96
Astana (Akmola), capital	D1	23
Astara	C3	45
Asti	B1	38
Astipálaia, island	C3	51
Astorga	C1	37
Astrakhan	E4	44
Astrolabe, reefs	C2	18
Asturias	C1	37
Asunción, capital	D4	75
Aswan	B2	56
Aswan High, dam	B3	56
Asyut	B2	56
At-Bashy	D2	23
Atacama, desert	B3	64
Atakpamé	B3	64
Ataq	B2	58
Atâr	B2	58
Atatürk, reservoir	D3	27
Atbara	B1	60
Atbara, river	C2	59
Atbarah, river	C2	59
Atbasar	C1	23
Ath	B2	33
Athabasca	D4	94
Athabasca, lake	A1	104
Athabasca, river	B4, D3, E2	94
Athens, capital	B3, Inset	51
Athens, Ga.	E2	126
Athi, river	C2	68
Athlone	C2	31
Áthos, mt.	C1	51
Ati	B4	59
Atiak	C3	94
Atikameg	C3	94
Atikameg Lake	B3	101
Atikokan	B3	101
Atitlán, lake	B5	85
Atlanta, capital, Ga.	E2	126
Atlantic City, N.J.	F2	126
Atlas, mts.	A1, B2	57
Atlin	F1	95
Atlin, lake	F1	95
Atrai, river	D2	21
Atrak, river	D2	22
Atrato, river	A3	78
Attapu	D4	11
Attawapiskat	D2	101
Attawapiskat, river	C2	101
Atuel, river	B4	74
Aua	C3	18
Aube, river	D3	34
Auburn	C5	34
Auch	C5	34
Auckland	B2	15
Augsburg	B4	40
Augusta, capital, Maine	G1	126
Augusta, Ga.	E2	126
Auki	B1	16
Aulac	E3	97
Aunuu, island	C1	18
Auob, river	C3	70
Aurangabad	C5	20
Aurillac	C4	34
Aurora	F3	102
Ausa, river	C1	39
Austin, capital, Tex.	D2	126
Australia		**14**
Australian Alps, mts.	D3	14
Australian Capital Territory	D3	14
Austria		**39**
Auvergne	C4	34
Auxerre	C3	34
Avalon, peninsula	E5	98
Aveiro	A2	36
Avellaneda	D3	74
Avellino	C2	38
Aviemore	C1	30
Avignon	D5	34
Ávila	D2	37
Avilés	D1	37
Avon, islands	A2	18
Avon, river	C3	30
Avonlea	E10	104
Awaji	B3	8

Name	Key	Page
Awaji, *island*	B3	8
Awasa	C3	60
Awash, *river*	C2	60
Awaso	A3	64
Awbari	B2	56
Awka	D4	65
Awwali, *river*	A2	26
Axel Heiberg, *island*	K1	99
Axim	A4	64
Ayacucho	C3	77
Ayagöz	E2	23
Aydin	A3	27
Ayer Chawan, *island*	A1	13
Ayer's Cliff	D6	103
Ayios Dhimítrios	Inset	51
Aylesbury	Inset III	30
Aylmer	E5	102
Aylmer	A6	103
Aylmer	G4	99
Aylmer, *lake*	E6	103
Ayn, al-	C2	25
Ayoûn el-Atroûs	C3	58
Ayr	B2	30
Aytos	F3	50
Ayutthaya, *region*	C2	58
Azare	F2	65
Azaz	A1	27
Azcapotzalco	Inset	84
Azerbaijan		45
Azerbaijan, *region*	B2	22
Azogues	B4	79
Azores, *islands*		5
Azov, *sea*	D3	22
Azraq ash-Shishan	B2	26
Azua	B2	89
Azuero, *peninsula*	B3	87
B		
Ba, *river*	B3	11
Baalbek	B1	26
Bab al-Mandab, *strait*	C1	60
Babahoyo	B3	79
Babanusah	B3	59
Babar, *island*	D2	13
Babbage, *river*	B1	105
Babda	A2	26
Babelthuap, *island*	C3	17
Babine, *lake*	J4	95
Babine, *river*	J3	95
Babruysk	D3	47
Babu Bheri	Inset II	20
Babuyan, *channel*	B2	12
Babuyan, *islands*	B2	12
Babylon, *ruins*	C2	24
Bac Lieu	A5	11
Bacabal	D2	81
Bacău	D2	43
Back, *river*	H3	99
Bačka Palanka	A2	49
Bacolod	B4	12
Bad Ems	A3	40
Bad Ischl	C3	39
Bad Kreuznach	A4	40
Bad Reichenhall	C5	40
Badajoz	C3	37
Badalona	H2	37
Badanah	B1	24
Badas	A2	13
Baddeck	G1	100
Baden	C1	35
Baden	E2	39
Baden	A3	96
Baden-Baden	B4	40
Baden-Württemberg	B4	40
Badger	D4	96
Badger	C5	98
Badou	B3	64
Bafatá	C1	62
Baffin, *bay*	L1	92
Baffin, *island*	M2	99
Baffin, *region*	N2	99
Bafilo	B2	64
Bafing, *river*	C2	62
Bafoulabé	A3	58
Bafoussam	B2	65
Baghdad, *capital*	B2	24
Baghlan	B2	22
Baglung	B2	19
Bagmati, *river*	C2	19
Bagoé, *river*	C1	63
Baguio	B2	12
Bagzane, *mt.*	B2	59
Bahamas		89
Bahawalpur	D4	21
Bahia	D3	81
Bahía Blanca	C4	74
Bahía Honda	A2	88
Bahía, *islands*	B1	86
Bahir Dar	B2	60
Bahoruco, *mts.*	A2	89
Bahr al-Arab, *river*	B3	59
Bahr al-Ghazal, *river*	C3	59
Bahr al-Jabal, *river*	C3	59
Bahr Salamat, *river*	B5	59
Bahrain		25
Bahrain, *gulf*	A2	25
Baia Mare	B2	43
Baicheng	F1	10
Baidyabati	Inset II	20
Baie Verte	C4	98
Baie-Comeau	H2	103
Baie-des-Sables	J3	103
Baie-St-Paul	F4	103
Baie-Ste-Anne	E1	97
Baie-Ste-Catherine	G3	103
Baieboro	G3	102
Bainsville	L2	102
Bair	B2	26
Baiti	B1	16
Baja	B2	43
Baja California	A1	84
Baja California Sur	B2	84
Bajadero	B2	90
Bajo Boquete	A2	87
Bakel	C2	62
Baker Brook	A1	97
Baker Lake	J4	99
Bakersfield, Calif.	B2	126
Bakhardok	C2	22
Bakhtaran	B3	22
Bakhtiari, *region*	B3	22
Bakony, *mts.*	A2	43
Baku, *capital*	C2	45
Bala	F2	102
Bala, *lake*	B3	30
Balabac, *island*	A5	12
Balabac, *strait*	A5	12
Balakän	B2	45
Balaklava	C4	47
Balaton, *lake*	A2	43
Balboa	C2	87
Baldur	B4	96
Baldy, *mt.*	A3	96
Balearic, *islands*	G3	37
Balearic, *sea*	G2	37
Baleia, *point*	E3	81
Balgonie	F10	104
Balhaf	B2	25
Balho	B1	60
Bali, *island*	C2	13
Baliceaux, *island*	B3	91
Balikesir	A2	27
Balikpapan	C2	13
Balkan, *mts.*	B2	50
Balkh	B1	22
Balkhash	D2	23
Balkhash, *lake*	D2	23
Ballancourt-sur-Essonne	Inset II	34
Ballarat, Vic.	D3	14
Ballerup	D3	32
Ballina	B1	31
Bally	Inset II	20
Ballymena	A2	30
Balmaceda	B8	76
Balmertown	B2	101
Balmoral	C1	97
Balranald	E4	84
Balsas, *river*	E4	84
Bălţi	A2	50
Baltic, *sea*		29
Baltimore, Md.	F2	126
Baluchistan, *region*	E4	22
Balykchy	E1	23
Balzers	B2	33
Bam	D4	22
Bamako, *capital*	B3	58
Bamangachi	Inset II	20
Bambadinca	C1	62
Bambana, *river*	B2	87
Bambari	B2	66
Bamberg	B4	40
Bamenda	B2	65
Bamian	B2	22
Ban Houayxay	A1	11
Ban Phai	C2	12
Banaba, *island*	A2	17
Banana	A2	67
Banana, *islands*	A1	63
Bananga	F7	20
Banbury	C3	30
Bancroft	H2	102
Banda Aceh	A1	13
Banda, *sea*	D2	13
Bandama Blanc, *river*	C2	63
Bandama Rouge, *river*	C2	63
Bandar Lampung	B2	13
Bandar Seri Begawan, *capital*	B2	13
Bandar-e Abbas	D4	22
Bandar-e Anzali	B2	22
Bandar-e Bushehr	C4	22
Bandar-e Khomeyni	B3	22
Bandar-e Torkeman	C2	22
Bandeira, *mt.*	D4	81
Bandra	Inset I	20
Bandundu	B2	67
Bandung	B2	13
Banff	C5	94
Bangalore	C6	20
Bangar	C2	13
Bangassou	B3	66
Banggi, *island*	D1	13
Banghiang, *river*	C3	11
Bangka, *island*	B2	13
Bangkok, *capital*	B3	12
Bangladesh		21
Bangor	B2	30
Bangor	B3	30
Bangor, Maine	G1	126
Bangui, *capital*	A3	66
Bangweulu, *lake*	B2	67
Bani	B2	89
Bani Suwayf	B2	56
Bani Walid	B1	56
Bani, *river*	B3	58
Baniyas	A2	27
Banja Luka	B1	48
Banjarmasin	C2	13
Banjul, *capital*	B2	62
Banks, *island*	G4	95
Banks, *island*	D2	99
Banks, *islands*	B1	18
Banks, *peninsula*	B3	15
Bann, *river*	A2	30
Bannockburn	H3	102
Bansang	D2	62
Bansbaria	Inset II	20
Banská Bystrica	B2	42
Bantry	B3	31
Bantry, *bay*	B3	31
Baoding	E2	10
Baoshan	C3	10
Baotou	E1	10
Baoulé, *river*	B3	58
Baqubah	B2	24
Baquerizo Moreno	Inset	79
Bar	A3	49
Bar-le-Duc	D2	34
Baraawe	B3	60
Barabinsk	D5	44
Baracaldo	E1	37
Barachois	M3	103
Baracoa	F3	88
Barahona	A2	89
Baraki Barak	B2	22
Baydhabo	A3	60
Barakpur	Inset II	20
Baram, *river*	D2	13
Barama, *river*	B2	80
Baranagar	Inset II	20
Baranavichy	C3	47
Barasat	Inset II	20
Barbados		91
Barbuda, *island*	E3	90
Barcelona	D1	79
Barcelona	H2	37
Barceloneta	B2	90
Bârda	B2	45
Bardaï	B2	59
Bardejov	C3	42
Bareilly	C3	20
Barents, *sea*	B3	44
Bargachia	Inset II	20
Bari	D2	38
Baril, *lake*	E2	94
Barinas	B2	79
Barind, *region*	B4	21
Baris	B3	56
Barisal	D6	21
Bark, *lake*	H2	102
Barkerville	M4	95
Barkly, *tableland*	C1	14
Barletta	D2	38
Barnaul	D6	44
Barnes, *ice cap*	O3	99
Barnsley	C3	30
Barnstaple	B3	30
Barnwell	D6	94
Baro, *river*	B2	60
Barouallie	B2	91
Barquisimeto	C1	79
Barra, *island*	A2	30
Barrancabermeja	B3	78
Barranquilla	B3	78
Barranquitas	C2	90
Barreiro	A3	36
Barrhead	C4	94
Barrie	F3	102
Barrière	M5	95
Barrington	B4	100
Barro	B1	62
Barrouallie	B2	91
Barrow, Alaska	Inset I	126
Barrow, *river*	C2	31
Barrow-in-Furness	B2	30
Barry's Bay	H2	102
Bartang, *river*	B1	23
Bartica	B2	80
Barú, *volcano*	A2	87
Baruun-Urt	D2	11
Bas-Caraquet	E1	97
Basarabeasca	B2	50
Basel	B1	35
Bashi, *channel*	B1	12
Basilan	B5	12
Basilan, *island*	B5	12
Basildon	Inset III	30
Basilicata	C2	38
Baskatong, *reservoir*	A5	103
Basque Country	E1	37
Bass, *strait*	C2	14
Bass Rock, *islet*	C2	30
Bassar	B2	64
Basse Santa Su	D2	62
Basse-Normandie	B2	34
Bassein	B3	12
Basseterre, *capital*	B2	90
Bassila	A3	64
Bastia	Inset I	34
Bastogne	D2	33
Bata	B3	66
Bataan, *peninsula*	B3	12
Batabanó, *gulf*	B2	88
Batan, *islands*	B1	12
Batang	C2	10
Batang Duri	C2	13
Batangafo	A2	66
Batangas	B3	12
Batdambang	B2	11
Bate, *bay*	Inset IV	14
Batéké, *plateau*	C5	66
Bath	C3	90
Bath	C3	30
Batha, *river*	C4	59
Bathsheba	B3	91
Bathurst	D1	97
Bathurst, *island*	J1	99
Batin, Wadi al-, *river*	A2	24
Batinah, al-, *region*	C1	25
Batman	E3	27
Baton Rouge, *capital, La.*	D2	126
Batouri	B3	65
Batroun	A1	26
Batticaloa	C4	19
Batticle	D2	98
Battle	A7	104
Battleford	B8	104
Batu Pahat	B2	13
Batumi	A4	45
Baubau	D2	13
Bauchi	B2	65
Bauria	Inset II	20
Bauru	E3	81
Bauska	C2	46
Bautzen	C3	40
Bavaria	B4	40
Bavarian Alps, *mts.*	B5	40
Bawiti, al-	A2	56
Bawku	B1	64
Bawlf	D5	94
Bay Bulls	E5	98
Bay de Verde	E5	98
Bay Roberts	E5	98
Bay St. Lawrence	G1	100
Bayamo	D3	88
Bayamón	C2	90
Bayamón, *river*	C2	90
Bayan Har, *range*	C2	10
Bayanhongor	C2	11
Bayda, al-	B2	25
Bayda, al-	D1	56
Bayda, al-	A3	60
Bayerischer Wald, *mts.*	C4	40
Bayeux	B2	34
Bayfield	D4	102
Baygorria, *lake*	B2	75
Bayjī, *lake*	D7	44
Bayonne	B5	34
Bayport	C3	100
Bayramaly	D3	22
Bayreuth	B4	40
Bays, *lake*	F2	102
Baza	E4	37
Bazardüzü Daği, *mt.*	B2	45
Bazin, *river*	A4	103
Beachside	D4	98
Beagle, *channel*	B7	74
Bear Lake	L4	95
Bear River	C2	100
Beata, *cape*	A3	89
Beata, *island*	A3	89
Beaton	O6	95
Beau Bassin	B2	69
Beauceville	F5	103
Beaufort West	B3	71
Beaufort, *sea*	B1	105
Beaulac	E6	103
Beaumont	C4	96
Beaumont, Tex.	D2	126
Beaupré	F4	103
Beauséjour	C4	96
Beauvais	C2	34
Beaver Creek	A4	105
Beaver Harbour	E3	100
Beaver Hill, *lake*	D2	96
Beaver Mines	C6	94
Beaver, *river*	A6	104
Beaver, *river*	D5	105
Beaverton	F3	102
Bécancour	D3	103
Bečan	B2	49
Béchar	A1	57
Bedeque, *bay*	B2	100
Bedford	C3	30
Bedford	D3	100
Bedford	D6	103
Bedok	B1	13
Beechy	C10	104
Beersheba	B2	26
Behala	Inset II	20
Bei'an	F1	10
Beihai	D3	10
Beijing, *capital*	E2	10
Beira	B3	68
Beirut, *capital*	A2	26
Beja	B3	36
Beja	B1	57
Bejaïa	B1	57
Bejaïa, *gulf*	B1	57
Béjar	D2	37
Bekaa, *valley*	A2	26
Békéscsaba	C2	43
Bekwai	B4	90
Bélabo	B2	65
Belair	B4	91
Belapurpada	Inset I	20
Belarus		47
Belasica, *mts.*	C2	48
Belaya Tserkov	C2	47
Beledweyne	B3	60
Belém	D2	81
Bélep, *islands*	C2	18
Belfast	B2	30
Belford Roxo	Inset I	81
Belfort	D3	34
Belfort, *gap*	D3	34
Belgaum	B5	20
Belgium		33
Belgrade, *capital*	B2	49
Beli Drim, *river*	B2	49
Bélinga	B1	66
Belitung, *island*	B2	13
Belize		85
Belize City	B2	85
Bella Coola	J5	95
Bella Unión	B1	75
Bellary	C5	20
Bellburns	C4	98
Belle Isle, *strait*	C3	98
Belle River	C3	102
Belle, *island*	B3	34
Belle, *island*	C3	98
Belle-Anse	C2	89
Belledune	D1	97
Belleview	A4	96
Belleville	H3	102
Bellingham, Wash.	A1	126
Bellingshausen, *sea*	B10	107
Bellinzona	D2	35
Belluno	C1	38
Bellville	A3	71
Belmont	B4	96
Belmopan, *capital*	B2	85
Beloeil	C6	103
Belo Horizonte	E3	81
Belomorsk	C3	44
Belukha, *mt.*	D1	126
Ben Eoin	G2	100
Ben Nevis, *mt.*	B1	30
Benavente	D1	37
Bender (Tighina)	B2	50
Benderbeyla	C2	60
Bendigo, Vic.	D3	14
Bengal, *bay*	E5	20
Bengbu	E2	10
Benghazi	D1	56
Bengkulu	B2	13
Bengough	E11	104
Benguela	B4	70
Beni Mellal	C1	57
Beni, *river*	A2	77
Benidorm	F3	37
Benin		64
Benin City	C4	65
Benin, *bight*	B5	65
Benito	A3	96
Benoit's Cove	B5	98
Benoni	C2	71
Bénoué, *river*	B2	65
Benson	G11	104
Bentiaba	B4	70
Bentley	C3	94
Benue, *river*	E3	65
Benxi	F1	10
Benzdorp	B3	80
Beqa, *island*	B3	17
Bequia, *island*	B2	91
Berat	A3	49
Berbera	B1	60
Berbérati	A3	66
Berbice, *river*	B3	80
Berdoba	C4	59
Berdyansk	D3	47
Berekua	B4	90
Berens River	C3	96
Berens, *island*	C3	96
Berens, *river*	C3	96
Beresford	D1	97
Berezniki	D4	44
Bergamo	B1	38
Bergen op Zoom	B3	32
Bergen, *sea*	Inset I	106
Bergerac	C4	34
Bergisch Gladbach	A3	40
Bering, *sea*	Inset I	126
Bering, *strait*	C11	44
Berkner, *island*	B12	107
Berlin, *capital*	C2	40
Bermejo, *river*	C2	74
Bermuda, *island*		82
Bern, *capital*	B2	35
Bernburg	B3	40
Bernese Alps, *mts.*	B2	35
Bernières	K6	103
Berounka, *river*	A3	42
Bertwell	H8	104
Berwick	C2	100
Berwick-upon-Tweed	C2	30
Besançon	D3	34
Besnard, *lake*	D5	104
Besor, *river*	B2	26
Bethanien	C4	70
Bethel, Alaska	Inset I	126
Bethierville	C5	103
Bethlehem	C2	71
Béticos, *mts.*	E4	37
Bétou	E2	66
Betsiamites	H3	103
Betsiamites, *river*	G2	103
Betsiboka, *river*	B2	69
Bette, *mt.*	B2	56
Beulah	A4	96
Beyla	D3	62
Beyneu	B2	23
Beyşehir, *lake*	B2	27
Béziers	C5	34
Bhadrakh	E4	20
Bhadreswar	Inset II	20
Bhagalpur	E3	20
Bhairahawa	B2	19
Bhaktapur	C2	19
Bhamapur	D5	20
Bhamo	C1	12
Bhandup	Inset I	20
Bharatpur	C3	20
Bhatapara	D4	20
Bhatpara	Inset II	20
Bhavnagar	B4	20
Bhayandar	Inset I	20
Bheri, *river*	B2	19
Bhima, *river*	C5	20
Bhimpur	Inset II	20
Bhiwandi	Inset I	20
Bhopal	C4	20
Bhubaneswar	E4	20
Bhuj	A4	20
Bhunya	B2	71
Bhutan		19
Biabou	B2	91
Biafra, *bight*	A3	65
Biak, *island*	E2	13
Biała Podlaska	F2	41
Białystok	F2	41
Biankouma	C3	63
Biarritz	B5	34
Bicaz, *reservoir*	D2	43
Biche, *lake*	E4	94
Bida	D3	65
Bidar	C5	20
Bié, *plateau*	C4	70
Biel	B1	35
Biel, *lake*	B1	35
Bielefeld	B2	40
Bielsko-Biała	D4	41
Bien Hoa	B4	11
Bienville, *lake*	A3	71
Big Beaver	E11	104
Big Bend	B2	71
Big Creek	L5	95
Big Fish, *river*	B1	105
Big Gull, *lake*	J3	102
Big Muddy, *lake*	F11	104
Big River	C2	104
Big Trout Lake	C2	101
Big, *island*	O4	99
Big, *river*	B2	98
Biggar	C8	104
Bignona	A3	62
Bigstone, *river*	D1	96
Bihać	A1	48
Bihar	E3	20
Bihor, *mts.*	B2	43
Bijagós, *islands*	A2	62
Bijapur	C5	20
Bijeljina	C1	48
Bikaner	B3	20
Bikar, *island*	C1	16
Bikini, *island*	B1	16
Bilaspur	D4	20
Biläsuvar	B3	45
Bilauktaung, *range*	B3, C3	12
Bilbao	E1	37
Billings, Mont.	C1	126
Billings, *reservoir*	Inset II	81
Bilma	C2	59
Biloku	B5	80
Biloxi, Miss.	E2	126
Biltine	C4	59
Bimbila	C2	64
Binche	C2	33
Bindloss	E6	94
Bindura	B1	69
Binga, *mt.*	B3	68
Bingen	A4	40
Binscarth	A4	96
Bint Jubayl	A2	26
Bintang	B2	62
Bintimane, *mt.*	B1	63
Bío-Bío, *river*	B6	76
Bioko, *island*	A1	66
Bir Gandús	A2	58
Bīr Morgrein	C1	58
Birak	B2	56
Birao	B1	66
Biratnagar	D3	19
Birch Cliff	K5	102
Birch Hills	E7	104
Birch River	A3	96
Birch, *mts.*	D2	94
Birchy Bay	D4	98
Bird, *island*	B2	91
Birendranagar	B2	19
Birganj	C2	19
Birjand	D3	22
Birkat Qarun, *lake*	B2	56
Birkenhead	B3	30
Birkirkara	B2	36
Birlad	D2	43
Birmingham	C3	30
Birmingham, Ala.	E2	126
Birni Nkonni	B3	59
Birobidzhan	E8	44
Birtle	A4	96
Biržai	C1	46
Birżebbuga	C3	36
Biscay, *bay*	B4	34
Bishkek, *capital*	D1	23
Bishnupur	Inset II	20
Bishop's Falls	D4	98
Biskra	C1	57
Bislig	C4	12
Bismarck, *archipelago*	A2	15
Bismarck, *capital, N. Dak.*	C1	126
Bismarck, *range*	A2	15
Bismarck, *sea*	A2	15
Bismuna, *lagoon*	C1	87
Bison, *lake*	B2	94
Bissau, *capital*	B2	62
Bissett	D3	96
Bissorä	B1	62
Bistcho, *lake*	A1	94
Bistrita	C2	43
Bistrița, *river*	C2	43
Bitam	A1	66
Bitola	B2	48
Bitumount	E2	94
Biu	G2	65
Biwa, *lake*	B3	8
Biysk	D6	44
Bizard, *island*	H5	103
Bizerte	B1	57
Bjorne, *peninsula*	L1	99
Black (Da), *river*	A2	11
Black Country, *region*	C3	30
Black Lake	E1	104
Black River	B2	88
Black Tickle	D2	98
Black Volta, *river*	A2, B3	64
Black, *forest*	A4	40
Black, *hills, S. Dak.*	C1	126
Black, *sea*		29
Blackburn	C3	30
Blackmans	B3	91
Blackpool	C3	30
Blacks Harbour	C3	97
Blackstone, *river*	B3	105
Blackville	D2	97
Blackwater, *river*	B2, C1	31
Blagoevgrad	B4	50
Blagoveshchensk	C3	49
Blagoveshchensk	D8	44
Blaine Lake	D8	104
Blainville	H5	103
Blanc, *mt.*	D4	34
Blanc, *reservoir*	C4	103
Blanc-Sablon	E3	101
Blanca, *bay*	C4	74
Blanda	B2	52
Blantyre	B3	68
Blarney	B3	31
Blatec	C2	48
Blenheim	B3	15
Blenheim	D5	102
Blida	B1	57
Bligh Water, *sound*	B2	17
Blind Bay	N6	95
Blind River	C1	102
Blitta	B2	64
Bloemfontein, *judicial capital*	C2	71
Blois	C3	34
Bloodvein, *river*	C3	96
Bloomfield	H4	102
Bloomington, Ind.	E2	126
Blossom Park	H6	102
Blow, *river*	B1	105
Blue Mountain, *peak*	C2	88
Blue Nile, *river*	C2	59
Blue Ridge	C4	94
Blue River	N5	95
Blue, *mts.*	E3	14
Blue, *mts.*	C2	88
Bluefields	B2	88
Bluefields	C3	87

	Key	Page
Bluenose, *lake*	E3	99
Bluffton	C5	94
Blyth	D4	102
Bo	B2	63
Bo Hai, *gulf*	E2	10
Boa Vista	B1	81
Boa Vista, *island*	D2	58
Boaco	B2	87
Bobcaygeon	G3	102
Bobo-Dioulasso	B3	64
Bocas del Toro	A2	87
Bocay	B1	87
Bocay, *river*	A2	87
Bocholt	A3	40
Bochum	A3	40
Bodaybo	D7	44
Bodo	E5	94
Bodø	C2	52
Boende	B2	67
Boggeragh, *mts.*	B2	31
Boggy, *peak*	D5	90
Bogor	B2	13
Bogotá, *capital*	B3	78
Bogra	C4	21
Bohemia, *region*	A3	42
Bohemian, *forest*	A3	42
Bohemian-Moravian, *heights*	B3	42
Bohol, *island*	C4	12
Bohol, *sea*	C4	12
Boiestown	C2	97
Boilleau	F3	103
Bois-des-Filion	H5	103
Boise, *capital, Idaho*	B1	126
Boissevain	A4	96
Boknafjord, *fjord*	B4	52
Boksburg	C2	71
Bol	A4	59
Bolama	B2	62
Bolands	D5	90
Bole	A2	64
Bolgatanga	B1	64
Bolívar, *mt.*	B2	79
Bolivia		77
Bolligen	B2	35
Bolnisi	C4	45
Bolobo	B2	67
Bologna	B1	38
Bolovens, *plateau*	D4	11
Bolsena, *lake*	B2	38
Bolsón de Mapimí, *depression*	D2	84
Bolton	C3	30
Bolton	F4	102
Bolu	B2	27
Bolzano	B1	38
Bom Jesus da Lapa	D3	81
Bombay	B5, Inset I	20
Bomu, *river*	C1	67
Bon Pays, *region*	B2	33
Bon, *cape*	C1	57
Bonaire, *island*		82
Bonao	B2	89
Bonaventure	L3	103
Bonaventure, *river*	L3	103
Bonavista	E5	98
Bonavista, *bay*	E5	98
Bondo	B1	67
Bondoukou	E2	63
Bondy	Inset II	34
Bongor	A5	59
Bonin, *islands*	Inset III	8
Bonn	A3	40
Bonnet Plume, *river*	C3	105
Bonny	D5	65
Bonnyville	E4	94
Bonshaw	B2	100
Bonthe	A2	63
Bööntsagaan, *lake*	B2	11
Boosaaso	B1	60
Boothia, *gulf*	K2	99
Boothia, *peninsula*	K2	99
Booué	A2	66
Bor	C2	49
Borås	B3	53
Bordeaux	B4	34
Borden	B2	100
Borden	C8	104
Borden, *island*	F1	99
Borden, *peninsula*	M2	99
Bordøy, *island*	Inset	32
Borgo Maggiore	B1	39
Borivli	Inset I	20
Borjomi	B4	45
Borneo, *island*	C1	13
Bornholm, *island*	E3	32
Bosanska Gradiška	B1	48
Bosanska Krupa	A1	48
Bosna, *river*	B1	48
Bosnia & Hercegovina		48
Boso, *peninsula*	D3	8
Bosporus, *strait*	B2	27
Bossangoa	A2	66
Bosten, *lake*	B1	10
Boston	C3	30
Boston Bar	M6	95
Boston, *capital, Mass.*	F1	126
Boswell	O6	95
Botany, *bay*	Inset IV	14
Boteti, *river*	A2	69
Botha	D5	94
Bothnia, *gulf*	B2, D2	53
Botna, *river*	B2	50
Botoşani	D2	43
Botrange, *mt.*	E2	33
Botswana		69
Botte Donato, *mt.*	D3	38
Bottrop	A3	40
Botwood	D4	98
Bouaflé	D3	63
Bouaké	B3	63
Bouar	A2	66
Boucherville	J5	103
Bouctouche	E2	97
Bougainville, *island*	B2	15
Boughton, *bay*	C2	100
Bougouni	B3	63
Boulder, Colo.	C2	126

	Key	Page
Boulogne-Billancourt	Inset II	34
Boulogne-sur-Mer	C1	34
Bouna	E2	63
Bourail	C2	18
Bourem	C2	58
Bourg-en-Bresse	D3	34
Bourges	C3	34
Bourgogne	C3	34
Bourke, N.S.W.	D3	14
Bournemouth	C4	30
Bousso	B5	59
Bow City	D6	94
Bow, *river*	D6	94
Bow, *river*	E6	104
Bowen, Qld.	D2	14
Bowling Green, Ky.	E2	126
Bowser, *lake*	H3	95
Bowsman	A3	96
Boyd's Cove	D4	98
Boyne	C2	31
Boyne, *river*	B4	96
Bozeman, Mont.	B1	126
Brabant Lake	G4	104
Brač, *island*	C3	48
Bracciano, *lake*	C2	38
Bracebridge	F2	102
Bradford	C3	30
Braga	A2	36
Bragança	B2	36
Bragg Creek	C6	94
Brahmanbaria	E5	21
Brahmaputra, *river*	F3	20
Brăila	D3	43
Braintree	Inset III	30
Brakpan	C2	71
Bralorne	L6	95
Bramalea	H5	102
Brampton	F4	102
Branco, *river*	B1	81
Brandberg, *mt.*	B2	70
Brandenburg	C2	40
Brandon	B4, C2	96
Brant	D6	94
Brantford	E4	102
Bras d'Or	G1	100
Brasília, *capital*	D3	81
Braşov	C3	43
Bratislava, *capital*	A2	42
Bratsk	D7	44
Braunau	C2	39
Brava, *coast*	H2	37
Brava, *island*	B4	58
Brazil		81
Brazilian, *highlands*	D3	81
Brazzaville, *capital*	C6	66
Brčko	B1	48
Brea, *point*	B3	90
Břeclav	C4	42
Brecon Beacons, *mts.*	B3	30
Breda	B3	33
Bredenbury	H10	104
Bregalnica, *river*	C2	48
Breidhafjördhur, *fjord*	A2	52
Bremen	B2	40
Bremerhaven	B2	40
Brenner, *pass*	B3	39
Brentwood	Inset III	30
Brescia	B1	38
Brest	A3	47
Brest	A2	34
Bretagne	B2	34
Breton	C4	94
Bria	B2	66
Briançon	D4	34
Briceni	A1	50
Bridge Lake	M5	95
Bridgeport, Conn.	F1	126
Bridgetown	B3	100
Bridgetown, *capital*	A4	91
Bridgewater	C3	100
Brienzersee, *lake*	B2	35
Brighton	C4	30
Brighton	H3	102
Brikama	B2	62
Brindisi	D2	38
Brisbane, Qld., *capital*	E2, Inset III	14
Brisbane, *river*	Inset III	14
Bristol	C3	30
Bristol	B2	97
Bristol, *channel*	B3	30
Britannia	E5	98
Britt	E2	102
Brive-la-Gallarde	C4	34
Brno	C3	42
Broadview	H10	104
Brochet	C1	96
Brock, *island*	F1	99
Brocket	D6	94
Brockville	K3	102
Brodfur, *peninsula*	L2	99
Broken Hill, N.S.W.	D3	14
Brokopondo	B2	80
Brolin	C3	30
Bromptonville	E6	103
Brookdale	B4	96
Brooks	E6	94
Brooks range, Alaska	Inset I	126
Broome, W.A.	B1	14
Broomhill	A4	96
Brossard	J6	103
Brownsville, Tex.	D3	126
Bruce Mines	B1	102
Bruce Peninsula N.P.	D2	102
Brugge	B1	33
Brugge-Ghent, *canal*	B1	33
Brûlé	B4	94
Brunei		13
Brunei, *bay*	C1	13
Brunei, *river*	B2	13
Brunswick	B2	40
Brunswick, Ga.	E2	126
Brunswick, *peninsula*	B9	76
Brussels	D4	102
Brussels, *capital*	C2	33
Bryan, Tex.	D2	126
Bryansk	D3	44
Bsharri	B1	26

	Key	Page
Bu Craa	B1	58
Bua, *river*	B2	68
Buada	B2	16
Buala	A1	16
Buba	C2	62
Bubanza	B2	61
Bubaque	B2	62
Bubiyan, *island*	C2	24
Bucaramanga	B3	78
Buchanan	A3	63
Buchanan	H9	104
Buchans	C5	98
Bucharest, *capital*	D3	43
Buck Creek	C4	94
Buck Lake	C5	94
Buckingham	A6	103
Budapest, *capital*	B2	43
Buea	A3	65
Buenaventura	A4	78
Buendía, *reservoir*	E2	37
Buene, *river*	A2	49
Buenos Aires, *capital*	D3	74
Buenos Aires, *lake*	A7	74
Buffalo Narrows	B5	104
Buffalo, *lake*	D5	94
Buffalo, *lake*	E4	99
Buffalo, N.Y.	F1	126
Bug, *river*	E2, F3	41
Bugeac, *region*	B3	50
Bugojno	B1	48
Buhayrat al-Asad, *lake*	Inset II	20
Buj-Buj	Inset II	20
Bujumbura, *capital*	B2	61
Buka, *island*	B2	15
Bukavu	C2	67
Bukhara	B3	23
Bukit Pagon, *mt.*	C3	13
Bukit Panjang	B1	13
Bukit Timah	B1	13
Bükk, *mts.*	C1	43
Bukoba	B1	68
Bula	A1	40
Bulawayo	B2	69
Bulembu	B1	71
Bulgan	C2	11
Bulgaria		50
Bulle	B2	35
Bulyea	F10	104
Bumba	B1	67
Bunbury, W.A.	A3	14
Bundaberg, Qld.	E2	14
Bungo, *channel*	B3	8
Bunia	C1	67
Bunsuru, *river*	D1	65
Buon Me Thuot	B4	11
Buqayq	C1	24
Buraydah	B2	24
Burco	B2	60
Burdekin, *river*	D1	14
Burdett	E6	94
Burdur, *lake*	B3	27
Burdwan	E4	20
Büren	B3	40
Burgas	F3	50
Burgeo	C5	98
Burgos	E1	37
Burhanpur	C4	20
Burin	D5	98
Burin, *peninsula*	D5	98
Buriram	C3	12
Burk's Falls	F2	102
Burke, *channel*	J5	95
Burkina Faso		64
Burlington	F4	102
Burlington, Vt.	F1	126
Burma (Myanmar)		12
Burnley	C3	30
Burns Lake	K4	95
Burntwood, *lake*	A2	96
Burntwood, *river*	B1, C1, D2	96
Bursa	B2	27
Burtnieku, *lake*	C2	46
Buru, *island*	D2	13
Burundi		61
Bururi	B2	61
Burutu	C5	65
Burwash Landing	B5	105
Bury	C3	30
Bury St. Edmunds	D3	30
Buryatiya, *republic*	D7	44
Bushmanland, *plain*	A2	71
Buta	C1	67
Butare	B2	61
Bute, *island*	B2	30
Butha-Buthe	B1	71
Butte, Mont.	B1	126
Buttonville	K5	102
Butuan	C4	12
Butwal	B2	19
Buurgplaatz, *mt.*	B1	33
Buxton	C3	30
Buyant-Uhaa	D3	11
Buyo, *lake*	C3	63
Büyük Menderes, *lake*	A3	27
Buzău	D3	43
Búzi, *river*	B2	68
Büzmeyin	C2	22
Byam Martin, *channel*	G1	99
Byam Martin, *island*	H1	99
Byarezina, *river*	D3	47
Byblos, *ruins*	A1	26
Bydgoszcz	C2	41
Byelaruskaya Hrada, *range*	C3	47
Bylot, *island*	N2	99
Bytom	D3	41
Byumba	C1	61

C

	Key	Page
Ca Mau	A5	11
Ca, *river*	A2	11
Caacupé	D4	75
Caaguazú	E4	75
Caazapá	D5	75
Cabanatuan	B3	12
Cabano	H4	103
Cabimas	B1	79
Cabinda	B1	70

	Key	Page
Cabo Rojo	A2	90
Cabora Bassa	B2	68
Cabora Bassa, *dam*	B2	68
Cabora Bassa, *lake*	A2	68
Caborca	B1	84
Cabrera	C1	89
Cabrera, *island*	H3	37
Çabri	B10	104
Čačak	B3	49
Cacao	B1	80
Cáceres	C3	81
Cáceres	C3	37
Cache Creek	M6	95
Cacheu	A1	62
Cacheu, *river*	B1	62
Cachimbo	C2	81
Cacine	B2	62
Cacouna	G4	103
Cadiz	B4	12
Cádiz	C4	37
Cádiz, *gulf*	C4	37
Cadotte Lake	B3	94
Caen	B2	34
Caerleon	C3	30
Caernarfon	B3	30
Caganyan de Oro	C4	12
Cagayan Sulu, *island*	A5	12
Cagayan, *islands*	B4	12
Cagayan, *river*	B2	12
Cagliari	B3	38
Cagliari, *gulf*	B3	38
Caguas	C2	90
Caha, *mts.*	B3	31
Cahors	C4	34
Cahul	B3	50
Caicos, *islands*	D4	89
Caidasm da Rainha	A3	36
Caille, *island*	B1	91
Cairns, Qld.	D1	14
Cairo, *capital*	B1	56
Cairo, III.	E2	126
Caja de Muertos, *island*	B3	90
Cajamarca	B2	77
Calabar	E5	65
Calabogie	J2	102
Calabozo	C2	79
Calabria	D3	38
Calafate	A7	74
Calais	C1	34
Calais	B3	94
Calais	B3	97
Calama	C2	76
Calamian, *islands*	A3	12
Calapan	B3	12
Călăraşi	D3	43
Calatayud	F2	37
Calatrava	B3	66
Calbayog	C3	12
Calcutta	E4, Inset II	20
Caledon, *river*	A1, C2	71
Caledonia	F4	102
Calgary	C5	94
Cali	A4	78
California	B2	126
California, *gulf*	B1	84
Callao	B3	77
Calling Lake	D3	94
Caltanissetta	C3	38
Calvi	Inset I	34
Calvinia	A3	71
Cam Ranh	B4	11
Camagüey	D2	88
Camagüey, *archipelago*	D2	88
Camberley	Inset III	30
Cambodia		11
Cambrai	C1	34
Cambrian, *mts.*	B3	30
Cambridge	D3	30
Cambridge Bay	G3	99
Cambridge-Narrows	C3	97
Cameron, *hills*	B1	94
Cameron, *mount*	A3	65
Cameroon		65
Cameroon, *island*	H1	99
Camiri	B4	77
Camopi	B2	80
Camopi, *river*	B2	80
Campana, *island*	A8	76
Campania	C2	38
Campbell River	K6	95
Campbellton	C1	97
Campbellton	A2	100
Campbellton	K4	103
Campbelltown, N.S.W.	Inset IV	14
Campbelltown, S.A.	Inset II	14
Campbeltown	B2	30
Campeche, *bay*	F4	84
Campeche, *state capital*	F4	84
Camper	B3	96
Camperville	A3	96
Campina Grande	E2	81
Campinas	D4	81
Campo Grande	C4	81
Campobasso	C2	38
Campobello, *island*	C4	97
Campos	D4	81
Campos Elísios	Inset I	81
Camrose	D4	94
Camsell Portage	A1	104
Camú, *river*	B1	89
Camuy	A1	90
Can Tho	A4	11
Caña Gorda, *beach*	B3	90
Canaan	B1	91
Canada		92
Canaima	E4	79
Çanakkale	A2	27
Canal Flats	P6	95
Canaray, *islands*	Inset I	37
Canaries	A2	91
Canary, *islands*		55
Canaveral, *cape, Fla.*	E3	126
Canberra, A.C.T., *natl. capital*	D3	14
Canchungo	A1	62
Cancún	G3	84
Candelaria	C2	90
Candiac	J6	103
Candle Lake	E7	104

	Key	Page
Cando	B8	104
Canelles, *river*	B3	91
Canelones	B3	75
Cangamba	D4	70
Cangzhou	E2	10
Caniapiscau, *lake*	C3	101
Caniapiscau, *river*	C2	101
Çankırı	C2	27
Cannes	D5	34
Canning	C2	100
Canning, *river*	Inset I	14
Canoe Narrows	B5	104
Canoe, *lake*	B5	104
Canora	H9	104
Canossa	B1	38
Canóvanas	D2	90
Canso	G2	100
Cantabria	D1	37
Cantábrica, *mts.*	C1	37
Canterbury	D3	30
Canterbury	B3	97
Canterbury, *bight*	B3	15
Canterbury, *plains*	B3	15
Canton, *island*	B2	17
Canwood	D7	104
Canyon Creek	C3	94
Cao Bang	B1	11
Cap-aux-Os	M3	103
Cap-Chat	K2	103
Cap-de-la-Madeleine	D5	103
Cap-Haïtien	C1	89
Cap-Pelé	E2	97
Cap-Rouge	K6	103
Cap-St-Ignace	F4	103
Cape Charles	D3	98
Cape Coast	B4	64
Cape Girardeau, Mo.	E2	126
Cape North	G1	100
Cape Race	E5	98
Cape Ray	B5	98
Cape St. George	B5	98
Cape Tormentine	E2	97
Cape Town, *legislative capital*	A3	71
Cape Verde		58
Cape York, *peninsula*	D1	14
Capitán Pablo Lagerenza	B1	75
Caplan	L3	103
Caprara, *point*	B2	38
Capreol	D1	102
Capri, *island*	C2	38
Capua	C2	38
Caquetá, *river*	B5	78
Car Nicobar, *island*	F7	20
Caracas, *capital*	C1	79
Caramoan, *peninsula*	B3	12
Carandiumã	Inset II	81
Caraquet	E1	97
Carberry	A4	96
Carbonara, *cape*	B3	38
Carbonear	E5	98
Carbonia	B3	38
Carcajou	B2	94
Carcross	C5	105
Cardamom, *mts.*	A3	11
Cárdenas	B1	88
Cardiel, *lake*	A6	74
Cardiff	B3	30
Cardigan	C2	100
Cardigan, *bay*	B3	30
Cardigan, *bay*	C2	100
Cardinal	K3	102
Cardinal, *lake*	B3	94
Caribbean, *sea*		82
Carievale	A4	96
Carleton	K3	103
Carleton Place	J2	102
Carlingford	C1	31
Carlingford, *lake*	C1	31
Carlisle	C2	30
Carlisle, *bay*	A4	91
Carlow	C2	31
Carlsbad, N. Mex.	H11	104
Carlyle	H11	104
Carmacks	B4	105
Carman	B4	96
Carmanville	C4	98
Carmarthen	B3	30
Carmelo	A2	75
Carnac	B3	34
Carnarvon	G2	102
Carnarvon	A2	71
Carnarvon, W.A.	A2	14
Carnduff	J11	104
Carnic Alps, *range*	C4	39
Carnsore, *point*	C3	31
Carolina	D2	90
Caroline	D4	94
Caroline, *islands*	B2	15
Caron	E10	104
Caroni, *river*	D2	79
Carora	C1	79
Carpathian, *mts.*		43
Carpentaria, *gulf*	C1	14
Carrantuohill, *mt.*	B3	31
Carriacou, *island*	C1	91
Carrick-on-Shannon	B2	31
Carroll	A4	96
Carrot River	G7	104
Carson City, *capital, Nev.*	B2	126
Carstairs	C5	94
Cartagena	B2	78
Cartagena	F4	37
Cartago	C3	86
Cartier	D1	102
Cartwright	D1	102
Cartwright	C2	98
Carúpano	D1	79
Carvoeiro, *cape*	A3	36
Carway	D6	94
Casa Grande, Ariz.	B2	126
Casablanca	C1	57
Casamance, *region*	B3	62
Casamance, *river*	B3	62

	Key	Page
Cascade	Inset	70
Cascade, *range*	A1	126
Cascapedia, *river*	K3	103
Cascumpec, *bay*	B2	100
Caserta	C2	38
Cashel	C2	31
Casilmiur, *river*	C3	79
Caslan	D4	94
Casper, Wyo.	C1	126
Caspian, *depression*	B2	23
Caspian, *sea*		7
Casselman	K2	102
Cassiar	H1	95
Cassiar, *mts.*	G1	95
Castel Gandolfo	C2	38
Castellón de la Plana	F3	37
Castelo Branco	B3	36
Castile and León	D1, E1	37
Castile-la Mancha	E3	37
Castile Bruce	B2	90
Castle Mountain	C5	94
Castlebar	B2	31
Castlegar	O6	95
Castries, *capital*	B1	91
Castro	B7	76
Cat, *island*	C2	89
Catacamas	C2	86
Catalina	E5	98
Catalonia	G2	37
Catamarca	C3	12
Catanduanes, *island*	C3	12
Catania	C2	90
Cataño	C2	90
Catanzaro	D3	38
Catio	B2	62
Catoche, *cape*	G3	84
Catumbela	B4	70
Cauca, *river*	B3	78
Caucasus, *mts.*	A1, A2	45
Caungula	C2	70
Caura, *river*	D2	79
Causapscal	J3	103
Cauto, *river*	E3	88
Cauvery, *river*	C6	20
Cavalla, *river*	C3	63
Cavally, *river*	C4	63
Cavan	C2	31
Cavendish	B2	100
Caviana, *island*	D1	81
Caxito	B2	70
Cayambe, *mt.*	C3	79
Cayenne, *capital*	B1	80
Cayer	C2	90
Cayey	C2	90
Cayman, *trench*	B2	88
Cayman, *islands*		82
Cayon	B1	90
Cazombo	E3	70
Ceará	E2	81
Cebollatí, *river*	C2	75
Cebu	B4	12
Cebu, *island*	B4	12
Cedar City, Utah	B2	126
Cedar Grove	E5	90
Cedar Rapids, Iowa	D1	126
Cedar, *lake*	A2	96
Cedros, *island*	A2	84
Ceduna, S.A.	C3	14
Ceerigaabo	B1	60
Cegléd	C2	43
Ceiba	B2	90
Ceiba	C2	90
Ceiba	D2	90
Celada	D2	90
Celaya	D3	84
Celebes (Sulawesi), *island*	D2	13
Celebes, *sea*	C1	13
Celje	C2	48
Celtic, *sea*	B3	31
Central African Republic		66
Central Butte	D10	104
Central Makran, *range*	C4	21
Central Siberian, *plateau*	C7	44
Centre	C3	100
Centre	C3	100
Centre de Flacq	D2	69
Centreville	E4	98
Ceram, *island*	D2	13
Ceram, *sea*	D2	13
Cerf, *island*	Inset	69
Cernavodă	E3	43
Cerro Castillo	B9	76
Cerro de Pasco	B3	77
Cervati, *mt.*	C2	46
Cēsis	C2	46
Cess, *river*	B3	63
Cessford	D6	94
České Budějovice	B4	42
Cetinje	A3	49
Ceuta	D5	37
Cévennes, *mts.*	C4	34
Ceyhan, *river*	D3	27
Chachapoyas	B2	77
Chaco Boreal, *region*	B2	75
Chad		59
Chad, *lake*	A4, C3	59
Chaeryŏng, *river*	B4	9
Chagai, *hills*	B4	21
Chaghcharan	C2	22
Chagres, *river*	B2	87
Chaguanas	A2	91
Chaitén	B7	76
Chaiyaphum	C3	12
Chalco	Inset	84
Chaleur, *bay*	D1	97
Chalna	C6	21
Châlons-sur-Marne	C3	20
Chambal, *river*	C3	20
Chambéry	D4	34
Chambeshi, *river*	C2	67
Chambord	D3	103
Chamelecon, *river*	A2	86
Chamonix-Mont-Blanc	D4	34
Champagne Castle, *mt.*	C2	71
Champagne-Ardenne	D2	34
Champaquí, *mt.*	C3	74
Champasak	B5	85

Key Page
Champlain D5 103
Chañaral B3 76
Chança, *river* B4 36
Chandannagar Inset II 20
Chandigarh C2 20
Chandler M3 103
Chandpur D5 21
Chandrapur C5 20
Chang (Yangtze), *river* D2, E2 10
Changane, *river* B4 68
Changchun F1 10
Changde E3 10
Changhua B1 9
Changi B1 13
Changjin B2 9
Changjin, *river* B2 9
Changsha E3 10
Changuinola A2 87
Changyŏn A3 9
Changzhi E2 10
Changzhou F2 10
Channel *islands*, Calif. A2 126
Channel-Port aux Basques B5 98
Chantilly C2 34
Chao Phraya, *river* B3 12
Chapada dos Parecis, *range* C3 81
Chapala, *lake* D3 84
Chaparé, *river* A3 77
Chapleau D3 101
Chaplin D10 104
Chardzhou D2 22
Charente, *river* B4 34
Chari, *river* A5 59
Charikar B1 22
Charity B2 80
Charleroi C2 33
Charles A1 96
Charlesbourg E5, Inset 103
Charleston, *capital*, W. Va. E2 126
Charleston, S.C. F2 126
Charlestown C3 90
Charlestown A3 91
Charleville Mézières D2 34
Charleville, Qld. D2 14
Charlie Lake M3 95
Charlo C1 97
Charlotte, N.C. E2 126
Charlottetown C3 98
Charlottetown B2 100
Charlotteville B1 91
Charny E5, K6 103
Charters Towers, Qld. D2 14
Chartres C2 34
Chase N6 95
Châteauguay C6, H6 103
Châteauroux C3 34
Châtellerault C3 34
Chatfield C4 96
Chatham Inset III 30
Chatham C5 102
Chatham, *sound* G4 95
Chatkal, *river* B2 23
Chatsworth E3 102
Chattanooga, Tenn. E2 126
Chau Doc A4 11
Chaumont D2 34
Chaves B2 36
Cheb A2 42
Cheboksary D4 44
Chech'ŏn C4 9
Chechnya, republic E4 44
Cheduba, *island* B2 12
Chegutu B2 69
Cheju Inset 9
Cheju, *island* Inset 9
Cheju, *strait* Inset 9
Chek Keng Inset 10
Chelan G8 104
Cheleken A2 22
Chelif, *river* B1 57
Chelles Inset II 34
Chełm F3 41
Chelmsford D3, Inset III 30
Cheltenham C3 30
Chelyabinsk D5 44
Chelyuskin, *cape* B7 44
Chembur Inset I 20
Chemin Grenier B3 69
Chemnitz C3 40
Chenab, *river* D3 21
Chenachane A2 57
Chene Inset I 20
Chénéville A6 103
Chengde E1 10
Chengdu D2 10
Chennai (Madras) D6 20
Cherbourg B2 34
Cherepovets D3 44
Cherkassy C2 47
Chernigov C1 47
Chernivtsi B2 47
Cherrapunji F3 20
Cherryville N6 95
Cherskiy C10 44
Cherskiy, *range* C8 44
Chesapeake, *bay* F2 126
Chesley D3 102
Chester C3 30
Chester C3 100
Chesterfield C3 30
Chesterfield Inlet K4 99
Chesterfield, *islands* A2 18
Cheticamp G1 100
Chetumal, *state capital* G4 84
Chetwynd M3 95
Cheviot, *hills* C2 30
Chevreuse Inset II 34
Cheyenne, *capital*, Wyo. C1 126
Chhukha A2 19
Chi, *river* C2 12
Chiai B2 9
Chiang Mai B2 12
Chiang Rai B2 12
Chiapa C1 76
Chiapas F4 84
Chiatura B3 45
Chiba D3 8
Chibougamau B2 103
Chibougamau, *lake* B2 103
Chicago, Ill. E1 126
Chicapa, *river* D3 70
Chichén Itzá, *ruins* G3 84
Chichester C4 30
Chichi, *island* Inset III 8
Chiclayo B2 77
Chico, *river* B6 74
Chiconcuac Inset 84
Chicoutimi E3 103
Chief, *river* L2 95
Chiem, *lake* C5 40
Chiesanuova B2 39
Chieti C2 38
Chifeng E1 10
Chignecto, *bay* C2 100
Chihuahua, *state capital* C2 84
Chilcotin, *river* K5 95
Chile 76
Chile Chico B8 76
Chililabombwe B2 67
Chilko, *lake* K5 95
Chillán B6 76
Chilliwack M6 95
Chiloé, *island* B7 76
Chilpancingo, *state capital* E4 84
Chilung B1 9
Chilwa, *lake* B2, C3 68
Chimalhuacán Inset 84
Chimay C2 33
Chimborazo, *mt.* B3 79
Chimbote B2 77
Chimoio B3 68
Chin, *hills* B2 12
China 10
Chinajá C4 85
Chinandega A2 87
Chincha Alta B3 77
Chinchaga, *river* A2 94
Chinde C3 68
Chindwin, *river* B1 12
Chingola B2 67
Chingoni C2 67
Chinhae C5 9
Chinhoyi B1 69
Chiniot D3 21
Chinju C5 9
Chinko, *river* B2 66
Chioggia C1 38
Chip, *lake* C4 94
Chipata C2 67
Chipewyan Lake D3 94
Chipman D2 97
Chira, *river* A5 79
Chirchiq, *river* C2 23
Chire, *river* B3 68
Chiredzi B2 69
Chiriquí, *gulf* A3 87
Chiriquí, *lagoon* B2 87
Chirner Inset I 20
Chirripó, *mt.* C3 86
Chirripó, *river* C2 86
Chisasibi A3 101
Chisholm C4 94
Chişinău, *capital* B2 50
Chita D7 44
Chitipa B1 68
Chitose Inset I 8
Chitral D2 21
Chitré B3 87
Chittagong E6 21
Chitungwiza B1 69
Chixoy, *river* C4 85
Choa Chu Kang A1 13
Choiceland F7 104
Choiseul A3 91
Choiseul, *island* A1 16
Choisy-le Roi Inset II 34
Chojnice C2 41
Choke, *mts.* B2 60
Cholet B3 34
Cholpon-Ata E1 23
Cholula E4 84
Choluteca B3 86
Choma B3 67
Chomo Lhari, *mt.* A1 19
Chon Buri B3 12
Chone A3 79
Chŏngch'ŏn, *river* A3 9
Ch'ŏngjin C2 9
Ch'ŏngju B4 9
Chŏngju A3 9
Chongqing D3 10
Chonju B5 9
Chonos, *archipelago* B7 76
Chontaleña, *mts.* B2 87
Chornobyl' C1 47
Chorzów D3 41
Choshui, *river* B2 9
Choybalsan D2 11
Christchurch B3 15
Christina, *river* E3 94
Christmas Island G2 100
Chu, *river* D1 23
Chubut, *river* A5 74
Chucunaque, *river* D2 87
Chugoku, *mts.* B3 8
Chukchi, *peninsula* C11 44
Chukchi, *range* C10 44
Chukchi, *sea* B11 44
Chukotka, autonomous okrug C10 44
Chumphon B4 12
Chunan B1 9
Ch'unch'ŏn B4 9
Chung Hau Inset 10
Chungho B1 9
Ch'ungju B4 9
Chungli B1 9
Chungqing, Ind. Mun. D3 10
Chungyang, *range* B2 9
Chuquicamata C2 76
Chur D2 35
Church Point A3 100
Churchbridge A4 96
Churchbridge J10 104
Churchill D1 96
Churchill Falls D3 98
Churchill, *lake* B4 104
Churchill, *river* D1 96
Churia, *mts.* B2 19
Chute-aux-Outardes H2 103
Chuuk, *islands* C2 15
Chuvashiya, republic D4 44
Ciales C2 90
Cibao, *valley* A1 89
Cicia, *island* C2 17
Cidra C2 90
Ciechánow E2 41
Ciego de Ávila D2 88
Cienfuegos C2 88
Cieza F3 37
Cijara, *reservoir* D3 37
Cikobia, *island* C1 17
Cilacap B2 13
Cilician Gates, *pass* C3 27
Cimone, *mt.* B1 38
Cincinnati, Ohio E2 126
Cirebon B2 13
Citlaltépetl, *mt.* E4 84
City View G6 102
Ciudad Acuña D2 84
Ciudad Bolívar D2 79
Ciudad Camargo C2 84
Ciudad Constitución B3 84
Ciudad del Carmen F4 84
Ciudad del Este E4 75
Ciudad Guayana D2 79
Ciudad Juárez C1 84
Ciudad Mante E3 84
Ciudad Obregón C2 84
Ciudad Real E3 37
Ciudad Rodrigo C2 37
Ciudad Valles E3 84
Ciudad Victoria, *state capital* E3 84
Ciudadela H2 37
Civitavecchia B2 38
Clair A1 97
Claire, *lake* D2 94
Clandeboye C4 96
Clara C2 31
Clarenville D5 98
Clark's Harbour B4 100
Clarksville, Tenn. E2 126
Clear Creek E5 102
Clear, *cape* B3 31
Clearwater M5 95
Clearwater, *river* E3 94
Clementsport B3 100
Clermont F4 103
Clermont-Ferrand C4 34
Clervaux B1 33
Clerve, *river* B1 33
Cleveland, Ohio E1 126
Clichy Inset II 34
Clifden A2 31
Clifford E4 102
Climax B11 104
Clinton M5 95
Clinton D4 102
Clinton Colden, *lake* G4 99
Cloncurry, Qld. D2 14
Clonmel C2 31
Cloridorme M2 103
Clovis, N. Mex. C2 126
Cloyne H3 102
Cluff Lake Mine A2 104
Cluj-Napoca B2 43
Cluny D3 34
Cluny D6 94
Clutha, *river* A4 15
Clyde River B4 100
Clyde River P2 99
Clyde, *estuary* B2 30
Clyde, *river* B2 30
Clydebank B2 30
Coacalco Inset 84
Coahuila D2 84
Coal River J1 95
Coal, *river* D5 105
Coaldale D6 94
Coalspur B4 94
Coamo C2 90
Coast, *mts.* F2, J5 95
Coast, *ranges* A1, A2 126
Coaticook E6 103
Coats Land, *region* B13 107
Coats, *island* M4 99
Coatzacoalcos F4 84
Cobán C4 85
Cobden J2 102
Cóbh B3 31
Cobham, *river* D2 96
Cobija A2 77
Cobourg G4 102
Coburg B3 40
Coburg, *island* N1 99
Cocagne E2 97
Cochabamba A3 77
Cochin (Kochi) C7 20
Cochrane B8 76
Cochrane D3 101
Cochrane, *lake* B8 76
Cochrane, *river* H2 104
Cockburn Harbour D4 89
Cockburn, *island* B2 102
Coclé del Norte B2 87
Coco C2 90
Coco, *islands* B3 12
Coco, *river* A2, C1 87
Cocos, *islands* 5
Cocotitlán Inset 84
Cod, *cape*, Mass. G1 126
Codri, *region* A3 50
Codrington E2 90
Codrington, *mt.* C17 107
Cody, Wyo. C1 126
Coe Hill H3 102
Coeroeni, *river* A3 80
Coeur d'Alene, Idaho B1 126
Coffee Bay C3 71
Cogalnic, *river* B2 50
Cognac B4 34
Coiba, *island* B3 87
Coihaique B8 76
Coimbatore C6 20
Coimbra A2 36
Cojedes, *river* C2 79
Colca, *river* C4 77
Colchester D3 30
Cold Lake E4 94
Coleraine A2 30
Coles Island D3 97
Coleville A9 104
Colihaut A2 90
Colima, *state capital* D4 84
Colina Inset 76
Coll, *island* A2 30
Collaguasi C2 76
Collingwood B3 15
Collingwood E3 102
Colmar D2 34
Cologne A3 40
Colombia 78
Colombier H3 103
Colombo, *capital* A5 19
Colón C2 87
Colón C2 88
Colonia A2 15
Colonia B3 75
Colonia Nueva Guinea B3 87
Colonsay E9 104
Colonsay, *island* A2 30
Colorado C2 86
Colorado C2 126
Colorado Springs, Colo. C2 126
Colorado, *plateau* B2 126
Colorado, *river* B4 74
Colorado, *river* B2 126
Columbia, *capital*, S.C. E2 126
Columbia, *mts.* M4 95
Columbia, *plateau* B1 126
Columbia, *river* B1 126
Columbus, *capital*, Ohio E2 126
Columbus, Ga. E2 126
Coma Pedrosa, *mt.* A1 36
Comayagua B2 86
Comayagua, *mts.* B2 86
Combermere H2 102
Comendador A2 89
Comerío C2 90
Comilla E5 21
Comino, *island* B1 36
Cominotto, *island* B1 36
Comitán F4 84
Committee, *bay* L3 99
Como B1 38
Como, *lake* B1 38
Comodoro Rivadavia B6 74
Comorin, *cape* C7 20
Comoros 67
Comox K6 95
Compiègne C2 34
Compton E6 103
Comrat B2 50
Con Son, *islands* B5 11
Conakry, *capital* B3 62
Concepción B6 76
Concepción D3 75
Concepción del Oro D3 84
Conchalí Inset 76
Conche D4 98
Conchos, *river* C2 84
Concord, *capital*, N.H. F1 126
Concordia D3 74
Condor C5 94
Congo, Dem Rep of 67
Congo, Rep of 66
Congo, *basin* D3 66
Congo, *river* D4 66
Congo, *river* B1 67
Conn, *lake* B1 31
Connecticut F1 126
Connemara, *region* B2 31
Consecon H4 102
Constance B5 40
Constance (Bodensee), *lake* D1 35
Constanţa E3 43
Constantine B1 57
Constitución B5 76
Consul A11 104
Contrecoeur C6 103
Contwoyto, *lake* G3 99
Conwy B3 30
Coober Pedy, S.A. C2 14
Cook's Harbour D3 98
Cook, *mt.* B3 15
Cook, *strait* B3 15
Cookshire E6 103
Cookstown F3 102
Coos Bay, Oreg. A1 126
Copán, *ruins* A2 86
Copenhagen, *capital* D3 32
Copiapó B3 76
Copiapó, *river* B3 76
Coppename, *river* A2 80
Coppermine, *river* F3 99
Coquí C3 90
Coquimbo B3 76
Coral, *sea* E1 14
Corantijn, *river* A2 80
Corazón C3 90
Corbeil-Essonnes Inset II 34
Corcovado, *gulf* B7 76
Corcovado, *mt.* Inset I 81
Córdoba C3 74
Córdoba D4 37
Córdoba, *range* B3 74
Corinth B3 51
Corinth, *gulf* B2 51
Corinth, *isthmus* B3 51
Corinto A2 87
Corisco, *bay* B4 66
Corisco, *island* B4 66
Cork B3 31
Cormack C4 98
Cormoran, *reef* B2 17
Cormorant A2 96
Cormorant, *lake* A2 96
Cornellá de Llogregat G2 37
Corner Brook C5 98
Corno, *mt.* C2 38
Cornwall B2 100
Cornwall L2 102
Cornwall, *island* K1 99
Cornwallis, *island* J1 99
Coro C1 79
Coromandel, *peninsula* C2 15
Coronach E11 104
Coronado, *bay* B3 86
Coronation, *gulf* F3 99
Coronel Oviedo D4 75
Coropuna, *mt.* C4 77
Corozal B1 85
Corozal C2 90
Corpus Christi, Tex. D3 126
Corregidor, *island* B3 12
Corrib, *lake* B2 31
Corrientes D2 74
Corse Inset I 34
Corsica, *island* Inset I 34
Cortina d'Ampezzo C1 38
Cortona B2 38
Corubal, *river* D1 62
Çoruh, *river* E2 27
Çorum C2 27
Corumbá C3 81
Corumbau, *point* E3 81
Corvallis, Oreg. A1 126
Cosenza D3 38
Coslada Inset II 37
Cosmoledo, *island group* A2 70
Costa Rica 86
Cotabato C5 12
Côte d'Ivoire 63
Cotentin, *peninsula* B2 34
Cotia Inset II 81
Coto Laurel B2 90
Cotonou B4 64
Cotopaxi, *mt.* B3 79
Cotswold, *hills* C3 30
Cottbus C3 40
Cotton Ground C2 90
Cotuí B1 89
Coubert Inset II 34
Couffo, *river* B4 64
Courantyne, *river* B3 80
Courland, *lagoon* A2 46
Courtenay K6 95
Courval D10 104
Coutts E6 94
Couva A2 91
Coventry C3 30
Covilhã B2 36
Cow Head C4 98
Cowan A3 96
Cowansville D6 103
Cowes C4 30
Cox's Bazar E7 21
Cox's Cove B4 98
Coyah B3 62
Coyoacán Inset 84
Cozumel, *island* G3 84
Cradock C3 71
Craigmyle D5 94
Craik E9 104
Craiova B3 43
Cranberry Portage A2 96
Cranbrook P6 95
Crane River B3 96
Crane Valley E11 104
Crapaud B2 100
Cravo Norte C3 78
Crawford Bay O6 95
Crawley Inset III 30
Crean, *lake* D6 104
Cree Lake D3 104
Cree, *river* E2 104
Cremona B1 38
Cremona C5 94
Cres, *island* B3 48
Cressday E6 94
Creston O6 95
Crete, *island* C4 51
Crete, *sea* C4 51
Créteil Inset II 34
Crewe C3 30
Crimean, *mts.* C4 47
Crimean, *peninsula* C3 47
Cristal, *mts.* A1 66
Cristóbal C2 87
Cristóbal Colón, *peak* B2 78
Crna Gora, *mts.* B3 49
Crna, *river* B2 48
Croatia 48
Crocker, *range* D2 13
Cromer A4 96
Crooked River G8 104
Crooked, *island* C4 89
Crooked, *river* L4 95
Cross Lake C2 96
Cross, *river* E4 65
Crotone D3 38
Cruz, *cape* D3 88
Cruzeiro do Sul A2 81
Crystal City B4 96
Cu Lao Thu, *island* B4 11
Cuajimalpa Inset 84
Cuamba C2 68
Cuando, *river* D4 70
Cuango, *river* D2 70
Cuanza, *river* C3 70
Cuareim, *river* B1 75
Cuauhtémoc C2 84
Cuautitlán Inset 84
Cuautitlán Izcalli Inset 84
Cuba 88
Cubal, *river* B4 70
Cubango, *river* D5 70
Cubatão Inset II 81
Cúcuta B3 78
Cuddalore C6 20
Cudworth E8 104
Cuenca B4 79
Cuenca E2 37
Cuernavaca, *state capital* E4 84
Cuiabá C3 81
Cuíto Cuanavale D5 70
Cuito, *river* D4 70
Cukorova, *region* C3 27
Culebra, *island* E2 90
Culebrinas, *river* A2 90
Culiacán, *state capital* C3 84
Cumaná D1 79
Cumberland K6 95
Cumberland House H7 104
Cumberland, *lake* H6 104
Cumberland, *peninsula* P3 99
Cumberland, *sound* P3 99
Cumbrian, *mts.* B2 30
Cunene, *river* B5, C4 70
Cuneo A1 38
Cupar B2 30
Cupar F10 104
Curaçao, *island* 82
Curaray, *river* C3 79
Curepipe C3 69
Curicó B4 76
Curitiba D4 81
Curral Velho D3 58
Curuzú Cuatiá D2 74
Cut Knife A8 104
Cuttack E4 20
Cuxhaven B2 40
Cuyo, *islands* B4 12
Cuyuni, *river* A2 80
Cuzco C3 77
Cyangugu A2 61
Cyclades, *islands* C3 51
Cypress River B4 96
Cyprus 27
Czar E5 94
Czech Republic 42
Częstochowa D3 41

D

Da Lat B4 11
Da Nang B3 11
Dabakala D2 63
Dabola C2 62
Dachang D3 10
Dachau B4 40
Dacotah C4 96
Dades, *river* C2 57
Dadu C4 21
Dafoe F9 104
Dagestan, republic E4 44
Dagupan B2 12
Dahlak, *archipelago* C2 60
Dahna, ad-, *desert* B1 24
Dahuk B1 24
Dajabón A1 89
Daka, *river* B2 64
Dakar, *capital* A2 62
Dakhla A2 58
Đakovica B3 49
Dalälven, *river* C2 53
Dalandzadgad C3 11
Dalhousie C1 97
Dalhousie K3 103
Dali D2 10
Dalian F2 10
Dallas C3 96
Dallas, Tex. D2 126
Dallol Bosso, *river* A3 59
Dalmatia, *region* B3 48
Daloa C3 63
Dalvík B2 52
Daly, *river* C1 14
Daman B4 20
Damanhur B1 56
Damascus, *capital* A3 27
Damaturu F2 65
Damavand, *mt.* C2 22
Damazin, ad- C3 59
Dame-Marie A2 89
Damietta B1 56
Damietta, *river* B1 56
Dammam, ad- C1 24
Dammartin-en-Goële Inset II 34
Dampier, W.A. A2 14
Damur, ad- A2 26
Danakil, *desert* C2 60
Danané B3 63
Dand A4 96
Dande, *river* B2 70
Dandeldhura A2 19
Dandong F1 10
Dangara A1 23
Dangme, *river* C2 19
Dangrek, *mts.* C3 12
Dangriga B2 85
Daniel's Harbour C4 98
Danjiangkou E2 10
Danlí B2 86
Danube, *river* 29
Danville D6 103
Danville, Va. F2 126
Dao Phu Quoc, *island* A4 11
Dapaong B1 64
Dapp D4 94
Daqing F1 10
Dar es-Salaam, *capital* C2 68
Dara A3 27
Dara B2 62
Đaravica, *mt.* B3 49
Darbhanga E3 20
Darhan C2 11
Darién, *mts.* D2 87
Dariense, *mts.* B2 87
Darjiling E3 20
Darling, *range* A3 14
Darling, *river* D3 14
Darlington C2 30
Darłowo C1 41
Darmstadt B4 40
Darnah D1 56
Darnley B2 100
Dartmoor, *plateau* B4 30
Dartmouth D3 100
Daru A2 15
Darwin, N.T., *capital* C1 14
Dashhowuz C2 22
Dasht-e Kavir, *desert* D3 22
Dasht-e Lut, *desert* D3 22
Datong E1 10
Daua, *river* F1 61
Daugavpils D3 46
Daule, *river* B3 79
Dauphin B1 91
Dauphin A3 96
Dauphin River B3 96
Dauphin, *lake* B3 96
Davao C5 12
Davao, *gulf* C5 12

	Key	Page
Davenport, Iowa	D1	126
David	A2	87
Davidson	D9	104
Davis Inlet	E3	98
Davis, strait	M2	92
Davos	D2	35
Dawa, river	C3	60
Dawhat as-Salwa, bay	B3	25
Dawkah	B2	25
Dawna, range	B2	12
Dawson	B3	105
Dawson Creek	M3	95
Dawson, bay	A2	96
Daymán, river	B1	75
Dayr az-Zawr	B2	27
Dayton, Ohio	E2	126
Daytona Beach, Fla.	E3	126
De Aar	B3	71
De Quincy Village	Inset	70
Dead Sea, lake	A2	26
Dead, sea	B2	26
Dean, channel	J5	95
Dean, river	K5	95
Dease Lake	G2	95
Death, valley, Calif.	B2	126
Deauville	C2	34
Debar	A2	48
Debden	D7	104
Debed, river	B2	45
DeBolt	A3	94
Debre Birhan	C2	60
Debre Markos	B2	60
Debrecen	C2	43
Decatur, Ill.	E2	126
Deccan, plateau	C5	20
Děčín	B2	42
Dédougou	C2	64
Dedza	B2	68
Dee, river	B3, C1	30
Deep River	H1	102
Deep, inlet	B1	98
Deepdale	A3	96
Deer Lake	C4	98
Deerfield	A4	100
Degeh Bur	D2	60
Dégelis	H4	103
Dehra Dun	C2	20
Dehiwala-Mt. Lavinia	A5	19
Dej	B2	43
Del Rio, Tex.	C3	126
Delacour	D5	94
Delap Cove	B3	100
Delaronde, lake	C6	104
Delaware	F2	126
Delburne	D5	94
Deleau	A4	96
Delft	B2	32
Delft, island	A2	19
Delfzijl	D1	32
Delgado	A2	86
Delhi	C3	20
Delhi	E5	102
Delicias	C2	84
Déline	D3	99
Delisle	C9	104
Deloraine	A4	96
Delos, island	C3	51
Delson	J6	103
Delta Beach	B4	96
Demerara, river	B3	80
Den Helder	B2	32
Denakil, desert	C1	60
Denare Beach	H6	104
Denbigh	H2	102
Dencross	C4	96
Dender, river	B2	33
Denigomodu	A2	16
Denmark		32
Denmark, strait	D2	106
Dennery	B2	91
Denpasar	C2	13
D'Entrecasteaux, islands	B2	15
D'Entrecasteaux, reefs	C1	18
Denver, capital, Colo.	C2	126
Denzil	A8	104
Dera Ghazi Khan	D3	21
Dera Ismail Khan	D3	21
Derby	C3	30
Derg, lake	B2	31
Derrick	B3	91
Derventa	B1	48
Derwent	E4	94
Des Moines, capital, Iowa	D1	126
Desaguadero, river	B2	74
Desaguadero, river	A3	77
Desberats	B1	102
Deschaillons	D5	103
Deschambault Lake	G6	104
Dese	C2	60
Deseado, river	B6	74
Deseronto	H3	102
Desna, river	C1	47
Desolación, island	B9	76
Desruisseau	B3	91
Dessau	C3	40
Destruction Bay	B5	105
Detmold	B3	40
Detroit, Mich.	E1	126
Deux Rivieres	G1	102
Deux-Montagnes	H5	103
Deva	B3	43
Deventer	D2	32
Devil's, island	B1	80
Devoll, river	B3	49
Devon, island	L1	99
Devonport, Tas.	D4	14
Dewberry	E4	94
Dezful	B3	22
Dháfni	Inset	51
Dhahran	C1	24
Dhaka, capital	C3	21
Dhamar	A2	25
Dhangarhi	B2	19
Dhankuta	D2	19
Dharan	D3	19
Dhaulagiri, mt.	B2	19
Dhofar, region	B3	25
Dhulagiri	Inset II	20
Dhuusamareeb	B2	60

	Key	Page
Diadema	Inset II	81
Dialakoto	B3	62
Diamond, island	B1	91
Dibrugarh	F3	20
Diefenbaker, lake	C10	104
Diekirch	B2	33
Dien Bien Phu	A2	11
Dieppe	C2	34
Dieppe	E2	97
Dieppe Bay Town	B1	90
Diffa	C3	59
Differdange	A2	33
Digby	B3	100
Digne	D4	34
Digul, river	E2	13
Dijon	D3	34
Dikhil	B2	60
Dikson	B6	44
Dili	D2	13
Dilijan	B2	45
Dillon	B5	104
Dilolo	B3	67
Dimbokro	D3	63
Dimitrovgrad	D3	50
Dimlang, mt.	F3	65
Dimona	B2	26
Dinagat, island	C4	12
Dinajpur	B3	21
Dinant	C2	33
Dinara, mt.	A2, C3	48
Dinaric Alps, mts.	A1, B3	48
Dinder, river	B1	60
Dingle	A2	31
Dingle, bay	A2	31
Dingli	B2	36
Dinsmore	C9	104
Diourbel	A2	62
Dipolog	B4	12
Dire Dawa	D2	60
Diriamba	A3	87
Dispur	F3	20
Diu	B4	20
Diuata, mts.	C4	12
Divo	D4	63
Divriği	D2	27
Diwaniyah, ad-	C2	24
Dixon Entrance, channel	F4	95
Dixonville	B3	94
Diyala, river	C2	24
Diyarbakır	E3	27
Djado	C1	59
Djambala	C5	66
Djanet	B2	57
Djelfa	B1	57
Djenné	C3	58
Djerba, island	C3	57
Djibouti		60
Djibouti, capital	C2	60
Djouah, river	B1	66
Djouf, el-, desert	B1, C3	58
Djougou	A3	64
Dnepr-Bug, canal	B3	47
Dneprodzerzhinsk	C2	47
Dnieper, river	C1, E3	47
Dniester, river	C2	47
Dnipropetrovsk	D2	47
Doaktown	C2	97
Doba	B5	59
Doboj	B1	48
Dobrich	F2	50
Dobruja, region	E3	43
Doctor Pedro P. Peña	A3	75
Dodecanese, islands	C3	51
Dodge City, Kans.	C2	126
Dodoma, capital	C2	68
Dodsland	B9	104
Doetinchem	D3	32
Dogo, island	B2	8
Dogondoutchi	A3	59
Doha, capital	D3	25
Doiran, lake	C2	48
Dolbeau	D3	103
Dôle	D3	34
Dolomites, range	B1	38
Domagnano	B1	39
Domeyko, mts.	C3	76
Dominica		90
Dominica, passage	A1	90
Dominican Republic		89
Dominion City	C4	96
Domont	Inset II	34
Domremy	E8	104
Domuyo, volcano	A4	74
Don Benito	D3	37
Doña Juana, mt.	B3	78
Donald Station	O5	95
Doncaster	C3	30
Dondo	B3	70
Donegal	B1	31
Donegal, bay	B1	31
Donets, basin	D2	47
Donetsk	D2	47
Dong Hoi	B3	11
Dong Nai, river	B4	11
Dongting, lake	E3	10
Dongwe, river	A2	67
Donnacona	E5	103
Dor, lake	C6	104
Dorado	C2	90
Dorchester	C4	30
Dordogne, river	C4	34
Dordrecht	B3	32
Dore Lake	C6	104
Dörgön, lake	B2	11
Dori	D1	64
Dorintosh	B6	104
Dorking	Inset III	30
Dornoch	B1	30
Dorohoi	D2	43
Dorothy	D5	94
Dorra	B1	60
Dortmund	A3	40
Dorval	H6	103
Dos Hermanas	D4	37
Dosquet	E5	103
Dosso	A3	59
Dothan, Ala.	E2	126
Douai	C1	34

	Key	Page
Douala	A3	65
Doubs, river	A1	35
Douglas	B2	30
Douglas, channel	H4	95
Douglastown	M3	103
Dourados	C4	81
Douro, river	B2	36
Dover	D3	30
Dover, capital, Del.	F2	126
Dover, strait	D4	30
Dovrefjell, mts.	B3	52
Dozen, island	B2	8
Drãa, river	A1, B2, C2	57
Draguignan	D5	34
Drake	E9	104
Drakensberg, mts.	B3, C3	71
Drammen	C4	52
Drava, river	A2	43
Drayton Valley	C4	94
Dresden	C3	40
Dresden	C5	102
Dreux	C2	34
Drin, river	A1	49
Drina, river	A2	49
Drobeta-Turnu Severin	B3	43
Drogheda	C2	31
Drumheller	D5	94
Drummond	B2	97
Drummondville	D6	103
Druskininkai	B2	46
Dryden	B3	101
Dschang	B2	65
Duars, plain	A3	19
Duarte, mt.	B1	89
Dubai	C2	25
Dubăsari	B2	50
Dubawnt, lake	H4	99
Dubawnt, river	H4	99
Dubbo, N.S.W.	D3	14
Dube, river	C3	63
Dublin, capital	C2	31
Dubrovnik	D4	48
Dubuque, Iowa	D1	126
Dubysa, river	B2	46
Duchess	E6	94
Duck Bay	A3	96
Duck Lake	D8	104
Dudelange	B2	33
Dudinka	C6	44
Dudley	C3	30
Duero, river	D2	37
Dufourspitze, mt.	B3	35
Dufrost	C4	96
Dugald	C4	96
Duisburg	A3	40
Dukhan	B3	25
Dulce, gulf	C4	86
Duluth, Minn.	D1	126
Dum-Dum	Inset II	20
Duma	A1	26
Dumaguete	B4	12
Dumbás	B3	52
Dumfries	B2	30
Dumjor	Inset II	20
Dún Laoghaire	C2	31
Dunaújváros	B2	43
Duncan	L7	95
Duncansby, cape	B1	30
Dundalk	C2	31
Dundee	C2	30
Dundurn	D9	104
Dunedin	B4	15
Dunfermline	B2	30
Dungarvan	C2	31
Dunkirk (Dunkerque)	C1	34
Dunkwa	B4	64
Dunlop	B2	96
Dunnegan	F1	100
Dunnville	F5	102
Dunqulah	C1	59
Dunsinane, mt.	B2	30
Dunstable	Inset III	30
Dunster	N4	95
Duqm	C2	25
Duque de Caxias	Inset I	81
Duque de York, island	A9	76
Durance, river	D5	34
Durango, Colo.	C2	126
Durango, state capital	D3	84
Durazno	B2	75
Durban	D2	71
Durham	C2	30
Durham	E3	102
Durham, N.C.	F2	126
Durmitor, mts.	A3	49
Durrës	A2	49
Dushanbe, capital	A1	23
Düsseldorf	A3	40
Dutse	E2	65
Dyce	A2	96
Dyje, river	B4	42
Dzaoudzi, territorial capital	C2	67
Dzavhan, river	B2	11
Dzhugdzhur, range	D8	44
Dzungaria, desert basin	B1	10
Dzyarzhynskaya Hara, mt.	C3	47

E

	Key	Page
Eagle, river	B2	98
Eagle, river	B2	105
Ear Falls	B2	101
East Angus	E6	103
East Antarctica	B1	107
East Braintree	D4	96
East China, sea		7
East Coast Bays	B2	15
East Coulee	D5	94
East Frisian, islands	A2	40
East Lake Ainslie	F1	100
East London	C3	71
East Point	B1	100
East Siberian, sea	B10	44
East York	K5	102
East, cape	C2	15
Eastbourne	D4	30
Eastend	B11	104
Eastern Ghats, mts.	C6	20
Easterville	B2	96
Eastmain	A3	101
Eastmain, river	B3	101
Eastport	E5	98
Eatonia	A9	104
Eau Claire, Wis.	D1	126
Eauripik, atoll	B2	15
Ebebiyín	D2	66
Eberswalde	C2	40
Ebolowa	B3	65
Ebon, island	B3	16
Ebor	A4	96
Ebro, river	F1	37
Ecatepec	Inset	84
Echo Bay	E3	99
Echo Bay	A1	102
Echternach	B2	33
Écija	D4	37
Ecuador		79
Ed	C3	60
Edam	C2	32
Edam	B7	104
Eddies Cove	C3	98
Eddystone	B3	96
Ede	C4	65
Ede	C2	32
Edéa	B3	65
Edgerton	E5	94
Edinburgh	B2	30
Edirne	A2	27
Edmonton, capital	D4	94
Edmundston	A1	97
Edmundston	H4	103
Édouard, lake	D4	103
Edrans	B4	96
Edson	B4	94
Edward, lake	A4	61
Edwards plateau, Tex.	C2	126
Eems, river	D1	32
Éfaté, island	C3	18
Egadi, islands	C3	38
Eganville	H2	102
Eger	C2	43
Egersund	B4	52
Eglinton, island	E1	99
Egmont, bay	A2	100
Egmont, cape	B2	15
Egmont, mt.	B2	15
Eğridir, lake	B2	27
Egypt		56
Eifel, plateau	A3	40
Eigg, island	A2	30
Eindhoven	C3	32
Einsiedeln	C1	35
Eiseb, river	D2	70
Eisenach	B3	40
Eisenhüttenstadt	C2	40
Eisleben	B3	40
Ejmiatsin	B2	45
Ejura	B3	64
Ekibastuz	D1	23
Ekwan, river	D2	101
El Cañuelo, ruins	C2	90
El Cerro del Aripo, mt.	A2	91
El Encanto	B5	78
El Ferrol	B1	37
El Macao	D2	90
El Paso, Tex.	C2	126
El Pital, mt.	A1	86
El Porvenir	C2	87
El Progreso	B2	86
El Salvador		86
El Seibo	C2	89
El Serrat	B1	36
El Tabo	Inset	76
El Tigre	D2	79
El Toro, mt.	Inset	76
El Trebolar	Inset	76
Elat	B3	26
Elâziğ	D2	27
Elba, island	B3	38
Elbasan	B2	49
Elbe, river	B2, C3	40
Elbert mt., Colo.	C2	126
Elbląg	D1	41
Elbow	D9	104
Elburz, mts.	C2	22
Elche	F3	37
Eldon	C2	100
Eldoret	C3	61
Elephant, island	C12	107
Elephanta, island	Inset I	20
Eleuthera, island	B2	89
Elevsís	Inset	51
Elfros	G9	104
Elgin	B1	30
Elgin	A4	96
Elgin	B2	97
Elgon, mt.	D3	61
Eli Malk, island	B3	17
Elie	C4	96
Elista	E4	44
Elk	F2	41
Elk Point	E4	94
Elkford	P6	95
Elkhorn	A4	96
Elkhovo	E3	50
Elko	B2	126
Elko, Nev.	B1	126
Ellef Ringnes, island	H1	99
Ellerts de Haan, mts.	A3	80
Ellesmere, island	M1	99
Ellice, river	G3	99
Ellinikón	Inset	51
Elliot Lake	C1	102
Ellisras	C1	71
Ellsworth Land, region	B10	107
Ellsworth, mts.	B10	107
Elm Creek	C4	96
Elma	D4	96
Elmina	B4	64
Elmira	C2	100
Elmira	E4	102
Elmsdale	A2	100
Elmvale	F3	102
Elnora	D5	94
Elqui, river	B3	76
Elrose	B9	104
Elsa	B4	105

	Key	Page
Elva	A4	96
Elvas	B3	36
Ely	D3	30
Ely, Nev.	B2	126
Embarcación	C1	74
Embarras Portage	E2	94
Embi	B2	23
Embu	D2	61
Emden	A2	40
Emerald, island	F1	99
Emerald, Qld.	D2	14
Emerson	C4	96
Emi Koussi, mt.	B3	59
Emilia-Romagna	B1	38
Emlembe, mt.	B1	71
Emmeloord	C2	32
Emmen	D2	32
Emporia, Kans.	D2	126
Ems, river	A2	40
Encarnación	E5	75
Enchant	D6	94
Ende	D2	13
Enderbury, island	B2	17
Enderby	N6	95
Enderby Land, region	C17	107
Endiang	D5	94
Enewetak, island	A1	16
Engadine, valley	D2	35
Engaño, cape	D2	89
Enggano, island	B2	13
Englee	C4	98
English, channel	C4	30
Englishtown	G1	100
Enguri, river	A3	45
Enid, Okla.	D2	126
Enilda	B3	94
Enna	C3	38
Ennadai, lake	H4	99
Ennery	C1	89
Ennis	B2	31
Ennistymon	B2	31
Enns	D3	39
Enns, river	D3	39
Enriquillo, lake	A2	89
Enschede	E2	32
Ensenada	A1	84
Ensenguly	C3	61
Entebbe	C3	61
Enugu	D4	65
Épi, island	C3	18
Épinal	D2	34
Episkopi	A2	27
Equatorial, channel	A5	19
Equatorial Guinea		66
Er Rif, range	C1	57
Erciyes Dağı, mt.	C2	27
Érd	B2	43
Erdenet	C2	11
Erebus, mt.	B5	107
Erenhot	E1	10
Erfurt	B3	40
Erg Chech, desert	C1	58
Erg Iguidi, desert	D1	58
Erickson	B4	96
Erie, lake	E5	102
Erie, Pa.	E1	126
Eriksdale	B4	96
Erimo, cape	Inset I	8
Eritrea		60
Erlangen	B4	40
Ermelo	C2	32
Erne, river	A2	30
Errigal, mt.	B1	31
Erromango, island	C4	18
Ersekë	B3	49
Erzen, river	A2	49
Erzgebirge, mts.	C3	40
Erzincan	D2	27
Erzurum	E2	27
Esbjerg	B3	32
Esch-sur-Alzette	B1	33
Eschen	B1	33
Escondido, river	B2	87
Escuintla	C5	85
Escuminac	K3	103
Esfahan	C2	22
Esil	C1	23
Esker	D3	98
Eskifjördhur	C2	52
Eskilstuna	C3	53
Eskimo Point	K4	99
Eskişehir	B2	27
Esla, river	D2	37
Esmeraldas	B2	79
Espanola	D1	102
Española, island	Inset	79
Esperance, W.A.	B3	14
Espichel, cape	A3	36
Espírito Santo	D3	81
Espiritu Santo, island	B2	18
Espoo	B2	53
Esquel	A5	74
Essaouira	B2	57
Essen	A3	40
Essequibo, river	B3, B5	80
Essex	C5	102
Esslingen	B4	40
Estados, island	C7	74
Estaire	E1	102
Estany d'Engolasters, lake	B2	36
Este, point	E2	90
Estelí	A2	87
Esterhazy	H10	104
Estevan	G11	104
Esther	E4	94
Eston	B9	104
Estonia		46
Estoril	A3	36
Estrela, mts.	B2	36
Esztergom	B2	43
Etchemin, river	L6	103
Ethelbert	A3	96
Ethiopia		60
Ethiopia, plateau	C2	60
Etna, mt.	C3	38
Etobicoke	J5	102
Etosha, pan	B1	70
Etrechy	Inset II	34
Etrek, river	B3	22

	Key	Page
Ettelbruck	B2	33
'Eua, island	C4	17
Euboea, island	B2	51
Eugene, Oreg.	A1	126
Eugenia, point	A2	84
Euphrates, river	C2	24
Eureka, Calif.	A1	126
Eutsuk, lake	J4	95
Evandale	C3	97
Evansville	C2	102
Evansville, Ind.	E2	126
Evenkiya, autonomous okrug	C6	44
Everest, mt.	C2	19
Everett, Wash.	A1	126
Evinayong	C2	66
Évora	B3	36
Évreux	C2	34
Évry	Inset II	34
Ewa	B1	16
Ewell	Inset III	30
Ewo	C4	66
Exeter	B4	30
Exeter	D4	102
Exmoor, plateau	B3	30
Extremadura	C3	37
Exuma, sound	C2	89
Eyasi, lake	B1	68
Eyebrow	D10	104
Eyl	C2	60
Eyre, lake	C3	14
Eyre, peninsula	C3	14
Eysturoy, island	Inset	32

F

	Key	Page
Fabyan	E5	94
Fada	C3	59
Fadiffolu, atoll	A2	19
Faenza	B1	38
Faeroe, islands	Inset	32
Fagamalo	B1	18
Făgăras	C3	43
Fagasa	B1	18
Fagatogo	B1	18
Fair, island	Inset	30
Fairbanks, Alaska	Inset I	126
Fairford	B3	96
Fairmont Hot Springs	P6	95
Fairweather, mt.	A1	95
Faisalabad	D3	21
Faizabad	D3	20
Fajardo	D2	90
Fakfak	E2	13
Falciano	C1	39
Falcon Lake	D4	96
Falelatai	B2	18
Falelima	A2	18
Falémé, river	C3	62
Faleniu	B1	18
Fălesti	B1	50
Falher	B3	94
Falkland, islands	C7	74
Fallujah, al-	B2	24
Falmouth	B2	88
Falmouth	E5	89
False Divi, point	D5	20
Falster, island	D4	32
Falun	C2	53
Famagusta	B1	27
Fan Si Pan, mt.	A1	11
Fangliao	B2	9
Fanø, island	B3	32
Farafangana	B3	69
Farafenni	A2	62
Farah	A2	22
Farah, river	A2	22
Faraulep, atoll	B2	15
Farewell, cape	A3	15
Farewell, cape	C3	106
Farghona	D2	23
Fargo, N. Dak.	D1	126
Faridpur	C5	21
Farim	B1	62
Farmington	M3	95
Farmington, N. Mex.	C2	126
Farnham	Inset III	30
Faro	B4	36
Faro	C4	105
Farquhar, island group	A6	103
Farrellton	A6	103
Fashir, al-	A2	59
Fatick	A2	62
Fatoto	C2	62
Fauquier	N6	95
Faxaflói, bay	A2	52
Faxälven, river	C2	53
Faya-Largeau	B2	59
Faylakah, island	C2	24
Fayyum, al-	B2	56
Fdérik	B2	58
Fehmarn, island	B1	40
Fehmarn, strait	C4	32
Feira de Santana	E3	81
Feldkirch	A3	39
Felidu, atoll	A3	19
Felixstowe	D3	30
Fen, river	E2	10
Fenelon Falls	G3	102
Fengshan	B2	9
Fengyüan	B1	9
Feni, islands	B2	15
Fens, region	D3	30
Feodosiya	D3	47
Fergana, valley	D2	23
Fergus	E4	102
Ferkéssédougou	B2	63
Ferlo, river	B2	62
Ferme-Neuve	A5	103
Fernandina, island	Inset	79
Fernie	P6	95
Ferrara	B1	38
Ferryland	E5	98
Fethiye	B3	27
Feuilles, river	B2	101
Feyzabad	C1	22
Fez	C1	57
Fianarantsoa	B3	69
Fichtelberg, mt.	C3	40

Key Page

Fichtelgebirge, *mts.* B4 40
Field O5 95
Field E1 102
Fier A3 49
Fife, *lake* E11 104
Fig Tree C3 90
Figueira da Foz A2 36
Figueres H1 37
Figuig D1 57
Fiji 17
Filadelfia B3 75
Filchner Ice Shelf
 glacier B12 107
Filfla, *island* B3 36
Fillmore G11 104
Fimbul Ice Shelf, *glacier* ..B14 107
Finisterre, *cape* B1 37
Finland 53
Finland, *gulf* C3 53
Finlay, *river* J2 95
Finn, *river* C1 31
Finnegan D5 94
Finnmark, *plateau* E2 52
Fireside J1 95
Firth, *river* A1 105
Firth A1 31
Fish, *river* C4 70
Fisher Branch C3 96
Fisherton C3 96
Fishguard B3 30
Fitzgerald E1 94
Fitzroy, *mt.* B8 76
Fitzroy, *river* B1 14
Five Islands C2 100
Flagstaff, Ariz. B2 126
Flat, *island* C1 69
Flatbush C4 94
Flaxcombe A9 104
Fleet E5 94
Fleetwood C3 30
Fleming A4 96
Flensburg B1 40
Flesherton E3 102
Fleur de Lys C4 98
Flevoland, *polder* C2 32
Flin Flon A2, C2 96
Flinders, *range* C3 14
Flinders, *river* D1 14
Flint, *island* D3 17
Flint, Mich. E1 126
Flodden Field, *plain* C2 30
Florence B2 38
Florence, S.C. F2 126
Florenceville B2 97
Florencia B4 78
Flores D3 85
Flores, *island* D2 13
Flores, *sea* C2 13
Floreşti B2 50
Floriano D4 81
Florianópolis D4 81
Florida B3 75
Florida D2 88
Florida B2 90
Florida E3 126
Florida Keys, Fla. E3 126
Florida, *straits* B1 88
Florø A3 52
Fly, *river* A2 15
Foam Lake G9 104
Foča B2 48
Focşani D3 43
Foggia C2 38
Fogo D4 98
Fogo, *island* B4 58
Foix C5 34
Folkestone D3 30
Fomboni A2 67
Fond du Lac, *river* F2 104
Fond-du-Lac C1 104
Fonseca, *gulf* B3, C2 86
Fontainebleau C2 34
Fontas M2 95
Fontvieille A2 35
Fonuafo'ou (Falcon), *island* ..B3 17
Fonualei, *island* C2 17
Forest D4 102
Forestville G3 103
Fork River A3 96
Forlì C1 38
Formentera, *island* G3 37
Formosa D2 74
Fornæs C3 32
Forres D2 30
Forsá C3 8
Forssa C3 53
Fort Albany D2 101
Fort Chipewyan E2 94
Fort Collins, Colo. C1 126
Fort Erie G5 102
Fort Frances B3 101
Fort Fraser K4 95
Fort Good Hope C3 99
Fort Lauderdale, Fla. E3 126
Fort Liard D4 99
Fort MacKay E2 94
Fort McMurray E3 94
Fort McPherson B3 99
Fort Myers, Fla. E3 126
Fort Nelson L2 95
Fort Nelson, *river* L1 95
Fort Norman C4 99
Fort Portal B3 61
Fort Providence E4 99
Fort Qu'Appelle G10 104
Fort Resolution F4 99
Fort Saskatchewan D4 94
Fort Severn C1 101
Fort Simpson D4 99
Fort Smith, Ark. D2 126
Fort Smith, *region* E4 99
Fort St. James K4 95
Fort St. John M3 95
Fort Steele P6 95
Fort Stockton, Tex. C2 126
Fort Vermilion C2 94
Fort Wayne, Ind. E1 126
Fort William B2 30
Fort Worth, Tex. D2 126
Fortaleza E2 81
Forteau C3 98
Forth, *estuary* C2 30
Forth, *river* B2 30

Key Page

Fortín Conde de Mirasol,
 fort E2 90
Fortín Ravelo B3 77
Fortune D5 98
Fortune Bridge C2 100
Fortune, *bay* D5 98
Foster, *river* E4 104
Fosterville B3 97
Foumban B2 65
Foumbouni A1 67
Four Falls B2 97
Foveaux, *strait* A4 15
Fox Island F2 100
Fox Lake E5 94
Fox Valley A10 104
Foxe, *basin* N3 99
Foxe, *channel* M3 99
Foxe, *peninsula* N4 99
Foyle, *inlet* C1 31
Foyle, *lake* A2 30
Foyle, *river* A2 30
Foz do Iguaçu C4 81
France 34
Frances, *lake* D5 105
Franceville B2 66
Franche-Comté D3 34
Francis G10 104
Francistown D2 69
Francois C5 98
François, *lake* K4 95
Frankenwald, *mts.* B3 40
Frankford H3 102
Frankfort, *capital*, Ky. ..E2 126
Frankfurt am Main B3 40
Frankfurt an der Oder ..C2 40
Franklin, *strait* J2 99
Franquelin J2 103
Franz Josef Land, *islands* ..A4 44
Fraser E1 95
Fraser Lake K4 95
Fraser, *river* L5, M4 95
Fraserburgh C1 30
Fraserdale D2 101
Fraserwood C4 96
Fray Bentos A2 75
Fredericia B3 32
Fredericton C3 97
Fredericton Jct. C3 97
Frederikberg D3 32
Frederiksberg D3 32
Frederikshavn C1 32
Fredrikstad C4 52
Freeport A2 89
Freeport A3 100
Freetown E5 90
Freetown, *capital* A1 63
Freiberg C3 40
Freiburg A5 40
Freirina B3 76
Fréjus D5 34
Fremantle, W.A. ..A3, Inset I 14
French Guiana 80
French River E1 102
Frenchman, *river* B11 104
Fresnillo D3 84
Fresno, Calif. B2 126
Fria B2 62
Fribourg B2 35
Friedrichshafen B5 40
Frigate, *island* C1 91
Frisches Haff, *bay* D1 41
Friuli-Venezia Giulia C1 38
Frobisher, *lake* C4 104
Frog, *lake* E4 94
Frome, *lake* D2 14
Frontier B11 104
Frosinone C2 38
Fruška Gora, *mts.* A2 49
Frutigen B2 35
Frýdek-Místek D3 42
Fua'amotu B4 17
Fuenlabrada ....Inset II 37
Fuerte Olimpo D2 75
Fuerte, *river* C2 84
Fuerteventura, *island* ..Inset I 37
Fuhayhil, al- C2 24
Fujairah, al- D2 25
Fuji, *mt.* C3 8
Fujian E3 10
Fujisawa C3 8
Fukue A3 8
Fukue, *island* A3 8
Fukui C2 8
Fukuoka A3 8
Fukushima D2 8
Fukuyama B3 8
Fulacunda B2 62
Fuladi, *mt.* B2 22
Fulda B3 40
Fulda, *river* B3 40
Fullarton A2 91
Funabashi D3 8
Funafuti, *capital* C3 16
Funafuti, *island* C3 16
Fundy, *bay* A3 100
Furnas, *reservoir* D4 81
Fürstenfeld E3 39
Fürth B4 40
Fushun F1 10
Futa Jalon, *plateau* B1 62
Futuna, *island* C4 18
Fuxin F1 10
Fuzhou E3 10
Fyn, *island* C3 32

G

Gaalkacyo B2 60
Gabarus G2 100
Gabès C3 57
Gabès, *gulf* C2 57
Gabon 66
Gaborone, *capital* B3 69
Gabriel, *island* C1 69
Gabrovo D3 50
Gabú C1 62
Gacko B2 48

Key Page

Gaeta C2 38
Gafsa B2 57
Gagnoa D3 63
Gagnon C3 101
Gagra A2 45
Gainesville, Fla. E3 126
Gainsborough J11 104
Gairdner, *lake* C3 14
Gaizina, *mt.* C2 46
Galahad E5 94
Galana, *river* E5 61
Galápagos, *islands* ....Inset 79
Galaţi E3 43
Galena Bay O6 95
Galicia C1 37
Galilee, *region* B1 26
Galle B5 19
Gallegos, *river* A7 74
Gallinas, *point* C1 78
Gällivare D1 53
Galoa B3 17
Galveston, Tex. D3 126
Galway B2 31
Galway, *bay* B2 31
Gam, *river* A1 11
Gambia, The 62
Gambia, *river* B2, C3, D2 62
Gambo D5 98
Gamprin B1 33
Gan, *river* E3 10
Gananoque J3 102
Gäncä B2 45
Gander D5 98
Gander Bay D4 98
Gandhinagar B4 20
Ganganagar B3 20
Ganges, *river* E3 20
Gangtok E3 20
Gansu C1, D2 10
Ganzhou E3 10
Gao D2 58
Gaoua C3 64
Gap D4 34
Garabil, *plateau* D3 22
Garabogazköl, *lake* A2 22
Garda, *lake* B1 38
Garden Hill D3 96
Garden Reach ....Inset II 20
Garden, *island* ......Inset I 14
Garden, *river* A1 102
Gardenton C4 96
Gardez B2 22
Gardner, *canal* H4 95
Gardner, *island* B2 17
Garissa E4 61
Garland A3 96
Garmisch-Partenkirchen ..B5 40
Garnish D5 98
Garonne, *river* C4 34
Garoowe B2 60
Garoua B2 65
Garry, *river* H3 99
Garson Lake A4 104
Garulia ....Inset II 20
Gary, Ind. E1 126
Gascoyne *river* A2 14
Gash, *river* B2 60
Gaspé M3 103
Gaspé, *peninsula* L3 103
Gaspereau Forks D2 97
Gatal, *cape* E4 37
Gateshead B2 76
Gatico B2 76
Gatineau A6 103
Gatineau Park A6 103
Gatineau, *river* A4, A5 103
Gatún, *lake* C2 87
Gau, *island* B3 17
Gauhati F3 20
Gaultois D5 98
Gavarr C2 45
Gävle C2 53
Gaya E4 20
Gaya A3 59
Gazanjyk B2 22
Gazelle, *peninsula* B2 15
Gaziantep D3 27
Gbarnga B2 63
Gdańsk D1 41
Gdańsk, *gulf* D1 41
Gdynia D1 41
Gêba, *river* C1 62
Geelong, Vic. D3 14
Geidam F1 65
Gege B2 71
Gejiu D3 10
Gela C3 38
Gelibolu (Gallipoli) A2 27
Gelsenkirchen A3 40
Gem D6 94
Gembloux C2 33
Gemena B1 67
General Eugenio A. Garay ..A2 75
General Santos C5 12
General, *river* C1 89
Genesee C4 94
Geneva A2 35
Geneva, *lake* A2 35
Genk D2 33
Gennargentu, *mts.* B2 38
Genoa B1 38
Genoa, *gulf* B1 38
Gentilly ....Inset II 37
Gentofte D3 32
George B3 71
George Town A2 13
George, *river* C2 101
Georgetown B2 91
Georgetown D2 62
Georgetown C2 100
Georgetown, *capital* B2 80
Georgia 45
Georgia E2 126
Georgian, *bay* E2 102
Gera C3 40
Geral, *range* C4 81

Key Page

Gerald A4 96
Geraldton C3 101
Geraldton, W.A. A2 14
Gerlachovka, *mt.* C2 42
Germany 40
Germiston C2 71
Gerona H2 37
Getafe ....E2, Inset II 37
Gevgelija C2 48
Geylegphug B3 19
Ghabah C2 25
Ghadamis A1 56
Ghaghara, *river* D3 20
Ghana 64
Ghanzi A2 69
Ghardaia B1 57
Gharyan B1 56
Ghat B2 56
Ghatkopar ....Inset 20
Ghaydah, al- C1 25
Ghazal, *river* B4 59
Ghazni B2 22
Ghent B1 33
Ghurdaqah, al- B2 56
Giant's Causeway, *headland* ..A2 30
Gibraltar 36
Gibraltar, *strait* D5 37
Gibson, *desert* B2 14
Giessen B3 40
Gifford, *river* M2 99
Gifu C3 8
Giglio, *island* B2 38
Gijón D1 37
Gikongoro B2 61
Gilbert Plains A3 96
Gilbert, *islands* A1 17
Gilbert, *river* D1 14
Gilgit E2 21
Gilliam D1 96
Gillingham D3 30
Gimie, *mt.* A2 91
Gimli C4 96
Giresun D2 27
Gironde, *river* B4 34
Gisborne C2 15
Gisenyi B1 61
Gitarama B2 61
Gitega B2 61
Giurgiu C4 43
Giza B2 56
Gizo A1 16
Gjirokastër B3 49
Gjøvik C3 52
Glace Bay H1 100
Gladstone B4 96
Gladstone, Qld. E2 14
Glâma, *river* C3 52
Glanville A2 90
Glasgow B2 30
Glasgow, Mont. C1 126
Glaslyn B7 104
Glastonbury C3 30
Gleichen D6 94
Glen Margaret D3 100
Glenboro B4 96
Glencoe D5 102
Glenella B4 96
Glenholme D2 100
Glenora G2 95
Glenwood D5 98
Glidden A9 104
Glifádha ....Inset 37
Glittertinden, *mt.* B3 52
Gliwice C3 41
Głogów C3 41
Gloucester C3 30
Gloucester K2 102
Glover, *reef* B2 85
Glovertown D5 98
Gmünd C3 60
Gobabis C2 70
Gobi, *desert* D1 10
Godavari, *river* C5 20
Godbout J2 103
Goderich D4 102
Godfrey J3 102
Godoy Cruz B3 74
Gods, *lake* D3 101
Gogama D3 101
Goiânia D3 81
Goiás D3 81
Golan Heights, *occ. terr.* ..A3 27
Gold Coast, Qld. E2 14
Gold River J6 95
Golden O5 95
Golden Lake H2 102
Golea, el- B2 57
Golfito C4 86
Golmud C2 10
Golyama Kamchiya, *river* ..C2 50
Goma C2 67
Gombe F2 65
Gomera, *island* ....Inset I 37
Gómez Palacio D2 84
Gonaïves C1 89
Gonâve, *gulf* B1 89
Gonâve, *island* B1 89
Gonder B1 60
Gongola, *river* F2 65
Goobies E5 98
Good Hope, *cape* A3 71
Goodlands B2 69
Goodlands A4 96
Goodsoil A6 104
Göppingen B4 40
Gorakhpur D3 20
Goražde B2 48
Gordon, *lake* E3 94
Gordondale A3 94
Gore B2 60
Gore Bay C2 102
Gori C4 45
Goris D3 45
Gorizia C1 38
Görlitz C3 40
Gorlovka D2 47

Key Page

Gorno-Altay, *republic* ..D6 44
Gorno-Altaysk D6 44
Goroka A2 15
Gorontalo D1 13
Gorzów Wielkopolski B2 41
Gosford, N.S.W. E2 14
Goshen F2 100
Goslar B3 40
Gospić B3 48
Gosport C4 30
Göta, *canal* B3 53
Göteborg och Bohus B3 53
Gotha B3 40
Gotland, *island* C3 53
Gotsu B3 8
Göttingen B3 40
Gouda B2 32
Goudiri C2 62
Gouin, *reservoir* B3 103
Goundam C2 58
Gouré C3 59
Govan E9 104
Governador Valadares D3 81
Gowd-e Zereh, *lake* A3 22
Göyçay B2 45
Gozo, *island* A1 36
Graaf-Reinet B3 71
Gračanica B1 48
Gracias A2 86
Grafton, N.S.W. E2 14
Graham Land, *region* ..C11 107
Graham, *island* F4 95
Graham, *island* K1 99
Grahamstown C3 71
Grampian, *mts.* C1 30
Gran Canaria, *island* ..Inset I 37
Gran Chaco, *region* B3 87
Granada B3 37
Granada B4 86
Granby D6 103
Grand Anse B1 91
Grand Bahama, *island* ..A2 89
Grand Bale C2 69
Grand Bank D5 98
Grand Bay C1 91
Grand Bend D4 102
Grand Bruit B5 98
Grand Canyon, Ariz. B2 126
Grand Centre E4 94
Grand Cess B3 63
Grand Erg Occidental,
 desert B1 57
Grand Erg Oriental, *desert* ..B1 57
Grand Falls B1 97
Grand Falls-Windsor D5 98
Grand Forks D11 104
Grand Forks, N. Dak. ..N6 95
Grand Island, Nebr. D1 126
Grand Junction, Colo. ..C2 126
Grand Manan, *island* ..C4 97
Grand Marais H5 94
Grand Narrows G2 100
Grand Pré C2 100
Grand Rapids B2 96
Grand Rapids, Mich. ..E1 126
Grand Roy B2 91
Grand Santi A1 80
Grand Turk, *capital* D4 89
Grand Turk, *island* D4 89
Grand Valley E4 102
Grand, *canal* C2 31
Grand, *harbor* B2 36
Grand, *lake* D2 97
Grand, *lake* C4 98
Grand, *river* C3 69
Grand-Etang F1 100
Grand-Mère D5 103
Grand-Remous A5 103
Grande Baleine, *river* ..A2 101
Grande de Añasco, *river* ..A2 90
Grande de Manatí, *river* ..C2 90
Grande de Matagalpa, *river* ..B3 94
Grande Prairie B7 74
Grande, *bay* B7 74
Grande, *range* C2 75
Grande, *river* B3 77
Grande, *river* D3 81
Grande, *river* B3 86
Grande-Anse B1 97
Grande-Rivière M3 103
Grande-Vallée M2 103
Grândola A3 36
Grandview A3 96
Granisle J4 95
Grantham D3 30
Granville Lake A1 96
Gras, *lake* F4 99
Grass, *river* A3, B2 96
Grassland D4 94
Grauspitz, *mt.* B2 33
Gravelbourg D11 104
Gravenhurst F3 102
Gravesend ....Inset III 30
Gravois, *point* B1 89
Graz D3 39
Great Abaco, *island* B1 89
Great Alföld, *plain* B2 43
Great Artesian, *basin* ..D2 14
Great Australian, *bight* ..B3 14
Great Bahama, *bank* B2 89
Great Barrier, *island* C2 15
Great Barrier, *reef* D1 14
Great *basin*, Nev. B2 126
Great Bear, *lake* D3 99
Great Britain 30
Great Dividing, *range* ..D1, D3 14
Great Exuma, *island* B3 89
Great Falls B1 97
Great Falls, Mont. B1 126
Great Fish, *river* C3 71
Great Inagua, *island* ..C4 89
Great Indian, *desert* B3 20
Great Karroo, *plateau* ..B3 71
Great Nicobar, *island* ..F7 20
Great Rift, *valley* 55
Great Ruaha, *river* C2 68
Great Salt, *lake*, Utah ..B1 126

Key Page

Great Sand Sea, *desert*......A2 56
Great Sandy, *desert* B2 14
Great Scarcies, *river* A1 63
Great Sea, *reef* B1 17
Great Slave, *lake* F4 99
Great Victoria, *desert* ..B2 14
Great Wall of China D2 10
Great Yarmouth D3 30
Great Zab, *river* B1 24
Great, *plains* C1 126
Greater Hinggan, *range* ..F1 10
Greater Sunda, *islands* ..B2 13
Gréboun, *mt.* B1 59
Gredos, *mts.* D2 37
Greece 51
Greeley, Colo. C1 126
Greely, *fjord* L1 99
Green Bay, Wis. E1 126
Green Lake C6 104
Green, *islands* B2 15
Greenland 106
Greenland, *sea* D2 106
Greenock B2 30
Greensboro, N.C. F2 126
Greenville B3 63
Greenville, S.C. E2 126
Greenwood N6 95
Greifswald C1 40
Grená C2 32
Grenada 91
Grenada, *island* B2 91
Grenadines, *islands* ..A3, B1, C1 91
Grenfell H10 104
Grenoble D4 34
Gretna C4 96
Greve D3 32
Grevenmacher B2 33
Grey River C5 98
Grey, *range* D2 14
Greymouth B3 15
Gribingui, *river* A2 66
Griffin G11 104
Griffith, N.S.W. D3 14
Grijalva, *river* F4 84
Grimsby C3 30
Grimsey, *island* B1 52
Grinnell, *peninsula* J1 99
Griqualand East, *region* ..C3 71
Griqualand West, *region* ..B2 71
Griquatown B2 71
Grise Ford M1 99
Griswold A4 96
Groningen B2 40
Groningen D1 32
Gronlid F7 104
Groote Eylandt, *island* ..C1 14
Grootfontein C1 70
Grootvloer, *pan* B2 71
Gros Islet B1 91
Gros Morne Natl. Park ..C4 98
Gros-Morne L2 103
Grosseto B2 38
Grossglockner, *mt.* B3 39
Groundbirch M3 95
Groznyy E4 44
Grudziądz D2 41
Grunthal C4 96
Guacanayabo, *gulf* D3 88
Guadalajara B2 37
Guadalajara, *state capital* ..D3 84
Guadalcanal, *island* A1 16
Guadalquivir, *river* D4 37
Guadalupe, *reservoir* ..Inset 84
Guadarrama, *mts.* D2 37
Guadeloupe, *island* 82
Guadiana, *river* C3 37
Guaillabamba, *river* C4 79
Guainía, *river* C4 78
Guajara Mirim B3 81
Guajira, *peninsula* C1 78
Guam, *island* 5
Guanacaste, *range* A1 86
Guanaja, *island* C1 86
Guanajuato, *state capital* ..D3 84
Guanare C2 79
Guánica ....Inset I 90
Guantánamo E3 88
Guaporé, *river* B3 81
Guaqui A3 77
Guaranda B3 79
Guaráu B2 36
Guarujá ....Inset II 81
Guarulhos ....Inset II 81
Guasave C2 84
Guatemala 85
Guatemala City, *capital* ..C5 85
Guaviare, *river* C2 79
Guayaguayare A2 91
Guayama C3 90
Guayambre, *river* B2 86
Guayaquil B3 79
Guayas, *river* B4 79
Guaymas B2 84
Guaynabo C2 90
Guben C3 40
Gudauta A2 45
Gudenå, *river* B2 32
Guecho E1 37
Guédiawaye A3 62
Guelph E4 102
Guelta Zemmur B1 58
Guéret C3 34
Guernica Y Luno E1 37
Guernsey, *island* ..Inset II 30
Guerrero D4 84
Guerrero Negro B2 84
Guiana, *highlands* D2 79
Guiers, *lake* B1 62
Guilarte, *mt.* B2 90
Guildford C3 30
Guilin E3 10

Key Page

Guimarães A2 36
Guinea 62
Guinea, *gulf* 55
Guinea-Bissau 62
Güiria D1 79
Guiyang D3 10
Guizhou D3 10
Gujranwala E3 21
Gujrat E3 21
Gulbarga C5 20
Gulbene D2 46
Gulf Coastal, *plain* D3 126
Gulistan C2 23
Gull Lake B10 104
Gull, *lake* C5 94
Gulu C2 61
Gumdag B2 22
Gummi C1 65
Gunisao, *river* C2 96
Gunnbjørn Fjeld, *mt.* D2 106
Gunton C4 96
Guntur D5 20
Gurabo D2 90
Guri, *reservoir* D2 79
Gusau D1 65
Gushgy D3 22
Gushgy, *river* D3 22
Gushikawa .....Inset II 8
Gustavo A. Madero .....Inset 84
Güstrow C2 40
Guyana 80
Guysborough F2 100
Gwadar B5 21
Gwai, *river* A2 69
Gwalior C3 20
Gwanda B2 69
Gweru B2 69
Gyda, *peninsula* B5 44
Gympie, Qld. E2 14
Gyöngyös B2 43
Győr A2 43
Gypsumville B3 96
Gyumri A2 45
Gyzylarbat B2 22

H

Ha Giang A1 11
Ha'apai, *island group* B3 17
Haapsalu B2 46
Haarlem B2 32
Habarut C1 25
Habay A2 94
Haboro .....Inset I 8
Hachijo, *island* C3 8
Hachinohe D1 8
Hachioji C3 8
Haddummati, *atoll* A4 19
Hadejia, *river* E1 65
Hadera B1 26
Haderslev B3 32
Hadhramaut, *district* B1 25
Haditha, al- B2 24
Haedo, *range* B2 75
Haeju A3 9
Hafford C8 104
Hafnarfjördhur A3 52
Hagen A3 40
Hague, *cape* B2 34
Haha, *island* .....Inset III 8
Haifa B1 26
Haifa, *bay* B1 26
Haikou E4 10
Hail B1 24
Hailar E1 10
Hainan D4 10
Haines Junction B5 105
Haiphong B2 11
Hairé Lao B1 62
Haiti 89
Hajdúböszörmény C2 43
Haji Ibrahim, *mt.* B1 24
Hajjah A1 25
Haka B2 12
Hakodate .....D1, Inset I 8
Halab (Aleppo) A1 27
Halaib D1 59
Halba B1 26
Halberstadt B3 40
Haldimand F5 102
Halfmoon Bay L6 95
Haliburton G2 102
Halifax C3 30
Halifax, *capital* D3 100
Halil, *river* D4 22
Halisahar .....Inset II 20
Hall Beach M3 99
Hall, *peninsula* P4 99
Halla-san, *mt.* .....Inset 9
Hallboro B4 96
Halle C2 33
Halle B3 40
Hallingdal, *valley* B3 52
Halmahera, *island* D1 13
Halmstad B3 53
Haltiatunturi, *mt* B1 53
Halton Hills F4 102
Hamadan B2 22
Hamah A2 27
Hamamatsu C3 8
Hamar C3 52
Hambantota C5 19
Hamburg B2 40
Hämeenlinna B2 53
Hameln B2 40
Hamersley, *range* A2 14
Hamhŭng B3 9
Hami C1 10
Hamilton B2 95
Hamilton B2 30
Hamilton F4 102
Hamilton, *inlet* B2 98
Hamiota A4 96
Hamm A3 40
Hammamat, *gulf* C1 57
Hammamat, al- C1 57
Hammerfest E1 52
Hammonds Plains D3 100
Hammondvale D3 97

Key Page

Hampden C4 98
Hampstead J5 103
Hampton D3 97
Hamun-e Jaz Murian, *lake* D4 22
Hamun-e Saberi, *lake* A2 22
Han, *river* E2 10
Han, *river* B4 9
Hanau B3 40
Handan E2 10
Hangayn, *mts.* B2 11
Hangö B3 53
Hangzhou F2 10
Hanley D9 104
Hannibal, Mo. D2 126
Hannover B2 40
Hanover D3 102
Hantzsch, *river* O3 99
Hanzhong D2 10
Haora .....E4, Inset II 20
Haparanda D1 53
Happy Valley-Goose Bay ..A2, E4 98
Har Us, *lake* B2 11
Harad C1 24
Harare, *capital* B1 69
Harbel A2 63
Harbin F1 10
Harbour Breton D5 98
Harbour Deep C4 98
Harbour, *island* B2 89
Harcourt D2 97
Hardangerfjord, *fjord* B4 52
Hardangervidda, *plateau* B3 52
Hardwood Lake H2 102
Hare Bay D5 98
Harer D2 60
Hargeysa A2 60
Hargrave A4 96
Harirud, *river* A2 22
Harlow .....Inset III 30
Härnösand C2 53
Harper C3 63
Harris C9 104
Harrisburg, *capital, Pa.* F1 126
Harrogate C2 30
Harstad D2 52
Hart, *ranges* L3 95
Hart, *river* B3 105
Hartford, *capital, Conn.* F1 126
Hartland B2 97
Hartley Bay H4 95
Hartney A4 96
Harwill C3 96
Harz, *mts.* B3 40
Hasa, al-, *region* C1 24
Hasakah, al- B1 27
Hashtadan, *region* E3 22
Haslemere .....Inset III 30
Hasselt D2 33
Hastings C2 15
Hastings D4 30
Hastings H3 102
Hat Yai B5 12
Hatillo B2 90
Hato Mayor C2 89
Hatteras *cape, N.C.* F2 126
Hattiesburg, Miss. E2 126
Haugesund B4 52
Haultain, *river* D4 104
Haute-Normandie C2 34
Havana, *capital* B1 88
Havel, *river* C2 40
Havelock H3 102
Havířov D3 42
Havre, Mont. C1 126
Havre-St-Pierre D3 101
Hawaii .....Inset II 126
Hawaii *island, Hawaii* .....Inset II 126
Hawalli C2 24
Hawar, *islands* B2 25
Hawea, *lake* A3 15
Hawf C1 25
Hawick C2 30
Hawke Harbour D2 98
Hawke's Bay C4 98
Hawke, *bay* C2 15
Hawkesbury L2 102
Hay River E4 99
Hay, *river* A2, B1 94
Hayes, *river* D1, D2 96
Hayma C2 25
Hayter E5 94
Hazelton J3 95
Hazelton, *mts.* H3 95
Hazlet B10 104
Hazm, al- A1 25
Hearst D3 101
Heart's Content E5 98
Heaslip A4 96
Heath Steele C1 97
Hebei E2 10
Hebrides, *sea* A1 30
Hebron E3 98
Hecate, *strait* G4 95
Hecla C3 96
Hecla and Griper, *bay* F1 99
Hedley M6 95
Heerenveen C2 32
Heerlen C4 32
Hefei E2 10
Hegang G1 10
Heha, *mt.* B2 61
Heidelberg B4 40
Heidenheim B4 40
Heilbronn B4 40
Heilong (Amur), *river* F1 10
Heilongjiang F1 10
Heimaey, *island* A3 52
Heinsburg E4 94
Heisler D5 94
Hekla, *volcano* B3 52
Hel D1 41
Helen, *reef* .....Inset 17
Helena, *capital, Mont.* B1 126
Helgoland, *island* A1 40
Hellín F3 37
Helmand, *river* A2 22
Helmsdale C1 30

Key Page

Helsingborg B3 53
Helsingør D2 32
Helsinki, *capital* B2 53
Heming Lake A2 96
Henan E2 10
Henashi, *cape* C1 8
Hengch'un B2 9
Hengelo D2 32
Hengyang E3 10
Henley Harbour D3 98
Hensall D4 102
Henzada B3 12
Herat A2 22
Herb Lake B2 96
Herbert C10 104
Heredia B2 86
Hereford C3 30
Heriot Bay K6 95
Hermitage-Sandyville D5 98
Hermon, *mt.* A3 27
Hermosillo, *state capital* B2 84
Hernád, *river* C1 43
Herne A3 40
Herning B2 32
Hertford .....Inset III 30
Herzliyya B1 26
Hess, *river* C4 105
Hesse B3 40
Hetauda C2 19
Hiatikulu B2 71
Hibbing, Minn. D1 126
Hicks Bay C2 15
Hidaka, *mts.* .....Inset I 8
Hidalgo E3 84
Hidalgo del Parral C2 84
Hieflau D3 39
Hierro, *island* .....Inset I 37
Higashiosaka B3 8
High Atlas, *ranges* B2 57
High Level B2 94
High River D6 94
High Tatra, *mts.* D4 41
High Wycombe .....Inset III 30
Highrock A1 96
Highrock, *lake* A1 96
Higüey D2 89
Hiiumaa, *island* B2 46
Hijaz, al-, *region* A1 24
Hilda E6 94
Hilden D2 100
Hildesheim B2 40
Hill Bank B2 85
Hillaby, *mt.* A3 91
Hillah, al- B2 24
Hillerød D3 32
Hillsborough C1 91
Hillsborough E3 97
Hillsborough, *bay* B2 100
Hilo, Hawaii .....Inset II 126
Hilton Beach B1 102
Hilversum C2 32
Himalayas, *mts.* 7
Himeji B3 8
Hinche C1 89
Hindelang B5 40
Hindu Kush, *range* B1 22
Hino, *cape* B3 8
Hinton B4 94
Hirakata B3 8
Hirakud, *reservoir* D4 20
Hirara .....Inset III 8
Hirmil, al- B1 26
Hirosake D1 8
Hiroshima B3 8
Hirtshals B2 32
Hisabpur .....Inset II 20
Hitachi D2 8
Hixon L4 95
Hjørring B2 32
Hkakabo Razi, *mt.* C1 12
Ho Chi Minh City B4 11
Hoa Binh A2 11
Hobart, *Tas., capital* D4 14
Hobsons, *bay* .....Inset V 14
Hobyo C3 60
Hoceima, al- D1 57
Hodgeville D10 104
Hodgson C3 96
Hódmezővásárhely C2 43
Hoeryŏng C1 9
Hof B3 40
Höfn C2 52
Hohe Tauern, *mts.* C3 39
Hohhot E1 10
Hokkaido, *island* .....D1, Inset I 8
Hoktemberyan B2 45
Holbæk C3 32
Holden D4 94
Holdfast E10 104
Holetown A3 91
Holguín E3 88
Holhol B2 60
Holland B4 96
Holman E2 99
Holon B1 26
Holstebro B2 32
Holton C2 98
Holyhead B3 30
Holyrood E5 98
Holywood B2 30
Homathko, *river* K5 95
Hombori Tondo, *mt.* C2 58
Hombori, *mts.* C2 58
Homer, Alaska .....Inset I 126
Homo, *bay* B2 18
Homs A2 27
Homyel E3 47
Hon Gai B2 11
Hondo C3 94
Hondo, *river* B1 85
Honduras 86
Honduras, *gulf* A1 86
Hong Kong, S.A.R. E3 10
Hong Kong, *island* .....Inset 10
Hongze, *lake* E2 10
Honiara, *capital* A1 16
Honolulu, *capital,*
Hawaii .....Inset II 126

Key Page

Honshu, *island* C2 8
Hoogeveen D2 32
Hoorn C2 32
Hope M6 95
Hope Bay C2 88
Hope Valley E5 94
Hopedale A1 98
Hopedale E3 98
Hopewell Cape E3 97
Horgën C1 35
Hormigueros A2 90
Hormuz, *strait* D4 22
Horn, *cape* C9 76
Horn, *cape* A1 52
Hornád, *river* C2 42
Hornavan, *lake* C1 53
Hornepayne D3 101
Horsburgh, *atoll* A2 19
Horse, *river* D3 94
Horsens B3 32
Horton, *river* D3 99
Hospitalet H2 37
Hoste, *island* C9 76
Hot Springs, Ark. D2 126
Hotan A2 10
Hotchkiss B2 94
Hottah, *lake* E3 99
Houghton, Mich. E1 126
Houmt Souk C3 57
Houston J4 95
Houston, Tex. D3 126
Hovd, *river* B2 11
Hove C4 30
Hoverla, *mt.* A2 47
Hövsgöl, *lake* C1 11
Howley C4 98
Hoy, *island* .....Inset I 30
Hradec Králové B2 42
Hrazdan B2 45
Hrazdan, *river* B2 45
Hrodna A3 47
Hron, *river* B2 42
Hsinchu B1 9
Hsinchuang B1 9
Hsintien B1 9
Hsinying B2 9
Hua Hin B3 12
Huacho B3 77
Huai, *river* E2 10
Huainan E2 10
Hualien B2 9
Huallaga, *river* B2 77
Huambo C4 70
Huancavelica B3 77
Huancayo B3 77
Huang (Yellow), *river* D2, E2 10
Huánuco B2 77
Huapí, *mts.* B2 87
Huaraz B2 77
Huascarán, *mt.* B2 77
Hubbards C3 100
Hubei E2 10
Hubley D3 100
Hubli-Dharwar C5 20
Hudaydah, al- A2 25
Huddersfield C3 30
Hudiksvall C2 53
Hudson Bay H8 104
Hudson's Hope M3 95
Hudson, *bay* J3 92
Hudson, *strait* O4 99
Hue B3 11
Huehuetenango B4 85
Huelva C4 37
Huesca F1 37
Hufuf, al- C1 24
Hugli, *river* .....Inset II 20
Hugli-Chunchura .....Inset II 20
Hüichŏn B2 9
Huila, *mt.* A4 78
Hüksan Chedo, *islands* A5 9
Hull A6 103
Hulun, *lake* E1 10
Hulwan B2 56
Humacao D2 90
Humber, *river* D3 30
Humboldt E8 104
Humenné C2 42
Humuya, *river* B2 86
Húnaflói, *bay* A2 52
Hunan E3 10
Hunedoara B3 43
Hungary 43
Hüngnam B3 9
Hünsruck, *mts.* A4 40
Hunter River B2 100
Huntington, W. Va. E2 126
Huntsville F2 102
Huntsville, Ala. E2 126
Hunyani, *river* B1 69
Huon B1 18
Huon, *peninsula* A2 15
Huron, *lake* E1 126
Hussar D5 94
Hutchinson, Kans. D2 126
Hvannadalshnúkur, *mt.* B3 52
Hvar, *island* C3 48
Hvíta, *river* A2 52
Hwange A2 69
Hyargas, *lake* B2 11
Hyderabad C5 20
Hyderabad C5 21
Hyesan C2 9
Hyland Post H2 95
Hyland, *river* D5 105
Hylo D4 94
Hyvinkää B2 53

I

Ialomiţa, *river* D3 43
Ialpug, *river* B2 50
Iaşi D2 43
Ibadan B3 65
Ibagué B3 78
Ibar, *river* B3 49
Ibaraki B3 8
Ibarra B2 79
Ibb A2 25

Key Page

Ibérico, *mts.* F2 37
Ibiza G4 37
Ibiza, *island* G3 37
Iboundji, *mt.* A2 66
Ibrahim, *river* A1 26
Ibri C1 25
Ica B3 77
Içá, *river* C1 81
Icacos, *key* D2 90
Ice Cap A1 98
Iceland 52
Ichŏn B2 9
Ichihara D3 8
Ichikawa C3 8
Ichilo, *river* B3 77
Ichinomiya C3 8
Idaho B1 126
Idaho Falls, Idaho B1 126
Iddesleigh E6 94
Idfu B3 56
Ídhra, *island* B3 51
Idlib A2 27
Idrija B2 48
Ife C4 65
Igarka C6 44
Igloolik M3 99
Igombe, *river* B1 68
Iguaçu, *falls* C4 81
Iguaçu, *river* C4 81
Iguala E4 84
Iguazú, *falls* E4 84
Ih Bogd Uul, *mt.* C3 11
Ihavandiffulu, *atoll* A1 19
Ihosy B3 69
Ilan B1 9
Iijoki, *river* C1 53
Iisalmi C2 53
Ijevan B2 45
Ijssel, *river* D2 32
Ijsselmeer, *sea* C2 32
Ijuw C2 16
Ikaría, *island* C3 51
Ikeja B4 65
Ikela C2 67
Iki, *island* A3 8
Ikorodu B4 65
Ila C4 65
Ilam B3 22
Ilam C2 19
Île-à-la-Crosse C5 104
Île-de-France C2 34
Ilebo C2 67
Ilesha C4 65
Ilford D2 96
Ilhéus E3 81
Ili, *river* C4 23
Iligan C4 12
Illampu, *mt.* A3 77
Illapel B4 76
Illimani, *mt.* A3 77
Illinois E1 126
Ilo C4 77
Iloilo B4 12
Ilorin C3 65
Imatra C2 53
Imbariê .....Inset I 81
Imbéry B2 90
Imeni Ismail Samani, *peak.* ..B1 23
Imi D3 60
Imjin, *river* B3 9
Imlili A2 58
Imperatriz D2 81
Imperial E9 104
Imperial Mills E4 94
Imperial, *river* B6 76
Impfondo D3 66
Imphal F4 20
Inari, *lake* C1 53
Inch'ŏn B4 9
Incles, *river* C1 36
Indalsälven, *river* B2 53
India 20
Indian Bay D4 96
Indian Brook G1 100
Indian Cabins B1 94
Indian Harbour D3 100
Indian Head G10 104
Indiana E1 126
Indianapolis, *capital, Ind.* E2 126
Indigirka, *river* D2 44
Indispensable, *reefs* B2 16
Indonesia 13
Indore C4 20
Indus, *river* C4, E2 21
Ingleside K3 102
Ingolstadt B4 40
Ingonish G1 100
Ingonish Beach G1 100
Ingushetiya, *republic* E4 44
Inhambane B5 68
Inhomirim .....Inset I 81
Inland, *sea* B3 8
Inn, *river* B3, C2 39
Inner Hebrides, *islands* A2 30
Inner Mongolia E1 10
Innisfail D5 94
Innisfil F3 102
Innsbruck B3 39
Inta D2 44
Interlaken B2 35
International Falls, Minn. D1 126
Inthanon, *mt.* B2 12
Inukjuak A2 101
Inuvik B3 99
Inuvik, *region* E1 10
Invercargill A4 15
Invermay G9 104
Inverness B1 30
Inverness F1 100
Inwood C4 96
Inyangani, *mt.* C2 69
Ioánnina B2 51
Ionian, *islands* B2 51
Ionian, *sea* A2 51
Iori, *river* C4 45
Iowa D1 126
Ipel', *river* B2 42
Ipiíba .....Inset I 81
Ipoh A2 13

Key Page

Ipoly, *river* B1 43
Ipswich D3 30
Iqaluit, *capital, Nunivut* P4 99
Iquique B2 76
Iquitos C1 77
Iracoubo B1 80
Iráklion C4 51
Iran 22
Iranshahr D5 22
Irapuato D3 84
Iraq 24
Irazú, *volcano* C3 86
Irbe, *strait* A3 46
Irbid A1 26
Irbil B1 24
Ireland 31
Iri B5 9
Irian Jaya, *region* E2 13
Iringa C2 68
Iriomote, *island* .....Inset II 8
Iriona C2 86
Irish, *sea* B3 30
Irkutsk D7 44
Iron Bridge B1 102
Iron Gate Reservoir B3 43
Iroquois Falls D3 101
Irrawaddy, *river* B2 12
Irtysh, *river* D1 23
Irtysh, *river* D5 44
Isabela A1 90
Isabela, *island* .....Inset 84
Isabelia, *mts.* B2 87
Ísafjördhur A1 52
Isangel C4 18
Isar, *river* C4 40
Ischia, *island* C2 38
Ise C3 8
Ise, *bay* C3 8
Isère, *river* D4 34
Isernia C2 38
Iseyin B4 65
Isherton B4 80
Ishigaki, *island* .....Inset II 8
Ishikari, *river* .....Inset I 8
Ishim D5 44
Ishim, *river* C1 23
Ishinomaki D2 8
Ishinomaki, *bay* D2 8
Ishizuchi, *mt.* B3 8
Isiro D1 67
Iskenderun D3 27
Iskür, *river* C2 50
Islamabad, *capital* D3 21
Island Lake D2 96
Island, *lake* D2 96
Islay, *island* A2 30
Isle aux Morts B5 98
Islington J6 102
Ismailiyah, al- B1 56
Isoka C2 67
Isparta B3 27
Israel 26
İstanbul B2 27
Istria, *peninsula* A2 48
Italy 38
İzmir A2 27
İzmit B2 27
Itabira D3 81
Itabuna E3 81
Itaipu .....Inset I 81
Itaipú, *reservoir* A4 75
Itajaí D4 81
Itanagar F3 20
Itapecerica da Serra .....Inset II 81
Itapeva .....Inset II 81
Itaquaquecetuba .....Inset II 81
Iténez, *river* B2 77
Itháki, *island* B2 51
Ittoqqortoormiit
(Scoresbysund) D2 106
Ituna G9 104
Ivalo C1 53
Ivano-Frankivsk A2 47
Ivanovo D3 44
Ivindo, *river* B1 66
Ivujivik A1 101
Iwaki D2 8
Iwakuni B3 8
Iwo C4 65
Iwo Jima, *island* .....Inset III 8
Ixelles C2 33
Ixtapa E4 84
Ixtapaluca .....Inset 84
Izabal, *lake* E4 85
Izhevsk D4 44
Izki C1 25
Izmail B3 47
Iztacalco .....Inset 84
Iztapalapa .....Inset 84
Izu, *islands* C3 8
Izu, *peninsula* C3 8
Izuhara A3 8

J

Jabal al-Akhdar, al-, *mts.* C1 25
Jabal al-Uwaynat, *mt.* D3 56
Jabal an-Nabi Shuayb, *mt.* A1 25
Jabal an-Nusayriyah, *mts.* A2 27
Jabal Katrinah, *mt.* B2 56
Jabal Ramm, *mt.* A3 26
Jabal Tuwayq, *mts.* B2 24
Jabal Zuqar, *island* A3 25
Jabalpur C4 20
Jaboatão E2 81
Jacaré-Acanga C2 81
Jackhead C3 96
Jackson's Arm C4 98
Jackson, *capital, Miss.* D2 126
Jackson, *port* .....Inset IV 14
Jackson, Wyo. B1 126
Jacksonville, Fla. E2 126
Jacmel C2 89
Jacques-Cartier, *river* E4 103
Jacquet River C1 97
Jadabpur .....Inset II 20
Jadida, el- B1 57
Jaén E4 37
Jaffna B2 19

	Key	Page
Jafr, al-	B2	26
Jagdalpur	D5	20
Jaghbub, al-	D2	56
Jahrah, al-	B2	24
Jamaica		**88**
Jaipur	C3	20
Jaipurhat	B3	21
Jakarta, capital	B2	13
Jakobstad	B2	53
Jajce	B1	48
Jalal-Abad	C2	23
Jalalabad	C2	22
Jalapa Enríquez, state capital	E4	84
Jalingo	F3	65
Jalisco	D4	84
Jalu	D2	56
Jaluit, island	B2	16
Jamaame	A3	60
Jamalpur	C4	21
Jambi	B2	13
James, bay	J3	92
Jammu	B2	20
Jamnagar	B4	20
Jampur	Inset II	20
Jämsä	C2	53
Jamshedpur	E4	20
Jamuna, river	C4	21
Jan Lake	H6	104
Jan Mayen, island		5
Janai	Inset II	20
Janakpur	C3	19
Janeville	D1	97
Jangy-Bazar	B2	23
Japan		**8**
Japan, sea	B2	8
Japanese Alps, mts.	C3	8
Japeri	Inset I	81
Japurá, river	A2	81
Jarama, river	Inset II	37
Jarash	A1	26
Jari, river	C1	81
Jarvie	D4	94
Jarvis	E5	102
Jask	D4	22
Jastrebac, mts.	B3	49
Jászberény	B2	43
Java, island	C2	13
Java, sea	C2	13
Javari, river	A2	81
Jawf, al-	A1	24
Jawf, al-	D3	56
Jawhar	B3	60
Jaya, mt.	E2	13
Jayapura	F2	13
Jayuya	B2	90
Jazirah, al-, region	B1	27
Jazzin	A2	26
Jebba	C3	65
Jebel Toubkal, mt.	C2	57
Jeddah	A2	24
Jeddore, lake	D5	98
Jefferson City, capital, Mo.	D2	126
Jejuí-Guazú, river	D4	75
Jejur	Inset II	20
Jekabpils	C2	46
Jelenia Góra	B3	41
Jelgava	B2	46
Jemseg	C3	97
Jena	B3	40
Jengish Chokusu, mt.	G1	23
Jenner	E6	94
Jenpeg	B2	96
Jérémie	A2	89
Jerez de la Frontera	C4	37
Jersey, island	Inset II	30
Jerudong	B2	13
Jerusalem, capital	B2	26
Jesenice	B2	48
Jessore	C5	21
Jésus, island	J5	103
Jetait	A1	96
Jhang Sadar	D3	21
Jhansi	C3	20
Jhelum	D3	21
Jhelum, river	D3	21
Ji'an	E3	10
Jiamusi	G1	10
Jiangsu	E2	10
Jiangxi	E3	10
Jiddah, island	A1	25
Jihlava	B3	42
Jilib	A3	60
Jilin	F1	10
Jilin	F1	10
Jima	B3	60
Jimaní	A2	89
Jiménez	D2	84
Jinan	E2	10
Jingdezhen	E3	10
Jining	E2	10
Jinja	C3	61
Jinotega	B2	87
Jinotepe	A3	87
Jinsha (Yangtze), river	C2	10
Jinzhou	F1	10
Jipijapa	A3	79
Jir Paraná	B3	81
Jirgatol	B1	23
Jiu, river	B3	43
Jiujiang	E3	10
Jixi	G1	10
Jizan	B2	24
Jizzakh	C2	23
João Pessoa	E2	81
Jobos	C3	90
Jodhpur	B3	20
Joe Batt's Arm	D4	98
Joensuu	C2	53
Joggins	C2	100
Johannesburg	C2	71
John D'or Prairie	C5	94
Johnsons Crossing	C5	105
Johor Baharu	B2	13
Johor, strait	B1	13
Joinville	D4	81
Joinville, island	C12	107

	Key	Page
Joka	Inset II	20
Joliet, Ill.	E1	126
Joliette	C5	103
Jolo	B5	12
Jolo, island	B5	12
Jonava	C2	46
Jones, sound	L1	99
Jonesboro, Ark.	D2	126
Jong, river	A2	63
Jönköping	B3	53
Jonquière	E3	103
Joplin, Mo.	D2	126
Jordan		26
Jordan, river	A2	26
Jos	E3	65
Jos, plateau	E2	65
Jotunheimen, mts.	B3	52
Jou	B4	63
Joussard	C3	94
Juan de Fuca, strait	L7	95
Juana Díaz	B2	90
Juàzeiro	D2	81
Juàzeiro do Norte	E2	81
Juba	C4	59
Juba, river	A3	60
Jubayl	A1	26
Jubayl, al-	C1	24
Jubilee, lake	D5	98
Júcar, river	F3	37
Juchitán de Zaragoza	F4	84
Judique	F2	100
Juigalpa	B2	87
Juiz de Fora	D4	81
Juliaca	C4	77
Julian Alps, mts.	A2	48
Juliana Top, mt.	A3	80
Jullundur	C2	20
Jumayliyah, al-	C2	25
Jumla	B2	19
Junagadh	B4	20
Junchrapara	Inset II	20
Jundiaí	B2	81
Juneau, capital, Alaska	Inset I	126
Jungfrau, mt.	B2	35
Juniper	B2	97
Juniyah	A2	26
Juozapines, mt.	C2	46
Jura, island	B2	30
Jura, mts.	A3	35
Jura, river	A2	46
Jurbarkas	B2	46
Jūrmala	B2	46
Jurong	A1	13
Juruá, river	B2	81
Juruena, river	C3	81
Juticalpa	B2	86
Juventud, island	B2	88
Južna, river	B3	49
Jvari	B3	45
Jwaneng	B3	69
Jyväskylä	C2	53

K

	Key	Page
K2 (Godwin Austen), mt.	A2	10
Ka Dake	B2	71
Ka, river	C2	65
Kabala	B1	63
Kabale	A4	61
Kabalo	C2	67
Kabardino-Balkariya, republic	E4	44
Kabelebo, river	A2	80
Kabompo, river	A2	67
Kabul, capital	B2	22
Kabul, river	B2	22
Kabwe	B2	67
Kachovka	C3	47
Kadavu, island	B3	17
Kadei, river	A3	66
Kadoma	B2	69
Kaduna	D2	65
Kaduna, river	D2	65
Kaduqli	B3	59
Kaédi	B3	58
Kaélé	B1	65
Kaeo	B2	15
Kaesŏng	B4	9
Kafan	D3	45
Kaffrine	B2	62
Kafr ad-Dawwar	B1	56
Kafu, river	B3	61
Kafue	B3	67
Kafue, river	B2	67
Kaga Bandoro	A2	66
Kagawong	C2	102
Kagera, river	B4, C1, C2	61
Kagitumba	C1	61
Kagoshima	A4	8
Kahayan, river	C2	13
Kahemba	B2	67
Kahnawake	H6	103
Kahntah	M2	95
Kahoolawe island, Hawaii	Inset II	126
Kai, islands	E2	13
Kaieteur, falls	B3	80
Kaifeng	E2	10
Kaikoura	B3	15
Kailahun	C3	62
Kailahun	B1	63
Kainji, river	B2	65
Kaiserslautern	A4	40
Kaitaia	B1	15
Kajaani	C2	53
Kakamega	C3	61
Kakata	A2	63
Kakeroma, island	Inset II	8
Kakhovka, reservoir	C3	47
Kakinada	D5	20
Kaladar	H3	102
Kalahari, desert	B3	69
Kalámai	B3	51
Kalamáki	Inset	51
Kálbäcär	B1	45
Kalemie	C2	67

	Key	Page
Kalgoorlie-Boulder, W.A.	B3	14
Kali	C1	62
Kali, river	B2	19
Kalimantan, region	C2	13
Kaliningrad	D3	44
Kalixälven, river	D1	53
Kallithéa	Inset	51
Kalmar	B3	53
Katagum, river	E3	65
Kalmykiya, republic	E4	44
Kalpeni, island	B7	20
Kalu, river	B5	19
Kalundborg	C3	32
Kalutara	A5	19
Kalwa	Inset I	20
Kamakwie	A1	63
Kaman	Inset I	20
Kamaran, island	A1	25
Kamarhati	Inset II	20
Kambia	A1	63
Kamchatka, peninsula	D10	44
Kamchiya, river	F2	50
Kamensk-Uralsky	D5	44
Kamet, mt.	C2	20
Kamina	C3	67
Kaminak, lake	J4	99
Kamloops	M6	95
Kampala, capital	C3	61
Kampong Cham	D4	11
Kampong Chhnang	C3	11
Kampong Saom	B5	11
Kampong Thum	C3	11
Kampot	C5	11
Kamsack	J9	104
Kamsar	A2	62
Kamui, cape	Inset I	8
Kananga	B2	67
Kanazawa	C2	8
Kanchenjunga, mt.	D2	19
Kanchipuram	C6	20
Kanchrapara	Inset II	20
Kandi	B2	64
Kandy	B4	19
Kane, basin	P1	99
Kangaroo, island	C3	14
Kangen, river	C3	59
Kanggye	B2	9
Kanghwa, bay	A4	9
Kangiqsualujjuaq	C2	101
Kangiqsujuaq	B1	101
Kangirsuk	B1	101
Kangnŭng	C4	9
Kangshan	B2	9
Kankan	D2	62
Kano	E1	65
Kanpur	D3	20
Kansaripara	Inset II	20
Kansas	C2	126
Kansas City, Kans.	D2	126
Kansas City, Mo.	D2	126
Kansay	A1	23
Kansk	D6	44
Kanté	B2	64
Kanuku, mts.	B4	80
Kanye	B3	69
Kaoko Veld, mts.	A1	70
Kaolack	A2	62
Kaoma	C2	67
Kaop'ing, river	B2	9
Kapfenberg	D3	39
Kapingamarangi, atoll	C2	15
Kapiskau, river	D2	101
Kaposvár	A2	43
Kapuskasing	D3	101
Kara	B2	64
Kara, sea	B5	44
Kara-Kum, canal	C2	22
Kara-Kum, desert	C2	22
Kara-Say	F2	23
Karabakh, canal	B2	45
Karachayevo-Cherkesiya, republic	E4	44
Karachi	C5	21
Karaj	C2	22
Karak, al-	A2	26
Karakol	C1	20
Karakoram, range	C1	20
Karaman	C3	27
Karasburg	C4	70
Karawanken, range	D4	39
Karbala	B2	24
Karcag	C2	43
Kardiva, channel	A2	19
Kärdla	B1	46
Kareliya, republic	C3	44
Kariba	B1	69
Kariba, lake	A1	69
Karibib	B2	70
Karisimbi, mt.	B1	61
Karkar, island	B2	15
Karkinit, bay	C3	47
Karlovac	A2	48
Karlovy Vary	A2	42
Karlskrona	C3	53
Karlsruhe	B4	40
Karlstad	B3	53
Karnali, river	B2	19
Karnaphuli, reservoir	F6	21
Karnaphuli, river	E6	21
Karonga	B1	68
Karpas, peninsula	C1	27
Kárpathos, island	C4	51
Kars	E2	27
Kartala, mt.	A1	67
Kartung	A2	62
Karun, river	B3	22
Karuzi	B2	61
Karviná	D3	42
Kasai, river	B2	67
Kasama	C1	67
Kasane	B4	69
Kasba, lake	H4	99
Kashi	A2	10
Kashiwa	C3	8
Kasinathpur	Inset II	20
Kaslo	O6	95
Kassala	D2	59
Kassel	B3	40

	Key	Page
Kasserine	B2	57
Kastamonu	C2	27
Kastoría	B1	51
Kastrup	D3	32
Kasugai	C3	8
Kasungu	B1	68
Kasur	E3	21
Katagum, river	E3	65
Katanga, plateau	B3	67
Katerini	B1	51
Kate's Needle, mt.	F2	95
Katherine, N.T.	C1	14
Kathgodam	C3	20
Kathiawar, peninsula	B4	20
Kathmandu, capital	C2	19
Katowice	D3	41
Katrine, lake	B2	30
Katsina	D1	65
Kattegat, strait	C2	32
Kau-Ur	B2	62
Kauai island, Hawaii	Inset II	126
Kaufbeuren	B5	40
Kaukau Veld, region	C2	70
Kaunas	B2	46
Kaura-Namoda	D1	65
Kavadarci	C2	48
Kavajë	A2	49
Kaválá	C1	51
Kavaratti, island	B6	20
Kavieng	B2	15
Kavir-e Namak, desert	D3	22
Kaw	B1	80
Kawagoe	C3	8
Kawaguchi	C3	8
Kawasaki	C3	8
Kawhia	B2	15
Kawthaung	C4	12
Kayangel, islands	C1	17
Kayes	A3	58
Kayser, mts.	A3	80
Kayseri	C2	27
Kazakh Upland, region	C2	23
Kazakhstan		**23**
Kazan	D4	44
Kazanlŭk	D2	50
Kazincbarcika	C1	43
Kearney	F2	102
Kearney, Nebr.	D1	126
Keban, reservoir	D2	27
Kebili	B3	57
Kebir, river	B1	26
Kebnekaise, mt.	C1	53
Kechika, river	J2	95
Kecskemét	B2	43
Kédainiai	B2	46
Kedgwick	B1	97
Kediri	C2	13
Kédougou	C3	62
Keele	C4	99
Keeley, lake	B6	104
Keetmanshoop	C4	70
Keewatin, region	J4	99
Kef, el-	B1	57
Kefallinía, island	A2	51
Keflavík	A3	52
Keg River	B2	94
Keila	C1	46
Kékes, mt.	C2	43
Kelang	A2	13
Kelani, river	B4	19
Kelliher	G9	104
Kelowna	N6	95
Kelsey	C1	96
Keluang	B2	13
Kelvington	G8	104
Kemano	J4	95
Kemerovo	D6	44
Kemi	B1	53
Kemijärvi	C1	53
Kemijoki, river	C1	53
Kemnay	A4	96
Kempenland, region	D1	33
Kemps Bay	B3	89
Kempt, lake	B4	103
Kempten	B5	40
Kemptville	K2	102
Kenaston	D9	104
Kendal	C2	30
Kendari	D2	13
Kenema	B2	63
Keng Tung	C2	12
Kenilworth	C3	30
Kenitra	C1	57
Kennetcook	D2	100
Keno	B4	105
Kenora	B3	101
Kensington	B2	100
Kenton	A4	96
Kentucky	E2	126
Kentville	A3	96
Kenya		**61**
Kenya, mt.		61
Keokradong, mt.	F7	21
Kerangan Nyatan	B3	13
Keratsínion	Inset	51
Kerch	D3	47
Kerch, strait	D3	47
Kerema	A2	15
Keremeos	N6	95
Keren	B2	60
Kerewan	B2	62
Kerguelen, islands		5
Kericho	C4	61
Kerinci, mt.	B2	13
Kerkennah, islands	C2	57
Kerki	C2	22
Kérkira	A2	51
Kérkira, island	A2	51
Kerman	D3	22
Kerman, region	D3	22
Kérouané	D3	62
Kerrobert	A9	104
Kerulen, river	D2	11
Keszthely	A2	43
Keta	C4	64
Ketchikan, Alaska	Inset I	126
Key Lake Mine	E3	104
Key West, Fla.	E3	126

	Key	Page
Keyano	B3	101
Khabarovsk	E8	44
Khabur, river	B1	27
Khakasiya, republic	D6	44
Khalándrion	Inset	51
Khalkidhikí, peninsula	B2	51
Khalkís	B2	51
Khaluf	C2	25
Khambhāt, gulf	B4	20
Khamis Mushayt	B2	24
Khan-Tengri, mt.	E2	23
Khanaqin	C2	24
Khania	B4	51
Khanka, lake	G1	10
Khanty-Mansiya, autonomous okrug	C5	44
Khanty-Mansiysk	C5	44
Kharagpur	E4	20
Kharg, island	C4	22
Kharijah, al-	B2	56
Kharijah, oasis	B2	56
Kharj, al-	B2	24
Kharkiv	D1	47
Khartoum North	C2	59
Khartoum, capital	C2	59
Khashm al-Qirbah	C2	59
Khashuri	B4	45
Khasi, hills	F3	20
Khaskovo	D4	50
Khatanga	B7	44
Khawr, al-	B1	25
Kherson	C3	47
Khíos, island	C2	51
Khiran, al-	C3	24
Khmelnytskyy	B2	47
Khojak, pass	C3	21
Khon Kaen	C2	12
Khor Angar	C1	60
Khorasan, region	D2	22
Khorat, plateau	C2	12
Khorixas	B2	70
Khorramabad	B3	22
Khorramshahr	B3	22
Khorugh	B2	23
Khouribga	C1	57
Khowst	B2	22
Khudzhand	A1	23
Khujayli	A2	23
Khulna	C6	21
Khums, al-	B1	56
Khuriya Muriya, islands	C3	25
Khust	A2	47
Khuzdar	C4	21
Khuzestan, region	B3	22
Khvoy	A2	22
Khyber, pass	D2	21
Kibungo	C2	61
Kibuye	A2	61
Kičevo	A2	48
Kidal	C1	58
Kidderminster	C3	30
Kiel	B1	40
Kiel, bay	B1	40
Kielce	E3	41
Kiev, capital	C1	47
Kiev, reservoir	C1	47
Kiffa	C3	58
Kifisiá	Inset	51
Kifissós, river	B2	51
Kigali, capital	B1	61
Kigoma	A1	68
Kii, channel	B3	8
Kii, peninsula	B3	8
Kikinda	B2	49
Kikkertavak, island	C3	98
Kikwit	B2	67
Kilchu	C2	9
Kildare	C2	31
Kilimanjaro, mt.	C1	68
Kilinochchi	B2	19
Kilkee	B2	31
Kilkenny	C2	31
Killala, bay	B1	31
Killaloe	H2	102
Killarney	B4	96
Killarney	D1	102
Killarney Lake	E5	94
Killdeer	D11	104
Killeen, Tex.	D2	126
Kilmarnock	B2	30
Kilombero, river	C2	68
Kilwa Kivinje	C2	68
Kimbe	B2	15
Kimberley	B2	71
Kimberley	O6	95
Kimberley	E3	102
Kimberley, plateau	B1	14
Kimch'aek	C2	9
Kimch'ŏn	C4	9
Kinabalu, mt.	D1	13
Kinabatangan, river	D1	13
Kinbasket, lake	B5	94
Kinbasket, lake	B5	94
Kincaid	C11	104
Kincardine	D3	102
Kindersley	A9	104
Kindia	A2	62
Kindu	C2	67
King Leopold, range	B1	14
King William, island	J3	99
King's Cove	E5	98
King's Landing	B3	97
King's Lynn	D3	30
King's Point	B4	98
Kingcome Inlet	J6	95
Kingman, Ariz.	A2	126
Kingston	B2	100
Kingston upon Hull	C3	30
Kingston upon Thames	Inset III	30
Kingston, capital	C3	88
Kingstown, capital	B2	91
Kingsville	F2	100
Kingussie	B2	30
Kinistino	E8	104
Kinkala	B2	66
Kinkora	B2	100
Kinloss	D3	102

	Key	Page
Kinmount	G3	102
Kinnairds, cape	C1	30
Kinosota	B4	96
Kinsarvik	B3	52
Kinsella	E5	94
Kinshasa, capital	A2	67
Kinyeti, mt.	C4	59
Kioa, island	C2	17
Kiosk	G1	102
Kipengere, range	B2	68
Kipling	H10	104
Kirakira	B2	16
Kirensk	D7	44
Kiribati		**17**
Kırıkkale	C2	27
Kiritimati (Christmas), island	D1	17
Kirkcaldy	B2	30
Kirkenes	F2	52
Kirkfield	G3	102
Kirkland Lake	D3	101
Kirkpatrick, mt.	A5	107
Kirkuk	B1	24
Kirkwall	Inset	30
Kirov	D4	44
Kirovakan	B2	45
Kirovograd	C2	47
Kirşehir	C2	27
Kirthar, range	C4	21
Kiruna	D1	53
Kisangani	C1	67
Kishi	B3	65
Kiskitto, lake	B2	96
Kiskőrei-víztároló, lake	C2	43
Kiskunhalas	B2	43
Kismayo	A4	60
Kissidougou	C3	62
Kississing, lake	A1	96
Kisumu	C4	61
Kita	B3	58
Kita, island	Inset III	8
Kitakami, river	D2	8
Kitakyushu	A3	8
Kitale	C3	61
Kitami	Inset I	8
Kitami, mts.	Inset I	8
Kitchener	E4	102
Kitgum	C2	61
Kíthira, island	B3	51
Kitikmeot, region	G3	99
Kitimat	H4	95
Kitwanga	H3	95
Kitwe	B2	67
Kivi, lake	C2	53
Kivu, lake	B1	61
Kızıl Irmak, river	C2	27
Kjølen, mts.	C1	53
Kladno	A2	42
Klagenfurt	D4	39
Klaipėda	A2	46
Klamath Falls, Oreg.	A1	126
Klarälven, river	B2	53
Klatovy	A3	42
Kleinburg	J5	102
Klemtu	H5	95
Kleve	A3	40
Kloulklubed	B3	17
Kluane, lake	B5	105
Knee, lake	D1	96
Knight, inlet	K6	95
Knockboy, mt.	B3	31
Knokke	B1	33
Knoxville, Tenn.	E2	126
Ko Chang, island	C3	12
Ko Kut, island	C4	12
Ko Phangan, island	B4	12
Ko Samui, island	B4	12
Ko Tarutao, island	B5	12
Kobe	B3	8
Koblenz	A3	40
Kobuleti	A4	45
Kočani	C2	48
Kočevje	B3	48
Kochi	B3	8
Kodiak, Alaska	Inset I	126
Kofarnihon, river	A2	23
Köflach	D3	39
Koforidua	B3	64
Kofu	C3	8
Køge	D3	32
Kohima	F3	20
Kohtla-Järve	D1	46
Koindu	B1	63
Koje-do, island	C5	9
Kokkina	A1	27
Kokkola	B2	53
Kokshetau	C1	23
Kola	A4	96
Kola, peninsula	C3	44
Kolari	B1	53
Kolda	B3	62
Kolding	B3	32
Kolhapur	B5	20
Kolín	B2	42
Kolkata (Calcutta)	E4, Inset II	20
Kołobrzeg	B1	41
Kolpashevo	D6	44
Kolshet	Inset I	20
Kolumadulu, atoll	A3	19
Kolwezi	C3	67
Kolyma, range	C10	44
Kolyma, river	C9	44
Komadugu Gana, river	F2	65
Komadugu Yobe, river	F1	65
Komárno	B3	42
Komárom	B2	43
Komati, river	B2	71
Komatsu	C2	8
Komi, republic		44
Komi-Permyat, autonomous okrug	D4	44
Komoé, river	E3	63
Komotiní	C1	51
Komsomolsk-na-Amure	D8	44
Konar, river	D2	21
Konduz	B1	22
Konduz, river	B1	22
Koné	C2	18
Kong, river	D4	11

	Key	Page
Konibodom	B1	23
Konin	D2	41
Konnagar	Inset II	20
Konotop	C1	47
Kontagora	C2	65
Kontum	B3	11
Konya	C3	27
Kootenay, lake	O6	95
Kootenay, river	P6	95
Kopaonik, mts.	B3	49
Kópavogur	A2	52
Koper	A3	48
Kopet, mts.	B2, D2	22
Korab	B2	49
Korab, mt.	A2	48
Korçë	B3	49
Korčula, island	C4	48
Korea, bay	A3	9
Korea, strait	C5	9
Korhogo	D2	63
Koriyama	D2	8
Korla	B1	10
Koro Toro	B4	59
Koro, island	B2	17
Koro, sea	B2	17
Koror, capital	B3	17
Koror, island	C3	17
Körös, river	C2	43
Korosten	B1	47
Kortrijk	B2	33
Koryak, range	C10	44
Koryakiya, autonomous okrug	C10	44
Kos, island	C3	51
Kosciusko, mt..	D3	14
Koshigaya	C3	8
Koshiki, islands	A4	8
Košice	C2	42
Kosovo, province	B3	49
Kosrae	D2	15
Kosrae, island	D2	15
Kossol, passage	C2	17
Kossol, reef	C2	17
Kossu, lake	D3	63
Koszalin	C1	41
Kota	C3	20
Kota Baharu	B1	13
Kota Kinabalu	D2	13
Kotcho, lake	M1	95
Kotka	C2	53
Kotlas	C4	44
Kotor, gulf	A3	49
Kotovsk	B2	47
Kotto, river	B2	66
Kouchibouguac	D2	97
Koudougou	C2	64
Koula-Moutou	B2	66
Koulikoro	B3	58
Koulountou, river	C3	62
Koumac	C2	18
Koungheul	B2	62
Kourou	B1	80
Kouroussa	D2	62
Kousséri	B1	65
Koutiala	B3	58
Kouto	C2	63
Kouvola	C2	53
Kovel	A1	47
Kowôn	B3	9
Kowloon	Inset	10
Kowt-e Ashrow	B2	22
Kozáni	B1	51
Kozhikode	C6	20
Kozloduy	B2	50
Kozu, island	C3	8
Kožuf, mts.	C2	48
Kpalimé	B3	64
Kpandu	C3	64
Kpémé	B3	64
Kra, isthmus	B4	12
Kracheh	E3	11
Kragujevac	B2	49
Kraków	D3	41
Kraljevo	B3	49
Kramatorsk	D2	47
Kranj	B2	48
Kranji	B1	13
Krasnodar	E3	44
Krasnoyarsk	D6	44
Krefeld	A3	40
Kremenchug	C2	47
Kretinga	A2	46
Kribi	A3	65
Krishna, river	C5	20
Kristiansand	B4	52
Kristianstad	B3	53
Kristiansund	B3	52
Kristinehamn	B3	53
Krk, island	B2	48
Krka, river	B2	48
Krong Kaoh Kong	A4	11
Kroonstad	C2	71
Krosnow	E4	41
Krško	C3	48
Krugersdorp	C2	71
Krujë	A2	49
Kruševac	B3	49
Kruševo	B2	48
Krychaw	E3	47
Kryvyi Rih	D2	47
Kuala Abang	B2	13
Kuala Belait	A2	13
Kuala Lumpur, capital	A2	13
Kuala Terengganu	B2	13
Kuantan	C2	13
Kuching	C2	13
Kuchino, island	A4	8
Kudymkar	D4	44
Kufstein	E3	99
Kugluktuk	F3	39
Kúito	C4	70
Kukës	B1	49
Kul, island	A4	22
Kula Kangri, mt.	B1	19
Kuldiga	A2	46
Kulmbach	B3	40
Kulob	A2	23
Kulpawn, river	B1	64
Kum, river	B4	9
Kumamoto	A3	8
Kumasi	B3	64
Kume, island	Inset II	8
Kumo	F2	65
Kunda	D1	46
Kunene, river	A1	70
Kunlun, mts.	B2	10
Kunming	D3	10
Kunsan	B5	9
Kuntaur	D2	62
Kuopio	C2	53
Kupa, river	B3	48
Kupang	D3	13
Kür, river	A2, C2	45
Kür-Aras, lowland	B2	45
Kurashiki	B3	8
Kuraymah	C1	59
Kürdzhali	D4	50
Kure	B3	8
Kuressaare	B2	46
Kurgan	D5	44
Kuril, islands	E9	44
Kurinwás, river	B2	87
Kurla	Inset I	20
Kurnool	C5	20
Kuršėnai	B1	46
Kursk	D3	44
Kuru, river	C2	19
Kuruman	B2	71
Kurume	A3	8
Kurunegala	B4	19
Kushiro	Inset I	8
Kushtia	C5	21
Kusông	A3	9
Kusti	C2	59
Kut, al-	C2	24
Kütahya	B2	27
Kutaisi	B3	45
Kutch, gulf	A4	20
Kutno	D2	41
Kuujjuaq	C2	101
Kuujjuarapik	A2	101
Kuwait		24
Kuwait, bay	B2	24
Kuwait, capital	B2	24
Kwa, river	B2	67
Kwahu, plateau	B3	64
Kwajalein, island	B2	16
Kwangju	B5	9
Kwango, river	B2	67
Kwekwe	B2	69
Kyaukpyu	B2	12
Kyle	B10	104
Kyle of Lochalsh	B1	30
Kyôngju	C5	9
Kyoto	B3	8
Kyrenia	B1	27
Kyrgyzstan		23
Kyrenia, range	B1	27
Kyushu, island	A3	8
Kyustendil	A3	50
Kyzyl	D6	44
Kyzyl-Kyya	C2	23
Kyzyl-Suu, river	C3	23
Kyzylkum, desert	B2	22

L

	Key	Page
La Asunción	D1	79
La Baie	F3	103
La Broquerie	C4	96
La Ceiba	B1	86
La Chaux-de-Fonds	A1	35
La Coma, river	B1	36
La Conception	B5	103
La Condamine	B1	35
La Coruña	B1	37
La Crete	B2	94
La Croix Maingot	A2	91
La Crosse, Wis.	D1	126
La Cruz	A1	86
La Digue, island	C1	70
La Doré	D3	103
La Esperanza	A2	86
La Goulette	C1	57
La Grande, river	B3	101
La Guadeloupe	F6	103
La Guaira Maiquetía	C1	79
La Have	C3	100
La Laguna	Inset I	37
La Libertad	A4	79
La Libertad	C3	85
La Loche	A4	104
La Louvière	C2	33
La Malbaie	F4	103
La Martre	K2	103
La Martre, lake	E4	99
La Montaña, region	C2	77
La Oroya	B3	77
La Palma	C2	87
La Palma, island	Inset I	37
La Paz	B2	86
La Paz, capital	A3	77
La Paz, state capital	B3	84
La Pérouse	B1	96
La Pérouse, strait	Inset I	8
La Plaine	B3	90
La Plata	D4	74
La Plata, river	C2	90
La Plonge, lake	C5	104
La Pocatière	F4	103
La Prairie	J6	103
La Rioja	B2	74
La Rioja	E1	37
La Rochelle	B3	34
La Romana	D2	89
La Ronge	C4	104
La Ronge, lake	E6	104
La Rosita	B2	87
La Serena	B3	76
La Spezia	B1	38
La Tortuga, island	C1	79
La Tuque	D4	103
La Unión	B7	76
La Unión	C2	86
La Vega	B1	89
La Virtud	A2	86
La-Roche-sur-Yon	B3	34
Labasa	B2	17
Labé	B2	62
Labe (Elbe), river	B2	41
Labelle	C3	100
Labi	A3	13
Laborec, river	C2	42
Laborie	B3	91
Labrador City	D3	98
Labrieville	G2	103
Labu	C2	13
Labuan, island	D2	13
Laç	A2	49
Lac du Bonnet	C4	96
Lac La Biche	E4	94
Lac La Hache	M5	95
Lac Mégantic	F6	103
Lac-aux-Sables	D5	103
Lac-Bouchette	D3	103
Lac-des-Aigles	H4	103
Lac-des-Îles	A5	103
Lac-Édouard	D4	103
Lac-Etchemin	F5	103
Lac-Nominingue	A5	103
Lac-Saguay	A5	103
Laccadive, islands	B6	20
Lachenaie	J5	103
Lachine	H6	103
Lachute	B6	103
Lacombe	D5	94
Ladhiqiyah, al- (Latakia)	A2	27
Ladoga, lake	C3	44
Ladysmith	C2	71
Ladywood	C4	96
Lae	A2	15
Lae, island	B2	16
Laem, mt.	B3	12
Læsø, island	C1	32
Lafayette, La.	D2	126
Lafia	E3	65
Lafleche	D11	104
Lafond	E4	94
Laghouat	B1	57
Lagodekhi	D4	45
Lagos	B4	65
Lagos	A4	36
Laguna de Bay, lake	B3	12
Lahave, river	C3	100
Lahij	A2	25
Lahn, river	B3	40
Lahore	E3	21
Lahti	C2	53
Laï	B5	59
Lairg	B1	30
Lajas	A2	90
Lajes	C4	81
Lakatoro	B3	18
Lake Alma	F11	104
Lake Charlotte	E3	100
Lake Edward	B2	97
Lake Harbour	O4	99
Lake Lenore	F8	104
Lake St. Peter	G2	102
Lakeba, island	C3	17
Lakeba, passage	C3	17
Lakefield	G3	102
Lakelse Lake	H4	95
Lakhpat	A4	20
Laki, volcano	B2	52
Lakselv	F1	52
Lalitpur	C2	19
Lamaline	D5	98
Lamap	B3	18
Lambaréné	A2	66
Lambton	E6	103
Lamèque	E1	97
Lamèque, island	E1	97
Lami	B3	17
Lamía	B2	51
Lammermuir, hills.	C2	30
Lamon, bay	B3	12
Lampa	Inset	76
Lampang	B2	12
Lampeter	B3	30
Lampman	H11	104
Lamu	F5	61
Lan, island	B2	9
Lanai island, Hawaii	Inset II	126
Lanark	J2	102
Lancaster	C2	30
Lancaster	L2	102
L'Ancienne-Lorette	K5	103
Land's End, promontory	B4	30
Lander, Wyo.	C1	126
Landes, region	B5	34
Landis	B8	104
Landshut	C4	40
Lang Son	B2	11
Langeburg, mts.	B3	71
Langeland, island	C4	32
Langenburg	J10	104
Langham	D8	104
Langkawi, island	A1	13
Langley	L6	95
Langruth	B4	96
Langstaff	K5	102
Langton	E5	102
Languedoc-Roussillon	C5	34
Lanigan	E9	104
Länkäran	C3	45
L'Annonciation	B5	103
Lansdowne	J3	102
Lansdowne House	A2	101
L'Anse-à-Valleau	M2	103
L'Anse-au-Loup	C4	98
L'Anse-aux-Gascons	M3	103
L'Anse-St-Jean	F3	103
Lansing, capital, Mich.	E1	126
Lantau, island	Inset	10
Lanús	D3	74
Lanzarote, island	Inset I	37
Lanzhou	D2	10
Lao Cai	A1	11
Laoag	B2	12
Laoang	C3	12
Laon	C2	34
Laos		11
Lapithos	B1	27
Lapland, region	B1	53
Lappeenranta	C2	53
Laptev, sea	B8	44
L'Aquila	C2	38
Larache	C1	57
Laramie, Wyo.	C1	126
Lares	B2	90
Larestan, region	C4	22
Large, island	C1	91
Lárisa	B2	51
Lark Harbour	B4	98
Larkana	C4	21
Larkhall	C4	96
Larnaca	B2	27
Larne	B2	30
Larochette	B2	33
Larrys River	F2	100
Larsen Ice Shelf, glacier	C12	107
Las Cruces, N. Mex.	C2	126
Las Minas, mt.	A2	86
Las Palmas	Inset I	37
Las Piedras	D2	90
Las Piedras	B3	75
Las Tablas	B3	87
Las Tunas	E3	88
Las Vegas, N. Mex.	C2	126
Las Vegas, Nev.	B2	126
L'Ascension	B5	103
Lashburn	A7	104
Lashio	C2	12
Lashkar Gah	A2	22
Last Mountain, lake	E9	104
Latacunga	B3	79
Late, island	C2	17
Latina	C2	38
Latium	C2	38
Lau, island group	C2	17
Laucala, island	C2	17
Laudat	B3	90
Lauder	A4	96
Launceston	B4	30
Launceston, Tas.	D4	14
Laurie River	A1	96
Laurier	B4	96
Lausanne	A2	35
Lautoka	A2	17
Laval	B2	34
Laval	C6, J5	103
Lavenham	B4	96
Lavoy	E4	94
Lavumisa	B3	71
Lawa, river	A2, B2	80
Lawn	D5	98
Lawrence Station	B3	97
Lawton, Okla.	D2	126
Layland	B4	96
Layou, river	B3	90
Lázaro Cárdenas	D4	84
Le Bic	H3	103
Le Creusot	D3	34
Le Havre	C2	34
Le Mans	C2	34
Le Puy	C4	34
Leader	A10	104
Leading Tickles	D4	98
Leaf Rapids	D1	96
Leamington	C5	102
l'Eau Claire, lake	B2	101
Lebanon		26
Lebanon, mts.	B1	26
Lebombo, mts.	C2, D1	71
Lebu	B6	76
Lecce	D2	38
Lech	B3	39
Lech, river	B4	40
Leduc	D4	94
Lee, river	B3	31
Leeds	C3	30
Leeuwarden	C1	32
Leeuwin, cape	A3	14
Leeward Group	B3	58
Lefka	A1	27
Lefkoniko	B1	27
Legacy	C3	86
Leganés	Inset II	37
Legazpi	B3	12
Legnica	C3	41
Leicester	C3	30
Leichhardt, river	D1	14
Leiden	B2	32
Leie, river	B3	33
Leikanger	B3	52
Leipzig	C3	40
Leiria	A3	36
Leitrim	H6	102
Leixões	A2	36
Lékéti, mts.	C5	66
Lélouma	B2	62
Lelystad	C2	32
Lempa, river	A1, B2	86
Lena, river	C8	44
Leneinsk	C2	23
Lenghu	C2	10
Lengoué, river	C3	66
Lenore	A4	96
Lens	C1	34
Lensk	C7	44
Léo	C3	64
Leoben	D3	39
Léogâne	C2	89
León	D3	84
León	A2	87
León	D1	37
Leone	B2	18
Leova	B2	50
Leoville	C7	104
Lepontine Alps, mts.	C2	35
Lepreau	C3	97
Lepsi	D2	23
Leribe	B1	71
Lérida	G2	37
Lerwick	Inset I	30
Les Cayes	B2	89
Les Éboulements	F4	103
Les Escaldes	B2	36
Les Escoumins	G3	103
Les Islets-Caribou	J2	103
Les Méchins	K3	103
Les Tantes, island	B1	91
Les Ulis	Inset II	34
Leskovac	B3	49
Lesosibirsk	D6	44
Lesotho		71
Lesser Caucasus, mts.	A2, B4	45
Lesser Hinggan, range	F1	10
Lesser Slave, lake	C3	94
Lesser Sunda, islands	C2	13
Lestrock	G9	104
Lésvos, island	C3	51
Leszno	C3	41
Lethbridge	D6	94
Lethbridge	E5	98
Lethem	B4	80
Leticia	C6	78
Letlhakeng	B3	69
Letterkenny	C1	31
Leuven	C2	33
Levack	D1	102
Levallois-Perret	Inset II	34
Leveque, cape	B1	14
Leverkusen	A3	40
Levice	B2	42
Levin	C4	15
Lévis	E5, L6	103
Levittown	B2	90
Lewes	D4	30
Lewis, island	A1	30
Lewisporte	D4	98
Lewiston, Idaho	B1	126
Lewiston, Maine	F1	126
Lexington, Ky.	E2	126
Leyte, island	C4	12
Lhasa	C3	10
Lhobrak, river	C2	19
Lhuntshi	C2	19
Lianyungang	E2	10
Liao, river	F1	10
Liaoning	F1	10
Liaoyang	F1	10
Liaoyuan	F1	10
Liard River	J1	95
Liard, river	K1	95
Libau	C4	96
Liberec	B2	42
Liberia		63
Liberia	A2	86
Libono	B1	71
Libreville, capital	A1	66
Libya		56
Libyan, desert	A2, D2	56
Lichfield	C3	30
Lichinga	B2	68
Lida	B3	47
Liechtenstein		35
Liège	D2	33
Lieksa	D2	53
Lienz	C4	39
Liepāja	A2	46
Lièvre, river	A5	103
Lifford	C1	31
Lifou, island	D2	18
Lifuka, island	C2	17
Liguria	B1	38
Ligurian, sea	B2	38
Lihir, group	B2	15
Likasi	C3	67
Likiep, island	B1	16
Lille	C1	34
Lille, strait	B3	32
Lillehammer	C3	52
Lillooet	M6	95
Lillooet, river	L6	95
Lilongwe, capital	B2	68
Lima, capital	B3	77
Lima, river	A2	36
Limassol	B2	27
Limbaži	B2	46
Limbe	A3	65
Limbourg	D2	33
Limerick	B2	31
Limfjorden, channel	B2	32
Límnos, island	C2	51
Limoges	C4	34
Limón	C3	86
Limón	D4	86
Limours	Inset II	34
Limousin	C4	34
Limpopo, river	C1	71
Linares	B5	76
Linares	E3	84
Linares	E3	37
Lincoln	C3	30
Lincoln, capital, Nebr.	D1	126
Lindau	B5	40
Lindbergh	E4	94
Linden	B3	80
Linden	D2	100
Lindi	C2	68
Lindsay	G3	102
Line, islands	D1	17
Lingayen, gulf	B2	12
Lingga, island	B2	13
Lingshi	A2	19
Linguère	B2	62
Linköping	C3	53
Linhe	D1	10
Linnhe, lake	B2	30
Linvanti, river	A1	69
Linwood	F2	100
Linz	D2	39
Lion, gulf	C4	34
Lionel Town	B3	88
Lions Head	D3	102
Lipa	B3	12
Lipari, islands	D3	38
Lipetsk	D3	44
Lippstadt	B3	40
Lipton	G10	104
Liptovský Mikuláš	B2	42
Lira	C2	61
Lisala	B1	67
L'Isalo, mts.	B3	69
Lisbon, capital	A3	36
Lisichansk	D2	47
L'Isle-Adam	Inset II	34
L'Isle-Verte	G3	103
Lismore, N.S.W.	E2	14
Listowel	E4	102
Litani	A2	26
Litani, river	A2, B3	103
Lithuania		46
Little Alföld, plain	A2	43
Little Andaman, island	F6	20
Little Bay	B5	98
Little Bras d'Or	G1	100
Little Current	D2	102
Little Fort	M5	95
Little Grand Rapids	D3	96
Little Inagua, island	C4	89
Little Rock, capital, Ark.	D2	126
Little Salmon, lake	C4	105
Little Scarcies, river	A1	63
Little Seldom	D4	98
Little Smoky, river	A4	94
Little St. Bernard, pass	D4	34
Little Zab, river	B1	24
Liuzhou	D3	10
Liverpool	C3	30
Liverpool	C3	100
Liverpool, bay	B3	30
Livingstone	B3	67
Livno	B2	48
Livorno	B2	38
Ljubljana, capital	B2	48
Ljusnanälven, river	B2	53
Llallagua	A3	77
Llandrindod Wells	B3	30
Llanos, plain	C2	79
Llanos, prairie	C3	78
Llanquihue, lake	B7	76
Lleyn, peninsula	B3	30
Llorts	B1	36
Lloyd, lake	B3	104
Lloydminster	E4	94
Lloydminster	A7	104
Lloyds, river	C5	98
Llullaillaco, volcano	B1	74
Lo Wu	Inset	10
Lo, river	A1	11
Loa, river	B2	76
Lobamba, capital	B2	71
Lobatse	B3	69
Lobaye, river	B4	66
Lobito	B4	70
Locarno	C2	35
Lockeport	B4	100
Lockport	C4	96
Lod (Lydda)	B2	26
Lodja	C2	67
Lodwar	C2	61
Łódź	D3	41
Loei	B2	12
Loess, plateau	C2	10
Lofoten, islands	C2	52
Logan, mt.	Inset III	14
Logan, Utah	B1	126
Logone, river	A5	59
Logroño	E1	37
Loi-kaw	C2	12
Loire, river	C3	34
Loíza	D2	90
Loja	B4	79
Loja	D4	37
Lokka, reservoir	C1	53
Lokoja	D4	65
Lokossa	A4	64
Lol, river	B3	59
Lolland, island	C4	32
Lom	B2	50
Lomami, river	C2	67
Lomas de Zamora	D4	74
Lomawai	A3	17
Lombardy	B1	38
Lombardy	J3	102
Lombok, island	C2	13
Lomé, capital	B3	64
Lomond, lake	B2	30
Łomża	F2	41
London	C3	102
London, capital	C3	30
London, capital	C3, Inset III	30
Londonderry	A2	30
Londrina	C4	81
Lone Butte	M5	95
Long Beach, Calif.	B2	126
Long Island, N.Y.	F1	126
Long Lake	C3	94
Long Range, mts.	B5, C4	98
Long Xuyen	A4	11
Long, island	C3	89
Longford	C3	31
Longlac	C3	101
Longreach, Qld.	D2	14
Longueuil	J5	103
Longview, Tex.	D2	126
Loon Lake	C3	94
Loon Lake	A6	104
Loop Head, cape	B2	31
Lop Buri	B3	12
Lop, lake	C1	10
Lorca	F4	37
Loreburn	D9	104
Lorengau	A2	15
Loreto	B2	84
Loretto	C4	96
Loretteville	K5	103
Lorient	B3	34
L'Original	L2	102
Lorne, estuary	A2	30
Lorraine	H5	103
Los Andes	B4	76
Los Angeles	B6	76
Los Ángeles, Calif.	B2	126
Los Chiles	B1	86
Los Mochis	C2	84
Los Reyes	Inset	84
Los Teques	C1	79
Lot, river	C4	34

	Key	Page
Louang Namtha	A1	11
Loubomo	B6	66
Louga	A2	62
Lough Erne, *lake*	A2	30
Loughborough, *lake*	J3	102
Lougheed, *island*	G1	99
Louisbourg	H2	100
Louisdale	F2	100
Louiseville	D5	103
Louisiade, *archipelago*	B3	15
Louisville	E2	126
Louisville, Ky.	E2	126
Lourdes	B5	34
Louri	C2	19
Louvres	Inset II	34
Lovech	C2	50
Lovell Village	B3	91
Lovettville	B4	94
Lowe Farm	C4	96
Lower Arrow, *lake*	N6	95
Lower Debert	D2	100
Lower Five Islands	C2	100
Lower Hutt	B3	15
Lower Montague	C2	100
Lower Post	H1	95
Lower Saxony	B2	40
Lower Tunguska, *river*	C6	44
Lower Woods Harbour	B4	100
Lowestoft	D3	30
Loyada	C2	60
Loyalty, *islands*	C2	18
Loyoro	D2	61
Lualaba, *river*	C2	67
Luanda, *capital*	B2	70
Luang, *mt.*	B2	11
Luang Prabang	B2	11
Luang Prabang, *range*	A3	11
Luang, *mt.*	B4	12
Luangwa	C3	67
Luangwa, *river*	C2	67
Luanshya	B2	67
Luapula, *river*	B2, C3	67
Luau	E3	70
Luba	A1	66
Lubango	B5	70
Lubbock, Tex.	C2	126
Lübeck	B2	40
Lubicon, *lake*	C3	94
Lublin	F3	41
Lubumbashi	C3	67
Lucapa	D2	70
Lucca	A2	88
Lucea	A2	88
Lucena	B3	12
Lucena	D4	37
Lučenec	E2	42
Lucern, *lake*	C2	35
Lucerne	C1	35
Lucie, *river*	A3	80
Luckenwalde	C2	40
Lucknow	D3	20
Lucknow	D4	102
Lucky Lake	C9	104
Luda Kamchiya, *river*	E3	50
Lüderitz	B4	70
Ludhiana	C2	20
Ludogorie, *region*	E2	50
Ludwigsburg	B4	40
Ludwigshafen am Rhein	B4	40
Luena	D3	70
Lugano	C3	35
Lugano, *lake*	C3	35
Luganville	B2	18
Lugenda, *river*	C2	68
Lugo	C1	37
Lugoj	A3	43
Luhansk	D2	47
Lukuga, *river*	C2	67
Lukulu	B1	67
Luleå	D1	53
Luleälven, *river*	D1	53
Lumphat	F2	11
Lumsden	E4	98
Lumsden	F10	104
Lumut	A2	13
Lund	B3	53
Lund	K6	95
Lundar	B4	96
Lundazi	C2	67
Lundi, *river*	B2	69
Lüneburg	B2	40
Lünen	A3	40
Lunenburg	C3	100
Lunga, *river*	B2	67
Lungwebungu, *river*	A2	67
Lunsar	A1	63
Luoyang	E2	10
Lupeni	B3	43
Luperón	B1	89
Luquillo	D2	90
Luremo	C2	70
Lúrio, *river*	C2	68
Lusaka, *capital*	B3	67
Lusambo	B2	67
Luseland	A8	104
Lushnjë	A3	49
Lusutfu, *river*	B2	71
Luton	C3	30
Lutsk	B1	47
Lützow-Holm, *bay*	C16	107
Luuq	C2	60
Luvua, *river*	B1, C2	67
Luwego, *river*	C2	68
Luxembourg		33
Luxembourg, *capital*	B2	33
Luxor	B2	56
Luzarches	Inset II	34
Luzhou	D3	10
Luzon, *island*	B3	12
Luzon, *strait*	B2	12
Lviv	A2	47
Lyddal	B1	96
Lyme, *bay*	C4	30
Lynn Lake	C1	96
Lyon	D4	34
Lytton	M6	95

M

	Key	Page
Ma, *river*	A2	11
Maan	A2	26

	Key	Page
Maas, *river*	C3, D3	32
Maastricht	C4	32
Mabaruma	B1	80
Maberly	J3	102
Mabou	F1	100
Mac Tier	F2	102
MacAlpine, *lake*	H3	99
Macao, S.A.R.	E3	10
Macapá	C1	81
Macas	B4	79
Maccan	C2	100
Macdonnell, *ranges*	C2	14
Macedonia, F.Y.R.		48
Maceió	E2	81
Macenta	D3	62
Macerata	C2	38
Macfarlane, *river*	C2	104
Macgregor	B4	96
Machakos	D4	61
Machala	B4	79
Machida	C3	8
Machupicchu, *ruins*	C3	77
MacKay, *lake*	L3	95
MacKay, Qld.	D2	14
Mackenzie	L3	95
Mackenzie, *bay*	B1	105
Mackenzie, *mts.*	C4	99
Mackenzie, *river*	B3, D4	99
Mackey	H1	102
Macklin	A8	104
Maclean, *strait*	G1	99
Macmillan, *river*	C4	105
Mâcon	D3	34
Macon, Ga.	E2	126
Madaba	A2	26
Madagascar		69
Madan	C4	50
Madang	A2	15
Madawaska	G2	102
Madden	C5	90
Madeira, *island*		55
Madeira, *river*	B2	81
Madhumati, *river*	C5	21
Madhupur Tract, *region*	D4	21
Madinat ath-Thawrah	B2	27
Madison, *capital, Wis.*	E1	126
Madiun	C2	13
Madoc	H3	102
Madre de Dios, *island*	A9	76
Madre de Dios, *river*	A2, C3	77
Madrid, *capital*	E2, Inset II	36
Madriu, *river*	B3	36
Madura, *island*	C2	13
Madurai	C7	20
Maebashi	C2	8
Maestra, *mts.*	D3	88
Maéwo, *island*	C2	18
Mafeking	A3	96
Mafeteng	A2	71
Mafia, *island*	C2	68
Mafikeng	C2	71
Mafra	A3	36
Mafraq, al-	B1	26
Magadalena de Kino	B1	84
Magadan	D9	44
Magburaka	B1	63
Magdagachi	D8	44
Magdalena	B2	77
Magdalena Contreras	Inset	84
Magdalena, *island*	B7	76
Magdalena, *river*	B3	78
Magdeburg	B2	40
Magelang	C2	13
Magellan, *strait*	B9	76
Maggiore, *lake*	B1	38
Magnetawan	F2	102
Magnitogorsk	D4	44
Magog	D6	103
Mahabharat, *range*	B2	19
Mahajamba, *river*	B2	69
Mahajanga	B2	69
Mahalapye	B2	69
Mahallah al-Kubra, al-	B1	56
Mahanadi, *river*	D4	20
Mahaska	C4	94
Mahbas, al-	C1	58
Mahdia	B3	80
Mahdia	C2	57
Mahé, *island*	C1, Inset	69
Mahébourg	C3	69
Mahilyow	D1	47
Mahim, *bay*	Inset I	20
Mai-Ndombe, *lake*	B2	67
Maidstone	D3	30
Maidstone	A7	104
Maiduguri	G2	65
Main Brook	C3	98
Main, *river*	B4	40
Main-à-Dieu	H1	100
Main-Danube, *canal*	B4	40
Maine	G1	126
Mainland, *island*	Inset I	30
Maintirano	A2	69
Mainz	B4	40
Maio, *island*	C3	58
Maipo, *river*	B4, Inset	76
Maipú	Inset	76
Maisí, *cape*	F3	88
Maisons-Laffitte	Inset II	34
Maitland Bridge	B3	100
Maíz, *islands*	C2	87
Maizuru	B3	8
Majardah, *river*	B1	57
Majé	Inset I	81
Majorca, *island*	H3	37
Majuro, *capital*	C2	16
Majuro, *island*	C2	16
Makamba	B3	61
Makassar, *strait*	C2	13
Makeni	B1	63
Makeyevka	D2	47
Makhachkala	E4	44
Makhaleng, *river*	A2	71
Makin, *island*	A1	17
Makkovik	B1	98
Makokou	B1	66
Makona, *river*	A1	63

	Key	Page
Makoua	C4	66
Makran Coast, *range*	B5	21
Makung	A2	9
Makurdi	E4	65
Malabar, *coast*	B6	20
Malabo, *capital*	A1	66
Malacca, *strait*	A1, A2	13
Malad	Inset I	20
Maladzyechna	C2	47
Málaga	D4	37
Malagarasi, *river*	B1	68
Malaita, *island*	B1	16
Malakal	C3	59
Malakula, *island*	B3	18
Malang	C2	13
Malanje	C3	70
Malanville	B2	64
Mälaren, *lake*	C3	53
Malatya	D2	27
Malawi		68
Malay, *peninsula*	A1	13
Malaysia		13
Malbaie, *river*	F4	103
Malbun	B3	33
Malcolm, *atoll*	A1	19
Malden, *island*	D2	17
Maldives		19
Male	E6	94
Male, *atoll*	A2	19
Male, *capital*	A2	19
Maleb	E6	94
Malegaon	B4	20
Mali		58
Mali Rajinac, *mt.*	B3	48
Malindi	F5	61
Mallaig	B1	30
Mallow	B2	31
Malmberget	D1	53
Malmédy	E3	32
Malmö	B3	53
Maloelap, *island*	C2	16
Malombe, *lake*	C2	68
Maloti, *mts.*	B2	71
Malta		36
Maltahöhe	B3	70
Malton	J5	102
Mamâri	C2	62
Mamawi, *lake*	E2	94
Mambéré, *river*	A2	66
Mamburao	B3	12
Mamiña	C2	76
Mamoré, *river*	B2	77
Mamou	B2	62
Mamry, *lake*	E1	41
Mamtalah, al-	B2	25
Mamuno	B2	46
Man	C3	63
Mana	B1	80
Mana, *river*	B1	80
Manado	D1	13
Managua, *capital*	A2	87
Managua, *lake*	A2	87
Manakara	B3	69
Manama, *capital*	B1	25
Manatí	C2	90
Manaus	C2	81
Manawan, *lake*	G5	104
Manbij	A1	27
Manchester	C3	30
Manchester, N.H.	F1	126
Manchurian, *plain*	F1	10
Mand, *river*	C4	22
Mandalay	C2	12
Mandalgov	C2	11
Mandara, *mts.*	B1	65
Mandaue	B4	12
Mandeville	B2	88
Mándra	Inset	51
Mandurah, W.A.	A3	14
Manfredonia	C2	38
Manga, *region*	C2	59
Mangalore	B6	20
Mango	B1	64
Mangoky, *river*	A3	69
Manicouagan, *reservoir*	C3	101
Manicougan Deux, *reservoir*	H2	103
Manigotagan	C3	96
Manila, *bay*	B3	12
Manila, *capital*	B3	12
Manisa	A2	27
Manito	A8	104
Manitoba, *lake*	B3, B4, D2	96
Manitou	B4	96
Manitoulin, *island*	C2	102
Manitouwadge	C3	101
Manitowaning	D2	102
Maniwaki	A5	103
Manizales	B3	78
Mankato, Minn.	D1	126
Mankayane	B2	71
Mankota	C11	104
Mankulam	B2	19
Mannar	A3	19
Mannar, *gulf*	C7	20
Mannar, *island*	A2	19
Mannheim	B4	40
Manning	B3	94
Mannville	E4	94
Mano, *river*	A2, B2	63
Manokwari	E2	13
Manono	C2	67
Manono, *island*	B2	18
Manor Park	H5	102
Manori, *point*	Inset I	20
Manouane	B4	103
Manp'o	B2	9
Mansa	B2	67
Mansa Konko	B2	62
Mansel, *island*	M4	99
Manson Creek	K3	95
Mansurah, al-	B1	56
Manta	A3	79
Manta, *bay*	A3	79
Mantaro, *river*	B3	77
Mantiqueira, *range*	D4	81
Mantova	B1	38
Mantua (Mantova)	B1	38
Manukau	B2	15

	Key	Page
Manus, *island*	A2	15
Manyara, *lake*	C1	68
Manzanillo	D3	88
Manzanillo	D4	84
Manzini	B2	71
Mao	A1	89
Mao	A4	59
Maple	J5	102
Maple Creek	A11	104
Maputo, *capital*	B5	68
Maquela do Zombo	C2	70
Mar Chiquita, *lake*	C3	74
Mar del Plata	D4	74
Mar, *range*	D4	81
Mara, *river*	C4	61
Maraba	D2	81
Maracaibo	B1	79
Maracaibo, *lake*	B2	79
Maracay	C1	79
Maradi	B3	59
Marajó, *island*	D2	81
Marakei, *island*	A1	17
Maramasike, *island*	B1	16
Maranhão	D2	81
Marano, *river*	C2	18
Marañón, *river*	B1, B2	77
Maras	D3	27
Marathon	C3	101
Marbella	D4	37
Marburg	B3	40
Marcelin	D8	104
Marche	C2	38
Marchena, *island*	Inset	79
Mardan	D2	21
Mardin	E3	27
Maré, *island*	D2	18
Maremma, *region*	B2	38
Margaree Forks	F1	100
Margaret, *lake*	C2	94
Margarita, *island*	D1	79
Margate	D3	30
Margherita, *peak*	A3	61
Maria	L3	103
Maria, *islands*	B3	91
Mariana	D3	81
Marianao	B1	88
Marías, *islands*	C3	84
Marib	B1	25
Maribor	C2	48
Marie Byrd Land, *region*	B8	107
Marie-Reine	B3	94
Mariehamn (Maarianhamina)	A2	53
Mariental	C3	70
Marigot	B2	90
Marijampolé	B2	46
Marinduque, *island*	B3	12
Marino	C2	18
Marion Bridge	G2	100
Maripasoula	B2	80
Mariscal Estigarribia	B3	75
Maritime Alps, *range*	D3	34
Maritsa, *river*	D3	50
Mariupol	D3	47
Mariy El, *republic*	D4	44
Marj Uyun	A2	26
Marj, al-	D1	56
Marka	A3	60
Markham	F4, K5	102
Markham, *river*	A2	15
Markstay	E1	102
Marl	A3	40
Marmara, *sea*	B2	27
Marmora	H3	102
Marne, *river*	C2, Inset II	34
Marneuli	C4	45
Maromokotro, *mt.*	B1	69
Marondera	B2	69
Maroni, *river*	A1	80
Maros, *river*	C2	43
Maroua	B1	65
Marovoay	B2	69
Marowijne, *river*	B2	80
Marquette, Mich.	E1	126
Marquis	B2	91
Marrakech	B2	57
Marsa al-Burayqah	C1	56
Marsabit	E2	61
Marsala	C3	38
Marsaxlokk, *bay*	C3	36
Marsden	A8	104
Marseille	D5	34
Marsh Harbour	B2	89
Marsoui	L2	103
Martaban, *gulf*	C3	12
Marten River	F1	102
Martensville	D8	104
Martin	B2	42
Martinique, *island*		82
Martins River	C3	100
Martorell	D2	90
Martoreli	D2	90
Martuni	C2	45
Mary	C3	22
Mary's Harbour	D3	98
Maryborough, Qld.	E2	14
Maryfield	J11	104
Maryland	F2	126
Marystown	D5	98
Masada, *ruins*	B2	26
Masai, *steppe*	C1	68
Masaka	B4	61
Masako	C5	9
Masan	C5	9
Masaya	A3	87
Masbate	B3	12
Masbate, *island*	C6	103
Mascouche	C6	103
Maseru, *capital*	A2	71
Masfut	D2	25
Mashhad	D2	22
Masindi	B3	61
Masirah, *gulf*	C2	25
Masirah, *island*	C2	25
Mask, *lake*	B2	31
Maskall	B2	85

	Key	Page
Massenya	B5	59
Masset	F4	95
Massey	C1	102
Massif Central, *plateau*	C4	34
Massif des Bongos, *range*	B2	66
Massy	Inset II	34
Masuda	A3	8
Masvingo	B2	69
Mat, *river*	B2	49
Matadi	A2	67
Matagalpa	B2	87
Matagami	A4	101
Matale	B4	19
Matam	C2	62
Matamoros	E2	84
Matane	J3	103
Matanzas	B1	88
Matapédia	K4	103
Matapédia, *river*	K4	103
Matara	B6	19
Mataram	C2	13
Mataró	H2	37
Matawa Place	D3	96
Matehuala	D3	84
Matelot	A2	91
Matera	D2	38
Mathura	C3	20
Matlock	C3	30
Mato Grosso	C3	81
Mato Grosso do Sul	C3	81
Mato Grosso, *plateau*	C3	81
Mátra, *mts.*	B2	43
Matrah	C1	25
Matru	A1	56
Matsoku, *river*	B2	71
Matsudo	C3	8
Matsue	B3	8
Matsumae	D1, Inset I	8
Matsumoto	C2	8
Matsuyama	B3	8
Mattawa	G1	102
Mattawin, *river*	C5	103
Matterhorn, *mt.*	B3	35
Matthew Town	C4	89
Matthews Ridge	A1	80
Mauá	Inset II	81
Maui, *island, Hawaii*	Inset II	126
Maule, *river*	B5	76
Maumturk, *mts.*	B2	31
Maun	A1	69
Mauna Loa, *mt., Hawaii*	Inset II	126
Maunabo	D2	90
Mauren	B1	33
Maurepas	Inset II	34
Mauritania		58
Mauritius		69
Mavinga	D5	70
May Pen	B3	88
Maya, *mts.*	A3	85
Mayaguana, *island*	C4	89
Mayaguana, *passage*	C4	89
Mayagüez	A2	90
Maydi	A1	25
Mayfair	C7	104
Maymont	C8	104
Maymyo	C2	12
Maynooth	C2	31
Maynooth	H2	102
Mayo	B4	105
Mayo, *lake*	C4	105
Mayombé, *massif*	B5	66
Mayon, *volcano*	B3	12
Mayotte, *island*	C2	67
Mayreau, *island*	B3	91
Mayumba	A2	66
Mazabuka	B2	67
Mazandaran, *region*	C2	22
Mazar-e Sharif	A1	22
Mazaruni, *river*	A2	80
Mazatenango	B5	85
Mazatlán	C3	84
Mažeikiai	B1	46
Mazoe, *river*	B1	69
Mazyr	D3	47
Mbabane, *capital*	B2	71
Mbahiakro	D3	63
Mbaké	A2	62
Mbala	C1	67
Mbale	D3	65
Mbalmayo	B3	65
Mbandaka	B2	67
M'banza Congo	B2	70
Mbanza-Ngungu	A2	67
Mbarara	B4	61
Mbemkuru, *river*	C2	68
M'Beni	A1	67
Mbéré, *river*	B2	65
Mbeya	B2	68
Mbini	C3	66
Mbini, *river*	C3	66
Mboro, *river*	D4	66
Mboune, *river*	B2	62
Mbour	A2	62
Mbuji-Mayi	B2	67
Mbuluzane, *river*	B2	71
Mbuluzi, *river*	B2	71
McAdam	B3	97
McAllen, Tex.	D3	126
McBride	M4	95
McCallum	C4	98
McCreary	B4	96
McDame	H1	95
McGee	B9	104
Mchinji	A2	68
McKerrow	D1	102
McKinley *mt., Alaska*	Inset I	126
McLeese Lake	L5	95
McLeod Lake	L4	95
McLeod Valley	C4	94
M'Clintock, *channel*	H2	99
McLure	M6	95
McMurdo, *sound*	B5	107
McRae	E4	94
Meacham	E8	104
Meadow Lake	B6	104
Meadow Portage	B2	96
Meaford	E3	102

	Key	Page
Mealy, *mts.*	A3	98
Meander River	B1	94
Mecca	A2	24
Mechelen	C1	33
Mecklenburg, *bay*	B1	40
Mecklenburg-Western Pomerania	C2	40
Mecsek, *mts.*	B2	43
Medan	A1	13
Medellín	B3	78
Medford, Oreg.	A1	126
Medgidia	E3	43
Mediaș	C2	43
Medicine Hat	D4	96
Medina	A1	24
Medina del Campo	D2	37
Medit	B2	13
Mediterranean, *sea*		29
Medley	E4	94
Medora	A4	96
Meductic	B3	97
Meelpaeg, *lake*	C5	98
Meerut	C3	20
Meghna, *river*	D5	21
Meghri	D4	45
Meighen, *island*	J1	99
Meiktila	B2	12
Meissen	C3	40
Mejicanos	A2	86
Mékambo	B1	66
Mekele	C1	60
Mékinac, *lake*	D4	103
Meknès	C1	57
Mekong, *delta*	C4	11
Mekong, *river*	A1, A4, C4, D3	11
Mékrou, *river*	B2	64
Melaka	B2	13
Melbourne, Fla.	E3	126
Melbourne, Vic., *capital*	D3	14
Meldrum Bay	B2	102
Meleb	C4	96
Melekeok	C3	17
Mélèzes, *river*	P4	99
Melfi	B5	59
Melfort	F8	104
Melilla	A4	96
Melipilla	Inset	76
Melita	A4	96
Melitopol	D3	47
Mellieha	B2	36
Mellieha, *bay*	B2	36
Melo	C2	75
Melrose	E2	100
Melun	Inset II	34
Melville	H10	104
Melville, *island*	C1	14
Melville, *island*	F1	99
Melville, *lake*	B2	98
Melville, *peninsula*	M3	99
Memmingen	B5	40
Memphis, Tenn.	D2	126
Memphrémagog, *lake*	D6	103
Menai, *strait*	B3	30
Ménaka	D2	58
Mende	C4	34
Mendoza	B3	74
Menihek	D3	98
Mennecy	Inset II	34
Menongue	C4	70
Mentawai, *islands*	A2	13
Menzel Bourguiba	B1	57
Meppel	D2	32
Mequinenza, *lake*	F2	37
Merano	B1	38
Merauke	F2	13
Mercedario, *mt*	A2	75
Mercedes	C3	12
Mergui	C4	12
Mergui, *archipelago*	C4	12
Mérida	C3	37
Mérida, *mts.*	B2	79
Mérida, *state capital*	G3	84
Meridian, Miss.	E2	126
Merigomish	E2	100
Merín, *lagoon*	D2	75
Merir, *island*	Inset	17
Merkys, *river*	C2	46
Meron, *mt.*	B1	26
Merredin, W.A.	A3	14
Merrick, *mt.*	B2	30
Merridale	A3	96
Merritt	M6	95
Mersch	B2	33
Mersey, *river*	C3	30
Mersin	C3	27
Merthyr Tydfil	B3	30
Meru	D3	61
Merume, *mts.*	A2	80
Mesaoria, *plain*	B1	27
Meseta, *plateau*	D3	37
Mesolóngion	B2	51
Mesopotamia, *region*	B2	24
Messina	D1	71
Messina	C3	38
Messina, *strait*	D3	38
Mesta, *river*	B4	50
Meta Incognita, *peninsula*	P4	99
Meta, *river*	C3	78
Métabetchouan	E3	103
Metcalfe	K2	102
Meteghan	A3	100
Métis-sur-Mer	J3	103
Metiskow	E5	94
Metz	D2	34
Meulan	Inset II	34
Meuse, *river*	D2	33
Mexiana, *island*	D1	81
Mexicali, *state capital*	A1	84
Mexico		84
Mexico City, *national capital*	E4, Inset	84
Mexico, *gulf*		82
Meymaneh	A1	22
Meyungs	B3	17
Mgwavuma, *river*	B3	71
Mhlume	B2	71
Miami	B4	96

	Key Page
Miami, Fla.	E3 126
Mianwali	D3 21
Miaoli	B1 9
Mica Creek	N5 95
Michalovce	C2 42
Miches	C2 89
Michigan	E1 126
Michigan, lake	E1 126
Michoacán	D4 84
Mico, river	B2 87
Micoud	B3 91
Micronesia	15
Midale	G11 104
Middelburg	C3 71
Middelburg	A3 32
Middle Andaman, island	F6 20
Middle Arm	C4 98
Middle Lake	E8 104
Middle Atlas, ranges	C1 57
Middle Musquodoboit	D2 100
Middlebro	D4 96
Middleburg	B3 100
Middleton	15
Middlesbrough	C2 30
Midi-Pyrénées	C5 34
Midland	F3 102
Midland, Tex.	C2 126
Midlands, region	C3 30
Miercurea Ciuc	C2 43
Mieres	D1 37
Mikkwa, river	C2 94
Mikkeli	C2 53
Mikomeseng	C2 66
Míkonos, island	C3 51
Mikura, island	C3 8
Miladummadulu, atoll	A1 19
Milagro	B4 79
Milan	B1 38
Milden	C9 104
Mildura, Vic.	D3 14
Miles City, Mont.	C1 126
Milestone	F10 104
Milford Haven	B3 30
Milford Sound	A3 15
Milh, river	B2 24
Mili, island	C2 16
Milk, river	E6 94
Mill Bay	L7 95
Mill Village	C3 100
Miller Lake	D2 102
Millet	D4 94
Milliken	K5 102
Milltown	D5 98
Millville	B2 97
Milne, bay	B3 15
Milo	D6 94
Milo, river	D3 62
Mílos, island	C3 51
Milton	B2 100
Milton	F4 102
Milverton	E4 102
Milwaukee, Wis.	E1 126
Mimico	J6 102
Miminegash	A2 100
Mina Baranis	C3 56
Mina Salman	B1 25
Minami, island	Inset III 8
Minas	C3 75
Minas Gerais	D3 81
Minas, channel	C2 100
Minatitlán	F4 84
Minch, strait	B1 30
Mindanao, island	C5 12
Mindelo	B2 58
Mindemoya	C2 102
Minden	G3 102
Mindoro, island	B3 12
Mindoro, strait	B3 12
Miner's Bay	G3 102
Miner, river	B3 105
Mingäçevir	B2 45
Mingäçevir, reservoir	B2 45
Minho, river	A1 36
Minicoy, island	B7 20
Minija, river	A2 46
Miniota	A4 96
Minitonas	A3 96
Mink Creek	A3 96
Minna	D3 65
Minneapolis, Minn.	D1 126
Minnedosa	B4 96
Minnesota	D1 126
Miño, river	C1 37
Minorca, island	H2 37
Minot, N. Dak.	C1 126
Minsk, capital	C3 47
Minto	B4 96
Minto	C2 97
Minto	B4 105
Minto, lake	B2 101
Minton	F11 104
Minya, al-	B2 56
Miquelon, island	M4 92
Mira	H1 100
Mirabel	B6 103
Mirador Nacional, mt.	C3 75
Miraflores	B4 78
Miragoâne	B2 89
Miramichi	D1 97
Miramichi, bay	E1 97
Miranda de Ebro	E1 37
Mirbat	B3 25
Mirebalais	C2 89
Miri	D2 13
Mirnyy	C7 44
Mirpur Khas	C5 21
Mirror	D5 94
Miscou, island	E1 97
Miscouche	B2 100
Misere	Inset 70
Misery, mt.	B1 90
Miskolc	C1 43
Misool, island	E2 13
Missinipe	F5 104
Mississauga	F4, J6 102
Mississippi	D2 126
Mississippi, lake	J2 102
Mississippi, river	D1 126
Missoula, Mont.	B1 126
Missouri	D2 126

	Key Page
Missouri, river	D1 126
Mistassibi, river	D1 103
Mistassini	D3 103
Mistassini, lake	B3 101
Mistassini, river	D2 103
Mistatim	G8 104
Mistelbach	E2 39
Misurata	C1 56
Mitchell	D4 102
Mitchell, mt., N.C.	E2 126
Mitchell, river	D1 14
Mitchinamécus, lake	A4 103
Mitilíni	C2 51
Mito	D2 8
Mitsamiouli	A1 67
Mittelland, canal	B2 40
Mitú	C4 78
Mitzic	A1 66
Miyake, island	C3 8
Miyako	C2 8
Miyako, island	Inset II 8
Miyakonojo	A4 8
Miyazaki	A4 8
Mizen Head, cape	B3 31
Mizo, hills	F4 20
Mizpe Ramon	B2 26
Mjøsa, lake	C3 52
Mkondvo, river	B2 71
Mliba	B2 71
Mo	C2 52
Moa, island	D2 13
Moa, river	B2 63
Moab, Utah	C2 126
Moala, island group	B3 17
Moanda	B2 66
Moba	C2 67
Mobaye	B3 66
Mobile, Ala.	E2 126
Moca	B1 89
Moca	A2 90
Moçambique	D2 68
Mocha, (Mukha, al-)	A2 25
Mocímboa da Praia	D1 68
Môco, mt.	C4 70
Mocoa	A4 78
Modena	B1 38
Moengo	B2 80
Moers	A3 40
Mogadishu, capital	B3 60
Mogami, river	C2 8
Mogi das Cruzes	Inset II 81
Mogilev Podolskiy	B2 47
Mogocha	D7 44
Mogotón, mt.	A2 87
Mohács	B2 43
Mohales Hoek	A3 71
Mohammedia	C1 57
Moher, cliffs	B2 31
Mojave, desert, Calif.	B2 126
Mojos	A2 77
Mokhotlong	C2 71
Mokolo	B1 65
Mokpo	B5 9
Mold	B3 30
Moldavia, region	D2 43
Molde	B3 52
Moldova	50
Moldoveanu, mt.	C3 43
Molepolole	B3 69
Molise	C2 38
Mollendo	C4 77
Molokai island, Hawaii	Inset II 126
Molopo, river	B2 71
Moloundou	C3 65
Molson, lake	C2 96
Molucca, sea	D2 13
Moluccas, islands	D2 13
Mombasa	E5 61
Mombetsu	Inset I 8
Mon Repos	B2 91
Møn, island	D4 32
Mona, passage	D2 89
Monaco	35
Monaco, capital	B1 35
Monaghan	C1 31
Monastery	F2 100
Monastir	C2 57
Mönchengladbach	A3 40
Monclova	D2 84
Moncton	E2 97
Mondego, cape	A2 36
Mondego, river	B2 36
Monforte	C1 37
Mongo	B4 59
Mongolia	11
Mongolian, plateau	C2 11
Mongomo	D3 66
Mongu	A3 67
Monitor	E5 94
Monjolo	Inset I 81
Monkey Bay	B2 68
Mono, river	A4, B2 64
Monopoli	D2 38
Monrovia, capital	A2 63
Mons	B2 33
Mont-Carmel	G4 103
Mont-Joli	H3 103
Mont-Laurier	A5 103
Mont-Royal	J5 103
Mont-Saint-Michel	B2 34
Mont-St-Pierre	L2 103
Mont-Tremblant-Village	B5 103
Montague	C2 100
Montalto, mt.	C3 38
Montana	B1 38
Montana	B1 126
Montargis	C2 34
Montauban	C4 34
Monte Carlo	B1 35
Monte Cristi	A1 89
Monte Plata	C2 89
Montebello	B6 103
Montecristo, island	B2 38
Montegiardino	B2 39
Montego Bay	B2 88
Montélimar	D4 34
Montelindo, river	C3 75

	Key Page
Montenegro, republic	A3 49
Montepulciano	B2 38
Monterey, Calif.	A2 126
Montería	B2 78
Montero	B3 77
Monterrey, state capital	D2 84
Montes Claros	D3 81
Montevideo, capital	B3 75
Montgomery, capital, Ala.	E2 126
Montluçon	C3 34
Montmagny	F5 103
Montmartre	G10 104
Montpelier, capital, Vt.	F1 126
Montpellier	C5 34
Montréal	C6, J5 103
Montréal, island	J5 103
Montreal, lake	E6 104
Montreal, river	E6 104
Montreuil	Inset II 34
Montreux	A2 35
Montrose	C2 30
Monywa	B2 12
Monza	B1 38
Moore Park	B4 96
Moose Factory	D2 101
Moose Jaw	E10 104
Moose Lake	A2 96
Moose, river	D2 101
Moosehorn	B3 96
Moosomin	J10 104
Moosonee	D2 101
Mopti	C3 58
Moquegua	C4 77
Moradabad	C3 20
Morant Bay	C3 88
Moratuwa	A5 19
Morava, river	A2, C3 42
Morava, river	B3 49
Moravia, region	C3 42
Moray, estuary	B1 30
Morden	B4 96
Mordoviya, republic	E4 44
Moree, N.S.W.	D2 14
Morehead	A2 15
Morelia, state capital	D4 84
Morell	C2 100
Morelos	E4 84
Morena, mts.	D3 37
Moresby, island	F5 95
Moreton, bay	Inset III 14
Morges	A2 35
Morghab, river	A1 22
Morghob, river	B1 23
Morghob, river	B1 23
Morice, lake	J4 95
Moricetown	J3 95
Morija	A2 71
Morinville	D4 94
Morioka	D2 8
Morlaix	B2 34
Morne Diablotin, mt.	B2 90
Moro, gulf	B5 12
Moro, river	A2 63
Morocco	57
Morogoro	C2 68
Morombe	A3 69
Morón	D2 88
Morón	C2 11
Morón de la Frontera	D4 37
Morondava	A3 69
Moroni, national capital	A1 67
Morotai, island	D1 13
Moroto	D2 61
Morpeth	D5 102
Morphou	A1 27
Morrin	D5 94
Morris	C4 96
Morrisburg	K3 102
Mors, island	B2 32
Morse	C10 104
Mortlach	D10 104
Mortlock, islands	C2 15
Moruga	A2 91
Moscow, capital	D3 44
Mosel, river	A4 40
Moselle, river	D2 34
Moshi	C1 68
Mosjøen	C2 52
Mosquitos, coast	C3 87
Moss	C4 52
Mossbank	E11 104
Mossel Bay	B3 71
Mossendjo	B5 66
Mossleigh	D6 94
Mossy, river	F6 104
Most	A2 42
Mostaganem	B1 57
Mostar	B2 48
Móstoles	Inset II 37
Mosul	B1 24
Motagua, river	D4 85
Motherwell	B2 30
Mouila	A2 66
Mould Bay	E1 99
Moule à Chique, cape	B3 91
Moulmein	C3 12
Moulouya, river	D1 57
Moundou	B5 59
Mount Carmel	A2 100
Mt. Forest	E4 102
Mount Gambier, S.A.	D3 14
Mount Hagen	A2 15
Mount Isa, Qld.	C2 14
Mt. Stewart	C2 100
Mountain Park	B5 94
Moura	B3 36
Mourne, mts.	A2 30
Mouscron	B2 33
Moussa Ali, mt.	B1 60
Mouths of the Danube, delta	E3 43
Mouths of the Ganges, delta	C7 21
Mouths of the Indus, delta	C5 21
Moyale	E2 61
Moyamba	A1 63
Moyie	P6 95
Moyobamba	B2 77

	Key Page
Moyowosi, river	B1 68
Mozambique	68
Mozambique, channel	55
Mozzoro	E2 81
Mpanda	B2 68
Mpika	C2 67
Mpoko, river	A2 66
Mporokoso	C1 67
Mqinvartsveri, mt.	C3 45
M'Ramani	B2 67
Mtkvari, river	C4 45
Mtskheta	C4 45
Mtwara	D3 68
Muang Khammouan	C3 11
Muang Không	C4 11
Muang Khôngxédôn	C4 11
Muang Paklay	A2 11
Muang Pakxan	B2 11
Muang Vangviang	B2 11
Muang Xaignabouri	A2 11
Muang Xay	A1 11
Muang Xépôn	D3 11
Muang Xon	B1 11
Muar	B2 13
Muara	C1 13
Mubende	B3 61
Mubi	G5 65
Muchinga, mts.	C2 67
Mudanjiang	F1 10
Mudawwarah, al-	B3 26
Mufulira	B2 67
Muğla	B3 27
Muharraq, al-, island	B1 25
Mühlhausen	B3 40
Mui Bai Bung, point	A5 11
Mukalla, al-	B2 25
Muko, island	Inset III 8
Mulaku, atoll	A3 19
Mulde, river	C3 40
Mulhacén, mt.	E4 37
Mulhouse	D3 34
Mull, island	A2 30
Mullaittivu	B2 19
Mullingar	C2 31
Multan	D3 21
Mulund	Inset I 20
Mulvihill	B4 96
Mumbai (Bombay)	B5, Inset I 20
Mumbai (Bombay), harbor	Inset I 20
Mumbra	Inset I 20
Mumbwa	B3 67
Mun, river	C3 12
Muna, island	D2 13
Munamägi, mt.	D3 46
Muncho Lake	K2 95
Munich	B4 40
Munsan	B4 9
Münster	A3 40
Munster, province	B2 31
Muonio	B1 53
Muonioälven, river	D1 53
Muoniojoki, river	B1 53
Mur, river	D3 39
Mura, river	C2 48
Muramvya	B2 61
Murat, river	E2 27
Murchison, river	A2 14
Murcia	F4 37
Murdochville	L3 103
Mures, river	B2 43
Murgab, river	D3 22
Muriel, lake	E4 94
Murilo, atoll	C2 15
Müritz, lake	C2 40
Murmansk	C1 44
Muroran	D1, Inset I 8
Muroto, cape	B3 8
Murray Harbour	C3 100
Murray River	C2 100
Murray, harbour	C2 100
Murray, river	A2 15
Murray, river	D3 14
Murrumbidgee, river	D3 14
Murska Sobota	D2 48
Mürz, river	D3 39
Murzuq	B2 56
Muş	E2 27
Müşa, river	B1 46
Musala, mt.	B3 50
Musan	C1 9
Muscat, capital	C1 25
Musgrave Harbour	E4 98
Musgrave, ranges	C2 14
Musgravetown	E5 98
Mushin	B4 65
Muskeg River	A4 94
Muskegon, Mich.	E1 126
Muskogee, Okla.	D2 126
Muskoka, lake	F2 102
Muskwa, ranges	J2 95
Musoma	B1 68
Musquodoboit Harbour	D3 100
Mussau, island	A2 15
Mustang	B2 19
Mustique, island	B3 91
Mustvee	D2 46
Musu-dan, point	C1 9
Mut	A2 56
Mutare	C2 69
Mutsamudu	B2 67
Mutsu	D1 8
Muyinga	C1 61
Muyun Kum, desert	D2 23
Muzaffarabad	D2 21
Muynoq	A2 23
Mwali (Mohéli), island	A2 67
Mwanza	B1 68
Mwene-Ditu	B2 67
Mweru, lake	B1, C3 67
Mwinilunga	B2 67
My Tho	B4 11
Myanmar (Burma)	12
Myingyan	B2 12
Myitkyina	C1 12
Mykolaïv	C3 47
Mymensingh	D4 21
Myrnam	E4 94

	Key Page
Mysore	C6 20
Mzimba	B2 68
Mzuzu	B2 68

N

	Key Page
N'dalatando	B3 70
N'Djamena, capital	A4 59
N'zeto	B2 70
Naas	C2 31
Nabatiyah at-Tahta, an-	A2 26
Naberezhnyye Chelny	D4 44
Nabeul	C1 57
Nabk, an-	B2 27
Nabouwalu	B2 17
Nacala	D2 68
Nacaome	B3 86
Nackawic	B3 97
Nadi	A2 17
Nadi, bay	A2 17
Nadur	B1 36
Naduri	B2 17
Næstved	C3 32
Nafud, an-, desert	B1 24
Nag Hammadi	B2 56
Naga	B3 12
Naga, hills	F3 20
Nagano	C2 8
Nagaoka	C2 8
Nagarote	A2 87
Nagasaki	A3 8
Nagorno-Karabakh, autonomous region	B2 45
Nagoya	C3 8
Nagpur	C4 20
Nagua	C1 89
Naguabo	D2 90
Nagykanizsa	A2 43
Naha	Inset II 8
Nahanni, river	D2 99
Nahariyya	B1 26
Naicam	F8 104
Naihati	Inset II 20
Nain	E3 98
Nairobi, capital	D4 61
Najaf, an-	B2 24
Najd, region	B1 24
Najin	D1 9
Najran	B2 24
Nakadori, island	A4 8
Nakano, island	A4 8
Nakfa	B1 60
Nakhichevan	A3 45
Nakhodka	E8 44
Nakhon Phanom	C2 12
Nakhon Ratchasima	C3 12
Nakhon Sawan	B3 12
Nakhon Si Thammarat	B4 12
Nakina	C2 101
Nakodu	B2 17
Nakskov	C4 32
Naktong, river	C5 9
Nakuru	C4 61
Nakusp	O6 95
Nal, river	Inset II 20
Nalikul	Inset II 20
Nam Dinh	B2 11
Nam Ngum, reservoir	B2 11
Nam Tok	B3 12
Namangan	D2 23
Namew, lake	F6 104
Namib, desert	A1, B3 70
Namibe	B5 70
Namibia	70
Namoluk, atoll	C2 15
Namonuito, atoll	C2 15
Nampö	A3 9
Nampa	B3 94
Nampula	C2 68
Namsos	C3 52
Namu, island	B2 16
Namuli, highlands	C2 68
Namur	C2 33
Namur, lake	B3 94
Namwala	B3 67
Nan	B2 12
Nan Ling, mts.	E3 10
Nan, river	B2 12
Nanaimo	L6 95
Nanchang	E3 10
Nanchong	D2 10
Nancy	D2 34
Nanda Devi, mt.	C2 20
Nanded	C5 20
Nanga Parbat, mt.	E2 21
Nanga-Eboko	B2 65
Nangi	Inset II 20
Nangnim-sanmaek, mts.	B3 9
Nanjing	E2 10
Nanning	D3 10
Nanole	Inset I 20
Nantbu	B2 9
Nanterre	Inset II 34
Nantes	B3 34
Nanticoke	E5 102
Nanumanga, island	B2 16
Nanumea, island	B2 16
Nanyang	E2 10
Nao, cape	G3 37
Napadogan	C2 97
Napaktulik, lake	F3 99
Napanee	J3 102
Napier	C2 15
Naples	C2 38
Naples, bay	C2 38
Napo, river	C1 77
Nara	B3 8
Nara, canal	C4 21
Narathiwat	B5 12
Narayanganj	D5 21
Narayani, river	B2 19
Narbonne	C5 34
Narcisse	C4 96
Nares, strait	O1 99
Narew, river	E2 41
Narmada, river	C4 20
Narrogin, W.A.	A3 14
Narrows, strait	C2 90

	Key Page
Narva	E1 46
Narva, river	D1 46
Narvik	D2 52
Naryan-Mar	C4 44
Naryn	E2 23
Naryn, river	E2 23
Nashshash, an-	C3 25
Nashville, capital, Tenn.	E2 126
Nashwaak Bridge	C2 97
Näsi, lake	B2 53
Nasik	B4 20
Nasiriyah, an-	C2 24
Nass, river	H3 95
Nassau, capital	B2 89
Nasser, lake	B3 56
Nata	B2 69
Natal	E2 81
Natalkuz, lake	K4 95
Natashquan	D3 101
Natitingou	A2 64
Natron, lake	C1 68
Natuna Besar, island	B1 13
Naucalpan de Juárez	Inset 84
Naujoji Akmenė	B1 46
Naumburg	B3 40
Nauru	16
Navabad	A1 23
Navarino, island	C9 76
Navarra	F1 37
Navojoa	C2 84
Navua	A3 17
Navua, river	A3 17
Nawabshah	C4 21
Nawoiy	C2 23
Náxos, island	C3 51
Nayarit	C3 84
Nazareth	B1 26
Nazca	C3 77
Naze	Inset II 8
Nazko	L5 95
Nazret	C2 60
Nchelenge	B1 67
Ndélé	B2 66
Ndendé	A2 66
Ndjolé	A2 66
Ndola	B2 67
Néa Liósia	Inset 51
Neagh, lake	B3 31
Neápolis	B3 51
Nebitdag	B2 22
Neblina, mt.	B1 81
Nebraska	D1 126
Nechako, river	K4 95
Neckar, river	B4 40
Necochea	D4 74
Neder Rijn, river	C3 32
Nee Soon	B1 13
Needles	N6 95
Neepawa	B4 96
Nefta	A3 57
Negele	C3 60
Negev, region	B2 26
Negombo	A4 19
Negra, lagoon	D2 75
Negra, point	A2 77
Negril	A2 88
Negro, river	B4 74
Negro, river	B2 81
Negro, river	C2 75
Negros, island	B4 12
Neguac	D1 97
Neiafu	C2 17
Neiba	A2 89
Neiba, mts.	A2 89
Neijiang	D3 10
Neil Harbour	G1 100
Neilburg	A8 104
Neisse, river	C3 40
Neiva	B4 78
Nekemte	B2 60
Nellore	C6 20
Nelson	B3 15
Nelson	O6 95
Nelson Forks	L1 95
Nelson House	B1 96
Nelson, river	C1, D1 96
Nelspruit	D2 71
Néma	D3 58
Nemeiben, lake	E5 104
Nemunas, river	A2, C2 46
Nemuro	Inset I 8
Nemuro, strait	Inset I 8
Nenagh	B2 31
Nendo, island	C2 16
Nenetsiya, autonomous okrug	C4 44
Nepal	19
Nepalganj	B2 19
Nepean	G6, K2 102
Nepisiguit, river	C1 97
Neretva, river	B2 48
Neris, river	C2 46
Ness, lake	B1 30
Nesselrode, mt.	E1 95
Nestaocano, river	C2 103
Netanya	B1 26
Netherlands	32
Nettilling, lake	O3 99
Netzahualcóyotl	Inset 84
Neubrandenburg	C2 40
Neuchâtel	A2 35
Neuchâtel, lake	A2 35
Neudorf	G10 104
Neufchâteau	D3 33
Neumünster	B1 40
Neunkirchen	A4 40
Neuquén	B4 74
Neusiedler, lake	E3 39
Neuss	A3 40
Neustadt	C2 40
Neustrelitz	C2 40
Nevada	B2 126
Nevada, mts.	E4 37
Nevers	C3 34
Neves	B4 63
Neves	Inset I 81
Nevėžis, river	B2 46
Nevis, island	C2 90
New Amsterdam	C2 80

Name	Key	Page
New Brigden	E5	94
New Britain, *island*	B2	15
New Caledonia, *island*	C2	18
New Delhi, *capital*	C3	20
New Denver	O6	95
New England, *range*	E3	14
New Ferolle	C4	98
New Fish Creek	B3	94
New Georgia Group, *islands*	A1	16
New Glasgow	E2	100
New Guinea, *island*	A2	15
New Hamburg	E4	102
New Hampshire	F1	126
New Hanover, *island*	B2	15
New Haven, Conn.	F1	126
New Ireland, *island*	B2	15
New Jersey	F1	126
New Kowloon	Inset	10
New Liskeard	E3	101
New Mexico	C2	126
New Minas	C2	100
New Orleans, La.	D3	126
New Plymouth	B2	15
New Providence, *island*	B3	89
New Richmond	L3	103
New Ross	C3	100
New Sandy Bay	B1	91
New Schwabenland, *region*	B16	107
New Siberian, *islands*	B9	44
New South Wales	D3	14
New Territories, *island*	Inset	10
New Waterford	G1	100
New Waterway, *channel*	B3	32
New York	F1	126
New York, N.Y.	F1	126
New Zealand		15
New, *river*	C4	90
New, *river*	B1	85
Newark, N.J.	F1	126
Newboro	J3	102
Newcastle	C2	90
Newcastle	C2	71
Newcastle upon Tyne	C2	30
Newcastle, N.S.W.	E3	14
Newcastle-under-Lyme	C3	30
Newdale	A4	96
Newell, *lake*	E6	94
Newman, W.A.	A2	14
Newmarket	D3	30
Newmarket	F3	102
Newport	C3	30
Newport News, Va.	F2	126
Newquay	B4	30
Newry	A2	30
Newtown St. Boswells	C2	30
Neyagawa	B3	8
Neyshabur	D2	22
Ngami, *lake*	A2	69
Ngaoundéré	B2	65
Ngara	B1	68
Ngaramasch	B4	17
Ngauruhoe, *mt.*	C2	15
Ngerkeel	B3	17
Ngemelis, *islands*	B3	17
Ngermechau	C2	17
Ngetbong	C2	17
Ngiro, *river*	D3	61
Ngonini	B1	71
Ngorongoro, *crater*	C1	68
Ngounié, *river*	A2	66
Ngozi	B1	61
Nguigmi	C3	59
Ngulu, *atoll*	A2	15
Nguru	F1	65
Ngwempisi, *river*	A2	71
Nha Trang	B4	11
Nhlangano	B3	71
Niagara Falls	F4	102
Niagara-on-the-Lake	F4	102
Niagassola	D1	62
Niamey, *capital*	A3	59
Niamtougou	B2	64
Niari, *river*	B5	66
Nias, *island*	A1	13
Nibok	B2	16
Nicaragua		87
Nicaragua, *lake*	B3	87
Nice	D5	34
Nicholls' Town	A2	89
Nickerie, *river*	A2	80
Nicobar, *islands*	F7	20
Nicola	M6	95
Nicolet	D5	103
Nicosia, *capital*	B1	27
Nicoya, *gulf*	B3	86
Nictau	B1	97
Nidže, *mts.*	B3	48
Niedere Tauern, *range*	D3	39
Niefang	C3	66
Nienburg	B2	40
Niéri Ko, *river*	C2	62
Nieuw Amsterdam	B2	80
Nieuw Nickerie	A2	80
Nigadoo	D1	97
Niğde	C3	27
Niger		59
Niger, *delta*	C5	65
Niger, *river*	B3	58
Nigeria		65
Nii, *island*	C3	8
Niigata	C2	8
Niihama	B3	8
Niihau, *island*, Hawaii	Inset II	126
Nijmegen	C3	32
Nikaia	Inset	51
Nikki	B3	64
Nikko	C2	8
Nikolayevsk-na-Amure	D9	44
Nikopol	C2	47
Niksar	A3	49
Nikšić	A3	49
Nilandu, *atoll*	A2	19
Nile, *river*	B2	56
Nilgiri, *hills*	C6	20
Niló̧polis	Inset I	81
Nimba, *mt.*	B3	63

Name	Key	Page
Nimba, *mts.*	B2	63
Nîmes	D5	34
Nine Mile River	D2	100
Ninette	B4	96
Ninga	B4	96
Ningbo	F3	10
Ningxia Hui	D2	10
Ninigo, *group*	A2	15
Niono	B3	58
Nioro du Rip	B3	62
Nioro du Sahel	B2	58
Niort	B3	34
Nipawin	F7	104
Nipigon	C3	101
Nipigon, *lake*	C3	101
Nipissing	F1	102
Nipissing, *lake*	F1	102
Niš	B3	49
Nišava, *river*	C3	49
Nishino, *island*	Inset III	8
Nishinomiya	B3	8
Nisling, *river*	B4	105
Nitra	B2	42
Niuafo'ou, *island*	B1	17
Niuatoputapu, *island*	C1	17
Niulakita, *island*	C4	16
Niutao, *island*	B2	16
Niverville	C4	96
Nizamabad	C5	20
Nizhnevartosk	C5	44
Nizhny Novgorod	D4	44
Nizhny Tagil	D4	44
Njazidja (Grande Comore), *island*	A1	67
Njombe, *river*	B2	68
Nkawkaw	B3	64
Nkhata Bay	B2	68
Nkhotakota	B2	68
Nkongsamba	A2	65
Noakhali	E6	21
Nobeoka	A3	8
Noel	D2	100
Nogales	B1	84
Nogales, Ariz.	B2	126
Nojima, *cape*	D3	8
Nok Kundi	B4	21
Nokaneng	A1	69
Nokomis	E9	104
Nola	A3	66
Nome, Alaska	Inset I	126
Nonacho, *lake*	G4	99
Nong Khai	C2	12
Nonsan	B4	9
Nonthaburi	B3	12
Nootka, *island*	J6	95
Norak	B1	23
Nord-Ostsee, *canal*	B1	40
Nord-Pas-de-Calais	C1	34
Nordenham	B2	40
Nordhausen	B3	40
Nordhorn	A2	40
Nordvik	B7	44
Norfolk	D5	94
Norfolk, Va.	F2	126
Norilsk	C6	44
Norland	G3	102
Normandin	D3	103
Norquay	H9	104
Norra Storfjället, *mt.*	C1	53
Norris Arm	D4	98
Norris Point	C4	98
Norrköping	C3	53
Norte, *key*	E2	90
N. Albanian Alps, *mts.*	A1, B3	49
North Andaman, *island*	F6	20
North Battleford	B8	104
North Bay	F1	102
North Cape	B1	100
North Carolina	F2	126
North China, *plain*	E2	10
North Comino, *channel*	B1	36
North Dakota	C1	126
North Downs, *hills*	C3	30
North Frisian, *islands*	B4	32
North Holland, *canal*	B2	32
North Korea		9
North Magnetic Pole	B13	106
North Malosmadulu, *atoll*	A2	19
N. Moose, *lake*	B2	96
North Ossetiya, *republic*	E4	44
North Platte, Nebr.	C1	126
North Portal	H11	104
North Rhine-Westphalia	A3	40
North Rustico	B2	100
North Saskatchewan, *river*	D8	104
North Sea, *canal*	B2	32
North Shields	C2	30
North Siberian, *lowland*	B6	44
North Star	B3	94
North Taranaki, *bight*	B2	15
N. Thompson, *river*	N5	95
North Uist, *island*	A1	30
North Wabasca, *lake*	D3	94
North West River	A2	98
North West, *cape*	A2	14
North York	K5	102
North, *cape*	F1	52
North, *channel*	A2	30
North, *channel*	B1	102
North, *island*	B2	15
North, *river*	B2	98
North, *sea*		29
Northallerton	C2	30
Northampton	C3	30
Northeast, *polder*	C2	32
Northeim	B3	40
Northern Divina, *river*	C4	44
Northern European, *plain*		
Northern Sporades, *islands*	B2	51
Northern Territory		14
Northgate	H11	104
Northumberland, *strait*	B3, D2	100
Northwest Gander, *river*	D5	98
Norton	C2	66
Norvegia, *cape*	B14	107
Norway		52
Norway House	C3	96
Norwegian, *bay*	K1	99

Name	Key	Page
Norwegian, *sea*	A2	52
Norwich	D3	30
Norwich	E4	102
Nossob, *river*	C3	70
Nosy Be, *island*	B1	69
Nosy Sainte Marie, *island*	B2	69
Noteć, *river*	C2, D2	41
Noto, *peninsula*	C2	8
Notre Dame de Lourdes	B4	96
Notre Dame Junction	D4	98
Notre Dame, *bay*	D4	98
Notre-Dame	E2	97
Notre-Dame, *river*	B2, C3	41
Notre-Dame-de-la-Merci	B5	103
Notre-Dame-de-la-Salette	A6	103
Notre-Dame-de-Lorette	D2	103
Notre-Dame-du-Bon-Conseil	D5	103
Notre-Dame-du-Lac	H4	103
Notre-Dame-du-Laus	A5	103
Nottingham	C3	30
Nottingham, *island*	N4	99
Nouadhibou	A2	58
Nouakchott, *capital*	A3	58
Nouméa, *capital*	C2	18
Nouvelle	K3	103
Nova Gorica	A3	48
Nova Iguaçu	Inset I	81
Novara	B1	38
Novaya Zemlya, *islands*	B4	44
Nové Zamky	B3	42
Novgorod	D3	44
Novi Pazar	B3	49
Novi Sad	A2	49
Novo Mesto	C3	48
Novokuznetsk	D6	44
Novosibirsk	D6	44
Novra	A3	96
Nowshak, *mt.*	D2	21
Nowy Sącz	E4	41
Nsanje	C3	68
Nsawam	B4	64
Nsok	D3	66
Nsoko	B3	71
Ntem, *river*	D2	84
Nu'ulua, *island*	D3	18
Nu'utele, *island*	D3	18
Nuba, *mts.*	C3	59
Nubian, *desert*	C1	59
Nueltin, *lake*	J4	99
Nueva Casas Grandes	C1	84
Nueva Gerona	B2	88
Nueva Loja	C2	79
Nueva Ocotepeque	A2	86
Nueva Palmira	A2	75
Nueva Rosita	D2	84
Nueva San Salvador	A2	86
Nuevitas	D2	88
Nuevo Laredo	E2	84
Nuevo León	D2	84
Nuevo Rocafuerte	D3	79
Nuguria, *islands*	B2	15
Nuhud, an-	B2	59
Nui, *island*	B2	16
Nuku'alofa, *capital*	B4	17
Nukufetau, *island*	C2	16
Nukulaelae, *island*	C3	16
Nukuoro, *atoll*	C2	15
Nukus	A2	23
Nullarbor, *plain*	B3	14
Numazu	C3	8
Ñuñoa	Inset	76
Nuoro	B2	38
Nuremberg	B4	40
Nutak	E3	98
Nuuk (Godthåb), *capital*	B2	106
Nuuuli	B1	18
Nuwara Eliya	B5	19
Nyaake	C3	63
Nyaba, *river*	B2	61
Nyala	B2	59
Nyanga, *river*	A2	66
Nyanza	B2	61
Nyasa (Malawi), *lake*	B2, B3	68
Nyborg	C3	32
Nyeri	D4	61
Nyetane, *river*	A2	71
Nyika, *plateau*	B2	68
Nyíregyháza	C2	43
Nykøbing	C4	32
Nyoman, *river*	B3	47
Nyong, *river*	B2	65
Nysa	C3	41
Nzérékoré	D4	62
Nzi, *river*	D3	63
Nzo, *river*	C3	63
Nzoia, *river*	C3	61
Nzwani (Anjouan), *island*	B2	67

O

Name	Key	Page
O'Leary	A2	100
Oahu, *island*, Hawaii	Inset II	126
Oak Lake	A4	96
Oak Point	C4	96
Oak Point	C3	97
Oak River	A4	96
Oakland, Calif.	A2	126
Oakner	A4	96
Oakview	B3	96
Oakville	A2	96
Oakville	F4	102
Oamaru	B4	15
Oaxaca, *state capital*	E4	84
Ob, *river*	C5	44
Oban	B2	30
Obed	B4	94
Oberammergau	B5	40
Oberhausen	A3	40
Oberpfälzer Wald, *mts.*	C4	40
Obi, *island*	D2	13
Obihiro	Inset I	8
Obo	C2	66
Obock	C2	60
Obuasi	B4	64
Occidental, *mts.*	B2, C4	77
Ocean Falls	J5	95
Ochamchire	A3	45
Ochil, *hills*	B2	30

Name	Key	Page
Ocho Rios	B2	88
Ochre River	B3	96
Ocoa, *bay*	B2	89
Ocotal	A2	87
Ocotlán	D3	84
Oda	B4	64
Odei, *river*	C1	96
Odemira	A4	36
Odense	C3	32
Odense, *fjord*	C3	32
Odenwald, *forest*	B4	40
Oder, *river*	B2, C3	41
Oderhaff, *lake*	C2	40
Odesa	C3	47
Odessa, Tex.	C2	126
Odienné	C2	63
Oeiras	A3	36
Oelemari, *river*	B3	80
Offa	C3	65
Offenbach	B3	40
Ofu, *island*	A1	18
Ogaden, *region*	D3	60
Ogbomosho	C3	65
Ogden, Utah	B1	126
Ogema	F11	104
Ogilvie, *mts.*	B3	105
Oglio, *river*	B1	38
Ogoki, *river*	C2	101
Ogooué, *river*	A2	66
Ogosta, *river*	B2	50
Ogražden, *mts.*	C2	48
Ogre	C2	46
Ogun, *river*	B3	65
Ohio	E1	126
Ohio, *river*	E2	126
Ohonua	C4	17
Ohrid	A2	48
Ohrid, *lake*	B2	49
Øibenhl	C3	66
Oise, *river*	C2, Inset II	34
Oistins	B5	91
Oita	A3	8
Ojinaga	D2	84
Ojos del Salado, *mt.*	B2	74
Oka, *river*	D4	44
Okahandja	C2	70
Okakarara	C2	70
Okanagan Falls	N6	95
Okanagan, *lake*	N6	95
Okara	D3	21
Okavango, *basin*	A1	69
Okavango, *river*	A1	69
Okayama	B3	8
Okazaki	C3	8
Okeechobee, *lake*, Fla.	E3	126
Okene	D4	65
Okha	D9	44
Okhotsk	D9	44
Okhotsk, *sea*	D9	44
Oki, *islands*	B2	8
Okinawa, *island*	Inset II	8
Okino Erabu, *island*	Inset II	8
Oklahoma	D2	126
Oklahoma City, *capital*, Okla.	D2	126
Okondja	B2	66
Okotoks	C6	94
Okushiri, *island*	C1, Inset I	8
Okwa, *river*	A2	69
Ólafsvík	A2	52
Olanchito	B2	86
Öland, *island*	C3	53
Olavarría	C4	74
Olbia	B2	38
Old Brahmaputra, *river*	C4	21
Old Crow	B2	105
Old Perlican	E5	98
Old Road	D5	90
Old Road Town	A2	90
Old Wives, *lake*	D10	104
Oldenburg	B2	40
Oldham	C3	30
Oldman, *river*	D6	94
Olds	C5	94
Olenek, *river*	C7	44
Oléron, *island*	B4	34
Olgilvie, *river*	B3	105
Ölgiy	A2	11
Olifants, *river*	A3, C1	70
Olinda	E2	81
Oliver	N6	95
Ollagüe, *volcano*	C2	76
Ollei	C2	17
Olmaliq	C2	23
Olomouc	C3	42
Olongapo	B3	12
Olosega, *island*	A1	18
Olsztyn	E2	41
Olt, *river*	C3	43
Oltenița	D3	43
Olympia, *capital*, Wash.	A1	126
Olympus *mt.*, Wash.	A1	126
Olympus, *mt.*	A2	27
Olympus, *mt.*	B1	51
Omagh	A2	30
Omaha, *beach*	B2	34
Omaha, Nebr.	D1	126
Oman		25
Oman, *gulf*	C1, D2	25
Omaruru	B2	70
Omatako, *river*	C1	70
Omboué	A2	66
Omdurman	C2	59
Omemee	G3	102
Ometepe, *island*	B3	87
Ominaca, *mts.*	J2	95
Ominaca, *mts.*	K3	95
Omiya	C3	8
Omo, *river*	C3	60
Omsk	D5	44
Omuta	A3	8
Onanole	B4	96
Ondame	B1	70
Ondangwa	B1	70
Ondava, *river*	B3	64
Ondjiva	C5	70
Ondo	C4	65
Öndörhaan	D2	11
Onefour	E6	94

Name	Key	Page
Onega, *lake*	C3	44
Onești	D2	43
Ongjin	A4	9
Ongole	C5	20
Onilahy, *river*	A3	69
Onion Lake	A7	104
Onitsha	D4	65
Ono, *island*	B3	17
Onon, *river*	D2	11
Onota, *island*	A1	16
Onsŏng	C1	9
Ontario		92
Ontario, *lake*	G4	102
Ontong Java, *island*	A1	16
Oostende	A3	33
Oostende-Brugge, *canal*	B1	33
Oosterschelde, *channel*	A3	32
Ootsa, *lake*	J4	95
Opava	C3	42
Opeongo, *lake*	G2	102
Opole	C3	41
Oporto (Porto)	A2	36
Opuwo	A1	70
Oqsu, *river*	C2	23
Oradea	B1	43
Oral	B2	44
Oran	A1	57
Orange Walk	B1	85
Orange, N.S.W.	D3	14
Orange, *river*	A3, B2	71
Orangeville	E4	102
Oranje, *river*	A3	70
Oranjemund	A4	70
Orapa	A2	69
Ordino	B2	36
Ordu	D2	27
Örebro	C3	53
Oregon	A1	126
Orellana, *lake*	D3	37
Orenburg	D4	44
Orense	C1	37
Øresund, *sound*	D3	32
Órganos, *mts.*	A2	88
Órgãos, *range*	Inset I	81
Orhei	B2	50
Orhon, *river*	B2, C1	11
Oriental, *mts.*	B2, C3	77
Oriental, *range*	C2	89
Orillia	F3	102
Orinoco, *river*	C3, D2	79
Orion	E6	94
Oristano	B3	38
Orizaba	E4	84
Orkney, *islands*	Inset I	30
Orlando, Fla.	E3	126
Orléans	C3	34
Orléans, *island*	F5, L5	103
Ormoc	C4	12
Orne, *river*	B2	34
Örnsköldsvik	C2	53
Orocué	C3	78
Oroluk, *atoll*	C2	15
Oromocto	C3	97
Oron	E5	65
Orontes, *river*	C2	27
Oroshá̧za	C2	43
Orrefors	C3	53
Orsha	E2	47
Orsk	D4	44
Ortegal, *cape*	C1	37
Orumiyeh (Urmia)	A2	22
Oruro	A3	77
Os, *river*	B2	50
Osaka	B3	8
Osasco	Inset II	81
Osh	C2	23
Oshakati	B1	70
Oshawa	G4	102
Oshima, *peninsula*	D1, Inset I	8
Oshogbo	C4	65
Osijek	C2	48
Osilinka, *river*	K3	95
Öskemen (Ust-Kamenogorsk)	E1	23
Oslo, *capital*	C4	52
Oslofjord, *fjord*	C4	52
Osnabrück	B2	40
Osorno	B7	76
Osoyoos	N6	95
Oss	C3	32
Osse, *river*	C4	65
Osterdalälven, *river*	B2	53
Östersund	B2	53
Ostrava	D3	42
Ostrołęka	E2	41
Osum, *river*	A3	49
Osumi, *islands*	A4	8
Osumi, *peninsula*	A4	8
Osumi, *strait*	A4	8
Oświęcim	D3	41
Otaru	Inset I	8
Otavalo	B2	79
Otavi	C1	70
Oti, *river*	B1, C2	64
Otjiwarongo	B2	70
Otranto	D2	38
Otranto, *strait*	A3	49
Otsu	B3	8
Ottawa	H5, K2	102
Ottawa, *river*	G1, G5 H5, K2	102
Otterlo	C2	32
Ötztal Alps, *range*	B4	39
Ou, *river*	B1	11
Ou, *river*	C2	8
Ouaddane	C2	66
Ouagadougou, *capital*	D2	64
Ouahigouya	C2	64
Ouaka, *river*	C2	66
Ouanary	C2	80
Ouargla	B1	57
Ouarra, *river*	D2	66
Ouarzazate	C2	57
Oudtshoorn	B3	71
Ouémé, *river*	B3	64
Ouesso	D3	66
Ouezzane	C1	57
Ouham, *river*	B2	66
Ouidah	B4	64
Oujda	D1	57

Name	Key	Page
Oulu	C1	53
Oulu, *lake*	C2	53
Oulujoki, *river*	C2	53
Oum er-Rbia, *river*	C1	57
Ounasjoki, *river*	B1	53
Oungre	G11	104
Our, *river*	B1	33
Ourthe, *river*	D2	33
Ouse, *river*	C2, D3	30
Outarde, *river*	H2	103
Outer Hebrides, *islands*	A1	30
Outjo	B2	70
Outlook	C9	104
Ouvéa, *island*	B2	17
Ovalau, *island*	B2	17
Ovalle	B4	76
Overflakkee, *island*	B3	32
Overflowing River	A2	96
Oviedo	A3	89
Oviedo	D1	37
Owando	C4	66
Owen Sound	E3	102
Owen Stanley, *range*	A2	15
Owendo	A1	66
Owensboro, Ky.	E2	126
Owerri	D5	65
Oxbow	H11	104
Oxford	C3	30
Oxford	C2	100
Oxford House	D1, D2	96
Oxford, *lake*	C2	96
Oyapock, *river*	B2	80
Oyem	A1	66
Oyo	B4	65
Ozama, *river*	C2	89
Ozark, *plateau*	D2	126
Özd	C1	43
Özgön	C2	23
Ozoir-la-Ferrière	Inset II	34
Ozurgeti	A4	45

P

Name	Key	Page
Pa-an	C3	12
Paamiut (Frederikshåb)	C2	106
Pabna	C4	21
Pacaraima, mts.	D3	79
Pacasmayo	B2	77
Pachuca, *state capital*	E3	84
Padang	B2	13
Paddle Prairie	B2	94
Paderborn	B3	40
Padma, *river*	D5	21
Padua (Padova)	B1	38
Paektu-san, *mt.*	C2	9
Pagadian	B5	12
Pago Pago, *capital*	B1	18
Pahang, *river*	B2	13
Paianía	Inset	51
Päijänne, *lake*	C2	53
Paint, *lake*	B1	96
Paisley	B2	30
Paita	A2	77
Pakaraima, mts.	A3	90
Pakistan		21
Pakowki, *lake*	E6	94
Paks	B2	43
Pakse	C4	11
Pala	A5	59
Palaiseau	Inset II	34
Palana	D10	44
Palanga	A2	46
Palangkaraya	C2	13
Palau		17
Palawan, *island*	A4	12
Paldiski	C1	46
Pale	B2	48
Palembang	B2	13
Palencia	D1	37
Palermo	C3	38
Palikir, *capital*	C2	15
Palk, *strait*	C7	20
Palliser, *cape*	C3	15
Palm, *island*	A4	91
Palma	H3	37
Palmas	D3	81
Palmer Land, *region*	B11	107
Palmerston	E4	102
Palmerston North	C3	15
Palmira	A4	78
Palmyra, *ruins*	B2	27
Palos, *cape*	F4	37
Palu	C2	13
Pamirs, mts.	B2	23
Pamirs, *region*	A2	10
Pampas, *plain*	C4	74
Pamplemousses	C2	69
Pamplona	F1	37
Panagyurishte	C3	50
Panaji	B5	20
Panama		87
Panama, *canal*	C2	87
Panamá, *capital*	C2	87
Panama, *gulf*	C2	87
Panay, *gulf*	B4	12
Panay, *island*	B4	12
PanⅮevo	B2	49
Panch'iao	B1	9
Pandan, *strait*	A2	13
Pandaruan, *river*	C2	13
Panev>ys	C2	46
Pangani, *river*	C1	68
Pangkalpinang	B2	13
Pangnirtung	Inset II	20
Panihati	Inset II	20
Panj	A2	23
Panj, *river*	B2	23
Panjakent	A1	23
Panjgur	B4	21
P'anmunjŏm	B2	9
Pantanal, *lowland*	C4	81
Pantelleria, *island*	C3	38
Pánuco, *river*	E3	84
Panzhihua	D3	10
Pápa	A2	43
Papagayo, *gulf*	A2	86
Paphos	A2	27
Papua, *gulf*	A2	15

Name	Key	Page
Papua New Guinea		15
Paquetville	D1	97
Pará	C2	81
Pará, river	C2	81
Paradise Hill	A7	104
Paradise River	C2	98
Paraguá, river	B2	77
Paraguai, river	C3	81
Paraguarí	D4	75
Paraguay		75
Paraguay, river	C2, C5	75
Paraíba	E2	81
Parakou	B3	64
Paramaribo, capital	B2	80
Paraná	C3	74
Paraná	C4	81
Paraná, river	D2	74
Paranaguá	D4	81
Paranam	B2	80
Pardubice	B2	42
Parent	B4	103
Parepare	C2	13
Paria, gulf	D1	79
Parima, range	B1	81
Paris, capital	C2, Inset II	34
Paris	E4	102
Parkhill	D4	102
Parkland	D6	94
Parksville	K6	95
Parma	B1	38
Parnaiba	D2	81
Parnaíba, river	D2	81
Pärnu	C2	46
Pärnu, river	C2	46
Paro	A2	19
Paropamisus, range	A2	22
Páros, island	C3	51
Parral	B6	76
Parrsboro	C2	100
Parry	D2	99
Parry Sound	E2	102
Parry, channel	J2	99
Parsnip, river	L4	95
Parson's Pond	C4	98
Pas de la Casa	C2	36
Pasadena	C5	98
Pasión, river	C3	85
Paso de los Toros	B2	75
Paso de Palmar, lake	B2	75
Passau	C4	40
Passero, cape	C3	38
Passo Fundo	C4	81
Pastavy	C2	47
Pastaza, river	B1	77
Pastillo	C3	90
Pasto	A4	78
Patagonia, region	A6	74
Patavilca	A2	77
Paterson, N.J.	F1	126
Patía, river	A4	78
Patiala	C2	20
Patillas	C2	90
Patna	E3	20
Patos, lagoon	C5	81
Pátrai	B2	51
Patricia	E6	94
Pattani	B5	12
Patuakhali	D6	21
Patuanak	C5	104
Patuca, mts.	C2	86
Patuca, river	C2	86
Pau	B5	34
Pauingassi	D3	96
Paulatuk	D3	99
Paulaya, river	C2	86
Paulo Afonso	E2	81
Pavaiai	B2	18
Pavia	B1	38
Pavilosta	A2	46
Pavlodar	D1	23
Pavlograd	C2	85
Payar	B2	62
Paye	Inset I	20
Payne, lake	B2	101
Paynton	B7	104
Pays De La Loire	B3	34
Paysandú	A2	75
Paz, river	C6	85
Pazardzhik	C3	50
Peace Point	D1	94
Peace River	C3	94
Peace, river	A3, C2	94
Peachland	N6	95
Pebane	C3	68
Pe~	B3	49
Pechora	C4	44
Pechora, river	C4	44
Pécs	B2	43
Pedernales	A2	89
Pedja, river	D2	46
Pedra Açú, mt.	Inset I	81
Pedra Lume	D2	58
Pedro Juan Caballero	E3	75
Pedro Santana	A1	89
Peebles	H10	104
Peel, river	B3, C2	105
Peerless Lake	C3	94
Pegasus, bay	B3	15
Pegu	C3	12
Peipus, lake	D2	46
Pekalongan	B2	13
Pekanbaru	B1	13
Pelee, island	C6	102
Peleliu, island	B4	17
Peleng, island	D2	13
Pelican Narrows	H5	104
Pelican Portage	D3	94
Pelican Rapids	A3	96
Pelican, lake	G5	104
Pelican, lake	A3	96
Pelly	J9	104
Pelly Bay	L3	99
Pelly Crossing	B4	105
Pelly, river	C4, C5	105
Pelotas	C5	81
Pematangsiantar	A1	13
Pemba	D2	68
Pemba, island	D2	68
Pemberton	L6	95
Pembina, river	B4	94
Pembina, river	B4	96
Pembroke	B3	30
Pembroke	H2	102
Penas, gulf	B8	76
Pendé, river	A2	66
Pendleton, Oreg.	B1	126
Penetanguishene	F3	102
P'enghu (Pescadores), islands	A2	9
Peniche	A3	36
Peninsular Malaysia, region	B2	13
Pennant	B10	104
Pennine Alps, mts.	B2	35
Pennines, mts.	C2	30
Pennsylvania	F1	126
Penonomé	B2	87
Penrith	C2	30
Pensacola, Fla.	E2	126
Pensacola, mts.	A11	107
Pentecost, island	C2	18
Penticton	N6	95
Peñuelas	B2	90
Penza	D4	44
Penzance	B4	30
Peoria, Ill.	E1	126
Perak, river	A2	13
Percé	M3	103
Perdue	C8	104
Pereira	B3	78
Péribonca, river	B3	101
Péribonka	D3	103
Périgueux	C4	34
Perim, island	A2	25
Peristéri	Inset	51
Perlas, archipelago	C2	87
Perlas, lagoon	C2	87
Perm	D4	44
Pernambuco	E2	81
Pernik	B3	50
Perpignan	C5	34
Perrot, island	G6	103
Persian, gulf	C1, C2, C3	24
Perth	B2	30
Perth	J3	102
Perth, W.A., capital	A3, Inset I	14
Perth-Andover	B2	97
Peru		77
Perugia	C2	38
Pervomaysk	C2	47
Pesaro	C2	38
Pescadores, channel	A2	9
Pescara	C2	38
Peshawar	D3	21
Peshkopi	B2	49
Petah Tiqwa	B1	26
Petare	C1	79
Petauke	C2	67
Petawawa	H2	102
Petén-Itzá, lake	D3	85
Peterborough	C3	30
Peterborough	G3	102
Peterhead	C1	30
Petersfield	C4	96
Petit Canouan, island	B3	91
Petit Martinique, island	C1	91
Petit Mustique, island	B3	91
Petit St. Vincent, island	A4	91
Petit-Rocher	D1	97
Petitcodiac	D3	97
Petite Riviere	C3	100
Petlura	A3	96
Petra, ruins	A2	26
Petrich	B4	50
Petrila	B3	43
Petrolia	C5	102
Petrólina	D2	81
Petropavl	C1	23
Petropavlovsk-Kamchatskiy	D9	44
Petrópolis	D4, Inset I	81
Petro∑ani	B3	43
Petrozavodsk	C3	44
Pevek	C10	44
Peyia	A2	27
Pforzheim	B4	40
Phan Rang	C4	11
Phan Thiet	B4	11
Phatthalung	B5	12
Phayao	B2	12
Phetchabun	C2	12
Phetchabun, range	B3	12
Phetchaburi	B3	12
Phichit	C2	12
Philadelphia, Pa.	F2	126
Philippine, sea	C3	12
Philippine, sea	B2	17
Philippines		12
Phitsanulok	B2	12
Phnom Penh, capital	C4	11
Phnum Tbeng Meanchey	C2	11
Phoenix, capital, Ariz.	B2	126
Phoenix, island	B2	17
Phoenix, islands	B2	17
Phôngsali	B1	11
Phou Bia, mt.	B2	11
Phra Nakhon Si Ayutthaya	B3	12
Phuket	B5	12
Phumi Samraong	B1	11
Phuntsholing	A3	19
Pianosa, island	B2	38
Piapot	A10	104
Piatra Neamœ	D2	43
Piauí	D2	81
Piave, river	C1	38
Pibor Post	C3	59
Pic de la Selle, mt.	D2	89
Picardie	C2	34
Pickle Lake	B2	101
Pico do Cano, volcano	B4	58
Picton	H3	102
Pictou	E2	100
Pidurutalagala, mt.	B4	19
Piedmont	A1	38
Piedra Sola	B2	75
Piedras Negras	D2	84
Pielinen, lake	C2	53
Pierceland	A6	104
Pierre, capital, S. Dak.	C1	126
Pierrefonds	G5	103
Pierreville	A2	91
Pierson	A4	96
Pie%t'any	A2	42
Pietermaritzburg	D2	71
Pietersburg	C1	71
Pigeon, lake	C4	94
Pigeon, lake	G3	102
Piggs Peak	B1	71
Pikangikum	B2	101
Pikes peak, Colo.	C2	126
Pikwitonei	C1	96
Pi∫a	C2	41
Pilar	C5	75
Pilaya, river	B4	77
Pilcomayo, river	B3, B4	77
Pilica, river	E3	41
Pílos	B3	51
Pilot Butte	F10	104
Pilot Mound	B4	96
Pinang, island	A2	13
Pinar del Río	A2	88
Pinawa	D4	96
Pindus, mts.	B2	51
Pine Bluff, Ark.	D2	126
Pine Dock	C3	96
Pine Falls	C4	96
Pine Point	F4	99
Pine River	A3	96
Pinehouse Lake	D5	104
Pines, island	D2	18
Ping, river	B2	12
P'ingtung	B2	9
Pingxiang	E3	10
Piniós, river	B2	51
Pink Mountain	L2	95
Pink, river	F4	104
Pinsk	C3	47
Pinta, island	Inset	79
Piotrków Trybunalski	D3	41
Pipestone	A4	96
Pipmuacan, reservoir	F2	101
Piracicaba	D4	81
Pirada	C1	62
Piraiévs	B3, Inset	51
Pirmasens	A4	40
Pirot	C3	49
Pirris, river	B3	86
Pisa	B2	38
Pisagua	B1	76
Pisco	B3	77
Pistoia	B2	38
Pite∑ti	C3	43
Pitlochry	B2	30
Pitseng	B2	71
Pitt, island	H4	95
Pittsburgh, Pa.	E1	126
Piura	A2	77
Placentia	D5	98
Placentia, bay	D5	98
Placenza	B1	38
Placetas	C2	88
Planken	B1	33
Plantagenet	K2	102
Plasencia	C2	37
Plaster Rock	B2	97
Plata, Río de la, estuary	D3	74
Plata, river	B3	75
Platte, river, Nebr.	C1	126
Plauen	C3	40
Playgreen, lake	B2	96
Pleasant Bay	G1	100
Pleiku	B4	11
Plenty, bay	C2	15
Plessisville	E5	103
Pleven	C2	50
Plevna	J3	102
Pljevlja	A3	49
Plo∫ne	C3	48
P∫ock	D2	41
Ploie∑ti	D3	43
Plovdiv	C3	50
Plum Coulee	C4	96
Plumas	B4	96
Plymouth	B1	91
Plymouth	B4	30
Píze√	A3	42
Po, river	A1, B1	38
Poá	Inset II	81
Pobé	B4	64
Pocatello, Idaho	B1	126
Podgorica	A3	49
Pogradec	B3	49
P'ohang	C4	9
Pohnpei, island	D2	15
Poinsett, cape	C2	107
Point Fortin	A2	91
Point Leamington	D4	98
Point Pedro	B2	19
Point Prim	B2	100
Point, lake	F3	99
Pointe au Baril	E2	102
Pointe du Bois	D4	96
Pointe Michel	B3	90
Pointe Sapin	D2	97
Pointe-a-la-Croix	K3	103
Pointe-Claire	H6	103
Pointe-des-Monts	J2	103
Pointe-Lebel	H2	103
Pointe-Noire	A6	66
Pointe-Verte	D1	97
Poisson Blanc, reservoir	A6	103
Poissy	Inset II	34
Poitiers	C3	34
Poitou-Charentes	C3	34
Pokemouche	E1	97
Pokhara	B2	19
Poland		41
Polar, plateau	A14	107
Polba	Inset II	20
Polis	A1	27
Polonnaruwa	B4	19
Polotsk	D2	47
Poltava	C2	47
Poltimore	A6	103
Pomeranian, bay	C1	40
Ponce	B2	90
Pond Cove	C3	98
Pond Inlet	N2	99
Pondicherry	C6	20
Ponferrada	C1	37
Ponoka	D5	94
Pont Cassé	B3	90
Pont-Rouge	E5	103
Pontchartrain, lake	Inset II	84
Pontevedra	B1	37
Pontianak	B2	13
Pontic, mts.	D2	27
Pontine, islands	C2	38
Pontine, marshes	C2	38
Pontoise	Inset II	34
Ponton	B2	96
Poole	C4	30
Poopó, lake	A3	77
Popayán	A4	78
Poperinge	A2	33
Poplar River	C3	96
Popomanaseu, mt.	B1	16
Popondetta	B2	15
Poprad	C2	42
Porcupine Plain	G8	104
Porcupine, river	B2	105
Pori	B2	53
Port Alberni	K6	95
Port Antonio	C2	88
Port au Choix	C4	98
Port au Port	B5	98
Port Augusta, S.A.	C3	14
Port Bickerton	F2	100
Port Blair	F6	20
Port Blandford	D5	98
Port Bruce	E5	102
Port Burwell	D3	98
Port Burwell	E5	102
Port Clements	F4	95
Port Colborne	F5	102
Port Coquitlam	L6	95
Port Dufferin	E3	100
Port Elgin	E3	97
Port Elgin	D3	102
Port Elizabeth	B2	91
Port Elizabeth	C3	71
Port Franks	D4	102
Port George	B2	100
Port Harcourt	D5	65
Port Hardy	J6	95
Port Hawkesbury	F2	100
Port Hedland, W.A.	A2	14
Port Hood	F1	100
Port Hope	G4	102
Port Hope Simpson	C3	98
Port Laoise	C2	31
Port Lincoln, S.A.	C3	14
Port Loko	A1	63
Port Loring	E2	102
Port Louis, capital	B2	69
Port Macquarie, N.S.W.	E3	14
Port Maria	C2	88
Port McNeill	J6	95
Port Moody	L6	95
Port Morant	C3	88
Port Moresby, capital	A2	15
Port Mouton	C4	100
Port Nolloth	A2	71
Port of Spain, capital	A2	91
Port Perry	G3	102
Port Pirie, S.A.	C3	14
Port Renfrew	K7	95
Port Rowan	E5	102
Port Said	B1	56
Port Saunders	C4	98
Port Stanley	E5	102
Port Sudan	D1	59
Port Talbot	B3	30
Port-au-Prince, bay	C2	89
Port-au-Prince, capital	C2	89
Port-Cartier	C3	101
Port-de-Paix	C1	89
Port-Gentil	A2	66
Port-Salut	B2	89
Portadown	A2	30
Portage	A2	100
Portage la Prairie	B4, D2	96
Portalegre	B3	36
Porter, lake	C4	104
Porters Lake	D3	100
Porth Edward	D3	71
Portimão	A4	36
Portland	A2	91
Portland Creek	C4	98
Portland, bight	B3	88
Portland, inlet	G4	95
Portland, Maine	F1	126
Portland, Oreg.	A1	126
Portneuf, river	G3	103
Portree	A1	30
Portsmouth	C4	30
Portsmouth	A2	90
Portsmouth, Va.	F2	126
Portugal		36
Porvenir	B9	76
Posadas	D2	74
Poste, river	A2	91
Postojna	B3	48
Postville	B2	98
Potaro, river	B3	80
Potenza	C2	38
Poti	A3	45
Potiskum	F2	65
Potnarvin	C4	18
Potosí	A3	77
Potrerillos	C3	76
Potsdam	C2	40
Pottuvil	C5	19
Pouch Cove	E5	98
Poutasi	C3	18
Pouthisat	B3	11
Pova×ská Bystrica	B2	42
Powassan	F1	102
Powell River	K6	95
Powerview	C4	96
Poyang, lake	E3	10
Poza Rica	E3	84
Po×arevac	B2	49
Poznań	B2	41
Pozo Colorado	C3	75
Pra, river	B4	64
Prachuap Khiri Khan	B4	12
Prague, capital	B2	42
Praia, capital	C4	58
Praslin	B2	91
Praslin, island	C1	70
Prato	B2	38
Prawda	D4	96
Preeceville	H9	104
Prelate	A10	104
Preparis, island	B3	12
Prescott	K3	102
Prescott, Ariz.	B2	126
Presidencia Roque Sáenz Peña	C2	74
Pre×ov	C2	42
Prespa, lake	B3	48
Presque Isle, Maine	G1	126
Prestea	A4	64
Preston	C3	30
Pretoria, administrative capital	C2	71
Préveza	B2	51
Prey Veng	D4	11
Priboj	A3	49
Priddis	C6	94
Prievidza	B2	42
Prijedor	A1	48
Prilep	B2	48
Priluki	C3	47
Primorsko	F3	50
Primrose, lake	A6	104
Prince Albert	E7	104
Prince Albert, hills	L3	99
Prince Albert, peninsula	E2	99
Prince Charles, island	N3	99
Prince George	L4	95
Prince of Wales, island	J2	99
Prince Patrick, island	E1	99
Prince Regent, inlet	K2	99
Prince Rupert	G4	95
Princes Town	A2	91
Princess Harbour	C3	96
Princess Margriet, canal	C1	32
Princess Royal, island	H4	95
Princeton	M6	95
Princeville	E5	103
Príncipe, island	C1	63
Prinzapolka	B2	87
Prinzapolka, river	B2	87
Pripyats, marshes	C3	47
Pripyats, river	C3	47
Pri×tina	B3	49
Privas	D4	34
Prizren	B3	49
Progresso	B1	85
Prokopyevsk	D6	44
Prokuplje	B3	49
Prome	B2	12
Prophet River	L2	95
Prost-jov	C3	42
Provence-Alpes-Côte-d'Azur	D4	34
Providence Bay	C2	102
Providence, capital, R.I.	F1	126
Providencia, island	Inset	78
Providenciales, island	C4	89
Provideniya	C11	44
Provo, Utah	B1	126
Pru, river	B3	64
Prut, river	B2	47
Przemyśl	F4	41
Psel, river	C1	47
Pskov	D3	44
Pskov, lake	D2	46
Ptsich, river	D3	47
Ptuj	B2	48
Pu'apu'a	B2	18
Pubnico	B4	100
Pucallpa	C2	77
Puck	D1	41
Puebla, state capital	E4	84
Pueblo, Colo.	C2	126
Puente Alto	Inset	76
Puerca, point	D2	90
Puerto Aisén	B8	76
Puerto Armuelles	A2	87
Puerto Ayacucho	C2	79
Puerto Bahía	E4	85
Puerto Barrios	B4	85
Puerto Bolívar	B4	79
Puerto Cabello	C1	79
Puerto Cabezas	C1	87
Puerto Carreño	D3	78
Puerto Cisnes	B7	76
Puerto Cortés	B2	85
Puerto Deseado	B6	74
Puerto Escondido	D4	84
Puerto Inírida	D4	78
Puerto Jiménez	B2	86
Puerto Leguízamo	B5	78
Puerto Lempira	D2	86
Puerto Maldonado	D3	77
Puerto Montt	B7	76
Puerto Natales	B9	76
Puerto Pinasco	D3	75
Puerto Plata	B1	89
Puerto Princesa	A2	90
Puerto Real	A2	90
Puerto Rico		90
Puerto Quepos	B3	86
Puerto Sandino	C4	18
Puerto Santa Cruz	B7	74
Puerto Suárez	B3	77
Puerto Vallarta	C3	84
Puerto Varas	B7	76
Puerto Williams	C9	76
Puertollano	D3	37
Puglia	C2	38
Pugwash	D2	100
Pujehun	B2	63
Pukatawagan	A1	96
Pukch'ńng	C2	9
Pukë	A1	49
Pula	A3	48
Pulangi, river	C5	12
Pu(awy	C2	41
Pulo Anna, island	Inset	17
Pulusuk, island	B2	15
Puná, island	A4	79
Punakha	A2	19
Pune	B5	20
Punggol	B1	13
P'ungsan	C2	9
Puno	C4	77
Punta, mt.	B2	90
Punta Arenas	B9	76
Punta del Este	C3	75
Punta Delgada	B9	76
Punta Gorda	B3	85
Punta Santiago	D2	90
Puntarenas	B3	86
Punto Fijo	B1	79
Purari, river	A2	15
Purbeck's Cove	C4	98
Purus, river	B2	81
Pusan	C5	9
Putao	C1	12
Putre	C1	76
Puttalam	A3	19
Puttgarden	B1	40
Putumayo, river	B5	78
Puvirnituq	A1	101
Puyo	C3	79
Puysegur, point	A4	15
Pyandzh, river	B1	23
P'yǒngsan	B3	9
P'yǒngsǒng	A3	9
P'yǒngyang	A3	9
P'yǒngyang, capital	A3	9
Pyrenees, range	C5	34

Q

Name	Key	Page
Qaanaaq (Thule)	B2	106
Qachas Nek	B3	71
Qadarif, al-	C2	59
Qaidam, basin	C2	10
Qalat	B2	22
Qalat Bishah	B2	24
Qaleh-ye Now	A2	22
Qaleh-ye Panjeh	C1	22
Qamea, island	C2	17
Qamishli, al-	B1	27
Qandahar	B2	22
Qaqortoq (Julianehåb)	C2	106
Qaraghandy (Karaganda)	D2	23
Qardho	B2	60
Qareh, river	B3	22
Qarokul, lake	B1	23
Qarshi	C3	23
Qaryah ash-Sharqiyah, al-	B1	56
Qasigiannguit (Christianshåb)	B2	106
Qasr as-Sabiyah	C2	24
Qatar		25
Qatranah, al-	B2	26
Qatrun, al-	B3	56
Qattarah, depression	A2	56
Qayrawan, al-	B1	57
Qayyarah, al-	B1	24
Qazvin	B2	22
Qelelevu, island	C2	17
Qeshm, island	D4	22
Qilian, range	C2	10
Qin Ling, mts.	D2	10
Qina	B2	56
Qingdao	F2	10
Qinghai	C2	10
Qinghai, lake	C2	10
Qinhuangdao	E2	10
Qiqihar	F1	10
Qiryat Gat	B2	26
Qiryat Shemona	B1	26
Qishn	C3	25
Qom	B2	22
Qormi	B2	36
Qostanay	C1	23
Qu'Appelle	G10	104
Qu'Appelle, river	D10	104
Quang Ngai	B3	11
Quantaq	C1	101
Quanzhou	E3	10
Quatre Bornes	B3	69
Quba	C2	45
Qubayyat, al-	B1	26
Québec, capital	E5, L6	103
Quebo	B2	62
Quebradillas	B2	90
Queen Charlotte	F4	95
Queen Charlotte, islands	G4	95
Queen Charlotte, sound	H5	95
Queen Charlotte, strait	H5	95
Queen Elizabeth, islands	H1	99
Queen Maud Land, region	B16	107
Queen Maud, mts.	A5	107
Queen Maude, gulf	H3	99
Queensland	D2	14
Queenstown	B1	13
Queenstown	A3	15
Queenstown	C3	71
Queenstown, Tas.	D4	14
Queguay Grande, river	B2	75
Queimados	Inset I	81
Quelimane	C3	68
Quellón	B7	76
Queluz	A3	36
Querétaro, state capital	D3	84
Quesnel	M5	95
Quesnel, lake	M5	95
Quetta	B2	21
Quetzaltenango	B5	85
Quevedo	B3	79
Quezon City	B3	12
Qui Nhon	B4	11
Quibala	C3	70

Name	Key	Page
Quibdó	A3	78
Quilchena	M6	95
Quill Lake	F8	104
Quill, lakes	F8	104
Quillota	B4	76
Quilpué	Inset	76
Quimbele	C2	70
Quimper	A2	34
Quinhámel	B2	62
Quintana Roo	G4	84
Quispamsis	D3	97
Quito, capital	B3	79
Qunaytirah, al-	A3	27
Qunfudhah, al-	A3	24
Qunghirot	A2	23
Quqon	D2	23
Qurghonteppa	A2	23
Qurnat as-Sawda, mt.	B1	26
Quthing	A3	71
Qyzylorda	C2	23

R

Name	Key	Page
Raahe	B2	53
Raanes, peninsula	L1	99
Raba	C2	13
Rába, river	A2	43
Rabat	B2	36
Rabat, capital	C1	57
Rabaul	B2	15
Rabbit Lake	C7	104
Rabbit Lake Mine	G2	104
Rabi, island	C2	17
Rach Gia	A4	11
Rachidia, er-	C2	57
Racine, Wis.	E1	126
Rădăuți	C2	43
Radium Hot Springs	O6	95
Radom	E3	41
Radviliškis	B2	46
Radville	F11	104
Rae	E4	99
Rafha	B1	24
Rafter	A1	96
Ragged, point	C3	91
Ragueneau	H2	103
Ragusa	C3	38
Rahimyar Khan	D4	21
Rainbow Lake	A2	94
Rainier mt., Wash.	A1	126
Raipur	D4	20
Rajang, river	C2	13
Rajbiraj	C3	19
Rajkot	B4	20
Rajpur	Inset II	20
Rajshahi	A2	19
Rakaposhi, mt.	E2	21
Raleigh, capital, N.C.	F2	126
Ralik, island chain	A1	16
Rama	B2	87
Ramadi, ar-	B2	24
Ramanbati	Inset II	20
Ramat Gan	B1	26
Ramea	C5	98
Ramla	B2	26
Ramon, mt.	B2	26
Ramree, island	A1	26
Ramtha, ar-	B1	26
Ramu	F2	61
Ramu, river	A2	15
Rancagua	B4	76
Rance, river	B2	34
Ranchi	E4	20
Rancho	B2	60
Randers	C2	32
Randonopolis	C3	81
Ranfurly	C4	96
Rangamati	F6	21
Ranger Lake	B1	102
Rangitikei, river	C2	15
Rangpur	C3	21
Ranong	B4	12
Rapel, river	B4	76
Rapid City	A4	96
Rapid City, S. Dak.	C1	126
Rapla	C1	46
Rapti, river	B2	19
Raqqah, ar-	B2	27
Ras al-Khafji	C1	24
Ras al-Khaymah	C2	25
Ras an-Naqb	A2	26
Ras Dashen, mt.	C1	24
Ras Musandam, cape	C1	25
Rasa, point	C5	74
Rashayya	A2	26
Rasht	B2	22
Ratak, island chain	A1	16
Ratchaburi	B3	12
Rathlin, island	A2	30
Ratingen	A3	40
Ratnapura	B5	19
Raukumara, range	C2	15
Rauma	B2	53
Raurkela	D4	20
Raut, river	B2	50
Ravenna	C1	38
Ravensburg	B5	40
Ravi, river	D3	21
Rawa, river	B4	80
Rawalpindi	D3	21
Rawdatayn, ar-	B2	24
Rawdon	D2	100
Rawson	B5	74
Raymore	F9	104
Rayong	B3	12
Rayside-Balfour	D1	102
Raz, point	A3	34
Razelm, lake	E3	43
Razgrad	E4	50
Ré, island	B3	34
Reading	C3	30
Reconquista	D2	74
Red (Hong), river	A2	11
Red Bay	C3	98
Red Deer	D5	94
Red Deer, lake	D5	94
Red Deer, river	D5, E6	94
Red Indian, lake	C5	98
Red Rose	C3	96
Red Sucker, lake	E2	96
Red Volta, river	B1, D3	64
Red Willow	D5	94
Red, river	C4	96
Red, river	D2	126
Red, sea	A1	24
Redange	A2	33
Redbridge	F1	102
Redding, Calif.	A1	126
Redonda, island	A6	90
Redstone	L5	95
Redvers	A4	96
Redwater	J11	104
Ree, lake	B2	31
Reed, lake	A2	96
Regensburg	C4	40
Reggio di Calabria	C3	38
Reggio nell'Emilia	B1	38
Reghin	C2	43
Regina	F10	104
Régina	B1	80
Registan, region	A2	22
Rehoboth	C3	70
Rehovot	B2	26
Reigate	Inset III	30
Reims	C2	34
Reina Adelaida, archipelago	B9	74
Reindeer, island	C3	96
Reindeer, lake	H3	104
Reindeer, river	G4	104
Reinosa	D1	37
Reliance	G4	99
Remagen	A3	40
Remich	B2	33
Rémire	B1	80
Remscheid	A3	40
Rencontre East	D5	98
Renfrew	J2	102
Rennell, island	B2	16
Rennes	B2	34
Rennie	D4	96
Renous	D2	97
Repentigny	K5	103
Reserve	H8	104
Resistencia	D2	74
Reșița	A3	43
Resolute	J2	99
Resolution, island	P4	99
Restigouche, river	B1	97
Reston	A4	96
Restoule	F1	102
Réunion, island		55
Reus	G2	37
Reuss, river	C2	35
Reutlingen	B4	40
Revelstoke	N6	95
Reventazón, river	C3	86
Revillagigedo, islands	B4	84
Rexdale	J5	102
Rexton	E2	97
Rey, island	C2	87
Reykjavik	B3	96
Reykjavík, capital	A2	52
Reynosa	E2	84
Rezekne	D2	46
Reznas, lake	D2	46
Rhaetian Alps, mts.	D2	35
Rharsa, salt marsh	A2	57
Rhine, canal	B1, B2	33
Rhine, river	A3, A4	40
Rhineland-Palatinate	A4	40
Rhode Island	F1	126
Rhodes	D3	51
Rhodes, island	D3	51
Rhodope, mts.	C4	50
Rhondda	B3	30
Rhône, river	D4	34
Rhône-Alpes	D4	34
Rhum, island	A1	30
Riaba	A1	66
Ribe	B3	32
Ribeira Brava	B2	58
Ribeira Grande	A1	58
Ribeirão Pires	Inset II	81
Ribeirão Prêto	D4	81
Riberalta	A2	77
Ribnica	B2	50
Rice, lake	G3	102
Richard, lake	C1	104
Richard-Toll	B1	62
Richards Bay	D2	71
Richards Landing	A1	102
Richardson, mts.	B1	105
Richardson, river	E2	94
Richelieu, river	C6	103
Richer	C4	96
Richibucto	E2	97
Richmond	D6	103
Richmond	L6	95
Richmond Hill	F4, K5	102
Richmond Park	D4	94
Richmond, capital, Va.	F2	126
Ricobayo, reservoir	D2	37
Rida	A2	25
Rideau, lake	J3	102
Rideau, river	H6	102
Riesa	C3	40
Rieti	C2	38
Riga, capital	C2	46
Riga, gulf	B2, B3	46
Rigolet	D5	98
Riiser-Larsen Ice Shelf, glacier	B14	107
Riiser-Larsen, peninsula	C16	107
Rijeka	B2	48
Rila, mts.	B3	50
Rimini	C1	38
Rimnicu Vilcea	C3	43
Rimouski	H3	103
Rincón, river	B2	87
Rincón del Bonete, lake	B2	75
Ringkøbing	B2	32
Río Blanco	B2	87
Rio Branco	B2	81
Río Claro	A2	91
Río Cuarto	C3	74
Rio de Janeiro	D4, Inset I	81
Río Gallegos	B4	74
Rio Grande	C5	81
Río Grande	D2	90
Rio Grande	A2	87
Rio Grande (Río Bravo), river	D2	84
Rio Grande do Norte	E2	81
Rio Grande do Sul	C4	81
Rio Verde	C3	81
Riobamba	B3	79
Ríohacha	B2	78
Rioni, river	B3	45
Riou, lake	D1	104
Rîșcani	A2	50
Rishiri, island	Inset I	8
Rishra	Inset II	20
Riske Creek	L5	95
Ritchies, archipelago	F6	20
River Cess	B3	63
River Hills	C4	96
River John	D2	100
Rivera	C1	75
Rivercrest	C4	96
Riverhurst	D10	104
Rivers	A4	96
Rivers Inlet	J5	95
Riverside, Calif.	B2	126
Riverside-Albert	E3	97
Riverton	C3	96
Riverview	E2	97
Rivière Bleue	G4	103
Rivière du Loup	C4	101
Rivière du Rempart	C2	69
Rivière Noire, mt.	B3	69
Rivière-à-Pierre	D4	103
Rivière-au-Renard	M3	103
Rivière-aux-Rats	C4	103
Rivière-du-Loup	G4	103
Rivière-du-Portage	E1	97
Rivière-Matawin	D5	103
Rivière-Ste-Marguerite	G3	103
Rivière-Verte	A1	97
Riyadh, capital	B1	24
Riyaq	B2	26
Roane	D3	34
Roanoke, Va.	F2	126
Roatán	B1	86
Roatán, island	B1	86
Robertsport	A2	63
Roberval	D3	103
Robinsonville	C1	97
Roblin	A3	96
Robore	C3	77
Robson, mt.	N4	95
Roca, cape	A3	36
Rocanville	J10	104
Rocha	C3	75
Rochdale	C3	30
Rochefort	B4	34
Rochester	D4	94
Rochester, Minn.	D1	126
Rochester, N.Y.	F1	126
Rock Island	D6	103
Rock, river	C2	68
Rockcliffe Park	H5	102
Rockford, Ill.	E1	126
Rockglen	E11	104
Rockhampton, Qld.	E2	14
Rockland	K2	102
Rocky Harbour	C4	98
Rocky Island, lake	B1	102
Rocky Mountain House	C5	94
Rocky, mts.		82
Rockyford	D5	94
Roddickton	C4	98
Rodez	C4	34
Rodney	D5	102
Roermond	D3	32
Roeselare	B2	33
Rogersville	D2	97
Roi, island	B1	16
Roi Et	C2	12
Rojo, cape	A3	90
Rokel, river	A1	63
Roland	C4	96
Rolling Hills	E6	94
Rollo, bay	C2	100
Rolphton	H1	102
Roma	A2	71
Roma, Qld.	D2	14
Roma, capital	C2	38
Romania		43
Rome, capital	C2	38
Rømø, island	B3	32
Roncador, cay	Inset	78
Roncador, range	C3	81
Ronde, island	B1	91
Rondônia	B3	81
Rongelap, island	B1	16
Rongerik, island	B1	16
Rønne	E3	32
Ronne Ice Shelf, glacier	B11	107
Roodeport	C2	71
Roosevelt, island	B6	107
Roosevelt Campobello Intl. Hist. Park	C4	97
Roper, river	C1	14
Roraima	B1	81
Roraima, mt.	A3	80
Rosa, mt.	A1	38
Rosalie	B3	90
Rosalind	D5	94
Rosario	C3	74
Roscommon	B2	31
Roscrea	B3	31
Rose Belle	C3	69
Rose Blanche	B5	98
Rose Hill	B2	69
Rose Valley	G8	104
Rose, island	B1	18
Roseau, capital	B3	90
Roseau, river	B4	96
Rosebud	D5	94
Rosemary	D6	94
Rosenfeld	C4	96
Rosenheim	C5	40
Rosenort	C4	96
Rosetown	B9	104
Rosetta, river	B1	56
Rosignol	B3	80
Roskilde	D3	32
Ross Ice Shelf, glacier	A6	107
Ross River	C4	105
Ross, island	B5	107
Ross, river	C4	105
Ross, sea	B6	107
Rosseau, lake	F2	102
Rossendale	B4	96
Rossignol, lake	B3	100
Rossland	O6	95
Rosslare	C2	31
Rosso	B3	58
Rosthern	D8	104
Rostock	C1	40
Rostov-na-Donu	E3	44
Roswell, N. Mex.	C2	126
Rotherham	C3	30
Rothesay	D3	97
Rotorua	C2	15
Rotterdam	B3	32
Roubaix	C1	34
Rouen	C2	34
Rouleau	F10	104
Round Lake Centre	H2	102
Round, island	D1	69
Round, pond	C5	98
Rounthwaite	B4	96
Routhierville	J3	103
Rouyn-Noranda	A4	101
Rovaniemi	C1	53
Rovigo	B1	38
Rovno	B1	47
Rowley, island	D5	94
Roxas	B4	12
Royal, canal	C2	31
Ruacana, falls	C2	70
Ruapehu, mt.	C2	15
Rub al-Khali (Empty Quarter), desert	C2	24
Rubtsovsk	D6	44
Ruda Śląska	D3	41
Rudnyy	C1	23
Rufiji, river	C2	68
Rufisque	A2	62
Rügen, island	C1	40
Ruggell	B1	33
Ruhengeri	B1	61
Ruhr, river	B3	40
Rukwa, lake	B2	61
Rukwa, lake	B2	68
Rum, cay	C3	89
Rumbek	B3	59
Runaway Bay	B2	88
Rundu	C1	70
Rungue	Inset	76
Rungwa, river	B2	68
Rupel, river	C1	33
Ruse	D2	50
Russell	A4	96
Russia		44
Rustavi	C4	45
Rutana	B2	61
Rutbah, ar-	B2	24
Rutherglen	F1	102
Rutland	N6	95
Ruvubu, river	B2	61
Ruvuma, river	C3	68
Ruways, ar-	B2, C1	25
Ruwenzori, range	B3	61
Ruyigi	C2	61
Ruzizi, river	A1, A2	61
Ružomberok	B2	42
Rwanda		61
Rweru, lake	C2	61
Ryazan	D3	44
Rybnik	D3	41
Ryotsu	C2	8
Rysy, mt.	E4	41
Ryukyu, islands	A4, Inset II	8
Rzeszów	F3	41

S

Name	Key	Page
's Hertogenbosch	C3	32
Saale, river	B3	40
Saar, river	A4	40
Saarbrücken	A4	40
Saaremaa, island	B2	46
Saarland	A4	40
Sab Abar	A3	27
Šabac	A2	49
Sabadell	H2	37
Sabana de la Mar	C1	89
Sabana Grande	B2	90
Sabaneta	A1	89
Sabha	B2	56
Sabie	B2	71
Sable cape, Fla.	E3	126
Sable River	B4	100
Sabzevar	D2	22
Sachigo, river	B2	101
Sackville	E3	97
Sacramento, capital, Calif.	A2	126
Sadah	A1	25
Sado, island	C2	8
Sado, river	A3	36
Safata, bay	B1	18
Safed Koh, range	D3	21
Safi	B1	57
Safotu	B1	18
Saga	A3	8
Sagaing	B2	12
Sagami, bay	C3	8
Sagamihara	C3	8
Saginaw, Mich.	E1	126
Sagua la Grande	C2	88
Saguenay, river	F3	103
Sagunto	F3	37
Sahara, desert		55
Saharanpur Panipat	C3	20
Şahbuz	A3	45
Sahel, region		55
Sahiwal	D3	21
Sai Kung	Inset	10
Saidpur	B3	21
Saimaa, lake	C2	53
St. Adolphe	C4	96
St. Alban's	D5	98
St. Albans	C3, Inset III	30
St. Albert	D4	94
St-Alexis-des-Monts	C5	103
St-Ambroise	E3	103
St. Ambroise	B4	96
St-André	B1	97
St-André	G4	103
St. Andrews	C2	30
St. Andrews	B3	97
St. Ann's Bay	B2	88
St. Anthony	D3	98
St-Antoine	C6	103
St-Apollinaire	E5	103
St-Augustin	E3	101
St. Augustine	A2	91
St. Augustine, Fla.	E3	126
St. Austell	B4	30
St. Barbe	D3	98
St. Bernard's	D5	98
St. Brendan's	E5	98
St. Bride's	D5	98
Saint-Brieuc	B2	34
St. Brieux	F8	104
St-Bruno	E3	103
St-Camille-de-Lellis	F5	103
St. Catharines	F4	102
St. Catherine's	E5	98
St. Catherine, mt.	B2	91
Saint Catherine's	C2	31
St-Charles, lake	K5	103
St. Clair, lake	C5	102
St. Clair, river	C5	102
St. Claude	B4	96
Saint-Cloud	Inset II	34
St. Cloud, Minn.	D1	126
St-Côme	C5	103
St-Constant	J6	103
St. Croix	B3	97
St-Cyprien	H4	103
St-David-de-Falardeau	E3	103
St. David's	B2	91
St. David's	B3	30
Saint-Denis	Inset II	34
St-Donat	B5	103
St. Edward	B2	100
St. Eleanors	B2	100
St. Elias, mts.	A5	105
St-Élie	B1	80
St-Émile	K5	103
St. Eustache	C4	96
St. Eustatius, island	Inset I	14
St-Eustache	H5	103
St-Fabien	H3	103
St-Fabien-de-Panet	F5	103
St-Félicien	D3	103
St-Félix-d'Otis	E3	103
St-François, lake	E6	103
St-François, river	D5	103
St.-Gédéon	F6	103
St. George	C3	97
St. George's	B5	98
St. George's, bay	B5	98
St. George's, capital	A2	91
St. George's, channel	B2	15
Saint George's channel	C3	31
St. George, Utah	B2	126
St-Georges	B5	98
St-Georges	F2	100
St-Georges	D4	103
St-Germain	G4	103
Saint-Germain-en-Laye	Inset II	34
St. Gotthard, pass	C2	35
St. Gotthard, tunnel	C2	35
St. Helens	C3	30
St-Henri-de-Taillon	E3	103
St-Hubert	H5	103
St-Hyacinthe	D6	103
St-Ignace-du-Lac	C5	103
St.-Isidore	D1	97
St.-Jacques	A1	97
St-Jacques-de-Leeds	E5	103
St-Jean, lake	C3	103
St. Jean Baptiste	C4	96
St-Jean-Chrysostome	L6	103
St-Jean-de-Matha	C5	103
St-Jean-Port-Joli	F4	103
St-Jean-sur-Richelieu	C6	103
St-Jérôme	B6	103
St. John, river	B2	97
St. John's	E5	98
St. John's, capital	D5	98
Saint John	C3	97
St. Joseph	A3	90
St. Joseph	C2	97
St. Joseph, lake	B1	102
St. Joseph, Mo.	D2	126
St-Joseph-de-Beauce	F5	103
St. Kitts (St. Christopher), island	B2	90
St. Kitts and Nevis		90
St-Lambert	J5	103
St. Labre	C4	96
St-Laurent	J5	103
Saint-Laurent du Maroni	A1	80
St. Lawrence	D5	98
St. Lawrence, cape	G1	100
St. Lawrence, gulf	L4	92
St. Lawrence Islands N.P.	J3	102
St. Lawrence, river	K4	92
St.-Lazare	A4	96
St-Léonard	B1	97
St. Lewis	D3	98
St. Lewis, river	C3	98
Saint-Lô	B2	34
St. Louis	A1	62
St. Louis	A2	100
St. Louis	E8	104
St. Louis, Mo.	D2	126
St-Louis, lake	H6	103
St-Louis-de-Kent	E2	97
St-Louis-de-Kent	E2	97
St. Lucia		91
St. Lucia, channel	B1	91
St-Ludger	F6	103
St-Ludger-de-Milot	E3	103
St. Malo	C4	96
St.-Malo	E6	103
Saint-Malo	B2	34
St-Marc	C1	89
St-Marc-du-Lac-Long	H4	103
St-Marcel	F5	103
St-Marcellin	H3	103
St. Margarets	D2	97
St. Martin	B3	96
St. Martin, lake	B3	96
St. Martins	D3	97
St. Mary's	E5	98
St. Marys	D4	102
St-Maurice, river	C4	103
St-Michel	F5	103
St-Michel-des-Saints	C5	103
St-Milaire	A1	97
St. Moritz	D2	35
St-Nazaire	B3	34
St-Nicolas	E5	103
St-Pacôme	G4	103
St-Pamphile	G5	103
St-Pascal	G4	103
St. Paul	E4	94
St. Paul, capital, Minn.	D1	126
St. Paul, river	A2	63
St. Paul's	C3	98
St. Paul's	A1	90
Saint Paul's, bay	B2	36
St. Peters	G2	100
St. Peters	C2	100
St. Peters, bay	C2	100
St. Peters, island	B2	100
St. Petersburg	D3	44
St. Petersburg, Fla.	E3	126
St-Philémon	F5	103
St. Pierre, island	M4	92
St-Pierre-Jolys	C4	96
St-Quentin	B1	97
St-Raphaël	F5	103
St-Rédempteur	K6	103
St-Rémi-d'Amherst	B5	103
St-Romuald	L6	103
St. Shotts	E5	98
St-Siméon	G4	103
St. Stephen	B3	97
St-Tite-des-Caps	F4	103
St-Tropez	D5	34
St-Vallier	F5	103
Saint Vincent, passage	B4	91
St. Vincent, gulf	Inset II	14
St. Vincent, island	B2	91
St. Vincent and the Grenadines		91
St. Walburg	A7	104
St-Zacharie	F5	103
Ste-Agathe-des-Monts	B5	103
Ste-Amélie	C4	96
Ste-Anne-des-Monts	K2	103
Ste-Anne-du-Lac	A5	103
Ste-Apolline	F5	103
Ste-Claire	F5	103
Ste-Croix	E5	103
Ste-Eulalie	D4	103
Ste-Foy	E5, K6	103
Ste-Luce	H3	103
Ste-Marie	E3	103
Ste-Monique	E3	103
Ste-Rose-du-Nord	F3	103
Ste-Thérèse	H5	103
Ste-Véronique	A5	103
Ste. Agathe	C4	96
Ste. Anne	C4	96
Ste. Rose du Lac	B3	96
Ste-Anne-de-Madawaska	A1	97
Saintes	B4	34
Sajama, mt.	A3	77
Sak, river	B3	71
Sakai	B3	8
Sakarya, river	B2	27
Sakha (Yakutiya), republic	C8	44
Sakhalin, island	I4	44
Saki	B3	8
Sakishima, islands	Inset II	8
Sakon Nakhon	C2	12
Sal Rei	B2	58
Sal, island	D2	58
Sala'ilua	A2	18
Salaberry-de-Valleyfield	B6	103
Salacgriva	C2	46
Salado, river	B3, C2	74
Salaga	B2	64
Salahiyah	A2	27
Salala	B3	25
Salamá	C4	85
Salamanca	D2	37
Salamís, island	Inset	51
Salar de Uyuni, salt flat	A4	77
Salaverry	B2	77
Salcedo	B1	89
Saldanha	A3	71
Saldus	B2	46
Salekhard	C5	44
Salelologa	B2	18
Salem	C6	20
Salem, capital, Oreg.	A1	126
Salerno	C2	38
Salerno, gulf	C2	38
Salford	C3	30
Salgótarján	B1	43
Salibia	B2	90
Salihorsk	C2	46
Salima	B2	68
Salina Cruz	E4	84
Salina, Kans.	D2	126
Salinas	C3	90
Salines, point	A2	91
Salisbury	C3	30

Name	Key	Page
Salisbury, island	N4	99
Salluit	A1	101
Sallum, as-	A1	56
Sally's Cove	C4	98
Salmon Arm	N6	95
Salmon River	A3	100
Salmon, Idaho	B1	126
Salmon, river	L4	95
Salo	B2	53
Salonta	A2	43
Saloum, river	B2	62
Salsette, island	Inset I	20
Salt Lake City, capital, Utah	B1	126
Salt Water, lake	Inset II	20
Salt, as-	A1	26
Salt, cay	D4	89
Salta	B1	74
Saltcoats	H9	104
Saltery Bay	K6	95
Saltillo, state capital	D2	84
Salto	B1	75
Salto del Guairá	E4	75
Salut, islands	B1	80
Salvador	E3	81
Salvage	E5	98
Salween, river	C2	10
Salyan	C3	45
Salzach, river	C3	39
Salzburg	C3	39
Salzburg Alps, range	C3	39
Salzgitter	B2	40
Samaná	C1	89
Samaná, bay	C1	89
Samaná, cape	C1	89
Samana, cay	C3	89
Samangan	B1	22
Samar, island	C4	12
Samar, sea	C3	12
Samara	D4	44
Samarian, hills	B1	26
Samarinda	C2	13
Samarqand	C3	23
Samarra	B2	24
Samawah, as-	C2	24
Sambalpur	D4	20
Sambre, river	C2	33
Samch'k	C4	9
Samina, river	B2	33
Samoa		18
Samokov	B3	50
Sámos, island	C3	51
Samothráki, island	C1	51
Samsø, island	C3	32
Samsø, strait	C3	32
Samsonvale, lake	Inset III	14
Samsun	D2	27
Samtredia	B3	45
Samur, river	B2	45
San	B3	58
San Andrés, island	Inset	78
San Angelo, Tex.	C2	126
San Antonio	B4, Inset	76
San Antonio	A3	85
San Antonio	C2	90
San Antonio Oeste	B5	74
San Antonio, cape	D4	74
San Antonio, cape	A2	88
San Antonio, Tex.	D3	126
San Baudilio de Llobregat	G2	37
San Bernardino, Calif.	B2	126
San Bernardo	Inset	76
San Blas, mts.	C2	87
San Borja	A2	77
San Carlos	B4	12
San Carlos	C3	75
San Carlos	B3	87
San Carlos de Bariloche	A5	74
San Carlos, river	B2	86
San Clara	A3	96
San Cristóbal	B2	77
San Cristóbal	B2	79
San Cristóbal	B2	89
San Cristóbal de las Casas	F4	84
San Cristóbal, island	B2	16
San Cristóbal, island	Inset	79
San Diego, Calif.	B2	126
San Felipe	D4	78
San Felipe	B1	84
San Félix	B3	76
San Fernando	B2	12
San Fernando	C4	37
San Fernando	B4	76
San Fernando	A2	91
San Fernando de Apure	C2	79
San Francique	A2	91
San Francisco	C3	74
San Francisco	B2	86
San Francisco de Macorís	B1	89
San Francisco, Calif.	A2	126
San Germán	A2	90
San Gimignano	B2	38
San Ignacio	B3	77
San Ignacio	B3	77
San Isidro	D2	90
San Jorge, gulf	B6	74
San José	B3	75
San José	C6	85
San José de Chiquitos	B3	77
San José de las Matas	A1	89
San José del Guaviare	B4	78
San Jose, Calif.	A2	126
San José, capital	B3	86
San José, river	B3	74
San Juan	B3	74
San Juan	B4	77
San Juan	A2	89
San Juan, capital	C2	90
San Juan, passage	D2	90
San Juan Bautista	D5	75
San Juan de Los Morros	C3	79
San Juan del Norte	C3	87
San Juan del Norte, bay	C3	87
San Juan del Sur	B3	87
San Juan, river	C3	87
San Juan, river	B3	87
San Lorenzo	D4	75
San Lorenzo	B2	79
San Lorenzo	B3	86
San Lorenzo	D2	90
San Lorenzo, cape	A3	79
San Lucas	C3	84
San Lucas, cape	B3	84
San Luis	B3	74
San Luis	D3	85
San Luis Potosí, state capital	D3	84
San Luis Río Colorado	B1	84
San Luis, lake	B2	77
San Marino		39
San Marino, capital	B1	39
San Marino, river	A1	39
San Martín, lake	A6	74
San Matías	C3	77
San Matías, gulf	C5	74
San Miguel	B2	86
San Miguel de Tucumán	C2	74
San Miguelito	C2	87
San Nicolás	C3	74
San Pablo	B3	12
San Pablo, river	B3	77
San Pawl il-Bahar	B2	36
San Pedro	D4	75
San Pedro de Atacama	C4	63
San Pedro de las Colonias	D2	84
San Pedro de Macorís	C2	89
San Pedro Sula	A2	86
San Pedro, river	C2	85
San Pietro, island	B3	38
San Rafael	B3	74
San Remo	A2	38
San Salvador de Jujuy	B1	74
San Salvador, capital	A2	86
San Salvador, island	Inset	79
San Salvador, island	C3	89
San Salvador, river	A2	75
San Sebastián	F1	37
San Sebastián	B2	90
San Severo	C2	38
San Valentín, mt.	B8	76
San Vicente	B2	86
San Vito, cape	C3	38
San, river	E2	11
San, river	F3	41
Sanaa, capital	A1	25
Sanaga, river	B2	65
Sanandaj	B2	22
Sanaw	C1	25
Sancti Spíritus	C2	88
Sand, river	E3	94
Sandakan	C2	13
Sanday, island	Inset I	30
Sandilands	C4	96
Sandougou, river	B3	62
Sandoy, island	Inset	32
Sandspit	A5	95
Sandur	Inset	32
Sandwich, bay	C2	98
Sandy Bay	H5	104
Sandy Cove	A3	100
Sandy Lake	D3	94
Sandy Lake	A4	96
Sandy Lake	B2	101
Sandy Point	B2	89
Sandy Point Town	A1	90
Sandy, island	B2	18
Sandy, island	B2	91
Sandy, lake	C4	98
Sanford	C4	96
Sangha, river	D2	66
Sangmélima	B3	65
Sangre Grande	A2	91
Sangro, river	C2	38
Sangudo	C4	94
Sankosh, river	B2	19
Sankrail	Inset II	20
Sankt Gallen	D1	35
Sankt Pölten	D2	39
Sankuru, river	B3	67
Sannar	C2	59
Sanski Most	A1	48
Sant Julià de Lòria	A3	36
Sant'Antioco, island	B3	38
Santa Ana	A2	77
Santa Ana	A2	86
Santa Ana, range	C1	75
Santa Ana, volcano	A2	86
Santa Bárbara	A2	86
Santa Barbara, Calif.	B2	126
Santa Catarina	C4	81
Santa Clara	C2	88
Santa Cruz	B3	77
Santa Cruz	A2	86
Santa Cruz de Tenerife	Inset I	37
Santa Cruz, island	Inset	79
Santa Cruz, islands	C2	16
Santa Cruz, river	A7	74
Santa Elena de Uairen	D3	79
Santa Elena, point	A4	79
Santa Fe	C3	74
Santa Fe, N. Mex.	C2	126
Santa Inés	B3	77
Santa Inés, island	B9	76
Santa Isabel	C3	90
Santa Isabel, island	A1	16
Santa Isabel, peak	A1	66
Santa Luzia, island	B2	58
Santa Maria	D2	58
Santa Maria	C4	81
Santa Maria di Leuca, cape	D3	38
Santa María, island	B2	18
Santa María, island	Inset	79
Santa Marta	B2	78
Santa Rita	B2	79
Santa Rosa	C4	74
Santa Rosa	B4	79
Santa Rosa de Copán	A2	86
Santa Rosa del Palmar	B3	77
Santa Rosalía	B2	84
Santana do Livramento	C5	81
Santander	E1	37
Santarém	A3	36
Santarém	C2	81
Santiago	B2	87
Santiago	A3	89
Santiago	B3	86
Santiago de Compostela	B1	37
Santiago de Cuba	E3	88
Santiago del Estero	C2	74
Santiago, capital	B4, Inset	76
Santiago, river	B1	77
Santo André	Inset II	81
Santo Antão, island	A1	58
Santo Domingo	B2	90
Santo Domingo de los Colorados	B3	79
Santo Domingo, capital	C2	89
Santo Tomás de Castilla	E4	85
Santos	D4, Inset II	81
Sanyati, river	B1	69
São Bernardo do Campo	Inset II	81
São Caetano do Sul	Inset II	81
São Domingos	A1	62
São Filipe	B4	58
São Francisco, river	D3	81
São Gonçalo	Inset I	81
São João de Meriti	Inset I	81
São José do Rio Prêto	D4	81
São Luís	D2	81
São Nicolau, island	B2	58
São Paulo	D4, Inset II	81
São Tiago, island	C3	58
São Tomé, capital	B4	63
São Tomé, island	B4	63
São Tomé, mt.	B4	63
São Tomé and Príncipe		63
São Vicente, cape	A4	36
São Vicente, island	A4	58
São Vincente	Inset II	81
Saona, island	D2	89
Saône, river	D3	34
Sapele	C5	65
Sapitwa, mt.	B3	68
Sapporo	Inset I	8
Sar, passage	B3	17
Sar-e Pol	B1	22
Sara Buri	B2	12
Sarajevo, capital	B2	48
Saramacca, river	B2	80
Sarandë	A4	49
Saransk	D4	44
Sarapiquí river	B2	86
Sarasota, Fla.	E3	126
Saratov	D4	44
Saravan	D4	11
Sarawak, state	C2	13
Saraya	D3	62
Sarbhang	B3	19
Sarcelles	Inset I	34
Sarda, river	A2	19
Sardinia, island	B2	38
Sargodha	D3	21
Sarh	B5	59
Sari	C2	22
Sariwln	A3	9
Sarjektjakko	C1	53
Sark, island	Inset II	30
Sarnia	C5	102
Saronic, gulf	Inset	51
ar Planina, mts.	B3	49
Sarstoon, river	A4	85
Sarstún, river	E4	85
Sary Tash	C3	23
Sarygamysh Koli, lake	B2	23
Saryshaghan	D2	23
Sasamungga	A1	16
Sasaram	D4	20
Sasebo	A3	8
Saskatchewan, river	G3	92
Saskatoon	D8	104
Sassandra	C4	63
Sassandra, river	C2, C4	63
Sassari	B2	38
Sassnitz	K1	40
Sata, cape	A4	8
Satpura, range	C4	20
Satsuma, peninsula	A4	8
Sattahip	B3	12
Satu Mare	B2	43
Sauble Beach	D3	102
Saudhárkrókur	B2	52
Saül	B2	80
Sault Ste. Marie	A1	102
Sault Ste. Marie, Mich.	E1	126
Sault-au-Mouton	G3	103
Saumur	B3	34
Saurimo	D3	70
Sauteurs	B2	91
Sava, river	B1, B2, C2	48
Savai'i, island	A2	18
Savalou	A3	64
Savan, island	B3	91
Savannah, Ga.	E2	126
Savannakhet	C3	11
Savé	B3	64
Savigny-sur-Orge	Inset II	34
Savinja, river	B2	48
Savona	B1	38
Savona	M6	95
Savonlinna	C2	53
Savu, sea	D2	13
Sawda, mt.	B2	24
Sawhaj	B2	56
Sawqirah	C2	25
Sawqirah, bay	C2	25
Saxony	C3	40
Saxony-Anhalt	C3	40
Sayabec	J3	103
Sayan, mts.	D6	44
Sayhut	C1	25
Sayward	K6	95
Saywun	B2	25
Sázava, river	B2	42
Scafell Pike, mt.	B3	30
Scarborough	C2	30
Scarborough	B1	91
Scarborough	F4, L5	102
Schaan	B2	33
Schaerbeek	C2	33
Schaffhausen	C1	35
Schefferville	D3	98
Schefferville	C3	101
Schelde, river	B2	33
Schellenberg	B1	33
Scheveningen	B2	32
Schiedam	B3	32
Schiermonnikoog, island	D1	32
Schleswig	B1	40
Schleswig-Holstein	B2	40
Schouwen, island	A3	32
Schreiber	C3	101
Schuler	E6	94
Schwäbisch Gmünd	C4	40
Schwedt	D2	40
Schweinfurt	B4	40
Schwerin	B2	40
Schweriner, lake	B2	40
Schwyz	C1	35
Scilly, islands	A4	30
Scone	A1	30
Sconser	A1	30
Scotstown	E6	103
Scott, island	C5	107
Scottsbluff, Nebr.	C1	126
Scugog, lake	G3	102
Scunthorpe	C3	30
Seaforth	D4	102
Seal Cove	C4	98
Seal, river	D1	96
Searchmont	A1	102
Seattle, Wash.	A1	126
Seawell	C4	91
Sebou, river	C1	57
Sebright	F3	102
Sechura, desert	A2	77
Seda, river	B3	36
Sedalia	E5	94
Sedan	D2	34
Sédhiou	B3	62
Sedley	F10	104
Seeley's Bay	J3	102
Sefadu	B1	63
Segbana	B2	64
Ségou	B3	58
Segovia	D2	37
Séguéla	C3	63
Segura, river	E3	37
Seinäjoki	B2	53
Seine, river	C2, Inset II	34
Sekake	B2	71
Sekondi-Takoradi	B4	64
Selebi-Phikwe	C2	69
Selenge Mörön, river	C2	11
Sélibaby	B4	58
Selínia	Inset	51
Selkirk	C4	96
Selvas, region	B2	81
Selwyn, mts.	C4	105
Seman, river	A3	49
Semara	B1	58
Semarang	C2	13
Sembabwane	B1	13
Sembawang	B1	13
Semeru, mt.	C2	13
Semey (Semipalatinsk)	E1	23
Semmering, pass	D3	39
Semois, river	D3	33
Sempach	C1	35
Sen, river	D2	11
Senaki	B3	45
Sendai	D2	8
Senegal		62
Senegal, river	B1, C2	62
Senkaku, islands	Inset II	8
Senmonorom	F3	11
Senne, river	C2	33
Senneterre	A4	101
Senta	B2	49
Seoul, capital	B4	9
Sepik, river	A2	15
Sept-Iles	C3	101
Septentrional, range	A1	89
Serangoon	B1	13
Serbia, republic	B2	49
Serengeti	A2	13
Serenje	C2	67
Sergino	B5	44
Sergipe	E3	81
Seria	A2	13
Serian	C2	13
Serov	D5	44
Serowe	B2	69
Serpent, island	D1	69
Sérrai	B1	51
Serranilla, bank	Inset	78
Serravalle	B1	39
Serrekunda	B2	62
Serule	B2	69
Sese, islands	C4	61
Sesheke	A3	67
Seti, river	A2	19
Sétif	C1	57
Setúbal	A3	36
Setúbal, bay	A3	36
Sevan, lake	C2	45
Sevastopol	C4	47
Seven Persons	E6	94
Seven Sisters Falls	D4	96
Severn, river	C3	30
Severn, river	B2	101
Severnaya Zemlya, islands	A6	44
Seville	C4	37
Sevran	Inset II	34
Sèvres	Inset II	34
Sewa, river	B2	63
Seward, Alaska	Inset I	126
Seychelles		70
Sfax	C2	57
Sfîntu Gheorghe	C3	43
Sha Tin	Inset	10
Shaanxi	D1	10
Shabwah	B1	25
Shache	A2	10
Shackleton Ice Shelf, glacier	C2	107
Shahr-e Kord	C3	22
Shaki	B3	65
Shalqar	B2	23
Sham, ash-	D1	25
Shamattawa	E2	96
Shamgong	B2	19
Shan, plateau	C2	12
Shanchung	B1	9
Shandong	E2	10
Shangani, river	A2	69
Shanghai	F2	10
Shannon	B2	31
Shannon, river	B2	31
Shantou	E3	10
Shantung	E2	10
Shanxi	F3	10
Shaoguan	E3	10
Shaoxing	F3	10
Shaoyang	E3	10
Sharbot Lake	J3	102
Sharjah	C2	25
Shashe, river	C2	69
Shashi	E2	10
Shatt al-Arab, river	C2	24
Shaunavon	B11	104
Shawinigan	D5	103
Sheberghan	B1	22
Shediac	E2	97
Sheerness	E5	94
Sheet Harbour	E3	100
Sheffield	C3	30
Sheguianda	D2	102
Sheho	G9	104
Shek Pik	Inset	10
Shelburne	B4	100
Shelburne	E3	102
Shelikhov, gulf	C9	44
Shell Lake	C7	104
Shellbrook	D7	104
Shelter Bay	N6	95
Shëngjin	A2	49
Shenyang	F1	10
Sherbro, island	A2	63
Sherbrooke	E2	100
Sherbrooke	E6	103
Sheridan, Wyo.	C1	126
Sherridon	A1	96
Sherwood Park	D4	94
Shetland, islands	Inset I	30
Sheva	Inset I	20
Shewa Gimira	B3	60
Shibar, pass	B2	22
Shibin al-Kawm	B1	56
Shijiazhuang	E2	10
Shikarpur	C4	21
Shikoku, island	B3	8
Shillong	F3	20
Shimizu	C3	8
Shimonoseki	A3	8
Shimonoseki, strait	A3	8
Shinano, river	C2	8
Shinas	C1	25
Shindand	A2	22
Shinyanga	B1	68
Shiono, cape	B3	8
Ship Cove	D3	98
Shippagan	E1	97
Shiraz	C4	22
Shire, river	B3	68
Shiretoko, cape	Inset I	8
Shizuoka	C3	8
Shkhara, mt.	B3	45
Shkodër	A1	49
Shkumbin, river	A2	49
Shoal Lake	A4	96
Sholapur	C5	20
Shostka	C1	47
Shreveport, La.	D2	126
Shrewsbury	C3	30
Shrirampur	Inset II	20
Shubenacadie	D2	100
Shubra al-Khaymah	B1	56
Shumen	E2	50
Shurugwi	B2	69
Shwebo	B2	12
Shymkent (Chimkent)	C2	23
Siahan, range	B4	21
Sialkot	E3	21
Siargao, island	C4	12
šiauliai	B2	46
Sibbald	E5	94
Siberia, region	C7	44
Sibiti	B5	66
Sibiu	C3	43
Sibu	C3	13
Sibuyan, island	B3	12
Sibuyan, sea	B3	12
Sicamous	N6	95
Sichuan	D2	10
Sicily, island	C3	38
Sicily, strait	B3	38
Sico, river	C2	86
Sicuani	C3	77
Sidi Bel Abbès	A1	57
Sidi Bou Zid	B2	57
Sidlaw, hills	B2	30
Sidney	L7	95
Sidon (Sayda)	A2	26
Sidra, gulf	C1	56
Sidvokodvo	B2	71
Siedlce	F2	41
Siegen	B3	40
Siempang	E1	11
Siemreab	B1	11
Siena	B2	38
Sieradz	D3	41
Sierra de Cayey, mts.	C2	90
Sierra de Loquillo, mts.	D2	90
Sierra Leone		63
Sierra Madre, mts.	B2	85
Sierra Madre, mts.	C5	85
Sierra Nevada de Santa Marta, mts.	B2	78
Sierra Nevada, mts., Calif.	A2	126
Sifton	B2	96
Siggiewi	B2	36
Sighetul Marmaœiei	A2	43
SighiΣoara	B2	43
Siguatepeque	B2	86
Siguiri	D2	62
Siirt	E3	27
Sikanni Chief	L3	95
Sikasso	B3	58
Sikhote Alin, range	E8	44
Sikkim (state)	E3	20
ªilal>	B2	49
Silay	B4	12
Silesia, region	C3	41
Silet	B2	57
Silgarhi	B2	20
Silhouette, island	C1	70
Siliana	B1	57
Silifke	C3	27
Silisili, mt.	B2	18
Silistra	F1	50
Silkeborg	B2	32
Silver City, N. Mex.	C2	126
Sima	B2	67
Simcoe, lake	E4	102
Simeulue, island	A1	13
Simferopol	C4	47
Simikot	B1	19
Simla	C2	20
Simon, lake	A6	103
Simonette, river	A4	94
Simonhouse	A2	96
Simpson, desert	D6	14
Sinai, peninsula	B2	56
Sinaloa	C3	84
Sincelejo	B2	78
Sinclair	A4	96
Sinclair Mills	M4	95
Sindhuli Garhi	C2	19
Siné, river	B2	62
Sines	A4	36
Singapore		13
Singapore, capital	B1	13
Singapore, island	B1	13
Singapore, strait	B2	13
Singen	B5	40
Singida	B2	68
Singur	Inset II	20
Sinp'o	C2	9
Sint-Niklaas	C1	33
Sint-Truiden	D2	33
Sin»iju	A2	9
Sió, river	B2	43
Siófok	B2	43
Sion	C3	35
Sioux City, Iowa	D1	126
Sioux Falls, S. Dak.	D1	126
Sioux Lookout	B2	101
Sipaliwini	A3	80
Siparia	A3	91
Siping	F1	10
Sipiwesk, lake	C1	96
Siple, island	B8	107
Siple, mt.	B8	107
Siquia, river	C2	87
Sirajganj	C4	21
Sirba, river	D2	64
Siret	D2	43
Siret, river	D2	43
Sirjan	D4	22
Sisaket	C3	12
Sisian	D3	45
Sisimiut (Holsteinsborg)	B2	106
Sisophon	C2	12
Siteki	B2	71
Sitka, Alaska	Inset I	126
Sittang, river	C2	12
Sittard	D3	32
Sittwe	B2	12
Siuna	B2	87
Siuri	D2	27
Siwah	A2	56
Sixaola, river	C3	86
Sjælland, island	C3	32
Skagen	C1	32
Skagerrak, strait	A3	32
Skaw, cape	C1	32
Skead	E1	102
Skeena, mts.	H3	95
Skeena, river	H4	95
Skeleton, coast	A1	70
Skellefteå	D2	53
Skellefteälven, river	D2	53
Skierniewice	E3	41
Skikda	B1	57
Skíros, island	B2	51
Skive	B2	32
Skjern, river	B3	32
Skookumchuck	P6	95
Skopje, capital	B2	48
Skovorodino	D8	44
Skownan	B2	96
Skye, island	A1	30
Slagelse	C3	32
Slaná, river	C3	43
Slatina	C3	43
Slave Lake	C3	94
Slave, river	F2	92
Slavonia, region	C2	48
Slavonska Po«ega	D2	48
Slavonski Brod	D2	48
Sliema	B2	36
Slieve Donard, mt.	B2	31
Sligo	B1	31
Sliven	D3	50
Slobozia	D3	43
Slough	Inset III	30
Slovakia		42
Slovenia		42
Slovenskérudohorie, mts.	B2	42
Sluch', river	B1	47
S{upsk	C1	41
Småland, region	B3	53
Smallwood, reservoir	D3	98
Smeaton	F7	104
Smederevo	B2	49
Smilovichi	C2	46
Smiltene	C2	46
Smith River	J1	95
Smithers	J4	95
Smithers Landing	J4	95
Smiths Cove	B3	100

Name	Key	Page
Smiths Falls	J3	102
Smithville	F4	102
Smoky, river	A3, A4	94
Smolensk	D3	44
Smolevichi	D2	47
Smolyan	C4	50
Smoothstone, lake	D6	104
Smoothstone, river	D6	104
Snake, river	C3	105
Snake, river	B1	126
Snaring	A4	94
Sneek	C1	32
Sněžka, mt.	B2	42
Śniardwy, lake	E2	41
Snow Lake	A2	96
Snowdon, mt.	B3	30
Snowdrift	F4	99
Snowflake	B4	96
Snug Harbour	D3	98
Snuol	E3	11
Soan-kundo, islands	B5	9
Sobaek, mts.	B5	9
Sobat, river	C3	59
Sobradinho, reservoir	D3	81
Sobral	D2	81
Soc Trang	A5	11
Sochi	A3	44
Socompa	C2	76
Socorro, N. Mex.	C2	126
Socotra, island	C2	25
Söderhamn	C2	53
Sofia, capital	B3	50
Sofia, river	B2	69
Sognafjord, fjord	B3	52
Soissons	C2	34
Sljøsln, bay	A3	9
Sokch'o	C3	9
Sokodé	B2	64
Sokoto, plains	C1	65
Sokoto	C1	65
Sokoto, river	C1	65
Sol, coast	D4	37
Sola	B1	18
Soldeu	B2	36
Solihull	C3	30
Solingen	A3	40
Solomon Is.		16
Solomon, sea	B2	15
Solosolo	C2	18
Solway, estuary	B2	30
Solwezi	B2	67
Somalia		60
Sombe, beach	E2	90
Sombor	A2	49
Sombra	C5	102
Somerset	B4	96
Somerset, island	K2	99
Someș, river	B2	43
Somme, river	C2	34
Somoto	A2	87
Son La	A2	11
Son, river	D4	20
Sonarpur	Inset II	20
Sønderborg	B4	32
Sondrio	B1	38
Songea	C3	68
Songhua, river	F1	10
Songkhla	B5	12
Songköl	D2	23
Sŏngnam	B4	9
Songnim	A3	9
Songwe, river	B1	68
Sonora	B1	84
Sonsonate	A2	86
Sonsoral, island	Inset	17
Sooke	L7	95
Sopron	A2	43
Sor, river	B3	36
Sorel	C5	103
Soria	E2	37
Sorø	C3	32
Soroca	B1	50
Sorocaba	D4	81
Sorong	E2	13
Soroti	C3	61
Sorraia, river	A3	36
Sorrento	C2	38
Sosnowiec	D3	41
Soso, bay	B3	17
Sota, river	B2	64
Sotk	C2	45
Sotouboua	B2	64
Soubré	C4	63
Soufrière	B4	90
Soufrière	A2	91
Soufrière, mt.	B1	91
Soufrière, volcano	A2	91
Souillac	C4	69
Soungrougrou, river	B1	71
Sources, mt.	B1	71
Souris	A4	96
Souris	C2	100
Souris, river	G11	104
Sous, plain	B2	57
Sous, river	B2	57
Sousúa	B1	89
South Africa		71
South Andaman, island	F6	20
S. Aultsivik, island	E3	98
South Australia	C2	14
South Baymouth	C2	102
South Bend, Ind.	E1	126
South Branch	B5	98
South Brook	C4	98
South Carolina		126
South China, sea	E4, Inset	10
South Comino, channel	B2	36
South Dakota	C1	126
South Downs, hills	C3	30
South Dum-Dum	Inset II	20
South Georgia, island		4
S. Gut St.-Anns		9
South Henik, lake	J4	99
S. Indian Lake	D1	96
South Korea		9
South Magnetic Pole	C3	107
South Male, atoll	A3	19
South Malosmadulu, atoll	A3	19
South Milford	B3	100

Name	Key	Page
S. Moose, lake	B2	96
South Orkney, islands	C12	107
South Ossetia, region	B3	45
South Pole	A17	107
South Rawdon	D3	100
South River	F2	102
South Ronaldsay, island	Inset I	30
South Saskatchewan, river	D8	104
South Shetland, islands	C12	107
South Shields	C2	30
South Taranaki, bight	B2	15
South Uist, island	A1	30
South West, cape	A4	15
South, island	A3	15
Southampton	C4	30
Southampton	D3	102
Southampton, island	L4	99
Southend	C4	104
Southend-on-Sea	D3	30
Southern Alps, mts.	A3	15
Southern Bug, river	B2	47
Southern Uplands, mts.	B2	30
Southland, plains	A4	15
Southport	C3	30
Southport	B2	100
Sovetskaya Gavan	E9	44
Soweto	C2	71
Soya, point	Inset I	8
Soyapango	A2	86
Soyo	B2	70
Sozh, river	E3	47
Spa	D2	33
Spain		37
Spandau	C2	40
Spanish	C1	102
Spanish Town	C3	88
Sparta	B3	51
Spartansburg, S.C.	E2	126
Spartivento, cape	D3	38
Sparwood	P6	95
Speightstown	A2	91
Spence Bay	K3	99
Spencer, gulf	C3	14
Spences Bridge	M6	95
Sperrin, mts.	A2	30
Spessart, mts.	B4	40
Spey, river	B1	30
Speyer	B4	40
Spiritwood	C7	104
Spišská Nová Ves	C2	42
Spithead, channel	C4	30
Split	C3	48
Split Lake	D1	96
Splügen, pass	D2	35
Spokane, Wash.	B1	126
Spoleto	C2	38
Spragge	C1	102
Sprague	D4	96
Spree, river	C3	40
Spring Bay	C2	102
Spring Coulee	D6	94
Spring Hall	A2	91
Springbok	A2	71
Springdale	C4	98
Springfield, capital, Ill.	E2	126
Springfield, Mass.	F1	126
Springfield, Mo.	D2	126
Springhill	C2	100
Springs	C2	71
Springside	H9	104
Springstein	C4	96
Springwater	B9	104
Spruce Grove	D4	94
Spy Hill	J10	104
Squamish	L6	95
Square Islands	D3	98
Sre Ambel	B4	11
Srebrenica	C1	48
Sredna Gora, mts.	C3	50
Sremska Mitrovica	A2	49
Sreng, river	B2	11
Sri Jayawardenepura, capital	A5	19
Sri Lanka		19
Srinagar	B2	20
Stafford	C3	30
Stand Off	D6	94
Standard	D5	94
Stanley	C2	97
Stanmore	E5	94
Stanovoy, range	D8	44
Stara Zagora	D3	50
Starbuck	C4	96
Starbuck, island	D2	17
Starnberg, lake	B5	40
Start, point	B4	30
Staubbach, falls	B2	35
Stavanger	A4	52
Stavropol	E4	44
Stayner	E3	102
Stead	C4	96
Steen River	B1	94
Stefanson, island	G2	99
Steinbach	C4	96
Steinkjer	C3	52
Stellarton	F2	100
Stellenbosch	A3	71
Stendal	B2	40
Stepanavan	B2	45
Stephenville	B5	98
Stettler	D5	94
Stevenage	Inset III	30
Stevenson, lake	C2	96
Stewart	H3	95
Stewart River	B4	105
Stewart, island	A3	15
Stewart, islands	B4, C3	105
Stewiacke	D2	100
Steyr	D2	39
Stikine	G3	95
Stikine, river	G2	95
Stirling	B2	30
Stirling	H3	102
Štip	C2	48
Stockerau	C2	39
Stockholm, capital	C3	53
Stoeng Treng	D2	11
Stoke-on-Trent	C3	30

Name	Key	Page
Stonecliffe	H1	102
Stoneham	E4	103
Stonewall	C4	96
Stoney Point	C5	102
Stony Mountain	C4	96
Stony Plain	D4	94
Stony Rapids	E1	104
Storå, river	B2	32
Storavan, lake	C1	53
Store, strait	C3	32
Storkerson, peninsula	G2	99
Stornoway	A1	30
Stornoway	E6	103
Storsjön, lake	B2	53
Storthoaks	A4	96
Stoughton	G11	104
Strakonice	A3	42
Stralsund	C1	40
Strangford	B2	30
Stranraer	B2	30
Strasbourg	D2	34
Strasbourg	F9	104
Stratford	D4	102
Stratford	E6	103
Stratford-upon-Avon	C3	30
Strathclair	A4	96
Strathlorne	F1	100
Strathnaver	L4	95
Strathroy	D5	102
Straubing	C4	40
Streymoy, island	Inset	32
Stromboli, island	C3	38
Stronsay, island	Inset I	30
Struga	A2	48
Struma, river	A3	50
Strumica	C2	48
Stryama, river	C3	50
Stuart, lake	K4	95
Stubbs	B2	91
Stuie	J5	95
Sturgeon, lake	C2	100
Sturgeon Falls	D3	101
Sturgis	H9	104
Stuttgart	B4	40
Subotica	A1	49
Suceava	D2	43
Suchiate, river	A5	85
Sucre, capital	A3	77
Sudan		59
Sudbury	E1	102
Sudd, region	B3	59
Suddie	B2	80
Sudeten, mts.	B3	41
Sudirman, range	E2	13
Suðuroy, island	Inset	32
Sue, river	B3	59
Suez	B2	56
Suez, canal	B1	56
Suez, gulf	B2	56
Sugandha	Inset II	20
Suhar	C1	25
Sühbaatar	C2	11
Suhl	B3	40
Suir, river	C2	31
Suita	B3	8
Sukabumi	B2	13
Sukang	B3	13
Sukhnah, as-	B2	27
Sukhothai	B2	12
Sukhumi	A3	45
Sukkur	C4	21
Sula, islands	D2	13
Sulaiman, range	C4	21
Sulaybikhat, as-	B2	24
Sulaymaniyah, as-	C1	24
Sulayyil, as-	B2	24
Sulima	B2	63
Sullana	A1	77
Sullivan, lake	E5	94
Sulu, archipelago	B5	12
Sulu, sea	A4	12
Sülüktü	A3	23
Sumatra, island	A2	13
Šumava, mts.	A3	42
Sumba, island	D2	13
Sumbar, river	B2	22
Sumbawa, island	C2	13
Sumbawanga	B3	68
Sumbe	B3	70
Summerford	D4	98
Summerland	N6	95
Summerside	C2	100
Summerville	E5	98
Summit Lake	K2	95
Summit Lake	L4	95
Šumperk	C3	42
Sumqayit	C2	45
Sumy	C1	47
Sun City	C2	71
Sun Kosi, river	C2	19
Sunch'ln	B5	9
Sundarbans, region	C7	21
Sunderland	C2	30
Sunderland	F3	102
Sundi	C1	63
Sundown	C4	96
Sundridge	F2	102
Sundsvall	C2	53
Sunnynook	E5	94
Sunset House	B3	94
Sunyani	B4	64
Sup'ung, reservoir	A2	9
Superior, lake	J4	92
Superior, Wis.	D1	126
Sur	C1	25
Sur (Tyre)	A2	26
Surab	C4	21
Surabaya	C2	13
Surakarta	C2	13
Surat	B4	20
Surat Thani	B4	12
Sûre, river	A2, B2	33
Surgut	C5	44
Surigao	C4	12
Surin	C3	12
Suriname		80
Suriname, river	B3	80
Surkhob, river	B1	23
Surma, river	E3	21

Name	Key	Page
Surprise	F1	95
Surt	C1	56
Surtsey, island	A3	52
Surud Ad, mt.	B1	60
Sussex	D3	97
Susuman	C9	44
Sutlej, river	D4	21
Sutton West	F3	102
Suva, capital	B3	17
Suvadiva, atoll	A4	19
Suwałki	F1	41
Suwanee, island	A4	8
Suwanose, island	A4	8
Suwar, as-	B2	27
Suwayda, as-	A3	27
Suwŏn	F1	9
Suzano	Inset II	81
Suzhou	F2	10
Svalbard, islands		5
Svay Rieng	D4	11
Svendborg	C3	32
Šventoji, river	C2	46
Svetozarevo	B3	49
Svilengrad	E4	50
Svishtov	D2	50
Svitavy	C3	42
Svobodnyy	D8	44
Swabian Jura, mts.	B4	40
Swains, island	A1	18
Swakopmund	B2	70
Swan Hills	C4	94
Swan Lake	B4	96
Swan River	A3	96
Swan, lake	A3	96
Swan, river	Inset I	14
Swansea	B3	30
Swaziland		71
Sweden		53
Swift Current	D5	98
Swift Current	C10	104
Swindon	C3	30
Świnoujście	B2	41
Switzerland		35
Swords	C2	31
Sydney	G1	100
Sydney	B2	17
Sydney, N.S.W., capital	E3, Inset IV	14
Syktyvkar	C4	44
Sylhet	E4	21
Syracuse (Siracusa)	C3	38
Syracuse, N.Y.	F1	126
Syrdarya, river	A1, C2	23
Syria		27
Syrian, desert	B1	26
Szczecin	B2	41
Szeged	C2	43
Székesfehérvár	B2	43
Szekszárd	B2	43
Szentes	C2	43
Szolnok	C2	43
Szombathely	A2	43

T

Name	Key	Page
Taabo, lake	D3	63
Tabar, islands	B2	15
Tabasará, mts.	B2	87
Tabasco	F4	84
Tabelbala	A2	57
Taber	D6	94
Tablas, island	B3	12
Tabligbo	B2	64
Taboão da Serra	Inset II	81
Tábor	B3	42
Tabora	B2	68
Tabou	C4	63
Tabriz	B2	22
Tabuaeran, island	D1	17
Tabuk	A1	24
Tabusintac	D1	97
Tacaná, volcano	A4	85
Tacloban	C4	12
Tacna	C4	77
Tacoma, Wash.	A1	126
Tacuarembó	C1	75
Tacuarembó, river	C1	75
Tacuarí, river	D2	75
Tadjoura	B2	60
Tadmur	B2	27
Tadoussac	G3	103
Taebaek-Sanmaek, mts.	C3	9
Taedong, river	B3	9
Taegu	C5	9
Taejŏn	B4	9
Tafahi, island	C1	17
Tafilah, at-	A2	26
Tafo	A2	64
Taganrog, gulf	D3	47
Tagish	C5	105
Tagish, lake	E1	95
Tagula, island	B3	15
Tagus, river	C3	37
Tahan, mt.	B2	13
Tahat, mt.	C2	57
Tahoua	B3	59
Tai, lake	F2	10
Tai, river	A2	10
T'aichung	B1	9
Taif, at-	B2	24
T'ainan	B1	9
Taipei, capital	B1	9
Taitao, peninsula	A8	76
T'aitung	B2	9
Taiwan		9
Taiwan, strait	E3	10
Taiyuan	E2	10
Taizz	A2	25
Tajikistan		23
Tajumulco, volcano	B4	85
Tak	B2	12
Taka, island	B1	16
Takamaka	Inset	70
Takamatsu	B3	8
Takara, island	A4	8
Takatsuki	B3	8
Takev	C5	11
Takipy	A1	96

Name	Key	Page
Takla Makan, desert	B2	10
Takla, lake	K3	95
Takua Pa	B4	12
Takutu, river	B4	80
Talagante	Inset	76
Talak, region	B2	59
Talamanca, range	C3	86
Talara	A1	77
Talas	C1	23
Talaud, islands	D1	13
Talavera de la Reina	D3	37
Talca	B5	76
Talcahuano	B6	76
Taldyqorghan	D2	23
Talish, mts.	C3	45
Tall Afar	B1	24
Tallahassee, capital, Fla.	E2	126
Tallinn, capital	C1	46
Taloqan	B1	22
Talsi	B2	46
Taltal	B2	76
Taltson, river	F4	99
Tamale	B2	64
Tamanrasset	B2	57
Tamarin	B3	69
Tamaulipas	E3	84
Tambacounda	C2	71
Tambo, river	C3, C4	77
Tâmega, river	B2	36
Tampa, Fla.	E3	126
Tampere	B2	53
Tampico	E3	84
Tampines	B1	13
Tampok, river	B2	80
Tamsagbulag	D2	11
Tamu	B1	12
Tamworth, N.S.W.	E3	14
Tan-Tan	B2	57
Tana, lake	B1	60
Tana, river	F4	61
Tana, river	F1	52
Tanabe	B3	8
Tanch'ln	C2	9
Tandil	D4	74
Tanega, island	A4	8
Tanen, range	B2	12
Tanezrouft, mts.	A2	57
Tanga	C2	68
Tanga, islands	B2	15
Tanganyika, lake	A2	68
Tanggula, range	C2	10
Tangier	E3	100
Tangier	C1	57
Tangshan	E2	10
Tanimbar, islands	E2	13
Tanjungpinang	B1	13
Tanna, island	C4	18
Tano, river	A3	64
Tanshui	B1	9
Tanta	B1	56
Tanzania		68
Taongi, island	B1	16
Taoudenni	C1	58
T'aoyüan	B1	9
Tapa	C1	46
Tapachula	F5	84
Tapajós, river	C2	81
Tapanahoni, river	B3	80
Tapeta	B2	63
Taquari, river	C3	81
Tara	D5	44
Tara, river	A2	49
Taraba, river	F3	65
Tarakan	C1	13
Taranto	D2	38
Taranto, gulf	D2	38
Tarapoto	B2	77
Tararua, range	C3	15
Tarat	B2	57
Tarbes	C5	34
Taree, N.S.W.	E3	14
Tarif	B2	25
Tarija	B4	77
Tarim, river	B1	10
Tarin Kowt	B2	22
Tarnobrzeg	E3	41
Tarnów	E3	41
Taroudant	C3	58
Tarragona	G2	37
Tarrasa	G2	37
Tarsus	C3	27
Tartu	D2	46
Tartus	A2	27
Tarvo	B3	77
Taseko, lake	L5	95
Tash Kömür	C2	23
Tashigang	C2	19
Tashir	B1	45
Tashkent, capital	C2	23
Tasikmalaya	B2	13
Tasman, bay	B3	15
Tasman, sea	D4	14
Tasmania	D4	14
Tata	C2	57
Tatabánya	B2	43
Tatamagouche	D2	100
Tataouine	C3	57
Tatar, strait	D9	44
Tatarstan, republic	D4	44
Tathlina, lake	E4	99
Tatla Lake	K5	95
Tatlayoko Lake	K5	95
Tatra, range	B2	42
Tau, island	A1	18
Taumaruni	C2	15
Taunggyi	C2	12
Taunton	C3	30
Taunus, mts.	B3	40
Taupo	C2	15
Taupo, lake	C2	15
Tauranga	C2	15
Taureau, reservoir	C5	103
Tauu, islands	B3	15
Tavan Bogd Uul, mt.	A1	11

Name	Key	Page
Taverny	Inset II	34
Taveuni, island	C2	17
Tavoy	C3	12
Tavoy, point	C3	12
Tawau	D2	13
Tawi Tawi, island	A5	12
Taxco	E4	84
Tay Ninh	B4	11
Tay, estuary	C2	30
Tay, lake	B2	30
Tay, river	B2	30
Taymouth	C2	97
Taymyr, peninsula	B6	44
Taymyriya, autonomous okrug	B6	44
Taza	C1	57
Tazin, lake	A1	104
Tazin, river	B1	104
Tbilisi, capital	C4	45
Tchamba	B2	64
Tchaourou	B3	64
Tchentlo, lake	K3	95
Tchibanga	A2	66
Te Anau, lake	A4	15
Tebicuary, river	D5	75
Tecomán	D4	84
Tecuci	D3	43
Tedzhen	C3	22
Tedzhen, river	C3	22
Teepee Creek	A3	94
Tees, river	C2	30
Teeswater	D3	102
Tefé	B2	81
Tegal	B2	13
Tegucigalpa, capital	B2	86
Tehek, lake	J4	99
Tehkummah	D2	102
Tehran, capital	C2	22
Tehuacán	E4	84
Tehuantepec, gulf	E4	84
Tehuantepec, isthmus	F4	84
Teifi, river	B3	30
Tekapo, lake	B3	15
Tekeze, river	B1	60
Tekirdağ	A2	27
Tekong, island	C1	13
Tel Aviv-Jaffa	B1	26
Tela	B2	86
Telavi	C4	45
Telde	Inset I	37
Telegraph Creek	G2	95
Teles Pires, river	C2	81
Telford	C3	30
Telkwa	J4	95
Telok Anson	A2	13
Telšiai	B2	46
Tema	C4	64
Temagami, lake	E1	102
Temburong, river	C2	13
Temirtau	D1	23
Tempisque, river	A2	86
Temuco	B6	76
Tena	C3	79
Téna Kourou, mt.	B3	64
Ténéré, desert	C1	59
Tenerife, island	Inset I	37
Tengiz, lake	C1	23
Tenkodogo	D3	64
Tennant Creek, N.T.	C1	14
Tennessee		E2 126
Tennessee, river	E2	126
Tenojoki, river	C1	53
Tenryu	C3	8
Teotihuacán	Inset	84
Tepexpan	Inset	84
Tepic, state capital	D3	84
Téra	A3	59
Terai, region	A2, C3	19
Teraina, island	D1	17
Teramo	C2	38
Teresina	D2	81
Teruel	F2	37
Termiz	C3	23
Termoli	C2	38
Ternate	D1	13
Terni	C2	38
Ternopil	B2	47
Terrace	H4	95
Terre Haute, Ind.	E2	126
Terrebonne	J5	103
Terreiro Velho	C1	63
Terrenceville	D5	98
Terschelling, island	C1	32
Teseney	A2	60
Teshio, river	Inset I	8
Tesiyn, river	B2	11
Teslin	B1	48
Teslin	C5	105
Teslin, lake	C5	105
Teslin, river	C5	105
Tessalit	D1	58
Tessaoua	B3	59
Testa del Gargano, point	D2	38
Tete	B3	68
Tête Jaune Cache	N5	95
Tétouan	C1	57
Tetovo	A1	48
Teulada, cape	B3	38
Teulon	C4	96
Tewkesbury	C3	30
Texarkana, Tex.	D2	126
Texas		126
Texcoco	Inset	84
Texel, island	B1	32
Teyateyaneng	A2	71
Tezoyuca	Inset	84
Tezzeron, lake	K4	95
Thaba-Tseka	B2	71
Thabana Ntlenyana, mt.	C2	71
Thai Nguyen	A2	11
Thailand		12
Thailand, gulf	B4, C4	12
Thames, river	C3, Inset III	30
Thamesville	D5	102
Thane	Inset I	20
Thanh Hoa	A2	11
Thanjavur	C6	20

	Key	Page
Thar, desert	C4	21
Thásos	C1	51
Thásos, island	C1	51
The Crane	C4	91
The Hague	B2	32
The Ovens	A2, C2	96
The Pas	D4	102
Thedford	D4	102
Thekulthili, lake	G4	99
Thelon, river	H4, J4	99
Theodore	H9	104
Thessalon	B1	102
Thessaloníki	B1	51
Thetford	D3	30
Thetford Mines	E5	103
Thicket	C4	91
Thicket Portage	C1	96
Thiès	A2	62
Thika	D4	61
Thimphu, capital	A2	19
Thingvellir	A2	52
Thio	C2	18
Thíra, island	C3	51
Thisted	B2	32
Thlewiaza, river	J4	99
Tholen, island	B3	32
Thomaston Corner	B3	97
Thompson	C1, D2	96
Thompson, river	M6	95
Thong Hoe	A1	13
Thorhild	D4	94
Thornhill	K5	102
Thorold	F4	102
Thrace, region	D4	50
Thracian, plain	C3	50
Three Kings, islands	B1	15
Thule, air base	B2	106
Thun	B2	35
Thunder Bay	C3	101
Thunersee, lake	B2	35
Thuringia	B3	40
Thuringian, forest	B3	40
Thurso	B1	30
Thurston, island	B9	107
Ti'avea	D2	18
Ti-n-Zaouâtene	B2	57
Tiáhuac	Inset	84
Tianjin	E2	10
Tibati	B2	65
Tiber, river	C2	38
Tiberias	B1	26
Tiberias (Galilee), lake	A1, B1	26
Tibesti, massif	B2	59
Tibet (Xizang)	B2	10
Tibet, plateau	B2	10
Tiburón, island	B2	84
Tichit	C3	58
Tichla	A2	58
Ticino, river	C2	35
Tide Head	C1	97
Tidjikdja	C3	58
Tien Shan, range	A1	10
Tierra del Fuego, island	C9	76
Tietê, river	Inset II	81
Tignish	A2	100
Tigre, river	B1	77
Tigris, river	B1	24
Tijuana	A1	84
Tikal	D2	85
Tikrit	B2	24
Tiksi	B8	44
Tiladummati, atoll	A1	19
Tilburg	C3	32
Tilbury	C5	102
Tillabéry	A3	59
Tilley	E6	94
Tillsonburg	E5	102
Tilomonte	C2	76
Tilston	A4	96
Timaru	B3	15
Timbuktu	C2	58
Timgad, ruins	B1	57
TimiΣoara	A3	43
Timmins	D3	101
Timor, island	D2	13
Timor, sea	B1	14
Tindouf	A2	57
Tingo María	B2	77
Tinkissa, river	C2	62
Tio	C2	60
Tipitapa, river	A2	87
Tipperary	B2	31
Tirana, capital	A2	49
Tiraspol	B2	50
Tiree, island	A2	30
TìrgoviΣte	C3	43
Tîrgu Jiu	B3	43
Tîrgu-MureΣ	C2	43
Tîrgu Neamœ	D2	43
Tîrgu Ocna	D2	43
Tirich Mir, mt.	D2	21
Tirso, river	B2	38
Tiruchchirappalli	C6	20
Tisa, river	B2	49
Tisdale	F8	104
Tista, river	C2	21
Tisza, river	C2	43
Titagarh	Inset II	20
Titano, mt.	B1	39
Titicaca, lake	A3, D4	77
Titov Veles	B2	48
Titova Mitrovica	B3	49
Tivaouane	A2	62
Tiverton	B4	30
Tiverton	D3	102
Tivoli	B2	91
Tiznit	B2	57
Tlaipan	Inset	84
Tlalnepantla	Inset	84
Tlaxcala, state capital	E4	84
Tlemcen	A1	57
Toa Payoh	B1	13
Toad River	K2	95
Toamasina	B2	69
Toba Kakar, range	C3	21
Tobago, cays	A4	91
Tobago, island	B1	91
Tobermory	D2	102
Tobi, island	Inset	17

	Key	Page
Tobin, lake	G7	104
Tobol, river	C1	23
Tobolsk	D5	44
Tobruk	D1	56
Tocantins	D3	81
Tocantins, river	D2	81
Toco	B2	91
Tocopilla	B2	76
Tofino	K6	95
Tofua, island	B3	17
Togo		64
Tokachi, river	Inset I	8
Tokaj	C1	43
Tokara, islands	A4	8
Tokat	D2	27
T!kch!k-kundo, islands	A4	9
Tokmok	D1	23
Tokorozawa	C3	8
Toktogul	C2	23
Toku, island	C2	17
Tokuno, island	Inset II	8
Tokushima	B3	8
Tokuyama	A3	8
Tokyo, capital	C3	8
Tôlanaro	B3	69
Toledo	D3	37
Toledo, mts.	D3	37
Toledo, Ohio	E1	126
Toliara	A3	69
Tolima, mt.	B3	78
Tolland	E4	94
Toltén, river	B6	76
Toluca, state capital	E4	84
Tolyatti	D4	44
Tom Price, W.A.	A2	14
Tomahawk	C2	91
Tomakomai	Inset I	8
Tomanivi, mt.	B2	17
Tombua	B5	70
Tomé	B6	76
Tomelloso	E3	37
Tomiko, lake	F1	102
Tomikawa	C3	8
Tomsk	D6	44
Tonalá	F4	84
Tonbridge	Inset III	30
Tone, river	C2	8
Tonga		17
Tongariro, mt.	C2	15
Tongatapu, island	B4	17
Tonghua	F1	10
Tongjos!n, bay	B3	9
Tongliao	F1	10
Tongsa	B2	19
Tongsa, river	B2	19
Tonkin, gulf	B2	11
Tonle Sap, lake	B2, C3	11
Tonle Sap, river	B2	11
Toowoomba, Qld.	D1	14
Topeka, Kans.	D2	126
Topley Landing	J4	95
Torbay	B4	30
Torbay	E5	98
Torghay, plateau	C1	23
Tormes, river	D2	37
Tornealven, river	D1	53
Torngat, mts.	D3	98
Tornio	B1	53
Torniojoki, river	B1	53
Toronto, capital	F4, K5	102
Tororo	D3	61
Torquay	G11	104
Torre del Greco	C2	38
Torrejón de Ardoz	Inset II	37
Torrelavega	D1	37
Torrens, lake	C2	14
Torrens, river	Inset II	14
Torrente	F3	37
Torreón	D2	84
Torres, islands	B1	18
Torres, strait	D1	14
Torrington	D5	94
Tórshavn	Inset	32
Tortosa	G2	37
Tortosa, cape	G2	37
Tortuga, island	C1	89
Tskhinvali	A3	45
Toru†	D2	41
Tõrva	C2	46
Tory Hill	G3	102
Tosa, bay	B3	8
Totness	A2	80
Tottori	D1	70
Touggourt	B1	57
Tougué	C2	62
Toulaman, river	B2	90
Touliu	B2	9
Toulon	D5	34
Toulouse	C5	34
Toungoo	C2	12
Toura, mts.	C2	63
Tourcoing	C1	34
Tournai	B2	33
Toussoro, mt.	B2	66
Toutes Aides	B3	96
Tovuz	A2	45
Towada, lake	D1	8
Townsville, Qld.	D1	14
Toxkan, river	E2	23
Toyama	C2	8
Toyama, bay	C2	8
Toyohashi	C3	8
Toyonaka	C3	8
Toyota	C3	8
Tozeur	B3	57
Tqvarcheli	A3	45
Trabzon	D2	27
Tracadie-Sheila	E1	97
Tracy	C3	97
Tracy	C5	103
Trafalgar	E2	100
Trail	O6	95
Tralee	B2	31
Tranås	B5	12
Transantarctic, mts.	B4	107
Transylvanian Alps, mts.	C3	43
Trapani	C3	38
Trasimeno, lake	C2	38
Trat	C3	12

	Key	Page
Traun, river	D2	39
Traverse City, Mich.	E1	102
Trebinje	B2	48
Treherne	B4	96
Treinta y Tres	C2	75
Trembleur, lake	K4	95
Trenche, river	C3	103
Trenaín	B2	42
Trent, river	C3	30
Trento	B1	38
Trenton	E2	100
Trenton	H3	102
Trenton, capital, N.J.	F1	126
Trepassey	E5	98
Tres Puntas, cape	B6	74
Treska, river	B2	48
Treviso	C1	38
Trier	A4	40
Triesen	B2	33
Triesenberg	B2	33
Trieste	C1	38
Trieste, gulf	A3	48
Triglav, mt.	A2	48
Tríkala	B2	51
Trim	C2	31
Trincomalee	C3	19
Trinidad	B2	77
Trinidad	B2	75
Trinidad	C2	88
Trinidad, island	A2	91
Trinidad, mts.	C2	88
Trinidad and Tobago		91
Trinity East	E5	98
Trinity, bay	E5	98
Triolet	C2	69
Tripoli (Tarabulus)	A1	26
Tripoli, capital	B1	56
Tripolitania, region	B1	56
Triton	D4	98
Trivandrum (Thiruvananthapuram)	C7	20
Trnava	A2	42
Trobriand, islands	B2	15
Trois-Pistoles	G3	103
Trois-Rivières	D5	103
Troisvierges	B1	33
Trollhättan	B3	53
Trombay	Inset I	20
Tromsø	D2	52
Trondheim	C3	52
Trondheimsfjord, fjord	B3	52
Trongisvágur	Inset	32
Troödos, mts.	A2	27
Trossachs	F11	104
Trout Creek	F1	102
Trout Lake	C3	94
Trout River	B4	98
Trout, lake	B4	94
Trout, lake	B2	101
Trouville	C2	34
Trowbridge	C3	30
Troyes	D2	34
Trujillo	B2	77
Trujillo	D3	79
Trujillo	B2	86
Trujillo	D3	37
Trujillo Alto	C2	90
Truro	B4	30
Truro	D2	100
Trutch	L2	95
Trutnov	B2	42
Tsaratanana, mts.	B1	69
Tsavo	E5	61
Tsedike, river	B3	71
Tsengwen, river	B2	9
Tsetserleg	C2	11
Tsévié	B3	64
Tshabong	A3	69
Tshane	A3	69
Tshaneni	B1	71
Tshikapa	B2	67
Tshuapa, river	B2	67
Tsiribihina, river	B2	69
Tsiroanomandidy	B2	69
Tsiteli-Tsqaro	D4	45
Tsu	A3	8
Tsugaru, strait	D1, Inset I	8
Tsumeb	C1	70
Tsumkwe	D1	70
Tsuruga	C3	8
Tsuruoka	C2	8
Tuam	B2	31
Tuas	A1	13
Tuasivi	B2	18
Tubarão	D4	81
Tübingen	B4	40
Tubmanburg	A2	63
Tucson, Ariz.	B2	126
Tucumcari, N. Mex.	C2	126
Tucupita	D2	79
Tucuruí, reservoir	D2	81
Tuen Mun	Inset	10
Tugela, river	D2	71
Tuguegarao	B2	12
Tuira, river	D2	87
Tuktoyaktuk	B3	99
Tuktut Nogait N.P.	D3	99
Tukums	B2	46
Tula	D3	44
Tula, ruins	D3	84
Tulcán	C2	79
Tulcea	E3	43
Tullamore	C2	31
Tulsa, Okla.	D2	126
Tulsequah	F2	95
Tulsipur	B2	19
Tultitlán	Inset	84
Tulun	D7	44
Tuma, river	B2	87
Tumaco	A4	78
Tumba, lake	B2	67
Tumbes	A1	77
Tumbler Ridge	M3	95
Tumen, river	C1	9
Tumuc-Humac, mts.	A2, B3	80
Tumucumaque, range	C1	81

	Key	Page
Tunbridge Wells	D3	30
Tundzha, river	E3	50
Tungsten	C4	99
Tunis, capital	C1	57
Tunis, gulf	C1	57
Tunisia		57
Tupelo, Miss.	E1	126
Tupiza	A4	77
Tupungato, mt.	B2	56
Tur, at-	C7	44
Tura	A2	23
Turan, lowland	A2	23
Turayf	A1	24
Turda	B2	43
Turfan, depression	C1	10
T»rgovishte	E2	50
Türi	C2	46
Turin	A1	38
Turin	D6	94
Turkana (Rudolf), lake	D2	61
Turkestan, mts.	A1	23
Turkey		27
Turkmenbashi	A2	22
Turkmenistan		22
Turks and Caicos Islands		89
Turks, islands	D4	89
Turku	B2	53
Turkwel, river	C2	61
Turnberry	A2	96
Turnbull	B2	96
Turneffe, islands	C2	85
Turnhout	C1	33
Turnor Lake	B4	104
Turnu MŒgurele	C4	43
Turquino, mt.	E3	88
Tursunzoda	A1	23
Turtle, lake	B7	104
Turtleford	B7	104
Tuscaloosa, Ala.	E2	126
Tuticorin	C7	20
Tutong	B2	13
Tutuila, island	AI, C2	18
Tuul, river	C2	11
Tuvalu		16
Tuxtla Gutiérrez, state capital	F4	84
Tuy Hoa	B4	11
Tuya, lake	G1	95
Tuz, lake	C2	27
Tuzla	B1	48
Tweed	H3	102
Tweed, river	C2	30
Twillingate	D4	98
Twin Butte	D6	94
Twin Falls, Idaho	B1	126
Two Creeks	A4	96
Tychy	D3	41
Tynda	D8	44
Tyndall	C4	96
Tyne Valley	B2	100
Tyne, river	C2	30
Tyrrhenian, sea	B2	38
Tyumen	D5	44
Tyva, republic	D6	44
Tywi, river	B3	30

U

	Key	Page
Uaboe	B1	16
Ubangi, river	B1	67
Ubayyid, al-	C2	59
Ube	A3	8
Úbeda	E3	37
Úbeda	E3	37
Uberaba	D3	81
Uberlândia	D3	81
Ubin, island	B1	13
Ubon Ratchathani	C3	12
Ucayali, river	C2	77
Uccle	C2	33
Uchiura, bay	Inset I	8
Uchquduq	B2	23
Ucluelet	K7	95
Udaipur	B4	20
Uddevalla	B3	53
Uddjaur, lake	C1	53
Udine	C1	38
Udmurtiya, republic	D4	44
Udon Thani	C2	12
Udu, point	C2	17
Uele, river	C1	67
Uelzen	B2	40
Ufa	D4	44
Uga, river	B2	70
Ugalla, river	B2	68
Uganda		61
Uíge	C2	70
Uitenhage	C3	71
Ujae, island	B2	16
Ujelang, island	A2	16
Ujjain	C4	20
Ujung Pandang	C2	13
Ukhta	C4	44
Ukhrul	G3	20
Ukerewe>	C2	46
Ukraine		47
Ulaan-Uul	C2	11
Ulaanbaatar, capital	C2	11
Ulaangom	B2	11
Ulan-Ude	D7	44
Ulansuhai, lake	D1	10
Ulchin	C2	9
Ulhas, river	Inset I	20
Uliastay	B2	11
Ulithi, atoll	B2	15
Ul»ng-do, island	C4	9
Ullapool	B1	30
Ullung, island	B4	40
Ulsan	C5	9
Ulster, province	C1	31
Ulu DaÆ (Mt. Olympus), mt.	B2	27
Ulúa, river	C2	86
Ulubaria	Inset II	20
Uluru (Ayers Rock)	C2	14
Uman	C2	47

	Key	Page
Umbeluzi, river	B2	71
Umboi, island	A2	15
Umbria	C2	38
Umeå	D2	53
Umeälven, river	C2	53
Umm al-Qaywayn	C1	25
Umm Bab	B3	25
Umm Qasr	C2	24
Umm Said (Musayid)	D4	25
Umniati, river	B2	69
Umtata	C3	71
Umuahia	C5	65
Umzingwani, river	B2	69
Una, river	A1	48
Unayzah	B1	24
Ungava, bay	L3	92
Ungheni	A2	50
Unión	C2	76
United Arab Emirates		25
United States		126
Unity	A8	104
Unst, island	Inset I	30
Upemba, lake	C3	67
Upernavik	B2	106
Upington	B2	71
Upolu, island	C2	18
Upper Arrow, lake	O6	95
Upper Liard	D5	105
Upper Lough Erne, lake	A	30
Upper Musquodoboit	E2	100
Upper Ohio	B4	100
Uppsala	C3	53
Ural	D4	44
Ural, mts.	B2	23
Uranium City	B1	104
Urawa	C3	8
Uranch	B2	23
Urmia, lake	A1	24
Uro%evac	B3	49
Uruapan	D4	84
Urubamba, river	C3	77
Uruguai, river	C4	81
Uruguay		75
Uruguay, river		74
Urukthapel, island	B3	17
Ürümqi	B1	10
Usak	B2	27
Ushuaia	B4	74
Usk, river	C3	30
Üsküdar	B2	27
Usmas, lake	B2	46
Ussuri, river	E8	44
Ussuriysk	C7	44
Ust-Ilimsk	D7	44
Ust-Kamchatsk	D10	44
Ust-Kut	D7	44
Ust-Ordynskiy Buryat, autonomous okrug	D7	44
Ust-Ordynskiy	C7	44
Uster	C1	35
Ústí nad Labem	B2	42
Ustica, island	C3	38
Ustka	C1	41
Ustyurt, plateau	A2, B2	23
Usulután	B2	86
Usumacinta, river	F4	84
Utah		126
Utah, beach	B2	34
Utan	Inset I	20
Utena	C2	46
Utikuma, lake	C3	94
Utila, island	B1	86
Utrecht	C2	32
Utsunomiya	C2	8
Uttaradit	B2	12
Utuado	B2	90
Utupua, island	C2	16
Uummannaq	B2	106
Uvira	C2	67
Uvs, lake	B1	11
Uwajima	B3	8
Uwaynat, al-	B2	56
Uyo	D5	65
Uyuni	A4	77
Uzbekistan		23
Uzhhorod	A2	47
U«ice	A3	49

V

	Key	Page
Vaal, reservoir	C2	71
Vaal, river	B2	71
Vaalserberg, mt.	D4	32
Vaasa	B2	53
Vác	B2	43
Vache, island	B2	89
Vadodara	B4	20
Vadsø	F1	52
Vaduz, capital	B2	33
Vágar, island	Inset	32
Vágur, island	Inset	32
Vahsh, river	A1	23
Vaitupu, island	C2	16
Vakhan, region	C1	22
Val Comeau	E1	97
Val Marie	C11	104
Val-d'Or	A4	101
Val-des-Bois	A6	103
Valcaño	D2	37
Valdecaño	D2	37
Valdepeñas	E3	37
Valdés, peninsula	C5	74
Valdivia	B6	76
Valemount	N5	95
Valença	A1	36
Valence	D4	34
Valencia	C1	79
Valencia	F3	37
Valencia, gulf	G3	37
Valenciennes	C1	34
Valera	B2	79
Valira d'Orient, river	B2	36
Valjevo	A2	49
Valka	C2	46
Valladolid	G3	84

	Key	Page
Valladolid	D2	37
Valle d'Aosta	A1	38
Valledupar	B2	78
Vallenar	B3	76
Valletta, capital	B3	36
Valley, river	A3	96
Valmiera	C2	46
Valparaíso	B4, Inset	76
Van	E2	27
Vancouver	L6	95
Vancouver, island	J6	95
Vanderhoof	K4	95
Vänern, lake	B3	53
Vanguard	C11	104
Vanier	H5	102
Vanier	L5	103
Vanikolo, islands	C2	16
Vanimo	A2	15
Vannes	B3	34
Vanrhynsdorp	A3	71
Vanscoy	D8	104
Vansittart, island	M3	99
Vantaa	B2	53
Vanua Balavu, island	C2	17
Vanua Lava, island	B1	18
Vanua Levu, island	B2	17
Vanuatu		18
Varanasi	D3	20
Vara«din	C2	48
Vardar, river	C2	48
Varde, river	B3	32
Vardenis	C2	45
Varkaus	C2	53
Varna	F2	50
Vasai	Inset I	20
Vasai, creek	Inset I	20
Vaslui	D2	43
Vassar	D4	96
Västerås	C3	53
Vatican City		39
Vatnajökull, ice cap	B2	52
Vättern, lake	B3	53
Vaudreuil	C6	103
Vaupés, river	B4	78
Vava'u, island	B4	17
Vavenby	N5	95
Vavuniya	B3	19
Vawkavysk	B3	47
Växjö	B3	53
Vayk	C3	45
Vega	C4	45
Vega Alta	C2	90
Vega Baja	C2	90
Vegreville	D4	94
Veimandu, channel	A3	19
Vejle	B3	32
Velika Morava, river	B2	49
Veliki, canal	A2	49
Veliko T»rnovo	D2	50
Vélingara	C3	62
Vélingara	B3	62
Vella Lavella, island	A1	16
Vellore	C6	20
Veneto	B1	38
Venezuela		79
Venezuela, gulf	B1	79
Venice	C1	38
Venice, gulf	C1	38
Venlo	D3	32
Venta, river	A2	46
Ventimiglia	A2	38
Ventspils	A2	46
Veracruz	E4	84
Vercelli	A1	38
Verde, river	C3	75
Verdun	D2	34
Verdun	J6	103
Vereeniging	C2	71
Verkhoyansk	C8	44
Verkhoyansk, range	C8	44
Vermillion, river	C4	103
Vermont	F1	126
Vernal, Utah	C1	126
Verner	E1	102
Vernon	N6	95
Vernon Bridge	C2	100
Vernon River	C2	100
Véroia	B1	51
Verona	B1	38
Verona	J3	102
Versailles	C2, Inset II	34
Vert, cape	A2	62
Verviers	D2	33
Vesoul	D3	34
Vesterålen, islands	C1	52
Vestmanna	Inset	32
Vestmannaeyjar	A3	52
Vesuvius, volcano	C2	38
Veszprém	A2	43
Vetauua, island	C2	17
Viana do Castelo	A2	36
Vianden	B2	33
Vibank	G10	104
Viborg	B2	32
Vicenza	B1	38
Vich	H2	37
Vichada, river	C3	78
Vichy	C3	34
Victoria	D6	76
Victoria	A1	36
Victoria	B2	100
Victoria Beach	C4	96
Victoria Beach	B3	100
Victoria Land, region	B5	107
Victoria Nile, river	C2	61
Victoria, capital	Inset	69
Victoria, capital	L7	95
Victoria, falls	B3	67
Victoria, lake	B4, C4	61
Victoria, peak	B3	85
Victoria, river	C1	14
Victoria, Tex.	D3	126
Victoriaville	E5	103
Vidin	A2	50
Viedma	C5	74

Name	Key	Page
Viedma, lake	A6	74
Vieille Case	A1	90
Vienna, capital	E2	39
Vienne, river	C3	34
Vientiane, capital	B3	11
Vieques	D2	90
Vieques, island	E2	90
Vieques, passage	D2	90
Vieques, sound	D2	90
Vierzon	C3	34
Viet Tri	A2	11
Vietnam		11
Vieux Fort	B3	91
Vigan	B2	12
Vignemale, mt.	B5	34
Vigo	B1	37
Vijayawada	D5	20
Vijosë, river	A3	49
Vila do Conde	A2	36
Vila Nova de Gaia	A2	36
Vila Real	B2	36
Vila Real de Santo Antonio	B4	36
Vila, capital	C3	18
Vilaine, river	B3	34
Vilanculos	C4	68
Vilcabamba, mts.	C3	77
Viljandi	C2	46
Vilkavi9kis	B2	46
Villa Ahumada	C1	84
Villa Hayes	D4	75
Villa María	C3	74
Villa Obregón	Inset	84
Villach	C4	39
Villahermosa, state capital	F4	84
Villalba	C2	90
Villarreal de los Infantes	F3	37
Villarrica	D4	75
Villavicencio	B3	78
Villazón	A4	77
Ville-Marie	C1	101
Villeneuve-Saint-Georges	Inset II	34
Villeroy	E5	103
Vilnius, capital	C2	46
Vilyuy, river	C7	44
Vilyuysk	C8	44
Viña del Mar	B4, Inset	76
Vincennes	Inset II	34
Vincente de Carvalho	Inset II	81
Vinces, river	B3	79
Vindelälven, river	C2	53
Vindhya, range	C4	20
Vinh	A2	11
Vinnitsa	B2	47
Vinson Massif, mt.	B10	107
Virden	A4	96
Virgin, river	C3	104
Virgin, islands		82
Virginia	F2	126
Virtsu	B2	46
Virunga, mts.	B1	61
Visakhapatnam	D5	20
Visayan, islands	B4	12
Visayan, sea	B4	12
Visby	C3	53
Viscount Melville, sound	F2	99
Viseu	B2	36
Vista	B4	98
Vista Hermosa	B4	78
Vistula, river	D2, E3	41
Viterbo	C4	96
Viterbo	C2	38
Viti Levu, island	A2	17
Vitoria	E1	37
Vitória	D4	81
Vitória da Conquista	D3	81
Vitsyebsk	E2	47
Vivian	C4	96
Vizcaíno, desert	B2	84
Vlaardingen	B3	32
Vladivostok	E8	44
Vlieland, island	B1	32
Vlissingen	A3	32
Vlorë	A3	49
Vltava, river	B3	42
Vöcklabruck	C2	39
Voinjama	B1	63
Vojvodina, province	A2	49
Volcano, islands	Inset III	8
Volga, river	E4	44
Volgograd	E4	44
Vologda	D3	44
Vólos	B2	51
Volta Redonda	D4	81
Volta, lake	C3	64
Volta, river	C3	64
Vonda	D8	104
Vorkuta	C5	44
Voronezh	D3	44
Vorotan, river	C3	45
Vorskla, river	C1	47
Võrts Järv, lake	D2	46
Võru	D2	46
Vosges, mts.	D2	34
Vostok, island	D3	17
Vranje	B2	49
Vratsa	B1	50
Vrbas	A2	49
Vrbas, river	B1	48
Vr%ac	B2	49
Vryburg	B2	71
Vukovar	B2	49
Vunaniu, bay	A3	17
Vung Tau-Con Dao	B4	11
Vunisea	B3	17

W

Name	Key	Page
Wa	A1	64
Waal, river	C3	32
Wabana	A2	15
Wabamun, lake	C4	94
Wabana	E5	98
Wabasca, river	C4	94
Wabe Gestro, river	C2	15
Wabe Shebele, river	D3	60
Wabowden	B2	96
Wabush	D4	98
Waco, Tex.	D2	126
Wad Madani	C2	59

Name	Key	Page
Waddan	C2	56
Waddenzee, sound	C1	32
Waddington, mt.	K5	95
Wadena	G9	104
Wadi al-Malik, river	B2	59
Wadi as-Sirhan, depression	B2	26
Wadi Halfa	C1	59
Wafrah, al-	B3	24
Wagga Wagga, N.S.W.	D3	14
Waigeo, island	E2	13
Waikato, river	C2	15
Waimamaku	B2	15
Waingapu	D2	13
Wairau, river	B3	15
Waitaki, river	B3	15
Wajh, al-	A1	24
Wajir	F3	61
Wakasa, bay	B3	8
Wakaw	E8	104
Wakayama	B3	8
Wakefield	C3	30
Wakkanai	Inset I	8
Wakomata, lake	B1	102
Wakrah, al-	D3	25
Walachia, region	B3	43
Wa{brzych	C3	41
Walcheren, island	A3	32
Walden	D1	102
Waldersee	B4	96
Waldheim	D8	104
Walensee, lake	D1	35
Walkerton	D3	102
Wallace	D3	100
Wallaceburg	C5	102
Walsall	C3	30
Walton	D4	102
Walvis Bay	B2	70
Wami, river	C2	68
Wanaka, lake	A3	15
Wanapitei, lake	E1	102
Wandering River	D3	94
Wando	B5	9
Wanganui	C2	15
Wanham	A3	94
Wapawekka, lake	F5	104
Wapawsik	B1	96
Wapiti, river	A4	94
Warangal	C5	20
Warbah, island	C1	24
Wardlow	E6	94
Ware	K2	95
Warman	D8	104
Warner	D6	94
Warren	C4	96
Warren	E1	102
Warren Landing	C2	96
Warri	C5	65
Warrington	C3	30
Warrnambool, Vic.	D3	14
Warsaw, capital	E2, C2	41
Warta, river	B2, C2	41
Warwick	C3	30
Wasa	P6	95
Wasaga Beach	F3	102
Wasagaming	B4	96
Wash, bay	D3	30
Washago	F3	102
Washington	A1	126
Washington, cape	A3	17
Washington, capital, D.C.	F2	126
Waskada	A4	96
Waskaganish	A3	101
Waskesiu Lake	D7	104
Waspam	C1	87
Water Valley	C5	94
Water, cays	A3	89
Waterborough	C3	97
Waterbury, lake	F2	104
Waterford	C2	31
Waterhen, lake	B3	96
Waterloo	E4	102
Waterloo	D6	103
Watertown, N.Y.	F1	126
Watford	Inset III	30
Watford	D5	102
Wathaman, lake	G3	104
Watrous	E9	104
Watsa	C1	67
Watson	F8	104
Watson Lake	D5	105
Wau	A2	15
Wavre	C2	33
Waw	B3	59
Wawa	D3	101
Wawa, river	B1	87
Wawanesa	B4	96
Weagamow Lake	B2	101
Webbwood	D1	102
Webequie	C2	101
Webi Shabeelle, river	B3	60
Wedgeport	A4	100
Weert	C3	32
Wei, river	D2	10
Weiden	C4	40
Weifang	E2	10
Weimar	B3	40
Weipa, Qld.	D1	14
Weitzel, lake	D3	104
Wekusko	B2	96
Wekusko, lake	B2	96
Weldiya	C2	60
Welkom	C2	71
Wellesley	A2	100
Wellington, capital	B3	15
Wellington, island	A8	76
Wells	C3	39
Welsford	C3	97
Welshpool	B3	30
Welwyn	A4	96
Wembere, river	B1	68
Wenchi	B3	64
Weno	C2	15
Weno, island	C2	15
Wenshan	D3	10
Wentworth	D2	100
Wentzel, lake	C1	94
Wenzhou	F3	10

Name	Key	Page
Werder	D3	60
Werra, river	B3	40
Weser, river	B2	40
Wesley	B2	90
Wesleyville	E4	98
West Antarctica	A8	107
West Devon	A2	100
West Frisian, islands	B1	32
West Ice Shelf, glacier	C1	107
West Palm Beach, Fla.	E3	126
West Point	A2	100
West Road, river	K4	95
West St. Modeste	C3	98
West Siberian, plain	C5	44
West Virginia	E2	126
Westbank	N6	95
Westbourne	B4	96
Western Australia	B2	14
Western Dvina, river	C2	46
Western Ghats, mts.	B5	20
Western Sahara		58
Western, channel	C5	9
Westerschelde, channel	A3	32
Westfield	C3	97
Westlock	D4	94
Westminster	Inset III	30
Weston	J5	102
Westport	B3	15
Westport	B3	31
Westport	J3	102
Westray	A2	96
Westray, island	Inset I	30
Wetar, island	D2	13
Wetaskiwin	D5	94
Wete	C1	68
Wetzlar	B3	40
Wewak	A1	15
Wexford	C2	31
Weyakwin	E6	104
Weyburn	G11	104
Weymouth	A3	100
Whakatane	C2	15
Whale Cove	K4	99
Whaletown	K6	95
Whangarei	B2	15
Wheatland	A4	96
Wheatley	C5	102
Wheeling, W. Va.	E1	126
Whistler	L6	95
Whitbourne	E5	98
Whitby	G4	102
White Fox	F7	104
White Lake	J2	102
White Nile, river	C3	59
White Rock	L6	95
White Sands	C3	100
White Volta, river	B1, D2	64
White, bay	C4	98
White, island	L3	99
White, river	A4	105
White, sea	C3	44
Whitecourt	C4	94
Whitefish Falls	D1	102
Whitefish, bay	A1	102
Whitehaven	B2	30
Whitehorse	C5	105
Whitelaw	A3	94
Whiteman, range	A2	15
Whitemouth	D4	96
Whitestone, river	B3	105
Whitewood	H10	104
Whitney	G2	102
Whitney mt., Calif.	B2	126
Wholdaia, lake	H4	99
Whyalla, S.A.	C3	14
Whycocomagh	F2	100
Wiarton	D3	102
Wichita Falls, Tex.	D2	126
Wichita, Kans.	D2	126
Wick	B1	30
Wicklow	C2	31
Wicklow Head, cape	D2	31
Wicklow, mts.	C2	31
Wiener Neustadt	E3	39
Wieprz, river	F3	41
Wiesbaden	B3	40
Wigan	C3	30
Wight, island	C3	30
Wilberforce	G2	102
Wilge, river	C2	71
Wilhelm, mt.	A2	15
Wilhelmina, canal	B3	32
Wilhelmina, mts.	A2	80
Wilhelmshaven	B2	40
Wilkes Land, region	C3	107
Wilkie	B8	104
William, river	B2	104
Williams Harbour	D3	98
Williams Lake	L5	95
Williamsport	C4	98
Williston, Lake	K3	95
Willow Bunch	E11	104
Willow Creek	A11	104
Willowbunch, lake	E11	104
Wilmington, Del.	F2	126
Wilmington, N.C.	F2	126
Wilmot	B3	100
Wiltondale	C4	98
Wiltz	A2	33
Winchester	C3	30
Winchester	K2	102
Wind, river	B3	105
Windermere	O6	95
Windermere	F2	102
Windfall	B4	94
Windhoek, capital	B2	70
Windsor	Inset III	30
Windsor	C3	100
Windsor	C5	102
Windsor	D6	103
Windward Group	B2	58
Windward Islands	B4	91
Windward, passage	F3	88
Winifred, lake	B4	94
Winisk	C1	101
Winisk, lake	C2	101
Winisk, river	C2	101

Name	Key	Page
Winkler	C4	96
Winneba	B4	64
Winnemucca, Nev.	B1	126
Winnipeg	C4, D2	96
Winnipeg Beach	C4	96
Winnipeg, lake	B3, C4, D2	96
Winnipeg, river	D4	96
Winnipegosis	B3	96
Winnipegosis, lake	A3	96
Winslow, Ariz.	B2	126
Winston-Salem, N.C.	E2	126
Winter Harbour	H6	95
Winterthur	C1	35
Wisconsin	D1	126
Wismar	B2	40
Witless Bay	E5	98
Witten	A3	40
Wittenberg	C3	40
Wittenberge	B2	40
Witu, island	A2	15
Wiwili	B2	87
W{adys{awowo	D1	41
W{oc{awek	D2	41
Woburn	F6	103
Wodzis{aw zl]ski	D3	41
Woking	A3	94
Wolf, lake	C5	105
Wolfsberg	D4	39
Wolfsburg	B2	40
Wolfville	C2	100
Wollaston Lake	G2	104
Wollaston, lake	H2	104
Wollaston, peninsula	E3	99
Wollongong, N.S.W.	E3	14
Wolseley	G10	104
Wolverhampton	C3	30
Wong, river	A2	19
Wonowon	M3	95
Wonsan	B3	9
Wood Islands	C3	100
Woodbridge	J5	102
Woodlands	B1	13
Woodlands	C4	96
Woodlark (Muyua), island	B2	15
Woodnorth	A4	96
Woodridge	C4	96
Woods, lake	B3	101
Woodstock	B2	97
Woodstock	A2	100
Woodstock	E4	102
Woody Point	C4	98
Woomera, S.A.	C3	14
Worcester	C3	30
Worcester	A3	71
Worcester, Mass.	F1	126
Worms	B4	40
Wotho, island	B1	16
Wotje, island	C1	16
Wrangel, island	B10	44
Wrath, cape	B1	30
Wreck Cove	D5	98
Wrentham	D6	94
Wrigley	G4	99
Wroc{aw	C3	41
Wuhan	E2	10
Wuhu	E2	10
Wukari	E4	65
Wum	B2	65
Wuppertal	A3	40
Würzburg	B4	40
Wutivi, mt.	B1	63
Wuwei	D2	10
Wuxi	F2	10
Wuzhong	D2	10
Wuzhou	E3	10
Wye, river	C3	30
Wyndham, W.A.	B1	14
Wynyard	F9	104
Wyoming	C1	126

X

Name	Key	Page
Xaçmaz	C2	45
Xai-Xai	B5	68
Xam Nua	C1	11
Xangongo	C5	70
Xankändi	B3	45
Xánthi	C1	51
Xau, lake	B2	69
Xi'an	D2	10
Xi, river	E3	10
Xiamen	E3	10
Xiangfan	E2	10
Xiangkhoang	B2	11
Xiangtan	E3	10
Xigaze	B3	10
Xingu, river	C3	81
Xining	D2	10
Xinjiang Uygur	B1	10
Xinxiang	E2	10
Xinyang	E2	10
Xochimilco	Inset	84
Xuddur	A3	60
Xuzhou	E2	10

Y

Name	Key	Page
Ya'an	D2	10
Yablonovyy, range	D7	44
Yabucoa	D2	90
Yacuiba	B4	77
Yafran	B1	56
Yaguarí, river	C1	75
Yaguarón, river	D2	75
Yahk	O6	95
Yakima, Wash.	A1	126
Yaku, island	A4	8
Yakutsk	C8	44
Yale	M6	95
Yalinga	B2	66
Yalta	C4	47
Yamagata	D2	8
Yamaguchi	A3	8
Yamal, peninsula	C5	44
Yamalo-Nenesiya, autonomous okrug	C5	44

Name	Key	Page
Yambio	B4	59
Yambol	E3	50
Yamoussoukro, capital	D3	63
Yampi, sound	B1	14
Yamuna, river	C3	20
Yan, river	B3	19
Yanbu al-Bahr	A1	24
Yangambi	C1	67
Yangd!k	B3	9
Yangon (Rangoon), capital	C3	12
Yangquan	E2	10
Yangtze, river	C2, D2	10
Yangzhou	E2	10
Yanji	F1	10
Yantai	F2	10
Yantra, river	D2	50
Yao	B3	8
Yaoundé, capital	B3	65
Yap, islands	A2	15
Yapen, island	E2	13
Yaque del Norte, river	A1	89
Yaque del Sur, river	A2	89
Yaqui, river	C2	84
Yare, river	D3	30
Yaren, capital	B3	16
Yariga, mt.	C2	8
Yarmouth	A4	100
Yaroslavl	D3	44
Yasawa, island group	A2	17
Yasuj	C3	22
Yata, river	A2	77
Yates	B4	94
Yatsushiro	A3	8
Yauco	B2	90
Yavarí, river	C1	77
Yaviza	D2	87
Yazd	C3	22
Yazd, region	C3	22
Ybbs, river	D2	39
Ye	C3	12
Yeboah	C3	30
Yecla	F3	37
Yeguas, point	D2	90
Yekaterinburg	D5	44
Yekepa	B2	63
Yell, island	Inset I	30
Yellow Grass	F11	104
Yellow, sea	F2	10
Yellowknife, capital	F4	99
Yemen		25
Yen Bai	A2	11
Yendi	B2	64
Yenisey, river	C6	44
Yeovil	C4	30
Yerevan, capital	B2	45
Yesilhrmak, river	D2	27
Yeu, island	B3	34
Yevlax	B2	45
Yevpatoriya	B4	47
Yevrey, autonomous oblast	E8	44
Yi, river	C2	75
Yialousa	C1	27
Yibin	D3	10
Yichang	E2	10
Yichun	F1	10
Yin Shan, mts.	E1	10
Yinchuan	D2	10
Yingkou	F1	10
Yining	B1	10
Ylikitka, lake	C1	53
Ylivieska	B2	53
Yoboki	B3	60
Yogyakarta	C2	13
Yojoa, lake	B2	86
Yokkaichi	C3	8
Yokohama	C3	8
Yokosuka	C3	8
Yola	G3	65
Yom, river	B2	12
Yomou	D4	62
Yonago	B3	8
Yonaguni, island	Inset II	8
Yonne, river	C2	34
Yopal	B3	78
York	C3	30
York	B2	100
York	K5	102
York Factory	E1	96
York, cape	D1	14
Yorkton	H9	104
Yoro	B2	86
Yoron, island	Inset II	8
Yoshino, river	B3	8
Yoshkar-Ola	D4	44
Y!su	B5	9
Yotvata	B3	26
Youghal	C3	31
Young	E9	104
Youngs Cove	D2	97
Ypané, river	D3	75
Ypoá, lake	D4	75
Ypres	A2	33
Ysyk-Köl, lake	E1	23
Yü Shan, mt.	F2	10
Yuan, river	D3	10
Yubari	Inset I	8
Yucatán, channel	A2	88
Yucatán, peninsula	G4	84
Yuen Long	Inset	10
Yueyang	E3	10
Yugoslavia		49
Yukon, river	D2	92
Yuma, Ariz.	B2	126
Yumen	C2	10
Yuna, river	B2	89
Yungas, region	A3	77
Yungho	B1	9
Yunnan	D3	10
Yurimaguas	B2	77
Yuscarán	B3	86
Yushu	C2	10
Yuzhno-Sakhalinsk	E9	44
Yverdon	A2	35

Z

Name	Key	Page
Zaanstad	B2	32

Name	Key	Page
Zabbar	C2	36
Zabid	A2	25
Zabol	E3	22
Zabrze	D3	41
Zacapa	D5	85
Zacatecas, state capital	D3	84
Zadar	B3	48
Zafra	C3	37
Zagazig	B1	56
Zaghouan	C1	57
Zagreb, capital	B2	48
Zagros, mts.	E4	22
Zahedan	E4	22
Zahlah	A2	26
Zaje∆ar	C3	49
Zákinthos, island	B3	51
Zakopane	D4	41
Zala, river	A2	43
Zalaegerszeg	A2	43
ZalŒu	B2	43
Zambales, mts.	B3	12
Zambezi	C2	67
Zambezi, river	A3, B3	67
Zambia		67
Zamboanga	B5	12
Zamboanga, peninsula	B5	12
Zamora	D2	37
Zamora	B5	79
Zamora, river	B4	79
Zamoj~	F3	41
Zanderij	B2	80
Zanjan	B2	22
Zanzibar	C2	68
Zao, mt.	D2	8
Zapadna Morava, river	B3	49
Zapatera, island	B3	87
Zaporizhzhia	D2	47
Zaqatala	B2	45
Zarafobod	A1	23
Zarafshon	B2	23
Zaragoza	F2	37
Zaranj	A2	22
Zareh Sharan	B2	22
Zaria	D2	65
Zarqa, az-	B1	26
Zarzis	C3	57
Zavidovi~i	B1	48
Zaysan	E2	23
Zaysan, lake	E2	23
Zebbug	A1	36
Zeebrugge	B1	33
Zefat	B2	26
Zenica	B1	48
Zeravshan, mts.	A2	23
Zeravshan, river	A1, B2	23
Zermatt	B2	35
Zestaponi	B3	45
Zeta, river	A3	49
Zevulun, plain	B1	26
Zêzere, river	B3	36
Zhambyl (Dzhambul)	D2	23
Zhangjiakou	E1	10
Zhangye	D2	10
Zhanjiang	E3	10
Zhejiang	E3	10
Zhelaniya, cape	B5	44
Zhengzhou	E2	10
Zhenjiang	E2	10
Zhezqazghan	C2	23
Zhitomir	B1	47
Zhlobin	D3	47
Zhob, river	C3	21
Zhoda	C4	96
Zhu, river	E3	10
Zhuzhou	E3	10
Zibo	E2	10
Zielona Góra	B3	41
Zigong	D3	10
Ziguinchor	A3	62
Zillah	C2	56
Zillertal Alps, range	B3	39
Zima, lake	A2	94
Zimbabwe		69
Zinder	B3	59
Zion	C3	90
Zittau	C3	40
Ziway, lake	C3	60
Zlatibor, mts.	A3	49
Zlín	C3	42
Znojmo	C4	42
Zomba	C3	68
Zonguldak	B2	27
Zorzor	B2	63
Zouar	B2	59
Zouîrât	B2	58
Zrenjanin	B2	49
Zug	C1	35
Zugdidi	A3	45
Zugspitze, mt.	B5	40
Zuid-Willemsvaart, canal	C3	32
Zújar, reservoir	D3	37
Zululand, region	D2	71
Zunyi	D3	10
Zürich	C1	35
Zürichsee, lake	C1	35
Zurrieq	B2	36
Zuwarah	B1	56
Zvishavane	B2	69
Zvolen	C3	42
Zvornik	B2	48
Zwedru	C3	63
Zwickau	C3	40
Zwolle	D2	32
Zyryanka	C9	44

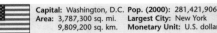

Capital: Washington, D.C. **Pop. (2000):** 281,421,906
Area: 3,787,300 sq. mi. **Largest City:** New York
9,809,200 sq. km. **Monetary Unit:** U.S. dollar

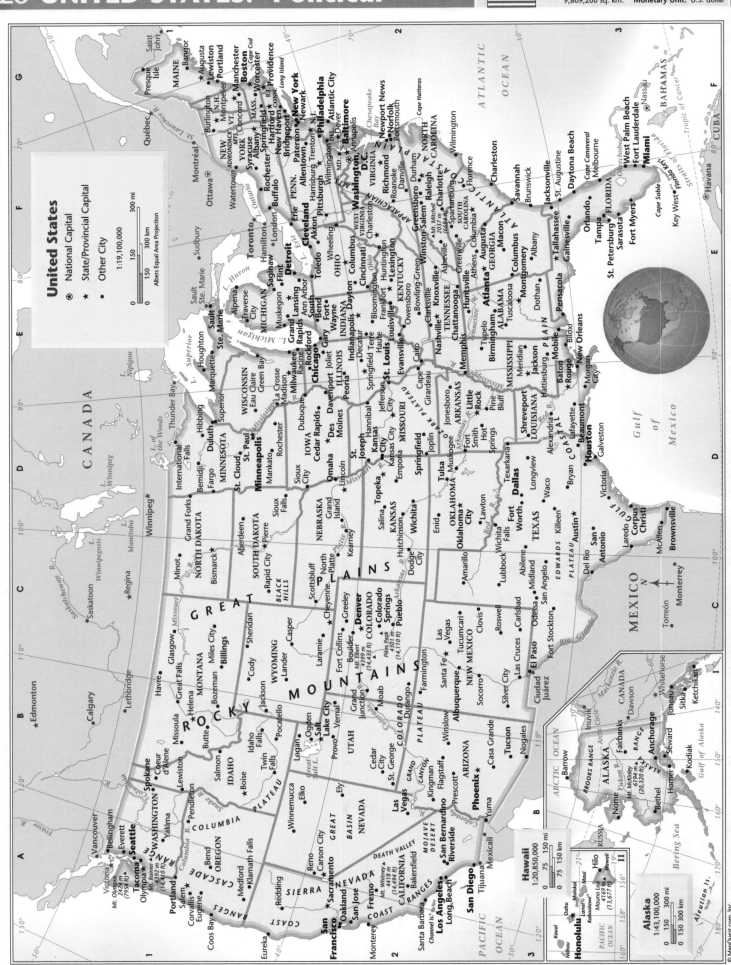

United States
⊛ National Capital
★ State/Provincial Capital
• Other City

1:19,100,000

0   150   300 mi

0   150   300 km

Albers Equal Area Projection

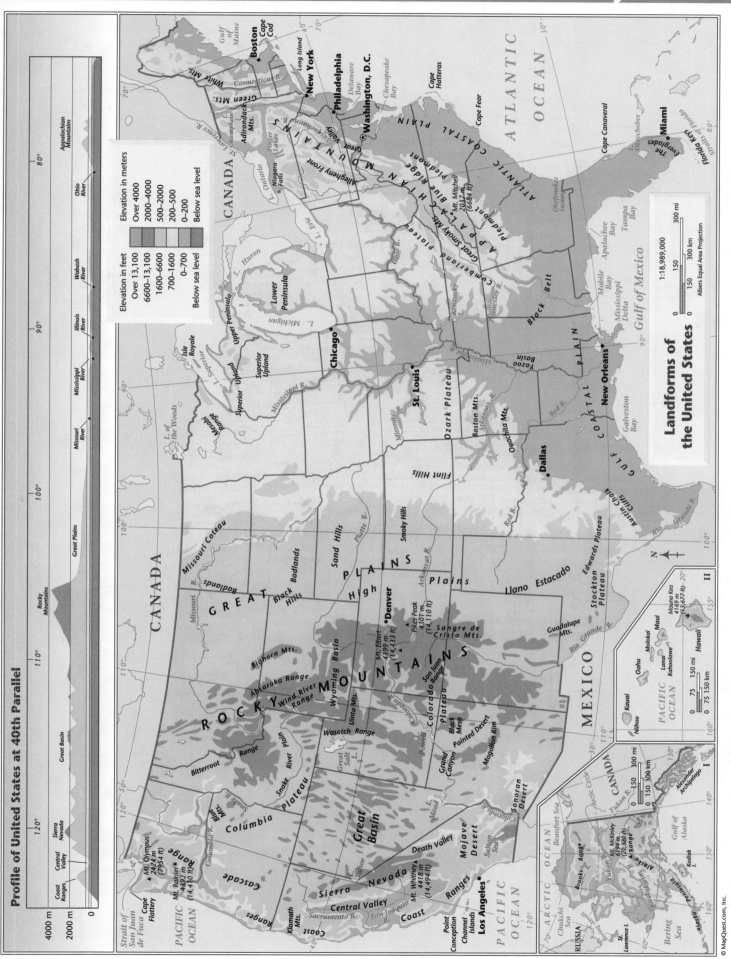

Landforms of the United States

1:18,989,000

Albers Equal Area Projection

Profile of United States at 40th Parallel

Elevation in meters
- Over 4000
- 2000–4000
- 500–2000
- 200–500
- 0–200
- Below sea level

Elevation in feet
- Over 13,100
- 6600–13,100
- 1600–6600
- 700–1600
- 0–700
- Below sea level

© MapQuest.com, Inc.

Capital: Montgomery
Area: 52,400 sq. mi.
135,800 sq. km.
Pop. (2000): 4,447,100
Largest City: Birmingham
242,820

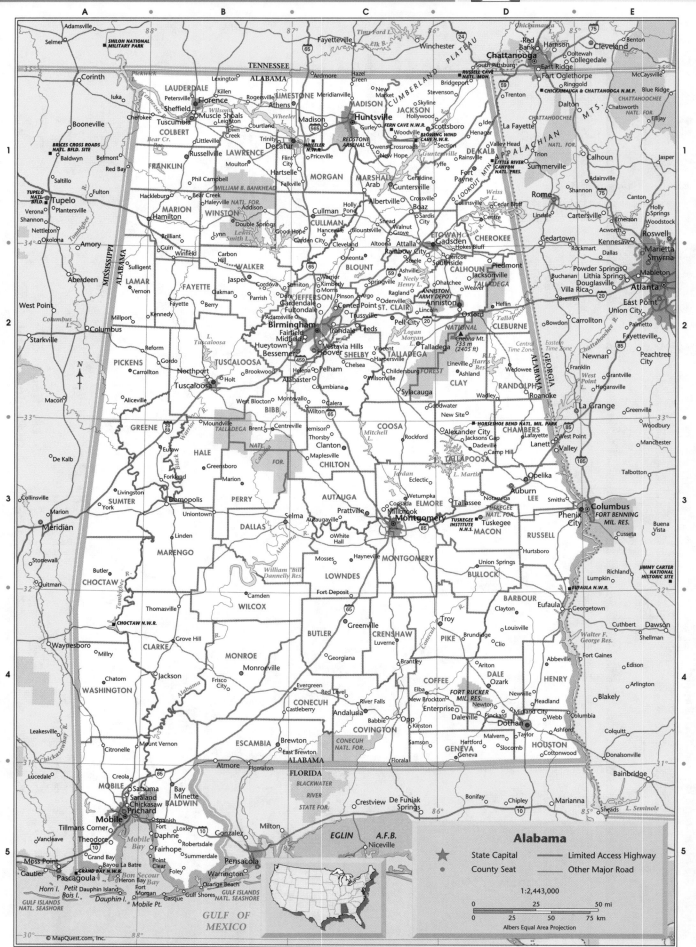

Alabama

★ State Capital
• County Seat

━━ Limited Access Highway
── Other Major Road

1:2,443,000

0   25   50 mi
0   25   50   75 km
Albers Equal Area Projection

© MapQuest.com, Inc.

Capital: Juneau
Area: 656,400 sq. mi.
1,700,000 sq. km.
Pop. (2000): 626,932
Largest City: Anchorage
260,283

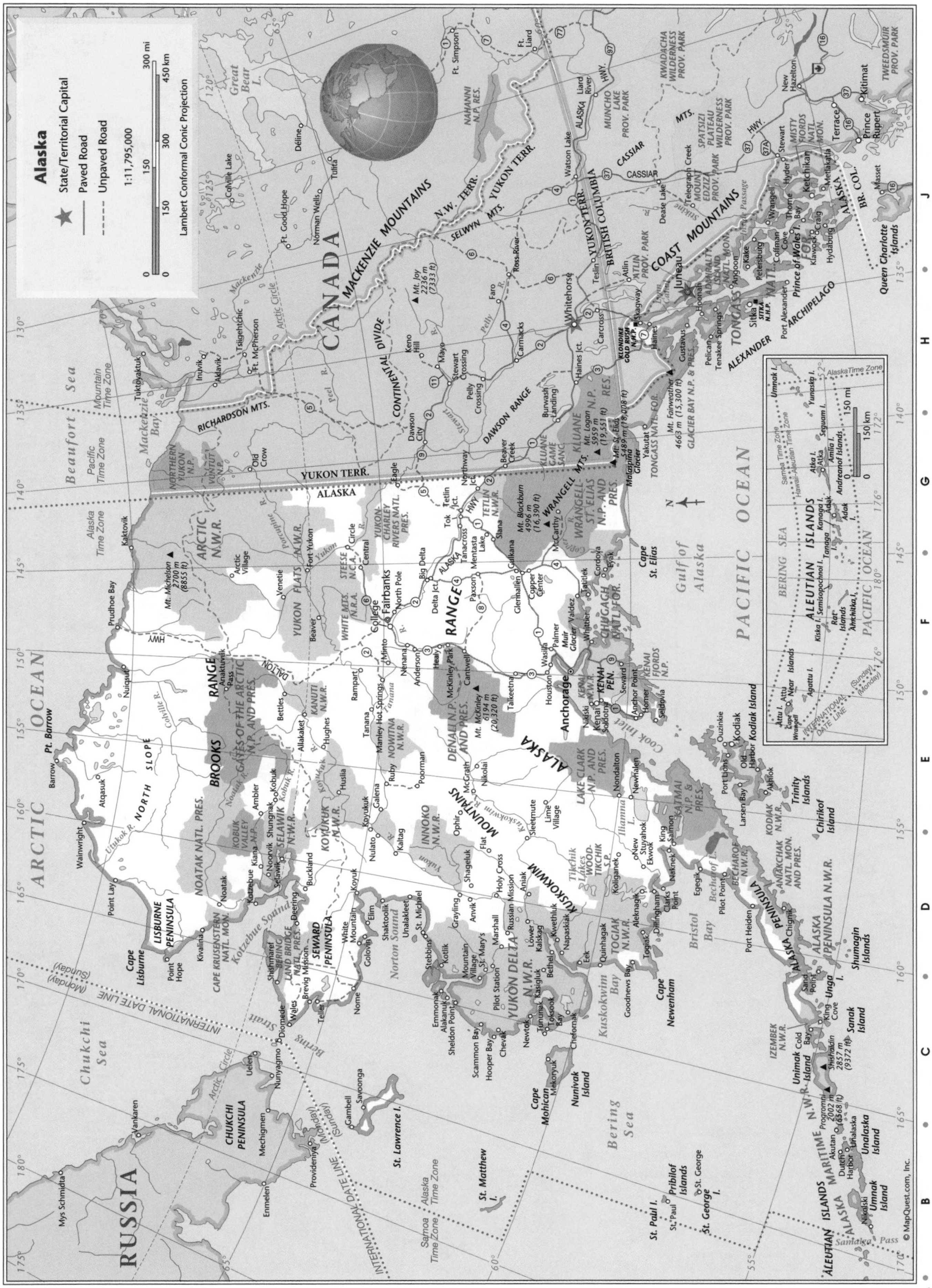

Alaska

★ State/Territorial Capital
— Paved Road
--- Unpaved Road

1:11,795,000

Lambert Conformal Conic Projection

300 mi
150
0
150 km
450

© MapQuest.com, Inc.

Capital: Phoenix	Pop. (2000): 5,130,632
Area: 114,000 sq. mi.	Largest City: Phoenix
295,300 sq. km.	1,321,045

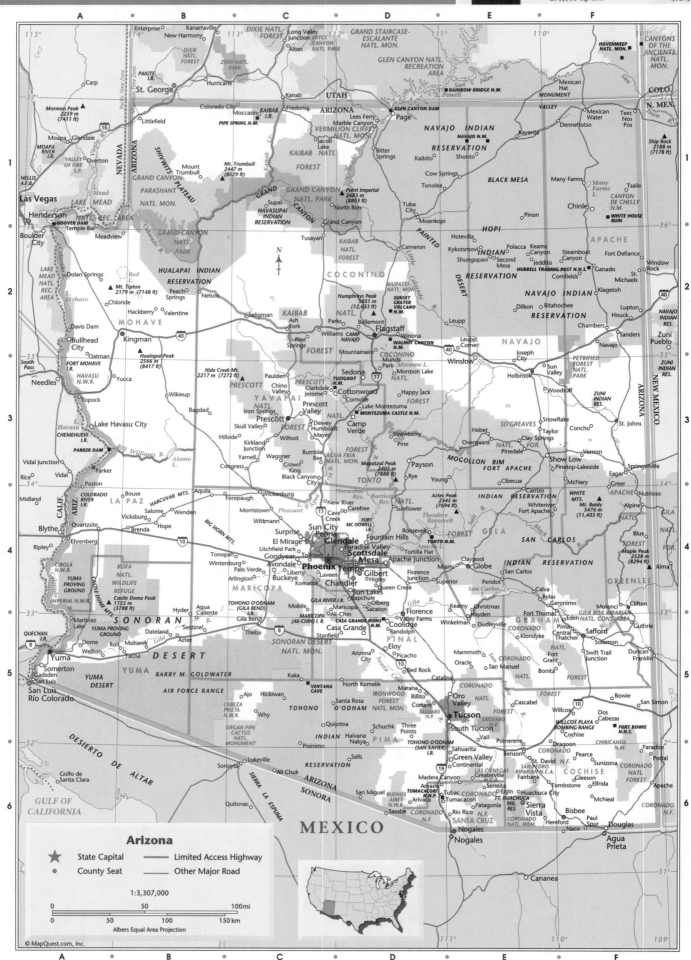

Arizona

★ State Capital
• County Seat
─── Limited Access Highway
─── Other Major Road

1:3,307,000

0   50   100mi
0   50   150 km

Albers Equal Area Projection

© MapQuest.com, Inc.

Capital: Little Rock
Area: 53,200 sq. mi.
137,700 sq. km.
Pop. (2000): 2,673,400
Largest City: Little Rock
183,133

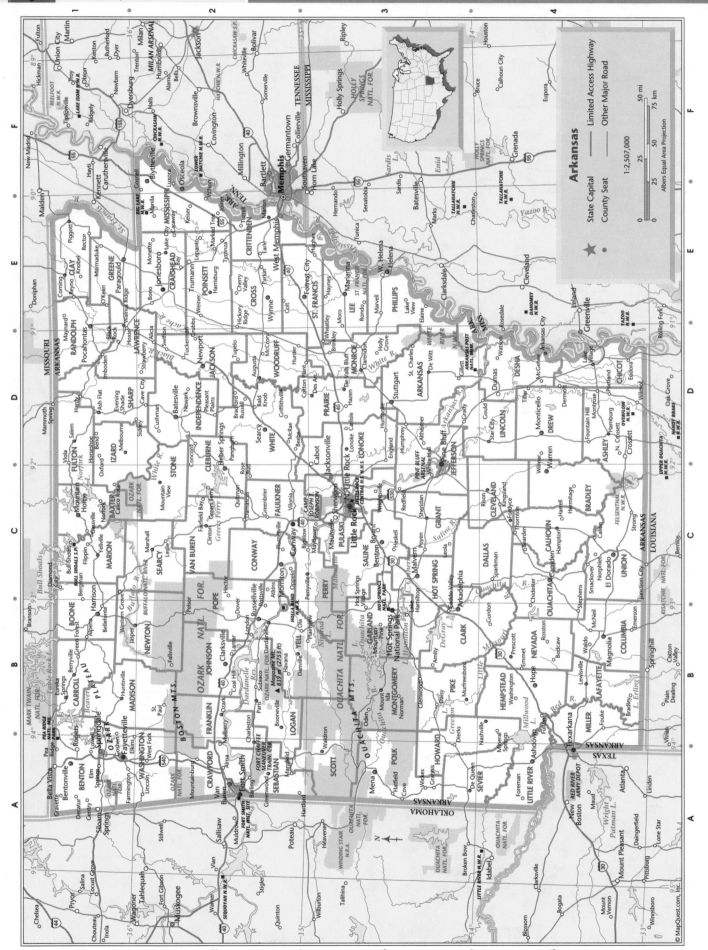

Arkansas

1:2,507,000

Albers Equal Area Projection

State Capital

County Seat

Limited Access Highway

Other Major Road

© MapQuest.com, Inc.

Capital: Sacramento	Pop. (2000): 33,871,648
Area: 163,700 sq. mi.	Largest City: Los Angeles
424,000 sq. km.	3,694,820

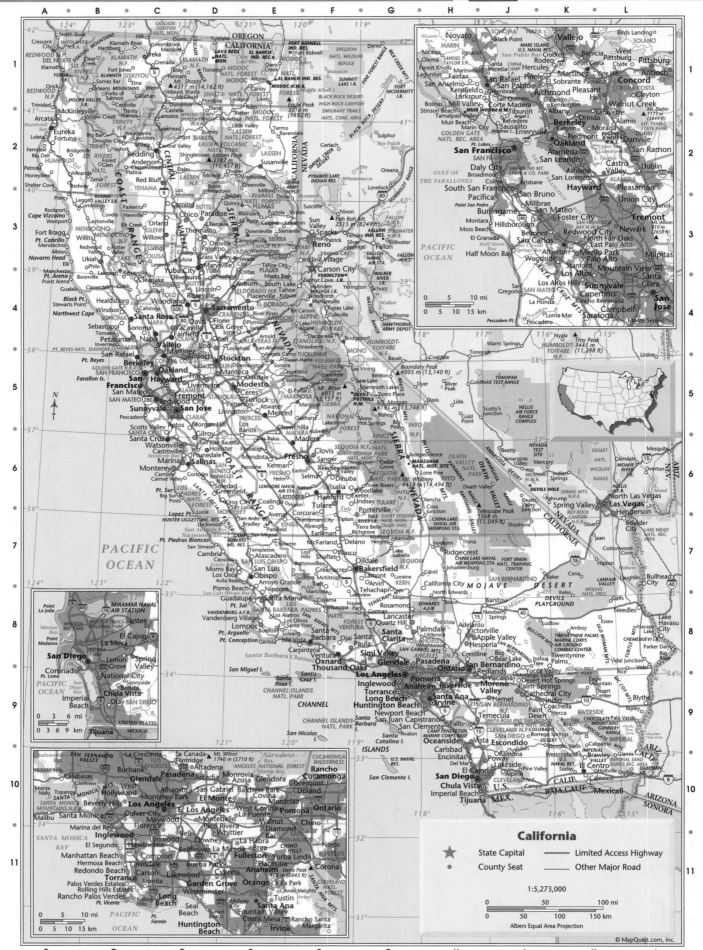

California

★ State Capital   ─── Limited Access Highway

• County Seat   ─── Other Major Road

1:5,273,000

0 50 100 mi

0 50 100 150 km

Albers Equal Area Projection

© MapQuest.com, Inc.

Capital: Denver
Area: 104,100 sq. mi.
269,600 sq. km.
Pop. (2000): 4,301,261
Largest City: Denver
554,636

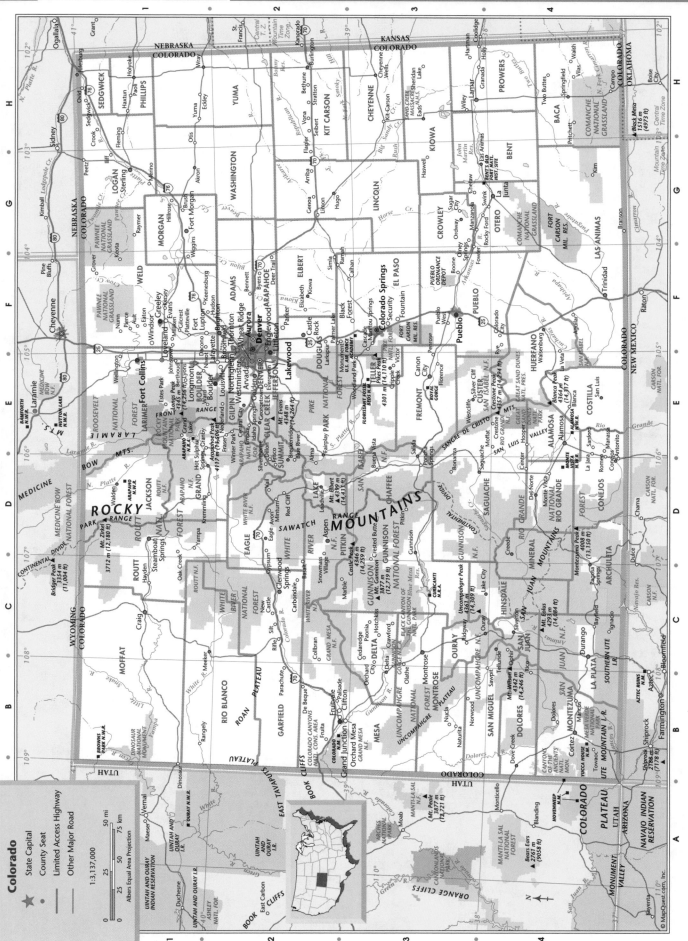

Colorado

★ State Capital
• County Seat
— Limited Access Highway
— Other Major Road

1:3,137,000

Albers Equal Area Projection

© MapQuest.com, Inc.

Capital: Hartford
Area: 5,500 sq. mi.
14,400 sq. km.

Pop. (2000): 3,405,565
Largest City: Bridgeport
139,529

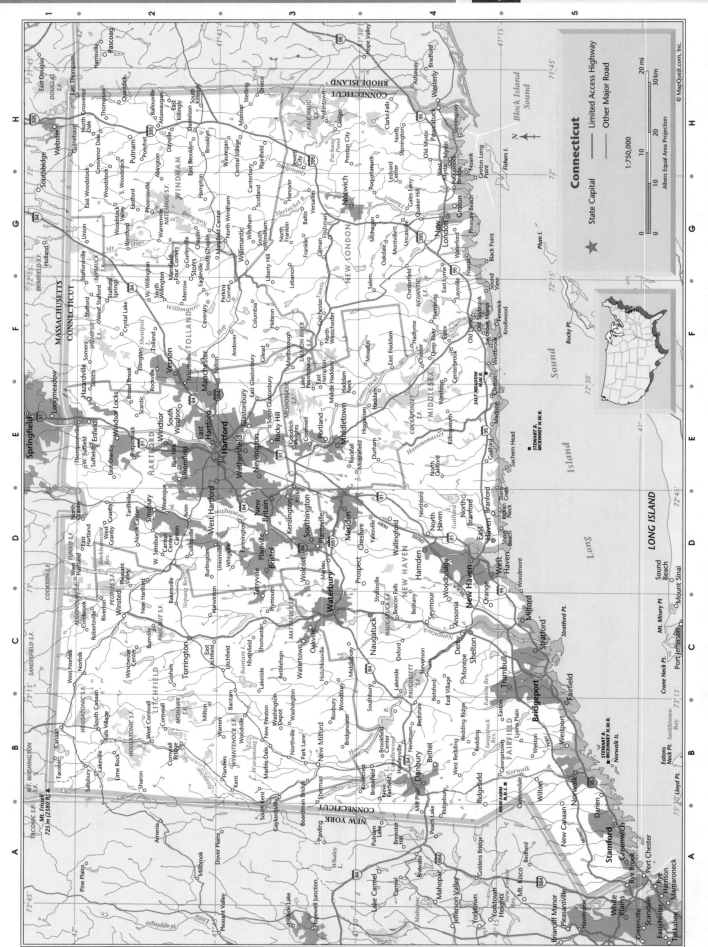

Connecticut

★ State Capital
— Limited Access Highway
— Other Major Road

1:750,000

Albers Equal Area Projection

© MapQuest.com, Inc.

Capital: Dover
Area: 2,500 sq. mi.
6,400 sq. km.
Pop. (2000): 783,600
Largest City: Wilmington
72,664

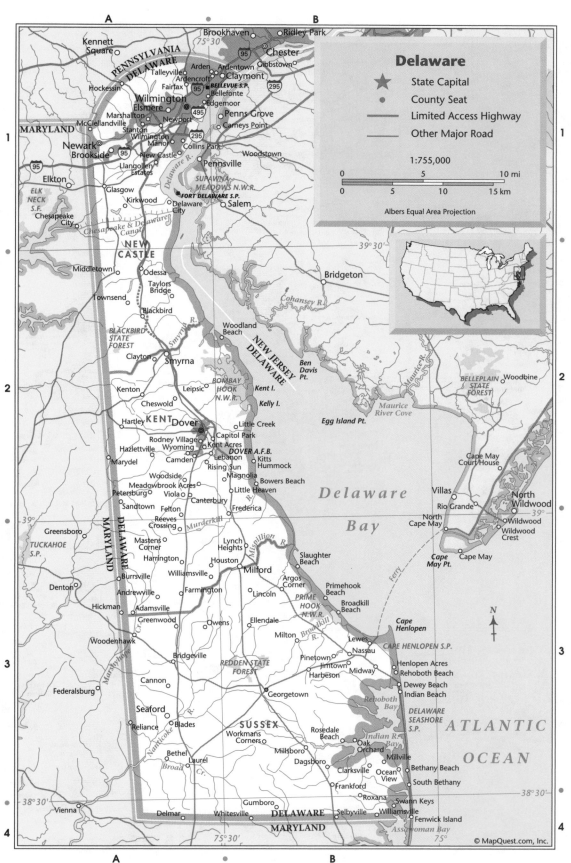

Delaware

★ State Capital
• County Seat
━━ Limited Access Highway
── Other Major Road

1:755,000

0   5   10 mi
0   5   10   15 km

Albers Equal Area Projection

© MapQuest.com, Inc.

Capital: Tallahassee
Area: 65,800 sq. mi.
170,300 sq. km.
Pop. (2000): 15,982,378
Largest City: Jacksonville
735,617

Florida

★ State Capital
• County Seat
— Limited Access Highway
— Other Major Road

1:3,135,000

0   25   50 mi
0 25 50 75 km
Albers Equal Area Projection

© MapQuest.com, Inc.

Capital: Atlanta
Area: 59,400 sq. mi.
153,900 sq. km.
Pop. (2000): 8,186,453
Largest City: Atlanta
416,474

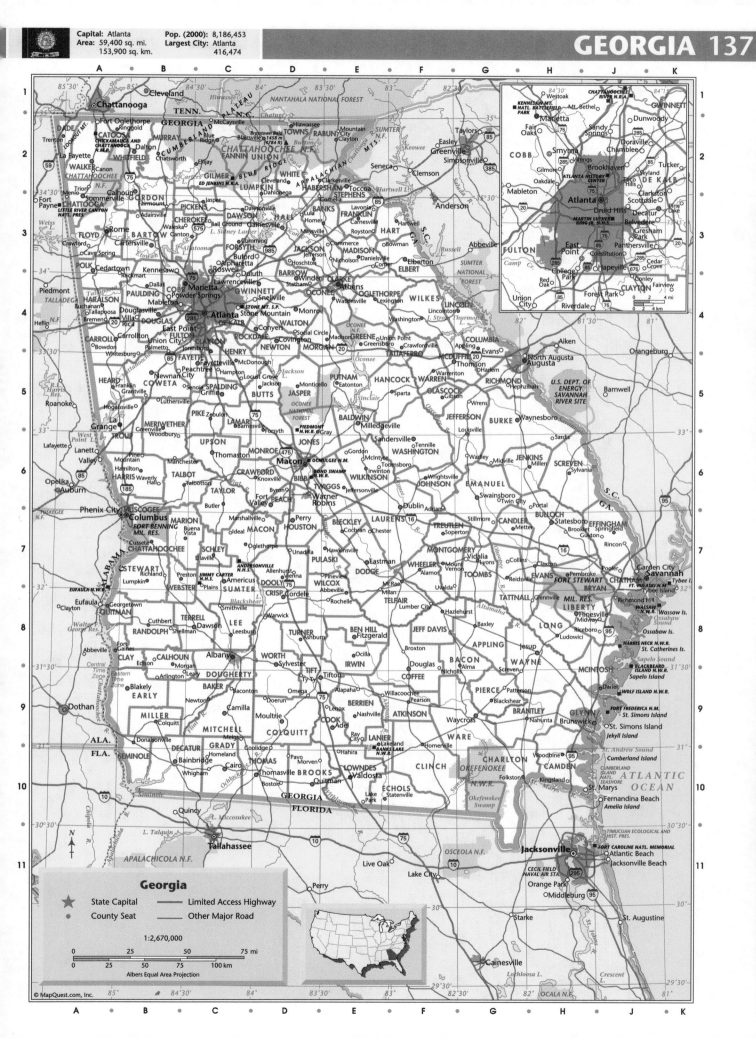

Georgia

★ State Capital
● County Seat
— Limited Access Highway
— Other Major Road

1:2,670,000

0   25   50   75 mi
0 25 50 75 100 km
Albers Equal Area Projection

© MapQuest.com, Inc.

Capital: Honolulu	**Pop. (2000):** 1,211,537
Area: 10,900 sq. mi.	**Largest City:** Honolulu
28,300 sq. km.	371,657

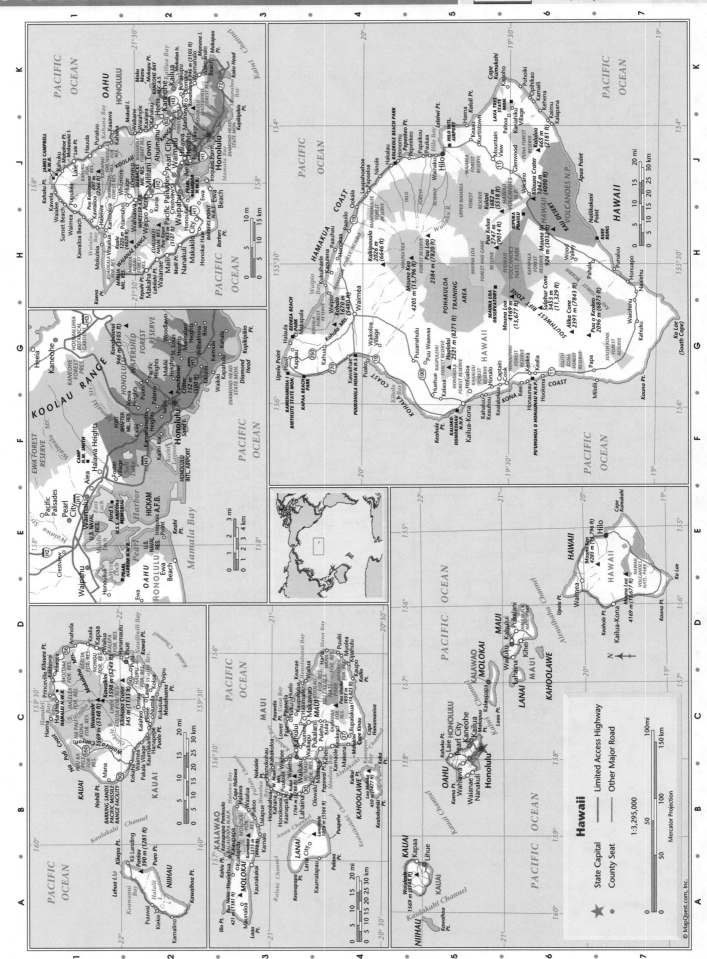

Capital: Boise
Area: 83,600 sq. mi.
216,500 sq. km.
Pop. (2000): 1,293,953
Largest City: Boise
185,787

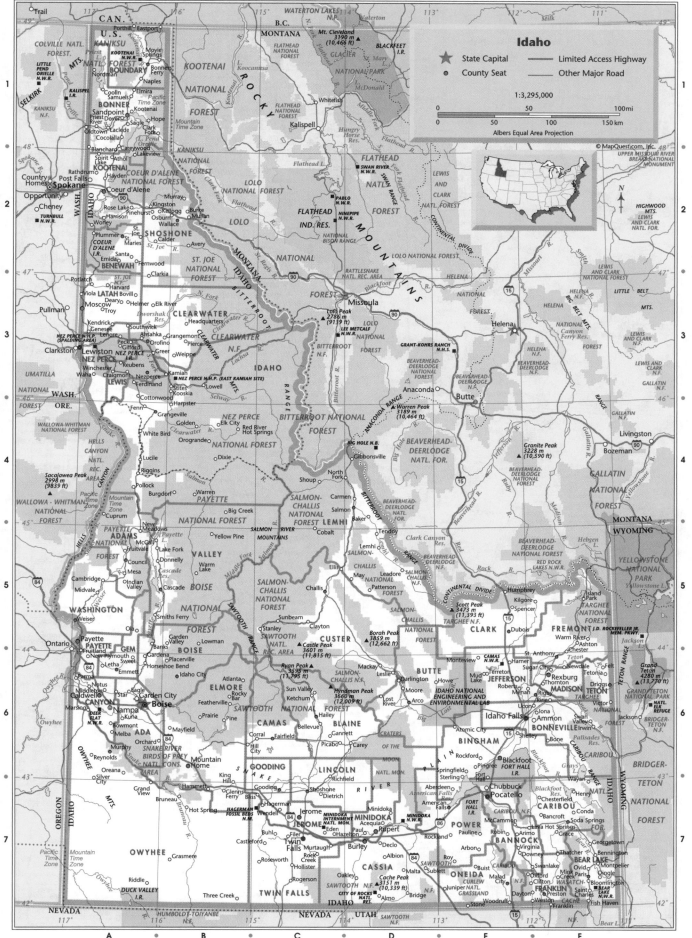

Idaho

★ State Capital — Limited Access Highway
● County Seat — Other Major Road

1:3,295,000

0   50   100mi
0   50   100   150 km

Albers Equal Area Projection

© MapQuest.com, Inc.

Capital: Springfield
Area: 57,900 sq. mi.
150,000 sq. km.
Pop. (2000): 12,419,293
Largest City: Chicago
2,896,016

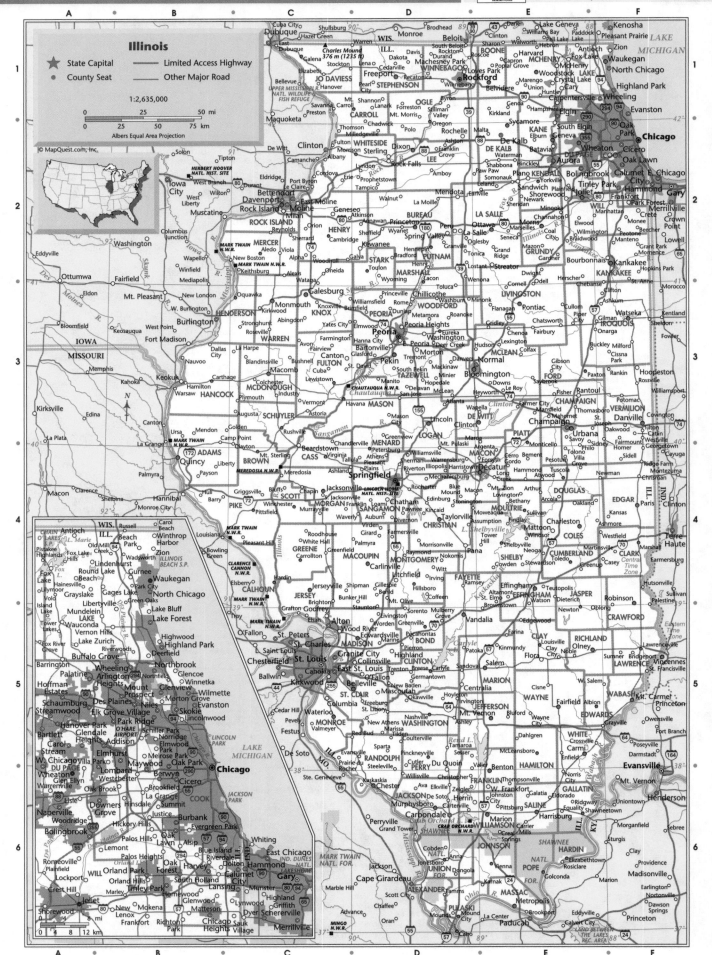

Illinois

★ State Capital   —— Limited Access Highway
● County Seat   —— Other Major Road

1:2,635,000

0   25   50 mi
0   25   50   75 km
Albers Equal Area Projection

© MapQuest.com, Inc.

Capital: Indianapolis
Area: 36,400 sq. mi.
94,300 sq. km.
Pop. (2000): 6,080,485
Largest City: Indianapolis
791,926

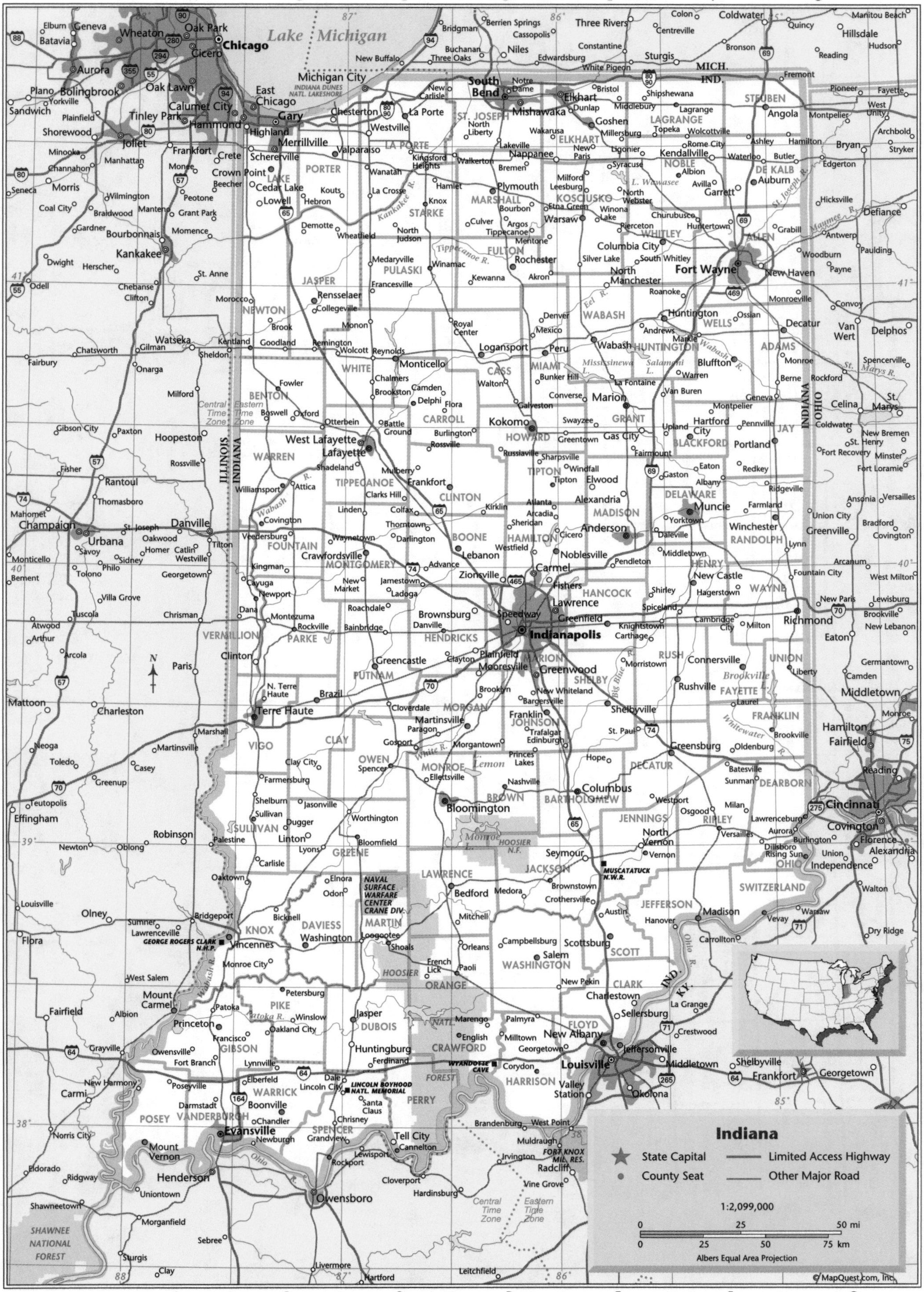

Lake Michigan

MICH.
IND.

Indiana

★ State Capital — Limited Access Highway
● County Seat — Other Major Road

1:2,099,000

0   25   50 mi

0   25   50   75 km

Albers Equal Area Projection

©MapQuest.com, Inc.

SHAWNEE NATIONAL FOREST

HOOSIER N.F.

NAVAL SURFACE WARFARE CENTER CRANE DIV.

GEORGE ROGERS CLARK N.H.P.

LINCOLN BOYHOOD NATL. MEMORIAL

MUSCATATUCK N.W.R.

WYANDOTTE CAVE

FORT KNOX MIL. RES.

Central Time Zone / Eastern Time Zone

Capital: Des Moines
Area: 56,300 sq. mi.
145,800 sq. km.
Pop. (2000): 2,926,324
Largest City: Des Moines
198,682

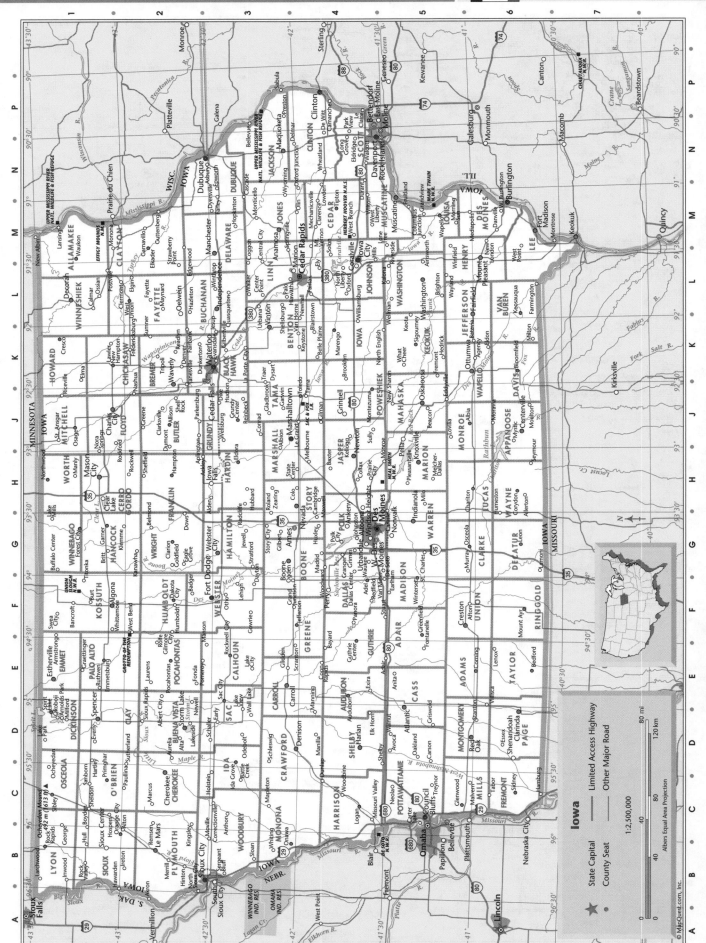

Iowa

State Capital ★
County Seat •

Limited Access Highway
Other Major Road

1:2,500,000

Albers Equal Area Projection

© MapQuest.com, Inc.

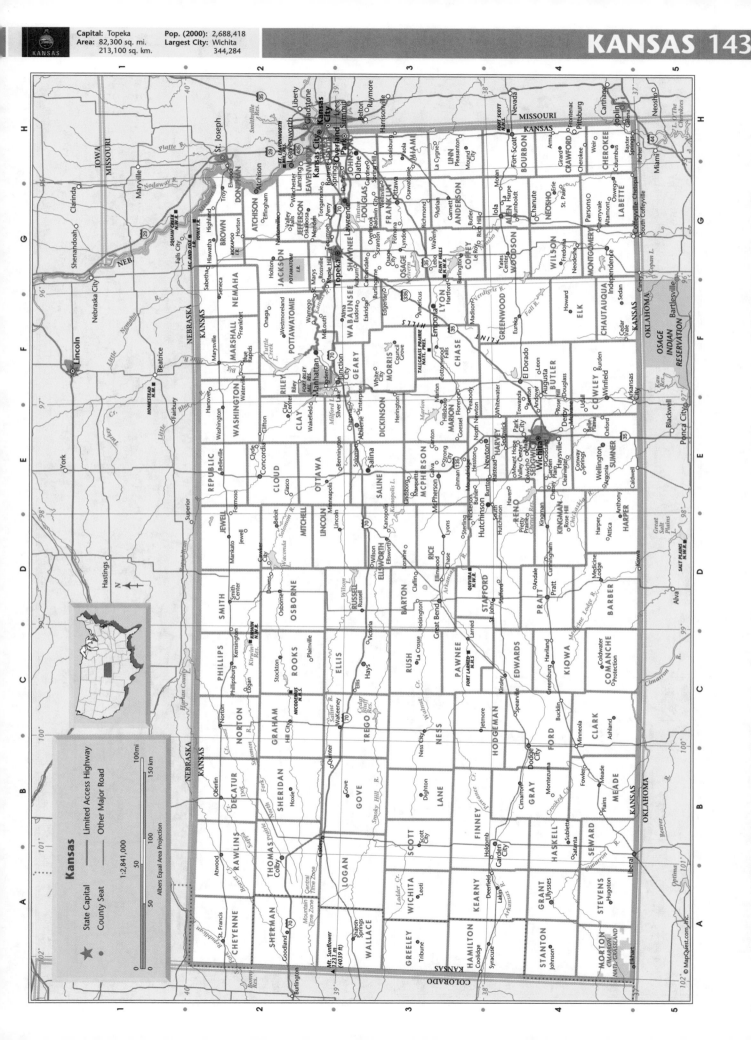

Capital: Topeka
Area: 82,300 sq. mi.
213,100 sq. km.
Pop. (2000): 2,688,418
Largest City: Wichita
344,284

Kansas
1:2,841,000
Albers Equal Area Projection

State Capital
County Seat
Limited Access Highway
Other Major Road

Capital: Frankfort
Area: 40,400 sq. mi.
104,700 sq. km.
Pop. (2000): 4,041,769
Largest City: Lexington
260,512

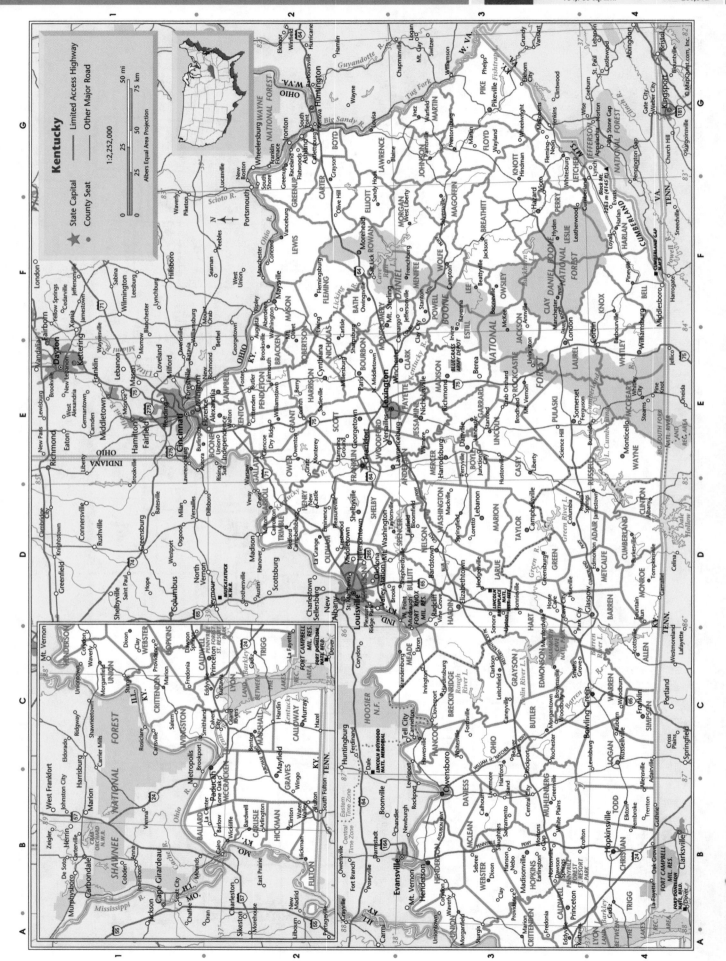

Kentucky

Limited Access Highway
Other Major Road

★ State Capital
● County Seat

1:2,252,000

50 mi
75 km

Albers Equal Area Projection

© MapQuest.com, Inc.

Capital: Baton Rouge
Area: 51,800 sq. mi.
134,300 sq. km.
Pop. (2000): 4,468,976
Largest City: New Orleans
484,674

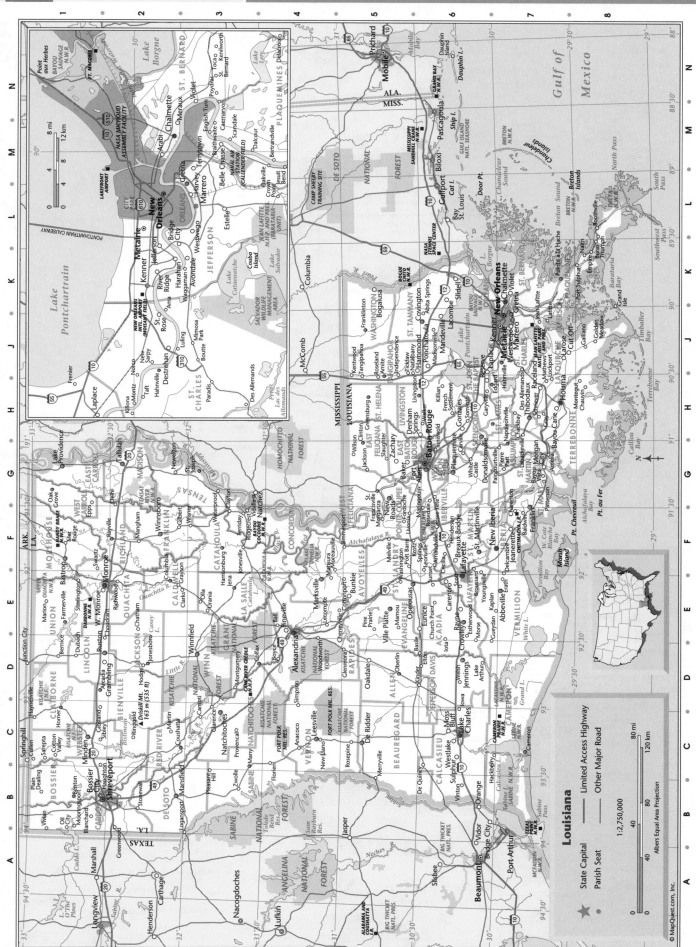

Louisiana

State Capital ★
Parish Seat •

Limited Access Highway
Other Major Road

1:2,750,000

Albers Equal Area Projection

© MapQuest.com, Inc.

Capital: Augusta
Area: 35,400 sq. mi.
91,700 sq. km.
Pop. (2000): 1,274,923
Largest City: Portland
64,249

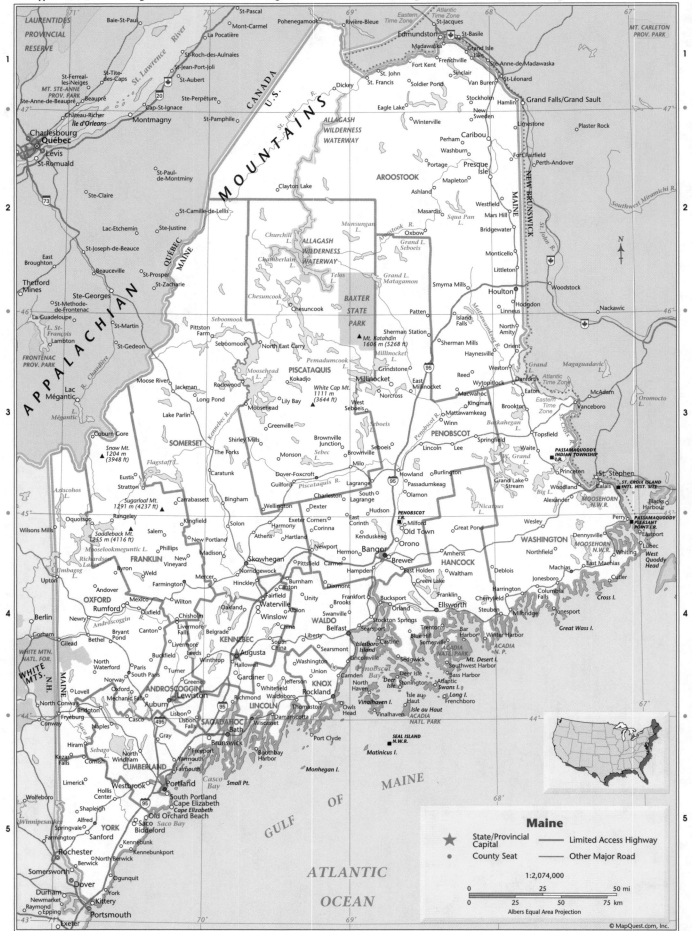

Maine

★ State/Provincial Capital
● County Seat
━━━ Limited Access Highway
━━━ Other Major Road

1:2,074,000

0   25   50 mi
0   25   50   75 km

Albers Equal Area Projection

© MapQuest.com, Inc.

Capital: Annapolis
Area: 12,400 sq. mi.
32,100 sq. km.
Pop. (2000): 5,296,486
Largest City: Baltimore
651,154

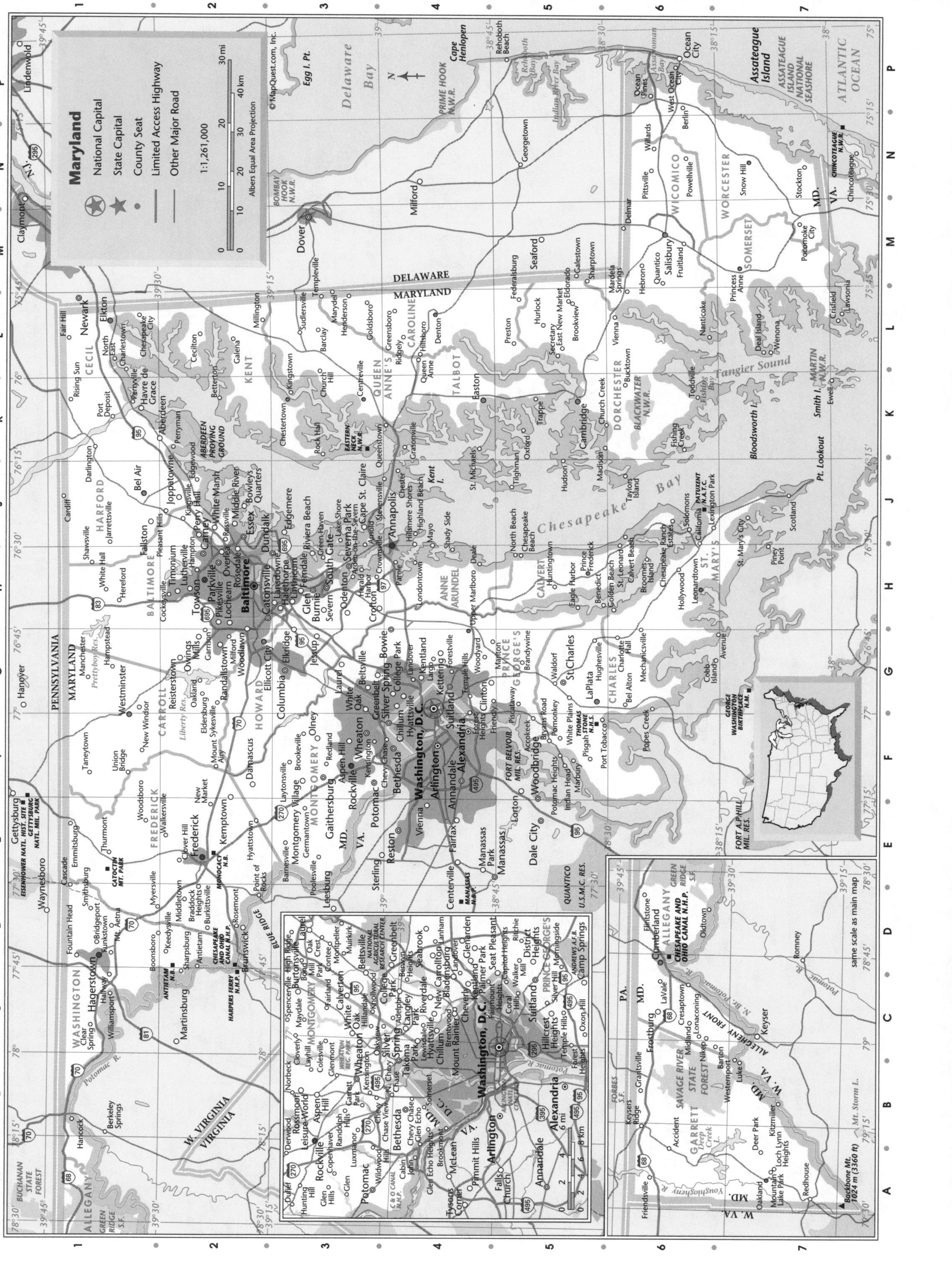

Maryland

- National Capital
- State Capital
- County Seat
- Limited Access Highway
- Other Major Road

1:1,261,000

Albers Equal Area Projection

30 mi
40 km

© MapQuest.com, Inc.

PENNSYLVANIA

DELAWARE
MARYLAND

W. VIRGINIA

VIRGINIA

Washington, D.C.

ATLANTIC OCEAN

Chesapeake Bay

Delaware Bay

same scale as main map

Capital: Boston
Area: 10,600 sq. mi. 27,300 sq. km.
Pop. (2000): 6,349,097
Largest City: Boston 589,141

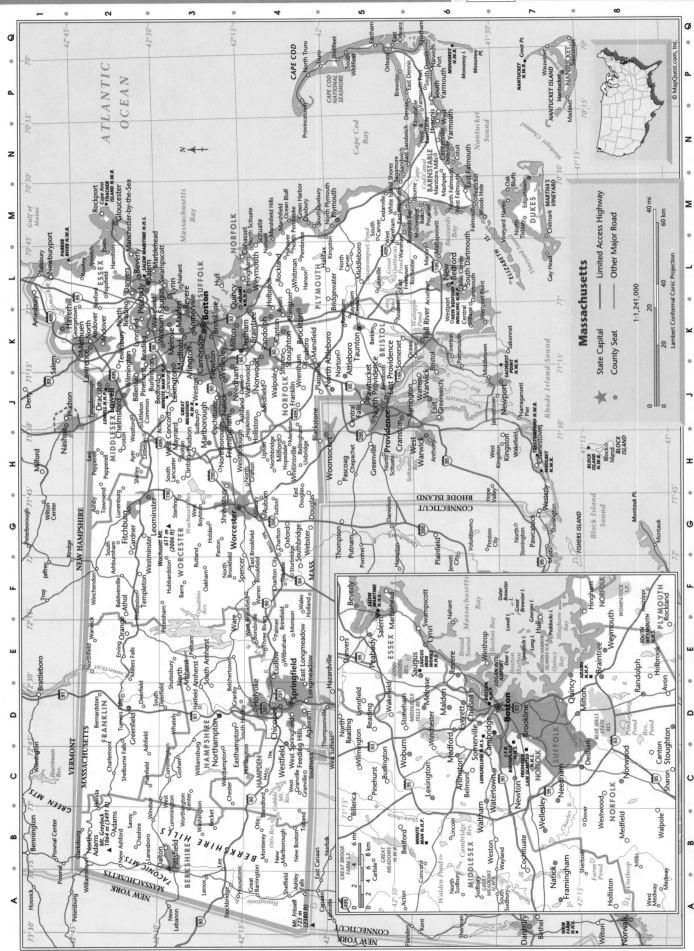

Massachusetts

1:1,241,000

Lambert Conformal Conic Projection

★ State Capital
○ County Seat

— Limited Access Highway
— Other Major Road

© 2002 MapQuest.com, Inc.

Capital: Lansing
Area: 96,700 sq. mi.
250,500 sq. km.
Pop. (2000): 9,938,444
Largest City: Detroit 951,270

Michigan

★ State Capital
● County Seat

━━━ Limited Access Highway
──── Other Major Road

1:3,205,000

0   50   100 mi
0 50 100 150 km

Albers Equal Area Projection

© MapQuest.com, Inc.

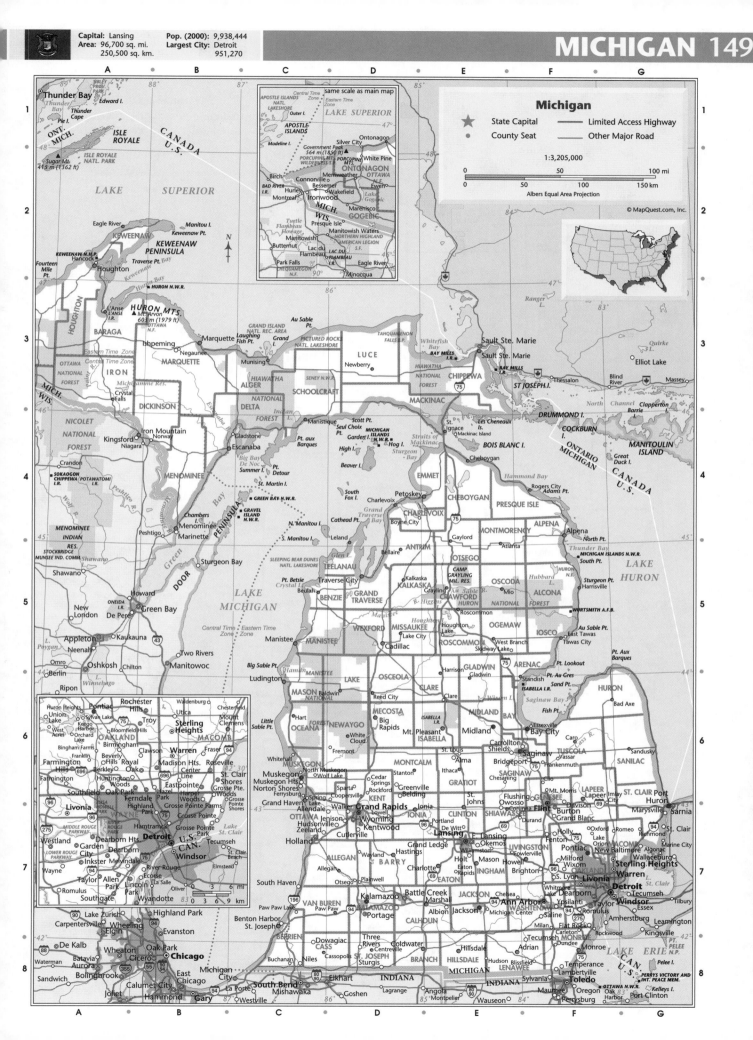

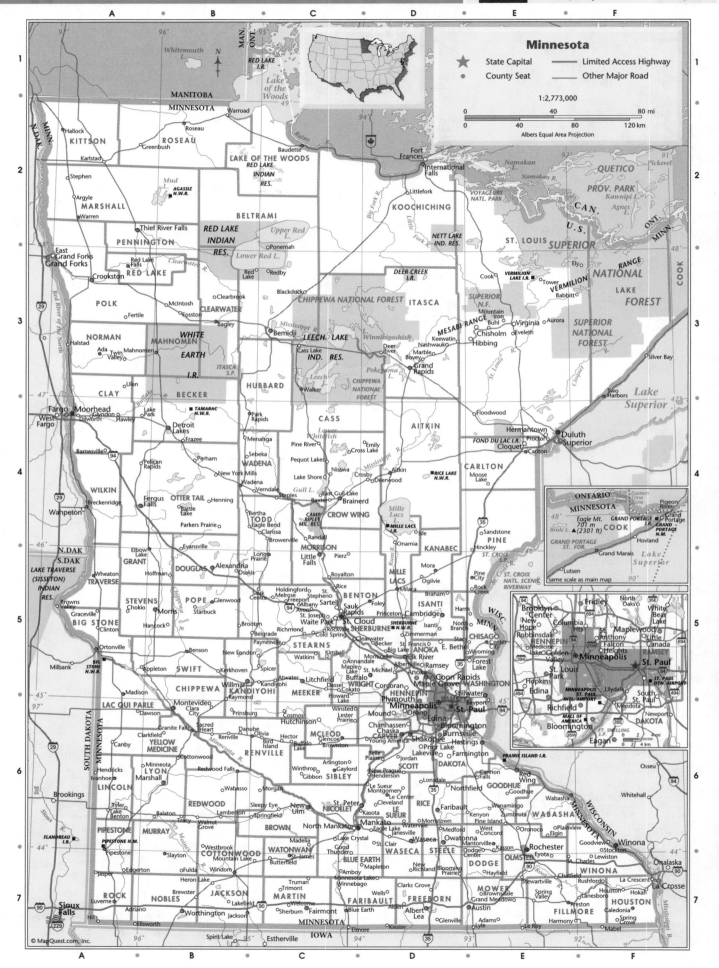

Capital: Jackson
Area: 48,400 sq. mi.
125,400 sq. km.
Pop. (2000): 2,844,658
Largest City: Jackson
184,256

Mississippi

★ State Capital
● County Seat
— Limited Access Highway
— Other Major Road

1:2,386,000

0 40 80 mi
0 40 80 120 km

© MapQuest.com, Inc.

TENN.
MISS.
ARK.
LA.
ALABAMA
LOUISIANA
MISSISSIPPI
Gulf of Mexico

Memphis, Germantown, Collierville, Forrest City, Southaven, Olive Branch, Byhalia, Horn Lake, Hernando, Walnut, Corinth, Burnsville, Iuka, Florence, Sheffield, De Soto, Marianna, Kossuth, Rienzi, Booneville, Red Bay, Russellville, Tuscumbia, Holly Springs, Ripley, Jumpertown, Blue Mountain, Dumas, Tishomingo, Golden, Marietta, West Helena, Helena, Coldwater, Senatobia, Abbeville, Myrtle, Baldwyn, Guntown, Saltillo, Tremont, Hamilton, Tunica, Como, Crenshaw, Oxford, New Albany, Blue Springs, Sherman, Fulton, Mantachie, Tula, Sledge, Sardis, Taylor, Ecru, Thaxton, Pontotoc, Algoma, Verona, Plantersville, Shannon, Nettleton, Smithville, Clarksdale, Lambert, Crowder, Pope, Water Valley, Toccopola, Tupelo, Amory, Hatley, Aberdeen, Caledonia, Alligator, Duncan, Tutwiler, Oakland, Charleston, Tillatoba, Coffeeville, Bruce, Pittsboro, New Houlka, Okolona, Houston, Vardaman, Derma, Woodland, Columbus, Shelby, Winstonville, Mound Bayou, Merigold, Drew, Glendora, Grenada, Slate Spring, Mantee, Walthall, West Point, Artesia, Rosedale, Pace, Renova, Doddsville, Duck Hill, Eupora, Maben, Mathiston, Starkville, Crawford, Brooksville, Cleveland, Boyle, Benoit, Shaw, Greenwood, Itta Bena, Carrollton, Winona, Kilmichael, Ackerman, Louisville, Macon, Indianola, Metcalfe, Leland, Moorhead, Sidon, Vaiden, French Camp, Weir, Noxapater, Shuqualak, Tuscaloosa, Arcola, Isola, Belzoni, Silver City, Tchula, Lexington, McCool, Ethel, Kosciusko, Durant, Sallis, Hollandale, Anguilla, Louise, Eden, Goodman, Pickens, Philadelphia, Scooba, De Kalb, Aliceville, Mayersville, Rolling Fork, Cary, Satartia, Bentonia, Flora, Yazoo City, Canton, Lena, Walnut Grove, Union, Collinsville, Decatur, Marion, Meridian, Demopolis, Tallulah, Vicksburg, Clinton, Madison, Ridgeland, Morton, Pelahatchie, Lake, Forest, Newton, Hickory, Chunky, Enterprise, Stonewall, Jackson, Pearl, Brandon, Polkville, Montrose, Louin, Paulding, Pachuta, Quitman, Winnsboro, Edwards, Raymond, Richland, Florence, Puckett, Raleigh, Sylvarena, Bay Springs, Shubuta, Port Gibson, Utica, Terry, Crystal Springs, Braxton, D'Lo, Mendenhall, Magee, Mize, Taylorsville, Heidelberg, Georgetown, Hazlehurst, Soso, Sandersville, Laurel, Waynesboro, Beauregard, Wesson, New Hebron, Mount Olive, Collins, Ellisville, Seminary, State Line, Fayette, Brookhaven, Monticello, Prentiss, Petal, Hattiesburg, Richton, New Augusta, Beaumont, McLain, Leakesville, Roxie, Meadville, Bude, Summit, McComb, Gloster, Liberty, Magnolia, Centreville, Woodville, Tylertown, Columbia, Purvis, Lumberton, Wiggins, Lucedale, Saraland, Prichard, Mobile, Poplarville, Picayune, Lyman, Vancleave, Tillmans Corner, Theodore, Daphne, Fairhope, Bogalusa, Kiln, Diamondhead, Lacombe, Gulfport, Ocean Springs, Biloxi, Gautier, Moss Point, Pascagoula, Long Beach, Pass Christian, Bay St. Louis, Waveland, Pearlington, D'Iberville, Slidell, Kenner, New Orleans, Chalmette

Counties: DE SOTO, TATE, MARSHALL, BENTON, TIPPAH, ALCORN, TISHOMINGO, PRENTISS, UNION, LEE, ITAWAMBA, TUNICA, PANOLA, LAFAYETTE, PONTOTOC, COAHOMA, QUITMAN, YALOBUSHA, CALHOUN, CHICKASAW, MONROE, BOLIVAR, TALLAHATCHIE, GRENADA, WEBSTER, CLAY, LEFLORE, CARROLL, MONTGOMERY, CHOCTAW, OKTIBBEHA, LOWNDES, SUNFLOWER, WASHINGTON, HUMPHREYS, HOLMES, ATTALA, WINSTON, NOXUBEE, ISSAQUENA, SHARKEY, YAZOO, LEAKE, NESHOBA, KEMPER, WARREN, MADISON, SCOTT, NEWTON, LAUDERDALE, HINDS, RANKIN, SMITH, JASPER, CLARKE, CLAIBORNE, COPIAH, SIMPSON, COVINGTON, JONES, WAYNE, JEFFERSON, PINE HILLS, JEFFERSON DAVIS, LAWRENCE, MARION, LAMAR, FORREST, PERRY, GREENE, ADAMS, FRANKLIN, LINCOLN, WILKINSON, AMITE, PIKE, WALTHALL, PEARL RIVER, STONE, GEORGE, JACKSON, HANCOCK, HARRISON

National Forests / Refuges: ST. FRANCIS N.F., HOLLY SPRINGS NATIONAL FOREST, TALLAHATCHIE N.W.R., DAHOMEY N.W.R., MATTHEWS BRAKE N.W.R., MORGAN BRAKE N.W.R., YAZOO N.W.R., PANTHER SWAMP N.W.R., HILLSIDE N.W.R., DELTA N.F., HANDY BRAKE N.W.R., OVERFLOW N.W.R., POVERTY POINT N.M., BIENVILLE NATIONAL FOREST, NOXUBEE N.W.R., MISS. CHOCTAW I.R., TOMBIGBEE N.F., DE SOTO NATIONAL FOREST, HOMOCHITTO NATIONAL FOREST, BAYOU COCODRIE N.W.R., ST. CATHERINE CREEK N.W.R., LAKE OPHELIA N.W.R., NATCHEZ N.H.P., VICKSBURG N.M.P., MERIDIAN N.A.S., CAMP SHELBY TRAIN. SITE, NASA STENNIS SPACE CTR., MISS. SANDHILL CRANE N.W.R., BOGUE CHITTO N.W.R., BAYOU SAUVAGE N.W.R., GRAND BAY N.W.R., GULF ISLAND NATL. SEASHORE

Water features: Sardis L., Enid L., Grenada L., Arkabutla L., Ross Barnett Res., Okatibbee L., Okatibbee L., Columbus L., Aliceville L., Pickwick L., Big Springs L., Woodall Mt. 246 m (806 ft), Mississippi River, Yazoo River, Big Black River, Pearl River, Tombigbee River, Pascagoula River, Leaf River, Chickasawhay River, Tensas River, Mississippi Sound, Lake Pontchartrain, Lake Borgne, Chandeleur Sound, Breton Sound, Gulf of Mexico, Horn I., Ship I., Cat I., Petit Bois I., Dauphin I., Mobile Bay, Mobile Pt.

Capital: Jefferson City
Area: 69,700 sq. mi.
180,500 sq. km.
Pop. (2000): 5,595,211
Largest City: Kansas City
441,545

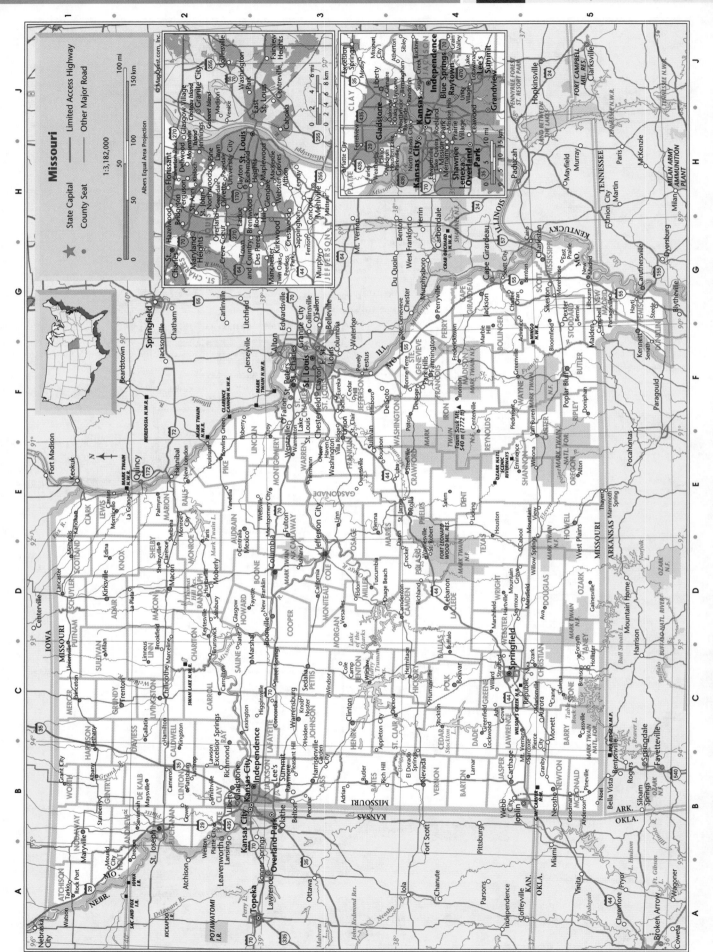

Capital: Helena
Area: 147,000 sq. mi.
380,800 sq. km.
Pop. (2000): 902,195
Largest City: Billings
89,847

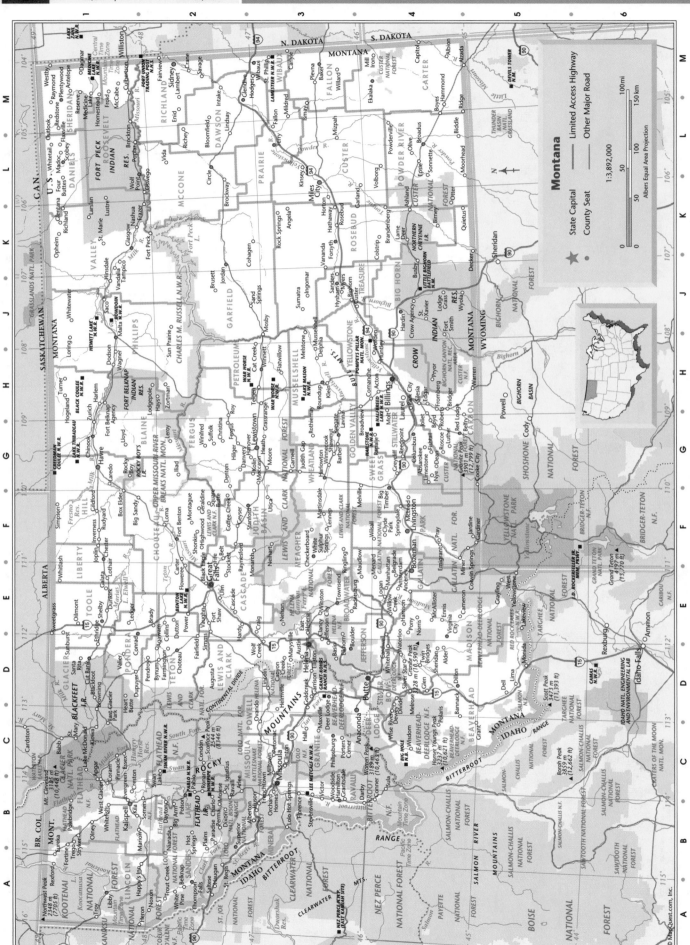

Montana
1:3,892,000
Albers Equal Area Projection

Limited Access Highway
Other Major Road

State Capital ★
County Seat ●

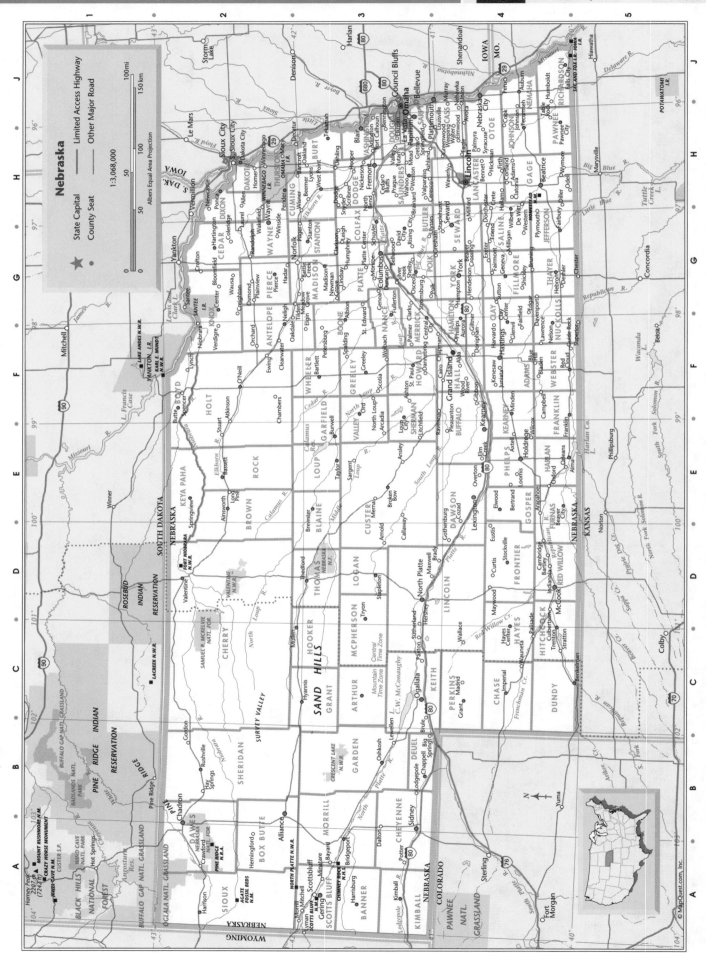

Capital: Lincoln
Area: 77,400 sq. mi.
200,300 sq. km.
Pop. (2000): 1,711,263
Largest City: Omaha
390,007

Nebraska

Limited Access Highway
Other Major Road

★ State Capital
• County Seat

1:3,068,000

Albers Equal Area Projection

Capital: Carson City
Area: 110,600 sq. mi.
286,400 sq. km.
Pop. (2000): 1,998,257
Largest City: Las Vegas
478,434

OREGON
IDAHO
NEVADA

Owyhee
120°
118°
116°
114°
42°

FORT MCDERMITT IND. RES.

Goose L.
FORT BIDWELL IND. RES.
Denio
McDermitt
DUCK VALLEY IND. RES.
Owyhee
Jarbidge
Jackpot
SAWTOOTH N.F.

Upper L.
SHELDON NATL. WILDLIFE REFUGE
Mountain City
HUMBOLDT-TOIYABE NATL. FOR.
Matterhorn 3304 m (10,839 ft)
Contact

MODOC NATL. FOR.
Vya
Massacre L.
FORT MCDERMITT IND. RES.
Orovada
Charleston
Pacific Time Zone
Mountain Time Zone

CALIFORNIA
Goose L.
SUMMIT LAKE IND. RES.
HUMBOLDT
Paradise Valley
OWYHEE DESERT
North Fork
Wilkins
GREAT SALT LAKE DESERT

WASHOE
BLACK ROCK DESERT-HIGH ROCK CANYON EMIGRANT TRAILS NATL. CONS. AREA
DESERT VALLEY
Midas
Jack Creek
ELKO
Montello

Golconda
Tuscarora
Wells
Cobre
Oasis
Pilot Peak 3263 m (10,704 ft)

Gerlach
Sulphur
Pronto
Winnemucca
Valmy
Dunphy
Elko
Deeth
Halleck
Arthur
Shafter
West Wendover

Empire
Mill City
Imlay
Humboldt
Battle Mountain
Carlin
Spring Creek
Lamoille
Ruby Dome 3471 m (11,387 ft)
TE-MOAK IND. RES.
HUMBOLDT-TOIYABE

Honey L.
Flanigan
PERSHING
Unionville
Beowawe
Jiggs
Ruby Valley
UTAH TEST AND TRAINING RANGE

SIERRA ARMY DEPOT
PYRAMID LAKE IND. RES.
Winnemucca L.
Oreana
Mt. Tobin 2979 m (9775 ft)
Crescent Valley
RUBY MTS.
RUBY LAKE N.W.R.
Currie

Pyramid L.
Sutcliffe
Dry L.
Lovelock
SHOSHONE RANGE
LANDER
GREAT BASIN
EUREKA
Goshute L.
Ruby L.
Lages
GOSHUTE IND. RES.
Ibapah Peak 3684 m (12,087 ft)

PLUMAS NATL. FOR.
Nixon
Cherry Creek
Tippett

Lemmon Valley
Wadsworth
FALLON N.W.R.
CHURCHILL
Dixie Valley
Austin
Newark L.
WHITE PINE
Steptoe
McGill
Mt. Moriah 3678 m (12,067 ft)

TAHOE N.F.
Sun Valley
Sparks
Fernley
Hazen
FALLON IND. RES.
STILLWATER N.W.R.
Eureka
Summit Mt. 3189 m (10,461 ft)
Ruth
Lane
Ely

Verdi
Reno
STOREY
Patrick
Stillwater
North Toiyabe Peak 3290 m (10,793 ft)
HUMBOLDT-
HUMBOLDT-TOIYABE NATL. FOR.
Preston
Lund
Majors Place
Wheeler Peak 3982 m (13,063 ft)
Baker

TOIYABE N.F.
Steamboat
Silver Springs
FALLON N.A.S.
Cold Springs
Middlegate
TOIYABE N.F.
Mt. Jefferson 3642 m (11,949 ft)
Minerva
GREAT BASIN N.P.

Incline Village
Virginia City
Dayton
Wabuska
Ione
YOMBA IND. RES.
Arc Dome 3588 m (11,773 ft)
Round Mountain
Currant
SCHELL CREEK RANGE
SNAKE RANGE
DESERT RANGE EXP. STA.

Carson City
LYON
Yerington
YERINGTON IND. RES.
Gabbs
YOMBA IND. RES.
HUMBOLDT-TOIYABE N.F.
Duckwater
DUCKWATER IND. RES.

Zephyr Cove
Minden
Gardnerville
Mason
Schurz
WALKER RIVER IND. RES.
SMOKY VALLEY
TOQUIMA RANGE
MONITOR RANGE
HOT CREEK RANGE
Adams-McGill Res.
Atlanta

South Lake Tahoe
WASHOE IND. RES.
Smith
Wellington
Topaz Lake
Mt. Grant 3426 m (11,239 ft)
Babbitt
MINERAL
HUMBOLDT-TOIYABE N.F.
Warm Springs
Nyala
GRANT RANGE
Sunnyside

ELDORADO N.F.
DOUGLAS
HAWTHORNE ARMY DEPOT
Hawthorne
Luning
Mina
NYE
HUMBOLDT-TOIYABE NATL. FOR
White R.

STANISLAUS NATL. FOR.
HUMBOLDT-TOIYABE NATL. FOR.
Basalt
Coaldale
Tonopah
Pioche
Ursine

YOSEMITE NATL. PARK
Mono L.
Mt. Montgomery
Boundary Peak 4005 m (13,140 ft)
ESMERALDA
Caselton
Panaca

Mt. Ritter 4010 m (13,157 ft)
Dyer
Silver Peak
Goldfield
TONOPAH TEST RANGE
LINCOLN
Tempiute
Rachel
Hiko
Caliente

DEVILS POSTPILE NATL. MON.
White Mt. Peak 4342 m (14,246 ft)
Lida
NELLIS AIR FORCE RANGE COMPLEX
Ash Springs
Alamo
Elgin
DIXIE NATL. FOR.

Mt. Morgan 4190 m (13,748 ft)
Gold Point
Scotty's Junction
NEVADA TEST SITE
PAHRANAGAT N.W.R.
Carp
PAIUTE IND. RES.

SIERRA NATL. FOR.
INYO NATL. FOR.
Beatty
DESERT NATL. WILDLIFE RANGE
Pacific Time Zone
Mountain Time Zone

Madera
KINGS CANYON N.P.
INYO NATL. FOR.
DEATH VALLEY
Amargosa Valley
Mercury
Indian Springs
Glendale
Moapa
Mesquite
Bunkerville

MANZANAR N.H.S.
Mt. Whitney 4418 m (14,494 ft)
MOAPA RIVER IND. RES.
Overton
VALLEY OF FIRE S.P.
GRAND CANYON-PARASHANT NATL. MON.

SEQUOIA NATL. PARK
SIERRA NEVADA
NEVADA
CALIFORNIA
DEATH VALLEY NATIONAL
ASH MEADOWS N.W.R.
DEVILS HOLE (DEATH VALLEY NATL. PARK)
SPRING MTS. N.R.A.
NELLIS A.F.B.
CLARK
L. Mead
Colorado R.

GIANT SEQUOIA NATL. MON. (South Unit)
Corcoran
Lindsay
SEQUOIA NATL. FOR.
CHINA LAKE NAVAL WEAPONS CENTER
Charleston Park
Pahrump
N. Las Vegas
Las Vegas
Paradise
Henderson
Hoover Dam
LAKE MEAD NATL. REC. AREA

Porterville
PARK
Spring Valley
Blue Diamond
Boulder City
Red L.

RED ROCK CANYON N.C.A.
Sloan
Goodsprings
Sandy
Nelson
BLACK MTS.

Amargosa R.
FORT IRWIN MIL. RES.
Jean
Cottonwood Cove
Searchlight

MOJAVE NATL.
Cal Nev Ari
L. Mohave
Kingman

Nevada

★ State Capital
● County Seat
— Limited Access Highway
— Other Major Road

1:3,364,000

0   50   100mi
0 50 100   150 km
Albers Equal Area Projection

MOJAVE DESERT
PRESERVE
FORT MOJAVE IND. RES.
Bullhead City

© MapQuest.com, Inc.

Capital: Concord	**Pop. (2000):** 1,235,786
Area: 9,400 sq. mi.	**Largest City:** Manchester
24,200 sq. km.	107,006

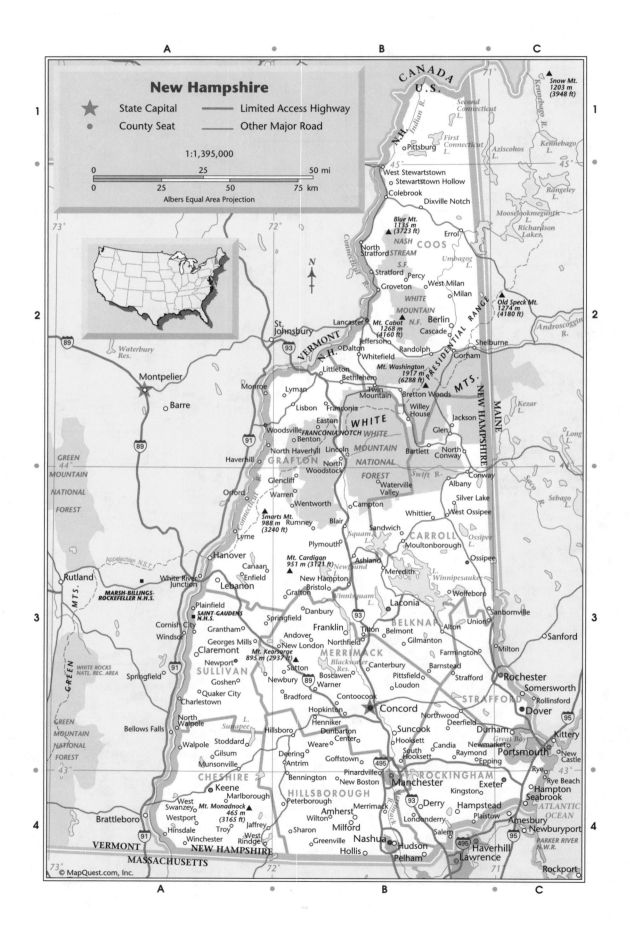

New Hampshire

★ State Capital — Limited Access Highway

• County Seat — Other Major Road

1:1,395,000

0 25 50 mi

0 25 50 75 km

Albers Equal Area Projection

© MapQuest.com, Inc.

Capital: Trenton
Area: 8,700 sq. mi.
22,600 sq. km.
Pop. (2000): 8,414,350
Largest City: Newark
273,546

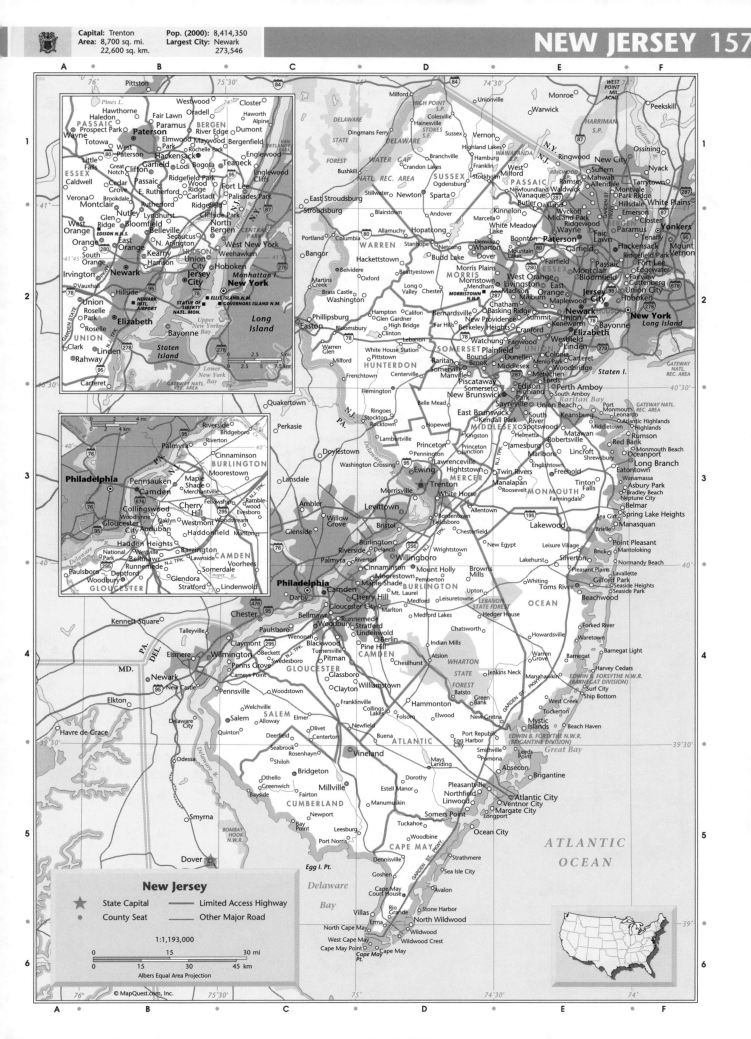

New Jersey

★ State Capital — Limited Access Highway
● County Seat — Other Major Road

1:1,193,000

0   15   30 mi
0   15   30   45 km
Albers Equal Area Projection

© MapQuest.com, Inc.

Capital: Santa Fe **Pop. (2000):** 1,819,046
Area: 121,600 sq. mi. **Largest City:** Albuquerque
314,900 sq. km. 448,607

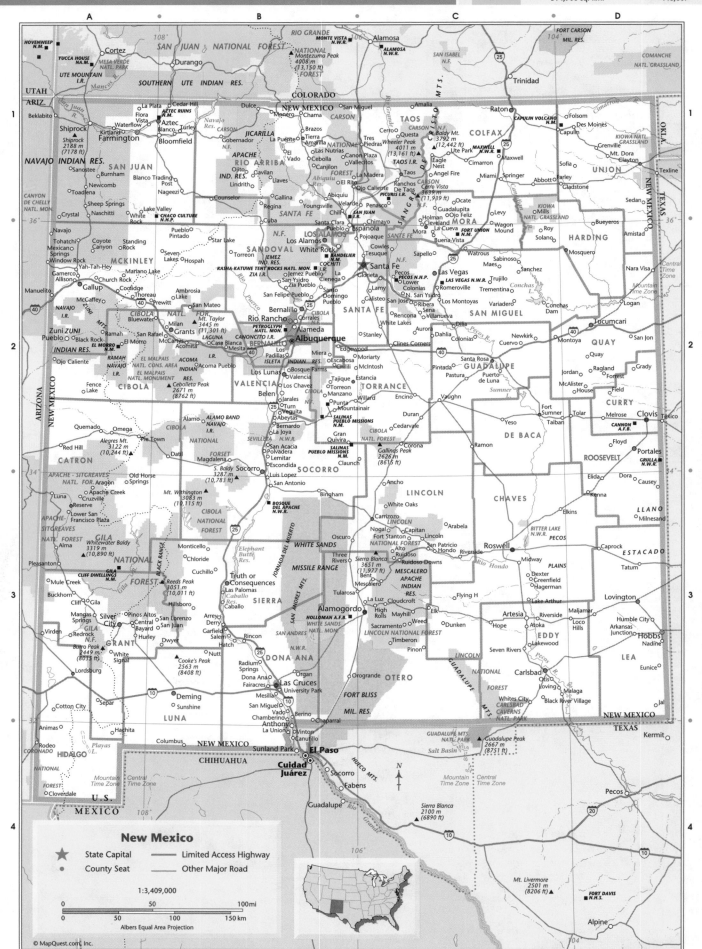

New Mexico

★ State Capital ── Limited Access Highway
• County Seat ── Other Major Road

1:3,409,000

0   50   100mi
0   50   100   150 km
Albers Equal Area Projection

© MapQuest.com, Inc.

Capital: Albany
Area: 54,700 sq. mi.
141,100 sq. km.

Pop. (2000): 18,976,457
Largest City: New York
8,008,278

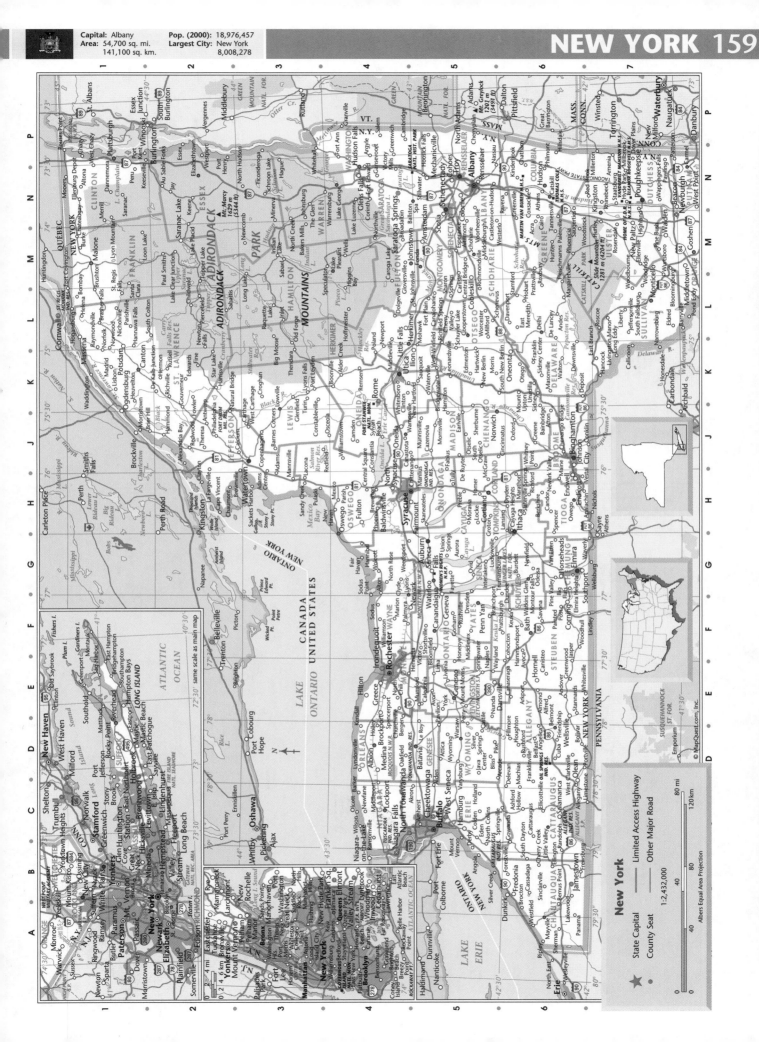

New York

State Capital
County Seat

Limited Access Highway
Other Major Road

1:2,432,000

Albers Equal Area Projection

©MapQuest.com, Inc.

Capital: Raleigh
Area: 53,800 sq. mi.
139,400 sq. km.
Pop. (2000): 8,049,313
Largest City: Charlotte
540,828

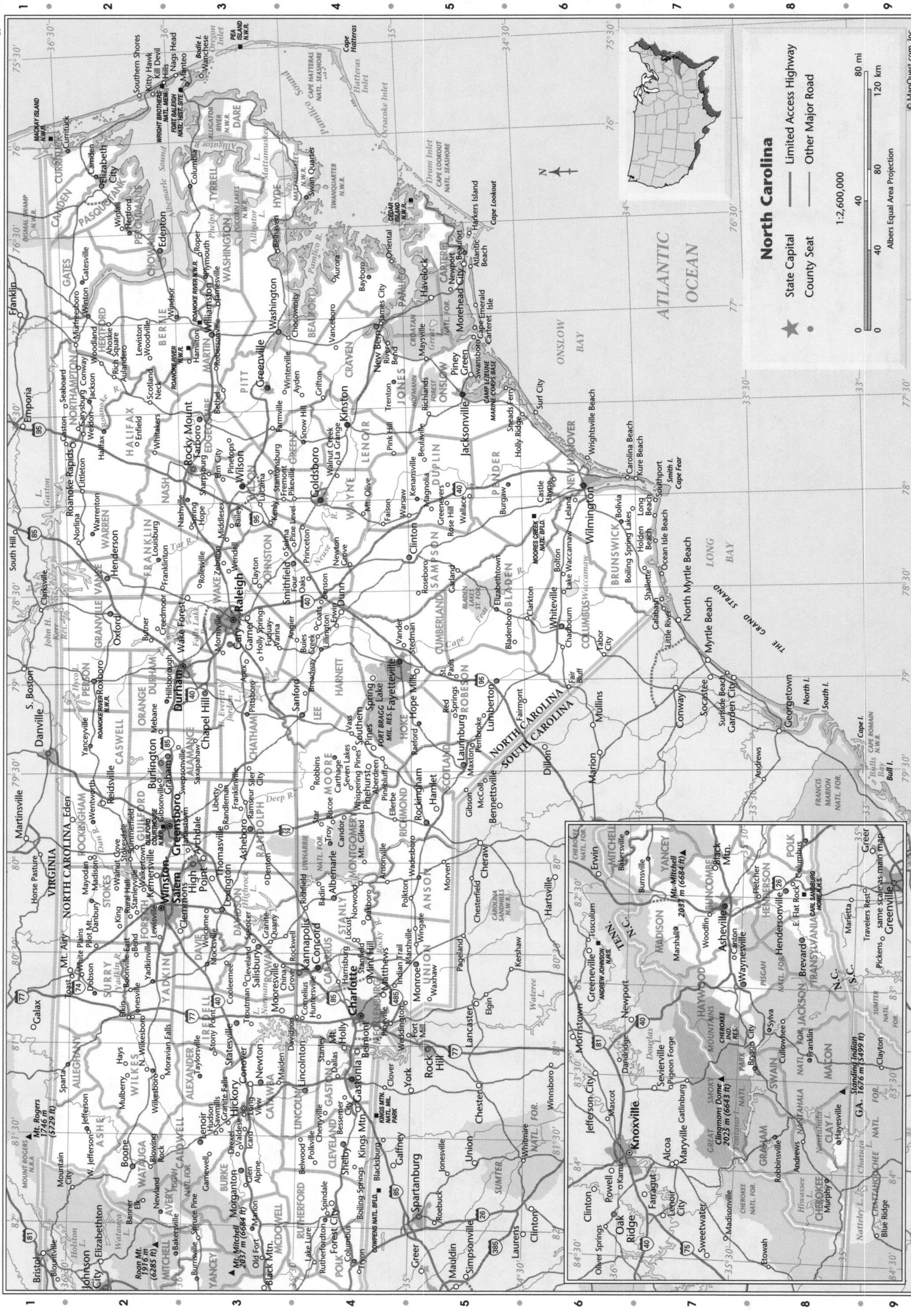

North Carolina

★ State Capital
• County Seat

— Limited Access Highway
— Other Major Road

1:2,600,000

Albers Equal Area Projection

80 mi
120 km

© MapQuest.com, Inc.

ATLANTIC OCEAN

VIRGINIA

NORTH CAROLINA

SOUTH CAROLINA

TENN.

GA.

Raleigh

Charlotte

Winston-Salem

Greensboro

Durham

Wilmington

Fayetteville

Asheville

Gastonia

Kannapolis

Concord

Salisbury

Statesville

Hickory

Rocky Mount

Wilson

Goldsboro

Kinston

Greenville

Washington

New Bern

Jacksonville

Morehead City

Elizabeth City

PAMLICO SOUND

ALBEMARLE SOUND

Cape Hatteras

Cape Lookout

ONSLOW BAY

LONG BAY

THE GRAND STRAND

Mt. Mitchell 2037 m (6684 ft)

Mt. Rogers 1746 m (5729 ft)

Clingmans Dome 2025 m (6643 ft)

Capital: Bismarck
Area: 70,700 sq. mi.
183,100 sq. km.
Pop. (2000): 642,200
Largest City: Fargo
90,599

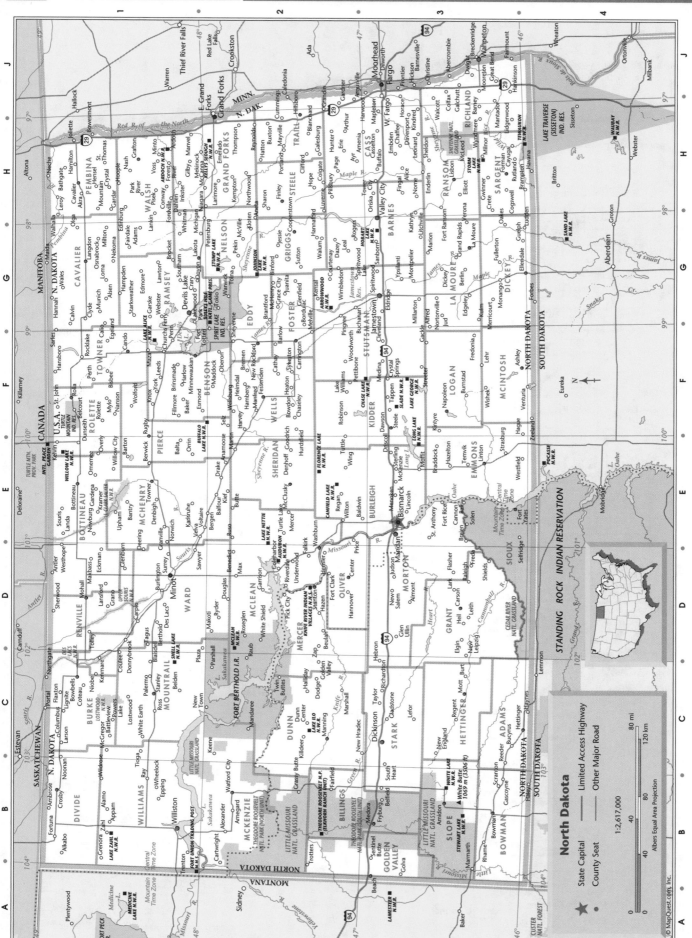

North Dakota

★ State Capital
• County Seat

— Limited Access Highway
— Other Major Road

1:2,617,000

Albers Equal Area Projection

© MapQuest.com, Inc.

Capital: Columbus
Area: 44,800 sq. mi.
116,100 sq. km.
Pop. (2000): 11,353,140
Largest City: Columbus
711,470

Capital: Oklahoma City   **Pop. (2000):** 3,450,654
Area: 69,900 sq. mi.   **Largest City:** Oklahoma City
181,000 sq. km.   506,132

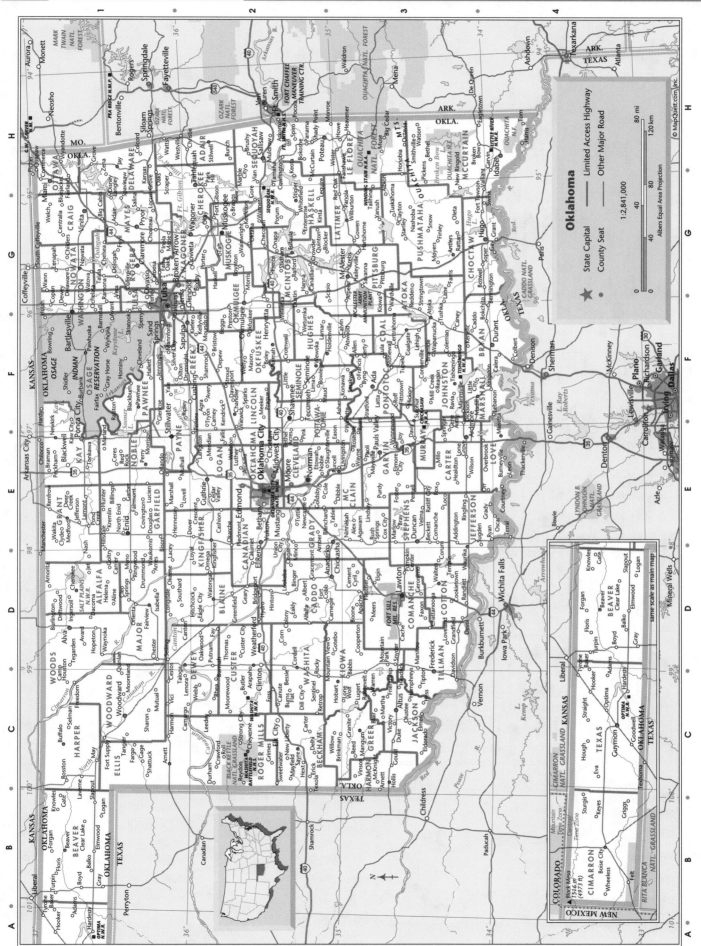

Oklahoma

★ State Capital — Limited Access Highway
• County Seat — Other Major Road

1:2,841,000

Albers Equal Area Projection

Capital: Salem
Area: 98,400 sq. mi.
254,800 sq. km.
Pop. (2000): 3,421,399
Largest City: Portland
529,121

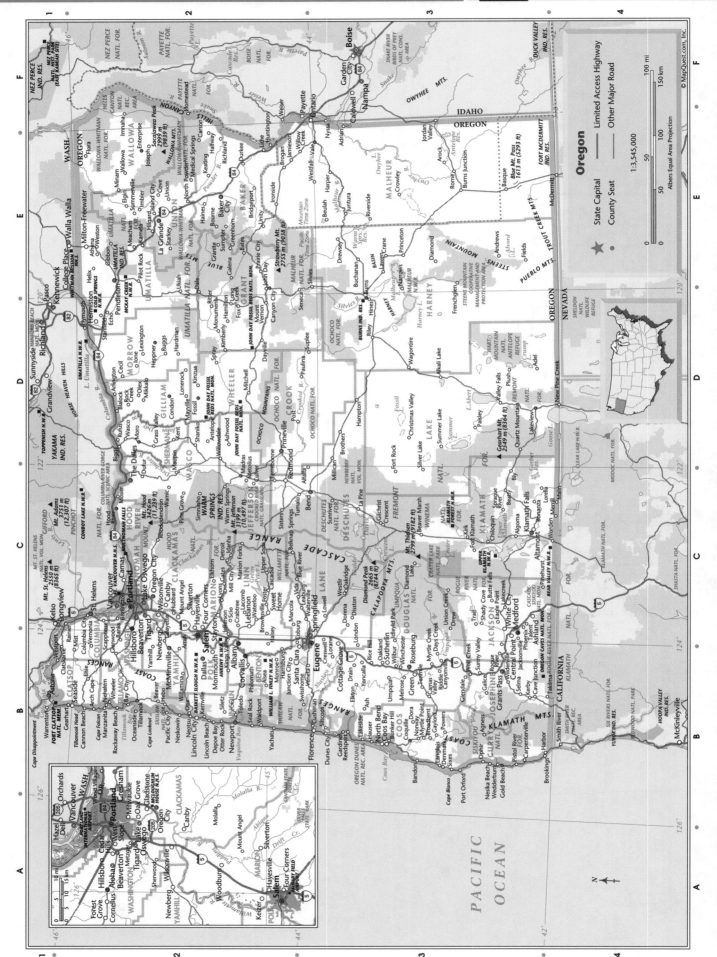

Capital: Harrisburg   Pop. (2000): 12,281,054
Area: 45,300 sq. mi.   Largest City: Philadelphia
117,300 sq. km.   1,517,550

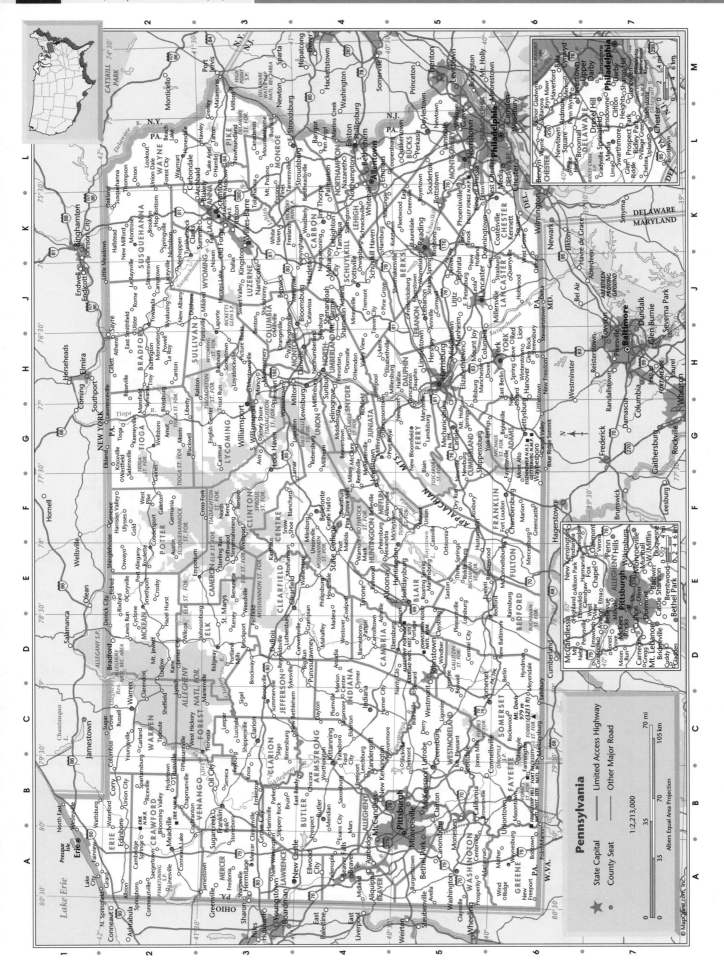

Pennsylvania

★ State Capital
• County Seat

—— Limited Access Highway
—— Other Major Road

1:2,213,000

Albers Equal Area Projection

Capital: Providence
Area: 1,500 sq. mi.
4,000 sq. km.
Pop. (2000): 1,048,319
Largest City: Providence
173,618

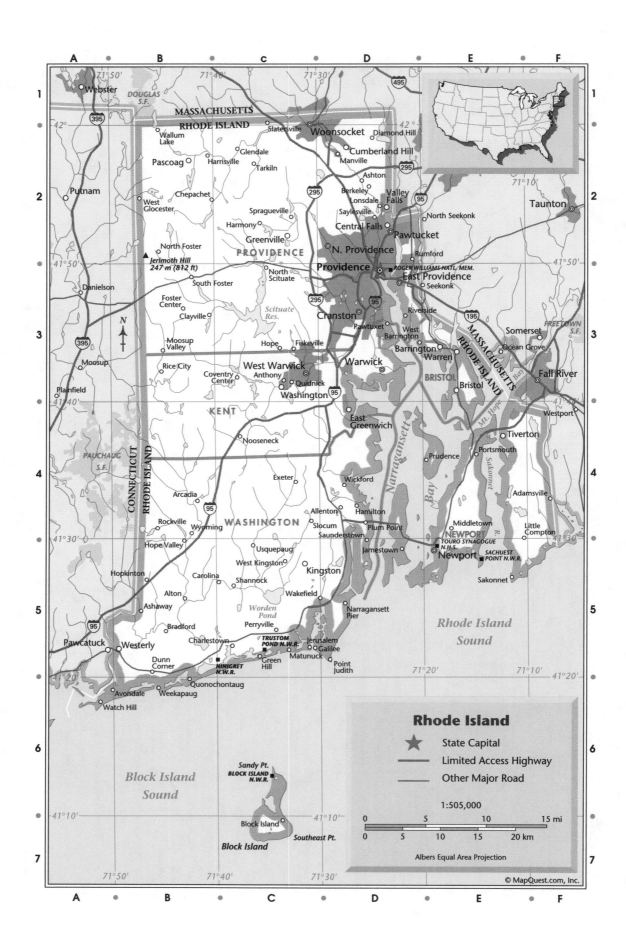

Webster
DOUGLAS S.F.
MASSACHUSETTS
RHODE ISLAND
Slatersville
Woonsocket
Diamond Hill
Wallum Lake
Glendale
Cumberland Hill
Manville
Pascoag
Harrisville
Tarkiln
Ashton
Putnam
Chepachet
Berkeley
Lonsdale
Valley Falls
North Seekonk
West Glocester
Spragueville
Saylesville
Central Falls
Pawtucket
Taunton
Harmony
PROVIDENCE
N. Providence
Rumford
Greenville
Jerimoth Hill
247 m (812 ft)
North Scituate
Providence
ROGER WILLIAMS NATL. MEM.
East Providence
Seekonk
Danielson
South Foster
Foster Center
Scituate Res.
Cranston
Pawtuxet
Riverside
West Barrington
RHODE ISLAND
MASSACHUSETTS
Somerset
FREETOWN S.F.
Clayville
Hope
Fiskeville
Barrington
Warren
Ocean Grove
Moosup Valley
Rice City
West Warwick
Warwick
BRISTOL
Bristol
Fall River
Moosup
Coventry Center
Anthony
Quidnick
Mt. Hope
Plainfield
Washington
Westport
KENT
East Greenwich
Narragansett Bay
PAUCHAUG S.F.
CONNECTICUT
RHODE ISLAND
Nooseneck
Wickford
Prudence
Portsmouth
Tiverton
Exeter
Sakonnet R.
Adamsville
Arcadia
Hamilton
Middletown
Little Compton
Rockville
Wyoming
WASHINGTON
Allenton
Slocum
Plum Point
NEWPORT
TOURO SYNAGOGUE N.H.S.
Hope Valley
Saunderstown
SACHUEST POINT N.W.R.
Usquepaug
Jamestown
Newport
Hopkinton
West Kingston
Kingston
Sakonnet
Carolina
Shannock
Alton
Wakefield
Ashaway
Worden Pond
Narragansett Pier
Bradford
Perryville
Rhode Island Sound
Pawcatuck
Westerly
Charlestown
TRUSTOM POND N.W.R.
Jerusalem
Galilee
Dunn Corner
NINIGRET N.W.R.
Green Hill
Matunuck
Point Judith
Avondale
Weekapaug
Quonochontaug
Watch Hill

Rhode Island

★ State Capital
— Limited Access Highway
— Other Major Road

1:505,000

0   5   10   15 mi
0   5   10   15   20 km

Block Island Sound
Sandy Pt.
BLOCK ISLAND N.W.R.
Block Island
Southeast Pt.
Block Island

Albers Equal Area Projection

© MapQuest.com, Inc.

Capital: Columbia
Area: 32,000 sq. mi.
82,900 sq. km.
Pop. (2000): 4,012,012
Largest City: Columbia
116,278

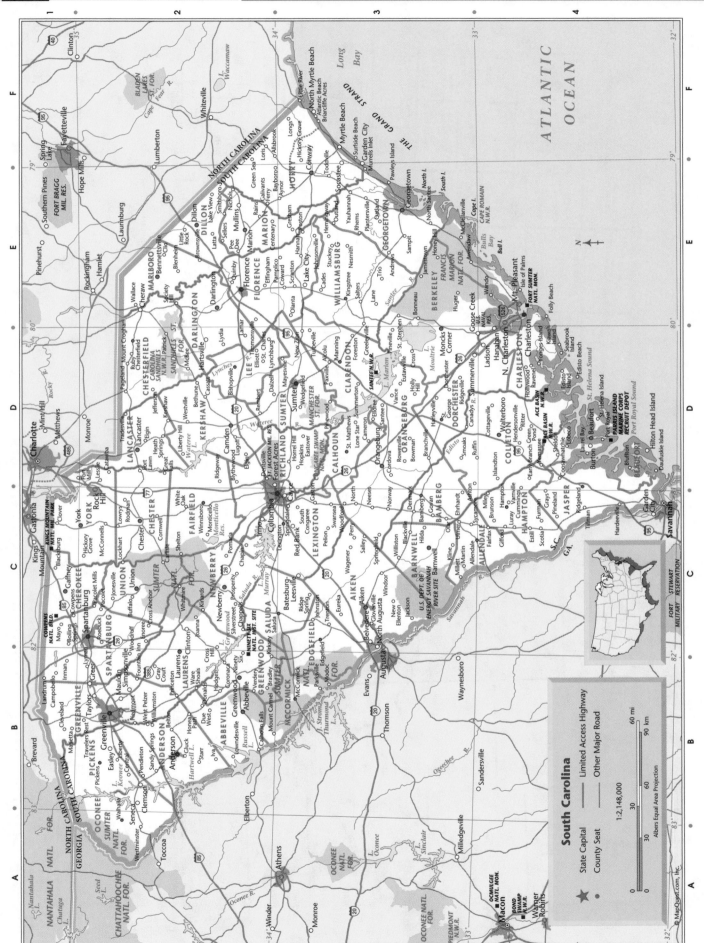

Capital: Pierre
Area: 77,100 sq. mi.
199,700 sq. km.

Pop. (2000): 754,844
Largest City: Sioux Falls
123,975

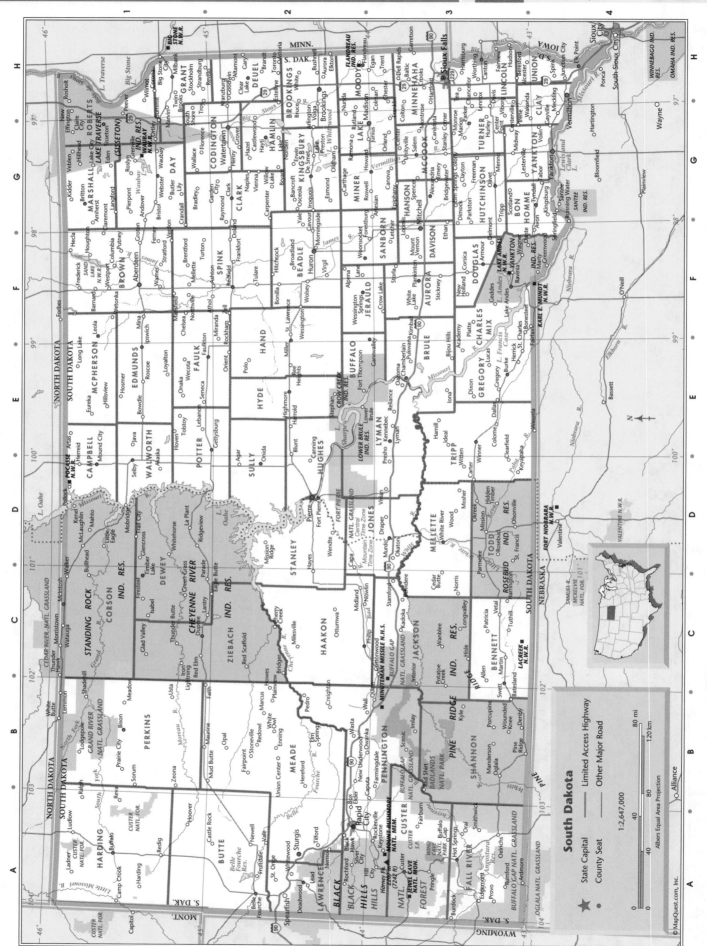

South Dakota

★ State Capital
• County Seat

Limited Access Highway
Other Major Road

1:2,647,000

Albers Equal Area Projection

©MapQuest.com, Inc.

Capital: Nashville
Area: 42,100 sq. mi.
109,200 sq. km.
Pop. (2000): 5,689,283
Largest City: Memphis
650,100

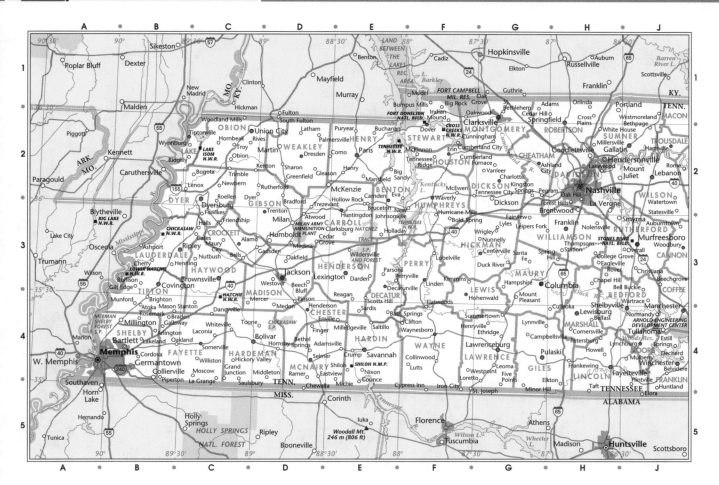

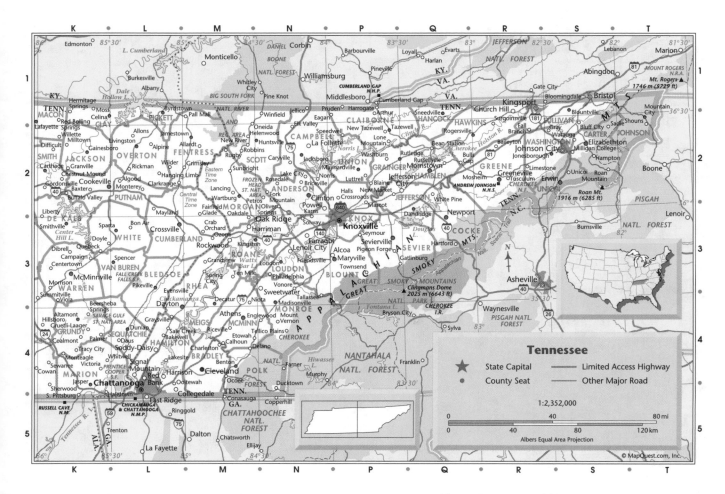

Tennessee

★ State Capital
● County Seat

— Limited Access Highway
— Other Major Road

1:2,352,000

0   40   80 mi
0   40   80   120 km

Albers Equal Area Projection

© MapQuest.com, Inc.

Capital: Austin
Area: 268,600 sq. mi.
695,700 sq. km.

Pop. (2000): 20,851,820
Largest City: Houston
1,953,631

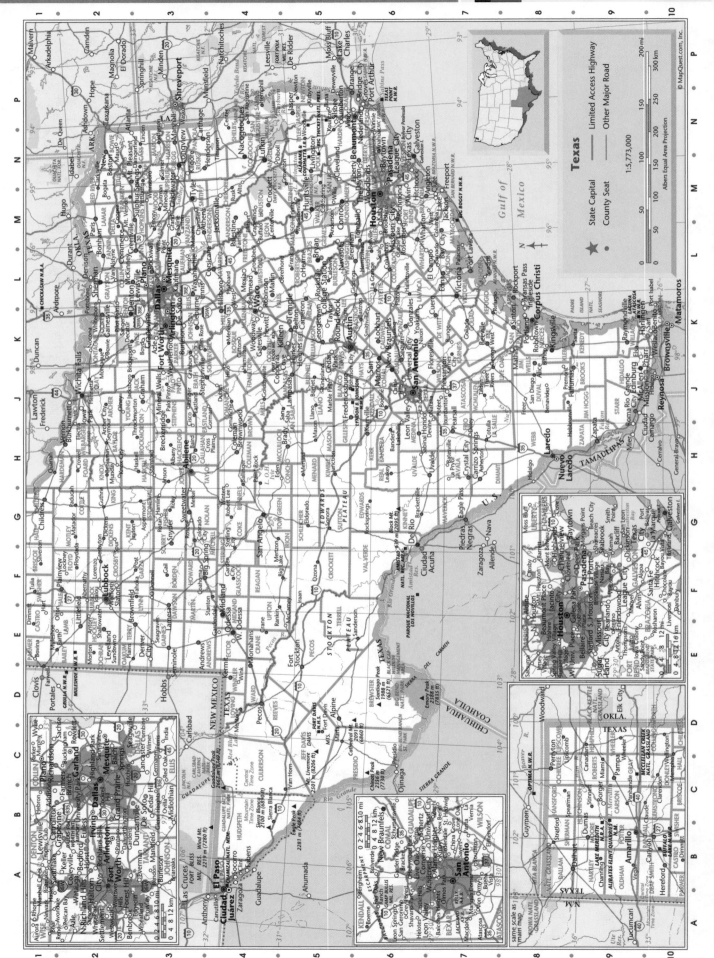

Texas

State Capital
County Seat

Limited Access Highway
Other Major Road

1:5,773,000

Albers Equal Area Projection

Gulf of Mexico

© MapQuest.com, Inc.

Capital: Salt Lake City
Area: 84,900 sq. mi.
219,900 sq. km.
Pop. (2000): 2,233,169
Largest City: Salt Lake City
181,743

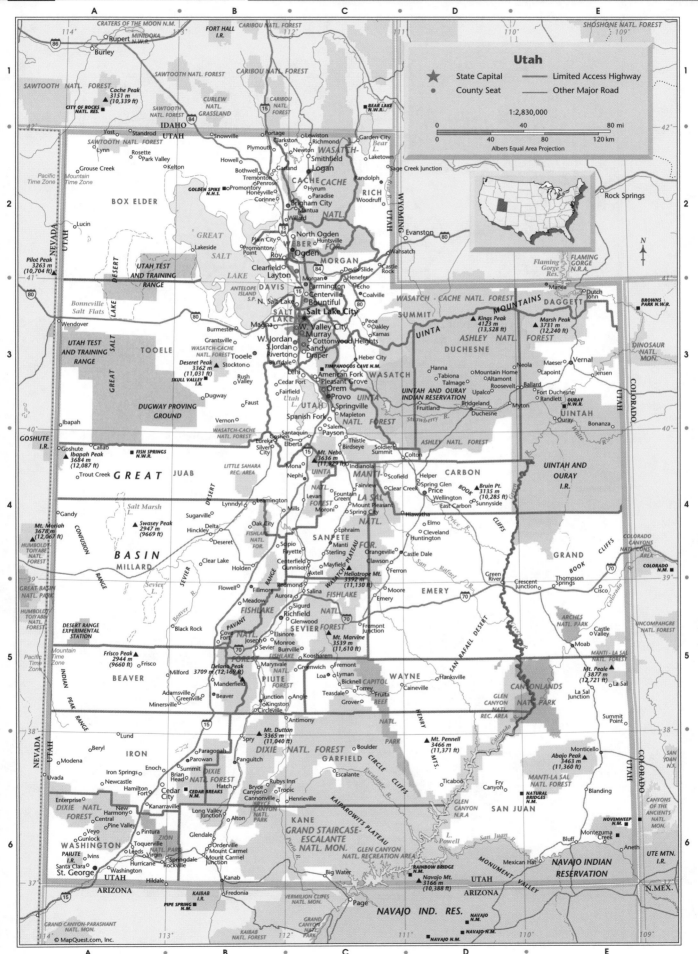

Utah

★ State Capital
● County Seat

━━ Limited Access Highway
── Other Major Road

1:2,830,000

0   40   80 mi
0   40   80   120 km
Albers Equal Area Projection

Capital: Montpelier
Area: 9,600 sq. mi.
24,900 sq. km.
Pop. (2000): 608,827
Largest City: Burlington
38,889

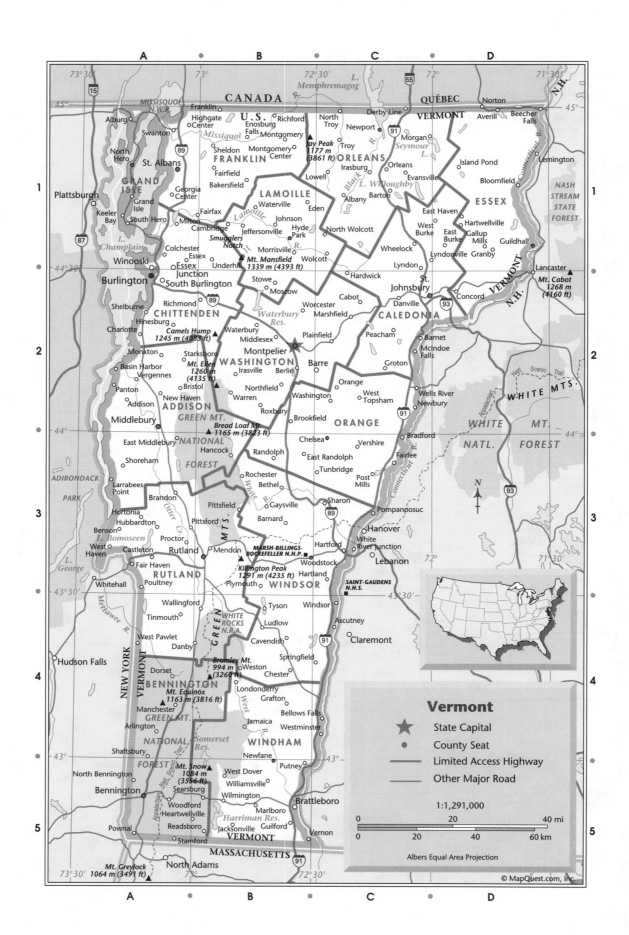

Vermont

★ State Capital
• County Seat
— Limited Access Highway
— Other Major Road

1:1,291,000

0   20   40 mi

0   20   40   60 km

Albers Equal Area Projection

© MapQuest.com, Inc.

Capital: Richmond
Area: 42,800 sq. mi.
110,800 sq. km.
Pop. (2000): 7,078,515
Largest City: Virginia Beach
425,257

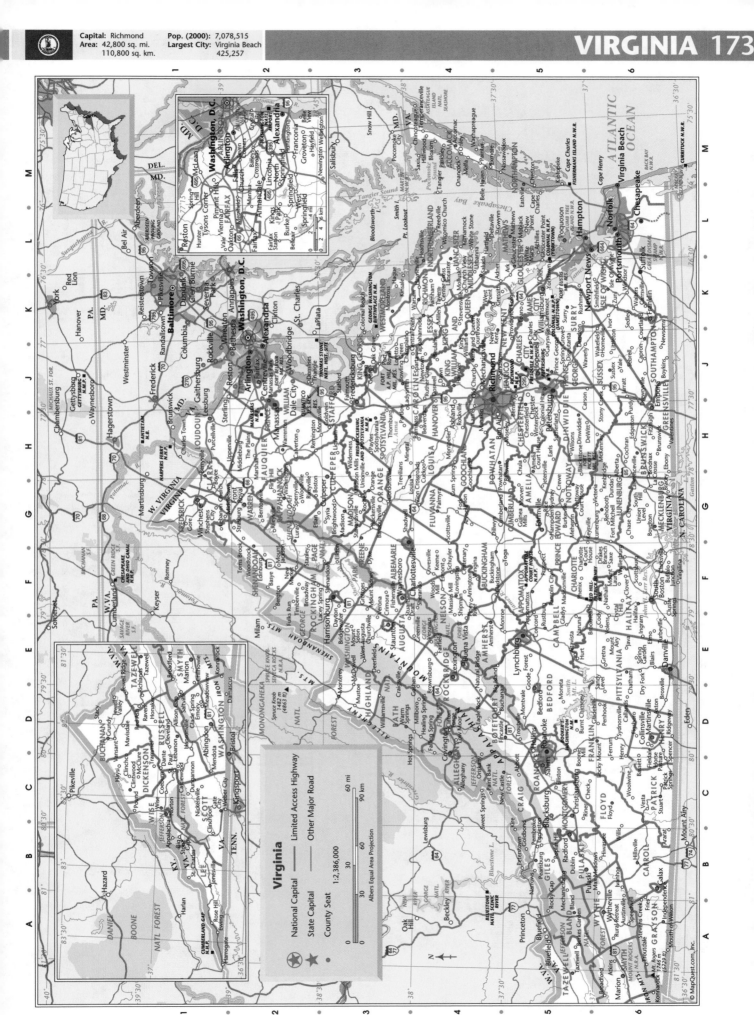

Virginia

National Capital ⚹
State Capital ★
County Seat •

Limited Access Highway
Other Major Road

1:2,386,000
Albers Equal Area Projection

© MapQuest.com, Inc.

Capital: Olympia	Pop. (2000): 5,894,121
Area: 71,300 sq. mi.	Largest City: Seattle
184,700 sq. km.	563,374

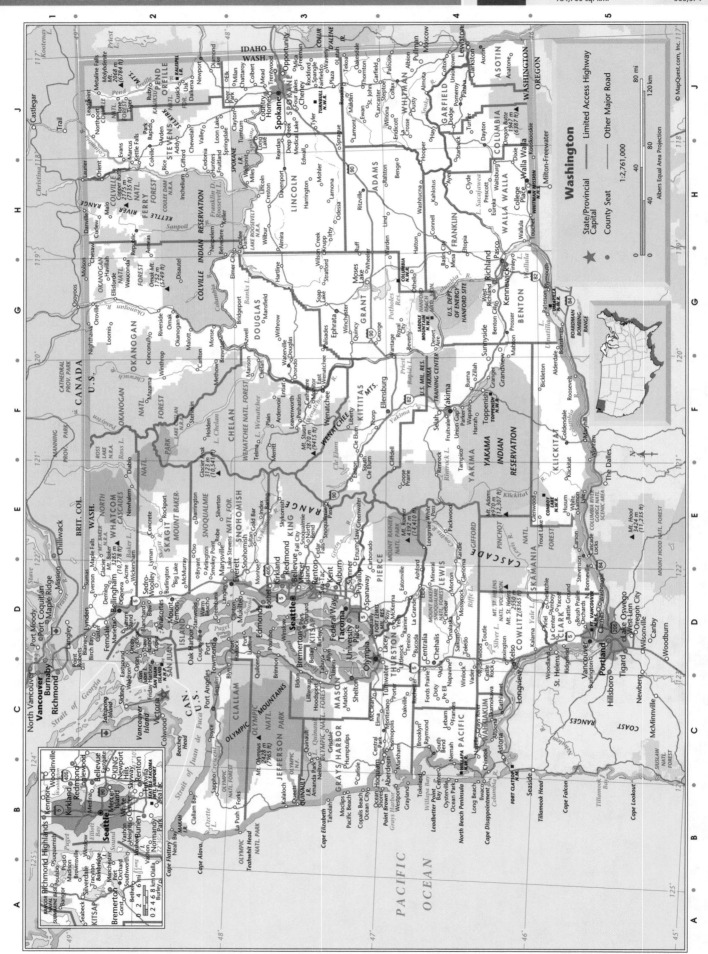

Washington

Scale 1:2,761,000

- ★ State/Provincial Capital
- • County Seat

— Limited Access Highway
— Other Major Road

Albers Equal Area Projection

© MapQuest.com, Inc.

Capital: Charleston
Area: 24,200 sq. mi.
62,800 sq. km.
Pop. (2000): 1,808,344
Largest City: Charleston
53,421

West Virginia

1:1,830,000
Albers Equal Area Projection

★ State Capital
• County Seat

— Limited Access Highway
— Other Major Road

© MapQuest.com, Inc.

WISCONSIN
1848

Capital: Madison
Area: 65,500 sq. mi.
169,600 sq. km.

Pop. (2000): 5,363,675
Largest City: Milwaukee
596,974

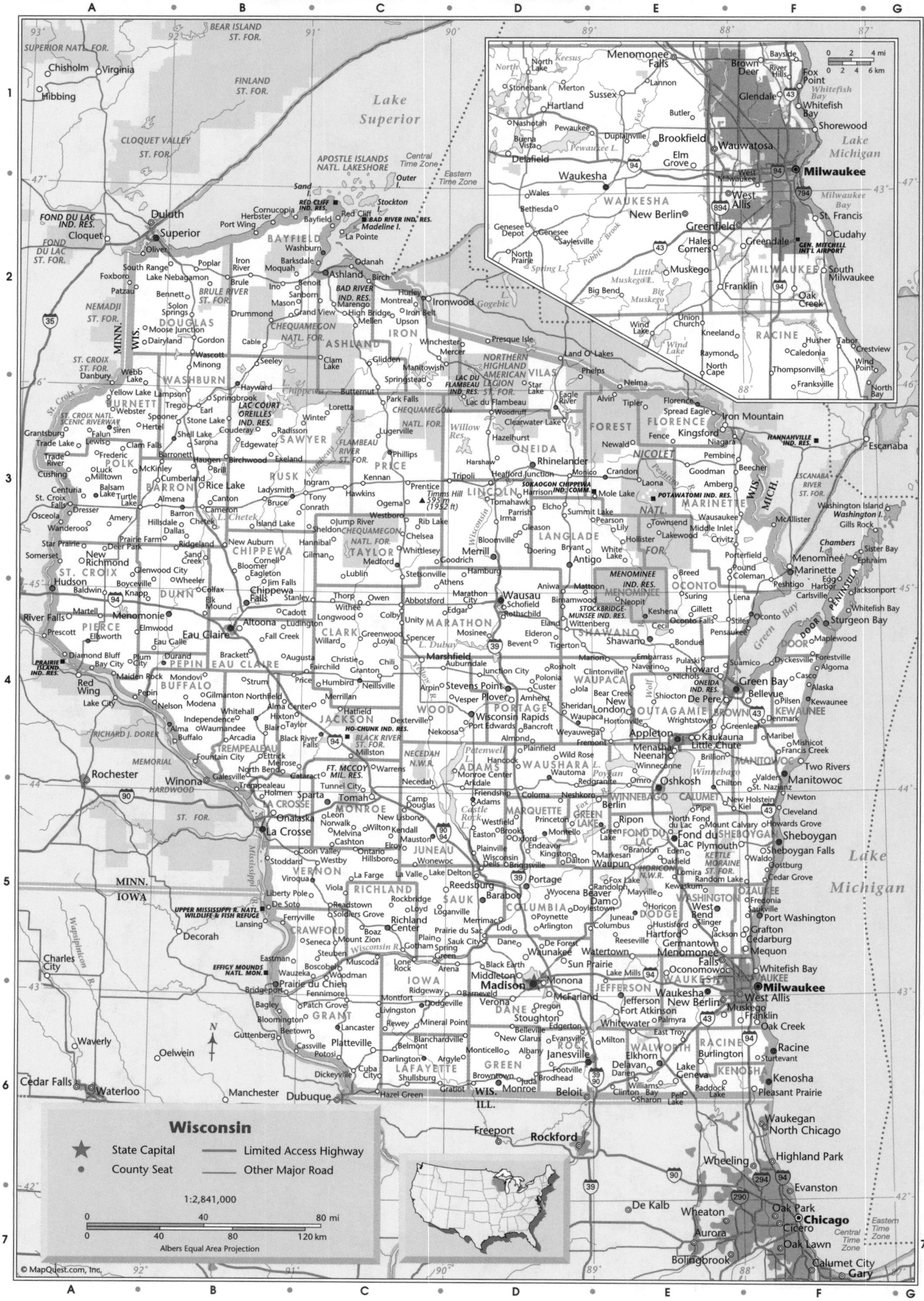

Wisconsin

★ State Capital
● County Seat
— Limited Access Highway
— Other Major Road

1:2,841,000

0   40   80 mi
0   40   80   120 km

Albers Equal Area Projection

© MapQuest.com, Inc.

Lake Superior

Lake Michigan

Apostle Islands Natl. Lakeshore

Central Time Zone / *Eastern Time Zone*

Milwaukee

Madison

Chicago

Rockford

Dubuque

Green Bay

Eau Claire

La Crosse

Superior   Duluth

Capital: Cheyenne **Pop. (2000):** 493,782
Area: 97,800 sq. mi. **Largest City:** Cheyenne
253,300 sq. km. 53,011

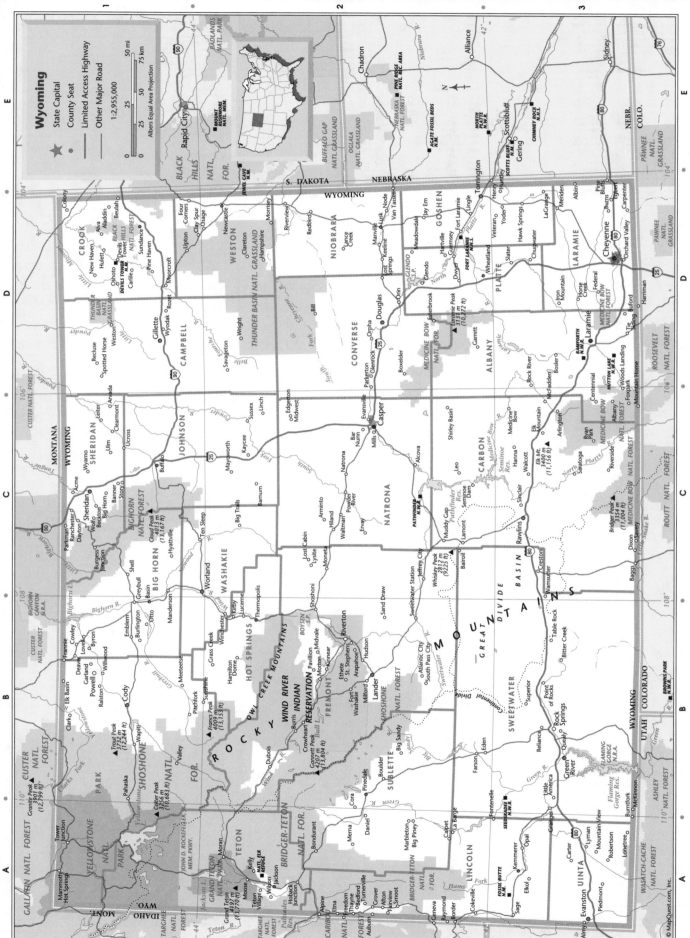

Wyoming

★ State Capital
● County Seat
── Limited Access Highway
── Other Major Road

1:2,955,000

50 mi
25
0

75 km
50
25
0

Albers Equal Area Projection

© MapQuest.com, Inc.

Abbreviations
N.H.P. ....National Historical Park
N.H.S. ....National Historic Site
N.M. ....National Monument
N.P. ....National Park
N.R.A. ....National Recreation Area

Alabama ....page 128

Cities and Towns
Abbeville D4
Adamsville C2
Alabaster C2
Albertville C1
Alexander City D3
Aliceville A2
Andalusia C4
Anniston D2
Arab C1
Ashford D4
Ashland D2
Asheville C2
Athens C1
Atmore B4
Attalla C1
Auburn D3
Bay Minette B5
Bayou La Batre A5
Bessemer C2
Birmingham C2
Blountsville C1
Boaz C1
Brent B3
Brewton B4
Bridgeport D1
Brundidge D4
Butler A3
Calera C2
Camden B4
Camp Hill D3
Carbon Hill B2
Carrollton A2
Center Point C2
Centre D1
Centreville B3
Chatom A4
Chelsea C2
Cherokee B1
Chickasaw A5
Childersburg C2
Citronelle A4
Clanton C3
Clayton D4
Clio D4
Collinsville D1
Columbiana C2
Cordova B2
Cottonwood D4
Creola A5
Crossville D1
Cullman C1
Dadeville D3
Daleville D4
Daphne B5
Decatur C1
Demopolis B3
Dora B2
Dothan D4
Double Springs B1
East Brewton B4
Elba C4
Enterprise D4
Eufaula D4
Eutaw B3
Evergreen C4
Fairfield C2
Fairhope B5
Falkville C1
Fayette B2
Flomaton B4
Florala C4
Florence B1
Foley B5
Fort Morgan A5
Fort Payne D1
Frisco City B4
Fultondale C2
Gadsden C2
Gardendale C2
Gasque B5
Geneva D4
Georgiana C4
Glencoe D2
Good Hope C1
Goodwater C2
Gordo B2
Grand Bay A5
Greensboro B3
Greenville C4
Grove Hill B4
Guin B2
Gulf Shores B5
Guntersville C1
Haleyville B1
Hamilton B1
Hanceville C1
Hartford D4
Hartselle C1
Hayneville C3
Hazel Green C1
Headland D4
Heflin D2
Helena C2
Henagar D1
Heron Bay A5
Hokes Bluff D2
Holt B2
Hoover C2
Hueytown B2
Huntsville C1
Irondale C2
Jackson A4
Jacksonville D2
Jasper B2
Jemison C3
Lafayette D3
Lanett D3
Leeds C2
Lincoln C2
Linden B3
Lineville D2
Livingston A3
Luverne C4
Madison C1
Marion B3
Meridianville C1
Midfield C2
Midland City D4
Millbrook C3
Mobile A5
Monroeville B4

Montevallo C2
Montgomery, capital C3
Moulton B1
Moundville B3
Muscle Shoals B1
New Hope C1
Newton D4
Northport B2
Oneonta C2
Opelika D3
Opp C4
Orange Beach B5
Oxford D2
Ozark D4
Parrish B2
Pelham C2
Pell City C2
Petersville B1
Phenix City D3
Phil Campbell B1
Piedmont D2
Pinson C2
Point Clear B5
Prattville C3
Priceville C1
Prichard A5
Ragland C2
Rainbow City D2
Rainsville D1
Reform A2
Roanoke D2
Robertsdale B5
Rockford C3
Russellville B1
Samson C4
Saraland A5
Sardis City C1
Satsuma A5
Scottsboro C1
Selma B3
Sheffield B1
Slocomb D4
Smiths D3
Southside C2
Spanish Fort B5
Springville C2
Stevenson D1
Sulligent B2
Sumiton B2
Sylacauga C2
Talladega C2
Tallassee D3
Taylor D4
Theodore A5
Thomasville B4
Thorsby C3
Tillmans Corner A5
Town Creek B1
Trinity B1
Troy D4
Trussville C2
Tuscaloosa B2
Tuscumbia B1
Tuskegee D3
Union Springs D3
Uniontown B3
Valley D3
Vernon A2
Vestavia Hills C2
Vincent C2
Warrior C2
Weaver D2
Wedowee D2
West Blocton B2
Wetumpka C3
Winfield B2
York A3

Other Features
Alabama, river B4
Appalachian, mts. D1
Bear Creek, reservoir B1
Black Warrior, river B3
Bon Secour, bay B5
Cahaba, river C4
Cheaha, mt. D2
Conecuh, river C4
Coosa, river D1
Dauphin, island A5
Guntersville, lake C1
Jordan, lake C3
Lewis Smith, lake B1
Logan Martin, lake D1
Lookout, mt. D1
Martin, lake D3
Mitchell, lake C3
Mobile, bay A5
Neely Henry, lake D2
Pickwick, lake A1
R.L. Harris, reservoir D2
Russell Cave Natl. Monument D1
Tallapoosa, river D3
Tennessee, river A1
Tombigbee, river A4
Tuscaloosa, lake B2
Tuskegee Institute Natl. Hist. Site D3
Weiss, lake D1
Wheeler, lake C1
William "Bill" Dannelly, reservoir B3
Wilson, lake B1

Alaska ....page 129

Cities and Towns
Adak ....Inset
Anchorage F2
Barrow D1
Bethel E2
Big Delta F2
College F2
Cordova F2
Craig J3
Delta Jct. F2
Dillingham E2
Fairbanks F2
Haines H3
Homer E3
Juneau, capital J3
Kenai E2
Ketchikan J3
Kodiak E3
Kotzebue C1
McKinley Park F2
Metlakatla J3
Nikiski E2
Nome B2
North Pole F2
Palmer F2
Petersburg J3
Prudhoe Bay F1
Seward F2

Sitka H3
Skagway H3
Soldotna E2
Talkeetna F2
Tok G2
Unalaska B4
Valdez F2
Wasilla F2
Whittier F2
Wrangell J3

Other Features
Adak, island ....Inset
Admiralty Island Natl. Monument J3
Agattu, island ....Inset
Alaska, gulf F3
Alaska, peninsula D3
Alaska, range E2
Aleutian, islands ....A4, Inset
Alexander, archipelago H3
Amchitka, island ....Inset
Amlia, island ....Inset
Andreanof, islands ....Inset
Aniakchak N.M. and Preserve D3
Atka, island ....Inset
Attu, island ....Inset
Barrow, point D1
Beaufort, sea H1
Bechanof, lake D3
Bering, sea B3
Bering, strait B2
Blackburn, mt. C3
Bristol, bay C3
Brooks, range D1
Cape Krusenstern N.M. C1
Chirikof, island D3
Chukchi, sea A1
Colville, river E1
Cook, inlet E3
Copper, river F2
Denali Natl. Park and Preserve E2
Fairweather, mt. H3
Gates of the Arctic N.P.
   and Preserve E1
Glacier Bay N.P. and Preserve H3
Iliamna, lake D3
Inside Passage, waterway J3
Kanaga, island ....Inset
Katmai Natl. Park and Preserve D3
Kenai, peninsula E3
Kenai Fjords Natl. Park F3
Kiska, island ....Inset
Klondike Gold Rush N.H.P. H3
Kobuk, river D1
Kobuk Valley Natl. Park D1
Kodiak, island E3
Kotzebue, sound C1
Koyukuk, river D1
Kuskokwim, bay C3
Kuskokwim, mts. D2
Kuskokwim, river D2
Lake Clark Natl. Park and Preserve E2
Lisburne, cape B1
Lisburne, peninsula C1
Logan, mt. G2
Lynn, canal H3
McKinley, mt. E2
Malaspina, glacier G3
Michelson, mt. G1
Mohican, cape B2
Muir, glacier F2
Near, islands ....Inset
Noatak, river D1
Norton, sound C2
Nunivak, island B3
Porcupine, river G1
Pribilof, islands B3
Prince of Wales, island J3
Progromni, volcano C4
Rat, islands ....Inset
St. Elias, mt. G2
St. George, island B3
St. Lawrence, island A2
St. Matthew, island A2
St. Paul, island B3
Samalga, pass B4
Sanak, island C4
Seguam, island ....Inset
Semisopochnoi, island ....Inset
Seward, peninsula C1
Shishaldin, volcano C4
Shumagin, islands D4
Sitka N.H.P. H3
Stikine, river J3
Tanaga, island ....Inset
Tanana, river E2
Tikchik, lakes D2
Trinity, islands E3
Unimak, island ....Inset
Unalaska, island B4
Unga, island D4
Unimak, island C4
Utukok, river C1
White Mts. Natl. Rec. Area F1
Wrangell, mts. G2
Wrangell-St. Elias N.P.
   and Preserve G2
Yukon, river D2
Yukon-Charley Rivers
   Natl. Preserve G2
Yunaska, island ....Inset

Arizona ....page 130

Cities and Towns
Ajo C5
Apache Junction C4
Avondale C4
Bagdad B3
Benson E6
Bisbee F6
Bitahochee E2
Buckeye C4
Bullhead City A2
Camp Verde D3
Carefree C4
Casa Grande D5
Catalina D4
Cave Creek C4
Chandler C4
Chinle F1
Chino Valley C3
Cibecue E3
Clarkdale C3
Claypool D4
Clifton F4
Colorado City C1
Cornville C3
Cow Springs E1
Crown King C3

Douglas F6
Dudleyville E5
Eagar F3
El Mirage C4
Eloy D5
Flagstaff D2
Florence D4
Fort Defiance F2
Fountain Hills C4
Ganado F2
Geronimo E4
Gila Bend C5
Gilbert D4
Globe E4
Goodyear C4
Grand Canyon C1
Greaterville E6
Green Valley E6
Guthrie F4
Happy Jack D3
Holbrook E3
Huachuca City E6
Kayenta E1
Kearny E4
Kingman A2
Kirkland Junction C3
Lake Havasu City A3
Lake Montezuma D3
Litchfield Park C4
Mammoth E5
Many Farms F1
Marana D5
Mesa D4
Miami E4
Nogales E6
Oracle E5
Oro Valley E5
Page D1
Paradise Valley D4
Parker A3
Payson D3
Peoria C4
Phoenix, capital C4
Pima E4
Pinetop-Lakeside F3
Prescott C3
Prescott Valley C3
Quartzsite A4
Queen Creek D4
Randolph D5
Sacaton D4
Safford F5
Sahuarita E6
St. David E6
St. Johns F3
San Carlos E4
Sanders F2
San Manuel E5
Scottsdale D4
Sedona D3
Sells D6
Show Low E3
Sierra Vista E6
Snowflake E3
Somerton A5
South Tucson E5
Springerville F3
Sun City C4
Sun Lakes D4
Superior D4
Surprise C4
Taylor E3
Tempe D4
Thatcher F5
Three Points D5
Tolleson C4
Tombstone E6
Tuba City D1
Tucson E5
Whiteriver F4
Wickenburg C4
Willcox F5
Williams C2
Window Rock F2
Winslow E3
Yuma A5

Other Features
Agua Fria, river C4
Alamo, lake B3
Apache, lake D4
Aztec Peak, mt. E4
Baldy, mt. F4
Bartlett, reservoir D4
Big Horn, mts. B4
Bill Williams, river A3
Black, mesa E1
Black, river F4
Canyon De Chelly N.M. F1
Casa Grande Ruins N.M. D5
Castle Dome, mts. A4
Castle Dome Peak, mt. A4
Chiricahua Natl. Monument F6
Colorado, river B2, D1
Coronado Natl. Mem. E6
Gila, river B5, D4, F4
Glen Canyon, dam D1
Glen Canyon Natl. Rec. Area C1
Grand, canyon C1
Grand Canyon Natl. Park B2, C1
Grand Canyon-Parashant N.M. B1
Harcuvar, mts. B4
Havasu, lake A3
Hide Creek, mt. C3
Hoover, dam A1
Hopi Indian Res. E2
Horseshoe, reservoir D4
Hualapai, mts. B3
Hubbell Trading Post N.H.S. F2
Humphreys Peak, mt. D2
Lake Mead Natl. Rec. Area B1
Little Colorado, river D2
Many Farms, lake F1
Maple Peak, mt. F4
Mazatzal Peak, mt. D3
Mohave, lake A2
Montezuma Castle N.M. D3
Monument, valley F1
Mormon, lake D3
Navajo Indian Res. E1, E2
Navajo Natl. Monument E1
Organ Pipe Cactus N.M. C5
Painted, desert D2
Parker, dam A3
Petrified Forest Natl. Park F3
Pipe Spring Natl. Monument C1
Pleasant, lake C4
Point Imperial, mt. D1
Powell, lake D1
Red, lake B2
Saguaro Natl. Monument E5
Salt, river E4

Arkansas ....page 131

Cities and Towns
Alicia D2
Alma A2
Arkadelphia B3
Arkansas City D4
Ashdown A4
Ash Flat D1
Atkins C2
Augusta D2
Bald Knob D2
Barling A2
Batesville D2
Bay E2
Beebe D2
Bella Vista A1
Benton C3
Bentonville A1
Berryville B1
Blytheville F2
Bodcaw B4
Booneville B2
Brinkley D3
Bryant C3
Bull Shoals C1
Cabot D3
Camden C4
Caraway E2
Carlisle D3
Cave City D2
Charleston A2
Clarendon D3
Clarksville B2
Clinton C2
Conway C2
Corning E1
Crossett D4
Daisy B3
Damascus C2
Danville B2
Dardanelle B2
De Queen A3
Dermott D4
Des Arc D3
De Valls Bluff D3
De Witt D3
Dierks A3
Dumas D4
Earle E2
El Dorado C4
England D3
Eudora D4
Eureka Springs B1
Fairfield Bay C2
Fallsville B2
Farmington A1
Fayetteville A1
Fordyce C4
Foreman A4
Forrest City E2
Fort Smith A2
Fountain Hill D4
Gentry A1
Glenwood B3
Gosnell F2
Gould D4
Gravette A1
Greenbrier C2
Green Forest B1
Greenwood A2
Griffithville C3
Gurdon B4
Hamburg D4
Hampton C4
Harrisburg E2
Harrison B1
Haskell C3
Hatfield A3
Hazen D3
Heber Springs C2
Helena E3
Hope B4
Horseshoe Bend D1
Hot Springs National Park B3
Hot Springs Village B3
Hoxie E1
Hughes E3
Hunter D2
Huntsville B1
Jacksonville C3
Jasper B1
Jonesboro E2
Lake City E2
Lake Hamilton B3
Lake Village D4
Lepanto E2
Lewisville B4
Lincoln A2
Little Rock, capital C3
Lonoke D3
Luxora F2
McCrory D2
McGehee D4
McNeil B4
McRae C2
Magnolia B4
Malvern C3
Manila E2
Marianna E2
Marion E2
Marked Tree E2
Marshall C2
Marvell E3
Maumelle C3
Mayflower C2
Melbourne D1
Mena A3
Monticello D4
Morrilton C2
Mountain Home C1

Mountain View C2
Mount Ida B3
Mulberry A2
Murfreesboro B3
Nashville B3
Newport D2
North Crossett D4
North Little Rock C3
Oden B3
Osceola F2
Ozark B2
Paragould E1
Paris B2
Parkin E2
Pea Ridge A1
Pelsor B2
Perryville C2
Piggott F1
Pine Bluff D3
Pocahontas E1
Prescott B4
Rector F1
Rison C4
Rogers A1
Rose Bud C2
Russell D2
Russellville B2
St. Charles D3
St. Paul B2
Salem D1
Searcy C2
Sheridan C3
Sherwood C3
Siloam Springs A1
Smackover C4
Springdale A1
Springhill B4
Star City D4
Stuttgart D3
Texarkana A4
Tillar D4
Trumann E2
Tuckerman D2
Tupelo D2
Van Buren A2
Waldo B4
Waldron A3
Walnut Ridge E1
Warren C4
Washington B4
West Fork A2
West Helena E3
West Memphis E2
White Hall C3
Wynne E2
Yellville C1

Other Features
Arkansas, river D3
Arkansas Post Natl. Mem. D3
Beaver, lake B1
Black, river B2
Boston, mts. B2
Buffalo, river B1
Buffalo Natl. River C2
Bull Shoals, lake C1
Cache, river E2
Catherine, lake C3
Dardanelle, reservoir B2
DeGray, lake B3
Erling, lake B4
Fort Smith Natl. Hist Site A2
Greers Ferry, lake C2
Greeson, lake B3
Hamilton, lake B3
Hot Springs Natl. Park B3
Little Missouri, river B4
Little Rock Central H.S N.H.S. B2
Magazine, mt. B2
Maumelle, lake C3
Millwood, lake B4
Mississippi, river F3
Nimrod, lake B3
Norfork, lake C1
Ouachita, lake B3
Ouachita, mts. A3
Ouachita, river B3, C4
Ozark, plateau B1
Pea Ridge Natl. Mil. Park A1
Red, river B4
St. Francis, river E1
Saline, river C3
Table Rock, lake B1
White, river C2, D3

California ....page 132

Cities and Towns
Adelanto H8
Alameda K2
Alamo L2
Albany K1
Alhambra D10
Alpine J10
Altadena D10
Alturas E1
Anaheim E11, H9
Anderson D2
Antioch D4, L1
Apple Valley H8
Aptos D5
Arcadia D10
Arcata A2
Arnold E4
Arroyo Grande E7
Arvin G7
Ashland K2
Atascadero E7
Atherton K3
Atwater E5
Auberry F5
Auburn E4
Avalon G9
Avenal E6
Azusa E10
Bakersfield G7
Baldwin Park E10
Barstow H8
Bell D10
Bellflower D11
Belmont K3
Belvedere J1
Benicia K1
Berkeley C5, K2
Beverly Hills C10
Big Bear Lake J8
Black Point J1
Bishop G5
Blythe L9
Bonita H8
Boron H8

	Key
Borrego Springs	J9
Brawley	K10
Brea	E11
Bridgeport	F4
Brisbane	J2
Broadmoor	J2
Buellton	E8
Buena Park	E11
Burbank	C10
Burlingame	J3
Burney	D2
Buttonwillow	F7
Calabasas	B10
Calexico	K10
California City	H7
Calipatria	K9
Calistoga	C4
Cambria	D7
Campbell	L4
Canyon	K2
Carlsbad	H9
Carmel	D6
Carmel Valley	D6
Carpinteria	F8
Carson	D11
Castroville	D6
Cathedral City	J9
Cayucos	E7
Central Valley	C2
Ceres	E5
Chester	D2
Chico	D3
Chino	F10
Chowchilla	E5
Chula Vista	C9, H10
Claremont	F10
Clayton	L1
Clearlake	C4
Cloverdale	B4
Clovis	F6
Clyde	L1
Coachella	J9
Coalinga	E6
Cobb	C4
Colfax	E3
Colusa	D3
Compton	D11
Concord	L1
Corcoran	F6
Corning	C3
Corona	F11
Coronado	B8
Corte Madera	J1
Costa Mesa	E11
Cottonwood	C2
Covina	E10
Cowan Heights	E11
Crescent City	A1
Crestline	H8
Crockett	K1
Culver City	C10
Cupertino	L4
Cypress	D11
Daly City	J2
Danville	L2
Davis	D4
Delano	F7
Del Mar	H10
Desert Hot Springs	J9
Diablo	L2
Diamond Bar	E10
Dinuba	F6
Dos Palos	E6
Downey	D11
Downieville	E3
Dublin	L2
Dunsmuir	C1
Earlimart	F7
East Los Angeles	D10
Easton	F6
East Palo Alto	K3
El Cajon	C8, J10
El Centro	K10
El Cerrito	K1
El Granada	J3
Elk Grove	D4
El Monte	D10
El Segundo	C11
El Sobrante	K1
Emeryville	K2
Encinitas	H9
Escondido	H9
Eureka	A2
Exeter	F6
Fairfax	H1
Fairfield	D4
Fallbrook	H9
Ferndale	A2
Firebaugh	E6
Florence	D11
Florin	D4
Fort Bragg	B3
Fortuna	A2
Foster City	K3
Fountain Valley	E11
Frazier Park	G8
Fremont	D5, L3
Fresno	F6
Fullerton	E11
Galt	D4
Garden Grove	E11
Gilroy	D5
Glendale	D10, G8
Glendora	E10
Glenview	B10
Gonzales	D6
Grass Valley	D3
Greenacres	F7
Greenbrae	J1
Greenfield	D6
Greenville	E2
Gridley	D3
Groveland	E5
Guadalupe	E8
Half Moon Bay	J3
Hanford	F6
Hawthorne	C11
Hayfork	B2
Hayward	C5, L2
Healdsburg	C4
Hemet	J9
Hercules	K1
Hermosa Beach	C11
Hesperia	H8
Hidden Hills	B10
Hillsborough	J3
Hollister	D6
Holtville	K10
Huntington Beach	E11, G9
Huron	E6
Ignacio	J1
Imperial Beach	B9, H10

	Key
Independence	G6
Indio	J9
Inglewood	C11, C9
Ingot	C2
Inyokern	H7
Ione	E4
Irvine	E11, H9
Isla Vista	F8
Jackson	E4
Joshua Tree	J8
Julian	J9
Kelseyville	C4
Kensington	K1
Kentfield	J1
Kerman	E6
Kernville	G7
Kettleman City	F6
King City	D6
La Canada-Flintridge	D10
La Crescenta	D10
Lafayette	K1
La Habra	E11
La Honda	K4
Lake Isabella	G7
Lakeport	C3
Lakeside	J10
Lakewood	D11
La Mesa	C8
La Mirada	D11
Lamont	G7
Lancaster	G8
La Puente	E10
Larkspur	J1
Laton	F6
Lawndale	C11
Lee Vining	F5
Lemon Grove	C8
Lemoore	F6
Lincoln	D4
Lindsay	F6
Littlerock	H8
Livermore	D5
Livingston	E5
Lockeford	D4
Lodi	D4
Loma Mar	K4
Lomita	C11
Lompoc	E8
Lone Pine	G6
Long Beach	D11, G9
Los Altos	K3
Los Altos Hills	K4
Los Angeles	D10, G8
Los Banos	E5
Los Molinos	C2
Los Osos	E7
Lynwood	D11
McCloud	C1
McFarland	F7
McKinleyville	A2
Madera	E6
Malibu	B10
Mammoth Lakes	G5
Manhattan Beach	C11
Manteca	D5
Marina	D6
Marina del Rey	C11
Marin City	J1
Marinwood	J1
Mariposa	F5
Markleeville	F4
Martinez	C4, K1
Marysville	D3
Maywood	D10
Mecca	J9
Mendota	E6
Menlo Park	K3
Merced	E5
Midway City	E11
Millbrae	J3
Mill Valley	J1
Milpitas	L3
Miranda	B2
Modesto	E5
Mojave	G7
Monrovia	E10
Montara	J3
Montclair	F10
Montebello	D10
Monte Nido	B10
Monterey	D6
Monterey Park	D10
Monte Sereno	L4
Moraga	K2
Moreno Valley	H9
Morgan Hill	D5
Morongo Valley	J8
Morro Bay	E7
Moss Beach	J3
Mountain View	K3
Mount Shasta	C1
Muir Beach	H1
Napa	C4
National City	C9
Needles	L8
Nevada City	D3
Newark	L3
Newberry Springs	J8
Newport Beach	H9
Nicasio	H1
Nice	C3
Nipomo	E8
Nipton	K7
Norco	F11
North Edwards	H7
North Fair Oaks	K3
Novato	H1
Oakdale	E5
Oakhurst	F5
Oakland	K2, C5
Oceanside	H9
Oildale	G7
Ojai	F8
Olema	H1
Olivehurst	D3
Ontario	F10, H8
Orange	E11
Orinda	K1
Orland	C3
Oroville	D3
Otay	C9
Oxnard	F8
Pacheco	L1
Pacifica	J2
Palermo	D3
Palmdale	G8
Palm Desert	J9
Palm Springs	J9
Palo Alto	K3
Palos Verdes Estates	C11
Paradise	D3
Pasadena	D10, G8

	Key
Patterson	D5
Petaluma	C4
Pico Rivera	D10
Piedmont	K2
Pine Valley	J10
Pinole	K1
Pismo Beach	E7
Pittsburg	L1
Placentia	E11
Placerville	E4
Pleasant Hill	L1
Pleasanton	L2
Pomona	E10, H8
Port Costa	K1
Porterville	G6
Portola	E3
Poway	H10
Prunedale	D6
Quartz Hill	G8
Quincy	E3
Ramona	J9
Rancho Cucamonga	F10
Rancho Palos Verdes	C11
Rancho Santa Margarita	F11
Rancho Rinconada	L4
Red Bluff	C2
Redding	C2
Redlands	H8
Redondo Beach	C11
Redwood City	C5, K3
Reedley	F6
Richgrove	F7
Richmond	J1
Ridgecrest	H7
Rio Dell	A2
Riverside	H9
Rodeo	K1
Rolling Hills	C11
Rolling Hills Estates	C11
Rosamond	G8
Roseville	D4
Sacramento, capital	D4
Salinas	D6
San Andreas	E4
San Anselmo	H1
San Bernardino	H8
San Bruno	J2
San Carlos	K3
San Clemente	F11
San Diego	B8, H10
San Francisco	C5, J2
San Gabriel	D10
Sanger	F6
San Gregorio	J4
San Jose	D5, L4
San Juan Bautista	D6
San Juan Capistrano	F11
San Leandro	K2
San Lorenzo	K2
San Luis Obispo	E7
San Mateo	C5, K3
San Pablo	J1
San Quentin	J1
San Rafael	C5, J1
San Ramon	L2
Santa Ana	E11, H9
Santa Barbara	F8
Santa Clara	L4
Santa Clarita	G8
Santa Cruz	C6
Santa Maria	E8
Santa Monica	C10
Santa Paula	F8
Santa Rosa	C4
Santa Venetia	J1
Santa Ynez	E8
Santee	C8
Saratoga	L4
Sausalito	J2
Scotts Valley	C5
Seal Beach	D11
Sebastopol	C4
Selma	F6
Shafter	F7
Shingletown	D2
Shoshone	J7
Simi Valley	G8
Soledad	D6
Solvang	E8
Sonoma	C4
Sonora	E5
South Lake Tahoe	F4
South San Francisco	J2
Spring Valley	C8
Squaw Valley	F6
Stanford	K3
Stinson Beach	H1
Stockton	D5
Sunnyvale	C5, L4
Sunol	L2
Sunset Beach	D11
Susanville	E2
Taft	F7
Tamalpais Valley	J1
Tehachapi	G7
Temecula	H9
Templeton	E7
Terra Bella	F7
Thermalito	D3
Thousand Oaks	G8
Tiburon	J1
Tipton	F6
Topanga	B10
Torrance	C11, G9
Tracy	D5
Truckee	E3
Tulare	F6
Turlock	E5
Tustin	E11
Twain Harte	E4
Twentynine Palms	J8
Ukiah	B3
Union City	L3
Upland	F10
Vacaville	D4
Vallejo	C4, K1
Vandenberg Village	E8
Ventucopa	F8
Ventura	F8
Victorville	H8
Villa Park	E11
Vine Hill	K1
Visalia	F6
Vista	H9
Walnut	E10
Walnut Creek	L1
Wasco	F7
Watsonville	D6
Weaverville	C2
Weed	C1
West Covina	E10
West Hollywood	C10

	Key
Westminster	E11
Westmorland	K9
West Pittsburg	L1
Westwood	E2
Wheatland	D3
Whittier	D10
Willits	B3
Willow Creek	B2
Willows	C3
Windsor	C4
Wofford Heights	G7
Woodlake	F6
Woodland	D4
Woodside	K3
Wrightwood	H8
Yorba Linda	E11
Yosemite Village	F5
Yreka	C1
Yuba City	D3
Yucaipa	H8
Yucca Valley	J8
Zenia	B2

Other Features

	Key
Alameda, river	L3
Alcatraz, island	J2
Allison, mt.	L3
Almanor, lake	D2
Amargosa, range	J6
Amargosa, river	J7
Angel, island	J1
Balboa, park	B8
Berryessa, lake	C4
Boundary, peak	G5
Bullion, mts.	J8
Cascade, range	D1
Central, valley	C2
Chabot, lake	K2
Channel, islands	E9, F9
Channel Islands Natl. Park	E9, F9
Chatsworth, reservoir	B10
Chino, river	F10
Chocolate, mts.	K9
Clair Engle, lake	C1
Clear, lake	C3
Clear Lake, reservoir	D1
Coast, ranges	C2, D6
Colorado, desert	J9
Colorado, river	L9
Cucamonga, river	F11
Death, valley	H6
Death Valley Natl. Park	H6
Devils Postpile Natl. Monument	F5
Diablo, mt.	L1
Eagle, lake	E2
Eagle, peak	E1
Eel, river	B2
Estero, bay	E7
Eugene O'Neill Natl. Hist. Site	K2
Farallon, island	H2
Farallones, gulf	H2
Giant Sequoia Natl. Mon.	F6, G6
Golden Gate Natl. Rec. Area	C5, J2
Goose, lake	E1
Grizzly, bay	L1
Half Moon, bay	J3
Honey, lake	E2
Humboldt, bay	A2
Imperial, valley	K9
Inyo, mts.	H6
Irvine, lake	F11
Joshua Tree Natl. Park	K8
Kern, river	G6
Kings, river	F6
Kings Canyon Natl. Park	G5
Klamath, mts.	B1
Klamath, river	B1
Lanfair, valley	K7
Lassen, peak	D2
Lassen Volcanic Natl. Park	D2
Lava Beds Natl. Monument	D1
McCoy, mts.	L9
Mad, river	B2
Manzanar Natl. Hist. Site	G6
Merced, river	E5
Middle Alkali, lake	F1
Mission, bay	B8
Mission Bay, park	B8
Mojave, desert	H7
Mojave, river	J8
Mono, lake	F5
Monterey, bay	D6
Morris, reservoir	E10
Muir Woods Natl. Monument	H1
Nacimiento, reservoir	D7
Napa, river	K1
Nicasio, reservoir	H1
Old Woman, mts.	K8
Oroville, reservoir	D3
Otay, river	C9
Panamint, range	H6
Panamint, valley	H6
Pescadero, river	J4
Pinnacles Natl. Monument	D6
Point Reyes Natl. Seashore	B4
Redwood Natl. Park	A1
Ritter, mt.	F5
Sacramento, river	C3
Salton, sea	K9
San Antonio, reservoir	D7
San Bernardino, mts.	H8
San Clemente, island	G10
San Diego, bay	B9
San Diego, river	B10
San Fernando, valley	B10
San Francisco, bay	J2
San Gabriel, mts.	G8
San Gabriel, reservoir	E10
San Joaquin, river	E5
San Luis Obispo, bay	E7
San Miguel, island	E8
San Nicolas, island	F9
San Pablo, bay	J1
San Rafael, mts.	F8
Santa Ana, mts.	F11
Santa Barbara, channel	E8
Santa Barbara, island	F9
Santa Catalina, island	G9
Santa Cruz, island	F8
Santa Cruz, mts.	D6
Santa Lucia, range	D6
Santa Monica, bay	B11
Santa Monica, mts.	B10
Santa Monica Mts. N.R.A.	B10
Santa Rosa, island	E8
Santa Rosa and San Jacinto Mountains N.M.	J9
Santiago, peak	F11
Sequoia Natl. Park	G6
Shasta, lake	C2
Shasta, mt.	C1

	Key
Sierra, peak	F11
Sierra Nevada, range	D3, G5
Siskiyou, mts.	B1
Smith River N.R.A.	B1
Tahoe, lake	E3
Tehachapi, mts.	G8
Telescope, peak	H6
Trinity, river	B2
Tule, river	F6
Turtle, mts.	L8
Upper, lake	E1
Upper San Leandro, reservoir	L2
Vizcaino, cape	B3
Whiskeytown-Shasta-Trinity N.R.A.	D1
White, mts.	G5
Whitney, mt.	G6
Wilson, mt.	D10
Yosemite Natl. Park	F5

Colorado .... page 133

Cities and Towns

	Key
Akron	G1
Alamosa	E4
Arvada	F2
Aspen	D2
Aurora	F2
Avon	D2
Bennett	F2
Berthoud	E1
Black Forest	F2
Boulder	E1
Breckenridge	D2
Brighton	F2
Broomfield	E1
Brush	G1
Buena Vista	D3
Burlington	H2
Canon City	E3
Carbondale	C2
Cedaredge	C3
Center	D4
Central City	E2
Cheyenne Wells	H3
Clifton	B2
Colorado Springs	F3
Conejos	D4
Cortez	B4
Craig	C1
Crawford	C3
Creede	D4
Cripple Creek	E3
Dacono	F1
Del Norte	D4
Delta	C3
Denver, capital	F2
Dolores	B4
Dove Creek	B4
Durango	C4
Eads	H3
Eagle	D2
Eaton	F1
Englewood	F2
Estes Park	E1
Evans	F1
Evergreen	E2
Fairplay	E2
Florence	E3
Fort Collins	E1
Fort Lupton	F1
Fort Morgan	G1
Fountain	F3
Frisco	D2
Fruita	B2
Fruitvale	B2
Georgetown	E2
Glenwood Springs	C2
Golden	E2
Grand Junction	B2
Greeley	F1
Gunnison	D3
Gypsum	D2
Haswell	G3
Hayden	C1
Holyoke	H1
Hot Sulphur Springs	D1
Hugo	G2
Idaho Springs	E2
Johnstown	F1
Julesburg	H1
Keota	F1
Kiowa	F2
Kit Carson	H3
Lafayette	E1
La Junta	G4
Lake City	C3
Lakewood	E2
Lamar	H3
Las Animas	G3
Leadville	D2
Limon	G2
Littleton	E2
Longmont	E1
Louisville	E1
Loveland	E1
Manitou Springs	E3
Meeker	C1
Milliken	F1
Monte Vista	D4
Montrose	C3
Niwot	E1
Northglenn	F2
Olathe	C3
Orchard City	C3
Orchard Mesa	B2
Ordway	G3
Ouray	C3
Pagosa Springs	C4
Palisade	B2
Palmer Lake	F2
Paonia	C3
Parker	F2
Platteville	F1
Pritchett	H4
Pueblo	F3
Pueblo West	F3
Rangely	B1
Rifle	C2
Rocky Ford	G3
Saguache	D3
Salida	E3
San Luis	E4
Security	F3
Silverthorne	D2
Silverton	C4
Snowmass Village	D2
Springfield	H4
Steamboat Springs	D1
Sterling	G1
Telluride	C4

	Key
Thornton	F2
Trinidad	F4
Vail	D2
Vilas	H4
Walden	D1
Walsenburg	E4
Wellington	E1
Westcliffe	E3
Westminster	F2
Wheat Ridge	F2
Wiley	H3
Windsor	F1
Woodland Park	E2
Wray	H1
Yuma	H1

Other Features

	Key
Animas, river	C4
Apishapa, river	F4
Arapahoe, peak	E1
Arapaho Natl. Rec. Area	E1
Arikaree, river	G2
Arkansas, river	F3
Bent's Old Fort Natl. Hist. Site	G3
Black Canyon of the Gunnison Natl. Park	C3
Blanca, peak	E4
Blue Mesa, reservoir	C3
Bonny, reservoir	H2
Canyons of the Ancients N.M.	B4
Castle, peak	D2
Colorado, plateau	A4
Colorado, river	C2
Colorado Natl. Monument	B2
Crestone, peak	E4
Cucharas, river	F4
Curecanti Natl. Rec. Area	C3
Dinosaur Natl. Monument	B1
Dolores, river	B3
Elbert, mt.	D2
Eolus, mt.	C4
Evans, mt.	E2
Florissant Fossil Beds N.M.	E3
Front, range	E1
Great Sand Dunes N.P.	E4
Green, river	B1
Gunnison, mt.	C3
Gunnison, river	B3
Hovenweep Natl. Monument	B4
John Martin, reservoir	G3
Laramie, mts.	E1
Laramie, river	E1
Little Snake, river	B1
Longs, peak	E1
Mancos, river	B4
Medicine Bow, mts.	D1
Mesa Verde Natl. Park	B4
Montezuma, peak	D4
North Fork Cimarron, river	H4
North Fork Smoky Hill, river	H1
North Platte, river	D1
Park, range	D1
Pikes, peak	E3
Purgatoire, river	G4
Rio Grande, river	E4
Roan, plateau	B2
Rocky, mts.	D1
Rocky Mt. Natl. Park	E1
Royal Gorge, canyon	E3
Sand Creek Massacre N.H.S.	H3
Sangre de Cristo, mts.	E3
San Juan, mts.	C4
San Luis, valley	E4
Sawatch, range	D2
South Fork Republican, river	H2
South Platte, river	E2, G1
Uncompahgre, peak	C4
U.S. Air Force Academy	F3
White, river	B1
Wilson, mt.	B4
Yampa, river	B1
Yucca House Natl. Monument	B4
Zirkel, mt.	D1

Connecticut .... page 134

Cities and Towns

	Key
Abington	G2
Andover	F3
Ansonia	C4
Attawaugan	H2
Avon	D2
Bakersville	D2
Ballouville	H2
Baltic	G3
Beacon Falls	C4
Berkshire	B4
Berlin	E3
Bethany	C4
Bethel	B4
Bethlehem	C3
Black Point	G4
Bloomfield	E2
Blue Hills	E2
Boardman Bridge	B3
Bolton	F2
Botsford	B4
Branford	D4
Bridgeport	C5
Bridgewater	B3
Bristol	D3
Broad Brook	E2
Brookfield	B4
Brookfield Center	B4
Brooklyn	H2
Burlington	D2
Burrville	C2
Cannondale	B5
Canterbury	H3
Canton	D2
Canton Center	D2
Centerbrook	F4
Central Village	H3
Chaplin	G2
Cheshire	D3
Chester	F4
Chesterfield	G4
Clarks Falls	H4
Clinton	E4
Colchester	F3
Colebrook	C2
Collinsville	D2
Columbia	F3
Cornwall	B2
Cornwall Bridge	B2
Coventry	F2
Cromwell	E3
Danbury	B4
Danielson	H2
Darien	B5
Dayville	H2

Key

Deep River F4
Derby C4
Durham E4
Eagleville F2
East Brooklyn H2
Eastford G2
East Glastonbury E3
East Granby E2
East Haddam F4
East Hampton E3
East Hartford E3
East Hartland D2
East Haven D4
East Killingly H2
East Litchfield C2
East Lyme G4
Easton B5
East Thompson H1
East Village C4
East Woodstock H2
Ellington F2
Enfield E2
Essex F4
Fairfield B5
Falls Village B2
Farmington D3
Fitchman G3
Flanders B3
Franklin G3
Gales Ferry G4
Gaylordsville B3
Georgetown B5
Gilead F3
Gilman G3
Glasgo H3
Glastonbury E3
Goodrich Heights E3
Goshen C2
Granby D2
Greenwich A5
Grosvenor Dale H2
Groton G4
Groton Long Point G4
Guilford E4
Gurleyville G2
Haddam E4
Haddam Neck F4
Hadlyme F4
Hamburg F4
Hamden D4
Hampton G2
Hanover G3
Hartford, *capital* E3
Harwinton C2
Hawleyville B4
Hazardville E2
Hebron F3
Higganum E4
Hotchkissville C3
Indian Neck D5
Jewett City H3
Kensington D3
Killingworth E4
Knollcrest B4
Knollwood F4
Lake Pocotopaug E3
Lakeside C3
Lakeside F4
Laysville F4
Lebanon F3
Ledyard Center G4
Liberty Hill F3
Lime Rock B2
Litchfield C2
Lyons Plain B5
Madison E4
Manchester E2
Mansfield Center G3
Mansfield Four Corners F2
Marble Dale B3
Marion D3
Meriden D3
Merrow F2
Middlebury C3
Middlefield E3
Middle Haddam E3
Middletown E3
Milford C5
Mill Plain A4
Milton B2
Mohegan G4
Monroe C4
Montville G4
Moosup H3
Mystic H4
Naugatuck C4
New Britain D3
New Canaan B5
New Fairfield B4
New Hartford C2
New Haven D4
Newington D3
New London G4
New Milford B4
Newtown B4
Niantic G4
Noank H4
Norfolk C2
North Branford D4
North Canton D2
Northfield C3
Northford D4
North Franklin G3
North Grosvenor Dale H2
North Guilford E4
North Haven D4
North Stonington H4
Northville B3
North Westchester F3
North Windham G3
Norwalk B5
Norwich G3
Oakdale G4
Oakville C3
Old Lyme F4
Old Mystic H4
Old Saybrook F4
Oneco H3
Orange C4
Oxford C4
Park Lane B3
Pawcatuck H4
Perkins Corner F4
Phoenixville G2
Plainfield H3
Plainville D3
Plantsville D3
Pleasant Valley C2
Pleasure Beach G4
Plymouth C3
Pomfret H2
Poquetanuck G4

Key

Poquonock E2
Poquonock Bridge G4
Portland E3
Preston City H3
Prospect D4
Putnam H2
Quaddick H2
Quaker Hill G4
Redding B4
Redding Ridge B4
Ridgebury A4
Ridgefield B4
Riverton C2
Robertsville C2
Rockfall E3
Rockville F2
Rocky Hill E3
Roxbury B3
Sachem Head E5
Salem F4
Salisbury B2
Scantic E2
Scitico E2
Scotland G3
Seymour C4
Sharon B2
Shelton C4
Sherman B3
Short Beach D5
Simsbury D2
Somers F2
Sound View F4
Southbury C4
South Canaan B2
South Chaplin G2
South Glastonbury E3
Southington D3
South Kent B3
South Killingly H2
South Willington F2
South Windham G3
South Windsor E2
Stafford F2
Stafford Springs F2
Staffordville F2
Stamford A5
Sterling H3
Stevenson C4
Stony Creek D5
Storrs F2
Straitsville C4
Stratford C5
Suffield E2
Taconic B1
Talcottville F2
Tariffville D2
Terryville C3
Thompson H2
Thompsonville E2
Tolland F2
Torrington C2
Trumbull C5
Uncasville G4
Union G2
Unionville D2
Vernon F2
Versailles G3
Voluntown H3
Wallingford D4
Warren B3
Warrenville G2
Washington B3
Washington Depot B3
Waterbury C3
Waterford G4
Watertown C3
Weatogue D2
Westbrook F4
West Cornwall B2
Westford G2
West Granby D2
West Hartford E2
West Hartland D1
West Haven D4
West Mystic H4
West Norfolk C1
Weston B5
Westport B5
West Redding B4
West Simsbury D2
West Stafford F2
West Suffield E2
West Willington F2
Wethersfield E3
Whigville D3
Willimantic G3
Wilton B5
Winchester Center C2
Windham G3
Windsor E2
Windsor Locks E2
Winsted C2
Winthrop F4
Wolcott D3
Woodbridge C4
Woodmont D5
Woodstock H2
Woodstock Valley G2
Woodville B3
Yalesville D4

Other Features

Appalachian Natl. Scenic Trail B2
Bantam, *lake* C3
Barkhamsted, *reservoir* D2
Candlewood, *lake* B4
Connecticut, *river* E4
Easton, *reservoir* B4
Farmington, *river* D2
Frissell, *mt.* B1
Gaillard, *lake* D4
Hammonasset, *river* E4
Hop, *river* F3
Housatonic, *river* B4
Long Island, *sound* D5
Mt. Hope, *river* G2
Natchaug, *river* G2
Naugatuck, *river* C4
Nepaug, *reservoir* C2
Norwalk, *river* B5
Norwalk, *islands* B5
Quinebaug, *river* H3
Saugatuck, *reservoir* B4
Shenipsit, *lake* F2
Shetucket, *river* G3
Thames, *river* G4
Waramaug, *lake* B3
Weir Farm Natl. Hist. Site B5
Willimantic, *river* F2
Yantic, *river* F3

Key

Delaware ....page 135

Cities and Towns

Adamsville A3
Andrewville A3
Argos Corner B3
Blackbird A2
Broadkill Beach B3
Brookside A1
Burrsville A3
Camden A3
Canterbury A3
Capitol Park A2
Clarksville B3
Claymont B1
Collins Park A1
Dover, *capital* A2
Edgemoor A1
Elsmere A1
Fairfax A1
Georgetown A3
Glasgow A1
Gumboro B4
Harbeson B3
Harrington A3
Hartley A2
Hazlettville A3
Hickman A3
Hockessin A1
Indian Beach B3
Jimtown B3
Kirkwood A1
Kitts Hummock B2
Laurel B4
Lewes B3
Lincoln B3
Little Heaven B2
Llangollen Estates A1
Lynch Heights B3
McClellandville A3
Marshallton A1
Marydel A3
Mastens Corner A3
Middletown A2
Midway B3
Milford B3
Millsboro B3
Milton B3
Nassau B3
Newark A1
New Castle A1
Oak Orchard B3
Owens A2
Petersburg A2
Pinetown B3
Primehook Beach B3
Reeves Crossing B3
Rehoboth Beach B3
Reliance A3
Rosedale Beach B3
Roxana B3
Sandtown A2
Seaford A3
Selbyville B4
Smyrna A2
Stanton A1
Swann Keys B4
Talleyville A1
Taylors Bridge A2
Whitesville B4
Williamsville B4
Williamsville B4
Wilmington A1
Wilmington Manor A1
Woodenhawk A3
Woodland Beach B2
Workmans Corners B3

Other Features

Broadkill, *river* B3
Chesapeake & Delaware, *canal* A1
Delaware, *bay* B2
Delaware, *river* A1
Henlopen, *cape* B3
Indian River, *bay* B3
Mispillion, *river* B3
Murderkill, *river* A3
Nanticoke, *river* A3
Rehoboth, *bay* B3
Smyrna, *river* A2

Key

Florida ....page 136

Cities and Towns

Alachua C2
Altamonte Springs D3
Anna Maria C4
Apalachicola A2
Apollo Beach C4
Apopka D3
Arcadia D4
Archer C2
Astor D2
Atlantic Beach D1
Auburndale D3
Aventura B3
Avon Park D4
Baldwin D1
Bal Harbour B3
Bartow D4
Bay Harbor Islands B3
Bayonet Point C3
Bee Ridge C4
Belle Glade E5
Belleview C3
Beverly Hills C3
Big Pine Key D7
Biscayne Park A3
Blountstown A1
Boca Raton E5
Bonifay A1
Bonita Springs D5
Boynton Beach E5
Bradenton C4
Brandon C4
Bristol A1
Bronson C2
Brooksville C3
Buckhead Ridge E4
Bunnell D2
Bushnell C3
Callaway A1
Cape Canaveral E3
Cape Coral D5
Carol City A3, E6
Chattahoochee A1
Chiefland C2
Chipley A1
Clearwater C4

Key

Clermont D3
Clewiston E5
Cocoa E3
Cocoa Beach E3
Coconut Grove A3
Cooper City A3
Coral Gables A3, E6
Coral Springs E5
Crawfordville A1
Crescent City D2
Crestview B6
Cross City B2
Crystal River C3
Dade City C3
Dania A3
Davie A2, E5
Daytona Beach D2
De Bary D3
Deerfield Beach E5
De Funiak Springs B6
De Land D2
Delray Beach E5
Deltona D3
Destin B6
Dunedin C3
Dunnellon C2
East Naples D5
Eastpoint A2
Edgewater D3
El Portal A3
Elfers C3
Englewood C5
Eustis D3
Fellsmere E4
Fernandina Beach D1
Flagler Beach D2
Florida City E6
Fort Lauderdale B2, E5
Fort Meade D4
Fort Myers D5
Fort Myers Beach D5
Fort Myers Villas D5
Fort Pierce E4
Fort Walton Beach B6
Frostproof D4
Gainesville C2
Gifford E4
Golden Gate D5
Gonzalez A6
Goulds E6
Greenacres City E5
Green Cove Springs D2
Gretna A1
Gulf Breeze A6
Haines City D3
Hallandale B3, E6
Havana A1
Hawthorne C2
Hialeah A3, E6
Hialeah Gardens A3
High Springs C2
Hilliard D1
Holiday C3
Holly Hill D2
Hollywood A3, E5
Holmes Beach C4
Homestead E6
Homosassa Springs C3
Hudson C3
Immokalee D5
Indian Harbour Beach E3
Indian Rocks Beach C4
Indiantown E4
Inverness C3
Jacksonville D1
Jacksonville Beach D1
Jasper C1
Jensen Beach E4
Jupiter E5
Kendall A4, E6
Key Biscayne A3
Key Largo E6
Keystone Heights D2
Key West D7
Kissimmee D3
La Belle D5
La Crosse C2
Lady Lake D3
Lake Buena Vista D3
Lake Butler C1
Lake City C1
Lakeland D3
Lake Mary D3
Lake Panasoffkee C3
Lake Wales D4
Lake Worth E5
Land O' Lakes C3
Lantana E5
Largo C4
Lauderdale Lakes B4
Lauderdale-by-the-Sea B2
Lauderhill A2
Lawtey C1
Layton D7
Leesburg D3
Live Oak C1
Longboat Key C4
Lutz C3
Lynn Haven C6
Macclenny C1
Madison B1
Marathon D7
Marco D6
Margate B4
Marianna C6
Marineland D2
Mayo B1
Merritt Island E3
Miami A3, E6
Miami Beach B3, E6
Miami Lakes A3, A5
Miami Shores A3, A5
Miami Springs A3, A5
Middleburg D1
Milton A6
Mims E3
Miramar A3, E6
Monticello B1
Moore Haven E4
Mount Dora D3
Naples D5
Naples Manor D5
Naples Park D5
Naranja E6
New Port Richey C3
New Smyrna Beach E2
Niceville B6
Noma A1
North Bay Village A3
North Fort Myers D5
North Miami A3, E6
North Miami Beach A3

Key

North Naples D5
North Port C4
Oakland Park B2, E5
Ocala C2
Ocoee D3
Okeechobee E4
Oldsmar C3
Olympia Hts. A3
Opa-Locka A3
Orange City D3
Orange Park D1
Orlando D3
Ormond Beach D2
Ormond-by-the-Sea D2
Otter Creek C2
Oviedo D3
Pace A6
Pahokee E5
Palatka D2
Palm Bay E3
Palm Beach E5
Palm Beach Gardens E5
Palm Coast D2
Palmetto C4
Palm Harbor C3
Panama City C6
Pembroke Park A3, E6
Pembroke Pines A3
Pennsaco A3
Pensacola A6
Perrine E6
Perry B1
Pierson D2
Pine Castle D3
Plantation A2, E5
Plant City C3
Polk City D3
Pomona Park D2
Port Charlotte C5
Port Orange E2
Port St. Joe C7
Port St. Lucie E4
Port Salerno E4
Punta Gorda C5
Quincy A1
Raiford C1
Ridge Manor C3
Riverview C4
Riviera Beach E5
Rockledge E3
Royal Palm Beach E5
St. Augustine D2
St. Augustine Shores D2
St. Cloud D3
St. Pete Beach C4
St. Petersburg C4
San Carlos Park D5
Sanford D3
Sanibel C5
Sarasota C4
Satellite Beach E3
Sebastian E4
Sebring D4
Silver Springs C2
Sneads A1
South Miami A3
South Venice C4
Springfield C6
Spring Hill C3
Starke C1
Stuart E4
Sunrise A3
Surfside B3
Sweetwater A3, E6
Tallahassee, *capital* A1
Tamarac A2, E5
Tampa C4
Tarpon Springs C3
Tavares D3
Tavernier E6
Temple Terrace C4
Titusville E3
Treasure Island C4
Trenton C2
Umatilla D3
Venice C4
Vero Beach E4
Vilano Beach D2
Virginia Gardens A3
Warrington A6
Wauchula D4
Webster C3
Weeki Wachee C3
Welaka D2
West Melbourne E3
West Miami A3
Weston E5
West Palm Beach E5
West Pensacola A6
Westwood Lakes A3
Wildwood D3
Williston C2
Wilton Manors B2
Winter Garden D3
Winter Haven D3
Winter Park D3
Woodville A1
Yulee D1
Zephyrhills C3

Other Features

Amelia, *island* D1
Apalachee, *bay* A2
Apalachicola, *bay* A2
Apalachicola, *river* A1
Aucilla, *river* B1
Big Cypress, *swamp* D5
Biscayne, *bay* B3, E6
Biscayne Natl. Park E6
Boca Chica Key, *island* D7
Caloosahatchee, *river* D5
Canaveral, *cape* E3
Canaveral Natl. Seashore E3
Castillo de San Marcos N.M. D2
Cedar Keys, *islands* C2
Charlotte, *harbor* C5
Chattahoochee, *river* A1
Choctawhatchee, *bay* B6
Crooked, *river* A1
De Soto Natl. Memorial C4
Deadman, *bay* B2
Dog, *island* A2
Dry Tortugas Natl. Park C7
Elliott Key, *island* E6
Escambia, *river* A6
Everglades, *swamp* A5, E6
Everglades Natl. Park E6
Fisher, *island* B3
Florida, *bay* E6
Florida, *straits* E7
Florida Keys, *islands* D7
Fort Caroline Natl. Memorial D1

Key

Fort Matanzas Natl. Monument D2
Gasparilla, *island* C5
George, *lake* D2
Gulf Islands Natl. Seashore A6
Homosassa, *bay* C3
Indian, *river* E4
Iron, *mt.* D4
Istokpoga, *lake* D4
John F. Kennedy Space Center E3
Key Biscayne, *island* B3
Key Largo, *island* E6
Kissimmee, *lake* D4
Lochloosa, *lake* C2
Marquesas Keys, *islands* C7
Mexico, *gulf* B5, B6
Ochlockonee, *river* A1
Okeechobee, *lake* E5
Okefenokee, *swamp* C1
Peace, *river* D4
Pensacola, *bay* A6
Ponce de Leon, *bay* D6
Romano, *cape* D6
Sable, *cape* D6
St. Andrews, *bay* B6
St. George, *island* A2
St. Johns, *river* D2
St. Joseph, *bay* C7
St. Marys, *river* D1
St. Vincent, *island* A2
San Blas, *cape* C7
Sands Key, *island* E6
Sanibel, *island* C5
Santa Rosa, *island* A6
Seminole, *lake* A1
Sugarloaf Key, *island* D7
Suwannee, *river* C1, C2
Talquin, *lake* A1
Tamiami, *canal* C4
Tampa, *bay* C4
Virginia Key, *island* B3
Waccasassa, *bay* C2
Withlacoochee, *river* B1
Yellow, *river* A6

Georgia ....page 137

Cities and Towns

Abbeville E8
Adairsville B3
Adel E9
Alamo F7
Albany C8
Alma G8
Alpharetta C3
Americus C7
Appling G4
Arlington B9
Ashburn D8
Athens E4
Atlanta, *capital* C4, J3
Augusta H5
Bainbridge B10
Barnesville C5
Baxley G8
Belvedere K3
Blackshear G9
Blairsville D2
Blakely B9
Blue Ridge C2
Boston D10
Bremen A4
Brookhaven J2
Brunswick H9
Buchanan A4
Buena Vista B7
Buford C3
Butler C6
Byron D6
Cairo C10
Calhoun B3
Camilla C9
Canton B3
Carnesville E3
Carrollton A4
Cartersville B3
Cedar Grove J3
Cedartown A3
Chamblee J2
Chatsworth B2
Clarkesville D3
Clarkston K2
Claxton G7
Clayton E2
Cleveland D3
Cochran E7
College Park H3
Colquitt B9
Columbus B6
Commerce E3
Conley J4
Constitution J3
Conyers D4
Cordele D7
Cornelia D3
Covington D4
Crawfordville F4
Cumming C3
Cusseta B7
Cuthbert B8
Dahlonega D2
Dallas B4
Dalton B2
Danielsville E3
Darien J9
Dawson C8
Dawsonville C3
Decatur K3
Donalsonville B9
Doraville K2
Douglas F9
Douglasville B4
Druid Hills J3
Dublin F6
Dunwoody J2
Eastman E7
East Point C4, H3
Eatonton E5
Elberton F3
Ellaville C7
Ellijay C2
Evans G4
Fair Oaks H2
Fairview K4
Fayetteville C5
Fitzgerald E8
Folkston G10
Forest Park J4
Forsyth D5
Fort Gaines A8
Fort Oglethorpe A1
Fort Valley D6

	Key
Franklin	A5
Gainesville	D3
Garden City	J7
Georgetown	A8
Gibson	F5
Gilmore	H2
Glennville	H8
Gordon	E6
Gray	D5
Greensboro	E4
Greenville	B5
Gresham Park	J3
Griffin	C5
Hahira	E10
Hamilton	B6
Hampton	C5
Hapeville	J3
Hartwell	F3
Hawkinsville	E7
Hazlehurst	F8
Hephzibah	G5
Hiawassee	D2
Hinesville	H8
Hogansville	B5
Homer	D3
Homerville	F9
Irwinton	E6
Jackson	D5
Jasper	C3
Jefferson	E3
Jeffersonville	E6
Jesup	H8
Jonesboro	C4
Kennesaw	B3
Kingsland	H10
Knoxville	D6
La Fayette	A2
La Grange	A5
Lakeland	E9
Lavonia	E3
Lawrenceville	D4
Leesburg	C8
Lexington	E4
Lincolnton	G4
Locust Grove	C5
Louisville	G5
Ludowici	H8
Lumber City	F8
Lumpkin	B7
Lyons	G7
Mableton	B4, G2
McDonough	C5
McIntyre	E6
Macon	D6
McRae	F7
Madison	E4
Manchester	B6
Marietta	B4, H1
Marshallville	D7
Metter	G7
Milledgeville	E5
Millen	H6
Monroe	D4
Monticello	D5
Morgan	B8
Moultrie	D9
Mount Vernon	F7
Mt. Bethel	J1
Nashville	E9
Newnan	B5
Newton	C9
Oakdale	H2
Ocilla	E8
Oglethorpe	C7
Panthersville	K3
Peachtree City	B5
Pearson	F9
Pembroke	H7
Perry	D7
Pooler	J7
Powder Springs	B4
Preston	B7
Quitman	E10
Red Oak	H4
Reidsville	G7
Richland	B7
Richmond Hill	J8
Rincon	J7
Ringgold	A2
Riverdale	J4
Rochelle	E8
Rockmart	A3
Rome	A3
Roswell	C3
Royston	E3
Sandersville	F6
Sandy Springs	J2
Savannah	J7
Scottdale	K3
Skyland	J2
Smyrna	H2
Snellville	D4
Social Circle	D4
Soperton	F7
Sparta	F5
Springfield	J7
St. Marys	H10
St. Simons Island	J9
Statenville	E10
Statesboro	H7
Statham	D4
Stone Mountain	C4
Summerville	A3
Swainsboro	G6
Sylvania	H6
Sylvester	D8
Talbotton	B6
Tennille	F6
Thomaston	C6
Thomasville	D10
Thomson	G5
Tifton	E9
Toccoa	E2
Toco Hills	J2
Trenton	A2
Trion	A2
Tucker	K2
Tybee Island	J9
Unadilla	D7
Union City	B4, H4
Union Point	E4
Valdosta	E10
Vidalia	G7
Vienna	D7
Villa Rica	B4
Wadley	G6
Warner Robins	D6
Warrenton	F5
Washington	F4
Watkinsville	E4
Waycross	G9
Waynesboro	G5

	Key
Westoak	H1
Winder	D3
Woodbine	H10
Wrens	G5
Wrightsville	F6
Zebulon	C5

Other Features

	Key
Alapaha, *river*	E9
Allatoona, *lake*	B3
Altamaha, *river*	G8
Andersonville Natl. Hist. Site	C7
Appalachian, *mts.*	D2
Blackshear, *lake*	D8
Blue, *ridge*	C2
Brasstown Bald, *mt.*	D2
Burton, *lake*	D2
Carters, *lake*	B2
Chattahoochee, *river*	A5, A9, G3
Chattahoochee River N.R.A.	J1
Chattooga, *river*	E2
Chatuge, *lake*	D1
Chickamauga and Chattanooga Natl. Military Park	A2
Coosa, *river*	D2
Cumberland, *island*	J10
Cumberland Island Natl. Seashore	J10
Ed Jenkins Natl. Rec. Area	C2
Etowah, *river*	B3
Flint, *river*	C9
Fort Frederica Natl. Monument	J9
Fort Pulaski Natl. Monument	K7
Hartwell, *lake*	F2
Jackson, *lake*	D5
Jekyll, *island*	J9
Jimmy Carter Natl. Hist. Site	C7
J. Strom Thurmond, *lake*	G4
Lookout Mt., *ridge*	A2
Martin Luther King Jr. N.H.S.	J3
Ocmulgee Natl. Monument	D6
Ochlockonee, *river*	C10
Ocmulgee, *river*	E7
Oconee, *lake*	E5
Oconee, *river*	F6
Ogeechee, *river*	F5
Ohoopee, *river*	G7
Okefenokee, *swamp*	G10
Ossabaw, *island*	J8
Russell, *lake*	F3
St. Catherines, *island*	J8
St. Marys, *river*	H10
St. Simons, *island*	J9
Sapelo, *island*	J9
Savannah, *river*	H5
Seminole, *lake*	B10
Sidney Lanier, *lake*	C3
Sinclair, *lake*	E5
Stone Mt. State Park	C4
Suwannee, *river*	F10
Tallapoosa, *river*	A4
Tybee, *island*	K7
Walter F. George, *reservoir*	A8
Wassaw, *island*	J8
Weiss, *lake*	A3
West Point, *lake*	A6
Withlacoochee, *river*	E10

Hawaii ....page 138

Cities and Towns

	Key
Ahuimanu	J2
Aiea	F1, J2
Captain Cook	G6
Crestview	E1, J2
Eleele	J5
Ewa	D2, J2
Ewa Beach	E2, J3
Foster Village	F1, J2
Haena	C1, J5
Halawa	B3
Halawa Heights	F1, J2
Haleiwa	H1
Hana	B3
Hanamaulu	D1
Hanapepe	J5
Hauula	J1
Heeia	G1, K2
Hilo	E7, J5
Holualoa	G5
Honalo	G5
Honokaa	H4
Honolulu, *capital*	C5, F2, J2
Iroquois Point	E2, J2
Kaanapali	B3, J1
Kahana	B3, J1
Kahului	C3, D6
Kailua	C5, K2
Kailua-Kona	D7, F5
Kalaheo	C2
Kalaoa	F5
Kalaupapa	B3
Kaneohe	C5, G1, K2
Kaunakakai	A3
Keaau	J5
Kealakekua	G6
Kealia	D1, G6
Kekaha	B2
Kihei	C4, D6
Kilauea	C1
Koloa	C2
Kualapuu	A3
Kula	C4
Lahaina	B3, D6
Laie	C5, J1
Lanai City	B3
Lawai	J5
Lihue	A5, D2
Maili	H2
Makaha	H2
Makakilo City	H2
Makawao	C3
Maunawili	K2
Mililani Town	H1
Mokuleia	H1
Mountain View	J5, H2
Nanakuli	H2
Pacific Palisades	E1, J2
Pahala	H6
Papaikou	J5
Pearl City	C5, E1, J2
Pepeekeo	K2
Pohakupu	K2
Pukalani	C3, D6
Pupukea	J1
Volcano	J5
Waialua	B3, H1
Waianae	B5, H2
Waihee	C3
Waikiki	G3
Waikoloa Village	G4

	Key
Wailua	C3, D1
Wailuku	C3, D6
Waimalu	E1, J2
Waimanalo	K2
Waimanalo Beach	K2
Waimea	C2, D6, H1
Waipahu	E1, J2
Waipio	H4
Waipio Acres	J2
Whitmore Village	J2

Other Features

	Key
Alenuihaha, *channel*	D6
Alika Cone, *mt.*	G6
Diamond Head, *point*	G3
Ford, *island*	E1
Haleakala Natl. Park	C4, D6
Hamakua, *coast*	H4
Hawaii, *island*	E7, H6
Hawaii Volcanoes Natl. Park	E7, H6
Hilo, *bay*	J5
Hualalai, *mt.*	G5
Kaala, *mt.*	H1
Kaena, *point*	B5, H1
Kahoolawe, *island*	B4, D6
Kahului, *bay*	C3
Kaikipauula, *mt.*	H4
Kailua, *bay*	K2
Kaiwi, *channel*	C5, K3
Ka Lae (South Cape), *cape*	D7, G7
Kalalua, *mt.*	J6
Kalaupapa, *peninsula*	B3
Kalaupapa Natl. Hist. Park	B3
Kaloko-Honokohau Natl. Hist. Park	F5
Kamakou, *mt.*	B3
Kau, *desert*	H6
Kauai, *channel*	B5, D2
Kauai, *island*	A5, B1
Kaulakahi, *channel*	A5, B1
Kawaikini, *mt.*	C1
Kiholo, *bay*	G4
Kilauea, *crater*	J6
Kilohana, *crater*	C2
Kinau, *point*	C4
Kipuka Puaulu, *mt.*	H6
Kohala, *coast*	F5
Kohala, *island*	G4
Kohala, *mts.*	G4
Kona, *coast*	F6
Konahuanui, *mt.*	G2, K2
Koolau Range, *mts.*	F1, J1
Kulani, *mt.*	J5
Kumukahi, *cape*	E7, K5
Lanai, *island*	B3, C6
Lehua, *island*	A1
Lua Makika, *mt.*	B4
Maalaea, *bay*	C4
Makaleha, *mts.*	C1
Makapuu, *point*	C5, K2
Mamala, *bay*	E2, J3
Maui, *island*	C3, D6
Mauna Iki, *mt.*	H6
Mauna Kea, *mt.*	E6, H5
Mauna Loa, *mt.*	D7, H6
Maunalua, *bay*	K3
Mokolii, *island*	J2
Mokuauia, *island*	J1
Mokulua, *island*	K2
Moku Manu, *island*	K2
Molokai, *island*	A3, C5
Molokini, *island*	C4
Na Pali, *coast*	B1
Niihau, *island*	A2, A5
Oahu, *island*	B5, D2, K1
Pearl, *harbor*	E1
Punchbowl, *crater*	G3
Pu'uhonua O Honaunau N.H.P.	G6
Puu Kainapuaa, *mt.*	J1
Puu Kaua, *mt.*	H2
Puukohola Heiau Natl. Hist. Site	G4
Puu Kukui, *mt.*	B3
Puu Kulua, *mt.*	H5
Puu Loa, *mt.*	H5
Puu O Keokeo, *mt.*	C6
Puu Ulaula, *mt.*	C4
Sand, *island*	F2
Sulphur Cone, *mt.*	G6
U.S.S. Arizona Memorial	E1
Upolu, *point*	D6, G3
Waiaeale, *mt.*	C5, C1
Waianae Range, *mts.*	H1
Wailuku, *river*	H5
Waimea, *canyon*	C2
West Maui	B3

Idaho ....page 139

Cities and Towns

	Key
Aberdeen	E7
American Falls	E7
Ammon	F6
Arco	D6
Banks	A5
Bellevue	C6
Bennington	F7
Blackfoot	E6
Boise, *capital*	A6
Bonners Ferry	A1
Buhl	C7
Burley	D7
Caldwell	A6
Cascade	A5
Challis	C5
Chubbuck	E7
Coeur d'Alene	A2
Council	A5
Driggs	F6
Dubois	E5
Eagle	A6
Emmett	A6
Fairfield	C6
Filer	C7
Fish Haven	F7
Fruitland	A6
Fruitvale	A5
Garden City	A6
Garden Valley	B5
Glenns Ferry	B7
Gooding	C7
Grangeville	A4
Hailey	C6
Hayden	A2
Idaho City	B6
Idaho Falls	E6
Jerome	C7
Kamiah	A3
Kellogg	A2
Ketchum	C6
Kuna	A6
Laclede	A1
Lewiston	A3

	Key
McCall	A5
Malad City	E7
May	D5
Middleton	A6
Montpelier	F7
Moscow	A3
Mountain Home	B6
Murphy	A6
Nampa	A6
New Plymouth	A6
Nezperce	A3
Orofino	A3
Osburn	A2
Paris	F7
Parma	A6
Patterson	D5
Pauline	A6
Payette	A5
Pinehurst	A2
Pocatello	E7
Post Falls	A2
Preston	F7
Priest River	A1
Rathdrum	A2
Rexburg	F6
Rigby	F6
Rupert	D7
St. Anthony	F6
St. Maries	A2
Salmon	D4
Sandpoint	A1
Shelley	E6
Shoshone	C7
Soda Springs	F7
Sugar City	F6
Sun Valley	C6
Thatcher	F7
Twin Falls	C7
Wallace	B2
Weiser	A5
Wendell	C7

Other Features

	Key
American Falls, *reservoir*	E7
Bear, *lake*	F7
Bear, *river*	F7
Big Lost, *river*	D6
Bitterroot, *range*	B3, D4
Blackfoot, *reservoir*	F7
Blackfoot, *river*	F6
Bruneau, *river*	B7
Cache, *mt.*	D7
Caribou, *range*	F6
Cascade, *reservoir*	A5
Castle, *mt.*	C5
Clearwater, *mts.*	B3
Clearwater, *river*	B4
Craters of the Moon N.M.	D6
Dworshak, *reservoir*	A3
Grays, *lake*	F6
Hagerman Fossil Beds N.M.	C7
Hells, *canyon*	A5
Hells Canyon Natl. Recreation Area	A4
Kootenai, *river*	A1
Lemhi, *river*	D5
Lochsa, *river*	B3
Middle Fork Salmon, *river*	C5
Minidoka Internment Natl. Mon.	C7
Nez Perce N.H.P.	A3, B3
North Fork Clearwater, *river*	B3
Owyhee, *mts.*	A6
Owyhee, *river*	A6
Palisades, *reservoir*	F6
Payette, *lake*	A5
Payette, *river*	A5
Pend Oreille, *lake*	A1
Pend Oreille, *river*	A1
Priest, *lake*	A1
Ryan, *mt.*	C6
St. Joe, *river*	A2
Salmon, *river*	B4
Salmon River, *mts.*	C5
Sawtooth, *range*	B5
Sawtooth Natl. Recreation Area	C5
Scott, *mt.*	A4
Snake, *river*	A4
South Fork Selway, *river*	B3
Teton, *river*	F6
Weiser, *river*	A5
Yellowstone Natl. Park	F5

Illinois ....page 140

Cities and Towns

	Key
Abingdon	C3
Addison	B5
Albion	E5
Aledo	C2
Alsip	B6
Altamont	E4
Alton	C5
Amboy	D2
Anna	D6
Antioch	A4, E1
Arcola	E4
Arthur	E4
Ashland	C4
Athens	D3
Atlanta	D3
Atwood	E4
Auburn	D4
Aurora	E2
Barrington	A5
Barry	B4
Bartlett	A5
Bartonville	D3
Batavia	E2
Beach Park	B4
Beardstown	C3
Beecher	B6
Belleville	D5
Belvidere	E1
Bement	E4
Benld	D4
Benton	E6
Berwyn	B6
Bethany	E4
Bloomington	D3
Blue Island	B6
Bolingbrook	A6, E2
Bourbonnais	F2
Braceville	E2
Braidwood	E2
Breese	D5
Bridgeport	F5
Brighton	C4
Brookfield	B6
Buffalo Grove	B5
Bunker Hill	D4
Burbank	B6
Bushnell	C3

	Key
Byron	D1
Cahokia	C5
Cairo	D6
Calumet City	C6, F2
Cambridge	C2
Canton	C3
Capron	E1
Carbondale	D6
Carlinville	D4
Carlyle	D5
Carmi	E5
Carol Stream	A5
Carpentersville	E1
Carrier Mills	E6
Carrollton	C4
Carterville	D6
Carthage	B3
Cary	E1
Casey	F4
Catlin	F3
Centralia	D5
Cerro Gordo	E4
Champaign	E3
Channahon	E2
Charleston	E4
Chatham	D4
Chenoa	E3
Chester	D6
Chicago	B5, F2
Chicago Heights	B6
Chillicothe	D3
Christopher	D6
Cicero	B6, F2
Clifton	F3
Clinton	E3
Coal City	E2
Colchester	C3
Collinsville	D5
Columbia	C5
Crest Hill	A6
Crete	F2
Crystal Lake	E1
Cuba	C3
Danville	F3
Decatur	E4
Deerfield	B5
De Kalb	E2
Delavan	D3
De Soto	D6
Des Plaines	B5
Dixon	D2
Dolton	B6
Downers Grove	A6
Du Quoin	D5
Dwight	E2
Earlville	E2
East Dubuque	C1
East Moline	C2
East Peoria	D3
East St. Louis	C5
Edwardsville	D5
Effingham	E4
Elburn	E2
Eldorado	E6
Elgin	E1
Elizabethtown	E6
Elk Grove Village	B5
Elmhurst	B5
Elmwood	D3
Elmwood Park	B5
Erie	C2
Eureka	D3
Evanston	B5, F1
Evergreen Park	B6
Fairbury	E3
Fairfield	E5
Farmer City	E3
Farmington	D3
Fisher	E3
Flora	E5
Forrest	E3
Forsyth	E4
Fox Lake	A4, E1
Fox Lake Hills	A4
Fox River Grove	A5
Frankfort	B6, F2
Freeburg	D5
Freeport	D1
Fulton	C2
Gages Lake	B4
Galena	C1
Galesburg	C3
Galva	C2
Geneseo	C2
Geneva	E1
Genoa	E1

	Key
Hoopeston	F3
Huntley	E1
Island Lake	A5
Jacksonville	C4
Jerseyville	C4
Johnston City	D6
Joliet	A6, E2
Jonesboro	D6
Justice	B6
Kankakee	F2
Kaskaskia	D6
Kewanee	D2
Kincaid	D4
Knoxville	C3
Lacon	D2
La Grange	B6
La Harpe	B3
Lake Bluff	B5
Lake Forest	B5
Lake Zurich	A5
Lanark	D1
La Salle	D2
Lansing	B6
Lawrenceville	F5
Lemont	B6
Lena	D1
Le Roy	E3
Lewistown	C3
Lexington	E3
Libertyville	B5
Lilymoor	A4
Lincoln	D3
Lincolnwood	B5
Lindenhurst	A4
Lisle	A6
Litchfield	D4
Lockport	A6
Lombard	B5
Louisville	E5
Loves Park	D1
Lynwood	C6
McHenry	E1
Machesney Park	D1
Mackinaw	D3
McLeansboro	E5
Macomb	C3
Macon	E4
Mahomet	E3
Manhattan	F2
Manito	D3
Manteno	F2
Marengo	E1
Marion	D6
Marissa	D5
Marley	E3
Maroa	E3
Marseilles	E2
Marshall	F4
Mascoutah	D5
Mason City	D3
Matteson	B6
Mattoon	E4
Maywood	B5
Melrose Park	B5
Mendota	D2
Metamora	D3
Metropolis	E6
Milan	C2
Milford	F3
Minonk	D3
Minooka	E2
Mokena	B6
Moline	C2
Momence	F2
Monmouth	C3
Monticello	E3
Morris	E2
Morrison	D2
Morton	D3
Morton Grove	B5
Mound City	D6
Mounds	D6
Mount Carmel	F5
Mount Carroll	D1
Mount Morris	D1
Mount Olive	D4
Mount Prospect	B5
Mount Pulaski	D3
Mount Sterling	C4
Mount Vernon	E5
Mount Zion	E4
Moweaqua	D4
Mundelein	A5
Murphysboro	D6
Naperville	A6
Nashville	D5
Neoga	E4
New Athens	D5
New Baden	D5
New Lenox	B6
Newton	E5
Niles	B5
Nokomis	D4
Normal	E3
Norridge	B5
Northbrook	B5
North Chicago	B4, F1
Northfield	B5
Oak Brook	B6
Oak Forest	B6
Oak Lawn	B6, F2
Oak Park	B5, F2
Oakwood	F3
Oblong	F4
O'Fallon	D5
Oglesby	D2
Okawville	D5
Old Mill Creek	B4
Olney	E5
Onarga	F3
Oquawka	C3
Oregon	D1
Orion	C2
Orland Hills	B6
Orland Park	B6
Ottawa	E2
Palatine	B5
Palestine	F4
Palos Heights	B6
Palos Hills	B6
Pana	D4
Paris	F4
Park City	B4
Park Forest	F2
Park Ridge	B5
Pawnee	D4
Paxton	E3
Pecatonica	D1
Pekin	D3
Peoria	D3
Peoria Heights	D3
Peotone	F2

Key

Peru D2
Petersburg D4
Pinckneyville D5
Pittsfield C4
Plainfield A6, E2
Plano E2
Polo D2
Pontiac E3
Princeton D2
Princeville D3
Prophetstown D2
Quincy B4
Rantoul E3
Red Bud D5
Richton Park B6
Riverdale B6
Riverton D4
Riverwoods B5
Roanoke D3
Robinson F4
Rochelle D2
Rochester D4
Rock Falls D2
Rock Island C2
Rockford D1
Rockton D1
Rome D3
Romeoville A6
Roodhouse C4
Roscoe D1
Rosiclare E6
Rossville F3
Round Lake Beach A4
Rushville C3
Russell B4
St. David C3
St. Elmo E4
St. Joseph E3
St. Libory D5
Salem E5
Sandoval D5
Sandwich E2
Sauk Village C6
Savanna C1
Savoy E3
Schaumburg A5
Schiller Park B5
Seneca E2
Sesser D5
Shawneetown E6
Shelbyville D4
Sheridan E2
Sherman D4
Shorewood A6, E2
Skokie B5
Somonauk E2
South Beloit D1
South Elgin E2
South Holland B6
South Jacksonville C4
Sparta D5
Spring Valley D2
Springfield, *capital* D4
Staunton D4
Steeleville D5
Sterling D2
Stockland F3
Stockton C1
Streamwood A5
Streator E2
Sullivan E4
Summit B6
Sycamore E2
Taylorville D4
Teutopolis E4
Tilton F3
Tinley Park B6, F2
Toledo E4
Tolono E4
Toluca D3
Toulon D2
Tower Lakes A5
Tremont D3
Trenton D5
Tuscola E4
Urbana E3
Vandalia D5
Vernon Hills B5
Vienna E6
Villa Grove E4
Villa Park B5
Virden D4
Virginia C4
Volo A4
Wadsworth B4
Walnut D2
Wapella E3
Warren D1
Warrensburg D4
Warrenville A6
Warsaw B3
Washington D3
Waterloo C5
Watseka F3
Wauconda A5
Waukegan B4, F1
Waverly D4
Westchester B6
West Chicago A5
West Frankfort E6
Westville F3
Wheaton A6, E2
Wheeling B5, F1
White Hall C4
Wilmette B5
Wilmington E2
Winchester C4
Winnebago D1
Winnetka B5
Winthrop Harbor B4
Woodridge A6
Wood River C5
Woodstock E1
Wyoming D2
Yorkville E2
Zeigler D6
Zion B4, F1

Other Features
Carlyle, *lake* D5
Chautauqua, *lake* C3
Chicago, *river* B5
Clinton, *lake* E3
Crab Orchard, *lake* D6
Des Plaines, *river* A6, B4
Du Page, *river* A6
Fox, *lake* A4
Fox, *river* D2
Illinois, *river* D3
Ind. Dunes Natl. Lakeshore C6
Kankakee, *river* E3
Kaskaskia, *river* E4

Key

Lincoln Home Natl. Hist. Site D4
Marie, *lake* A4
Michigan, *lake* F1
O'Hare, *airport* B5
Ohio, *river* D6
Orland, *lake* B6
Rend, *lake* D5
Rock, *river* D2
Sangamon, *river* C3
Shelbyville, *lake* E4
Spoon, *river* C3
Wabash, *river* E6

Indiana ....page 141

Cities and Towns
Albany F4
Albion F2
Alexandria E4
Anderson E4
Angola G1
Arcadia D4
Argos D2
Atlanta D4
Attica B4
Auburn F2
Aurora G6
Austin E7
Avilla F2
Bargersville D5
Batesville F6
Bedford D7
Berne G3
Bicknell B7
Bloomfield C6
Bloomington C6
Bluffton F3
Boonville B8
Bourbon D2
Brazil B5
Bremen D2
Brookston C3
Brookville F6
Brownsburg D5
Brownstown D7
Butler G2
Cambridge City F5
Cannelton C9
Carmel D5
Chandler B8
Charlestown E8
Chesterton B1
Churubusco F2
Cicero D4
Clayton C5
Clinton B5
Cloverdale C5
Columbia City E2
Columbus E6
Connersville F5
Corydon D8
Covington B4
Crawfordsville C4
Crothersville E7
Crown Point B2
Culver D2
Dale C8
Daleville E4
Danville C5
Darmstadt A8
Decatur G3
Delphi C3
Demotte B2
Dunlap E1
East Chicago B1
Eaton F4
Edinburgh E6
Elkhart E1
Ellettsville C6
Elwood E4
English D8
Evansville A9
Fairmount E4
Farmland F4
Ferdinand C8
Fishers D5
Flora C3
Fort Branch A8
Fort Wayne F2
Fowler B3
Frankfort C4
Franklin D6
Fremont G1
French Lick C7
Galveston D3
Garrett F2
Gary B1
Gas City E4
Geneva G3
Georgetown E8
Goshen E1
Greencastle C5
Greenfield E5
Greensburg F6
Greentown E3
Greenwood D5
Hagerstown F5
Hammond A1
Hanover F7
Hartford City F4
Hebron B2
Highland B1
Hope E6
Huntertown F2
Huntingburg C8
Huntington F3
Indianapolis, *capital* D5
Jasonville B6
Jasper C8
Jeffersonville E8
Kendallville F2
Kentland B3
Kingsford Heights C2
Knox C2
Kokomo D3
Kouts B2
Lafayette C4
Lagrange F1
Lakeville D1
La Porte C1
Lawrence D5
Lawrenceburg G6
Lebanon D4
Liberty F5
Ligonier E2
Lincoln City B8
Linton B6
Logansport C3
Loogootee C7
Lowell B2
Madison F7

Key

Marion E3
Martinsville D6
Merrillville B2
Michigan City C1
Middlebury E1
Milan F6
Milford E2
Mishawaka D1
Mitchell D7
Monon C3
Monticello C3
Montpelier F3
Mooresville D5
Mount Vernon A9
Mulberry C4
Muncie F4
Nappanee D2
Nashville D6
New Albany E8
Newburgh B9
New Carlisle C1
New Castle F5
New Haven F2
Newport B5
New Whiteland D5
Noblesville D4
North Judson C2
North Liberty D1
North Manchester E2
North Terre Haute B5
North Vernon E6
Notre Dame D1
Oakland City B8
Odon C7
Orleans D7
Osgood F6
Ossian F3
Otterbein B3
Oxford B3
Paoli D7
Pendleton E4
Peru D3
Petersburg B8
Plainfield D5
Plymouth D2
Portland G4
Princeton A8
Redkey F4
Rensselaer B3
Richmond G5
Rising Sun G7
Rochester D2
Rockport B9
Rockville B5
Rushville F5
Salem D7
Schererville B2
Scottsburg E7
Sellersburg E8
Seymour E7
Shadeland C4
Shelbyville E5
Sheridan D4
Shoals C7
South Bend D1
South Whitley E2
Speedway D5
Spencer C6
Sullivan B6
Syracuse E2
Tell City C9
Terre Haute B6
Thorntown C4
Tippecanoe D2
Tipton D4
Union City G4
Upland F4
Valparaiso B2
Veedersburg B4
Vernon E7
Versailles F6
Vevay F7
Vincennes A7
Wabash E3
Wakarusa E1
Walkerton D2
Warsaw E2
Washington B7
Waterloo G2
Westfield D4
West Lafayette C4
Westport E6
Westville C1
Williamsport B4
Winamac C2
Winchester G4
Winona Lake E2
Woodburn G2
Worthington C6
Yorktown F4
Zionsville D5

Other Features
Big Blue, *river* E5
Brookville, *lake* F5
Eel, *river* D2
George Rogers Clark N.H.P. A7
Indiana Dunes Natl. Lakeshore B1
Kankakee, *river* C2
Lemon, *lake* D6
Lincoln Boyhood Natl. Memorial C8
Maumee, *river* G2
Michigan, *lake* B1
Mississinewa, *lake* E3
Monroe, *lake* D6
Ohio, *river* A9
Patoka, *lake* B8
St. Joseph, *river* G2
Salamoni, *lake* E3
Tippecanoe, *river* C4
Wabash, *river* A8
Wawasee, *lake* E2
White, *river* C6
Whitewater, *river* F6

Iowa ....page 142

Cities and Towns
Ackley H2
Adel F4
Akron A2
Albia J5
Algona F1
Allison J2
Alta D2
Altoona H4
Ames G3
Anamosa M3
Ankeny H4
Asbury N3
Atlantic D5

Key

Audubon E4
Avoca D5
Batavia K5
Bayard E4
Bedford E6
Belle Plaine K4
Bellevue P3
Belmond G2
Bettendorf P4
Bloomfield K6
Boone G3
Brighton L5
Britt G1
Brooklyn K4
Burlington M6
Camanche P4
Carlisle G5
Carroll E3
Carter Lake C5
Cascade N3
Cedar Falls K3
Cedar Rapids L4
Center Point L3
Centerville J6
Chariton H5
Charles City J1
Cherokee C2
Clarinda D6
Clarion G2
Clarksville J2
Clear Lake H1
Clinton P4
Colfax H4
Columbus Junction M5
Coon Rapids E4
Coralville L4
Corning E6
Corydon H6
Council Bluffs C5
Cresco K1
Creston F5
Dakota City F2
Dallas Center G4
Davenport N4
Decorah L1
Denison D4
Denver K2
Des Moines, *capital* G4
De Witt N4
Dubuque N2
Dunlap D4
Durant N4
Dyersville M3
Eagle Grove G2
Eldora H3
Eldridge N4
Elgin L2
Elkader M2
Emmetsburg E1
Epworth N3
Estherville E1
Evansdale K3
Fairfield L6
Farley M3
Fayette L2
Forest City G1
Fort Dodge F2
Fort Madison M6
Garner G1
Gilmore City F2
Glenwood C5
Greenfield F5
Grimes G4
Grinnell J4
Grundy Center J3
Guthrie Center E4
Guttenberg M2
Hampton H2
Harlan D4
Hartley D1
Hawarden B1
Hiawatha L3
Holstein C3
Hudson K3
Hull B1
Humboldt F2
Huxley G4
Ida Grove D3
Independence L3
Indianola G5
Iowa City L4
Iowa Falls H2
Jefferson F4
Jesup K3
Johnston G4
Kalona L5
Keokuk M7
Keosauqua L6
Knoxville H5
Lake City E3
Lake Mills G1
Lake View D3
Lamoni G6
La Porte City K3
Laurens E2
Le Claire P4
Le Mars B2
Lenox E6
Leon G6
Logan C4
Lovilia J5
Madrid G4
Manchester M3
Manly H1
Manning D4
Manson E3
Mapleton C3
Maquoketa N3
Marengo K4
Marion L3
Marshalltown J3
Mason City H1
Mediapolis M5
Melcher-Dallas H5
Milford D1
Missouri Valley C4
Monona M1
Monroe H4
Montezuma J4
Monticello M3
Mount Ayr F6
Mount Pleasant L6
Mount Vernon M4
Moville B3
Muscatine M5
Nashua J2
Nevada H3
New Hampton K1
New London M6
Newton H4
Nora Springs J1
North Liberty L4

Key

Northwood H1
Norwalk G5
Oakland D5
Oelwein L2
Ogden F3
Onawa B3
Orange City B1
Osage J1
Osceola G5
Oskaloosa J5
Ottumwa K5
Park View N4
Parkersburg J2
Pella J5
Perry G4
Pleasantville H5
Pocahontas E2
Polk City G4
Postville L1
Prairie City H4
Primghar C1
Red Oak D5
Reinbeck J3
Remsen C2
Rock Rapids B1
Rock Valley B1
Rockwell City E3
Sac City E3
Sanborn C1
Sergeant Bluff B3
Sheldon C1
Shell Rock J2
Shenandoah D6
Sibley C1
Sidney C6
Sigourney K5
Sioux Center B1
Sioux City B2
Spencer D1
Spirit Lake D1
Storm Lake D2
Story City G3
Strawberry Point L2
Stuart F4
Sumner K2
Tama J4
Tipton M4
Toledo J4
Traer K3
Urbandale E6
Villisca D6
Vinton K3
Walcott N4
Wapello M5
Washington L5
Waterloo K3
Waukee G4
Waukon M1
Waverly K2
Webster City G2
West Branch M4
West Burlington M6
West Des Moines G4
West Liberty M4
West Union L2
Williamsburg K4
Wilton M4
Windsor Heights G4
Winterset F5
Woodbine C4

Other Features
Big Sioux, *river* A1
Boone, *river* G2
Cedar, *river* K3
Chariton, *river* H6
Clear, *lake* H1
Coralville, *lake* L4
Des Moines, *river* F3
Effigy Mounds Natl. Monument M1
Floyd, *river* B2
Fox, *river* L3
Herbert Hoover Natl. Hist. Site M4
Iowa, *river* K4
Little Sioux, *river* D2
Maple, *river* D2
Mississippi, *river* M2
Missouri, *river* B4
Rathbun, *lake* J6
Red Rock, *lake* J5
Saylorville, *reservoir* G4
Skunk, *river* L5
Spirit, *lake* D1
Storm, *lake* D2
Turkey, *river* L2
Wapsipinicon, *river* K2
West Nishnabota, *river* K2

Kansas ....page 143

Cities and Towns
Abilene E3
Adrian G3
Alma F3
Andover D4
Anthony D4
Arkansas City E4
Arma H4
Ashland C4
Atchison G2
Atwood B2
Augusta F4
Baldwin City G3
Baxter Springs H4
Belle Plaine E4
Belleville E2
Beloit D2
Bonner Springs H2
Buhler D3
Burlington G3
Butler F4
Caldwell E4
Caney G4
Carbondale G3
Chanute G4
Chapman E3
Cheney D4
Cherryvale G4
Chetopa G4
Cimarron B4
Clay Center E2
Clearwater D4
Clifton E2
Coffeyville G4
Colby A2
Coldwater C4
Columbus H4
Concordia E2
Conway Springs E4
Coolidge A3
Cottonwood Falls F3

Key

Council Grove F3
Derby E4
De Soto H3
Dighton B3
Dodge City B4
Douglass E4
El Dorado F4
Elkhart A4
Ellinwood D3
Ellis C3
Ellsworth D3
Emporia F3
Erie G4
Eudora G3
Eureka F4
Florence F3
Fort Scott H4
Fredonia G4
Frontenac H4
Galena H4
Garden City B4
Gardner H3
Garnett G3
Girard H4
Goddard D4
Goodland A2
Gove B3
Great Bend D3
Greensburg C4
Halstead D3
Harper D4
Hays C3
Haysville E3
Herington E3
Hesston E3
Hiawatha G2
Hill City C2
Hillsboro E3
Hoisington D3
Holcomb B4
Holton G2
Horton G2
Howard F4
Hoxie B2
Hugoton A4
Humboldt G4
Hutchinson E3
Independence G4
Iola G4
Iuka D4
Jetmore C3
Johnson A4
Junction City F2
Kansas City H2
Kansas City H2
Kingman D4
Kinsley C4
La Crosse C3
Lakin A4
Lansing H2
Larned C3
Lawrence G3
Leavenworth H2
Leoti A3
Liberal B4
Lincoln D2
Lindsborg E3
Lorraine D3
Louisburg H3
Lyndon G3
Lyons D3
McPherson E3
Maize E4
Manhattan F2
Mankato D2
Marion E3
Marysville F2
Meade B4
Medicine Lodge D4
Minneapolis E2
Mound City H3
Moundridge E3
Mulvane E4
Neodesha G4
Ness City C3
Newton E3
North Newton E3
Norton C2
Oakley B2
Oberlin B2
Ogden F2
Olathe H3
Osage City G3
Osawatomie H3
Osborne D2
Oskaloosa G2
Oswego G4
Ottawa G3
Overland Park H3
Paola H3
Park B2
Park City E4
Parsons G4
Peabody E3
Phillipsburg C2
Pittsburg H4
Plainville C2
Pratt D4
Rich Hill G3
Rose Hill E4
Rose Hill E4
Russell D3
Sabetha G2
St. Francis A2
St. John D3
St. Marys F2
Salina E3
Scott City B3
Sedan F4
Sedgwick E3
Seneca G2
Sharon Springs A3
Silver Lake F2
Smith Center D2
South Hutchinson E3
Spring Hill H3
Stafford D3
Sterling D3
Stockton C2
Sublette B4
Syracuse A3
Tecumseh G3
Tonganoxie H2
Topeka, *capital* G2
Towanda F4
Tribune A3
Troy G2
Ulysses A4
Valley Center E4
Valley Falls G2
Wakeeney C3
Wamego F2

	Key
Washington	E2
Waterville	F2
Wellington	E4
Wellsville	G3
Westmoreland	F2
Wichita	E4
Winfield	F4
Yates Center	G4

Other Features

	Key
Arkansas, *river*	A4, D3
Big Blue, *river*	F2
Cedar Bluff, *reservoir*	C3
Cheney, *reservoir*	E4
Chikaskia, *river*	D4
Cimarron, *river*	A4
Clinton, *lake*	G3
Fall, *river*	F4
Flint Hills	F4
Fort Larned Natl. Hist. Site	C3
Fort Scott Natl. Hist. Site	H4
Kanapolis, *lake*	E3
Kansas, *river*	F2
Kirwin, *reservoir*	C2
Little Blue, *river*	E1
Marion, *lake*	E3
Medicine Lodge, *river*	C4
Melvern, *lake*	G3
Milford, *lake*	F2
Missouri, *river*	G1
Neosho, *river*	G3
Nicodemus Natl. Hist. Site	C2
North Fork Solomon, *river*	B2
Republican, *river*	D1
Saline, *river*	C2
Smoky Hill, *river*	B3
Solomon, *river*	D2
South Fork Republican, *river*	A2
Sunflower, *mt.*	A2
Tuttle Creek, *lake*	F2
Verdigris, *river*	F3
Waconda, *lake*	D2
Wilson, *lake*	D3

Kentucky .... page 144

Cities and Towns

	Key
Aberdeen	F2
Albany	D4
Alexandria	E2
Allensville	B4
Ashland	G2
Auburn	C4
Augusta	E2
Barbourville	F4
Bardstown	D3
Bardwell	B2
Beattyville	F3
Beaver Dam	C3
Bedford	D2
Benton	B2
Berea	E3
Berry	E2
Booneville	F3
Bowling Green	C4
Brandenburg	C3
Brooks	D2
Brooksville	E2
Brownsville	C3
Burkesville	D4
Burlington	E1
Butler	E2
Cadiz	B4, C2
Calhoun	C3
Calvert City	C2
Campbellsville	D3
Campton	F3
Carlisle	E2
Carrollton	D2
Carrsville	C1
Catlettsburg	G2
Cave City	D3
Central City	B3
Clay City	F3
Clinton	B2
Columbia	D3
Concord	F2
Corbin	E4
Corinth	E2
Covington	E1
Crestwood	D2
Cumberland	G4
Cynthiana	E2
Danville	E3
Dawson Springs	B3, C1
Dixon	B3, C1
Dry Ridge	E2
Earlington	B3
Eddyville	A3, C2
Edmonton	D3
Ekron	C3
Elizabethtown	D3
Elkton	B4
Eminence	D2
Fairfield	D3
Falmouth	E2
Flatwoods	G2
Flemingsburg	F2
Florence	E2
Foster	E2
Frankfort, *capital*	E2
Franklin	C4
Frenchburg	F3
Fulton	B2
Georgetown	E2
Glasgow	D3
Gratz	E2
Grayson	G2
Greensburg	D3
Greenup	G2
Greenville	B3
Guthrie	B4
Hardinsburg	C3
Harlan	F4
Harrodsburg	E3
Hartford	C3
Hawesville	C3
Hazard	G3
Henderson	B2
Hickman	B2
Hindman	G3
Hiseville	D3
Hobson	D3
Hodgenville	D3
Hopkinsville	B4
Horse Cave	D3
Hyden	F3
Independence	E2
Inez	G3
Irvine	F3
Jackson	F3
Jamestown	D4
Jeffersontown	D2
Jeffersonville	F3
Jenkins	G3
Junction City	E3
La Fayette	B4, D2
La Grange	D2
Lancaster	E3
Lawrenceburg	E2
Leatherwood	F3
Lebanon	D3
Leitchfield	C3
Lewisport	C3
Lexington	E2
Liberty	E3
Livermore	B3
Livingston	E3
London	E3
Louisa	G2
Louisville	D2
McKee	F3
Mackville	D3
Madisonville	B3
Manchester	F3
Marion	A3, C1
Mayfield	B2
Maysville	F2
Middlesboro	F4
Middletown	D2
Monterey	E2
Monticello	E4
Morehead	F2
Morganfield	B3, C1
Morgantown	C3
Mt. Olivet	E2
Mt. Sterling	F2
Mt. Vernon	E3
Mt. Washington	D2
Muldraugh	C3
Munfordville	D3
Murray	C2
Nebo	B3
New Castle	D2
Nicholasville	E3
Oak Grove	D2
Okolona	D2
Olive Hill	F2
Owensboro	B3
Owenton	E2
Owingsville	F2
Paducah	C2
Paris	E2
Patesville	C3
Phelps	G3
Pikeville	G3
Pine Knot	E4
Pineville	F4
Pleasure Ridge Park	D2
Prestonsburg	G2
Princeton	B3, C2
Providence	B3, C1
Raceland	G2
Radcliff	D3
Richmond	E3
Rochester	C3
Russell Springs	D3
Russellville	C4
St. Matthews	D2
Salyersville	F3
Sandy Hook	F2
Scottsville	C4
Sebree	B3
Shelbyville	D2
Shepherdsville	D3
Slaughters	B3
Smithland	C1
Somerset	E3
South Shore	G2
Springfield	D3
Stanford	E3
Stanton	F3
Sturgis	A3, C1
Taylorsville	D2
Tompkinsville	D4
Valley Station	D2
Vanceburg	F2
Versailles	E2
Vicco	F3
Vine Grove	D3
Walton	E2
Warsaw	E2
West Liberty	F3
Wheelwright	G3
Whitesburg	G3
Whitley City	E4
Wickliffe	B2
Williamsburg	E4
Williamstown	E2
Wilmore	E3
Winchester	E3
Woodbury	C3
Zion	B3

Other Features

	Key
Barkley, *lake*	B4, C2
Barren, *river*	C3
Barren River, *lake*	C4
Big Sandy, *river*	H2
Big South Fork Natl. River and Rec. Area	E4
Buckhorn, *lake*	F3
Cave Run, *lake*	F2
Cumberland, *lake*	E4
Cumberland, *river*	E4
Cumberland Gap Natl. Hist. Park	F4
Dale Hollow, *lake*	D4
Fish Trap, *river*	G3
Green, *river*	B3, D3
Green River, *lake*	D3
Kentucky, *lake*	C2
Kentucky, *river*	D2, E3
Licking, *river*	F2
Lincoln Birthplace Natl. Hist. Site	D3
Mammoth Cave Natl. Park	C3
Nolin River, *lake*	C3
Ohio, *river*	F2
Rough, *river*	C3
Rough River, *lake*	C3
Tennessee, *river*	C3
Tug Fork, *river*	G3

Louisiana .... page 145

Cities and Towns

	Key
Abbeville	E7
Abita Springs	J6
Alexandria	E4
Ama	Inset
Amelia	G7
Amite	J5
Arabi	Inset
Arcadia	D1
Arnaudville	F6
Avondale	Inset
Baker	G5
Baldwin	F7
Ball	E4
Basile	D6
Bastrop	F1
Baton Rouge, *capital*	G6
Bayou Cane	H7
Bayou Vista	G7
Belle Chasse	Inset
Bentley	E3
Bernice	D1
Bertrandville	Inset
Bogalusa	K5
Bossier City	B1
Boyce	D4
Braithwaite	Inset
Breaux Bridge	F6
Bridge City	Inset
Broussard	F6
Bunkie	E5
Buras	K8
Caernarvon	Inset
Cameron	C7
Carencro	E6
Carville	G6
Cecilia	F6
Chalmette	Inset, K7
Charenton	F7
Chauvin	H8
Church Point	E6
Clinton	G5
Colfax	D3
Columbia	E2
Cottonport	E5
Coushatta	C2
Covington	J6
Crowley	E6
Crown Point	Inset
Cullen	C1
Cut Off	J7
Dalcour	Inset
Delcambre	F7
Delhi	G2
Denham Springs	H5
De Quincy	C6
De Ridder	C5
Des Allemands	J7
Destrehan	Inset
Donaldsonville	H6
Edgard	H6
Elton	D6
English Turn	Inset
Erath	E7
Estelle	Inset
Eunice	E6
Farmerville	E1
Ferriday	F3
Franklin	F7
Franklinton	J5
Frenier	Inset
Galliano	J8
Garyville	H6
Glenmora	D5
Golden Meadow	J8
Gonzales	H6
Grambling	D1
Grand Isle	K8
Gray	H7
Greensburg	H5
Greenwood	B2
Gretna	Inset, J7
Gueydan	E6
Hackberry	C6
Hahnville	Inset, J7
Hammond	J5
Harahan	Inset
Harrisonburg	E2
Harvey	Inset
Haughton	C1
Haynesville	C1
Henderson	F6
Homer	C1
Houma	H7
Independence	J5
Inniswold	G6
Iota	D6
Iowa	C6
Jackson	G5
Jeanerette	F7
Jean Lafitte	J7
Jefferson	Inset
Jena	E3
Jennings	D6
Jesuit Bend	Inset
Jonesboro	D2
Jonesville	E3
Kaplan	E6
Kenilworth	Inset
Kenner	Inset, J7
Kentwood	J5
Kiliona	Inset
Kinder	D6
Krotz Springs	F5
Labadieville	H7
Lacombe	K6
Lafayette	E6
Lafitte	J7
Lake Arthur	D6
Lake Charles	C6
Lake Providence	G1
Laplace	Inset, J6
Larose	J7
Lecompte	E4
Leesville	C4
Livingston	H5
Lockport	J7
Logansport	B3
Luling	Inset
Mamou	E5
Mandeville	J6
Mansfield	B3
Mansura	E5
Many	C3
Marion	E1
Marksville	E4
Marrero	Inset, J7
Melder	D4
Melville	F5
Meraux	Inset, J7
Metairie	Inset, J7
Mimosa Park	Inset
Minden	C1
Monroe	E2
Montegut	H8
Montz	Inset
Morgan City	G7
Moss Bluff	C6
Napoleonville	G7
Natalbany	J5

	Key
Natchitoches	C3
Newellton	G2
New Iberia	F6
New Llano	C4
New Orleans	Inset, J7
New Roads	G5
New Sarpy	Inset
Norco	D5
Oakdale	D5
Oak Grove	G1
Oakville	Inset
Oberlin	D5
Oil City	B1
Olla	E3
Opelousas	E5
Paincourtville	G6
Paradis	Inset
Patterson	G7
Plaquemine	G6
Point a la Hache	K7
Ponchatoula	J6
Port Allen	G5
Port Barre	F5
Port Sulphur	K8
Poydras	Inset
Raceland	H7
Rayne	E6
Rayville	G2
Reserve	H6
Richwood	E2
Ringgold	C2
River Ridge	Inset
Ruston	D1
St. Bernard	Inset
St. Francisville	G5
St. Joseph	G3
St. Martinville	F6
St. Rose	Inset
Scarsdale	Inset
Schriever	H7
Scott	E6
Shreveport	B2
Simmesport	F5
Slidell	K6
Springhill	C1
Stonewall	B2
Sulphur	C6
Sunset	E6
Swartz	F1
Taft	Inset
Tallulah	G2
Terrytown	Inset
Thibodaux	H7
Toca	Inset
Vidalia	G3
Ville Platte	E5
Vinton	B6
Violet	Inset, K7
Vivian	B1
Waggaman	Inset
Walker	H5
Washington	E5
Welsh	D6
Westlake	C6
West Monroe	E1
Westwego	Inset, J7
White Castle	G6
Winnfield	D3
Winnsboro	F2
Zachary	G5
Zwolle	B3

Other Features

	Key
Atchafalaya, *bay*	G8
Atchafalaya, *river*	F5
Barataria, *bay*	K8
Bistineau, *lake*	C1
Black, *river*	F4
Borgne, *lake*	Inset, K6
Breton, *islands*	L8
Caddo, *lake*	A1
Caillou, *bay*	G8
Calcasieu, *lake*	C7
Caney, *lake*	E2
Cane River Creole Natl. Hist. Park	D3
Catahoula, *lake*	E3
Chandeleur, *islands*	M7
Driskill, *mt.*	C2
Grand, *lake*	D7
Jean Lafitte N.H.P. and Preserve	J7
Little, *river*	D2
Marsh, *island*	F7
Mississippi, *river*	G3
Ouachita, *river*	F1
Pearl, *river*	K5
Pontchartrain, *lake*	Inset, J6
Red, *river*	C3
Sabine, *lake*	B7
Sabine, *river*	B5
Terrebonne, *bay*	H8
Timbalier, *bay*	J8
Toledo Bend, *reservoir*	B4
Vermilion, *bay*	F7
West Cote Blanche, *bay*	F7
White, *lake*	E7

Maine .... page 146

Cities and Towns

	Key
Alfred	B5
Amherst	D4
Athens	C4
Auburn	B5
Augusta, *capital*	B4
Bangor	D4
Bar Harbor	D4
Bass Harbor	D4
Bath	B5
Belfast	C4
Berwick	B5
Biddeford	B5
Boothbay Harbor	C5
Brewer	D4
Bridgton	B4
Brunswick	C4
Bucksport	D4
Calais	E3
Camden	C4
Cape Elizabeth	B5
Caribou	D2
Chisholm	B4
Clinton	C4
Conway	A4
Damariscotta	C4
Dexter	C4
Dixfield	B4
Dover-Foxcroft	C3
East Millinocket	D3
Eastport	E3
Ellsworth	D4
Fairfield	C4

	Key
Falmouth	B5
Farmington	B4
Fort Fairfield	E2
Fort Kent	D1
Frankfort	D4
Franklin	D4
Freeport	B5
Frenchboro	D4
Frenchville	D1
Fryeburg	B4
Gardiner	B4
Greene	B4
Hallowell	B4
Hampden	D4
Houlton	E2
Howland	D3
Kennebunk	B5
Kittery	B5
Lewiston	B4
Lincoln	D3
Lisbon Falls	B4
Livermore Falls	B4
Machias	E4
Madawaska	D1
Madison	C4
Mars Hill	E2
Mechanic Falls	B4
Mexico	B4
Milbridge	E4
Milford	D4
Millinocket	D3
Milo	D3
Norridgewock	C4
North Amity	E3
North Berwick	B5
North Conway	A4
North East Carry	C3
North Windham	B4
Norway	B4
Oakland	C4
Old Orchard Beach	B5
Old Town	D4
Orono	D4
Oxford	B4
Patten	D3
Portland	B5
Presque Isle	D2
Richmond	C4
Rockland	C4
Rumford	B4
Saco	B5
Sanford	B5
Skowhegan	C4
South Paris	B4
South Portland	B5
Springvale	B5
Thomaston	C4
Van Buren	E1
Waldoboro	C4
Waterville	C4
Westbrook	B5
Westfield	E2
Wilsons Mills	A4
Wilton	B4
Winslow	C4
Winthrop	C4
Wiscasset	C4
Woodland	E3
Yarmouth	B5
York	B5

Other Features

	Key
Acadia Natl. Park	D4
Androscoggin, *river*	B4
Appalachian, *mts.*	A3
Aroostook, *river*	D2
au Haut, *island*	D4
Azischohs, *lake*	A3
Baskahegan, *lake*	E3
Baxter State Park	D2
Big, *lake*	E3
Casco, *bay*	C4
Chamberlain, *lake*	C2
Chesuncook, *lake*	C2
Churchill, *lake*	C2
Cross, *island*	E4
Deer, *island*	D4
Elizabeth, *cape*	B4
Flagstaff, *lake*	B3
Grand, *lake*	E3
Grand Matagamon, *lake*	D2
Grand Seboeis, *lake*	D2
Great Wass, *island*	E4
Islesboro, *island*	D4
Katahdin, *mt.*	D3
Kennebec, *river*	C4
Long, *island*	D4
Maine, *gulf*	C5
Matinicus, *island*	D4
Mattawamkeag, *river*	D3
Millinocket, *lake*	D3
Monhegan, *island*	C4
Moosehead, *lake*	C3
Mooselookmeguntic, *lake*	B4
Mt. Desert, *island*	D4
Munsungan, *lake*	D2
Nicatous, *lake*	D3
Pemadumcook, *lake*	C3
Penobscot, *bay*	D4
Penobscot, *river*	D3
Piscataquis, *river*	C3
Richardson, *lakes*	B4
Saco, *bay*	B5
Saco, *river*	B4
St. Croix, *river*	E3
St. John, *river*	C1
Saddleback, *mt.*	B4
Sebago, *lake*	B5
Sebec, *lake*	C3
Seboeis, *lake*	D3
Seboomook, *lake*	C2
Snow, *mt.*	B3
Sugarloaf, *mt.*	B4
Swans, *island*	D4
Telos, *lake*	C2
Umbagog, *lake*	A4
Vinalhaven, *island*	D4
West Grand, *lake*	E3
West Quoddy Head, *peninsula*	E4
White Cap, *mt.*	C3

Maryland .... page 147

Cities and Towns

	Key
Aberdeen	K2
Accident	A6
Accokeek	F5
Adelphi	C4
Annapolis, *capital*	J4
Arden-on-the-Severn	H3
Arnold	J3

	Key
Aspen Hill	B3, F3
Avenue	G7
Baltimore	H2
Bel Air	K2
Beltsville	C3, G3
Berlin	P6
Berwyn Heights	C4
Bethesda	B4, F4
Bladensburg	C4
Boonsboro	D1
Bowie	G4
Bowleys Quarters	J2
Braddock Heights	D2
Brandywine	G5
Brentwood	C4
Brunswick	D2
Bucktown	K6
Burtonsville	C3
Cabin John	A4
California	J6
Calverton	C3
Cambridge	K5
Cape St. Claire	J3
Camp Springs	C5
Carney	H2
Cascade	D1
Catonsville	H2
Centreville	K3
Chesapeake Beach	H5
Chesapeake Ranch Estates	H6
Chestertown	K3
Cheverly	C4
Chillum	C4, G4
Clinton	C5
Clover Hill	E2
Cloverly	C3
Cockeysville	H2
Colesville	C3
College Park	C4, G4
Columbia	G3
Contee	D3
Copenhaver	A3
Coral Hills	C5
Cresaptown	C6
Crisfield	L7
Crofton	H3
Crownsville	H3
Cumberland	D6
Damascus	F2
Deale	H4
Delmar	M6
Denton	L4
Derwood	A3
District Heights	D5
Dufief	A3
Dundalk	H2
Easton	K4
Edgemere	J3
Edgewood	J2
Eldersburg	G2
Eldridge	G3
Elkton	L1
Ellicott City	G3
Emmitsburg	E1
Essex	J2
Fair Hill	L1
Fallston	J1
Federalsburg	L5
Ferndale	H3
Forest Heights	B5, G4
Forestville	G4
Fountain Head	D1
Frederick	E2
Friendship	A6
Frostburg	C6
Fruitland	M6
Gaithersburg	F3
Garrison	G2
Germantown	F3
Glen	A3
Glenarden	H3
Glen Burnie	H3
Glen Echo Heights	B4
Glen Hills	A3
Glenmont	B3
Golden Beach	H6
Grantsville	B6
Grasonville	K4
Green Haven	H3
Greenbelt	D4, G3
Greensboro	L4
Hagerstown	D1
Halfway	C1
Hampstead	H2
Hampton	H2
Hancock	B1
Havre de Grace	K1
Herald Harbor	H3
High Ridge	D3
Hillandale	C4
Hillcrest Heights	C5
Hillsmere Shores	J4
Hughesville	G5
Hunting Hill	A3
Hurlock	L5
Hyattstown	F2
Hyattsville	C4, G4
Indian Head	F5
Jarrettsville	J1
Jessup	H3
Joppatowne	J2
Kemptown	E2
Kensington	B3, F3
Kentland	D4, G4
Kettering	H4
Keysers Ridge	B6
Kingstown	K3
Kingsville	J2
Knollwood	C4
Lake Shore	J3
Landover	C4, G4
Langley Park	C4
Lanham	G4
Lansdowne	H3
LaPlata	G5
Largo	G4
Laurel	D3, G3
LaVale	C6
Lawsonia	L7
Layhill	B3
Leonardtown	H6
Lewisdale	C4
Lexington Park	J6
Linthicum	H3
Lochearn	H2
Londontown	H4
Lutherville	H2
Luxmanor	B3
Manchester	G1
Marlton	G5
Maydale	C3
Middle River	J2

184 MARYLAND–MINNESOTA

Key
Middletown D2
Milford G2
Montgomery Village F3
Montpelier D3
Mount Aetna D1
Mountain Lake Park A7
Mount Airy F2
Mount Rainier C4
Muirkirk D3
New Carrollton D4
Norbeck B3
North Chevy Chase B4
North East L1
Oak Crest D3
Oakland A7
Oakland G2
Oakview C3
Ocean City P6
Ocean Pines P6
Odenton H3
Olney F3
Overlea H2
Owings Mills G2
Oxon Hill C5
Palmer Park D4
Parkville H2
Parole H4
Perry Hall J2
Perryman K2
Perryville K1
Pikesville H2
Pleasant Hills J2
Pocomoke City M7
Poolesville E3
Potomac A3, F3
Potomac Heights F5
Preston L5
Prince Frederick H5
Princess Anne M7
Randallstown G2
Randolph Hills B3
Redhouse A7
Reisterstown G2
Rising Sun K1
Ritchie D5
Riverdale C4
Riviera Beach H3
Rock Hall K3
Rockville A3, F3
Rosedale H2
Rossmoor Leisure World B3
Rossville J2
St. Charles G5
St. Michaels K4
Salisbury M6
Seabrook D4
Seat Pleasant D5
Severn H3
Severna Park H3
Shady Side H4
Shawsville H1
Silver Hill C5
Silver Spring B4, F4
Snow Hill N7
South Gate H3
Spencerville C3
Stevensville J3
Suitland C5, G4
Sykesville G2
Takoma Park C4
Taneytown F1
Temple Hills C5, G4
Thurmont E1
Timonium H2
Towson H2
Upper Marlboro H4
Waldorf G5
Walker Mill D5
Walkersville E2
Westernport B7
Westminster F1
West Ocean City P6
Wheaton B3, F3
White Marsh J2
White Oak C3, G3
White Plains G5
Wildwood Hills A3
Williamsport C1
Woodlawn G2
Woodyard G4

Other Features
Allegheny Front, *mt. ridge* C7
Antietam Natl. Battlefield D2
Appalachian Natl. Scenic Trail D2
Assateague Island Natl. Seashore P7
Assawoman, *bay* P6
Backbone, *mt.* A7
Chesapeake, *bay* J5
Chesapeake and Ohio Canal N.H.P. A4, D2
Chester, *river* K3
Chincoteague, *bay* N7
Choptank, *river* K5
Deep Creek, *lake* A6
Liberty, *reservoir* G2
North Branch Potomac, *river* C7
Nanticoke, *river* L6
Patapsco, *river* H3
Patuxent, *river* H4
Potomac, *river* G6
Susquehanna, *river* J1
Thomas Stone Natl. Hist. Site F5
Wicomico, *river* G6
Youghiogheny, *river* A6

Massachusetts ....page 148

Cities and Towns
Abington L4
Acton A5, J3
Acushnet L6
Adams B2
Amesbury L1
Amherst D3
Andover K2
Arlington C6, K3
Ashby G2
Ashfield C2
Ashland J3
Assinippi F8
Assonet K5
Athol F2
Attleboro J5
Auburn G4
Avon D8, K4
Ayer H2
Baldwinville F2
Barnstable N6
Becket B3
Bedford B5, J3
Belchertown E3
Bellingham J4
Belmont C6
Berkley K5
Bernardston D2
Beverly F5, L2
Billerica B5, J2
Blackstone H4
Blandford C4
Bliss Corner L6
Bolton H3
Bondsville E4
Boston, *capital* D6, K3
Boxford L2
Braintree E8, K4
Brewster P5
Bridgewater L5
Brimfield F4
Brockton K4
Brookfield F4
Brookline C7, K3
Burlington C5, K2
Buzzards Bay M5
Cambridge D6, K3
Canton C8, K4
Carlisle B5
Cedarville M5
Centerville N6
Central Village K6
Charlton G4
Charlton City G4
Chatham Q6
Chelmsford J2
Chelsea D6
Cheshire B2
Chester C3
Chicopee D4
Chilmark M7
Clarksburg B2
Clinton H3
Cochituate B7, J3
Cohasset L4
Concord B6, J3
Cotuit N6
Dalton B3
Danvers E5, L2
Dartmouth K6
Dedham C7, K4
Dennis P6
Douglas H4
Dover B8, J4
Dracut J2
Duxbury M4
East Brookfield F4
East Dennis P6
East Douglas H4
East Falmouth M6
East Freetown L5
Eastham Q5
Easthampton D3
East Longmeadow D4
East Orleans Q5
East Pepperell H2
East Wareham M5
Edgartown M7
Erving E2
Essex L2
Everett D6
Fall River K6
Falmouth M6
Feeding Hills D4
Fiskdale F4
Fitchburg G2
Florida B2
Foxboro K4
Framingham A7, J3
Franklin J4
Gardner G2
Gay Head L7
Georgetown L2
Gloucester M2
Granby D3
Granville C4
Great Barrington A4
Greenfield D2
Green Harbor M4
Halifax L5
Hamilton L2
Hanover L4
Hanson L4
Haverhill K1
Hingham F8, L4
Holbrook E8, K4
Holland F4
Holliston A8, J4
Holyoke D4
Hopedale H4
Hopkinton H4
Hubbardston G3
Hudson H3
Hull F7, L3
Huntington C4
Hyannis N6
Ipswich L2
Kingston M5
Lakeville L5
Lawrence K2
Lee B3
Lenox A3
Leominster G2
Lexington C6, K3
Lincoln B6
Littleton H2
Littleton Common J2
Longmeadow D4
Lowell J2
Ludlow E4
Lunenburg H2
Lynn E6, L3
Lynnfield D5, K2
Madaket P7
Malden D6, K3
Manchester-by-the-Sea L2
Mansfield K4
Marblehead F5, L3
Marion L6
Marlborough H3
Marshfield M4
Marshfield Hills M4
Mashpee N6
Mattapoisett L6
Maynard J3
Medfield B8, J4
Medford D6, K3
Medway A8
Melrose D6, K3
Mendon H4
Methuen K2
Middleboro L5
Milford H4
Millis B8
Milton D7, K3
Monson E4
Monterey B4
Monument Beach M6
Nahant E6, L3
Nantucket P7
Natick B7, J3
Needham C7, K3
New Ashford B2
New Bedford L6
New Boston B4
Newburyport L1
New Marlborough B4
Newton C7, K3
North Adams B2
North Amherst D3
Northampton D3
North Andover K2
North Attleboro J5
Northborough H3
Northbridge H4
North Brookfield F3
North Carver L5
North Falmouth M6
Northfield E2
North Grafton H4
North Pembroke L4
North Plymouth M5
North Reading D5, K2
North Scituate L4
North Sudbury A6
North Tisbury M7
Norton K5
Norwell L4
Norwood C8, K4
Oakham F3
Ocean Bluff M4
Ocean Grove K6
Orange E2
Orleans Q5
Osterville N6
Otis B4
Oxford G4
Palmer E4
Paxton G3
Peabody E5, L2
Pelham E3
Pembroke L4
Pepperell H2
Petersham F3
Phillipston F2
Pinehurst C5, K2
Pittsfield B3
Plainfield C2
Plainville J4
Plymouth M5
Pocasset M6
Provincetown P4
Quincy E7, K3
Randolph D8, K4
Raynham K5
Raynham Center K5
Reading D5, K2
Rehoboth K5
Revere E6, K3
Rochester L6
Rockland E8, L4
Rockport M2
Rutland G3
Sagamore M5
Salem F5, L2
Salisbury L1
Sandwich N5
Saugus E6, K3
Savoy B2
Scituate L4
Sharon C8, K4
Sheffield A4
Shelburne Falls D2
Sherborn B8
Shirley H2
Shrewsbury H3
Shutesbury E3
Somerset K5
Somerville D6, K3
South Amherst D3
Southbridge F4
South Carver M5
South Deerfield D3
South Dennis P6
South Duxbury M4
South Lancaster H3
South Sudbury A7
South Wellfleet P5
South Yarmouth P6
Spencer G4
Springfield D4
Sterling G3
Stoneham D5
Stoughton D8, K4
Sturbridge F4
Sudbury A6, J3
Sutton G4
Swampscott E6, L3
Taunton K5
Teaticket M6
Templeton F2
Tewksbury K2
Three Rivers E4
Tolland B4
Topsfield L2
Truro P5
Turners Falls D2
Tyngsborough J2
Upton H4
Uxbridge H4
Vineyard Haven M7
Wakefield D5, K2
Wales F4
Walpole C8, J4
Waltham C6, B6
Ware F3
Wareham M5
Warren F4
Warwick E2
Washington B3
Watertown C6
Wauwinet P7
Wayland B7
Webster G4
Wellesley B7, J3
West Barnstable N6
Westborough H3
West Boylston G3
West Brookfield F4
West Concord J3
West Cummington C3
West Falmouth M6
Westfield D4
Westford J2
West Granville C4
Westhampton C3
West Medway A8
Westminster G2
Weston B6, J3
Westport K6
Westport Point K6
West Springfield D4
West Wareham L5
Westwood C8, K4
West Yarmouth P6
Weymouth E8, L4
Whately D3
White Island Shores M5
Whitinsville H4
Whitman L4
Wilbraham E4
Williamstown B2
Wilmington C5, K2
Winchendon F2
Winchester C6
Windsor B2
Winthrop E6
Woburn C5, K3
Worcester G3
Worthington Center C3
Wrentham J4
Yarmouth Port P6

Other Features
Adams Natl. Hist. Park E8, L4
Ann, *cape* M2
Berkshire, *hills* B4
Boston, *bay* E6
Boston, *harbor* E7
Boston Harbor Islands N.R.A. E7
Boston Natl. Hist. Park D6
Buzzards, *bay* M6
Cape Cod, *bay* N5
Cape Cod, *canal* M5
Cape Cod Natl. Seashore P5
Charles, *river* B7
Chicopee, *river* D4
Cobble Mt., *reservoir* C4
Cod, *cape* P4
Connecticut, *river* E2
Deer, *island* E7
Elizabeth, *islands* L7
Frederick Law Olmsted N.H.S. C7
Georges, *island* E7
Greylock, *mt.* B2
Hingham, *bay* E7
Housatonic, *river* A4
J.F.K. Birthplace Natl. Hist. Site D7
Long, *island* E7
Longfellow Natl. Hist. Site D6
Lowell Natl. Hist. Park J2
Maine, *gulf* M1
Martha's Vineyard, *island* M7
Massachusetts, *bay* F6, M3
Merrimack, *river* K1
Minute Man Natl. Hist. Park B6, J3
Monomoy, *island* P6
Muskeget, *channel* N7
Nantucket, *island* P7
New Bedford Whaling N.H.P. L6
Neponset, *river* C7
Otis, *reservoir* B4
Peddocks, *island* E7
Quabbin, *reservoir* F3
Quincy, *bay* E7
Salem Maritime N.H.S. F5, L2
Saugus Iron Works N.H.S. E6
Shawsheen, *river* B6
Spectacle, *island* E7
Swift, *river* E4
Taconic, *mts.* A2
Wachusett, *reservoir* G3
Wachusett, *river* G3
Walden, *pond* B6

Michigan ....page 149

Cities and Towns
Adrian E8
Albion E7
Algonac G7
Allegan D7
Allendale C7
Allen Park A7
Alma E6
Alpena F4
Ann Arbor F7
Atlanta E5
Bad Axe G6
Baldwin D6
Battle Creek D7
Bay City F6
Belding D6
Bellaire D5
Belleville F7
Benton Harbor C7
Berkley A6
Bessemer C2
Beulah C5
Beverly Hills A6
Big Rapids D6
Birmingham A6
Blissfield F8
Bloomfield Hills A6
Boyne City D4
Bridgeport F6
Brighton F7
Buchanan C8
Burton F6
Cadillac D5
Carleton F7
Caro F6
Carrollton F6
Cassopolis C8
Cedar Springs D6
Center Line B6
Centreville D8
Charlevoix D4
Charlotte E7
Cheboygan E4
Chelsea E7
Chesaning E6
Chesterfield C6
Christmas C3
Clare E6
Clawson B6
Clio F6
Coldwater D8
Connorville C2
Coopersville D6
Crystal Falls A3
Cutlerville D7
Davison F6
Dearborn A7, F7
Dearborn Hts. A7
Detroit B7, F7
De Witt E7
Dowagiac C8
Dundee F8
Durand F7
Eagle River A2
East Lansing E7
Eastpointe B6
East Tawas F5
Eaton Rapids E7
Ecorse B7
Escanaba B4
Essexville F6
Farmington A6
Farmington Hills A6
Fenton F7
Ferndale B6
Ferrysburg C6
Flat Rock F7
Flint F6
Flushing F6
Fowlerville E7
Frankenmuth F6
Franklin A6
Fraser B6
Fremont D6
Garden City A7
Gaylord E4
Gladstone B4
Gladwin E6
Grand Blanc F7
Grand Haven C6
Grand Ledge E7
Grand Rapids D7
Grayling E5
Greenville D6
Grosse Pointe B7
Grosse Pointe Farms B6
Grosse Pointe Park B7
Grosse Pointe Shores B6
Grosse Pointe Woods B6
Hamtramck B7
Hancock A2
Harper Woods B6
Harrison E5
Harrisville F5
Hart C6
Hastings D7
Hazel Park B6
Highland Park B7
Hillsdale E8
Holland C7
Holly F7
Holt E7
Houghton A2
Houghton Lake E5
Howell F7
Hudson E8
Hudsonville D7
Huntington Woods A6
Huron Heights A6
Imlay City F6
Inkster A7
Ionia D6
Iron Mountain A4
Ironwood C2
Ishpeming B3
Ithaca E6
Jackson E7
Jenison D7
Kalamazoo D7
Kalkaska D5
Keego Harbor A6
Kentwood D7
Kingsford A4
Lake City D5
Lake Orion F7
Lambertville F8
L'Anse A3
Lansing, *capital* E7
Lapeer F6
Lincoln Park A7
Livonia A7, F7
Lowell D7
Ludington C6
Madison Hts. B6
Manistee C5
Manistique C4
Marenisco D2
Marine City G7
Marquette B3
Marshall E7
Marysville G7
Mason E7
Melvindale A7
Menominee B4
Merriweather D2
Michigan Center E7
Midland E6
Milan F7
Milford F7
Mio E5
Monroe F8
Mount Clemens B6
Mount Morris F6
Mount Pleasant E6
Munising C3
Muskegon C6
Muskegon Hts. C6
Negaunee B3
New Baltimore G7
Newberry D3
Niles C8
North Muskegon C6
Norton Shores C6
Norway B4
Oak Park A6
Okemos E7
Ontonagon D1
Orchard Lake A6
Otsego D7
Owosso E6
Oxford F7
Paw Paw C7
Paw Paw Lake C7
Petoskey E4
Plainwell D7
Pontiac A6, F7
Portage D7
Port Huron G7
Portland E7
Rapid River C4
Reed City D6
Richmond G7
River Rouge B7
Rochester Hills A6
Rockford D6
Rockwood F7
Rogers City F4
Romeo F7
Romulus F7
Roscommon E5
Roseville B6
Royal Oak B6
Saginaw F6
St. Clair G7
St. Clair Shores B6
St. Ignace E4
St. Johns E6
St. Joseph C7
St. Louis E6
Saline F7
Sandusky G6
Sault Ste. Marie E3
Shields E6
Silver City D1
Skidway Lake E5
Southfield A6
Southgate A7
South Haven C7
South Lyon F7
Sparta D6
Spring Lake C6
Standish F6
Stanton D6
Sterling Heights F7
Sturgis D8
Sylvan Lake A6
Tawas City F5
Taylor A7, F7
Tecumseh F7
Temperance F8
Three Rivers D7
Traverse City D5
Troy B6
Union Lake A6
Utica B6
Vassar F6
Wakefield C2
Waldenburg B6
Walker D7
Warren B6, F7
Wayland D7
Wayne A7
West Acres A6
West Branch E5
Westland A7
White Cloud D6
Whitehall C6
White Pine D2
Whitmore Lake F7
Williamston E7
Wixom F7
Wolf Lake C6
Wyandotte B7
Wyoming D7
Ypsilanti F7
Zeeland C7

Other Features
Arvon, *mt.* A3
Au Sable, *river* E5
Beaver, *island* D4
Big Bay De Noc, *bay* C4
Big Sable, *point* C5
Bois Blanc, *island* E4
Cass, *river* F6
Chambers, *island* B4
Detroit, *river* B7
Drummond, *island* F4
Erie, *lake* G8
Escanaba, *river* B3
Glen, *lake* D5
Gogebic, *lake* D2
Government Peak, *mt.* D1
Grand, *island* C3
Grand Island Natl. Rec. Area C3
Grand Traverse, *bay* D4
Green, *bay* B5
Hamlin, *lake* C5
Hammond, *bay* E4
Higgins, *lake* E5
High, *island* D4
Hog, *island* D4
Houghton, *lake* E5
Hubbard, *lake* F5
Huron, *bay* A3
Huron, *lake* G5
Huron, *mts.* A3
Indian, *lake* C3
Isle Royale, *island* A1
Isle Royale Natl. Park A2
Keweenaw, *bay* A3
Keweenaw, *peninsula* A2
Keweenaw, *point* B2
Keweenaw Natl. Hist. Park A2
Lookout, *point* F5
Manistee, *river* D5
Manitou, *island* B2
Menominee, *river* B4
Michigamme, *reservoir* A3
Michigan, *lake* C5
North Manitou, *island* C4
Paint, *river* A3
Pictured Rocks Natl. Lakeshore C3
Porcupine, *mts.* D2
Saginaw, *bay* F6
St. Clair, *lake* G7
St. Martin, *island* C4
Sleeping Bear Dunes Natl. Lakeshore C5
South Fox, *island* D4
South Manitou, *island* C4
Straits of Mackinac E4
Sturgeon, *bay* D4
Superior, *lake* A2
Thunder, *bay* F5
Whitefish, *bay* E3
Wixom, *lake* E6

Minnesota ....page 150

Cities and Towns
Ada A3
Aitkin D4
Albany C5
Albert Lea D7
Albertville D5
Alexandria B5
Annandale C5
Anoka D5
Appleton A5
Arlington C6
Aurora E3
Austin E7
Babbitt F3
Bagley B3
Barnesville A4
Baudette C2
Baxter C4
Bayport E6
Belle Plaine D6
Bemidji C3
Benson B5
Big Lake D5
Bird Island C6

Minnesota

Cities and Towns

Name	Key
Blooming Prairie	D7
Bloomington	D6
Blue Earth	C7
Brainerd	C4
Breckenridge	A4
Brooklyn Center	E5
Buffalo	D5
Burnsville	D6
Caledonia	F7
Cambridge	D5
Canby	A6
Cannon Falls	E6
Carlton	E4
Center City	E5
Chanhassen	D6
Chaska	D6
Chatfield	E7
Chisholm	E3
Clara City	B6
Clarks Grove	D7
Clearwater	C5
Cloquet	E4
Cokato	C5
Cold Spring	C5
Columbia Hts.	E5
Coon Rapids	D5
Corcoran	D5
Crookston	A3
Crosby	D4
Crystal	D6
Dawson	A6
Detroit Lakes	B4
Dilworth	A4
Dodge Center	E6
Duluth	E4
Eagan	F6
Eagle Lake	D6
East Bethel	D5
East Grand Forks	A3
Edina	D6
Elbow Lake	B5
Elk River	D5
Ely	F3
Evansville	B4
Eveleth	E3
Eyota	E7
Fairmont	C7
Falcon Heights	F5
Faribault	D6
Farmington	D6
Fergus Falls	A4
Foley	D5
Forest Lake	E5
Fosston	B3
Fridley	F5
Gaylord	C6
Glencoe	C6
Glenwood	B5
Golden Valley	E5
Goodview	F6
Grand Forks	A3
Grand Marais	F5
Grand Portage	F4
Grand Rapids	D3
Granite Falls	B6
Hallock	A2
Hastings	E6
Hawley	A4
Hayfield	E7
Hermantown	E4
Hibbing	E3
Hokah	F7
Hopkins	E5
Hovland	F4
Howard Lake	C5
Hutchinson	C6
International Falls	D2
Ivanhoe	A6
Jackson	B7
Janesville	D6
Jordan	D6
Kasson	E6
Kenyon	E6
La Crescent	F7
Lake Crystal	C6
Lakefield	B7
Lakeville	D6
Le Center	D6
Le Sueur	D6
Lewiston	F7
Litchfield	C5
Little Canada	F5
Little Falls	C5
Long Prairie	C5
Lonsdale	D6
Lutsen	E5
Luverne	A7
McIntosh	B3
Madelia	C6
Madison	A5
Mahnomen	B3
Mankato	D6
Mantorville	E6
Maple Grove	D5
Maple Lake	C5
Mapleton	D7
Maplewood	F5
Marshall	B6
Melrose	C5
Mendota	F6
Milaca	D5
Minneapolis	D6
Minneota	B6
Montevideo	B6
Montgomery	D6
Monticello	D5
Moorhead	A4
Mora	D5
Morris	B5
Mound	D6
Mountain Iron	E3
Mountain Lake	C7
New Hope	E5
New Prague	D6
New Ulm	C6
Niswa	C4
North Branch	E5
Northfield	D6
North Mankato	C6
North Oaks	F5
Olivia	C6
Orono	D6
Oronoco	E6
Ortonville	A5
Osakis	B5
Owatonna	D6
Park Rapids	B4
Paynesville	C5
Pelican Rapids	A4
Perham	B4
Pigeon River	F4
Pine City	E5
Pine Island	E6
Pipestone	A7
Plainview	E6
Plymouth	D5
Preston	E7
Princeton	D5
Prinsburg	B6
Prior Lake	D6
Proctor	E4
Ramsey	D5
Red Lake Falls	A3
Red Wing	E6
Redwood Falls	B6
Renville	B6
Richfield	E5
Robbinsdale	E5
Rochester	E6
Roseau	B2
Rushford	F7
St. Anthony	F5
St. Charles	E7
St. Cloud	C5
St. Francis	D5
St. James	C7
St. Joseph	C5
St. Louis Park	E5
St. Michael	D5
St. Paul, capital	D6
St. Peter	D6
Sandstone	E4
Sartell	C5
Sauk Centre	C5
Sauk Rapids	C5
Shakopee	D6
Silver Bay	F3
Slayton	B7
Sleepy Eye	C6
South St. Paul	F5
Spring Valley	E7
Springfield	C6
Staples	C4
Stewartville	E7
Stillwater	E5
Thief River Falls	A2
Tracy	B6
Truman	C7
Two Harbors	F3
Tyler	A6
Virginia	E3
Wabasha	E6
Wadena	B4
Waite Park	C5
Walker	C3
Warren	A2
Warroad	B2
Waseca	D6
Waterville	D6
Wells	D7
Wheaton	A5
White Bear Lake	F5
Willmar	B5
Windom	B7
Winnebago	C7
Winona	F6
Winsted	C6
Winthrop	C6
Worthington	B7
Wyoming	E5
Young America	D6
Zimmerman	D5
Zumbrota	E6

Other Features

Name	Key
Big Fork, river	D2
Brule, lake	E4
Buffalo, river	A4
Chippewa, river	B5
Clearwater, river	B3
Cloquet, river	E3
Des Moines, river	B6
Eagle, mt.	F4
Grand Portage Natl. Monument	F4
Gull, lake	C4
Lake of the Woods, lake	C1
Leech, lake	C3
Little Fork, river	D2
Lower Red, lake	B3
Lower Whitefish, lake	C4
Mall of America	F6
Mesabi, range	D3
Mille Lacs, lake	D4
Minnesota, river	B6
Mississippi, river	C3
Mud, lake	B2
Namakan, lake	E2
Pipestone Natl. Monument	A6
Pokegama, lake	D3
Rainy, river	A3
Red River of the North, river	A3
Root, river	E7
Rum, river	D5
St. Croix, river	E4
St. Louis, river	E3
Superior, lake	F3
Upper Red, lake	C2
Vermilion, range	F3
Voyageurs Natl. Park	E2
Winnibigoshish, lake	D3

Mississippi .... page 151

Cities and Towns

Name	Key
Aberdeen	D2
Ackerman	C2
Alligator	B1
Amory	D2
Ashland	D1
Baldwyn	D1
Bassfield	C4
Batesville	C1
Bay St. Louis	C5
Bay Springs	C4
Beauregard	B4
Belmont	D1
Belzoni	B2
Biloxi	D5
Blue Springs	D1
Booneville	D1
Brandon	C3
Braxton	C3
Brookhaven	B4
Bruce	C2
Calhoun City	C2
Canton	B3
Carrollton	C2
Carthage	C3
Centreville	A4
Charleston	B1
Clarksdale	B1
Cleveland	B2
Clinton	B3
Coahoma	B1
Coffeeville	C2
Coldwater	C1
Collins	C4
Collinsville	D3
Columbia	B4
Columbus	D2
Como	C1
Corinth	D1
Crystal Springs	B4
Decatur	C3
De Kalb	D3
Diamondhead	C5
D'Iberville	D5
Doddsville	B2
Drew	B2
Durant	C2
Eden	B3
Edwards	B3
Ellisville	C4
Eupora	C2
Falcon	B1
Fayette	A4
Flora	B3
Florence	C3
Forest	C3
Friars Point	B1
Fulton	D1
Gautier	D5
Glendora	B2
Gloster	A4
Golden	D1
Goodman	C3
Greenville	A2
Greenwood	B2
Grenada	C2
Gulfport	C5
Hattiesburg	C4
Hazlehurst	B4
Hernando	C1
Hollandale	B2
Holly Springs	C1
Horn Lake	C1
Houston	D2
Indianola	B2
Itta Bena	B2
Iuka	D1
Jackson, capital	B3
Jonestown	B1
Kiln	C5
Kosciusko	C2
Kossuth	D1
Laurel	C4
Leakesville	D4
Learned	B3
Leland	B2
Lena	C3
Lexington	B2
Liberty	B4
Long Beach	C5
Louisville	C2
Lucedale	D5
Lula	B1
Lumberton	C4
Lyman	C5
McComb	B4
McCool	C2
Macon	D2
Madison	B3
Magee	C4
Magnolia	B4
Mantee	C2
Marion	D3
Marks	B1
Mayersville	A3
Meadville	B4
Mendenhall	C4
Meridian	D3
Monticello	B4
Montrose	C3
Moorhead	B2
Morton	C3
Moss Point	D5
Mound Bayou	B2
Natchez	A4
Nettleton	D1
New Albany	D1
New Augusta	C4
Newton	C3
Ocean Springs	D5
Okolona	D1
Olive Branch	C1
Oxford	C1
Paden	D1
Pascagoula	D5
Pass Christian	C5
Paulding	C3
Pearl	B3
Pearlington	C5
Pelahatchie	C3
Petal	C4
Philadelphia	C3
Picayune	C5
Pickens	C3
Pittsboro	C2
Polkville	C3
Pontotoc	D1
Pope	C1
Poplarville	C5
Port Gibson	B4
Prentiss	C4
Purvis	C4
Quitman	D3
Raleigh	C3
Raymond	B3
Richland	B3
Ridgeland	B3
Ripley	D1
Rolling Fork	B3
Rosedale	A2
Ruleville	B2
Sallis	C2
Saltillo	D1
Sardis	C1
Satartia	B3
Seminary	C4
Senatobia	C1
Shannon	D1
Shaw	B2
Shelby	B2
Shubuta	D4
Silver Creek	B4
Slate Spring	C2
Southaven	C1
Starkville	D2
Summit	B4
Sumner	B2
Sylvarena	C3
Taylorsville	C4
Tchula	B2
Tillatoba	C2
Toccopola	C1
Tunica	B1
Tupelo	D1
Tutwiler	B1
Tylertown	B4
Union	C3
Vaiden	C2
Vancleave	D5
Verona	D1
Vicksburg	B3
Walthall	C2
Water Valley	C1
Waveland	C5
Waynesboro	D4
Wesson	B4
West	C2
West Point	D2
Wiggins	C3
Winona	C2
Woodland	C2
Woodville	A4
Yazoo City	B3

Other Features

Name	Key
Arkabutula, lake	B1
Big Black, river	B3
Big Springs, lake	D1
Big Sunflower, river	B2
Bogue Chitto, river	B4
Buttahatchee, river	D2
Cat, island	C5
Chickasawhay, river	D4
Coldwater, river	B1
Columbus, lake	D2
Enid, lake	C1
Grenada, lake	C2
Gulf Island Natl. Seashore	D5
Homochitto, river	A4
Horn, island	D5
Leaf, river	C4
Mississippi, river	B1
Mississsppi, sound	D5
Natchez Natl. Hist. Park	A4
Noxubee, river	D2
Okatibbee, lake	D3
Pascagoula, river	C3
Pearl, river	C3
Petit Bois, island	D5
Pickwick, lake	D1
Pontotoc, mt. ridge	D1
Ross Barnett, reservoir	C3
Sardis, lake	C1
Ship, island	D5
Tallahatchie, river	B1
Tombigbee, river	D1
Tupelo Natl. Battlefield	D1
Vicksburg Natl. Mil. Park	B3
Woodall, mt	D1
Yazoo, river	B2

Missouri .... page 152

Cities and Towns

Name	Key
Adrian	B3
Affton	H3
Albany	B1
Alton	E5
Anderson	B5
Appleton City	B3
Ashland	D3
Atherton	J4
Aurora	C5
Ava	D5
Barnett	D3
Belton	B3
Benton	G5
Bernie	G5
Bethany	B1
Birmingham	J4
Bloomfield	G5
Blue Springs	J4
Bolivar	C4
Bonne Terre	F4
Boonville	D3
Bowling Green	E2
Branson	C5
Brentwood	H2
Bridgeton	H2
Brookfield	C2
Buckner	J4
Buffalo	C4
Butler	B3
Cabool	D4
California	D3
Calverton Park	H2
Camdenton	D4
Cameron	B2
Campbell	F5
Canton	E1
Cape Girardeau	G4
Carrollton	C2
Carthage	B4
Caruthersville	G5
Cassville	C5
Cedar Hill	F3
Centerville	F4
Centralia	D2
Chaffee	G4
Charleston	G5
Chesterfield	F3
Chillicothe	C2
Claycomo	J4
Clayton	F3, H2
Clinton	C3
Columbia	D3
Concord	H3
Concordia	C3
Crestwood	H3
Creve Coeur	H2
Cuba	E3
Dellwood	H2
Desloge	F4
De Soto	F3
Des Peres	H2
Dexter	G5
Dixon	D3
Doniphan	F5
East Prairie	G5
Edina	D1
Eldon	D3
El Dorado Springs	B4
Elsberry	F2
Eminence	E4
Eureka	F3
Excelsior Springs	B2, J3
Farley	H3
Farmington	F4
Fayette	D2
Fenton	G3
Ferguson	H2
Festus	F3
Florissant	H2
Forsyth	C5
Fredericktown	F4
Fulton	D3
Gainesville	D5
Galena	C5
Gallatin	C2
Gladstone	B2, J3
Glasgow	D2
Glasgow Village	H2
Glendale	H3
Grain Valley	J4
Granby	B5
Grandview	J4
Grant City	B1
Greenfield	C4
Greenville	F4
Hamilton	C2
Hannibal	E2
Harrisonville	B3
Hartville	D4
Hayti	G5
Hazelwood	H2
Hermann	E3
Hermitage	C4
Higginsville	C2
Hillsboro	F3
Holden	C3
Hollister	C5
Houston	E4
Huntsville	D2
Independence	B2, J4
Ironton	F4
Jackson	G4
Jefferson City, capital	D3
Jennings	H2
Joplin	B4
Kahoka	E1
Kansas City	B2, H4
Kennett	F5
Keytesville	D2
Kingston	C2
Kinloch	H2
Kirksville	D1
Kirkwood	H3
Knob Noster	C3
Ladue	H2
Lake Lotawana	J4
Lake St. Louis	F3
Lamar	B4
Lancaster	D1
La Plata	D1
Lathrop	B2
Lawson	B2
Lebanon	D4
Lee's Summit	B3, J4
Lemay	H3
Lexington	C2
Liberty	B2, J3
Licking	E4
Lilbourn	G5
Linn Creek	D3
Linneus	C2
Louisiana	E2
Mackenzie	H3
Macon	D2
Malden	G5
Manchester	G3
Mansfield	D4
Maplewood	H3
Marble Hill	G4
Marceline	D2
Marionville	C5
Marshall	C2
Marshfield	D4
Maryland Heights	H2
Maryville	B1
Mattese	H3
Maysville	B2
Mehlville	H3
Memphis	D1
Mexico	E2
Milan	C1
Millard	D1
Moberly	D2
Monett	C5
Monroe City	E2
Montgomery City	E3
Monticello	E1
Mosby	J3
Mound City	A1
Mountain Grove	D4
Mountain View	E4
Mt. Vernon	C4
Murphy	H3
Neosho	B5
Nevada	B4
New Haven	E3
New London	E2
New Madrid	G5
Nixa	C4
North Kansas City	H4
Northwoods	H2
Oaks	J4
O'Fallon	F3
Olivette	H2
Oregon	A2
Osage Beach	D3
Osceola	C3
Overland	H2
Owensville	E3
Ozark	C4
Pacific	F3
Pagedale	H2
Palmyra	E2
Paris	D2
Park Hills	F4
Parkville	H4
Peculiar	B3
Peerless Park	G3
Perryville	G4
Pevely	F3
Piedmont	F4
Pierce City	C5
Pine Lawn	H2
Pineville	B5
Platte City	B2, H3
Plattsburg	B2
Pleasant Hill	B3
Poplar Bluff	F5
Portageville	G5
Potosi	F4
Princeton	C1
Randolph	J4
Raymore	B3
Raytown	J4
Republic	C4
Rich Hill	B3
Richland	D4
Richmond	C2
Richmond Heights	H2
Riverside	H4
Rock Hill	H2
Rock Port	A1
Rolla	E4
St. Ann	H2
St. Charles	F3, G2
St. Clair	F3
Ste. Genevieve	F3
St. James	E3
St. John	H2
St. Joseph	B2
St. Louis	F3, H2
St. Peters	F3
St. Robert	D4
Salem	E4
Salisbury	D2
Sappington	H3
Sarcoxie	B4
Savannah	B2
Scott City	G4
Sedalia	C3
Senath	F5
Seymour	D4
Shelbina	D2
Shelbyville	D2
Shirley	F4
Sikeston	G5
Slater	C2
Smithville	B2
Springfield	C4
Stanberry	B1
Steele	G5
Steelville	E4
Stockton	C4
Stoutsville	E2
Sugar Creek	J4
Sullivan	E3
Sweet Springs	C3
Tarkio	A1
Thayer	E5
Town and Country	G2
Trenton	C1
Troy	F3
Tuscumbia	D3
Union	E3
Unionville	C1
Unity Village	J4
University City	H2
Van Buren	E5
Vandalia	E2
Versailles	D3
Vienna	E3
Villa Ridge	F3
Waldron	H3
Warrensburg	C3
Warrenton	E3
Warsaw	C3
Washington	E3
Watson	A1
Waynesville	D4
Weatherby Lake	H3
Webb City	B4
Webster Groves	H3
Wellsville	E2
Wentzville	E3
West Plains	E5
Weston	B2
Willard	C4
Willow Springs	E4
Windsor	C3

Other Features

Name	Key
Bull Shoals, lake	D5
Eleven Point, river	E5
Fox, river	E1
G.W. Carver Natl. Monument	B5
Grand, river	B1
Harry S. Truman, reservoir	C3
Lake of the Ozarks, lake	D3
Mark Twain, lake	E2
Meramec, river	E4
Mississippi, river	G4
Missouri, river	C2
Osage, river	B4, D3
Ozark Natl. Scenic Riverways	E4
Platte, river	B2
St. Francis, river	F4
Stockton, lake	C5
Table Rock, lake	C5
Taum Sauk, mt.	F4
Thomas Hill, reservoir	D2
Weldon, river	C2

Montana .... page 153

Cities and Towns

Name	Key
Anaconda	D3
Baker	M3
Belgrade	E4
Big Timber	F4
Billings	H4
Boulder	D3
Bozeman	E4
Bridger	H4
Broadus	L4
Butte	D3
Chester	F1
Chinook	G1
Choteau	D2
Circle	L2
Columbus	G4
Conrad	E1
Crow Agency	J4
Cut Bank	D1
Deer Lodge	D3
Dell	D5
Dillon	D4
East Helena	E3
Ekalaka	M4
Evergreen	B1
Forsyth	K3
Fort Benton	F2
Gardiner	F5
Glasgow	K1
Glendive	M2
Great Falls	E2
Hamilton	B3
Hardin	J4
Harlowton	G3
Hathaway	K3
Havre	G1
Helena, capital	D3
Kalispell	B1
Lame Deer	K4
Laurel	H4
Lewistown	G2
Libby	A1
Lincoln	D3
Livingston	F4
Lolo Hot Springs	B3
Malta	J1
Miles City	L3

MONTANA (continued)

Name	Key
Missoula	C3
Orchard Homes	B3
Philipsburg	C3
Plentywood	M1
Polson	B2
Pony	C4
Red Lodge	E4
Roman	B2
Roundup	H3
Rudyard	F1
St. Regis	A2
Scobey	L1
Shelby	E1
Sidney	M2
Somers	B1
Stanford	F2
Superior	B2
Terry	L3
Thompson Falls	A2
Townsend	E3
West Yellowstone	E5
Whitefish	B1
Wibaux	M3
Wolf Point	L1

Other Features

Name	Key
Bighorn, river	J4
Bighorn Canyon Natl. Rec. Area	H4
Bitterroot, range	B3
Bull, mts.	H3
Canyon Ferry lake	E3
Clark Fork, river	D3
Cleveland, mt.	C1
Custer Battlefield Natl. Monument	J4
Elwell, lake	E1
Flathead	B2
Flathead river	B1
Fort Peck, lake	K2
Fresno, reservoir	F1
Glacier Natl. Park	C1
Granite Peak	D4
Granite Peak, mt.	G4
Grant-Kohrs Ranch N.H.S.	D3
Homer Youngs Peak, mt.	C4
Hungry Horse, reservoir	C1
Koocanusa, lake	A1
Kootenai, river	A1
Little Missouri, river	M5
Madison, river	E4
Marias, river	E1
Middle Fork, river	C1
Milk, river	D1
Missouri, river	G2
Musselshell, river	H3
Northwest Peak, mt.	A1
Pompeys Pillar Natl. Mon.	H3
Powder, river	L3
Rocky, mts.	C2
St. Mary, river	C1
St. Regis, river	B2
Scarface Peak, mt.	C2
South Fork, river	C2
Swan, river	C2
Teton, river	E2
Tongue, river	K4
Upper Missouri River Breaks N.M.	G2
Warren Peak, mt.	C4
Yellowstone, river	L3
Yellowstone Natl. Park	F5

Nebraska .... page 154

Cities and Towns

Name	Key
Ainsworth	E2
Albion	E3
Alliance	B2
Alma	E4
Ashland	H3
Atkinson	F2
Auburn	J4
Aurora	F4
Bartlett	F3
Bassett	E2
Beatrice	H4
Beaver City	E4
Bellevue	J3
Benkelman	C4
Blair	H3
Brewster	E3
Bridgeport	A3
Broken Bow	E3
Burwell	F2
Butte	F2
Center	G2
Central City	F3
Chadron	B2
Chapman	F3
Chappell	B3
Clay Center	F4
Columbus	G3
Cozad	E4
Crete	H4
Dakota City	H2
David City	G3
Elkhorn	H3
Elwood	E4
Exeter	G4
Fairbury	G4
Falls City	J4
Franklin	F4
Fremont	H3
Fullerton	F3
Geneva	G4
Gering	A3
Gibbon	F4
Gordon	B2
Gothenburg	D4
Grand Island	F4
Grant	C4
Greeley	F3
Gretna	H3
Guide Rock	F4
Harrisburg	A3
Harrison	A2
Hartington	G2
Hastings	F4
Hayes Center	C4
Hebron	G4
Holdrege	E4
Hyannis	C4
Imperial	C4
Kearney	E4
Kimball	A3
La Vista	A3
Leigh	G3
Lexington	E4
Lincoln, capital	H4
Loomis	E4
Loup City	F3
McCook	D4
Madison	G3
Milford	G4
Minden	F4
Mitchell	A3
Mullen	C2
Nebraska City	J4
Neligh	F2
Nelson	F4
Norfolk	G2
North Platte	D3
Oakland	H3
Ogallala	C3
Omaha	J3
O'Neill	F2
Ord	F3
Osceola	G3
Oshkosh	B3
Papillion	H3
Pawnee City	H4
Paxton	C3
Pender	H2
Pierce	G2
Plainview	G2
Plattsmouth	J3
Plymouth	H4
Ponca	H2
Prague	H3
Ravenna	F3
Red Cloud	F4
Rushville	B2
St. Paul	F3
Schuyler	G3
Scottsbluff	A3
Seward	G4
Sidney	B3
South Sioux City	H2
Springfield	H3
Springview	E2
Stanton	G3
Stapleton	D3
Stockville	D4
Superior	F4
Sutton	G3
Syracuse	H4
Taylor	E3
Tecumseh	H4
Tekamah	H3
Thedford	D3
Trenton	C4
Tryon	D3
Valentine	D2
Valley	H3
Wahoo	H3
Waverly	H4
Wayne	G2
West Point	H3
Wilber	H4
Wisner	H3
Wymore	H4
York	G4

Other Features

Name	Key
Agate Fossil Beds N.M.	A2
Arikee, river	B5
Big Blue, river	G3
C.W. McConaughy, lake	C3
Calamus, reservoir	E3
Calamus, river	E2
Cedar, river	E2
Chimney Rock Natl. Hist. Site	A3
Elkhorn, river	E2, G3
Harlan Co., lake	E4
Homestead Natl. Monument	H4
Lewis and Clark, lake	G2
Little Blue, river	G4
Loup, river	F3
Middle Loup, river	D3
Missouri, river	J4
Niobrara, river	B2, E2
North Loup, river	C2, E3
North Platte, river	B3
Pine, mt. ridge	B2
Pine Ridge Natl. Rec. Area	A2
Platte, river	D4, G3
Republican, river	D4
Sand, hills	C3
Scotts Bluff Natl. Monument	A3
South Fork Republican, river	B5
South Loup, river	E3

Nevada .... page 155

Cities and Towns

Name	Key
Alamo	C3
Battle Mountain	B1
Beatty	B3
Boulder City	C4
Carlin	B1
Carson City, capital	A2
Elko	C1
Ely	C2
Eureka	C2
Fallon	A2
Fernley	A2
Gardnerville	A2
Goldfield	B3
Hawthorne	A2
Henderson	C3
Incline Village	A2
Las Vegas	C3
Laughlin	C4
Lovelock	A1
McGill	C2
Mesquite	C3
Minden	A2
North Fork	C1
North Las Vegas	C3
Pahrump	B3
Paradise	C3
Pioche	C3
Reno	A2
Silver Peak	B3
Sparks	A2
Spring Creek	C1
Spring Valley	C3
Sun Valley	A2
Tonopah	B2
Virginia City	A2
Wells	C1
West Wendover	C1
Winnemucca	B1
Yerington	A2
Zephyr Cove	A2

Other Features

Name	Key
Arc Dome, mt.	B2
Black Rock, desert	A1
Boundary Peak, mt.	A3
Colorado, river	C4
Desert, valley	A1
Egan, range	C2
Goshute, lake	C1
Grant, mts.	C2
Grant, mt.	A2
Great Basin	B2
Great Basin Natl. Park	C2
Hoover Dam	C3
Hot Creek, range	B2
Humboldt, river	B1
Independence, mts.	C1
Jefferson, mt.	B2
Lake Mead Natl. Rec. Area	C3
Marys, river	C1
Matterhorn, mt.	C1
Mead, lake	C3
Mohave, lake	C4
Monitor, range	C2
Moriah, mt.	C2
North Toiyabe Peak, mt.	B2
Owyhee, desert	B1
Owyhee, river	B1
Pilot Peak, mt.	C1
Pyramid, lake	A1
Quinn, river	B1
Ruby, mts.	C1
Ruby Dome, mt.	C1
Rye Patch, reservoir	A1
Schell Creek, range	C2
Shoshone, mts.	B2
Shoshone, range	B2
Smoky, valley	B2
Snake, range	C2
Summit, mt.	B2
Tahoe, lake	A2
Tobin, mt.	B1
Toiyabe, range	B2
Toquima, range	B2
Tuscarora, mts.	B1
Virgin, river	C3
Walker, river	A2
Wheeler Peak, mt.	C2
White, river	C3

New Hampshire .... page 156

Cities and Towns

Name	Key
Albany	B3
Amherst	B4
Antrim	B3
Barnstead	B3
Bartlett	B2
Benton	B2
Berlin	B2
Blair	B3
Bradford	B3
Bretton Woods	B2
Bristol	B3
Candia	B3
Cascade	B2
Claremont	A3
Concord, capital	B3
Contoocook	B3
Conway	B2
Cornish City	A3
Dalton	B2
Deerfield	B3
Deering	B3
Derry	B4
Dixville Notch	B2
Dover	C3
Dunbarton Center	B3
Durham	C3
Easton	B2
Enfield	A3
Epping	B3
Exeter	C4
Farmington	B3
Franklin	B3
Gilmanton	B3
Glencliff	B2
Gorham	B2
Groveton	B2
Hampstead	B4
Hampton	C4
Hanover	A3
Haverhill	A2
Henniker	B3
Hillsboro	B3
Hinsdale	A4
Hollis	B4
Hooksett	B3
Hudson	B4
Jackson	B2
Jaffrey	A4
Jefferson	B2
Keene	A4
Laconia	B3
Lancaster	B2
Lebanon	A3
Littleton	B2
Loudon	B3
Lyman	B2
Manchester	B4
Meredith	B3
Merrimack	B4
Milan	B2
Milford	B4
Monroe	A2
Munsonville	A3
Nashua	B4
Newbury	A3
New Castle	C3
New London	B3
Newmarket	C3
Newport	B3
North Conway	B2
Northfield	B3
North Haverhill	A2
North Walpole	A3
North Woodstock	B2
Orford	A3
Ossipee	B3
Pelham	B4
Percy	B2
Peterborough	B4
Pinardville	B4
Pittsfield	B3
Plymouth	B3
Portsmouth	C3
Quaker City	A3
Randolph	B2
Raymond	B3
Rochester	B3
Rye	C4
Sandwich	B3
Sharon	B4
Shelburne	B2
Silver Lake	B3
Somersworth	C3
South Hooksett	B3
Springfield	A3
Stewartstown Hollow	B2
Strafford	B3
Stratford	B2
Suncook	B3
Sutton	B3
Tilton	B3
Warner	B3
Waterville Valley	B3
Westport	A4
West Rindge	B4
West Stewardstown	B2
Whittier	B3
Willey House	B2
Winchester	A4
Wolfeboro	B3
Woodsville	A2

Other Features

Name	Key
Appalachian Natl. Scenic Trail	A3
Blackwater, reservoir	B3
Blue, mt.	B2
Cabot, mt.	B2
Cardigan, mt.	B3
Connecticut, river	A3
First Connecticut, lake	B1
Franconia, notch	B2
Great, bay	C3
Indian, lake	B1
Kearsarge, mt.	B3
Merrimack, river	A4
Monadnock, mt.	A4
Newfound, lake	B3
Ossipee, lake	B3
Presidential, mt. range	B2
Saint-Gaudens Natl. Hist. Site	A3
Second Connecticut, lake	B1
Smarts, mt.	A3
Squam, lake	A3
Sunapee, lake	A3
Swift, river	B3
Umbagog, lake	B2
Washington, mt.	B2
White, mt.	B2
Winnipesaukee, lake	B3
Winnisquam, lake	B3

New Jersey .... page 157

Cities and Towns

Name	Key
Absecon	E5
Allendale	E1
Allentown	D3
Alloway	C4
Alpine	C1
Asbury Park	E3
Atlantic City	E5
Atlantic Highlands	D4
Atsion	D4
Avalon	D5
Barrington	B3
Basking Ridge	D2
Batsto	D4
Bay Point	C5
Bayonne	E2
Bayside	C5
Beachwood	E4
Beattyestown	D2
Beckett	C4
Belle Mead	D3
Belleville	E2
Bellmawr	B3, C4
Belmar	E3
Belvidere	C2
Bergenfield	B1
Berkeley Heights	E2
Berlin	D4
Bernardsville	D2
Blackwood	C4
Blairstown	D2
Bloomfield	E2
Bogota	B2
Boonton	E2
Bordentown	D3
Bound Brook	D2
Bradley Beach	E3
Brass Castle	C2
Brick	E3
Bridgeboro	C3
Bridgeton	C5
Brielle	E3
Brigantine	E5
Brookdale	B1
Browns Mills	D4
Budd Lake	D2
Buena	D4
Burlington	D3
Butler	E2
Caldwell	A1
Camden	B3, C4
Cape May	D6
Cape May Court House	D5
Carlstadt	B1
Carneys Point	C4
Carteret	E2
Cedar Grove	B1
Centerton	C4
Centreville	D2
Chatham	E2
Cherry Hill	B3, C4
Chesilhurst	D4
Chesterfield	D3
Cinnaminson	B3, D4
Clark	A2
Clayton	C4
Cliffside Park	B1
Clifton	E2
Clinton	D2
Closter	C1
Colesville	D1
Collings Lakes	D4
Collingswood	B3
Colonia	E2
Cranford	E2
Deerfield	C4
Delanco	D3
Denville	D2
Deptford	B4
Dover	D2
Dumont	C1
Dunellen	E2
East Brunswick	E3
East Orange	E2
East Rutherford	B1
Eatontown	E3
Edgewater	B1
Edison	E2
Egg Harbor City	D4
Elizabeth	E2
Elmer	C4
Elmwood Park	B1
Elwood	D4
Emerson	E2
Englewood	C1
Englewood Cliffs	C1
Englishtown	E3
Erma	D6
Estell Manor	D5
Evesboro	C3
Ewing	D3
Fair Lawn	B1, E2
Fairfield	E2
Fairton	C5
Fairview	F2
Fanwood	E2
Farmingdale	E3
Fellowship	C3
Fieldsboro	D3
Flemington	D3
Folsom	D4
Fords	E2
Forked River	E4
Fort Lee	C1
Franklin	D1
Franklinville	C4
Freehold	E3
Frenchtown	C2
Garfield	E2
Gilford Park	E4
Glassboro	C4
Glen Gardner	D2
Glen Ridge	E2
Glendora	B4
Gloucester City	B3, C4
Goshen	D5
Great Notch	E2
Green Bank	D4
Greenwich	C5
Guttenberg	F2
Hackensack	D2
Hackettstown	D2
Haddon Heights	B3
Haddonfield	B3
Hainesville	B1
Haledon	B1
Hamburg	D1
Hammonton	D4
Hampton	D2
Harrison	B2
Haworth	C1
Hawthorne	E2
Hedger House	D4
High Bridge	D2
Highland Lakes	E1
Highland Park	E2
Highlands	F3
Hightstown	D3
Hillsdale	E1
Hillside	B2
Hoboken	E2
Hopatcong	D2
Hopewell	D3
Howardville	D4
Indian Mills	D4
Irvington	E2
Jamesburg	E3
Jenkins Neck	D5
Jersey City	E2
Keansburg	D2
Kearny	E2
Kendall Park	D3
Kenilworth	E2
Kinnelon	E2
Lakehurst	E3
Lakewood	E3
Lambertville	D3
Lavallette	E4
Lawnside	B3
Lawrenceville	D3
Leeds Point	E5
Leisure Village	E3
Leisuretowne	D4
Leonardo	E3
Lincroft	E3
Linden	E2
Lindenwold	B4, C4
Linwood	D5
Little Falls	B1
Livingston	E2
Lodi	B1
Long Branch	F3
Long Valley	D2
Lyndhurst	B2
Madison	E2
Mahwah	E1
Manahawkin	E4
Manalapan	E3
Manasquan	E3
Manumuskin	D5
Manville	D2
Maple Shade	B3, C4
Maplewood	E2
Marcella	E2
Margate City	E5
Marlboro	E3
Marlton	C3, D4
Matawan	E3
Mays Landing	D5
Maywood	B1
Medford Lakes	D4
Mendham	D2
Menlo Park	E2
Merchantville	B3
Metuchen	E2
Middlesex	E2
Middletown	E3
Midland Park	E2
Milford	C2
Millburn	E2
Millville	C5
Monmouth Beach	F3
Montclair	E2
Montvale	E1
Moorestown	C3, D4
Morris Plains	E2
Morristown	E2
Mountain Lakes	D2
Mount Holly	D4
Mount Laurel	D4
Mystic Islands	E4
National Park	B3
Neptune City	E3
Netcong	D2
Newark	E2
New Brunswick	E3
New Egypt	D3
Newfield	C4
New Gretna	E4
Newfoundland	E1
New Providence	E2
Newton	D1
Normandy Beach	E3
North Arlington	B2
North Bergen	B2
North Cape May	D6
Northfield	D5
North Wildwood	D5
Nutley	B2
Oakland	E1
Oaklyn	B3
Ocean City	D5
Oceanport	E3
Ogdensburg	D1
Olivet	C4
Oradell	C1
Orange	E2
Othello	C5
Oxford	D2
Palisades Park	B2
Palmyra	B3, C3
Paramus	B1, E2
Park Ridge	E1
Passaic	E2
Paterson	E2
Paulsboro	A4, C4
Pemberton	D4
Pennington	D3
Penns Grove	C4
Pennsauken	B3
Pennsville	B4
Perth Amboy	E2
Phillipsburg	C2
Piscataway	E2
Pine Hill	C4
Pitman	C4
Pittstown	D2
Plainfield	E2
Pleasant Plains	E3
Pleasantville	D5
Point Pleasant	E3
Pomona	D5
Port Monmouth	E3
Port Norris	C5
Princeton	D3
Princeton Junction	D3
Prospect Park	B1
Quinton	C4
Rahway	A2
Ramblewood	C3
Ramsey	E1
Raritan	D2
Red Bank	E3
Ridgefield	B1
Ridgefield Park	B1, E2
Ridgewood	E2
Ringoes	D3
Ringwood	E1
Rio Grande	D5
River Edge	C1
Riverside	C3, D3
Riverton	B3, C3
Robertsville	E3
Rochelle Park	B2
Rocktown	D3
Roselle	A2
Roselle Park	A2
Rumson	F3
Runnemede	B4, C4
Rutherford	B1
Salem	C4
Sayreville	E3
Seabrook	C5
Sea Girt	E3
Sea Isle City	D5
Seaside Heights	E4
Seaside Park	E4
Secaucus	B2
Ship Bottom	E4
Shrewsbury	E3
Silverton	E3
Smithville	E5
Somerdale	B4
Somers Point	D5
Somerset	E2
Somerville	D2
South Amboy	E3
South Orange	A2
South River	E3
Sparta	D1
Spotswood	E3
Spring Lake Heights	E3
Stanhope	D2
Stillwater	D1
Stockholm	D1
Stratford	B4, C4
Strathmere	D5
Summit	E2
Surf City	E4
Sussex	D1
Swedesboro	C4
Teaneck	B1
Tenafly	F2
Tinton Falls	E3
Toms River	E4
Totowa	B1
Trenton, capital	D3
Tuckahoe	D5
Tuckerton	E4
Turnersville	C4
Twin Rivers	E3
Union	E2
Union Beach	E3
Union City	E2
Upton	D4
Vauxhall	A2
Ventnor City	E5
Vernon	E1
Verona	A1
Villas	D5
Vineland	C5
Voorhees	C4
Waldwick	E1
Wanamassa	E3
Wanaque	E1
Waretown	E4
Warren Glen	C2
Warren Grove	E4
Washington	D2
Washington Crossing	D3
Watchung	E2
Wayne	A1, E2
Weehawken	B2
Welchville	C4
Wenonah	C4
Westfield	E2
West Milford	E1
Westmont	B3
West New York	B2
West Orange	E2
West Paterson	B1
Westville	B3
Westwood	B1
Wharton	D2
White Horse	D3
White House Station	D2
White Meadow Lake	D2

	Key
Whiting	E4
Wildwood	D6
Wildwood Crest	D6
Williamstown	D4
Willingboro	D3
Woodbine	D5
Woodbridge	E2
Woodbury	B4, C4
Woodlynne	B3
Wood Ridge	B1
Woodstown	C4
Woodstream	C3
Wrightstown	D3
Wyckoff	E1

Other Features

	Key
Cape May, point	D6
Cooper, river	B4
Delaware, bay	C5
Delaware, river	D3
Delaware Water Gap N.R.A.	D1
Edison Natl. Hist. Site	B2
Gateway Natl. Rec. Area	F3
Great, bay	E5
Hudson, river	C2
Morristown Nat. Hist. Park	D2
Pines, lake	B1
Raritan, bay	E3
Statue of Liberty N.M.	B2

New Mexico ....page 158

Cities and Towns

	Key
Acoma Pueblo	B2
Acomita	B2
Alameda	B2
Alamogordo	C3
Albuquerque	B2
Anthony	B4
Artesia	C3
Aztec	B1
Bayard	A3
Belen	B2
Bernalillo	B1
Bloomfield	B1
Bosque Farms	B2
Carlsbad	C3
Carrizozo	C3
Central	A3
Chaparral	B3
Chimayo	C1
Clayton	D1
Clovis	D2
Corrales	B2
Deming	B3
Dulce	B1
Elida	D3
Elk	C3
Elkins	C3
Espanola	B2
Estancia	B2
Eunice	D3
Fairacres	B3
Farmington	A1
Floyd	D2
Fort Sumner	C2
Gallup	A2
Grants	B2
Greenfield	C3
Hobbs	D3
Hurley	A3
Jal	D3
Jemez Pueblo	B2
Kirtland	A1
La Luz	C3
Las Cruces	B3
Las Vegas	C2
Lordsburg	A3
Los Alamos	B2
Los Chavez	B2
Los Lunas	B2
Los Padillas	B2
Lovington	D3
Lower Colonias	C2
Lower San Francisco Plaza	A3
Maxwell	C1
Mayhill	C3
Mesilla	B3
Milan	B2
Mora	C2
Moriarty	B2
Mosquero	D2
Navajo	A2
Polvadera	B2
Portales	D2
Questa	C1
Ranchos De Taos	C1
Raton	C1
Reserve	A3
Rio Rancho	B2
Roswell	C3
Ruidoso	C3
Sabinoso	C2
San Felipe Pueblo	B2
San Miguel	B1
San Miguel	B3
Santa Fe, capital	C2
Santa Rosa	C2
Santo Domingo Pueblo	B2
Shiprock	A1
Silver City	A3
Socorro	B2
Springer	C1
Sunland Park	B4
Taos	C1
Tesuque	C2
Tierra Amarilla	B1
Truth or Consequences	B3
Tucumcari	D2
Tularosa	B3
University Park	B3
Ute Park	C1
Valencia	A1
Waterflow	A2
Zuni Pueblo	A2

Other Features

	Key
Abiquiu, reservoir	B1
Alegres, mt.	A2
Aztec Ruins Natl. Monument	B1
Baldy, mt.	C1
Bandelier Natl. Monument	B2
Black, mt. range	B3
Burro, mts.	A3
Caballo, reservoir	B3
Canadian, river	C1
Capulin Volcano N.M.	D1
Carlsbad Caverns Natl. Park	C3
Cebolleta, mt.	B2
Cerro Vista, mt.	C1
Chaco Culture Natl. Hist. Park	B1

	Key
Cimarron, river	D1
Conchas, lake	C2
Continental Divide, mt. ridge	B2
Cooke's, mt.	B3
Elephant Butte, res.	B3
El Malpais Natl. Monument	B2
El Morro Natl. Monument	A2
Fort Union Natl. Monument	C2
Gallinas, mt.	C2
Gila, river	A3
Gila Cliff Dwellings N.M.	A3
Guadalupe, mts.	C3
Jornada Del Muerto	B3
Kasha-Katuwe Tent Rocks N.M.	B2
Llano Estacado, plateau	D3
Navajo, reservoir	B1
Navajo Indian Res.	A1
Pecos, river	C2, C3
Pecos, plains	C3
Pecos N.H.P.	C2
Petroglyph Natl. Monument	B2
Playas, lake	A4
Reeds, mt.	B3
Rio Grande, river	C1
Rio Hondo, river	C3
Rio Puerco, river	B2
Salinas Pueblo Missions N.M.	B2
San Andres, mts.	B3
Sangre De Cristo, mts.	C1
San Juan, river	A1
Shiprock, mt.	A1
Sierra Blanca, mt.	C3
South Baldy, mt.	B3
Sumner, lake	C2
Taylor, mt.	B2
Wheeler, mt.	C1
White Sands Natl. Monument	B3
Whitewater Baldy, mt.	A3
Withington, mt.	B3
Zuni, mts.	A2

New York ....page 159

Cities and Towns

	Key
Adams	H3
Adams Center	H3
Akron	C4
Albany, capital	N5
Albion	D4
Alden	D5
Alfred	E6
Allegany	D6
Altamont	M5
Amsterdam	M5
Angola	B5
Arcade	D5
Astoria	A3
Athens	N6
Attica	D5
Auburn	G5
Avon	E5
Bainbridge	J6
Baldwinsville	H4
Ballston Spa	N4
Batavia	D4
Bath	F6
Beacon	N7
Bedford-Stuyvesant	A4
Belle Harbor	A4
Belmont	D6
Bensonhurst	A4
Big Flats	G6
Binghamton	J6
Bloomfield	F5
Bolivar	D6
Boonville	K4
Breezy Point	A4
Brentwood	C1
Brewerton	H4
Bridgehampton	E1
Brighton Beach	A4
Broadalbin	M4
Brockport	E4
Brocton	B6
Bronx	A3, B1
Bronxville	A2
Brooklyn	A4, B2
Buffalo	C5
Cairo	M6
Calcium	J2
Caledonia	E5
Cambridge	P4
Camden	J4
Canajoharie	L5
Canandaigua	F5
Canarsie	A4
Canastota	J4
Canisteo	E6
Canton	K1
Carmel	N7
Carthage	J3
Castleton-on-Hudson	N6
Catskill	N6
Cayuga Heights	H6
Cazenovia	J5
Cedarhurst	B4
Central Square	H4
Chatham	N6
Cheektowaga	C5
Chittenango	J4
Churchville	E4
Clayton	H2
Clinton	K4
Clyde	G4
Cobleskill	L5
Cohoes	N5
College Point	A3
Colonie	N5
Coney Island	A4
Cooperstown	L5
Corinth	N4
Corning	F6
Cortland	H5
Coxsackie	N6
Cuba	D6
Dannemora	N1
Dansville	E5
Delhi	L5
De Ruyter	J5
Deposit	K6
Dolgeville	L4
Dover Plains	N7
Dryden	H6
Dundee	G6
Dunkirk	B6
East Atlantic Beach	B4
Eastchester	A2
East Hampton	E1
East Islip	C1
East New York	A4
East Northport	C1

	Key
East Patchogue	D1
Eden	C5
Elizabethtown	N2
Ellenville	M7
Elmira	G6
Elmira Heights	G6
Elmont	B4
Endicott	H6
Endwell	H6
Fairmount	H4
Far Rockaway	B4
Fayette	G5
Fine	K2
Flatbush	A4
Flushing	A3
Fonda	M5
Fort Edward	N4
Fort Plain	L5
Franklin Sq.	B4
Franklinville	D6
Fredonia	B6
Freeport	C2
Frewsburg	B6
Friendship	D6
Fulton	H4
Geneseo	E5
Geneva	G5
Glen Cove	B4
Glens Falls	N4
Gloversville	M4
Goshen	M7
Gouverneur	K2
Gowanda	C6
Granville	P4
Gravesend	A4
Great Neck	B1
Greece	E4
Greene	J6
Greenport	E1
Greenwich	P4
Groton	H5
Hamburg	C5
Hamilton	J5
Hampton Bays	E1
Hancock	K7
Harlem	A3
Hempstead	B4
Herkimer	L4
Hicksville	C1
Highland	N7
Hilton	E4
Holbrook	C1
Holland	C5
Holley	D4
Homer	H5
Hoosick Falls	P5
Hornell	E6
Horseheads	G6
Houghton	D6
Howard Beach	A4
Hudson	N6
Hudson Falls	N4
Huntington Station	C1
Hurley	M7
Ilion	K4
Inwood	B4
Irondequoit	E4
Ithaca	H6
Jamaica	B2
Jamestown	B6
Johnson City	J6
Johnstown	M4
Keeseville	P1
Kew Gardens	A4
Kinderhook	N6
Kingston	N7
Lake George	M2
Lake Placid	M4
Lake Pleasant	M4
Lakewood	B6
Lancaster	H5
Larchmont	B2
Lawrence	B4
Le Roy	D5
Levittown	C1
Liberty	L7
Lima	E5
Lindenhurst	C2
Little Falls	L4
Little Valley	C6
Livingston Manor	L7
Livonia	E5
Lockport	C4
Long Beach	B2
Long Eddy	K7
Long Island City	A3
Long Lake	M3
Loon Lake	M1
Lowville	K3
Lynbrook	B4
Lyons	G4
Malone	M1
Mamaroneck	B2
Manhasset Hills	B3
Manhattan	A3
Manlius	J4
Manorhaven	B3
Massapequa	C2
Massena	L1
Mastic	D1
Mastic Beach	D1
Mattituck	E1
Mayville	A6
Mechanicville	N5
Medina	D4
Mexico	H4
Middleburgh	M5
Middleport	D4
Middletown	M7
Millbrook	N7
Mineola	B1
Mohawk	K5
Monroe	M7
Montauk	F1
Monticello	L7
Montour Falls	G6
Moravia	H5
Mount Kisco	B1
Mount Morris	E5
Mount Vernon	B1, C5
Munnsville	J5
Nassau	N5
Newark	F4
Newburgh	M7
New City	B1
Newfane	C4
New Hartford	K4
New Hyde Park	B4
New Paltz	M7
New Rochelle	B2
New York	B2
Niagara Falls	B4

	Key
Norfolk	L1
North Collins	C5
North Hills	B3
North Syracuse	H4
North Tonawanda	C4
Norwich	J5
Norwood	L1
Nunda	E5
Nyack	B1
Oakfield	D4
Ogdensburg	K1
Olcott	C4
Olean	D6
Oneida	J4
Oneonta	K6
Ossining	B1
Oswego	H4
Owego	H6
Oxford	J6
Ozone Park	A4
Painted Post	F6
Palmyra	F4
Pawling	N7
Peekskill	B1
Pelham	A3
Pelham Manor	A3
Penn Yan	F5
Perry	D5
Peru	N1
Philadelphia	J2
Philmont	N6
Phoenix	H4
Pine Bush	M7
Plattsburgh	P1
Port Henry	P2
Port Jefferson	D1
Port Morris	A3
Port Washington	B3
Potsdam	L1
Poughkeepsie	N7
Pulaski	H3
Queens	B4
Randolph	C6
Ransomville	C4
Ravena	N6
Red Hook	N7
Rensselaer	N5
Rhinebeck	N7
Richfield Springs	L5
Riverhead	D1
Rochester	E4
Rockaway Point	A4
Rocky Point	D1
Rome	K4
Rosendale	M7
Rouses Point	P1
Rye	B2
Sackets Harbor	H3
Sag Harbor	E1
St. George	A2
St. Johnsville	L5
Salamanca	C6
Sands Point	B3
Saranac Lake	M2
Saratoga Springs	N4
Saugerties	N6
Sayville	D2
Schenectady	N5
Schoharie	M5
Scotia	N5
Seneca Falls	G5
Sherburne	K5
Shortsville	F5
Sidney	K6
Silver Creek	B5
Skaneateles	H5
Sodus	G4
Southampton	E1
South Fallsburg	L7
Southold	E1
Southport	G6
Spencerport	E4
Springville	C5
Stillwater	N5
Stony Brook	C1
Suffern	A1
Syracuse	H4
Throgs Neck	A3
Ticonderoga	P3
Troy	N5
Trumansburg	G5
Tupper Lake	M2
Unadilla	K6
Utica	K4
Valley Stream	B4
Victory Mills	N4
Voorheesville	N5
Walden	M7
Walton	K6
Wampsville	J4
Wappingers Falls	N7
Warrensburg	N4
Warsaw	D5
Warwick	A1
Waterloo	G5
Watertown	J3
Waterville	K5
Watkins Glen	G6
Waverly	G6
Wayland	E5
Weedsport	G4
Wellsville	E6
West Carthage	J3
Westfield	A6
West Point	N7
West Seneca	C5
Whitehall	P3
White Plains	B1
Whitesboro	K4
Whitestone	A3
Williamsburg	A4
Wilson	C4
Wolcott	G4
Woodmere	B4
Woodstock	M6
Yonkers	B1
Yorktown Heights	B1

Other Features

	Key
Adirondack, mts.	L2
Adirondack Park	M2
Appalachian Natl. Scenic Trail	A1
Black, lake	J2
Black, river	K6
Cannonsville, reservoir	K6
Catskill, mts.	L6
Cayuga, lake	G5
Champlain, lake	P1
Chenango, river	J6
Cranberry, lake	L2
Delaware, river	K7

	Key
Eleanor Roosevelt N.H.S.	N7
Erie, canal	J4
Erie, lake	A5
Fire Island Natl. Seashore	D2
Fishers, island	F1
Fort Stanwix Natl. Monument	J4
Galloo, island	H3
Gardiners, island	F1
Gateway Natl. Rec. Area	B2
Genesee, river	D6
George, lake	N3
Governors Island Natl. Mon.	A4
Great Sacandaga, lake	M4
Hinckley, reservoir	K4
Home of F.D.R. Natl. Hist. Site	N7
Hudson, river	M3
Indian, lake	M3
J.F.K. Int'l Airport	A4
Keuka, lake	F5
Long, island	E1
Long, lake	M3
Long Island, sound	C1
Marcy, mt.	M3
Martin Van Buren Natl. Hist. Site	N6
Mettawee, river	P3
Mohawk, river	L4
Oneida, lake	J4
Ontario, lake	E3
Pepacton, reservoir	L6
Piseco, lake	L4
St. Lawrence, river	K1
Salmon River, reservoir	J4
Saratoga, lake	N4
Saratoga Natl. Hist. Park	N4
Schoharie, reservoir	M6
Schroon, lake	N3
Slide, mt.	M7
Staten, island	A2
Stony, island	H3
Susquehanna, river	J6
Thomas Cole Natl. Hist. Site	N6
Thousand, islands	H2
Tupper, lake	L2
Unadilla, river	K5
Upper Saranac, lake	M2
Vanderbilt Mansion N.H.S.	N7
West Point Military Academy	A1
Women's Rights N.H.P.	G5

North Carolina ....page 160

Cities and Towns

	Key
Aberdeen	G4
Ahoskie	L2
Albemarle	E4
Andrews	C8
Angier	H3
Apex	H3
Archdale	F3
Asheboro	F3
Asheville	E7
Atlantic Beach	M5
Ayden	L4
Badin	E4
Bakersville	A2
Bayboro	M4
Beaufort	M5
Belhaven	M3
Belmont	C4
Benson	H4
Bessemer City	C4
Bethel	L3
Biscoe	F4
Black Mt.	A5
Bladenboro	H5
Blowing Rock	B2
Boiling Spring Lakes	J6
Boiling Springs	B4
Bolivia	J6
Boone	B2
Brevard	E8
Bryson City	C8
Buies Creek	H4
Burgaw	K5
Burlington	G2
Burnsville	A3
Butner	H2
Camden	N2
Canton	E7
Carolina Beach	K6
Carthage	G4
Cary	H3
Chadbourn	H6
Chapel Hill	G3
Charlotte	D4
Cherryville	C4
China Grove	D3
Clayton	J3
Clemmons	E2
Clinton	J5
Coats	H4
Columbia	N3
Columbus	A4
Concord	D4
Conover	C3
Cornelius	D4
Creedmoor	H2
Cullowhee	D8
Currituck	N2
Dallas	C4
Danbury	E2
Davidson	D3
Denton	E3
Dobson	D2
Drexel	B3
Dunn	H4
Durham	H2
E. Flat Rock	E8
Eden	F2
Edenton	N2
Elizabeth City	N2
Elizabethtown	H5
Elkin	D2
Elm City	K3
Emerald Isle	M5
Enfield	K2
Erwin	H4
Fairmont	G5
Farmville	K3
Fayetteville	H4
Fletcher	E8
Forest City	B4
Four Oaks	H4
Franklin	C8
Franklinton	H2
Fremont	K3
Fuquay-Varina	H3
Gamewell	B3
Garner	H3
Gastonia	C4
Gatesville	M2

	Key
Gibsonville	F2
Goldsboro	K4
Graham	G2
Granite Falls	C3
Granite Quarry	E3
Greensboro	F2
Greenville	L4
Grifton	L4
Halifax	K2
Hamlet	F5
Harkers Island	M5
Harrisburg	D4
Havelock	M5
Hayesville	C8
Hays	C2
Henderson	J2
Hendersonville	E8
Hertford	N2
Hickory	C3
High Point	E3
Hillsborough	G2
Hope Mills	H5
Hudson	C3
Huntersville	D4
Icard	C3
Indian Trail	D4
Jackson	L2
Jacksonville	L5
Jamestown	F3
Jefferson	C2
Jonesville	D2
Kannapolis	D4
Kenansville	K5
Kenly	J3
Kernersville	E2
Kill Devil Hills	P2
King	E2
Kings Mt.	C4
Kinston	K4
Kitty Hawk	P2
La Grange	K4
Laurinburg	G5
Leland	J6
Lenoir	B3
Lewisville	E2
Lexington	E3
Liberty	F3
Lillington	H4
Lincolnton	C4
Locust	E4
Long Beach	J7
Long View	C3
Louisburg	J2
Lumberton	G5
Madison	F2
Maiden	C3
Manteo	P3
Marion	B3
Marshall	A7
Marshville	E5
Matthews	D4
Maxton	G5
Mayodan	F2
Mebane	F2
Mint Hill	D4
Mocksville	D3
Monroe	D5
Mooresville	D3
Moravian Falls	C2
Morehead City	M5
Morganton	B3
Mt. Airy	D2
Mt. Gilead	F4
Mt. Holly	C4
Mt. Olive	K4
Mulberry	C2
Murfreesboro	L2
Murphy	B8
Nags Head	P3
Nashville	K3
New Bern	L4
Newland	B2
Newport	M5
Newton	C3
Norwood	E4
North Wilkesboro	C2
Oxford	H2
Pembroke	G5
Pinehurst	G4
Pinetops	K3
Pineville	D4
Piney Green	L5
Pittsboro	G3
Plymouth	M3
Polkville	B4
Raeford	G5
Raleigh, capital	H3
Randleman	F3
Red Springs	G5
Reidsville	F2
River Bend	L4
Roanoke Rapids	K2
Robbinsville	C8
Robersonville	L3
Rockingham	F5
Rockwell	E3
Rocky Mount	K3
Rolesville	J3
Rose Hill	J5
Roseboro	H5
Roxboro	H2
Rural Hall	E2
Rutherfordton	B4
Salisbury	D3
Sanford	G4
Sawmills	C3
Scotland Neck	L3
Selma	J3
Seven Lakes	F4
Sharpsburg	K3
Shelby	B4
Siler City	G3
Smithfield	J3
Sneads Ferry	L5
Snow Hill	K4
Southern Pines	G4
Southern Shores	P2
Southport	J7
Sparta	C1
Spencer	E3
Spindale	B4
Spring Lake	H4
Spruce Pine	A3
St. Pauls	G5
Stanley	C4
Stanleyville	E2
Statesville	D3
Stokesdale	F2
Stony Point	C3
Summerfield	F2
Swan Quarter	N4
Sylva	D8

	Key
Tabor City	H6
Tarboro	K3
Taylorsville	C3
Thomasville	E3
Toast	D2
Trenton	L4
Troutman	D3
Troy	F4
Valdese	B3
Wadesboro	E5
Wake Forest	H3
Wallace	K5
Wanchese	P3
Warrenton	J2
Warsaw	J5
Washington	L3
Waxhaw	D5
Waynesville	D7
Weddington	D4
Welcome	E3
Weldon	K2
Wendell	J3
Wentworth	F2
W. Jefferson	C2
Whiteville	H6
Wilkesboro	C2
Williamston	L3
Wilmington	K6
Wilson	K3
Windsor	M2
Winfall	N2
Wingate	E5
Winston-Salem	E2
Winterville	L3
Winton	M2
Woodfin	E7
Wrightsville Beach	K6
Yadkinville	D2
Yanceyville	G2
Zebulon	J3

Other Features

	Key
Albemarle, sound	N3
Alligator, lake	N3
Alligator, river	N3
B. Everett Jordan, lake	G3
Bodie, island	P3
Cape Fear, river	H5
Cape Hatteras Natl. Seashore	P4
Cape Lookout Natl. Seashore	N5
Chatuga, lake	C8
Clingmans Dome, mt.	C7
Dan, river	F2
Deep, river	F3
Falls Lake, reservoir	H3
Fear, cape	K7
Fontana, lake	C7
Fort Raleigh Natl. Hist. Site	P3
Gaston, lake	K1
Great, lake	L5
Great Smoky Mts. Natl. Park	C7
Hatteras, cape	P4
Hatteras, inlet	P4
Highrock, lake	E3
Hiwassee, lake	B8
Hyco, lake	G2
John H. Kerr, reservoir	H1
Lookout, cape	M5
Mattamuskeet, lake	N3
Mitchell, mt.	A3
Nantahala, lake	C8
Neuse, river	J4
Norman, lake	D3
Ocracoke, inlet	N4
Oregon, inlet	P3
Pamlico, river	M4
Pamlico, sound	P4
Phelps, lake	N3
Roan, mt.	A2
Roanoke, river	K2
Rocky, river	E4
Smith, island	K7
Standing Indian, mt.	C8
Tar, river	J2
Waccamaw, lake	J6
Wright Brothers Natl. Memorial	P2
Yadkin, river	D2

North Dakota ....page 161

Cities and Towns

	Key
Ashley	F3
Beach	A3
Belcourt	F1
Beulah	D2
Bismarck, capital	E3
Bowman	B3
Cando	F1
Carrington	F2
Casselton	H3
Cavalier	H1
Center	D2
Cooperstown	G2
Crosby	B1
Devils Lake	G1
Dickinson	C3
Ellendale	G3
Fargo	J3
Fessenden	F2
Finley	H2
Forman	H3
Fort Yates	E3
Garrison	D2
Grafton	H1
Grand Forks	H2
Harvey	F2
Hazen	D2
Hettinger	C3
Hillsboro	H2
Jamestown	G2
Lakota	G1
La Moure	G3
Langdon	G1
Larimore	H2
Linton	E3
Lisbon	H3
McClusky	E2
Mandan	E3
Mayville	H2
Mohall	D1
Mott	C3
Napoleon	F3
New Rockford	F2
New Town	C1
Oakes	G3
Park River	H1
Rolla	F1
Rugby	F1
Stanley	C1
Stanton	D2
Steele	F3

	Key
Tioga	C1
Towner	E1
Valley City	H3
Wahpeton	J3
Washburn	D2
Watford City	B2
West Fargo	J3
Williston	B1

Other Features

	Key
Cannonball, river	D3
Devils, lake	G1
Fort Union Trading Post N.H.S.	A1
Green, river	B2
Heart, river	D3
Intl. Peace Garden	E1
James, river	F2
Jamestown, reservoir	G2
Knife, river	C2
Knife River Indian Villages N.H.S.	D2
Little Missouri, river	B3
Long, lake	E3
Maple, river	G3, H2
Missouri, river	D2
Oahe, lake	E3
Pembina, river	G1
Sakakawea, lake	C2
Sheyenne, river	E2, G2, H3
Souris, river	D1
Theodore Roosevelt N.P.	B2, B3
White Butte, mt.	B3
Wild Rice, river	H3

Ohio ....page 162

Cities and Towns

	Key
Aberdeen	C8
Ada	C4
Akron	G3
Alliance	H4
Ansonia	A5
Antrim	H5
Antwerp	A3
Arabia	F8
Arcanum	A6
Archbold	A2
Arlington	C4
Ashland	F4
Ashtabula	J2
Athens	F7
Aurora	H3
Avon Lake	F2
Baltimore	E6
Barberton	G3
Barnesville	H6
Batavia	B7
Bay Village	G9
Beachwood	J9
Bedford	J9
Bedford Heights	J9
Bellaire	J5
Bellefontaine	C4
Bellevue	E3
Bellville	E4
Berea	C9
Berlin Heights	F3
Bethel	B8
Beverly	G6
Blanchester	C7
Blissfield	G5
Blue Ash	C9
Bluffton	C4
Boardman	J3
Bowling Green	C3
Bradford	B5
Bremen	F6
Brewster	G4
Bridgetown	B9
Broadview Heights	H10
Brook Park	G9
Brooklyn	H9
Brookville	B6
Brunswick	G3
Bryan	A3
Bucyrus	E4
Burton	H3
Cadiz	J5
Caldwell	G6
Cambridge	G5
Camden	A6
Canal Fulton	G4
Canal Winchester	E6
Canfield	J3
Canton	H4
Cardington	D4
Carey	D4
Carrollton	H4
Cedarville	C6
Celina	A4
Centerburg	E5
Chagrin Falls	H3
Chardon	H2
Chesterhill	G7
Cheviot	B9
Chillicothe	E7
Cincinnati	A7
Circleville	E6
Cleveland	G2
Cleveland Heights	G2
Cleves	A9
Clyde	E3
Coldwater	A5
Columbiana	J4
Columbus, capital	D6
Columbus Grove	B4
Congress	F4
Conneaut	J2
Cortland	J3
Coshocton	G5
Covington	B5
Crestline	E4
Creston	G4
Crooksville	F6
Cuyahoga Falls	H3
Dalton	G4
Dayton	B6
De Graff	C5
Deer Park	C9
Defiance	B3
Delaware	D5
Delhi Hills	B9
Delphos	B4
Delta	C2
Deshler	C3
Dover	H4
Dresden	F5
Dublin	D5
Dunkinsville	D8
E. Cleveland	H8
East Liverpool	J4
East Palestine	J4

	Key
Eaton	A6
Edgerton	A3
Elida	B4
Elyria	F3
Euclid	G2
Fairborn	C6
Fairfield	A7
Fairport Harbor	H2
Fairview Park	C9
Findlay	C4
Fitchville	F3
Forest	C4
Forest Park	B8
Forestville	B7
Fort Recovery	A5
Fort Shawnee	B4
Fostoria	D3
Franklin	B6
Fredericktown	E5
Fremont	D3
Fresno	G5
Gahanna	E5
Galion	E4
Gallipolis	F8
Gambier	F5
Garfield Hts.	H9
Geneva	J2
Genoa	D2
Georgetown	C8
Germantown	B6
Gibsonburg	D3
Grafton	F3
Granville	E5
Green	G4
Green Springs	D3
Greenfield	D7
Greenville	A5
Greenwich	E3
Grove City	D6
Hamilton	A7
Hannibal	D6
Harrisburg	D6
Harrison	A9
Heath	F5
Hebron	F6
Hicksville	A3
Hillsboro	C7
Hiram	H3
Holgate	B3
Hubbard	J3
Huron	E3
Independence	H9
Jackson	E7
Jackson Center	B5
Jefferson	J2
Jeffersonville	C6
Johnstown	E5
Keene	G5
Kent	H3
Kenton	C4
Kettering	B6
Kimbolton	G5
Kirtland	H2
Lakewood	G9
Lancaster	E6
Lebanon	B7
Leipsic	C3
Lewisburg	A6
Lexington	E4
Lima	B4
Lisbon	J4
Lodi	G3
Logan	F6
London	D6
Lorain	F3
Loudonville	F4
Louisville	H4
Loveland	B7
Lucasville	E8
Lyndhurst	J8
McArthur	F7
McConnelsville	G6
Macedonia	J10
Macksburg	H6
Madeira	C9
Manchester	C8
Mansfield	E4
Maple Hts.	J9
Marietta	H7
Marion	D4
Martins Ferry	J5
Marysville	D5
Mason	B7
Massillon	G4
Maumee	C2
Mayfield Hts.	J9
Mechanicsburg	C5
Medina	G3
Mentor	H2
Miamitown	B9
Middleburg Heights	G9
Middlefield	H3
Middletown	B6
Milan	E3
Milford	B7
Millersburg	G4
Minerva	H4
Minster	B5
Monfort Heights	B9
Monroe	B7
Montgomery	C9
Montpelier	A2
Mount Gilead	E4
Mount Healthy	B9
Mount Orab	C7
Mount Sterling	D6
Mount Vernon	E5
Napoleon	B3
Nelsonville	F7
Newark	F5
New Baltimore	B9
New Boston	E8
New Bremen	B5
New Carlisle	B6
Newcomerstown	G5
New Concord	G6
New Lebanon	B6
New Lexington	F6
New London	F3
New Paris	A6
New Philadelphia	H5
New Richmond	B8
Newtown	C9
Niles	J3
North Baltimore	C3
North Canton	H4
North College Hill	B9
North Kingsville	J2
North Olmsted	G3
North Royalton	H10
Northfield	H9
Northridge	C6

	Key
Norwalk	E3
Norwood	C9
Oak Harbor	D2
Oak Hill	E8
Oberlin	F3
Olmsted Falls	G9
Oregon	D2
Orrville	G4
Orwell	J2
Otsego	G5
Ottawa	B3
Painesville	H2
Parma	G3
Parma Heights	H9
Pataskala	E6
Paulding	A3
Peebles	D8
Pepper Pike	J9
Perrysburg	C2
Pickerington	E6
Piketon	E7
Pioneer	A2
Piqua	B5
Plain City	D5
Plymouth	E4
Pomeroy	F7
Port Clinton	E2
Portsmouth	E8
Powhatan Point	J6
Ravenna	H3
Reading	B7
Reynoldsburg	E6
Richmond Heights	J8
Richwood	D5
Ripley	C8
Rittman	G4
Roseville	F6
Russells Point	C5
Sabina	C7
Sagamore Hills	J9
St. Bernard	C9
St. Clairsville	J5
St. Henry	A5
St. Louisville	F5
St. Marys	B4
St. Paris	C5
Salem	J4
Salineville	J4
Sandusky	E3
Selma	C6
Seven Hills	H9
Shadyside	J6
Shaker Hts.	J9
Sharonville	C9
Shelby	E4
Shreve	F4
Sidney	B5
Silverton	C9
Smithville	G4
Solon	J9
Somerset	F6
South Charleston	C6
South Euclid	J8
South Point	E9
Springdale	C9
Springfield	C6
Steubenville	J5
Strasburg	G4
Streetsboro	H3
Strongsville	G3
Stryker	B3
Sugarcreek	G5
Sunbury	E5
Sylvania	C2
The Village of Indian Hill	C9
Tiffin	D3
Tipp City	B6
Toledo	C2
Troy	B5
Twinsburg	J10
Uhrichsville	H5
University Hts.	J9
Upper Sandusky	D4
Urbana	C5
Utica	F5
Van Wert	A4
Vandalia	B6
Venedocia	B4
Vermilion	E3
Versailles	B5
Wapakoneta	B4
Warren	J3
Warrensville Heights	J9
Warsaw	G5
Washington Court House	D6
Waterville	C2
Wauseon	B2
Waverly	E7
Waynesville	B6
Wellington	E7
Wellston	E7
Wellsville	J4
West Alexandria	A6
West Jefferson	D6
West Lafayette	G5
West Liberty	C5
West Milton	B6
West Salem	F4
West Union	C8
West Unity	B2
Westerville	E5
Westlake	G9
Weston	C3
Wheelersburg	E8
Wickliffe	J8
Wilkesville	F7
Willard	E3
Williamsburg	B7
Williamsport	D6
Williamsport	E4
Wilmington	C7
Woodsfield	H6
Woodville	D3
Wooster	G4
Wyoming	C9
Xenia	C6
Yellow Springs	C6
Youngstown	J3

Other Features

	Key
Clendening, lake	H5
Cuyahoga Valley N.P.	G3, H9
Dayton Aviation N.H.P.	B6
Erie, lake	G1
First Ladies Natl. Hist. Site	H4
Hocking, river	F7
Hopewell Culture N.H.P.	E7
James A. Garfield N.H.P.	H2
Kelleys, island	E2
Mohican, river	F4
Muskingum, river	G6
Ohio, river	J6

	Key
Salt Fork, lake	H5
Sandusky, river	D3
Scioto, river	D4
Senecaville, lake	H6
William H. Taft Natl. Hist. Site	C9

Oklahoma ....page 163

Cities and Towns

	Key
Ada	F3
Agawam	C3
Alva	D1
Anadarko	D3
Antlers	G3
Apache	D3
Arapaho	C2
Ardmore	E3
Arkoma	H2
Atoka	F3
Barnsdall	F1
Bartlesville	F1
Beaver	B1
Bethel Acres	E2
Bixby	G2
Blackwell	E1
Blanchard	E2
Boise City	B4
Bristow	F2
Broken Arrow	G2
Broken Bow	H3
Buffalo	C1
Cache	D3
Calera	F4
Carnegie	D2
Catoosa	G1
Chandler	F2
Checotah	G2
Chelsea	G1
Cherokee	D1
Cheyenne	C2
Chickasha	E2
Choctaw	E2
Chouteau	G1
Claremore	G1
Cleveland	F1
Clinton	D2
Coalgate	F3
Collinsville	G1
Comanche	E3
Commerce	H1
Cordell	D2
Corum	D3
Coweta	G2
Cushing	F2
Davis	E3
Dewey	F1
Drumright	F2
Durant	F4
Eagletown	H3
Edmond	E2
Elk City	C2
Enid	E1
Eufaula	G2
Fairfax	F1
Fairview	D1
Farris	G3
Fittstown	F3
Floris	B1
Forgan	B1
Fort Gibson	G2
Frederick	D3
Geary	D2
Glenpool	G2
Granite	C3
Grove	H1
Guthrie	E2
Guymon	C4
Harmon	C1
Hartshorne	G3
Haskell	G2
Healdton	E3
Heavener	H3
Hennessey	E1
Henryetta	F2
Hobart	C2
Holdenville	F2
Hollis	C3
Hominy	F1
Hooker	A1
Hugo	G3
Idabel	H4
Inola	G1
Jay	H1
Jenks	G1
Joy	E3
Kingfisher	E2
Konawa	F3
Krebs	G3
Laverne	C1
Lawton	D3
Lenora	C1
Lindsay	E3
Locust Grove	G1
Lone Grove	E3
Loveland	D3
Lovell	E1
McAlester	G3
McCurtain	H2
McKnight	C3
Madill	F3
Mangum	C3
Mannford	F1
Marietta	E4
Marlow	E3
Medford	E1
Midwest City	E2
Minco	E2
Moore	E2
Muldrow	H2
Muskogee	G2
Mustang	E2
Newcastle	E2
Newkirk	E1
Norman	E2
Nowata	G1
Oakhurst	F1
Okeene	D1
Okemah	F2
Oklahoma City, capital	E2
Okmulgee	G2
Owasso	G1
Panama	H2
Pawhuska	F1
Pawnee	F1
Perkins	E2
Perry	E2
Picher	H1
Piedmont	E2
Ponca City	E1
Poteau	H2
Prague	F2

	Key
Pryor Creek	G1
Purcell	E2
Roll	C2
Sallisaw	H2
Sand Springs	F1
Sapulpa	F2
Sayre	C2
Seminole	F2
Shattuck	C1
Shawnee	F2
Skiatook	F1
Slaughterville	E2
Snyder	D3
Sparks	F2
Spiro	H2
Stanley	G3
Stigler	G2
Stillwater	E1
Stilwell	H2
Stratford	F3
Stroud	F2
Sulphur	F3
Tahlequah	H2
Talihina	G3
Tecumseh	F2
Tishomingo	F3
Tonkawa	E1
Tulsa	G1
Turley	G1
Tuttle	E2
Vian	H2
Vinita	G1
Wagoner	G2
Walters	E3
Wanette	E3
Warner	G2
Warren	C3
Watonga	D2
Watova	G1
Waukomis	D1
Waurika	D3
Weatherford	D2
Westville	H1
Wetumka	F2
Wewoka	F2
Wilburton	G3
Wilson	E3
Woodward	C1
Wynnewood	E3
Yale	F1
Yukon	E2

Other Features

	Key
Arkansas, river	F1
Black Mesa, mt.	B4
Broken Bow, lake	H3
Canadian, river	C2
Canton, lake	D1
Chickasaw Natl. Rec. Area	C1
Cimarron, river	C1
Fort Gibson, lake	G1
Hugo, lake	G3
Illinois , river	H2
Kaw, lake	F1
Keystone, lake	F1
North Canadian, river	C1
Oklahoma City Natl. Memorial	E2
Oologah, lake	G1
Ouachita, mts.	C3
Red, river	F4
Sooner, lake	F1
Texoma, lake	F4
Washita Battlefield N.H.S.	C2
Winding Stair Natl. Rec. Area	H3

Oregon ....page 164

Cities and Towns

	Key
Albany	B2
Aloha	A2
Altamont	C3
Ashland	C3
Astoria	B1
Baker City	E2
Bandon	B3
Beaverton	A2, C2
Bend	C2
Brookings	B3
Brownsville	C2
Burns	D2
Canby	A2, C2
Canyon City	E2
Cedar Hills	A2
Central Point	C3
Clatskanie	B1
Condon	D2
Coos Bay	B3
Coquille	B3
Cornelius	A2
Corvallis	B3
Cottage Grove	B3
Creswell	B3
Crowley	E3
Dallas	B2
Eagle Point	C3
Elgin	E2
Enterprise	E2
Eugene	B2
Florence	B3
Forest Grove	A2
Fossil	D2
Four Corners	A2, C2
Glendale	B3
Gold Beach	B3
Grants Pass	B3
Green	B3
Gresham	B2
Harbor	B3
Harrisburg	B2
Hayesville	A2, C2
Heppner	D2
Hermiston	D2
Hillsboro	A2, C2
Hines	D3
Homestead	F2
Hood River	C2
Hubbard	C2
Jacksonville	C3
Jefferson	C2
John Day	E2
Junction City	B2
Juntura	E3
Keizer	B2
Klamath Falls	C3
Lafayette	B2
Lakecreek	C3
La Grande	E2
Lake Oswego	A2, C2
Lakeside	B3
Lakeview	D3
Lebanon	C2

Key

Lexington D2
Lincoln Beach B2
Lincoln City B2
McMinnville C2
Madras C2
Meacham E2
Medford C3
Metzger A2
Mill City C2
Milton-Freewater E2
Milwaukie A2
Molalla A2
Monument D2
Moro D2
Mount Angel A2, C2
Mount Vernon D2
Myrtle Creek B3
Myrtle Point B3
Newberg A2, C2
Newport B2
North Bend B3
Nyssa F3
Oak Grove A2
Oakridge C3
Ontario F2
Oregon City A2, C2
Pendleton E2
Philomath B2
Phoenix C3
Pilot Rock E2
Portland A2, C2
Post D2
Prineville D2
Rainier C1
Redmond C2
Reedsport B3
Riley D3
Rogue River B3
Roseburg B3
Rufus D2
St. Helens D2
Stanfield E2
Salem, *capital* A2, B2
Santa Clara B2
Scappoose C2
Seaside B2
Seneca E2
Shady Cove C3
Sherwood A2
Silverton A2, C2
Springfield C2
Stayton C2
Sunriver C3
Sutherlin B3
Sweet Home C2
Talent C3
The Dalles A2, C2
Tigard A2, C2
Tillamook B2
Toledo B2
Umpqua B3
Union E2
Vale E3
Veneta B2
Vernonia B2
Waldport B2
Warm Springs C2
Warrenton B1
Waterloo C2
West Slope A2
White City C3
Willamina B2
Wilsonville A2, C2
Woodburn A2
Wood Village B2

Other Features

Abert, *lake* D3
Blue, *mts.* E2
Calapooya, *mts.* C3
Cascade, *range* C3
Cascade-Siskiyou Natl. Mon. C3
Clackamas, *river* C2
Coast, *mt. ranges* B2
Columbia, *river* D2
Coos, *bay* B3
Crater, *lake* C3
Crater Lake Natl. Park C3
Crescent, *lake* C3
Crooked, *river* D2
Davis, *lake* C3
Deschutes, *river* C2
Diamond Peak, *mt.* C3
Gearhart Mtn., *mt.* D3
Green Peter, *lake* C2
Harney, *basin* D3
Harney, *lake* D3
Hells, *canyon* F2
Hells Canyon Natl. Rec. Area F2
Hood, *mt.* C2
Jefferson, *mt.* C2
John Day, *river* D2
John Day Fossil Beds N.M. D2
Klamath, *mts.* B3
Lookout, *cape* B2
McLoughlin house N.H.S. A2
Malheur, *lake* E3
Malheur, *river* E3
Molalla, *river* B2
Multnomah, *waterfalls* C2
Ochoco, *mts.* D2
Oregon Caves Natl. Monument B3
Oregon Dunes Natl. Rec. Area B3
Owyhee, *lake* E3
Owyhee, *river* E2
Powder, *river* E2
Pudding, *river* A3
Pueblo, *mts.* E3
Rogue, *river* B3
Sacajawea Peak, *mt.* E2
Silvies, *river* D3
Siuslaw, *river* B3
Snake, *river* F2
South Umpqua, *river* B3
Steens, *mts.* E3
Strawberry Mt., *mt.* E2
Summer, *lake* D3
Thielsen, *mt.* C3
Tillamook, *bay* B2
Trout Creek, *mts.* E3
Umatilla, *lake* D2
Upper Klamath, *lake* C3
Waldo, *lake* C3
Wallowa, *mts.* E2
Willamette, *river* A2

Pennsylvania ....page 165

Cities and Towns

Albion A2
Aliquippa A4
Allensville F4
Allentown L4
Allison Park E6
Altoona E4
Ambridge A4
Annville H5
Archbald K2
Ardmore M6
Arnot G2
Ashland J4
Athens H2
Austin E2
Avalon D7
Avis G3
Bala Cynwyd M6
Baldwin E7
Bangor L4
Barnesboro D4
Beaver A4
Beaver Falls A4
Beavertown G4
Bedford E5
Bellefonte F4
Belleville F4
Bellevue D7
Bellwood E4
Berlin D6
Berwick J3
Berwyn L6
Bethel Park A5, D7
Bethlehem L4
Birdsboro K5
Blairsville C5
Blakely K3
Bloomsburg J4
Blossburg G2
Boalsburg F4
Boothwyn L7
Boswell D5
Boyertown K5
Bradford D2
Brentwood E7
Bridgeville D7
Brockport D3
Brockway D3
Brodheadsville L4
Brooklyn K2
Brookville C3
Broomall L6
Brownsville B5
Bryn Mawr L6
Burgettstown A5
Butler B4
California B5
Cambridge Springs A2
Canonsburg A5
Canton H2
Carbondale K2
Carlisle G5
Carnegie D7
Carroll Valley G6
Carrolltown D4
Castle Shannon E7
Catawissa J4
Chambersburg F6
Chelsea L7
Chester L6, L7
Clairton B5
Clarion C3
Clarks Summit K2
Claysburg E5
Clearfield E3
Clifton Heights L7
Clymer C4
Coatesville K6
Columbia H5
Connellsville B6
Conyngham J4
Coopersburg L5
Coraopolis D7
Cornwall J5
Corry B2
Coudersport E2
Crafton D7
Cresson D5
Crosby E2
Cuddy D7
Curwensville D4
Dallas K3
Danville H4
Darby M7
Delmont C5
Denver J5
Derry C5
Dillsburg G5
Dormont D7
Dover H5
Downingtown K5
Doylestown L5
Drexel Hill M7
DuBois D3
Duncannon G5
Duquesne E7
Dushore J2
East Greenville K5
East Lansdowne M7
Easton L4
East Petersburg J5
East Stroudsburg L3
Ebensburg D4
Eddystone L7
Edinboro A2
Effinwild E6
Elizabethtown H5
Elizabethville H4
Elkland G2
Ellwood City A4
Elysburg H4
Emlenton B3
Emmaus L4
Emporium E2
Emsworth D7
Ephrata J5
Erie A1
Etna E7
Evans City A4
Everett E5
Exton K5
Fayetteville F6
Fleetwood K5
Ford City B4
Forest City K2
Forest Grove H2
Forksville J2
Fox Chapel E7
Freeland K3
Freeport B4
Galeton F2
Gettysburg G6
Girard A1
Gladden D7
Gladwyne M6
Glenolden M7
Glen Riddle L7
Glen Rock H6
Gradyville L7
Greencastle F6
Greensburg B5
Greenville A3
Gregg D7
Grove City A3
Hallstead K2
Hamburg K4
Hanover H6
Harmarville E6
Harrisburg, *capital* H5
Harrisville A3
Harveys Lake J3
Haverford M6
Havertown M6
Hazel Hurst D2
Hazleton K4
Hermitage A3
Herndon H4
Hershey H5
Highland D6
Holidaysburg E5
Homer City C4
Honesdale L2
Huntingdon E5
Hyndman D6
Indiana C4
Indianola E6
Jersey Shore G3
Jim Thorpe K4
Johnsonburg D3
Johnstown D5
Kane D2
Kennett Square K6
King of Prussia L6
Kingston K3
Kittanning B4
Kutztown K5
Lake City A1
Lancaster J5
Lansdale L5
Lansdowne M7
Laporte J3
Latrobe C5
Lebanon J5
Leechburg B4
Lehighton K4
Levittown M5
Lewisburg H4
Lewistown G4
Ligonier C5
Lima L7
Linglestown H5
Lititz J5
Littlestown G6
Lock Haven G3
Lykens H4
McCandless A4, D6
McConnellsburg E6
McKees Rocks D7
McKeesport B5
Macungie K4
Mahanoy City J4
Manchester H5
Manheim J5
Mansfield G2
Mars A4
Martinsburg E5
Marysville H5
Masontown B6
Matamoras M3
Meadville A2
Mechanicsburg G5
Media L6, L7
Mercer A3
Mercersburg F6
Meridian B4
Merion M6
Meyersdale C6
Middleburg G4
Middletown H5
Midland A4
Mifflinburg G4
Mifflintown G4
Mifflinville J4
Milford M3
Millersburg H4
Millersville J6
Millheim G4
Millvale E7
Milroy F4
Milton H3
Minersville J4
Monessen B5
Monroeville B5, F7
Mont Alto F6
Montgomery H3
Montoursville H3
Montrose K2
Moon Run D7
Moscow K3
Mt. Carmel J4
Mt. Holly Springs G5
Mount Joy H5
Mt. Lebanon D7
Mt. Nebo D6
Mt. Oliver E7
Mt. Pleasant B5
Mt. Pocono L3
Mount Union F6
Muncy H3
Munhall E7
Myerstown J5
Nanticoke J3
Nanty Glo D5
Nazareth L4
Nesquehoning K4
New Bloomfield G5
New Castle A4
New Freedom H6
New Holland J5
New Kensington B4, F6
New Oxford G6
Newport G5
Newtown M5
Newtown Square M7
Newville F6
New Wilmington A3
North East B1
Northampton L4
North Springfield A1
Northumberland H4
Oakmont E7
Oil City B3
Old Forge K3
Orwigsburg J4
Oxford J6
Palmerton K4
Patton D4
Pen Argyl L4
Penn Hills E7
Penn Wynne M6
Perkasie L5
Philadelphia L6, M7
Philipsburg E4
Phoenixville K5
Picture Rocks H3
Pine Grove J4
Pittsburgh B5, E7
Pittston K3
Pleasantville B2
Pleasantville D5
Point Marion B6
Polk B3
Port Allegany E2
Port Matilda E4
Portage D5
Portland Mills D3
Pottstown K5
Pottsville J4
Powell H2
Prospect Park L7
Punxsutawney D4
Quakertown L5
Quarryville J6
Radnor L6
Rainsburg D6
Reading K5
Red Lion H6
Renovo F3
Reynoldsville D3
Ridgway D3
Ridley Park L7
Roaring Spring E5
St. Marys D3
Saxonburg B4
Sayre H2
Schnecksville K4
Schuylkill Haven J4
Scottdale B5
Scranton K3
Selinsgrove H4
Shamokin H4
Sharon A3
Sharon Hill M7
Sharpsville A3
Sheffield C2
Shenandoah J4
Shippensburg F5
Shoemakersville K5
Shrewsbury H6
Sinking Spring J5
Slatington K4
Slippery Rock A3
Smethport E2
Somerset C5
Souderton L5
South Williamsport G3
Spring Grove H6
Springdale F6
Springfield L7
State College F4
Stewartstown H6
Strasburg J6
Stroudsburg L4
Sugarcreek B3
Sunbury H4
Susquehanna K2
Swarthmore L7
Sykesville D3
Tamaqua K4
Tionesta C3
Titusville B2
Tobyhanna L3
Towanda J2
Tower City H4
Tremont J4
Trevorton H4
Troy H2
Tunkhannock K2
Tyrone E4
Union City B2
Uniontown B6
Upland L7
Valley View H4
Vandergrift B4
Verona E7
Village Green L7
Villanova L6
Warren C2
Washington A5
Waterford B2
Watsontown H3
Waymart L3
Wayne L6
Waynesboro F6
Waynesburg A6
Weatherly K4
Wellsboro G2
Wesleyville A1
West Chester K6
West Grove K6
West Mifflin E7
West Pike F2
West View E7
Whitehall K4
White Horse L6
Wilcox D2
Wilkes-Barre K3
Wilkinsburg E7
Williamsport G3
Willow Grove L5
Windber D5
Womelsdorf J5
York H6
York Springs G5
Youngsville C2
Zelienople A4

Other Features

Allegheny, *reservoir* D2
Allegheny, *river* A3
Allegheny Natl. Rec. Area D2
Allegheny Portage Railroad N.H.S. E5
Appalachian, *mts.* F5
Clarion, *river* C3
Conemaugh, *river* C6
Davis, *mt.* C6
Delaware, *river* L2
Delaware Water Gap N.R.A. M3
Eisenhower Natl. Hist. Site G6
Erie, *lake* A1
Friendship Hill Natl. Hist. Site B6
Gettysburg Natl. Mil. Park G6
Johnstown Flood Natl. Memorial D5
Juniata, *river* F5
Lehigh, *river* L3
Ohio, *river* A4
Presque Isle, *island* A1
Raystown, *lake* E5
Schuylkill, *river* K5
Steamtown Natl. Hist. Site K3
Susquehanna, *river* J2
Tioga, *river* G2
Valley Forge Natl. Hist. Park L5

Rhode Island ....page 166

Cities and Towns

Adamsville F4
Allenton D4
Alton B5
Anthony C3
Arcadia B4
Ashaway B5
Ashton D2
Avondale A6
Barrington E3
Berkeley D2
Bradford B5
Bristol E3
Carolina C5
Central Falls D2
Charlestown C5
Chepachet B2
Clayville B3
Coventry Center C3
Cranston D3
Cumberland Hill D2
Diamond Hill D2
Dunn Corner B5
East Greenwich D3
East Providence D3
Exeter C4
Fiskeville C3
Foster Center B3
Galilee C5
Glendale C2
Green Hill C5
Greenville C2
Hamilton D4
Harmony C2
Harrisville B2
Hope C3
Hope Valley B5
Hopkinton B5
Jamestown D3
Jerusalem C5
Kingston C5
Little Compton E4
Lonsdale D2
Matunuck C5
Middletown E4
Moosup Valley B3
Narragansett Pier D5
Newport D4
Nooseneck C4
North Foster B2
North Providence D2
North Scituate C3
Pascoag B2
Pawtucket D2
Pawtuxet D3
Perryville C5
Plum Point D5
Portsmouth E4
Providence, *capital* D3
Prudence E4
Quidnick C3
Quonochontaug B6
Rice City B3
Riverside D3
Rockville B4
Rumford D2
Sakonnet E5
Saunderstown D5
Saylesville D2
Shannock C5
Slatersville C2
Slocum C4
South Foster B3
Spragueville C2
Tarkiln B2
Tiverton E4
Usquepaug C5
Valley Falls D2
Village Green L7
Wakefield C5
Wallum Lake B2
Warren E3
Warwick D3
Washington C3
Watch Hill A6
Weekapaug B6
West Barrington D3
Westerly A6
West Glocester B2
West Kingston C5
West Warwick C3
Woonsocket C1
Wyoming B4

Other Features

Block, *island* C7
Block Island, *sound* B6
Mt. Hope, *bay* E4
Narragansett, *bay* D4
Rhode Island, *sound* E5
Roger Williams Natl. Mem. D3
Sakonnet, *river* E4
Scituate, *reservoir* C3
Touro Synagogue N.H.S. E5

South Carolina ....page 167

Cities and Towns

Abbeville B2
Aiken C3
Allendale C4
Anderson B2
Andrews E3
Bamberg D3
Barnwell C3
Batesburg-Leesville C3
Beaufort D4
Belton B2
Belvedere C3
Bennettsville E2
Bishopville D2
Blacksburg C1
Blackville C3
Boiling Springs C1
Brownsville E2
Buffalo C2
Burton D4
Calhoun Falls B2
Camden D2
Cayce C3
Central B2
Charleston E4
Cheraw E2
Chester C2
Chesterfield D2
Clemson B2
Clinton C2
Clover C1
Columbia, *capital* D3
Conway E3
Cowpens C1
Darlington E2
Denmark D2
Dentsville D2
Dillon E2
Easley B2
Edgefield C3
Elgin D2
Enoree C2
Estill C4
Fairfax C4
Florence E2
Folly Beach E4
Forest Acres D2
Foreston D3
Fort Mill D1
Fountain Inn B2
Furman C4
Gaffney C1
Garden City F3
Georgetown E3
Gifford C4
Gloverville C3
Goose Creek D3
Great Falls D2
Greeleyville E3
Greenville B2
Greenwood B2
Greer B2
Hampton C4
Hanahan D4
Hardeeville C5
Harleyville D3
Hartsville D2
Hickory Grove C2
Hickory Grove F3
Hilda C3
Hilton Head Island D4
Holly Hill D3
Hollywood D4
Honea Path B2
Horrel Hill D2
Inman B1
Irmo C2
Isle of Palms E4
Jackson C3
Jefferson D2
Joanna C2
Johnsonville E3
Johnston C3
Kershaw D2
Kiawah Island D4
Kingstree E3
Kline C3
Ladson D4
Lake City E3
Lancaster D2
Landrum B1
Lane E3
Latta E2
Laurel Bay D4
Laurens C2
Lexington C3
Liberty B2
Little River F3
Little Rock E2
Loris F2
Lugoff D2
Lyman B2
Lynchburg D2
McBee D2
McClellanville E3
McCormick B3
Manning D3
Marion E2
Mauldin B2
Mayesville D2
Mayo C1
Moncks Corner D3
Mt. Pleasant E4
Mullins E2
Murrells Inlet F3
Myrtle Beach F3
Neeses C3
New Ellenton C3
Newberry C2
Nichols E2
Ninety Six B2
North Augusta C3
North Charleston D4
North Myrtle Beach F3
Norway C3
Olanta E3
Olar C3
Orangeburg D3
Pacolet C2
Pacolet Mills C2
Pageland D2
Pamplico E3
Patrick D2
Pelion C3
Pendleton B2
Pickens B2
Piedmont B2
Pinewood D3
Pomaria C2
Port Royal D4
Ravenel D4
Red Bank C3
Ridgeland C4
Ridgeville D3
Ridgeway D2
Rock Hill D1
Roebuck C2
Rowesville D3
Ruby D2
St. George D3
St. Matthews D3
St. Stephen E3
Salley C3
Salters E3
Saluda C3
Santee D3
Sellers E2
Seneca B2
Simpsonville B2
Socastee F3
Society Hill E2
South Congaree C3
Spartanburg C2
Springfield C3
Starr B2
Stuckey E3

	Key
Summerville	D3
Sumter	D3
Surfside Beach	F3
Swansea	C3
Sycamore	C3
Taylors	B2
Timmonsville	E2
Travelers Rest	B2
Trenton	C3
Turbeville	D3
Union	C2
Varnville	C4
Wagener	C3
Walhalla	A2
Walterboro	D4
Ware Shoals	B2
Westminster	A2
Whitmire	C2
Williamston	B2
Williston	C3
Winnsboro	C2
Woodruff	B2
Yemassee	D4
York	C2

Other Features

	Key
Bull, *island*	E4
Bulls, *bay*	E4
Cape, *island*	E3
Congaree Swamp N.M.	D3
Cowpens Natl. Bfld.	C1
Edisto, *river*	D3
Fort Sumter Natl. Monument	E4
Greenwood, *lake*	C2
Hartwell, *lake*	B2
J. Strom Thurmond, *lake*	B3
Keowee, *lake*	B2
Kings Mt. Natl. Mil. Park	C1
Long, *bay*	F3
Lynches, *river*	D2
Marion, *lake*	D3
Monticello, *reservoir*	C2
Moultrie, *lake*	D3
Murray, *lake*	C2
Ninety Six Natl. Hist. Site	B2
North, *island*	E3
Port Royal, *sound*	D4
Russell, *lake*	B2
St. Helena, *sound*	D4
Saluda, *river*	C2
Santee, *river*	E3
Savannah, *river*	C3
South, *island*	E3
The Grand Strand	F3
Wateree, *lake*	D2
Wateree, *river*	D2

South Dakota .... page 168

Cities and Towns

	Key
Aberdeen	F1
Alexandria	G3
Armour	F3
Belle Fourche	A2
Beresford	H3
Black Hawk	A2
Box Elder	A2
Britton	G1
Brookings	H2
Burke	E3
Canton	H3
Chamberlain	E3
Cherry Creek	C2
Clark	G2
Clear Lake	H2
Custer	A3
Deadwood	A2
Dell Rapids	H3
De Smet	G2
Dupree	C1
Elk Point	H4
Faulkton	E1
Flandreau	H2
Fort Pierre	D2
Freeman	G3
Gettysburg	E1
Hartford	H3
Highmore	E2
Hot Springs	A3
Howard	G2
Huron	F2
Ipswich	E1
Kadoka	C3
Lake Andes	F3
Lead	A2
Lemmon	B1
Lennox	G3
Leola	F1
Madison	G2
Martin	C3
Milbank	H1
Miller	E2
Mitchell	F3
Mobridge	D1
Murdo	D3
Onida	E2
Parker	G3
Parkston	G3
Philip	C2
Pierre, *capital*	D2
Pine Ridge	B3
Plankinton	F3
Platte	F3
Rapid City	A2
Redfield	F2
Rosebud	D3
Salem	G3
Selby	D1
Sioux Falls	H3
Sisseton	G1
Spearfish	A2
Sturgis	A2
Timber Lake	C1
Tyndall	G4
Vermillion	H4
Volga	H2
Wagner	F3
Watertown	G2
Webster	G1
Wessington Springs	F2
White River	D3
Winner	E3
Woonsocket	F2
Wounded Knee	B3
Yankton	G4

Other Features

	Key
Andes, *lake*	F3
Angostura, *reservoir*	A3
Bad, *river*	C2
Badlands Natl. Park	B3
Belle Fourche, *reservoir*	A2
Belle Fourche, *river*	A2
Big Sioux, *river*	H2
Big Stone, *lake*	H1
Black, *hills*	A2
Bois de Sioux, *river*	H1
Cheyenne, *river*	C2
Francis Case, *lake*	F3
Grand, *river*	C1
Harney Peak, *mt.*	A3
James, *river*	F1
Jewel Cave Natl. Monument	A3
Keya Paha, *river*	D3
Lewis and Clark, *lake*	G4
Little Missouri, *river*	A1
Little White, *river*	D3
Minuteman Missile N.H.S.	B3, C3
Missouri, *river*	E3
Moreau, *river*	B1
Mount Rushmore Natl. Memorial	A3
North Fork Grand, *river*	B1
Oahe, *lake*	D2
Pine, *ridge*	B3
Sharpe, *lake*	E2
South Fork Grand, *river*	A1
Traverse, *lake*	H1
Vermillion, *river*	G3
Waubay, *lake*	G1
White, *river*	D3
Whitewood, *river*	G2
Wind Cave Natl. Park	A3

Tennessee .... page 169

Cities and Towns

	Key
Adamsville	E4
Alamo	C3
Alcoa	P3
Algood	L2
Altamont	K4
Arlington	B4
Ashland City	G2
Athens	M4
Bartlett	B4
Baxter	K2
Bells	C3
Benton	M4
Bethel Springs	D4
Bethpage	J2
Blaine	P2
Blountville	S1
Bluff City	S2
Bolivar	D4
Brentwood	H2
Bristol	S1
Brownsville	C3
Bruceton	E2
Buffalo Valley	K2
Byrdstown	K1
Camden	E2
Campaign	K3
Carthage	K2
Caryville	N2
Celina	K1
Centerville	G3
Charlotte	G2
Chattanooga	L4
Church Hill	R1
Clarksville	G1
Cleveland	M4
Clinton	N2
Collegedale	L4
Collierville	B4
Columbia	G3
Conasauga	M4
Cookeville	L2
Covington	B3
Cowan	J4
Crossville	L3
Dandridge	Q2
Dayton	L3
Decatur	M3
Decaturville	E3
Decherd	J4
Dickson	G2
Dover	F2
Dresden	D2
Dunlap	L4
Dyer	C2
Dyersburg	C2
East Ridge	L4
Elizabethton	S2
Englewood	N4
Erin	F2
Erwin	S2
Estill Springs	J4
Etowah	M4
Fairfield Glade	M2
Farragut	N3
Fayetteville	H4
Forest Hills	H4
Frankewing	H4
Franklin	H3
Gainesboro	K2
Gallatin	J2
Gatlinburg	P3
Germantown	B4
Gleason	D2
Goodlettsville	H2
Granville	K2
Graysville	L4
Greeneville	R2
Greenfield	D2
Grimsley	M2
Gruetli-Laager	K4
Halls	C3
Halls Crossroads	P2
Hampshire	G3
Harriman	M3
Hartsville	J2
Henderson	D4
Hendersonville	H2
Humboldt	D3
Huntingdon	E3
Huntsville	N2
Jackson	D3
Jacksboro	N2
Jamestown	M2
Jasper	K4
Jefferson City	Q2
Jellico	N1
Johnson City	S2
Jonesborough	S2
Karns	N3
Kenton	C2
Kingsport	R1
Kingston	M3
Kingston Springs	G2
Knoxville	P3
Lafayette	J1
La Follette	N2
Lake City	N2
Lakewood	H2
La Vergne	H2
Lawrenceburg	G4
Lebanon	H2
Lenoir City	N3
Lewisburg	H4
Lexington	E3
Linden	F3
Livingston	L2
Loretto	G4
Loudon	N3
Lynchburg	J4
McEwen	F2
McKenzie	D2
McKinnon	F2
Madisonville	N3
Manchester	J4
Martin	D2
Maryville	P3
Mascot	P2
Maynardville	P2
Medon	D4
Memphis	A4
Middleton	D4
Milan	D3
Millersville	H2
Milligan College	S2
Millington	B4
Monterey	L2
Morristown	Q2
Mosheim	R2
Mountain City	T1
Mount Juliet	H2
Mount Pleasant	G3
Munford	B4
Murfreesboro	J3
Nashville, *capital*	H2
Newbern	C2
New Johnsonville	F2
New Tazewell	P2
Nolensville	H3
Norris	N2
Oak Hill	H2
Oak Ridge	N2
Oliver Springs	N2
Oneida	M2
Overall	H2
Paris	E2
Parsons	E3
Pegram	G2
Pigeon Forge	P3
Pikeville	L3
Portland	H1
Powell	N2
Pulaski	G4
Reagan	E3
Red Bank	L4
Ridgely	C2
Ripley	B3
Rockwood	M3
Rogersville	R2
Rutherford	D2
Rutledge	Q2
Savannah	E4
Selmer	D4
Sevierville	P3
Sewanee	K4
Shelbyville	J4
Signal Mountain	L4
Smithville	K3
Smyrna	H3
Sneedville	Q1
Soddy-Daisy	L4
Somerville	C4
South Fulton	D2
South Pittsburg	K4
Sparta	L3
Spencer	L3
Spring City	M3
Spring Hill	H3
Springfield	H1
Stanton	C4
Surgoinsville	R2
Sweetwater	N3
Taft	H4
Tazewell	P2
Tellico Plains	N4
Tennessee Ridge	F2
Tiptonville	C2
Tracy City	K4
Trenton	D3
Trimble	C2
Tullahoma	J4
Tusculum	R2
Union City	C2
Wartburg	M2
Waverly	F2
Waynesboro	F4
Westmoreland	J1
White House	H2
White Pine	Q2
Whitwell	K4
Winchester	J4
Woodbury	J3

Other Features

	Key
Andrew Johnson Natl. Hist. Site	R2
Appalachian, *mts.*	N4
Appalachian Natl. Scenic Trail	Q3
Barkley, *lake*	F1
Big South Fork Natl. River and Rec. Area	M1
Center Hill, *lake*	K3
Cherokee, *lake*	Q2
Chickamauga & Chattanooga Natl. Mil. Park	L5
Chickamauga, *lake*	M3
Clinch, *river*	Q2
Clingmans Dome, *mt.*	Q3
Cumberland, *river*	G2
Dale Hollow, *lake*	L1
Douglas, *lake*	Q3
Duck, *river*	H3
Great Smoky, *mts.*	P3
Great Smoky Mts. Natl. Park	Q3
Holston, *river*	R2
Kentucky, *lake*	E2
Mississippi, *river*	B3
Norris, *lake*	P2
Roan, *mt.*	P2
Shiloh Natl. Mil. Park	E4
Tennessee, *river*	E5, K5
Watts Bar, *lake*	M3
Woods, *reservoir*	J4

Texas .... page 170

Cities and Towns

	Key
Abernathy	F2
Abilene	H3
Addison	C1
Alamo Heights	B7
Albany	H3
Algoa	F9
Alice	J8
Alpine	D5
Alvin	M6
Amarillo	B9
Anahuac	N6
Anderson	M5
Andrews	E3
Angleton	M6
Anson	H3
Anthony	A3
Aransas Pass	K8
Archer City	J2
Arlington	L3
Asherton	H7
Aspermont	G2
Atascosa	A7
Athens	M3
Atlanta	N2
Austin, *capital*	L5
Avondale	A1
Azle	K3
Bacliff	C9
Baird	H3
Balch Springs	C2
Balcones Heights	A7
Ballinger	H4
Bandera	H6
Barrett	F8
Bastrop	K5
Batesville	H7
Bay City	M7
Bayou Vista	G10
Baytown	N6
Beaumont	N5
Beaumont Place	F8
Beaver	C8
Bedford	B2
Beeville	K7
Bellaire	E8
Bellmead	K4
Belton	K4
Benavides	J8
Benbrook	A2
Benjamin	H2
Bergheim	A6
Big Lake	F4
Big Spring	F3
Bishop	K8
Boerne	J6
Bogata	M2
Bonham	L2
Borger	C9
Bovina	E1
Bowie	K2
Bracken	B6
Brackettville	G6
Brady	H4
Breckenridge	J3
Brenham	L5
Briar	A1
Bridge City	P5
Bridgeport	K2
Brookshire	M6
Brookside Village	F9
Brownfield	E2
Brownsville	K10
Brownwood	J4
Bryan	L5
Buckingham	C1
Buena Vista	B7
Buffalo	L4
Bulverde	A6
Buna	P5
Bunker Hill Village	E8
Burkburnett	J1
Burleson	A3
Burleson	K3
Burnet	J5
Caldwell	L5
Cameron	L5
Canadian	D9
Canton	M3
Canutillo	A4
Canyon	B9
Carrizo Springs	H7
Carrollton	B1
Carthage	N3
Castle Hills	A6
Castle Hills	A7
Cedar Hill	B3
Cedar Park	K5
Center	N4
Centerville	M4
Chandler	M3
Channelview	F8
Channing	B9
Childress	G1
Chocolate Bayou	F10
Cisco	J3
Clarendon	C10
Clarksville	M2
Claude	C9
Cleburne	K3
Cleveland	M5
Clifton	K4
Cloverleaf	F8
Clute	M6
Cockrell Hill	B2
Coldspring	M5
Coleman	H4
College Station	L5
Colleyville	A2
Colorado City	G3
Columbus	L6
Comanche	J4
Combine	D2
Commerce	L2
Conroe	M5
Converse	B6
Cooper	M2
Copperas Cove	K4
Corpus Christi	K8
Corsicana	L3
Cotulla	H7
Crane	E4
Crockett	M4
Crosby	F8
Crosbyton	F2
Crowell	H2
Crowley	A3
Crystal City	H7
Cuero	K6
Daingerfield	N2
Dalhart	B8
Dallas	L3
Dalworthington Gardens	B2
Danbury	F10
Dayton	N5
Decatur	K2
Deer Park	F8
Del Rio	G6
Denison	L2
Denton	K2
Denver City	E3
De Soto	L3
Devine	J6
Diboll	N4
Dickens	G2
Dickinson	F9
Dilley	H7
Dimmitt	E1
Dublin	J4
Dumas	B9
Duncanville	A3
Eagle Lake	L6
Eagle Pass	G7
Eastland	J3
Eden	H4
Edgecliff	A3
Edinburg	J9
Edna	L7
El Campo	L6
Eldorado	G4
Electra	J1
Elgin	K5
Elsa	J9
El Paso	A4
Emory	M3
Ennis	L3
Euless	B2
Everman	A3
Fabens	A4
Fair Oaks Ranch	A6
Fairfield	L4
Falfurrias	J8
Farmers Branch	B1
Farwell	D1
Ferris	C3
Flatonia	K6
Floresville	J6
Floydada	F2
Forest Hill	A2
Fort Davis	D5
Fort Stockton	E5
Fort Worth	K3
Franklin	L4
Fredericksburg	J5
Freeport	M7
Freer	J8
Friendswood	F9
Gail	F3
Gainesville	L2
Galena Park	F8
Galveston	N6
Ganado	L6
Garden City	F4
Garden Ridge	B6
Gardendale	B7
Garland	C2
Gatesville	K4
George West	J7
Georgetown	K5
Germann	C3
Giddings	L5
Gilmer	N3
Gladewater	N3
Glen Rose	K3
Glenn Heights	B3
Goldthwaite	J4
Goliad	K7
Gonzales	K6
Gorman	J3
Graham	J2
Granbury	K3
Grand Prairie	B2
Grand Saline	M3
Grapeland	M4
Grapevine	B1
Grapevine	K3
Greenville	L2
Groesbeck	L4
Groves	P6
Groveton	M4
Guthrie	G2
Hallettsville	L6
Haltom City	A2
Hamilton	J4
Hamlin	G3
Harker Heights	K4
Harlingen	K9
Haskell	H2
Hearne	L5
Hebbronville	J8
Helotes	A6
Hemphill	P4
Hempstead	L5
Henderson	N3
Henrietta	J2
Hereford	B10
Hewitt	K4
Hico	J4
Hidalgo	J9
Highland Park	C2
Highlands	F8
Hillsboro	K3
Hitchcock	F9
Hitchcock	M6
Hollywood Park	A6
Houston	M6
Hubbard	K4
Huntsville	M5
Hurst	A2
Hutchins	C2
Idalou	F2
India	C3
Ingleside	K8
Iowa Park	J1
Irving	B2
Jacinto City	F8
Jacksboro	J2
Jacksonville	M4
Jasper	P5
Jayton	G2
Jefferson	N3
Jersey Village	E8
Johnson City	J5
Jourdanton	J7
Juliff	E9
Junction	H5
Karnes City	K7
Katy	M6
Kaufman	L3
Keller	A2
Kermit	D4
Kerrick	B8
Kerrville	H5
Kilgore	N3
Killeen	K4
Kingsland	J5
Kingsville	K8
Kirby	B7
Kirbyville	P5
Knox City	H2
Kountze	N5
La Grange	L6
Lake Jackson	M7
Lakehills	J6
La Marque	G9
Lamesa	E3
Lampasas	J4
Lancaster	B3
La Porte	F9
La Pryor	H7
Laredo	H8
League City	M6
Leakey	H6
Leon Springs	A6
Leon Valley	J6
Levelland	E2
Lewisville	L2
Liberty	N5
Lipscomb	D8
Littlefield	E2
Live Oak	B6
Livingston	N5
Llano	J5
Lockhart	K6
Lockney	F1
Longview	N3
Lubbock	F2
Lufkin	N4
Luling	K6
Lumberton	N5
Mabank	L3
McAllen	J9
McCamey	E4
Macdona	A7
McKinney	L2
Madisonville	M5
Mangus Corner	A7
Mansfield	B3
Manvel	F9
Marble Falls	J5
Marfa	C5
Marlin	L4
Marshall	N3
Mason	H5
Matador	G1
Mathis	K8
Memphis	C10
Menard	H5
Mentone	D4
Meridian	K4
Merkel	G3
Mertzon	G4
Mesquite	L3
Mexia	L4
Miami	C9
Midland	E4
Midlothian	B4
Mineola	M3
Mineral Wells	J3
Mission	J9
Missouri City	M6
Monahans	E4
Mont Belvieu	G8
Montague	K2
Morgans Point	G8
Morton	E2
Moss Bluff	G8
Mt. Houston	F8
Mt. Pleasant	N2
Mt. Vernon	M2
Muleshoe	E1
Munday	H2
Murphy	C1
Nacogdoches	N4
Nassau Bay	F9
Navasota	L5
Nederland	N6
New Berlin	B7
New Boston	N2
New Braunfels	J6
Newton	P5
Nixon	K6
Nocona	K2
North Houston	E8
North Richland Hills	A2
Odessa	E4
Olmos Park	A7
Olney	J2
Olton	E1
Orange	P5
Ovilla	B3
Ozona	G4
Paducah	G1
Paint Rock	H4
Palacios	L7
Palestine	M4
Palo Pinto	J3
Pampa	C9
Panhandle	C9
Pantego	B2
Paris	M2
Parita	B7
Parker	C1
Pasadena	M6
Pearland	F9
Pearsall	H7
Pecos	D4
Pelican Bay	A2
Perryton	C8
Pharr	J9
Pilot Point	L2
Pittsburg	N2
Plains	E2
Plainview	F1
Plano	L2
Pleasanton	J7
Port Arthur	P6
Port Bolivar	G9
Port Isabel	K9
Portland	K8
Port Lavaca	L7
Post	F2
Poteet	J6
Premont	J8
Presidio	C6
Quanah	H1
Quitman	M3
Ranger	J3
Rankin	E4
Raymondville	K9
Red Oak	B3
Refugio	K7
Reno	A2
Richardson	C1
Richland Hills	A2

	Key
Richmond	M6
Rio Grande City	J9
Roanoke	A1
Robert Lee	G4
Robinson	K4
Robstown	K8
Roby	G3
Rockdale	L5
Rockport	K7
Rocksprings	G5
Rockwall	L3
Roma	H9
Roscoe	G3
Rosenberg	M6
Rosharon	E9
Rotan	G3
Round Rock	K5
Rowlett	C2
Rusk	M4
Sabinal	H6
Sachse	C1
St. Hedwig	B7
San Angelo	G4
San Antonio	J6
San Augustine	N4
San Benito	K9
Sanderson	E5
San Diego	J8
Sandy Point	E9
Sanger	K2
San Geronimo	A6
San Leon	G9
San Marcos	K6
San Saba	J4
Sansom Park	A2
Sarita	K8
Satsuma	E8
Sayers	B7
Schertz	C6
Schumansville	B6
Seabrook	F9
Seadrift	L7
Seagoville	C2
Seagraves	E3
Sealy	L6
Seguin	K6
Selma	B6
Seminole	E3
Seymour	H2
Shallowater	E2
Shavano Park	A6
Sherman	L2
Shoreacres	G9
Sierra Blanca	B4
Silsbee	N5
Silverton	F1
Sinton	K7
Slaton	F2
Smith Point	G9
Smithville	K5
Snyder	G3
Socorro	A4
Sonora	G5
South Houston	F9
Southlake	A1
Southside Place	E8
Southton	B7
Spearman	C8
Spring Valley	E8
Spur	G2
Stafford	E9
Stamford	H3
Stanton	F3
Stephenville	J3
Sterling City	G4
Stratford	B8
Sugar Land	E9
Sulphur Springs	M2
Sundown	E2
Sunnyvale	C2
Sweetwater	G3
Tahoka	F2
Taylor	K5
Temple	K4
Texarkana	N2
Texas City	N6
The Woodlands	M5
Thompsons	E9
Three Rivers	J7
Throckmorton	H2
Tilden	J7
Tomball	M5
Trinity	M5
Trophy Club	A1
Tulia	F1
Tyler	M3
Universal City	J6
University Park	C2
Uvalde	H6
Van Alstyne	L2
Van Horn	C4
Vega	B9
Vernon	H1
Victoria	L7
Vidor	N5
Von Ormy	A7
Waco	K4
Waskom	N3
Watauga	A2
Waxahachie	L3
Weatherford	K3
Webster	F9
Wellington	D10
Weslaco	K9
West	M6
West Columbia	M6
West Odessa	E4
Westover Hills	A2
West University Place	E8
Westworth	A2
Wharton	L6
Wheatland	A3
Wheeler	D9
White Settlement	A2
Whitesboro	L2
Wichita Falls	J2
Willis	M5
Wills Point	L3
Wilmer	C2
Windcrest	B6
Winnie	N6
Winnsboro	M3
Winters	H4
Wolfforth	F2
Woodville	N5
Woodway	K4
Wylie	K6
Yoakum	K6
Zapata	H9
Zuehl	B7

Other Features	Key
Alibates Flint Quarries N.M.	B9
Amistad, reservoir	F6
Amistad Natl. Rec. Area	G6
Balcones, escarpment	A6
Big Bend Natl. Park	D6
Big Thicket Natl. Preserve	N5
Black, mt.	G6
Canadian, river	C9
Cathedral, mt.	D5
Chamizal Natl. Mem.	A4
Chinati Peak, mt.	C6
Dallas-Fort Worth Intl. Airport	B2
Davis, mts.	C5
Eagle Peak, mt.	B5
Edwards, plateau	G5
Emory Peak, mt.	D6
Falcon, reservoir	H9
Fort Davis Natl. Hist. Site	C5
Galveston, bay	G9
Galveston, island	N6
Guadalupe, mts.	C3
Guadalupe Mts. Natl. Park	C4
Guadalupe Peak, mt.	C4
Kemp, lake	H2
Lake Meredith Natl. Rec. Area	C9
Livermore, mt.	C5
Livingston, lake	M5
Lyndon B. Johnson N.H.P.	J5
Meredith, lake	C9
Nueces, river	J7
O.H. Ivie, lake	H4
Padre Island Natl. Seashore	K8
Pecos, river	E4
Pelican, island	G9
Red, river	H1
Red Bluff, lake	D4
Rio Grande	D5
Sabine, pass	P6
Sabine, river	P5
Sam Rayburn, reservoir	N4
Santiago Peak, mt.	D6
Sierra Del Carmen, mt.	D6
Stockton, plateau	E5
Toledo Bend, reservoir	P4

Utah .... page 171

Cities and Towns

	Key
American Fork	C3
Beaver	B5
Bicknell	C5
Blanding	E6
Bluffdale	C3
Bountiful	C2
Brigham City	C2
Castle Dale	C4
Cedar City	A6
Centerville	C3
Clearfield	B2
Coalville	C3
Cottonwood Heights	C3
Delta	B4
Draper	C3
Duchesne	D3
East Carbon	D4
Enoch	A6
Ephraim	C4
Farmington	C3
Ferron	C4
Fillmore	B5
Garland	B2
Grantsville	B3
Gunnison	C4
Heber City	C3
Helper	D4
Hildale	A6
Huntington	D4
Hurricane	A6
Hyrum	C2
Ivins	A6
Junction	B5
Kanab	B6
Lapoint	E3
Layton	C2
Lehi	C3
Lewiston	C2
Loa	C5
Logan	C2
Long Valley Junction	B6
Maeser	E3
Magna	B3
Manila	E3
Manti	C4
Mapleton	C4
Moab	E5
Monroe	B5
Monticello	E6
Morgan	C2
Mount Pleasant	C4
Murray	C3
Myton	D3
N. Salt Lake	C3
Nephi	C4
North Ogden	C2
Ogden	C2
Orangeville	C4
Orem	C3
Panguitch	B6
Parowan	B6
Payson	C3
Plain City	B2
Pleasant Grove	C3
Price	D4
Provo	C3
Randolph	C2
Richfield	B5
Richmond	C2
Riverton	C3
Roosevelt	D3
Roy	B2
St. George	A6
Salem	C3
Salina	C5
Salt Lake City, capital	C3
Sandy	C3
Santa Clara	A6
Santaquin	C4
Smithfield	C2
South Jordan	C3
Spanish Fork	C3
Springville	C3
Sugarville	B4
Tooele	B3
Tremonton	B2
Vernal	E3
Washington	A6
Wellington	D4
West Jordan	C3
West Valley City	C3
Willard	B2

Other Features	Key
Abajo Peak, mt.	E6
Arches Natl. Park	E5
Bear, lake	C2
Bear, river	C2
Beaver, river	B5
Bonneville Salt Flats	A3
Bruin Point, mt.	D4
Bryce Canyon Natl. Park	B6
Canyonlands Natl. Park	E5
Capitol Reef Natl. Park	C5
Cedar Breaks Natl. Monument	B6
Colorado, river	E5
Delano Peak, mt.	B5
Deseret Peak, mt.	B3
Dinosaur Natl. Monument	E3
Dutton, mt.	B5
Escalante, river	C6
Flaming Gorge, reservoir	E2
Flaming Gorge Natl. Rec. Area	E2
Frisco Peak, mt.	A5
Glen Canyon Natl. Rec. Area	D6
Golden Spike Natl. Hist. Site	B2
Grand Staircase-Escalante N.M.	C6
Great, basin	A4
Great Salt, lake	B2
Great Salt Lake, desert	A3
Green, river	D4
Heliotrope, mt.	C4
Henry, mts.	D6
Ibapah Peak, mt.	A4
Kings Peak, mt.	D3
Marsh Peak, mt.	E3
Marvine, mt.	C5
Monument, valley	D6
Natural Bridges Natl. Monument	E6
Navajo, mt.	D6
Navajo Indian Res.	E6
Nebo, mt.	C4
Paria, river	C6
Pavant, range	B5
Peale, mt.	E5
Pennell, mt.	D6
Powell, lake	D6
Price, river	D4
Rainbow Bridge Natl. Monument	D6
Salt Marsh, lake	A4
San Juan, river	D6
San Rafael, river	D4
Sevier, desert	B4
Sevier, lake	A5
Strawberry, river	D3
Swasey Peak, mt.	A4
Timpanogos Cave N.M.	C3
Uinta, mts.	D3
Utah, lake	C3
Wasatch, plateau	C5
White, river	E3
Zion Natl. Park	A6

Vermont .... page 172

Cities and Towns

	Key
Addison	A2
Albany	C1
Ascutney	C4
Averill	D1
Bakersfield	B1
Barnard	B3
Barnet	C2
Barre	C2
Basin Harbor	A2
Beecher Falls	D1
Bellows Falls	C4
Bennington	A5
Benson	A3
Berlin	B2
Bethel	B3
Bloomfield	D1
Bradford	C3
Brandon	A3
Brattleboro	B5
Bristol	A2
Brookfield	B2
Burlington	A1
Cabot	C2
Cambridge	B1
Castleton	A3
Cavendish	B4
Charlotte	A2
Chelsea	C3
Colchester	A1
Concord	D2
Danby	B4
Danville	C2
Dorset	A4
East Burke	D1
East Haven	D1
East Middlebury	A3
East Randolph	B3
Eden	B1
Enosburg Falls	B1
Essex	A1
Essex Junction	A1
Evansville	C1
Fair Haven	A3
Fairfax	B1
Fairfield	B1
Fairlee	C3
Franklin	B1
Gallup Mills	D1
Gaysville	B3
Georgia Center	A1
Grafton	B4
Granby	D1
Grand Isle	A1
Groton	C2
Guildhall	D1
Guilford	B5
Hancock	B3
Hanover	C2
Hardwick	C2
Hartford	C3
Hartland	C3
Hartwellville	D1
Heartwellville	A5
Highgate Center	A1
Hinesburg	A1
Hortonia	A3
Hubbardton	A3
Hyde Park	B1
Irasburg	C1
Irasville	B2
Jacksonville	B5
Jamaica	B4
Jeffersonville	B1
Johnson	B1
Keeler Bay	A1
Larrabees Point	A3
Lemington	D1

	Key
Londonderry	B4
Lowell	C1
Lyndon	C1
Lyndonville	C1
McIndoe Falls	C2
Marlboro	B5
Mendon	B3
Middlebury	A2
Middlesex	B2
Milton	A1
Monkton	A2
Montgomery	B1
Montgomery Center	B1
Montpelier, capital	B2
Morgan	C1
Morrisville	B1
Moscow	B2
Newbury	C2
Newfane	B4
New Haven	A2
Newport	C1
North Bennington	A5
Northfield	B2
North Hero	A1
North Wolcott	C1
Norton	D1
Orange	C2
Panton	A2
Peacham	C2
Pittsfield	B3
Pittsford	A3
Plainfield	C2
Plymouth	B3
Pompanoosuc	C3
Post Mills	C3
Poultney	A3
Pownal	A5
Proctor	A3
Putney	B5
Randolph	B3
Readsboro	B5
Richford	B1
Richmond	A2
Rochester	B3
Roxbury	B2
Rutland	B3
St. Albans	A1
St. Johnsbury	C2
Searsburg	B5
Shaftsbury	A4
Sharon	C3
Shelburne	A2
Sheldon	B1
Shoreham	A3
South Burlington	A2
South Hero	A1
Springfield	C4
Stamford	A5
Starksboro	A2
Swanton	A1
Tinmouth	A4
Troy	C1
Tunbridge	C3
Tyson	B4
Underhill	B1
Vergennes	A2
Vernon	B5
Vershire	C3
Warren	B2
Washington	C2
Waterbury	B2
Waterville	B1
Wells River	C2
West Burke	D1
West Dover	B5
West Haven	A3
Westminster	C4
Weston	B4
West Pawlet	A4
West Topsham	C2
Wheelock	C1
White River Junction	C3
Williamsville	B5
Wilmington	B5
Windsor	C4
Winooski	A1
Wolcott	C1
Woodford	A5
Woodstock	B3
Worcester	B2

Other Features

	Key
Appalachian Natl. Scenic Trail	A5
Black, river	C1
Bomoseen, lake	A3
Bread Loaf, mt.	B2
Bromley, mt.	B4
Camels Hump, mt.	B2
Champlain, lake	A1
Connecticut, river	C3
Ellen, mt.	B2
Equinox, mt.	A4
Green, mts.	B4
Harriman, reservoir	B5
Jay Peak, mt.	B1
Killington Peak, mt.	B3
Lamoille, river	J4
Mansfield, mt.	B1
Marsh-Billings-Rockefeller N.H.P.	A3
Mettawee, river	A3
Missisquoi, river	B1
Seymour, lake	C1
Smugglers Notch, pass	B1
Snow, mt.	B5
Somerset, reservoir	B4
Waterbury, reservoir	B2
West, river	B4
White, river	B3
White Rocks N.R.A.	B4
Willoughby, lake	C1

Virginia .... page 173

Cities and Towns

	Key
Abingdon	D1
Accomac	M4
Achilles	L5
Alberta	H6
Alexandria	J2
Allison Gap	D1
Altavista	F4
Amelia Court House	H5
Amherst	E4
Annandale	M2
Appalachia	A6
Appomattox	F5
Arlington	J2
Ashland	H4
Baileys Crossroads	M2
Bassett	C6
Basye	F2

	Key
Bedford	D5
Belleair	L2
Belle Haven	M4
Belle View	M2
Bensley	J5
Berryville	H1
Big Stone Gap	B1
Blacksburg	B5
Blackstone	H5
Bland	A5
Bloxom	M4
Bluefield	A5
Bon Air	H4
Bowling Green	J3
Boyce	G1
Boydton	G6
Boykins	J6
Bridgewater	F3
Bristol	D2
Brodnax	G6
Brookneal	F5
Brunswick	H6
Buckingham	F4
Buena Vista	E4
Burke	L2
Burkeville	G5
Callands	D6
Cape Charles	L5
Castlewood	C1
Centreville	J2
Charles City	J5
Charlotte Court House	F5
Charlottesville	F4
Chase City	G6
Chatham	E6
Cheriton	M5
Chesapeake	L6
Chester	J5
Chesterfield	H5
Chilhowie	E1
Chincoteague	M4
Christiansburg	C5
Chula	H5
Claremont	K5
Clifton Forge	D4
Clinchco	C1
Clintwood	C1
Coeburn	C1
Collinsville	D6
Colonial Beach	K3
Colonial Hts.	J5
Concord	J6
Courtland	J6
Covington	C4
Crewe	G5
Crimora	F3
Crystal City	M2
Crystal Hill	F6
Culpeper	G3
Cumberland	G4
Dale City	J2
Danville	E6
Dendron	K5
Dillwyn	G4
Dinwiddie	H5
Drakes Branch	F5
Dublin	B5
Dumfries	J2
Dungannon	C1
Eastville	M5
Elkton	F3
Emory	D1
Emporia	H6
Ewing	A1
Fairfax	J2
Fairfax Station	L2
Falls Church	M2
Falmouth	J3
Farmville	G5
Ferrum	D6
Figsboro	D6
Fincastle	D4
Fishersville	F3
Flint Hill	G2
Floyd	C6
Forest	E5
Fort Mitchell	G6
Franconia	M2
Franklin	K6
Fredericksburg	J3
Fries	B6
Front Royal	G2
Galax	B6
Gate City	C1
Glade Spring	D1
Gloucester	K5
Gloucester Point	L5
Goochland	H4
Gordonsville	G3
Goshen	D4
Gretna	E6
Grottoes	F3
Groveton	M2
Grundy	F6
Halifax	F6
Hampton	L5
Hanover	J4
Harrisonburg	F3
Harrogate	A6
Heathsville	L4
Hollins	D5
Hopewell	J5
Horse Pasture	D6
Huntington	M2
Hurt	E6
Independence	A6
Isle of Wight	K6
Jetersville	G5
Jonesville	B1
Kenbridge	G6
King and Queen Courthouse	K4
King George	J3
Kings Park	L2
King William	J4
Lancaster	L4
Lawrenceville	H6
Lebanon	D1
Leesburg	H1
Lexington	E4
Lincolnia	M2
Louisa	G4
Lovingston	F4
Lunenburg	G6
Luray	F2
Lynchburg	E5
McLean	M1
Madison	G3
Manakin	H4
Manassas	J2
Manassas Park	L2
Mantua	M2
Marion	A6

	Key
Martinsville	D6
Mathews	L5
Mechanicsville	A5
Mechanicsville	J4
Meherrin	G5
Millboro	D4
Monterey	D3
Montross	K3
Mount Jackson	F2
Narrows	B5
New Castle	C4
New Kent	K4
New Market	F2
Newport News	L6
Newsoms	J6
Norfolk	L6
North Springfield	M2
Norton	C1
Nottoway Court House	G5
Oakton	L2
Onancock	M4
Orange	G3
Palmyra	G4
Pearisburg	B5
Petersburg	J5
Peterstown	J5
Pimmit Hills	M1
Poquoson	L5
Portsmouth	L6
Powhatan	H4
Prince George	J5
Pulaski	B5
Purcellville	H1
Radford	B5
Raven	D1
Reston	J2
Richlands	D1
Richmond, capital	J4
Ridgeway	D6
Roanoke	D5
Rocky Mount	D6
Rustburg	E5
Ruther Glen	J4
Salem	C5
Saltville	D1
Saluda	K4
Shenandoah	F3
Smithfield	K6
South Boston	F6
South Hill	G6
Spotsylvania	H3
Springfield	M2
Spring Hill	M1
Stafford	J3
Stanardsville	G3
Staunton	E3
Sterling	J1
Stony Creek	J6
Strasburg	G2
Stuart	C6
Stuarts Draft	E3
Suffolk	K6
Surry	K5
Sussex	J6
Tappahannock	K4
Tazewell	A5
Timberville	F2
Triangle	J2
Tysons Corner	M1
Vale	L1
Verona	E3
Victoria	G6
Vienna	L1
Virginia Beach	M6
Warm Springs	D3
Warrenton	H2
Warsaw	K4
Washington	G2
Waverly	J5
Waynesboro	F3
Weber City	C1
Wellington	M3
West Point	K4
West Springfield	M2
Williamsburg	K5
Winchester	G1
Wise	C1
Woodbridge	J2
Woodstock	F2
Wytheville	A6
Yorktown	K5

Other Features

	Key
Allegheny, mts.	D3
Anna, lake	H3
Appalachian, mts.	C4
Appomattox Court House N.H.P.	F5
Arlington Natl. Cem.	L1
Assateague Island Natl. Seashore	M4
Booker T. Washington N.M.	D5
Charles, cape	M5
Chesapeake, bay	L5
Colonial Natl. Hist. Park	K5
Fredericksburg & Spotsylvania Natl. Mil. Park	H3
Gaston, lake	G6
George Washington Birthplace N.M.	K3
Henry, cape	M6
Iron, mts.	A5
James, river	K5
John H. Kerr, reservoir	F6
Manassas Natl. Battlefield Park	H2
Mount Rogers Natl. Rec. Area	A6
Petersburg Natl. Battlefield	J5
Potomac, river	K3
Rappahannock, river	J3
Rogers, mt.	A5
Shenandoah, mts.	E3
Shenandoah, river	F3
Shenandoah Natl. Park	G2
Smith Mtn., lake	D5
York, river	K5

Washington .... page 174

Cities and Towns

	Key
Aberdeen	C4
Amboy	D5
Anacortes	D2
Arlington	D2
Asotin	J4
Auburn	D3
Bangor	A1
Battle Ground	D5
Bellingham	D1
Belvedere	H2
Benton City	G4
Bethel	A2
Birch Bay	D1
Blaine	D1
Boardman	A1

Washington (Cities and Towns) — Key

Bothel ...D3
Bremerton ...D3
Brewster ...G2
Bridgeport ...G3
Bucoda ...D4
Burien ...B2
Burlington ...D2
Camas ...D5
Cashmere ...F3
Castle Rock ...D4
Cathlamet ...C4
Central Park ...C3
Centralia ...D4
Chehalis ...D4
Chelan ...F3
Cheney ...J3
Chewelah ...J2
Clarkston ...J4
Cle Elum ...F3
Clinton ...D3
Colfax ...J4
College Place ...H4
Colville ...J2
Connell ...H4
Cosmopolis ...C4
Country Homes ...J3
Coupeville ...D2
Davenport ...H3
Dayton ...J4
Deer Park ...J3
Dusty ...J4
Eastgate ...B2
Easton ...E3
Eastsound ...D2
East Wenatchee ...F3
Eatonville ...D3
Edmonds ...D3
Ellensburg ...F3
Elma ...C3
Elmer City ...H3
Enumclaw ...E3
Ephrata ...G3
Everett ...D2
Everson ...D2
Fall City ...E3
Federal Way ...D3
Ferndale ...D2
Fords Prairie ...C4
Forks ...B3
Four Lakes ...J3
Friday Harbor ...C2
Fruitvale ...F4
Goldendale ...F5
Gorst ...A2
Grandview ...G4
Granger ...F4
Hoquiam ...C3
Inglewood ...C2
Kelso ...D4
Kenmore ...B1
Kennewick ...G4
Kent ...D3
Kettle Falls ...H2
Kirkland ...D3
Lacey ...D3
La Grande ...D4
Lake Stevens ...D2
Leavenworth ...F3
Lexington ...D4
Longmire ...E4
Longview ...D4
Lynden ...D2
Mabton ...G4
McKenna ...D3
McMurray ...D2
Markham ...C4
Marysville ...D2
Medical Lake ...J3
Medina ...B2
Mercer Island ...D3
Merritt ...E4
Monroe ...D3
Montesano ...C4
Moses Lake ...G3
Mount Vernon ...D2
Mukilteo ...D3
Newhalem ...E2
Newport ...J2
Newport Hills ...B2
Normandy Park ...B2
North Bend ...E3
Oak Harbor ...D2
Ocean Park ...B4
Ocean Shores ...B3
Okanogan ...G2
Olalla ...B2
Olympia, capital ...D3
Omak ...G2
Opportunity ...J3
Orchards ...D5
Oroville ...G2
Othello ...G4
Oysterville ...B4
Pasco ...G5
Plymouth ...G5
Pomeroy ...J4
Port Angeles ...C2
Porter ...C4
Port Hadlock ...D2
Port Ludlow ...D3
Port Orchard ...D3
Port Townsend ...D2
Poulsbo ...D3
Prosser ...G4
Pullman ...J4
Puyallup ...D3
Quincy ...G3
Raymond ...C4
Redmond ...D3
Renton ...D3
Republic ...H2
Richland ...G4
Richmond Highlands ...B1
Ridgefield ...D5
Ritzville ...H3
St. John ...J4
Seabeck ...A2
Sea-Tac ...D3
Seattle ...D3
Sedro-Woolley ...D2
Selah ...F4
Sequim ...C2
Shelton ...C3
Silverton ...E2
Skyway ...B2
Smokey Point ...D2
Snohomish ...D3
Snoqualmie ...E3
South Bend ...C4
Southworth ...B2
Spanaway ...D3
Spokane ...J3
Stanwood ...D2
Stevenson ...E5
Sultan ...E3
Sumas ...D2
Sumner ...D3
Sunnyside ...F4
Suquamish ...A1
Tacoma ...D3
Tekoa ...J3
Tenino ...D4
Tiger ...J2
Toppenish ...F4
Tracyton ...A2
Trentwood ...J3
Tukwila ...B2
Tumwater ...D4
Union Gap ...F4
University Place ...D3
Vancouver ...D5
Vashon ...B2
Walla Walla ...H4
Wapato ...F4
Warden ...G4
Washougal ...D5
Waterville ...F3
Wenatchee ...F3
Westport ...B4
West Richland ...G4
White Center ...B2
White Salmon ...E5
Winslow ...D3
Woodinville ...B1
Woodland ...D5
Yakima ...F4
Yelm ...D4
Zillah ...F4

Other Features

Adams, mt. ...E4
Bainbridge, island ...B2
Baker, mt. ...E2
Banks, lake ...G3
Cascade, range ...E4
Chelan, lake ...F2
Chewuch, river ...F2
Columbia, river ...G2
Copper Butte, mt. ...H2
Cowlitz, river ...E4
Disappointment, cape ...B4
Elliott, bay ...B2
Flattery, cape ...B2
Franklin D. Roosevelt, lake ...H2
Glacier Peak, mt. ...E2
Grays, harbor ...B4
Green, river ...E3
Hanford Reach Natl. Mon. ...G4
Hood, canal ...C3
Kettle River, range ...H2
Klickitat, river ...E4
Lake Chelan Natl. Rec. Area ...F2
Lake Roosevelt Natl. Rec. Area ...H2
Lewis, river ...E4
Mt. Baker Natl. Rec. Area ...E2
Mount Rainier Natl. Park ...E4
Mt. St. Helens Natl. Vol. Mon. ...D4
North Cascades Natl. Park ...E2
Okanogan, river ...G2
Olympic, mts. ...C3
Olympic Natl. Park ...C3
Olympus, mt. ...C3
Omak, mt. ...G2
Orcas, island ...D2
Oregon Butte, mt. ...J4
Ozette, lake ...B2
Pasayten, river ...F2
Pend Oreille, river ...J2
Potholes, reservoir ...G3
Priest Rapids, lake ...G4
Puget, sound ...B1, D2
Rainier, mt. ...E4
Riffe, lake ...D4
Rimrock, lake ...E4
Ross, lake ...F2
Ross Lake Natl. Rec. Area ...F2
Sacajawea, lake ...H4
St. Helens, mt. ...D4
San Juan, island ...C2
Sanpoil, river ...H2
Selkirk, mts. ...J2
Skagit, river ...E2
Skykomish, river ...E3
Snake, river ...J4
Spokane, river ...H3
Strait of Juan de Fuca ...B2
Stuart, mt. ...F3
Umatilla, lake ...G5
Vashon, island ...B2
Wallula, lake ...H4
Washington, lake ...B1
Wenatchee, lake ...F3
Wenatchee, mts. ...F3
Wenatchee, river ...F3
White, pass ...E4
Whitman Mission Natl. Hist. Site ...H4
Willapa, bay ...B4
Yakima, river ...F4
Yale, lake ...D4

West Virginia ...page 175

Cities and Towns

Ansted ...D4
Barboursville ...B4
Beckley ...D5
Belington ...G2
Berkeley Springs ...K1
Bluefield ...D6
Bradley ...D5
Bridgeport ...F2
Buckhannon ...F3
Charles Town ...L2
Charleston, capital ...C4
Chester ...K4
Circleville ...F3
Clarksburg ...F2
Clay ...D4
Clendenin ...D4
Craigsville ...E4
Davis ...H2
East Liverpool ...K4
Edray ...F4
Eleanor ...C3
Elizabeth ...E2
Elkins ...G3
Fairmont ...F2
Fayetteville ...D4
Fort Ashby ...J2
Franklin ...H3
Gary ...C6
Glenville ...E3
Grafton ...F2
Grantsville ...D3
Hamlin ...B4
Harpers Ferry ...L2
Harrisville ...D2
Hinton ...E5
Huntington ...B4
Hurricane ...B4
Inwood ...K2
Kenova ...A4
Keyser ...J2
Kingwood ...G2
Lewisburg ...F5
Logan ...C5
Madison ...C4
Mannington ...F1
Marlinton ...F4
Marmet ...C4
Martinsburg ...L2
Matewan ...B5
Middlebourne ...E1
Milton ...B4
Montgomery ...D4
Moorefield ...J2
Morgantown ...G1
Moundsville ...K6
Mt. Hope ...D5
Mullens ...D5
Newburg ...G2
New Cumberland ...K4
New Haven ...C3
New Martinsville ...E1
New Milton ...E2
Nitro ...C4
Oak Hill ...D5
Oceana ...C5
Orma ...D3
Paden City ...E1
Parkersburg ...C2
Parsons ...G2
Pennsboro ...E2
Petersburg ...H3
Peterstown ...E6
Philippi ...F2
Pineville ...C5
Point Pleasant ...B3
Princeton ...D6
Rainelle ...E5
Ravenswood ...C3
Reedy ...D3
Richwood ...E4
Ripley ...C3
Romney ...J2
Ronceverte ...F5
Rupert ...E5
St. Albans ...C4
St. Marys ...D2
Salem ...E2
Shady Spring ...D5
Shepherdstown ...L2
Shinnston ...F2
Sistersville ...E1
Slanesville ...J2
South Charleston ...C4
Spencer ...D3
Summersville ...E4
Sutton ...E3
Terra Alta ...G2
Union ...E5
Vienna ...C2
Wayne ...B4
Webster Springs ...F4
Weirton ...K5
Welch ...C6
Wellsburg ...K5
Wellsville ...K4
West Milford ...F2
Weston ...F2
West Union ...E2
Wheeling ...K5
White Sulphur Springs ...F5
Whitesville ...C5
Williamson ...B5
Williamstown ...D2
Winfield ...C3

Other Features

Allegheny, mts. ...G4
Big Sandy, river ...B5
Bluestone, lake ...E5
Bluestone Natl. Scenic River ...E5
Gauley River Natl. Rec. Area ...D4
Greenbrier, river ...E5
Harpers Ferry Natl. Hist. Park ...L2
Kanawha, river ...B3
New River Gorge Natl. River ...D5
Ohio, river ...E1
Potomac, river ...J2
Shenandoah, river ...H4
Spruce Knob, mt. ...G3
Spruce Knob-Seneca Rocks N.R.A. ...H3
Sutton, lake ...E3

Wisconsin ...page 176

Cities and Towns

Abbotsford ...C4
Adams ...D5
Algoma ...F4
Alma ...B4
Altoona ...B4
Amery ...A3
Antigo ...D3
Appleton ...E4
Arcadia ...B4
Ashland ...C2
Augusta ...B4
Baldwin ...A4
Balsam Lake ...A3
Baraboo ...D5
Barronett ...A3
Bayside ...F1
Beaver Dam ...E5
Belleville ...D6
Bellevue ...F4
Beloit ...D6
Bennett ...B2
Berlin ...E5
Bethesda ...D2
Big Bend ...H2
Black River Falls ...C4
Bloomer ...B3
Bloomville ...D3
Boscobel ...C5
Breed ...E3
Brillion ...E4
Brodhead ...D6
Brookfield ...E1
Brown Deer ...F1
Bryant ...D3
Buena Vista ...D1
Burlington ...E6
Butler ...E1
Cadott ...B4
Cameron ...B3
Canton ...B3
Carlisville ...F4
Cedarburg ...F5
Cedar Grove ...F5
Chelsea ...C3
Chetek ...B3
Chili ...C4
Chilton ...E4
Chippewa Falls ...B4
Cleveland ...F5
Clinton ...E6
Clintonville ...E4
Colby ...C4
Coloma ...D5
Columbus ...D5
Conrath ...B3
Cornell ...B3
Cornucopia ...B2
Crandon ...E3
Crestview ...F2
Cuba City ...C6
Cudahy ...F2
Darlington ...C6
De Forest ...D5
De Pere ...E4
Delafield ...E1
Delavan ...E6
Denmark ...F4
Dodgeville ...C6
Duplainville ...E1
Durand ...B4
Eagle River ...D3
Easton ...D5
East Troy ...E6
Eau Claire ...B4
Edgar ...C4
Edgerton ...D6
Elkhorn ...E6
Ellsworth ...A4
Elm Grove ...E1
Elroy ...C5
Evansville ...D6
Fennimore ...C6
Florence ...E3
Fond du Lac ...E5
Forestville ...F4
Fort Atkinson ...E6
Fox Lake ...E5
Fox Point ...F1
Fredonia ...F5
Friendship ...D5
Galesville ...B4
Genesee ...D2
Genesee Depot ...E5
Germantown ...E5
Gillett ...E4
Glendale ...F1
Grafton ...F5
Green Bay ...F4
Greendale ...F2
Greenfield ...F2
Green Lake ...E4
Greenleaf ...E4
Hales Corners ...E2
Hamburg ...D3
Harrison ...D3
Hartford ...E5
Hartland ...D1
Hayward ...B2
Hillsboro ...C5
Hollister ...E3
Holmen ...B5
Horicon ...E5
Hortonville ...E4
Howard ...E4
Howards Grove ...F5
Hudson ...A4
Hurley ...C2
Husher ...F2
Jackson ...E5
Janesville ...D6
Jefferson ...E6
Juda ...D6
Jump River ...C3
Juneau ...E5
Kaukauna ...E4
Kenosha ...F6
Keshena ...E4
Kewaskum ...E5
Kewaunee ...F4
Kiel ...E5
Kneeland ...E5
Lac du Flambeau ...D3
La Crosse ...B5
Ladysmith ...B3
Lake Delton ...D5
Lake Geneva ...E6
Lake Mills ...E5
Lampson ...B3
Lancaster ...C6
La Pointe ...C2
Little Chute ...E4
Lodi ...D5
Lomira ...E5
McFarland ...D5
Madison, capital ...D5
Maiden Rock ...A4
Manitowish ...D2
Manitowoc ...F4
Marathon City ...D4
Marinette ...F3
Markesan ...E5
Marshfield ...C4
Mason ...B2
Mattoon ...D3
Mauston ...C5
Mayville ...E5
Medford ...C3
Menasha ...E4
Menomonee Falls ...E5
Menomonie ...B4
Mequon ...F5
Merrill ...D3
Middleton ...D5
Milton ...D6
Milwaukee ...F5
Mineral Point ...C6
Mishicot ...F4
Modena ...B4
Mole Lake ...E3
Mondovi ...B4
Monona ...D5
Monroe ...D6
Montello ...D5
Montfort ...C6
Mosinee ...D4
Muscoda ...C5
Muskego ...E6
Neenah ...E4
Neillsville ...C4
Nekoosa ...D4
New Berlin ...E6
New Glarus ...D6
New Holstein ...E5
New Lisbon ...C5
New London ...E4
New Richmond ...A3
Newton ...F5
Niagara ...F3
North Fond du Lac ...E5
North Lake ...D1
North Prairie ...D2
Oak Creek ...F6
Oconto ...F4
Oconto Falls ...E4
Odanah ...C2
Omro ...E4
Onalaska ...B5
Oostburg ...F5
Oregon ...D6
Osceola ...A3
Oshkosh ...E4
Paddock Lake ...E6
Palmyra ...E6
Park Falls ...C3
Pell Lake ...E6
Peshtigo ...F3
Pewaukee ...E1
Phillips ...C3
Platteville ...C6
Pleasant Prairie ...F6
Plover ...D4
Plymouth ...F5
Polonia ...D4
Portage ...D5
Port Edwards ...D4
Porterfield ...F3
Port Washington ...F5
Port Wing ...B2
Poynette ...D5
Prairie du Chien ...B5
Prairie du Sac ...D5
Prescott ...A4
Princeton ...D5
Pulaski ...E4
Racine ...F6
Randolph ...D5
Random Lake ...F5
Raymond ...F2
Reedsburg ...D5
Rhinelander ...D3
Rice Lake ...B3
Richland Center ...C5
Ridgeway ...D5
Ripon ...E5
River Falls ...A4
River Hills ...F1
Rothschild ...D4
St. Croix Falls ...A3
St. Francis ...F2
Sauk City ...D5
Saukville ...F5
Saylesville ...D2
Schofield ...D4
Shawano ...E4
Sheboygan ...F5
Sheboygan Falls ...F5
Shell Lake ...B3
Shorewood ...F1
Slinger ...E5
South Milwaukee ...F2
Sparta ...C5
Spencer ...C4
Spooner ...B3
Spread Eagle ...E3
Spring Green ...C5
Stanley ...C4
Stevens Point ...D4
Stonebank ...D1
Stoughton ...D6
Sturgeon Bay ...F4
Sturtevant ...F6
Summit Lake ...D3
Sun Prairie ...D5
Superior ...A2
Sussex ...E1
Tabor ...F2
Thompsonville ...F2
Thorp ...C4
Tomah ...C5
Tomahawk ...D3
Tony ...C3
Two Rivers ...F4
Verona ...D6
Viroqua ...C5
Wales ...D2
Wanderoos ...A3
Washburn ...C2
Watertown ...E5
Waukesha ...E6
Waunakee ...D5
Waupaca ...D4
Waupun ...E5
Wautoma ...D4
Wauwatosa ...E1
Wauzeka ...C5
West Allis ...F6
West Bend ...E5
Westby ...C5
West Milwaukee ...F2
Weyauwega ...E4
Whitehall ...B4
Whitewater ...E6
Williams Bay ...E6
Wind Lake ...E2
Wind Point ...G2
Winneconne ...E4
Wisconsin Dells ...D5
Wisconsin Rapids ...D4
Wrightstown ...E4

Other Features

Apostle Islands Natl. Lakeshore ...C1
Big Muskego, lake ...E2
Castle Rock, lake ...D5
Chetek, lake ...B3
Chippewa, lake ...B3
Door, peninsula ...F4
Dubay, lake ...D4
Flambeau, river ...C3
Green, bay ...F4
Madeline, island ...C2
Michigan, lake ...G5
Mississippi, river ...B5
Outer, island ...C1
Peshtigo, river ...E3
Petenwell, lake ...D4
Pewaukee, lake ...D1
Poygan, lake ...E4
St. Croix Natl. Scenic Riverway ...A3
Sand, island ...C1
Spring, lake ...C2
Stockton, island ...C1
Superior, lake ...C1
Timms Hill, mt. ...C3
Winnebago, lake ...E4
Wisconsin, river ...D3
Wolf, river ...E3
Yellow, river ...C4

Wyoming ...page 177

Cities and Towns

Afton ...A2
Basin ...B1
Boxelder ...D2
Buffalo ...C1
Byron ...B1
Casper ...C2
Cheyenne, capital ...D3
Cody ...B1
Cokeville ...A2
Deaver ...B1
Douglas ...D2
Evanston ...A3
Evansville ...C2
Gillette ...D1
Glenrock ...C2
Green River ...B3
Greybull ...B1
Jackson ...A2
Kemmerer ...A3
Lander ...B2
Laramie ...D3
Lovell ...B1
Lusk ...D2
Lyman ...A3
Medicine Bow ...C2
Mills ...C2
Newcastle ...D2
Pinedale ...B2
Powell ...B1
Rawlins ...C3
Reliance ...B3
Riverton ...B2
Rock Springs ...B3
Saratoga ...C3
Sheridan ...C1
Sundance ...D1
Thermopolis ...B2
Torrington ...D2
Wamsutter ...C3
Wheatland ...D2
Worland ...C1

Other Features

Absaroka, range ...A1
Belle Fourche, river ...D2
Big Sandy, river ...B3
Bighorn, lake ...B1
Bighorn, mts. ...C1
Bighorn Canyon Natl. Rec. Area ...B1
Bridger Peak, mt. ...C3
Clarks Fork Yellowstone, river ...B1
Cloud Peak, mt. ...C1
Colter Peak, mt. ...A1
Continental Divide, mt. ridge ...B2
Devils Tower Natl. Monument ...D1
Elk, mt. ...C3
Flaming Gorge, reservoir ...B3
Flaming Gorge Natl. Rec. Area ...B3
Fort Laramie Natl. Hist. Site ...D2
Fossil Butte Natl. Monument ...A3
Francs Peak, mt. ...B2
Gannett Peak, mt. ...B2
Grand Teton, mt. ...A2
Grand Teton Natl. Park ...A2
Great Divide, basin ...C3
Green, river ...B3
Greybull, river ...B1
Jackson, lake ...A2
Laramie, mts. ...C2
Laramie, river ...D3
Laramie Peak, mt. ...D2
Little Bighorn, river ...C1
Little Missouri, river ...D1
Little Powder, river ...D1
Little Snake, river ...C3
Medicine Bow, river ...C2
North Platte, river ...D2
Norwood, river ...B1
Owl Creek, mts. ...B2
Pathfinder, reservoir ...C2
Powder, river ...D1
Rocky, mts. ...B2
Seminoe, reservoir ...C3
South Fork Cheyenne, river ...D2
South Fork Powder, river ...C2
Sweetwater, river ...B2
Teton, river ...A2
Tongue, river ...C1
Trout Peak, mt. ...B1
Whiskey Peak, mt. ...C2
Wind, river ...B2
Wind River, range ...B2
Yellowstone, lake ...A1
Yellowstone Natl. Park ...A1